Jewish American
Women Writers

JEWISH AMERICAN WOMEN WRITERS
A Bio-Bibliographical and Critical Sourcebook

Ann R. Shapiro
EDITOR-IN-CHIEF

Sara R. Horowitz
ADVISORY EDITOR FOR FICTION

Ellen Schiff
ADVISORY EDITOR FOR DRAMA

Miriyam Glazer
ADVISORY EDITOR FOR POETRY

Greenwood Press
WESTPORT, CONNECTICUT
LONDON

Library of Congress Cataloging-in-Publication Data

Jewish American women writers : a bio-bibliographical and critical
    sourcebook / Ann R. Shapiro, editor-in-chief . . . [et al.] : foreword
    by Sarah Blacher Cohen.
      p. cm.
    Includes bibliographical references and index.
    ISBN 0–313–28437–7 (alk. paper)
    1. American literature—Jewish authors—Bio-bibliography.
  2. Jewish authors—United States—Biography—Dictionaries.
  3. Jewish women—United States—Biography—Dictionaries.
  4. American literature—Women authors—Bio-bibliography.
  5. American literature—Jewish authors—Dictionaries. 6. Women
authors, American—Biography—Dictionaries. 7. American literature—
Women authors—Dictionaries. I. Shapiro, Ann R.
    PS153.J4J48   1994
    016.8109'8924—dc20   93–40618

British Library Cataloguing in Publication Data is available.

Copyright © 1994 by Ann R. Shapiro

Library of Congress Catalog Card Numbers: 93–40618
ISBN: 0–313–28437–7

First published in 1994

Greenwood Press, 88 Post Road West, Westport, CT 06881
An imprint of Greenwood Publishing Group, Inc.

Printed in the United States of America

The paper used in this book complies with the
Permanent Paper Standard issued by the National
Information Standards Organization (Z39.48–1984).

10 9 8 7 6 5 4 3 2 1

To all those women past and present whose voices
may at last be heard and recorded

"The voice of a woman is an impropriety."
(Talmud Bali, Berachot 24a)

CONTENTS ⎯⎯⎯⎯⎯⎯⎯⎯⎯⎯⎯⎯⎯⎯⎯⎯⎯⎯⎯⎯⎯⎯

FOREWORD _____

Kadia Molodowsky writes in "Women's Songs" of her desire to emancipate her poetry from the confinement of the Yiddish literary tradition, but she is unable to escape from its all-consuming influence, its haunting presence. Molodowsky is determined to part company with the tradition's lacrymose vision, its oppressive pessimism, which prevents her spirit from soaring. But the grandmothers' "whimperings race like the autumn wind past" her and their "words are the silken cord still binding" her thoughts. A number of the woman writers whom General Editor, Ann Shapiro, and advisory editors, Sara Horowitz, Ellen Schiff, and Miriyam Glazer, have with great discernment invited to their tastefully furnished house of fiction also wanted to leave the sacred wine behind and cut the Jewish literary cord. But their grandmothers have called them back, and, according to the astute critics in this volume, many of these fiction writers, poets, and dramatists have returned to their old Jewish and Judaic roots; some have unearthed new ones. And as such they have flourished.

Thus, in varying degrees, they have embraced their identity as Jewish writers and have not, like Lionel Trilling, resented critics of their work who discovered in it either "faults or virtues" that they called Jewish. Yet their self-acceptance as Jewish writers has not guaranteed these women a place in the Jewish literary canon. For Cynthia Ozick admonishes us that *halakhah*, Jewish law, prescribes that Jewish women be "omitted—by purposeful excision"—from the creative "endeavor of the Jewish people" (138). What she claims we have left, then, is a "Jewish half-genius" who can listen to the "Voice of the Lord of History . . . with only half an ear, speaking with only half a tongue, and never understanding that we have made ourselves partly deaf and partly dumb" (140). We owe an enormous debt of gratitude to Ann Shapiro and her scholarly cohorts for being such keen tracers of missing or lost Jewish women writers and for cogently assessing their unique contributions. By uncovering the multifaceted

wisdom concealed behind the *mechitza*, the ritual partition in Orthodox synagogues or temples separating men from women, they have helped restore the
"Jewish half-genius."

Sarah Blacher Cohen

WORKS CITED

Molodowsky, Kadia. "Women's Songs, I." Trans. Adrienne Rich. *Treasury of Yiddish
Poetry*. Ed. Irving Howe and Eliezer Greenberg. New York: Holt, Rinehart &
Winston, 1969. 284.

Ozick, Cynthia. "Notes towards Finding the Right Question." *Lilith Magazine* 6 (1979).
Rpt. *On Being a Jewish Feminist*. Ed. Susanna Heschel. New York: Schocken,
1983. 120–51.

PREFACE

This volume explores the extraordinary achievement of Jewish American women novelists, poets, and playwrights who have written in the English language. A reference work, composed mainly of entries alphabetically arranged by writer, the book not only supplies information on biography, bibliography, and a survey of criticism on each writer, but it also provides an analysis of the writer's work by a scholar in Jewish American literature, women's literature, or a related field. In addition, there is a special chapter on some of the important writers of autobiographies that document the experience of Jewish women in America. An introduction defining the scope of Jewish American women's literature and additional bibliographical information complete the work.

Every effort was made to provide a representative selection of writers. Recent anthologies and bibliographies of American women's literature and Jewish women's literature were consulted, along with critical works and anthologies of Jewish American writing (although most of the authors and editors of works on Jewish Americans have shown little interest in women's enormous contribution). The preliminary list was then circulated among contributors and other scholars who had expertise in specialized areas, and writers were added and deleted accordingly. Sometimes a particular entry was included because an individual contributor was enthusiastic about a writer who she or he felt deserved wider recognition. Thus, in a very real sense, this book was a collaborative effort among the many people—women and men—who gave unstintingly of their time because they thought this anthology was needed.

While the book that has emerged is large, there is no claim that it presents the canon of Jewish American women's literature. It would be presumptuous to state there were any such canon because many of the writers are living and writing today, and even those who wrote many years ago have often not been recognized until recently. There are a core of writers represented here who would be on anybody's list of Jewish American women writers, but there are also some who are very young and have not as yet produced a great deal. And there are others whose work has been out of print until recently and has, therefore, only just become accessible.

In addition to the writers discussed here, Jewish American women have made an enormous contribution to Yiddish literature. While literature written in Yiddish is outside the parameters of the present volume, this literature has been explored elsewhere by such writers as Norma Fain Pratt and Kathryn Hellerstein.[1] It should also be noted that several of the writers who are included draw on the traditions of Yiddish writing and storytelling.

Although all of the writers discussed in this volume have written novels, poetry, or plays, many of these writers also write in other genres, and a few are probably even better known for their literary, social, or political criticism. Nonetheless, the focus of the entries is on *belles lettres.*

I am indebted to all the contributors who not only worked diligently on their own entries, but who provided additional guidance on new contributors and graciously shared their knowledge of people and issues. I am also deeply grateful to each of the writers who provided information on her life and work in interviews and letters, read the finished entry to ensure accuracy of detail, and made helpful suggestions about other writers and sources of information. An unexpected bonus was the friendships that developed between a number of writers and contributors, creating an ever-widening community of writers and scholars in this relatively new field.

My most heartfelt thanks are reserved for my indefatigable advisory editors, Sara Horowitz, Advisory Editor for Fiction, and Ellen Schiff, Advisory Editor for Drama. They provided expert advice on the content of the volume, assisted in finding contributors, and read and added editorial comments to all entries in their areas of expertise. While I must take full responsibility for the final product, their assistance throughout the book's long gestation was paramount. Special thanks also go to Miriyam Glazer for her assistance with poetry entries.

I am also grateful to the NEH for the opportunity to participate in a summer seminar on Jewish American Writers. Very special thanks are due the seminar director, Professor Mark Krupnick, whose continuing support has been invaluable since the inception of this book.

Finally, I thank the President, Administrative Officers, and Sabbaticals Committee at the State University of New York, at Farmingdale, who provided me with a sabbatical so that I could complete this work.

NOTE

1. In her essay "Culture and Radical Politics: Yiddish Women Writers, 1890–1940" (1980), Norma Fain Pratt discusses the lives and work of about fifty Yiddish women writers who immigrated to the United States during the first half of the twentieth century. Kathryn Hellerstein focuses on Yiddish women poets in two essays, "Women Poets in Yiddish" (1988) and "Songs of Herself: A Lineage of Women Yiddish Poets" (1990).

Jewish American
Women Writers

INTRODUCTION _____

THE BRAIDED TRADITION: ETHNICITY, HISTORY, AND ETHICS

In the absence of a canon, one is tempted to talk of tradition, but even here there are difficulties because tradition is not a single, continuous strand. Rather, the tradition of Jewish American women's writing must be viewed as a large braid with many intersecting strands. These strands include narratives by and about the immigrant generations; Holocaust and survivor literature; works motivated by either religion or ethnicity or both; narratives focused on gender issues; and literature that explores ethical concerns, sometimes, but not necessarily in a religious context.

One strand is the story of the immigrant at the turn of the century, when the largest single wave of Jews fled pogroms and poverty in the *shtetlach* of Europe to find a better life in the New World. Limited language skills and preoccupation with daily life prevented this generation from making a large contribution to literature in English, but two women writers, Mary Antin and Anzia Yezierska, managed to produce works of lasting interest.

While the largest immigration of Jews occurred at the turn of the century, immigration has been ongoing, and literature written by new immigrants continues to be written, for example, by such Holocaust survivors as Ilona Karmel, Irena Klepfisz, and Lore Segal. Moreover, even where the writer is not a first-generation immigrant but the child or grandchild of immigrants, the experience of immigration and assimilation often figures prominently in her life and work. In recent years, such writers as Gertrude Stein and Edna Ferber have been reassessed as ethnic writers, significantly motivated by a need to assimilate in an alien culture.[1] Even contemporary fiction bears the impress of the conflict between Old World values and modern American life, notably in works by Lynne Sharon Schwartz, E. M. Broner, and Grace Paley.

Another important strand is represented by imaginative re-creation of history. Especially compelling is the Holocaust, which has become a subject both for those who escaped and for those whose response, though historically based, is necessarily imagined.[2] Norma Rosen, Marge Piercy, and Cynthia Ozick are among those who have made important contributions in this area. Other writers reach even further back in history to find inspiration in the Old Testament, which becomes a living source for Elizabeth Swados and Shirley Kaufman, among others.

But by far the largest number of writers represented here are secular Jewish women who are not mainly concerned with any of the issues mentioned above. Many of them, however, create identifiably Jewish characters who express concerns of Jews of a particular time and place. For example, Edith Konecky's Allegra/Rachel must confront the peculiarities of an alien American Jewish value system embraced by a generation in urban America, while younger writers like Rebecca Goldstein and Allegra Goodman invent characters who are modern intellectuals imbued with a Jewish tradition that is sometimes difficult to reconcile with their lives in contemporary America.

While all of the writers noted so far are recognizably Jewish, there are many other writers whose work may be marginally connected or not connected at all to clearly identifiable Jewish themes. Inevitable questions arise: Why is this writer or this work considered Jewish? Is it sufficient to be born into a family with genetic, ethnic, or religious ties to Judaism? Is it necessary that a work reflect Jewishness in content, context, or language? While such questions are important, there are no definitive answers either in literature or in politics. In making choices for the present volume, I was guided in particular by the views of Elie Wiesel and Evelyn Torton Beck, whose all-encompassing definitions of the Jewish writer favor inclusion rather than exclusion.

Elie Wiesel emphatically affirms the significance of Judaism for all Jewish writers:

Whether he celebrates the triumphs or the torments of his people or whether he denigrates them, whether he clings to his past or detaches himself from it, he will reflect his background in more than one way. Jew by conviction or Jew in spite of himself, the Jewish writer *cannot* be anything else. What is most ironic is that even his rejection of his Jewishness identifies him.

A Jewish writer is, in the final analysis, a Jew who has chosen the art of writing to extol or to condemn a certain way of living, believing, fighting, or in one word: being. He remains a Jew even if he writes against Jews. Except that in this case, he will be an apologetic Jew and an inauthentic writer. (xiii)

Although Wiesel does not indicate that the Jewish writer may, in fact, be ''she'' as well as ''he,'' I think that he is mainly accurate in his broad definition. Nonetheless, writers who converted from Judaism or whose parent converted, such as Denise Levertov, were excluded.

In her definition of ''Jew,'' Evelyn Torton Beck emphasizes ethical concerns and suggests other crucial aspects of Jewishness:

Being Jewish informs a woman's consciousness from the time she is young until she grows old, no matter how far from religion her family may be. . . . To be born a Jew is to be born into a group with its own religious practices and beliefs, as well as a particular value system and code of ethics . . . some of us have created our own woman-identified Jewish rituals. Some are avowed atheists. Yet all of us are Jews. Some are struggling with denials and erasures, forced assimilations, silences and shame. Others take pride and pleasure and great joy from our Jewish identities. For some, this identity lies in the link with radical political traditions: Jewish activism in the Bund (Yiddish abbreviation for ''General Jewish Workers Union in Lithuania, Poland and Russia,'' a Jewish socialist party founded in Russia in 1897), the American labor union movement, the civil rights movement, the anti-war movement, the feminist movement, the struggle for gay and lesbian rights. . . . Our shared wisdom, shared fears and hopes, shared sense of history, shared languages and literature; our oral story-telling tradition. (xvii–xviii)

An extraordinary number of the writers included here exemplify Beck's notion that Jewish women writers are largely motivated by ethical concerns; indeed, many are political activists. Jewish writers are a peculiar ethnic group in that their ethnicity is closely tied to a religion rich in ethical precepts. One must at least ask whether writers such as Lillian Hellman, Rosellen Brown, Joanne Greenberg, Fannie Hurst, Karen Malpede, Adrienne Rich, Irena Klepfisz, Tess Slesinger, Tillie Olsen, and Helen Yglesias write out of what Beck identifies as ''a particular value system and code of ethics.''

In the effort to present the commonalities among Jewish American women writers, it is at the same time necessary to recognize their wide diversity. The writers represented here include communists and proponents of the American dream; assimilated Jews and those who celebrate their faith and ethnicity; radical feminists and traditional wives and mothers; lesbians who have come out and lesbians who have not, as well as straight women; orthodox believers and atheists. Some are well known and others barely recognized. All have made a contribution to the braid of many strands that represents Jewish American women's writing.

BEHIND THE *MECHITZA*

No one identifies a book as the story of white, Christian, male heterosexuals. It is only the marginal who have to identify themselves or remain invisible. This painful fact has certainly been noted by Jewish male literary critics. Sanford Pinsker, for example, observed with chagrin ''one can turn the 1,000 plus pages of the first edition of *The Literary History of the United States* (1948) without encountering a single Jewish-American fictionist'' (ix). Since 1948 a number of volumes have been published by Jewish men not only affirming, but celebrating the existence of Jewish male writers in American literature. But these books exclude women in the same way that earlier American literary histories excluded Jewish men. While the omission of women is not, of course, unique to Jewish American literature, one might have expected that the very men who objected to the omission of Jews from American literature would logically have included women as well as men in their new anthologies and critical works.

On the contrary, as Jewish women in an orthodox synagogue must sit behind a *mechitza*, separated from the men who are performing the service, so in Jewish American literary history and criticism, women have been kept behind a metaphoric *mechitza* separating them from the men who are acknowledged as the legitimate participants in this subgenre of American literature. Jewish women writers still remain nearly invisible in most collections of Jewish American literature.

A cursory survey of anthologies and literary histories suggests that the situation is improving, but only marginally. In 1950, Harold V. Ribalow edited *This Land, These People*, an anthology of twenty-five writers—twenty-four men and one woman. Nineteen sixty-four saw the publication of Azriel Eisenberg's *The Golden Land: A Literary Portrait of American Jewry, 1654 to the Present*, a massive anthology of eighty-eight works, only eight by women. In the same year, Irving Malin's *Breakthrough: A Treasury of Contemporary American-Jewish Literature* included only Grace Paley and Muriel Rukeyser among twenty-eight male writers. Then in 1965, Malin published *Jews and Americans*, which included no women. There were also no women in Max Schulz's *Radical Sophistication: Studies in Contemporary Jewish-American Novelists* (1969) or in *The Rise of American Jewish Literature* (1970), edited by Charles Angoff and Meyer Levin. In *The Literature of American Jews* (1974), Theodore Gross included only Muriel Rukeyser and Grace Paley among twentieth-century writers. Irving Howe edited *Jewish American Stories* (1977), selecting stories by four women and twenty-six men. And as if to prove nothing much has changed regarding women writers, Sanford Pinsker, in *Jewish-American Fiction, 1917–1987* (1992) writes, "Merely to sound their names—Henry Roth, Delmore Schwartz, Isaac Rosenfeld, Bernard Malamud, Philip Roth, Saul Bellow, Cynthia Ozick—is to realize how important, how 'established,' Jewish-American writers have become" (ix).

The problem in the historic excising of the contribution of Jewish American women writers is that what remains is a misrepresentation. If we read the experience only of men, we know little about American Jewry. As Irena Klepfisz and Melanie Kaye/Kantrowitz point out, "women's contributions to Jewish material and cultural survival are vast" but sexism "prevents our contributions from being named, recorded, honored, so that a tradition gets passed along which tries as much as possible to pretend women had nothing to do with it" (11).

If the men have failed to notice the women behind the *mechitza*, the women themselves have decided to take matters into their own hands to make sure that their voices would be heard. In 1980 Julia Wolf Mazow edited *The Woman Who Lost Her Names: Selected Writings by American Jewish Women*. This was followed by Evelyn Torton Beck's *Nice Jewish Girls: A Lesbian Anthology* (1980) and *The Tribe of Dina: A Jewish Women's Anthology* (1986), edited by Melanie Kaye/Kantrowitz and Irena Klepfisz. Joyce Antler added *America and I: Short*

Stories by American Jewish Women Writers (1990) and Sylvia Barack Fishman edited *Follow My Footprints: Changing Images of Women in American Jewish Fiction* (1992), which includes works by eleven men and ten women. The most recent anthology at this writing is *Writing Our Way Home* (1992), edited by Ted Solotoroff and Nessa Rapoport. This book is unique among Jewish American collections not only because it is edited by a man and a woman, but because it contains more stories by women than by men.

In addition to the anthologies, a good deal of scholarly criticism of Jewish American women writers has been produced in the last several years. Mary Dearborn broke new ground in 1986 with *Pocahontas's Daughters: Gender and Ethnicity in American Culture*, a book that discusses Jewish women writers, although it is not limited to them. Rose Kamel published *Aggravating thecon-* *science: Jewish American Literary Mothers in the Promised Land* in 1988. And in 1992, two more works were added: Diane Lichtenstein's *Writing Their Nations: The Tradition of Nineteenth-Century American Jewish Women Writers* and Ellen Serlen Uffen's *Strands of the Cable: The Place of the Past in Jewish American Women's Writing*. In the same year Norma Rosen contributed to the dialogue on Jewish American women with her book of personal essays, *Accidents of Influence: Writing as a Woman and a Jew in America*. In addition, two special issues of *Studies in American Literature*[3] have been devoted to women writers, and a number of articles have appeared in books and other periodicals.

It is hoped that the present volume should, at the very least, make clear that the contribution of Jewish American women to literature has been enormous and important. To paraphrase Muriel Rukeyser, if being a Jew in the twentieth century is a gift,[4] then being a Jew and a woman at the dawn of the twenty-first century is not only a gift but a new opportunity.

THE POETICS OF JEWISH AMERICAN WOMEN'S LITERATURE OR THE NOT-SO-SACRED TEXTS

While Jewish American women have written partially out of an experience that they shared with American and Jewish American men and also with other women, they have also invented new iconographies, themes, paradigms, and myths.

In American literature, famous writers have penned canonized works about whaling voyages and bear hunting; they have also covered reams of paper with stories of fathers and sons. We have been taught to read the stories of male experience. But what happens when men in general and Jewish men in particular encounter such a story as Tillie Olsen's ''I Stand Here Ironing''? The story was first published in Olsen's 1961 collection *Tell Me a Riddle*, along with the now equally well-known title story. But Olsen would probably have remained obscure were it not for the rise of the women's movement during the 1970s, when she became almost a cult figure for the new feminist criticism.

Olsen's iconography of the iron moving over the dress on the ironing board—

an integral part of her own domestic life—belongs to the everyday life of most women and few men. And the subject—the relationship between a mother and a daughter—is more significant to women than to men reared in a Jewish American milieu that Irving Howe identified as "the world of our fathers." As Annette Kolodny points out, "male readers who find themselves outside of and unfamiliar with symbolic systems that constitute female experience in women's writings will necessarily dismiss those systems as undecipherable, meaningless, or trivial. And male professors will find no reason to include such works in the canon of 'major authors' " (148).

In direct opposition to the literature written by women, the contemporary male Jewish literary canon has long focused on Philip Roth, Saul Bellow, and Bernard Malamud, sometimes playfully identified as the Hart, Schafner, and Marx of Jewish American literature. Roth and Bellow, in particular, have advanced the notion that Jewish American literature is unequivocally male. At the end of *The Counterlife*, for example, Roth announces, "Circumcision confirms that there is an us, and an us that isn't solely him and me." He continues, "it's fitting to conclude with my erection, the circumcised erection of the Jewish father" (324). What is odd about Roth's iconography, of course, is that he seems innocently unaware that he has excluded not only non-Jews from the newly discovered "us," but also all Jewish women. Norman Finkelstein says of this passage that "this is genuine modern midrash" (1940). If so, one must ask not only what is it about but for whom is it written.

The falsification of Jewish literary history and criticism is perpetuated by scholars who develop paradigms based only on reading Bellow, Roth, and other male writers. In women's fiction, there are no Jewish mothers like Mrs. Portnoy or Jewish American Princesses like Brenda Patimkin. No one is searching for the "ultimate *shiksa*" (Jaher), as the male protagonists of Roth and Bellow frequently do. Nor can we embrace Leslie Fiedler's notion that the search for America in American Jewish fiction is an erotic encounter between the Jewish "Don Juan and the *shiksa*" (21). The world of our mothers is still largely uncharted territory.

That territory can be explored in several ways. If we look back at the literary histories that mainly describe male experience, we need to rethink every chapter to include the experience of the Jewish woman. For example, the immigrant experience recorded by Abraham Cahan is not the same experience as that of Anzia Yezierska[5]; assimilation poses different problems for Henry Roth and Edna Ferber; the alienation of which Delmore Schwartz writes is distinct from the alienation conceptualized by Adrienne Rich; the problems of urbanization were different for Tess Slesinger and Albert Halper; Israel may be the promised land for some, but at least one American feminist, Marcia Freedman, describes herself as an "exile in the Promised Land" in her book by that title; and whatever *halakhah* might mean for a male writer, it has been infinitely more complicated for the Jewish woman, who often saw herself as excluded from the Covenant entirely. Holocaust literature is especially problematic because, as

Marlene Heinemann has observed, "Even the most impartial and sensitive male survivor will be unable to provide an insider's picture of women's experiences in the Nazi camps, since male and female prisoners were segregated in separate camps" (3).

We must invent new paradigms and myths to describe the writing of Jewish American women. Elaine Showalter writes, "Too many literary abstractions which claim to be universal have in fact described only male perceptions, experience, and options, and have falsified the social and personal contexts in which literature is produced and consumed" (Showalter, *Toward a Feminist Poetics* 127). Thematically some distinct patterns emerge. For example, consider the analogue of the search for the ultimate *shiksa* in the search for the *shaygets*, or WASP male, notable especially in the fiction of Anzia Yezierska, where some version of John Dewey is the love object of the female heroine seeking assimilation. While Yezierska's preoccupation with the Gentile male was perhaps obsessive, it is not unique. Other Jewish women writers whose heroines are attracted to Gentile lovers include Emma Wolf, Erica Jong, Anne Roiphe, Nessa Rapoport, and Wendy Wasserstein.

As for the Jewish mother stereotype, Adrienne Rich suggests, "the 'Jewish mother' is only one creation of the enforced withdrawal of nineteenth- and twentieth-century women from all roles save one." She suggests the result for the Jewish daughter is quite different from that of the Jewish son, for whom the mother is an object of "blame and ridicule." Instead, the Jewish daughter suffers from "matrophobia," a term she borrows from Lynn Sukenick, which means "fear . . . of *becoming one's mother*"; daughters struggle "to become individuated and free" (*Of Woman Born* 237–38).[6] Ellen Schiff finds further complications in the contemporary relationship between the Jewish mother and her daughter because rapid changes in women's roles have left both mothers and daughters without role models (111–12).

Even as new meanings are applied to old myths, it is necessary to keep in mind that women writers share themes that have been developed in male Jewish literature, particularly the problem of the outsider in a world where anti-Semitism takes new forms in every generation. But the problem is compounded for women, who are not only outsiders in a Gentile world but outsiders in the double partriarchy of secular society and Judaism.

Paula Hyman has observed, "within the framework of traditional Judaism, women are not independent, legal entities." Instead, they are categorized in law with "the minor, the deaf-mute, and the idiot" (106). Thus exiled, Jewish women writers have created new women's worlds where men may enter but only on the periphery. E. M. Broner creates such a world in the stone house in Jerusalem, which is the setting for *A Weave of Women*; while Cynthia Ozick imagines a female mayor of New York; Ruth Puttermesser, who attempts to fulfill her woman's mission—to repair New York City—with the help of a female *golem* ("Puttermmesser and Xanthippe").

Even more troublesome than women's exclusion from full legal protection is their exclusion from sacred study. If we accept Harold Bloom's notion that "an obsession with study, a condition of text-centeredness . . . held the great Diaspora Jewries together" (321), then we are faced with the dilemma that women have been exiled from Judaism itself, since many traditional Talmudists prohibit women from reading, no less writing, sacred texts. Rabbi Eliezer ben Hyrcanus wrote, "The words of the Torah should be burnt rather than be taught to women" (*Jerusalem Talmud*, Sota 3:4). And with reference to women's participation in religious services, in *Megilla* 23a it is written that "a woman should not read the Torah out of respect for the congregation." Similarly, the Woman of Valor described in Proverbs 31 is housekeeper and breadwinner, but reading and study are reserved for her husband.

While the modern Jewish woman is no longer necessarily bound by such precepts, Jewish women have even in the recent past been discouraged from writing. Malke Lee, a Yiddish poet who immigrated to America in 1921, wrote that her father burned her poetry because, as Norma Fain Pratt recounts, "he believed it was against God's will that a girl write" (73). And Hinde Zaretsky, another Yiddish writer of the same generation, tells how her grandmother slapped her when she was commended in school for what she termed "my first intuitive experience with imaginative writing" (Interview with Hinde Zaretsky, qtd. in Pratt 73).

If girls are no longer punished for writing, traditional Jewish women still suffer the indignity of being excluded from the study and "text-centeredness" which Harold Bloom cites as the central concern of Judaism. Cynthia Ozick lamented, "And the rabbi speaks the word 'Jew.' I can be sure that he is not referring to me, for to him 'Jew' means 'male Jew'. . . . When my rabbi says, 'A Jew is called to the Torah,' he never means me or any other living Jewish woman" (qtd. in Broner "Honor and Ceremony" 236–37).

But regardless of rabbinic preconceptions, Cynthia Ozick has provided a rationale for a woman to be both Jew and writer in her advocacy of a new liturgy, which she states will be "touched by the Covenant" (173). She points out that in the past, Torah was preserved by "augmenting it" and foresees "fresh Talmudic modes that, in our age, take the urgent forms of imaginative literature" (1975). And despite Ozick's quarrel with what she considers Bloom's notion of "literature as idol," Ozick's new liturgy seems to have much in common with what Bloom calls "high literature" (325), a literature that he specifically attributes to Ozick. Both Ozick and Bloom further suggest that the new Jewish language will be English.[7] The implications propounded by these two leading Jewish literary theorists have enormous implications for Jewish American women writing today, including, of course, Ozick herself. If women were excluded from Jewish textuality in the past, it now becomes possible for them to participate through literature in English in the new liturgy of the future.

Although neither Ozick nor Bloom is deliberately making a case for feminism—Jewish or otherwise—Jewish feminist writers and critics have been articulating similar arguments in their conscious efforts to create a literature and a poetics that will allow women to participate fully in what Ozick calls "a new culture-making" (174). The sacred texts of Judaism are themselves being mined by women, who find new meanings and write new *midrash*. For example, consider the biblical story of Dina, which captured the imagination of Irena Klepfisz and Melanie Kaye/Kantrowitz when they edited their anthology, *The Tribe of Dina*. While the Dina of the Old Testament is silent and passive when she is raped and when her brothers murder her rapist and his clan, Klepfisz and Kantrowitz suggest that her modern sisters can tell their own stories. Dina (Dinah) also is the source of Ita Sheres's book *Dinah's Rebellion* in which Sheres creates new *midrasah* to tell the story of Dinah that was omitted from the Old Testament.

Claire Satlof, in an article on the new Jewish feminist poetic, suggests, "Books and stories by such American Jewish feminists as Esther Broner, Joanne Greenberg, Rhoda Lerman, Cynthia Ozick, Nessa Rapoport and others[8] self-consciously attempt to end the division of the world into a male-controlled spiritual realm and an everyday, profane woman's world," and she further suggests that "any Jewish feminists' attempt to create a literature of their own must ground itself in the area of Jewish ritual activity—the area most immediately in need of change" (187).

E. M. Broner in particular is concerned with creating new ritual. In *A Weave of Women*, she creates many female rituals, including an elaborate ritual for a newborn girl, a hymenotomy, intended as analogous to the ritual circumcision (*brit milah*) of the newborn boy. The point of this ritual goes beyond the *brit milah* in introducing the notion that the girl will not be "judged by her hymen but by the energies of her life" (25). In other words, not only must the birth of a baby girl be celebrated just as is the birth of a baby boy, but the ritual further implies that women must go beyond their sex roles to exercise their full humanity. Thus, Broner's *Weave* and other feminist texts write new *midrash* as they create new ritual.

Although the expansion of the tradition through literature is a cause for celebration among feminists, it should not be construed as acceptance by the academy. I recall discussing the hymenotomy in a National Endowment for the Humanities (NEH) seminar and hearing a quiet murmuring near me—the voice of an Orthodox Jewish man whispering, "But it isn't Jewish." If men, in general, have difficulty entering women's texts, the problem is augmented for Jewish men, who may challenge the very authenticity of the writing of Jewish American women, which departs from not only the literary tradition, but from the Jewish tradition that has shaped men's lives.

The issue of a Jewish woman's poetics is further complicated by the difficulty of some writers accepting the notion of themselves as either Jewish writers or women writers because to them, such classification implies marginalization or ghettoization. At one time Adrienne Rich objected to the notion of Jewish writer, but in her more recent work, she has reversed this position, affirming her Jewishness as woman and writer.[9] Cynthia Ozick, on the other hand, has denied that the term "woman writer" is meaningful because the writer is above all free and can think herself into "a male, or a female, or a stone, or a raindrop, or a block of wood, or a Tibetan, or the spine of a cactus" (285). Nonetheless, I would argue that her writing belies her assertion. She does not write as a Tibetan or a spine of a cactus; she writes inescapably as a Jewish woman. It is, I believe, as impossible for her to renounce the implications of femaleness as it would be to renounce the Jewishness she readily embraces. It should be noted, however, that Ozick has been welcomed by male critics into the pantheon of Jewish American writers, while other woman who write more specifically about female experience have not.

For some Jewish writers, female experience in literature informs language and style as well as content. Rachel Blau duPlessis, in contrasting male and female writing states, "these differing experiences do surely produce (some) different consciousnesses, different cultural experiences, different relations to realms of symbols and symbol users. Different 'language,' metaphorical; different uses of the grammatical and expressive resources of language (verb parts, questions, intonation, pronouns)" (1273). E. M. Broner suggests further that a woman's writing should be non-hierarchical and collaborative as well as non-linear: "The narrative style has always been a male style—one man tells his stories and the rest of us listen. I thought it radical that I interrupted a tale, as in *Her Mothers*, or had multiple women's voices, multiple narrators, as in *Weave* ("Of Holy Writing" 269).[10]

Other aspects of language have become critical for both Jewish and non-Jewish theologians and writers. The point is made that the privilege of naming was given to Adam and that privilege continues to be a male prerogative. Jewish theologian Judith Plaskow writes, "As Mary Daly has said, women have had our power of *naming* stolen from us. From the day that God brought the animals to Adam in the garden of Eden to see what *he* would call them, it has been through the words of men that we have known and addressed the world" (4). The problem is underscored in fiction by Nessa Rapoport in her story "The Woman Who Lost Her Names," where a woman loses her very identity in a marriage in which the husband appropriates the right to change his wife's name and then to name their newborn daughter.[11]

In summary, the need to "re-vision"[12] not only language but all female experience is a central concern of most of the writers included here. Norma Rosen's protagonist Hannah, identifying with her biblical namesake, thinks, "Let Him hear for a change a woman's voice. Arguments with men God sometimes seemed to enjoy—with Abraham, with Moses, with Lot, with Jonah. Up to a point. But with women? About this there was no news"(138). As the pages that follow make clear, there is a good deal of news from women, who have been raising their voices in anger and in song, now more than ever, in the hope that they will be heard not only by God but also by men and women.

NOTES

1. Mary Dearborn's *Pocahontas's Daughters* includes a chapter on Gertrude Stein as ethnic writer, while Diane Lichtenstein has a chapter on Edna Ferber's ethnicity in *Writing Our Nations.*

2. For a discussion of the Holocaust as described in literature by those who did not experience it directly, see Lillian Kremer, *Witness Through the Imagination.*

3. See *Studies in American Jewish Literature* 3 (1983) and 11.2 (Fall 1992).

4. In "Letter to the Front," VII (1944), Rukeyser writes, "To be a Jew in the twentieth century/Is to be offered a gift."

5. In "Cultural Mediation and the Immigrant's Daughter: Anzia Yezierska's *Bread Givers*," Gay Wilentz elaborates on the point that male critics have "set up a male paradigm for immigrant experience."

6. Other excellent analyses of Jewish mothers and daughters include Erika Duncan's "The Hungry Jewish Mother" and Sonya Michel's "Mothers and Daughters in American Jewish Literature: The Rotted Cord."

7. Ozick declared, "even now for Jews already there are traces (in the form of novels) of a Jewish liturgical literature written in English" (1977). And Harold Bloom stated, "English is becoming *the* Jewish language in that surely more Jews can use it whether as a first or second language than can use any other language" (328).

8. Satlof qualifies her generalization in a footnote indicating that although all of these writers would not identify themselves as Jewish feminists (certainly Ozick would not), they are grouped because they are "participating in a specifically Jewish feminist movement."

9. In *Dramatic Encounters*, Louis Harap quotes Adrienne Rich's statement, "I have never felt myself to be a Jewish writer" (68), but in her essay "Split at the Root: An Essay on Jewish Identity" (1982) and her poem *Sources* (1983), she affirmed her Jewishness as an integral part of herself.

10. These ideas about language are not unique to the writers mentioned here. Similar arguments are made by Deena Metzger, Sheila de Bretteville, and Julia Kristeva (Qtd. in *Feminist Criticism*, 363).

11. See entry on Nessa Rapoport in this volume.

12. The word was coined by Adrienne Rich, who defined it as "the act of looking back, of seeing with fresh eyes of entering an old text from a new critical direction. . . . " (*On Lies* 35).

WORKS CITED

Angoff, Charles, and Meyer Levin, eds. *The Rise of American Jewish Literature: An Anthology of Selections from the Major Novels.* New York: Simon and Schuster, 1970.

Antler, Joyce, ed. *America and I: Short Stories by American Jewish Women Writers.* Boston: Beacon, 1990.

Auden, W. H. "Introduction." *Red Ribbon on a White Horse.* By Anzia Yezierska. New York: Persea, 1981. 11–19.

Beck, Evelyn Torton, ed. *Nice Jewish Girls: A Lesbian Anthology.* Trumansburg, NY: Crossing Press, 1982.

Bloom, Harold. *Agon: Towards a Theory of Revision*. New York: Oxford University Press, 1982.

Broner, E. M. "Honor and Ceremony in Women's Rituals." *The Politics of Women's Spirituality: Essays on the Rise of Spiritual Power within the Feminist Movement.* Ed. Charlotte Spretnak. Garden City, NY: Anchor, 1982. 234–44.

———. Interview with Nancy Jo Hoy. "Of Holy Writing and Priestly Voices." *Massachusetts Review* 24 (1983):254–69.

———. *A Weave of Women*. Bloomington: Indiana University Press, 1978.

Dearborn, Mary. *Pocahontas's Daughters: Gender and Ethnicity in American Culture.* New York: Oxford University Press, 1986.

Duncan, Erika. "The Hungry Jewish Mother." *The Lost Tradition: Mothers and Daughters in Literature*. Ed. Cathy N. Davidson and E. M. Broner. New York: Frederick Ungar, 1980. 231–41.

DuPlessis, Rachel Blau. "For the Etruscans." *The Future of Difference*. Ed. Alice Jardine and Hester Eisenstein. Boston: G. K. Hall, 1981. Revised in Showalter, *Feminist Criticism*. 271–91.

Eisenberg, Azriel Louis, ed. *The Golden Land: A Literary Portrait of American Jewry, 1654 to the Present*. New York: T. Yoseloff, 1965.

Fiedler, Leslie. "Genesis: The American-Jewish Novel through the Twenties." *Midstream* 4 (Summer 1958):21–33.

Finkelstein, Norman. *The Ritual of New Creation: Jewish Tradition and Contemporary Literature*. Albany: SUNY Press, 1992.

Fishman, Sylvia Barack, ed. *Follow My Footprints: Changing Images of Women in American Jewish Fiction*. Hanover, NH: University Press of New England, 1992.

Freedman, Marcia. *Exile in the Promised Land*. Ithaca, NY: Firebrand Press, 1990.

Gittenstein, R. Barbara. "American-Jewish Poetry: An Overview." *Handbook of American Jewish Literature: An Analytical Guide to Topics, Themes, and Sources*. Ed. Lewis Fried. Westport, CT: Greenwood, 1988. 123–41.

Greenberg, Blu. *On Women and Judaism: A View from Tradition*. Philadelphia: Jewish Publication Society, 1981.

Gross, Theodore, ed. *The Literature of American Jews*. New York: Macmillan, 1974.

Harap, Louis. *Dramatic Encounters: The Jewish Presence in Twentieth-Century American Drama, Poetry, and Humor*. Westport, CT: Greenwood, 1987.

Heinemann, Marlene E. *Gender and Destiny: Women Writers and the Holocaust*. Westport, CT: Greenwood, 1986.

Howe, Irving, ed. *Jewish American Stories*. New York: New American Library, 1977.

Hyman, Paula. "The Other Half: Women in the Jewish Tradition." *The Jewish Woman: New Perspectives*. Ed. Elizabeth Koltun. New York: Schocken, 1976. 105–13.

Jaher, Frederick Cople. "The Quest for the Ultimate *Shiksa*." *American Quarterly* 35 (Winter 1983):518–42.

Jones, Ann Rosalind. "Writing the Body. Toward an Understanding of l'Ecriture Feminine," *Feminist Studies* 7.2 (1981). Rpt. in Showalter, *Feminist Criticism* 144–67.

Kamel, Rose Yalow. *Aggravating the Conscience: Jewish-American Literary Mothers in the Promised Land*. New York: Peter Lang, 1988.

Kay/Kantrowitz, Melanie, and Irena Klepfisz, eds. *The Tribe of Dina: A Jewish Women's Anthology*. Boston: Beacon, 1989.

Kolodny, Annette. "Dancing Through the Minefield: Some Observations on the Theory, Practice, and Politics of a Feminist Literary Criticism." *Feminist Studies* 6 (1980). Rpt. in Showalter, *Feminist Criticism*, 144–67.

Kremer, Lillian. *Witness Through the Imagination: Jewish American Holocaust Literature*. Detroit: Wayne State University Press, 1991.

Lichtenstein, Diane. *Writing Their Nations: The Tradition of Nineteenth-Century American Jewish Women Writers*. Bloomington: Indiana University Press, 1992.

Malin, Irving, ed. *Breakthrough: A Treasury of Contemporary American-Jewish Literature*. New York: McGraw-Hill, 1964.

———. *Jews and Americans*. Carbondale: Southern Illinois University Press, 1965.

Mazow, Julia Wolf, ed. *The Woman Who Lost Her Names: Selected Writings by American Jewish Women*. San Francisco: Harper & Row, 1980.

Metzger, Deena. "In Her Image." *Heresies* 1 (May 1977):2.

Michel, Sonya. "Mothers and Daughters in American Jewish Literature: The Rotted Cord." *The Jewish Woman: New Perspectives*. Ed. Elizabeth Koltun. New York: Schocken, 1984. 272–82.

Olsen, Tillie. *Tell Me a Riddle*, 1961. Rpt. New York: Delta, 1989.

Ozick, Cynthia. *Art and Ardor*. New York: Knopf, 1983.

———. "Puttermesser and Xanthippe." *Levitation: Five Fictions*. New York: Knopf, 1981. 75–158.

Pinsker, Sanford. *Jewish-American Fiction, 1917–1987*. New York: Twayne, 1992.

Plaskow, Judith. "The Jewish Feminist: Conflict in Identities." *The Jewish Woman: New Perspectives*. Ed. Elizabeth Koltun. New York: Schocken, 1976. 3–10.

Ribalow, Harold V., ed. *This Land, These People*. New York: Beechurst, 1950.

Rich, Adrienne. *On Lies, Secrets and Silence*. London: Virago, 1980.

———. *Of Woman Born: Motherhood as Experience and Institution*. 1976. Rpt. New York: Bantam, 1977.

Rosen, Norma. *Accidents of Influence: Writing as a Woman and a Jew in America*. Albany: SUNY Press, 1992.

Roth, Philip. *The Counterlife*. New York: Penguin, 1989.

Rubin, Stephen J. "American Jewish Autobiography." *Handbook of American Jewish Literature: An Analytical Guide to Topics, Themes and Sources*. Ed. Louis Fried. Westport, CT: Greenwood, 1988. 287–313.

Satlof, Claire. "History, Fiction, and the Tradition: Creating a Jewish Feminist Poetics." *On Being a Jewish Feminist: A Reader*. Ed. Susanna Heschell. New York: Schocken, 1983. 186–206.

Schiff, Ellen. "The Greening of American-Jewish Drama." *Handbook of American-Jewish Literature: An Analytical Guide to Topics, Themes and Sources*. Ed. Lewis Fried. Westport, CT: Greenwood, 1988. 91–122.

Schulz, Max F. *Radical Sophistication: Studies in Contemporary Jewish-American Novelists*. Athens: Ohio University Press, 1969.

Sheres, Ita. *Dinah's Rebellion: A Biblical Parable for Our Time*. New York: Crossroad, 1990.

Showalter, Elaine, ed. *Feminist Criticism: Essays on Women, Literature, and Theory*. New York: Pantheon, 1985.

———. "Toward a Feminist Poetics." *Women's Writing and Writing About Women*.

Ed. Mary Jacobus. London: Croom Helm, 1979. Rpt. in Showalter, *Feminist Criticism.* 125–43.

Solataroff, Ted and Nessa Rapoport. *Writing Our Way Home: Contemporary Stories by American Jewish Writers.* New York: Schocken, 1992.

Sukenick, Lynn. ''Feeling and Reason in Doris Lessing's Fiction.'' *Contemporary Literature* 14.4:519.

Uffen, Ellen Serlen. *Strands of the Cable: The Place of the Past in Jewish American Women's Writing.* New York: Peter Lang, 1992.

Wiesel, Elie. ''Foreword.'' *The Literature of American Jews.* Ed. Theodore Gross. New York: Macmillan, 1974. xiii–xiv.

Wilentz, Gay. ''Cultural Mediation and the Immigrant's Daughter: Anzia Yezierska's *Bread Givers.*'' *MELUS* 17.3 (Fall 1991–1992): 33–41.

MARY ANTIN (1881–1949)

Kirsten Wasson

BIOGRAPHY

In 1881 Mary Antin was born in Polotsk, Russia, into a world rife with disruption and violence. In this same year, pogroms and other anti-Semitic violence broke out and continued to escalate in the years preceding the Antin family's immigration in 1892 to the United States. In her autobiography, *The Promised Land*, Antin recounts such travesties as pogroms led by local priests and the forced induction of Jewish boys into the Russian army.

Her father, though trained to be a religious scholar, was uninterested in such a career and tried his hand unsuccessfully at various businesses. It was her mother, as the owner and manager of a store inherited from Mary's grandfather, who supported the family in Mary's younger years. Mary's parents were unusually progressive on the subject of their children's educations, and Mary and her sister were provided with both a Hebrew instructor and a teacher who tutored them in secular topics.

The Antin family's relative affluence came to a dramatic closure when both parents became ill and unable to work; it was this downfall that contributed significantly to the father's decision to leave for the United States. He went alone, leaving his family behind for three years until he could afford to bring over his wife and children. Mary was eleven when she immigrated; she kept a record of the five-week journey in letters written to relatives; these letters were translated a few years later into English and published as a memoir, *From Polotsk to Boston*.

Mary's father had little success in business in Boston, and as the family became more and more dependent on Mary's brother's earnings, her father became more and more bitter at the necessity of working odd jobs. Mary, meanwhile, achieved greater and greater successes in school and moved on to high school—Boston's Girls' Latin School. A loner, Mary must have experienced isolation from her classmates as well as alienation from her family as she worked diligently and alone. Mary did remain in contact with an elementary school teacher, an encouraging and influential Miss Dillingham, with whom she corresponded for years after graduation. And she became something of a regular visitor to the home of Rev. Edward Everett Hale, who, in turn, introduced her to a number of other wealthy Bostonians.

It was through the Hale Settlement House that she met her husband, Amadeus William Grabau (1870–1946), a geologist and paleontologist. Mary married him in 1901 and moved to New York City, where she attended Columbia Teachers College, but never earned a degree. She was close friends with Josephine (sister of Emma) Lazarus at this time, and it was to her that Antin dedicated *The Promised Land* in 1912, two years after Josephine died.

The book was a best-seller for years and was translated into German and Portuguese. Antin became a lecturer on the subject of immigration; she toured across the country until 1918, when she suffered a mental collapse. Two years later her husband moved to Peking for his work and remained there until his death. With their daughter, Mary moved back to Boston in 1920. She spent much of the rest of her life devoted to a religious community in western Massachusetts, Gould Farm, which operated under many of the assumptions of the early nineteenth-century transcendentalists—self-sufficiency and the doctrine of correspondence between the tangible world and the human mind.

MAJOR THEMES

The dominant themes of Mary Antin's two autobiographies and book-length essay, *They Who Knock at Our Gates*, are immigration, assimilation, and identity in America. In the introduction to *The Promised Land*, Antin imagines her own identity as existing in two halves, one of which she pronounces dead—so thorough has been her own assimilation: "I have been made over . . . I am just as much out of the way as if I were dead, for I am absolutely other than the person whose story I have to tell . . . " (xix). This statement of self annihilation denies connections to a past and she proclaims herself "reborn"; as a "made over" immigrant, Antin adopts a rhetoric of conversion in depicting the course of her life's events. She asserts an overwhelming allegiance to American history and the ideology of freedom, democracy, and opportunity in "the Promised Land."

She draws a number of romantic parallels between Jewish and American history, comparing the Declaration of Independence to Mosaic Law, reading the American Revolution "as a chapter in sacred history," setting Thomas Jefferson "in a class with Joshua," and regarding citizenship "as a holy order" (*They Who Knock* 27). This mythologizing of the New World "promise" helps Antin to develop a continuity between her experiences in Russia and the United States. She loosely frames her life's events in terms of Israelite history, presenting Russian anti-Semitism as the bondage that precedes her family's "Exodus." At the Passover service she attends the year before the family immigrates, she and others decree, "Next year—in America!" (141).

In granting American ideals and cultural landmarks a place in religious history, she also outlines her argument for continuing the tradition of providing refuge and freedom for the tired, the poor, the homeless. In *They Who Knock*, she highlights the contradictions inherent in the coexistence of the national mythology of the land of immigrants with American nativism and restrictionist policy. In the name of "the gospel of brotherhood," Antin argues for tolerance toward the "new immigrants" of the late nineteenth and early twentieth century, and she offers her own success as an example of the pride that assimilation can bring to the individual and the nation.

Antin's case against nativist attitudes is being made to a potentially nativist audience; her voice resonates with resentment at her outsider status, as well as assurances to the reader that she belongs on the inside. An example of Antin's ambivalence toward her native-born audience is the use of the third person in discussing the plight of the immigrant in *They Who Knock at Our Gates*. While she makes a strong argument against the fallacies in logic and prejudice at the root of restrictionist policies, rarely does she acknowledge her own position or experience as an immigrant. She argues from the position of the "we" who need to recognize that "Ellis Island is another name for Plymouth Rock" (98). She appeals to the reader's pride in American traditions of individualism and the self-made man without suggesting that her relationship to these traditions is anything other than that of a native-born insider.

There are, however, cracks in the "conversion" that Antin maintains in presenting her identity. While *The Promised Land* is written from the stance of one proclaiming to be "absolutely other" than the girl with the old world past, the autobiography expresses a potent nostalgia for the landscape of Antin's childhood in Russia. This nostalgia provides an alternative vision to the text's glorification of assimilation and its wholesale subscribing to "the American way." There is a tension in the autobiography between a voice that pledges allegiance to the promised land and a voice that remembers an old world past of community and ritual.

Antin's nostalgia, in part, is for the larger role that Judaism played in their life when she and her family lived in the Pale, the settlement to which Jews were confined in Russia. As members of the oppressed Diaspora in Eastern Europe, Antin's family identified with Talmudic codes and traditions of Jewish identity as a strategy of survival. Antin herself was an early skeptic, and she recounts her days of religious tutoring with both fondness and humor, presenting herself as something of a rebel whose attitude toward religious convention "depended on my mood" (126). The structure that spiritual matters gave family life in Antin's early home is unavoidably lost in the migration.

Antin's nostalgia also centers around memories of her mother, friends, and relatives who formed a female community in the face of patriarchal religious law. We are presented with the image of a mother who had a great deal of economic power and local status; Antin's mother, Hannah Hayye acted as manager of her father's store and was equipped with an extensive education. Despite the secondary roles women customarily played in this world, she imparts to her daughter a sense of belonging and fluency within traditional patriarchal definitions of female identity. For instance, Antin writes of one of her earliest memories that her mother "sang lullabies on lofty themes. I heard the names of Rebecca, Rachel, and Leah as early as the name of father, mother, nurse" (40).

Along with introducing her daughter to the biblical matriarchs, Hannah Hayye introduces Maryashe (Mary's name before passing through the gates at Ellis Island) to the realm of female rituals within Judaism. Attending the *mikveh*, for instance, is characterized by the pleasure and sanctity of sensual experience outside the presence of men. Another of Mary's memories of this female community recalls an occasion of nude swimming, a moment that does not have religious meaning instilled in it; yet, the experience is recounted as occurring at a place that "was sacred." This particular spot, she explains, "belonged to the women" (89). Antin's geography of self includes a number of such important locations, where identity is inscribed through bonds between women, uninhibited by cultural codes designed to silence female expression.

For all her deference to the notion of the melting pot and her own "melt down" within it, then, Antin revives elements of her past with a vigorous memory. She does not allow the history and romance of the American myth to erase a connection to her childhood and its important moments of self-discovery.

Furthermore, just as she speaks out against the discrimination and violence against Jews in Russia, so, too, does she criticize the exploitation of the poor in capitalist America. While her attitude toward "the land of opportunity" is one of gratitude—even at times of worship—Antin questions governmental policy towards immigration, and in doing so she critiques "the sins of untrammelled capitalism" and the ethics of politicians making policy that encourages divisiveness. In *They Who Knock*, she argues against the notion that immigrants take away work from native-born Americans; instead, she points a finger at the uneven distribution of wealth and opportunities created by capitalism and at the travesty of child labor.

It is from personal experience that Antin speaks when she refers to working-class life. Although she is identified as the child in her family most worthy of a complete education, Mary's sisters and brothers all work outside of the home well before they have the chance to finish school, and her father and mother are constantly on the edge of poverty. In *The Promised Land*, on the one hand, Antin embraces the American educational system as a force of transmogrification in her life. On the other hand, she is explicit in her criticism of the limitations placed on even so promising a pupil as herself, for the immigrant student suffers the frustration and pain of leading a double life.

Antin's life in the promised land is not the unified forward motion that a casual reading might suggest; she leads two lives, in and out of the ghetto, and her narrative traverses back and forth over the line between the realm of her aspirations—at school and the Hale Settlement House, where she is befriended by Edward Everett Hale, "The Grand Old Man of Boston"—and the world of her family who lead the lives of working-class immigrants (344). Mary's successes provoke pride, a form of compensation for the Antins' sense of failure, but their position as tenants of the promised land is tenuous: Their apartments become increasingly miserable, and the family becomes increasingly dependent on the children's earnings. As it is depicted in *The Promised Land*, the Antin's adopted home, which they expected to be a locus of "rebirth," becomes less and less capable of renewing life and fulfilling promises.

In the conclusion of the autobiography, Mary's source of renewal and hope is no longer simply America as idea, but the American landscape, in fact, the earth itself. Throughout the book, water imagery figures prominently in Antin's attention to her environment—a river that runs through the Pale, the water in which the women bathe, and, of course, the ocean that divides Mary's past from her future. Her fascination with water's paradoxical powers of continuity and division point to the ocean's symbolic effect: Water exists much like the evolving self in that it is in constant flux, contained only by language that nominates it as existing with a single "body."

During her crossing to America, Antin identifies the ocean as a place where one can hear "all the voices of the world." This description suggests the expansiveness, the multiplicity of experience, to which Antin is drawn. The memoir closes with Mary's pondering her life's meaning after a day at the shore, which she visited in an outing of the Hale House natural history club. She carries with her a jar of ocean water she has collected; she stands on the land where promises of rebirth and conversion are fulfilled, yet she carries along with her the sea and its connection to an earlier self and multivocality. She asks a question about her existence in this closing scene and provides an answer that has little to do with national codes of self and success: "How shall I number the days of my life, except by the stars of the night, except by the salt drops of the sea?" (364). The almost biblical intonation here points to a poetic, transcendentalist vision of the universe and the human place on earth. The processes of a lifetime are perceived in terms of changes and continuities in the physical environment rather than in culturally inscribed measurements of identity.

And yet Antin's jar of sea water is contained; symbolically, this containment implies the restrictions placed on the multiplicity of the immigrant self. The tension evident in the final scene is indicative of the text's subtle ambivalence toward assimilation and its inscriptions of identity. The sea water sealed in a jar has been "adopted"; it is a piece of the ocean that can be transported. However, the jar cannot transport the ocean's tide, its constant evolutions of movement, its "voices." Similarly, Antin's converted self is only one piece of her identity; her autobiography, which speaks from the position of conversion, cannot fully define or describe her life's experience.

SURVEY OF CRITICISM

Mary Dearborn's *Pocahontas's Daughters* contains the most detailed and lengthy discussion to date of Mary Antin's work. Her discussion of Antin's participation in American mythologies of the ethnic woman is insightful; particularly original is her observation that Antin plays the role of "mediator" with her reader. Dearborn's perceptions are limited on one count—her argument that Antin "thoroughly internalized the dominant culture's vision of the ethnic and the foreign . . . *The Promised Land* seems to lack any alternative, protesting voice" (42). While it is true that such a voice is often unavailable, as in the initial passage asserting conversion, Antin's text is more complex than the monolithic pledge of allegiance many critics have considered it.

Allen Guttman's brief mention of Antin in *The Jewish Writer in America* is a case in point. And in an otherwise attentive introduction to the autobiography, "The Youngest of America's children in Mary Antin's *The Promised Land*," Richard Tuerk refers to "the naivete of . . . [Antin's] view that America is the Promised Land" (33). Similarly, Evelyn Avery calls *The Promised Land* a "romantic immigrant view of America" (53), and Sarah Blacher Cohen, in *"The Promised Land*: A Breach of Promise," points to Antin's "eagerness to become assimilated" (34). Steven Rubin provides an alternative reading, concluding that the book reveals "an uncertain relationship between the author's present identity and her past self" (41).

Sally Ann Drucker addresses *The Promised Land* from a historian's perspective and makes a number of valuable comparisons between Antin's life and work and that of Anzia Yezierska and Elizabeth Stern. The most complete biographical study of Antin is written by Sam Bass Warner, Jr., in his historical account of fourteen twentieth-century Bostonians.

NOTE

1. I am indebted to Sam Bass Warner, Jr., for his thorough and thoughtful *Province of Reason*, which is the source of much of the biographical information included here.

BIBLIOGRAPHY

Works by Mary Antin

The Promised Land. New York: Houghton Mifflin, 1912. Reprinted by Princeton University Press, 1969.
"The Lie." *Atlantic Readings Series*. Boston: Atlantic Monthly Press, 1913:177–90.
They Who Knock at Our Gates, A Complete Gospel of Immigration. Boston: Houghton Mifflin, 1914.
"The Soundless Trumpet." *Atlantic Monthly* (May 1937):560–69.
"House of One God." *Common Ground* 1 (Spring 1941):36–42.

Works about Mary Antin

Avery, Evelyn. "Oh My Mishpocha: Some Jewish Women Writers from Antin to Kaplan View the Family." *Studies in American Jewish Literature* 5 (1986):44–53.

Cohen, Sarah Blacher. "Mary Antin's *The Promised Land*: A Breach of Promise." *Studies in American Jewish Literature* 3 (Fall 1977):45–54.

Dearborn, Mary. *Pocahontas's Daughters: Gender and Ethnicity in American Culture.* New York and London: Oxford University Press, 1986.

Drucker, Sally Ann. " 'It Doesn't Say So in Mother's Prayerbook': Autobiographies in English by Immigrant Jewish Women." *American Jewish History* 79.1 (Autumn 1989):55–71.

Guttman, Allen. *The Jewish Writer in America: Assimilation and the Crisis of Identity.* New York and London: Oxford University Press, 1971.

Rubin, Steven J. "Style and Meaning in Mary Antin's *The Promised Land*: A Reevaluation." *Studies in American Jewish Literature* 5 (1986):35–43.

Tuerk, Richard. "The Youngest of America's Children in Mary Antin's *The Promised Land*." *Studies in American Jewish Literature* 5 (1986):29–34.

Warner, Sam Bass, Jr. *Province of Reason*. Cambridge and London: Harvard University Press, 1984.

ANN BIRSTEIN (1927–   )

Ludger Brinker

BIOGRAPHY

In many respects Ann Birstein's childhood was not a typical one for a child born to immigrant Jewish parents in New York in the late twenties. Her father, Bernard Birstein, was an Orthodox rabbi who, despite protests from members of his congregation, resolutely opened a small synagogue on West 47th Street in Manhattan to Broadway actors and transformed it into what came to be widely known as "The Actors Temple." Living in a household that had many personal contacts with Jewish celebrities such as Eddie Cantor and Sophie Tucker while growing up in the Gentile environment of Hell's Kitchen gave Birstein a view of social conflict not often encountered in other Jewish writers' reminiscences of the same period. The tensions between the influences and demands of a strictly religious household and the secular possibilities inherent in living in the middle of Manhattan, Birstein would later successfully explore in her work.

Like many women growing up in an Orthodox household at the time, Birstein was not required to know much about Orthodox ritual and belief other than those functions traditionally performed by women. But thanks to her father's relative worldliness and his respect for her literary abilities even as a teenager, she helped write some of his sermons and blessings. Birstein's formal education was entirely secular. After high school, she majored in English at Queens College where she received a B.A., *magna cum laude*, in 1948. She then did graduate work at the Kenyon School of English and later at the Sorbonne in Paris, but she did not continue because she was already launched on a literary career. While at Queens College, Birstein had been encouraged by one of her advisers to enter a literary competition sponsored by a publishing house and, on the basis of a novel manuscript for which she had precociously written a chapter each week, was awarded the "Dodd Mead Intercollegiate Literary Fellowship." As part of the award, her first novel, *Star of Glass*, was published in 1950.

In addition to *Star of Glass*, Ann Birstein's works include five other novels, *The Troublemaker* (1955), *The Sweet Birds of Gorham* (1966), *Dickie's List*

(1973), *American Children* (1980), and *The Last of the True Believers* (1988), a collection of three novellas published under the title *Summer Situations* (1972), a biography of her father, *The Rabbi on Forty-Seventh Street* (1982), short stories, articles, and reviews published in *The New Yorker, McCall's, Mademoiselle, Vogue,* and *The New York Times Book Review.* She also coedited *The Works of Anne Frank* (1959), served as movie critic for *Vogue* for six years, and published numerous articles, from reminiscences about the Yiddish theater to a travel piece on Hong Kong for *Inside,* a quarterly magazine published by the Jewish Federation of Philadelphia.

Birstein married the critic Alfred Kazin in 1952. Their daughter Cathrael was born in 1955. She devoted herself to being a wife and a mother as well as a writer. But as her fiction documents, Birstein was early involved in the growing women's movement. While the main characters of her novels and stories tend to remain married (Birstein herself was divorced in 1982), her female protagonists grow in self-awareness and independence. Birstein also continued to work as a journalist and as a teacher, teaching creative writing at various colleges and universities, among them the Iowa Writers Workshop. Well known in New York intellectual and artistic circles, she is a member of the English Department of Barnard College; in addition, she founded "Writers on Writing at Barnard," a series of summer workshops for emerging writers, which she has directed since 1987. Currently, Birstein is working on two novels.

MAJOR THEMES

Birstein's technique in her fiction of intensely looking behind the social tapestry makes her an often savagely funny and ironic novelist of manners of the contemporary Jewish urban scene.

Both *Star of Glass* and *The Troublemaker,* Birstein's first two novels, are studies of generational mother-daughter conflicts set against an Eastern European, immigrant, Jewish background, a subject familiar to all readers of American Jewish literature since Anzia Yezierska. Against her parents' wishes, Fay Rosen, the protagonist of *Star of Glass,* begins to work as a secretary in a poor synagogue run by a dictatorial rabbi, and she eventually comes to a clearer understanding of the importance of Judaism in her life. This gradual process of return to traditional religious values occurs despite the fact that both of her immigrant parents consider religion old fashioned and out of date for what they believe is the modern American life-style they have adopted. Their concept of genteel American life is derived more from soap operas than from real firsthand knowledge; the parents are unmasked as stereotypical social climbers, and their foibles are gleefully exposed by Birstein's keen satirical pen. But Fay, learning from the example of a pious older couple who worship at the synagogue, finds the courage to emancipate herself from her scheming mother who wants her to marry a businessman and not waste her life at a religious institution, especially one neither fashionable nor financially stable. It is ironic that the temple rabbi, Jacob Wax, does not himself believe in the religious messages he melodramatically delivers to his congregation. Instead, he uses his position of authority to manipulate people, dominate his wife and younger brother, and aggrandize himself. In the end, Fay stands up to her mother and asserts her independence but loses her chance for a fulfilling relationship with Harry, the rabbi's younger brother, because of the rabbi's unyielding control over all members of his household.

The Troublemaker also emphasizes the conflicts between an Old World mother and the emerging consciousness of her New World daughter, although here the children not the parents are socially pretentious. In addition, the novel allows Birstein to explore various types within the Jewish immigrant community. While the father is a religious man and fund-raiser for a Jewish philanthropic organization; one uncle is a Communist and is not permitted to visit the family; while an aunt timidly wants to break away from the constraints of a traditional Jewish marriage by spending a half-hour daily in a neighborhood café. In the figure of *Zayde*, the mother's invalid father, the theme of generational conflict gains an even greater depth; shipped from one daughter to another, *Zayde* gives the novelist the opportunity to explore intensely the breakdown of traditional family bonds and pieties in the New World.

Despite the fact that both novels are set in Jewish immigrant households, *Star of Glass* in the late forties and *The Troublemaker* in the early forties just before the United States entered World War II, the Holocaust is not mentioned, though it is implicitly present in the background. Only in her fifth novel, *American Children*, published in 1980 but set in 1946-1947, does Birstein return to the parent-child conflict and introduces, in the figure of a distant cousin, Josef, a Holocaust survivor and displaced person. But even though the narrator, Lois Ackerman, is eager for her father, who bears an Old-World grudge against Josef's entire family, to offer Josef a home with them, the survivor's tragic history is far removed from her day-to-day concerns. His history remains in the background, and when he expresses a sexual interest in Lois, he is quickly and unceremoniously dispatched to other relatives and is forgotten.

Star of Glass, *The Troublemaker*, and *American Children* are narratives of emancipation, of the gradual loosening of ties between children and parents— here, specifically between mothers and daughters. The fact that the parents are immigrants and the children consider themselves to be typical Americans makes these works emblematic of an entire genre of American literature; not only is it poignantly Jewish but also entirely American, because such narratives are found in the literature of almost every American ethnic group.

A college novel of another kind, *The Sweet Birds of Gorham*, depicts the one-year tenure of Daisy Lerner—as curious and unconventional as Henry James's Daisy Miller—as writing instructor at Gorham College, the fictional counterpart of an amalgamation of Amherst and Smith colleges. The novel is a savagely funny exposé of the foibles and pretensions of various faculty members at a small, provincial college in the late fifties.

Birstein's other fictions describe marital claustrophobia. Their tone is often one of ironic embitterment, focusing frequently on the pettiness of human interaction even in the most intellectual households. Despite efforts by the frustrated female protagonists to liberate themselves from the strictures of their environment, more often than not their attempts at liberation fail, and they pick up the pieces of their marriages without enthusiasm but also without being able to perceive viable alternatives.

Sandra Baxter, the protagonist of *Dickie's List*, is the emotionally and intellectually unfulfilled wife of a New York quality publishing house editor. There seem to be two major sources for Sandra's never fully articulated discontent: the corruption of publishing by commercial considerations and her family's Jewishness.

The world of publishing houses, where commercial considerations are more important than the willingness to take risks, forms the background of the novel. Sandra—and, one cannot help but suspect, Birstein as well—is shocked that rather than publish an unknown woman's first, and supposedly brilliant, novel, Dickie's house decides to pay a quarter-of-a-million-dollar advance for an unredeemably terrible book that bears an uncanny resemblance to Norman Mailer's *Why Are We in Vietnam*? That this move is a necessary gamble on Dickie's part to keep an important novelist on his list does not occur to Sandra, whose disenchantment turns into a lament about earlier, but never specified, times when, in her opinion, publishing was a vocation and not a business.

Sandra's Jewish background matters to her only when she is in direct personal contact with members of her family. But even then, she wonders, "Why did people assume Jews were warm, when they were only heated?" (161). This comment certainly applies to her mother and her sister Leah. Sandra's relationship with them is fraught with the weight of Jewish history in the United States. Both of these women are "alrightniks" who wanted to become Americanized as soon as possible and, who, like Fay Rosen's mother, wanted to leave Eastern Europe, Judaism, and Jewishness far behind. For both of them Sandra's status, her large Upper West Side apartment with a river view and maid, and her successful marriage, signify that their deprivations on Sandra's behalf have been successful. They cannot understand Sandra's discontent, her boredom. Sandra is not ashamed of her Jewishness, but rather is tired of its claims on her, even though, she thinks, "it seems to be coming back into style" (160). She cannot identify with traditional Judaism but also does not want to deny the fact that she is Jewish. In that respect she is typical of many second-generation American Jewish women of Birstein's generation and background. On the one hand, they were encouraged by the school system as well as by their elders, who were determined to create a better world for their "American children," to strip away most ethnic ties and pieties; on the other hand, they would always be reminded of that ethnic origin by the world at large.

Since neither religion nor ethnicity offers a viable choice for her, Sandra Baxter, instead, becomes a passionate observer of and enthusiastic participant in the social scene, her easygoing manners an asset to her husband's business calculations. Few writers are better equipped to describe Sandra's world than Ann Birstein. The New York literary party in which reputations are made or lost forms the fascinating background against which all actions of *Dickie's List* are set. But what comes through most clearly is a general sense of dullness, a deadly dullness that both repels and fatally attracts Sandra. At the end of the novel, the never-ending literary cocktail party that Sandra's life has consisted of may be over, but the reader is left to guess what kind of life may be in store for her. Birstein does not supply easy answers; a return to traditional Judaism is never envisaged, nor is there a hint that Sandra might identify more strongly with the secular elements of her Jewish heritage. In the end, she is an ethnic-at-large, to borrow Jerre Mangione's phrase, without any particular vision to give meaning to the term.

The New York intellectual scene is explored somewhat differently in *The Last of the True Believers*, which follows the career of the Gentile protagonist, Sunny Mansfield, from budding author to young faculty wife to frustrated middle-aged woman to successful writer. Sunny Mansfield, blonde, blue-eyed, and Protestant, is Birstein's ironic response to writers like Philip Roth and their fictional obsession with the *shikse*. It is only in this novel that the author allows her protagonist to take the final, until then only contemplated but never acted upon, step: divorce. But Sunny's conversion to Judaism does not bring about a discussion of Judaism or its relevance in the characters' lives. Sunny takes her newly found religion seriously, we are told, but her husband does not. The recent return to Jewishness and Judaism, reflected in American Jewish literature, has no place in Birstein's intellectual New York. Birstein herself would say she cannot return because she never left. Her biography of her father, an orthodox New York rabbi, is a celebration of a man of faith.

SURVEY OF CRITICISM

There is a dearth of academic criticism of Birstein's work. To date, no essays on her fiction have been published in scholarly journals, nor has there been any sustained discussion of her work in the context of larger studies of Jewish American literature. The only long essay, Françoise Brousse's published conference contribution, is not on the fiction, but on the Birstein's biography of her father, *The Rabbi on Forty-Second Street*. Thus, any attempt for a systematic critical evaluation must rely solely on book reviews.

Reviews of *Star of Glass*, the winner of the Intercollegiate Literary Fellowship, are mixed. The reviewer for the *New York Herald Tribune Book Review* comments that "the story, frequently funny or touching, seems an honest and thoughtful picture of situations that must be seething in countless new-American homes" ("Tangled Lives" 15). Midge Decter, writing her first review in *Commentary*, despite some reservations, admires the fact that Birstein has created "a new type of rabbi for fiction, and an honest type" (404).

Birstein's second novel, *The Troublemaker*, published five years after *Star of*

Glass, was generally well received and elicited more critical comments than its predecessor. All the reviewers agree that this novel pits Old World attitudes against New World values. For Jane Cobb, the novel presents American Jewish life so faithfully that "one can find the whole family, any time, on any street in New York" (27).

The reception of *The Sweet Birds of Gorham* represents a critical break-through of sorts. Most reviews are longer and more detailed—both in praise and criticism—than those of the first two novels, and critics seem to take Birstein more seriously as an artistic presence to be reckoned with than before. The reviewer for the *Times Literary Supplement* offers comments that "Miss Birstein's weakness is that she does not fully realize where her primary strength is," but offsets this criticism with the comment that the novel is "disarmingly deadpan, but sensitively created" ("Four More" 1178). Most other reviews focus on the work's setting at a fictional New England college and place it in the tradition of the college novel. As such, "the métier, as one of Miss Birstein's academicians might call it, is nicely drawn" (30), comments Martin Levin. The longest and most thoughtful review comes from the pen of Malcolm Bradbury who compares the novel's protagonist, Daisy, to Henry James's heroine of the same name. He concludes that the novel, taken in its entirety, is "intelligent, well-textured, and elegant, an excellent sentimental tale, full of all kinds of sharp observation, and thoroughly pleasing to read" (43).

By the time Birstein published the three novellas "Love in the Dunes," "How I Spent My Summer Vacations," and "When the Wind Blew" under the title *Summer Situations* in 1972, she had become well known in New York academic and intellectual circles. This is reflected in the fact that, within one week, the book was twice reviewed in the *New York Times*, first by Anatole Broyard and then by Sally Beauman in the *New York Times Book Review*. Beauman notes that, "choosing a difficult area to explore—the thin line where aspirations teeter over into pretensions—she creates a world of social and sexual disappointments, where almost all her characters are wryly aware of reality's stubborn refusal to live up to their fantasies and expectations" (7). Diane Johnson agrees and adds that Birstein "may end by being a bit too cheerful and dry, but given the facts of female life and male reviewing, that is probably a sound choice" (12).

The next book, *Dickie's List*, published just one year after *Summer Situations*, received widespread attention. Lois Gould in the *New York Times Book Review* writes that Sandra, the novel's heroine, is "a classic girl-child of the century. Mama raised her to play moon to some Dickie's son. Now, after years of total eclipse, all she wishes is that she could see a little better in the dark" (5). But Gould sees the ending of the novel in a positive light: "Miss Birstein leaves no doubt that for Sandra—and hopefully for many Sandras—the cocktail party is finally over" (5).

Birstein's next two published books, *American Children* and *The Rabbi on Forty-Second Street*, look backward to the world of the author's youth. *American*

Children is a college novel which focuses on the students. Barbara Raskin admires the way in which Birstein adroitly combines the college novel with the "Upper West Side Jewish American Princess (J.A.P.) genre" (B7). Ann Hulbert notes that, traditionally "a WASP-y genre, the ironic collegiate memoir here turns out to be more innocently funny than sophisticatedly mean" (40). All critics concur that Birstein, within the limits she has set herself, has written a successful book. Christopher Lehmann-Haupt is typical when he observes that, "Miss Birstein's tone is light and gently satirical, her mode is picaresque, and she writes with such fluidity that her novel seems to end only moments after it has begun" (C25).

It is, however, Birstein's biography of her father, *The Rabbi on Forty-Second Street*, that has commanded the most overwhelmingly positive critical responses from reviewers. Brousse's scholarly essay describes the book's loving, imaginative reconstruction of the author's father's life in the context of the forces of Americanization and the Jewish experience. American reviewers commend Birstein on the great imaginative powers she brings to her subject. The reviewer for the *New Yorker* sets the tone with the comment that it is a "delightful biography," and that "occasional lapses into the speculation about scenes she could not have witnessed violate only the letter, not the spirit, of biography" ("Books" 142). The most eloquent and thoughtful praise comes from Barbara Grizzuti Harrison who calls the work, "Beautifully written, it's funny, it's a joy to read—and it taught me things that I am glad to know and will be happy to remember" (376). She compares the biography to folklore and myth and concludes that "its uniqueness and specificity are exactly what makes it accessible; the more Birstein's family history differs from mine, the more I recognize myself and my family in her and hers" (376).

Birstein's most recent novel, *The Last of the True Believers*, is a return to the familiar territory of the New York intellectual world. Jennifer Regan lauds the novel for its "eyewitness sensitivity and accuracy," because "it's right up to date in its coverage of the battle of the sexes" (E10). Elaine Kendall maintains that "Birstein revives the familiar saga with style and wit, renews it with wonderfully tart observations on the Eastern literary-academic Establishment" (V14). Kendall's statement, "Though you may know the country, revisiting it can be surprisingly rewarding" (V14), best sums up the critical opinion.

BIBLIOGRAPHY

Works by Ann Birstein

Fiction

Star of Glass. New York: Dodd, Mead, 1950.
The Troublemaker. New York: Dodd, Mead, 1955.
The Sweet Birds of Gorham. New York: McKay, 1966.

Summer Situations. New York: Coward, 1972.
Dickie's List. New York: Coward, 1973.
American Children. New York: Doubleday, 1980.
The Last of the True Believers. New York: Norton, 1988.

Nonfiction

(with Alfred Kazin) *The Works of Anne Frank*. New York: Doubleday, 1959.
The Rabbi on Forty-Second Street. New York: Dial, 1982.

Works about Ann Birstein

Adams, Phoebe. "Potpourri." *Atlantic Monthly* June 1966:138.
Beauman, Sally. "A World of Social and Sexual Disappointments." *New York Times Book Review* 5 March 1972:7ff.
"Books—Briefly Noted." *New Yorker* 26 April 1982: 142.
Bradbury, Malcolm. "Bird's-Eye View." *Reporter* 30 June 1966:40ff.
Brousse, Françoise. "Sois Juif Dans Ta Temeure, Sois Homme Hors De Chez Toi: *The Rabbi on Forty-Second Street*, d'Ann Birstein." *Le Facteur Religieux en Amérique du Nord No 7: Religion et Memoire Ethnique au Canada et aux Etats-Unis*. Ed. Jean Beranger and Pierre Guillaume. Talence: Centre de Recherches Amer. Anglophone. Maison des Sciences de l'Homme d'Acquitaine, 1986. 241–58.
Broyard, Anatole. "Three Misspent Vacations." *New York Times* 28 February 1972:29.
Cobb, Jane. "Cookie's Growing Pains." *New York Times Book Review* 13 February 1955:26–27.
Decter, Midge. "A Rabbi, New Style." *Commentary* October 1950:402–4.
"Four More." *Times Literary Supplement* 15 December 1966:1178.
Gould, Lois. "A Literary Who's Who." *New York Times Book Review* 2 September 1973:4–5.
Harrison, Barbara Grizzuti. "The Rabbi Rejoiced." *Commonweal* 18 June 1982:376–78.
Hulbert, Ann. "Brief Review." *The New Republic* 29 March 1980:40.
Johnson, Diane. "When Is a Book for Women Only?" *Book World* 5 March 1972:12.
Kendall, Elaine. "Portrait of the Artist as a Young Ms." *Los Angeles Times* 2 September 1988:V12ff.
Lehmann-Haupt, Christopher. "Books of the Times." *New York Times* 27 February 1980:C25.
Levin, Martin. "Reader's Report." *New York Times Book Review* 10 April 1966:30.
Price, R.G.G. "A Fitful Backward Glance." *Punch* 28 December 1966:970.
Raskin, Barbara. "Upper West Side Story." *Washington Post Book World* 3 March 1980: B7.
Regan, Jennifer. "A Pot Boiler That's Fit for Public TV." *Buffalo News* 23 October 1988:E10.
"Tangled Lives." *New York Herald Tribune Book Review* 10 December 1950:15.

E. M. BRONER (1930–   )

Ann R. Shapiro

BIOGRAPHY

Born in Detroit to Russian immigrants, Beatrice (Weckstein) and Paul B. Masserman, Esther Masserman grew up in a traditional Jewish family in which, according to Marilyn French, she "suffered from the second-best status often accorded girls" (Introduction, *Weave* xi). When she graduated from high school at sixteen, Broner went to New York but returned to Michigan to attend Wayne State University, where she received her B.A. in 1950 and her M.F.A. in 1962. While in college, she married Robert Broner, with whom she had four children. In 1978, she received her Ph.D. from Union Institute and has taught or has been artist-in-residence at Ohio State University, Tulane/Sophie Newcomb, Oberlin College, UCLA, Columbia University, New York University, CUNY, and Sarah Lawrence College. She has also taught at Haifa University in Israel.

While raising her family and studying, she began writing plays and short stories. In 1967, she published her first verse play, *Summer Is a Foreign Land*. This was followed by a novella and stories, *Journal/Nocturnal and Seven Stories* (1968). She wrote two novels, *Her Mothers* (1975) and *A Weave of Women* (1978), and is currently working on a third novel, *The Repair Shop*. Her interest in writing for the theater is also reflected in the production of several plays and radio scripts, as well as plays in reading.[1] In addition, she and Cathy N. Davidson compiled and edited an anthology of women's writing, *The Lost Tradition: Mothers and Daughters in Literature* (1980). Broner's most recent book to date is *The Telling*, a nonfiction work that includes the coauthored *The Women's Haggadah* and a history of the community of women in New York, which since 1976, has performed a woman's Passover service called the "Third Seder."

Broner has not only written feminist literature, but she has long been a political activist working for peace and for women's issues. In Israel she demonstrated regularly with the Women in Black, an *ad hoc* group of Israeli and Palestinian women against the occupation in the territories and prayed with the Women of the Wall, a group that attempted to hold a service with a Torah reading at the women's part of the Western Wall. In New York, she attends the meetings of the Women's Action Coalition.

She has also been a representative to several international conferences: United Nations Institute for Training and Research, "Creative Women in Changing Societies" (Copenhagen 1980), and the B'nai Brith Women/ADL International Women's Meeting (Paris 1984), where she delivered a keynote address. She was sent to the United Nations' "End of the Decade, Decade of the Woman" (Nairobi 1985); there she articulated a view of the women's movement that runs through much of her fiction and nonfiction: "It [the women's movement] honors the mothers and foremothers in our neglected lineage, and it goes forward into yet unstudied connections" ("The Road to Nairobi" 36).

Besides participating in formal organizations, Broner has tried, alone and with others, to initiate changes in Jewish worship and ceremony so that women can participate equally with men. After the death of her father in 1987, she attempted to say *Kaddish*, a daily ritual required of Jewish sons, who must attend a *minyan*. Because Orthodox Jewish tradition precludes the participation of women in a *minyan*, she was called *zona* [whore] and forced to pray behind a variety of makeshift partitions, but she prevailed, finally earning the respect of several of the congregants (Broner, "Mornings and Mourning: a Kaddish Journal"). Undaunted by the indignities she suffered in her efforts to pray in a small American synagogue, she later joined other Jewish women in Israel to pray at the Western Wall in defiance of the ultra-Orthodox Jews, who responded with physical and verbal abuse because of their belief that women must not have a Torah, stand in a group, or pray audibly. She recently explained, "I am distant from the male-dominated culture, the over-culture, as well as separate from the genderizing of the liturgy of Jewish culture" ("Alienated from the Whole").

Commenting on the publication by Harper SF of *The Telling*, Broner observed, "In the old days when I would read my *Women's Haggadah* to a group, I would be booed—in synagogues, Jewish Centers. Now HarperSF thinks it's hot on the spirituality list. So one goes from being attacked to being admired—but it's taken a while for that to occur" (Letter to the author. 5 July 1992).

MAJOR THEMES

Taken together, Broner's work reveals a Jewish woman's search for a place in an alien patriarchal world. Broner's heroines, like Broner herself, are always seeking a legitimate way to participate in a society where male values prevail and men are valued over women. Underlying the search is a conviction that a woman must establish her matrilineage—her connections to her biological mother and her foremothers—so that she can realize her full humanity. For Broner, it is not women's role to serve men but to stand alongside them in the family, the synagogue, and the secular state and to reform those institutions so that they serve women and men better. But despite her serious concerns, Broner insists "laughter is integral to my art" because through humor we make pain and hatred "ironic and impersonal" ("Broner on Broner" 110, 113).

Broner's earliest published works, *Summer Is a Foreign Land* (1966) and the stories which were collected in *Journal/Nocturnal and Seven Stories* (1968), reflect her dissatisfaction with American Jews, who appear to have lost sight of the spiritual goals of Judaism in the process of assimilation. She describes *Summer Is a Foreign Land* as "a recounting of an exodus in honor of the pioneers who came to Ellis Island and those of their American descendants who chose to make themselves uncomfortable in a comfortable world" (1). The pioneer of the play is Baba, who remembers that she was once a young, strong nurse in Russia, but now is "a nothing in this place/of heated rooms, hot water bottles, no samovars, no walks in my fur cape." She concludes, "I sit in summer in this foreign land" (151). Only Baba's grandson completes the exodus—"the private exodus, where one goes out of the land of bondage whether that be the homeland or the home life" (7). The daughters and granddaughter remain obedient wives and mothers, apparently content to settle for America's eternal "summer." Several years later, Broner would tell an interviewer, "The obedient daughter, the obedient wife, the wife, the obedient citizen. We have to go beyond all that" ("Of Holy Writing" 257). It remained for Broner to write the story of women's escape from bondage in a new women's Haggadah.

The failure of American Jews to realize the promise of the Exodus also pervades the lives of the characters in *Journal/Nocturnal and Seven Stories*. The nameless female protagonist of "Journal/Nocturnal," like Baba, is freed only in dreams. Her life is described in a page divided down the middle, where daytime experience is on the left side of the page and nightime experience is on the right. While the woman is tied to husband, home, children, and community volunteerism in the journal section, in the nocturnal section, she imagines she is Gentile and her lover is a Nazi rapist.

Like "Journal/Nocturnal," the seven stories also deal mainly with empty lives—the spiritual failure, especially of Jews in America. "The New Nobility," which won the O. Henry Prize, is a story of five young men and a woman who are alienated in the 1960s, unable to find meaning in the era of Vietnam and the aftermath of McCarthyism. The female protagonist, horrified by Judge Kaufman, who condemned the Rosenbergs to die, becomes "an anti-Semite" and moves with her husband to the Midwest (259).

Three of the stories, "The Lone Ranger," "The Shva," and "Each Face Extinct," deal with Jewish racist attitudes toward blacks—a racism which suggests that the meaning of the Exodus has been forgotten in America. In "The Enemies," Broner extends her concerns about Jewish racism to Arab–Jewish relations. In that story, a Jewish woman attempts to give business to an Israeli salesman only to learn that he is Arab and not Jewish—that he has, in fact, been the victim of Jews.

Broner's two novels, *Her Mothers* (1975) and *A Weave of Women* (1978), represent sequential stages in her lifelong quest for meaning in women's lives.

Both works are personal and political. In *Her Mothers*, she examines her American and biblical foremothers in an effort to understand the contemporary Jewish woman. Unable to find role models in either the American or the ancient Jewish tradition, Broner created a feminist utopia in *A Weave of Women*.

The title, *Her Mothers*, comes from Virginia Woolf's *A Room of One's Own*: "A woman writing thinks back through her mothers." Broner shares Woolf's belief that women learn to write by reading the writing of other women, that indeed all woman's writing is made possible because of earlier efforts by women. While Broner appropriates Woolf's reference to "her mothers" to mean what Woolf intended, she also means more. The mothers of Broner's novel include Beatrix Palmer, who is searching for her daughter and also for her past. This lost past consists of her own women classmates and her foremothers in nineteenth-century American literature and the Old Testament. Beatrix is frustrated in her search because role models are absent, much of the record is lost, and what remains is a history of exploitation and lies. The novel laments what Broner would later call women's "neglected lineage" ("Road to Nairobi" 36).

But *Her Mothers* is also the search for the missing daughter—a search that would occupy Broner again in *A Weave of Women* and in the anthology she edited with Cathy Davidson, *The Lost Tradition: Mothers and Daughters in Literature*. In all three works, Broner was exploring variations of the Demeter/Persephone myth, the story of the earth mother who loses her daughter.[2] According to Broner, the "intent is to make a new mythos, a search like the *Odyssey*, only mother searching daughter" (Letter to the author. 10 December 1992). The search for the daughter proves more satisfying than the search through history. If the past was bleak, the future still holds promise. Not only does Beatrix find her daughter, but her daughter is pregnant with a baby girl, thus providing the connections to the future that Beatrix could not find in the past. Beatrix's lifelong quest ends with an image of a baby girl, singing because she is finally unafraid, an idea which Broner would later develop in *A Weave of Women*. At the end of *Her Mothers*, *Unafraid Women*, clearly the fictional name for *A Weave of Women*, is yet to be published. Since Broner, like Beatrix, has learned from her mothers only a history of defeat, she will need to create a better society in the future. And that society is depicted in *A Weave of Women*.

The loosely connected events in *Weave* are told by multiple female voices because, as Broner explains elsewhere, "There is no chief story teller of women's history—we make history together" ("Of Holy Writing" 269). She describes the prose style used here and in her earlier works, "Journal/Nocturnal" and *Her Mothers*, as "an elegiac style, almost a kind of Homeric prose to suggest a search, a holy pilgrimage, an enlargement of woman and her pain, her search, her triumphs—when at last they come" ("Of Holy Writing" 255).

Thematically, *A Weave of Women* forms a continuum with the earlier works which depict past abuse of women. While the past is often recalled in *Weave*, the novel creates a new world where women support each other. Broner explains, "the women are finally housed, the generations responsible for one another, making family together" (Letter to the author. 10 December 1992).

By the time she published *Weave*, Broner was already engaged in creating new feminist rituals with other women in New York, Los Angeles, and Israel. In explaining the importance of ritual, she wrote, "Ritual displays cultural authority. . . . The patriarchal world would remove woman from ritual ("Honor and Ceremony" 235). Broner's object in *A Weave of Women* is to create a women's community, not in the New Jerusalem, as America was once called, but in ancient Jerusalem, in Israel, the place of birth and rebirth. There, women from several nations representing diverse religions and social backgrounds gather in order to create a feminist utopia unencumbered by preconceptions of a patriarchal culture. The community is held together by women's rituals that underscore important events in the women's lives. While some of these rituals are new, others are variations on existing Jewish ritual so that women are included, as they are not included in traditional Judaism. In creating this ritual, Broner is, in effect, embracing the *midrashic* tradition, a tradition of Jewish storytelling which adds new stories to those of the past as a way of creating continuity—a continuity which traditional Judaism has provided mainly for men. In the end, the community of women is disbanded but not destroyed. The image that closes the novel is the "caravan of women that encircles the outskirts of the city . . . our mothers of the desert" (294). If the promised land has still not been attained, there is, nonetheless, affirmation in the continuing exodus of women seeking freedom from past bondage.

Broner's most recently published work includes autobiographical short stories and personal essays written out of the pain of watching her mother become increasingly debilitated before she died, leaving her daughter a legacy of memories to make palpable through writing.

For the last six years, Broner has also been writing *The Repair Shop*, a novel that expands on the Jewish notion, *tikkun*. A young woman rabbi and a group of street people bring what Broner calls "magic and reality" to the city in order to fight evil. While men are lovers, mentors, or aids (some are the auxiliary police), it is the activist women, led by the rabbi, who provide sanctuary and hope.

SURVEY OF CRITICISM

Journal/Nocturnal and Seven Stories received mixed reviews, especially the title story, which impressed some critics and irritated others. James R. Frakes, writing in the *New York Times*, praised "Journal/Nocturnal" for "wit, honest poignancy, psychological accuracy, a daring attempt to combine the ancient subject of adultery with contemporary issues," but he complained about the form as "presenting a problem in reading skills that not even McLuhan has considered." He found Broner's "striking talents" better illustrated in the short stories, citing "The Enemies," "The Schva," and "The New Nobility" (56).

Adele Z. Silver, in the *Saturday Review*, praised the "supple style" and the handling of poetic images in *Journal/Nocturnal* but found "the topicality of the plot and the irritating namelessness of its characters smother the story's real artistic interest." She preferred some of the shorter stories and cited Broner's individual gifts as "imagery, sympathy, an obliqueness of vision" (66). Only Elizabeth Dalton, writing for *Commentary*, was unequivocal in her praise for *Journal/Nocturnal*, where for her the style and language work to convey the emotional crisis of the protagonist (69–74).

Her Mothers earned the praise of Leah Napolin, who reviewed it for *Ms.*, as a "bitter, fearless, and uproariously funny work" (105–06). Scholar Cathy Davidson pointed out, "Like Broner's other works, *Her Mothers* is a technically ingenious book" (27).

The most extended published discussion of Broner's early works is found in Rose Yalow Kamel's *Aggravating the Conscience*, in which Kamel makes a case for Broner as a major writer of Jewish American women's literature defining the genre together with Anzia Yezierska, Tillie Olsen, and Grace Paley.

With *A Weave of Women*, Broner finally attracted the interest of both literary critics and scholars. While Jane Larkin Crain, writing in the *New York Times Book Review*, complained that *Weave* was "stuffed with all the cant of contemporary sexual politics" (26), other critics and scholars have been impressed by its technical innovation and its development of Jewish feminist themes. John Leonard declared in the *New York Times*, " 'A Weave of Women' is an astonishment. E. M. Broner seeks nothing less than to achieve a kind of epic poem, a recapitulation of the rhythms of female consciousness" (C6). And Sheila Schwartz and Nancy Lynn Schwartz declared *Weave* is "an extraordinary novel . . . which should become a classic" (481–82).

Cathy N. Davidson and Ann R. Shapiro found in *Weave* a work that demands our attention because it breaks new ground both in style and content. Davidson calls the novel "a technically innovative work, written in prose but also by turns poetic, lyrical and dramatic" (28). Shapiro was especially impressed with Broner's exploration of secular American feminism and feminist Judaism to create a unique literary work that defies genre specifications. The women's voices not only rage at the patriarchal world, but they also sing harmoniously in the new world they attempt to create.

NOTES

1. She has had her play, *The Body Parts of Margaret Fuller* (1976), produced at Wayne State University Hilberry Theater, and has been playwright-in-residence at McCarter Theatre, Princeton, New Jersey. In addition, she had plays in reading at the 92nd Street Y in New York: *Letters to My TV Past*, a one-act, and the two-act, *The Olympics*. She has also had *Half-a-Man* in reading at the Los Angeles Theatre Works and at the Center Players in Detroit. Two produced radio scripts for National Public Radio are *Above the Timber Line* and *The Cousins*.

2. See Broner's interpretation of the Demeter/Persephone myth in the introduction to *The Lost Tradition: Mothers and Daughters in Literature*, p. 2 and in her interview with Nancy Jo Hoy, pp. 254–55.

BIBLIOGRAPHY

Works by E. M. Broner

In addition to the works listed below, Broner has written religious ceremonies, unpublished plays (see Note 1) and a variety of reviews and articles.

Fiction

Summer Is a Foreign Land (play). Detroit: Wayne State University Press, 1966.
Journal/Nocturnal and Seven Stories. New York: Harcourt, Brace, 1968.
Her Mothers. Bloomington: Indiana University Press, 1975.
A Weave of Women. Bloomington: Indiana University Press, 1978.
"Carefree Hours." *Frontiers: A Journal of Womens Studies* 12.2 (1991):130–36.
"My Mother's Madness." *Ms.* July–Aug. 1991:49–54.
"Song." *The North American Review* September 1991:28–32.
The Repair Shop. Forthcoming.

Selected Nonfiction

"Broner on Broner: The Writing of Humor, or a Funny Thing Happened to Me on the Way to a Tragedy." *Regionalism and the Female Imagination* 3 (1977–78):110–19.
With Cathy Davidson. eds. *The Lost Tradition: Mothers and Daughters in Literature*. New York: Ungar, 1980.
"Honor and Ceremony in Women's Rituals." *The Politics of Women's Spirituality: Essays on the Rise of Spiritual Power within the Feminist Movement*. Ed. Charlotte Spretnak. Garden City, NY: Anchor, 1982. 234–44.
Interview with Nancy Jo Hoy. "Of Holy Writing and Priestly Voices." *Massachusetts Review* 24(1983):254–69.
"The Road to Nairobi." *Moment* Nov. 1984:35–39.
"The Four Questions of Women." *Ms.* April 1985:54–56.
"The Nairobi Difference." *Moment* Oct. 1985:24–27ff.
"Mornings and Mourning: A Kaddish Journal." *Tikkun* Sept.–Oct. 1989:19–22ff.
"The Playpen of the Patriarchs: Why We Need a Conference on the Empowerment of Jewish Women. *Lilith* (Spring 1989):35.
"Ghost Stories." *Tikkun* Nov.–Dec. 1990:82–83.
"Alienated from the Whole and Separated from the Part" (Bordeaux: University of Michel Montaigne, 1992).
Letter to the author. 5 July 1992.
Letter to the author. 10 December 1992.
The Telling. San Francisco: HarperSanFrancisco, 1992.

Works about E. M. Broner

Crain, Jane Larkin. "Three Novels: 'A Weave of Women.' " *New York Times Book Review* 13 Aug. 1978:26.

Dalton, Elizabeth. "Books in Review: 'Journal/Nocturnal and Seven Stories.' " *Commentary* Apr. 1969:69–74.

Davidson, Cathy N. "E. M. Broner" in *Twentieth-Century American-Jewish Fiction Writers*. Ed. Daniel Walden. *Dictionary of Literary Biography*. Detroit: Gale, 1984:26–28.

Duncan, Erika. "The Hungry Jewish Mother." *The Lost Tradition: Mothers and Daughters in Literature*. Eds. Cathy N. Davidson and E. M. Broner. New York: Ungar, 1980. 231–41.

Frakes, James R. "Density Clarified: 'Journal/Nocturnal.' " *New York Times Book Review*, 29 Sept. 1968:56.

Kamel, Rose Yalow. *Aggravating the Conscience: Jewish-American Literary Mothers in the Promised Land*. New York: Peter Lang, 1988. 151–184.

Leonard, John. "Books of the Times: 'A Weave of Women.' " *New York Times*, 25 July 1978:C6.

Napolin, Leah. "Demons Tweaking Her Funny Bone." *Ms.* July 1976:105–06.

Schwartz, Sheila, and Nancy Lynn Schwartz. "The House of Women." *Nation* 14 Nov. 1978:481–82.

Shapiro, Ann R. "The Novels of E. M. Broner: A Study in Secular Feminism and Feminist Judaism." *Studies in American Jewish Literature* Spring 1991:93–103.

Silver, Adele Z. "Parched Souls and Full Hearts." *Saturday Review* 23 November 1968: 66.

ROSELLEN BROWN (1939–   )

Karen Wilkes Gainey

BIOGRAPHY

Rosellen Brown, author of four novels, numerous short stories, and two books of poetry, was born on May 12, 1939, in Philadelphia, the daughter of David and Blossom Lieberman Brown. Brown's parents left Philadelphia only a few weeks after her birth, the first in a series of moves during her childhood. Brown suggests that her preoccupation with "those who belong somewhere" and "those that don't" may have come from feeling like "the new girl a few times too often, and being a little too shy to do it very well" (Interview with Pearlman, 105). She continues, "Add to the mix the fact that we've lived in places where being Jewish, in search of a Jewish community at the same time we've wanted to belong to the community at large, has added layers of discomfort and isolation, and you've got good grounds for a persistent if modest itch of alienation" (Interview with Pearlman, 105).

Brown grew up in what she calls a very "assimilated" Jewish family; the family was not observant, did not attend synagogue, and neither of her brothers had a *bar mitzvah*. Brown remembers, however, that they were very conscious of their Jewish heritage; she stresses the strong sense of Jewish social justice that her parents instilled in her and her brothers and their frequent discussion of "Jewish issues and questions." Brown recalls that her mother insisted on a "white tablecloth and candles" on Friday nights, a practice her mother believes resulted in Brown and her brothers marrying Jews. Brown acknowledges that she has become more observant since her marriage to Marvin Hoffman in 1963. She remembers being reluctant when her husband wanted to celebrate Passover soon after they were married, but she acquiesced, even to acquiring a set of special dishes and utensils, and found that she actually enjoyed the rituals (Telephone interview).

Brown received a B.A. in English from Barnard College in 1960 and an M.A. in English and American Literature from Brandeis University in 1962. While at Brandeis, Brown was a Woodrow Wilson Fellow and was subsequently asked by the Wilson Foundation to help start Honors programs in disadvantaged colleges—mostly black schools in the South. She and Hoffman, a psychology teacher, accepted the offer and taught at Tougaloo College in Mississippi from 1965–67, an experience that provided material for several of her books. *Some Deaths in the Delta* (1970), a book of social-protest poems set in Mississippi, is obviously based on that experience. Brown has acknowledged that Gerda, the leading character of *The Autobiography of My Mother* (1976), was based on one of her colleagues at Tougaloo, Ernst Borinski, a German Jewish immigrant who had fled Germany in 1938, leaving his family behind. These years in the South during the Civil Rights movement also fostered her interest in portraying everyday life in the midst of extraordinary pressures and led her directly to write *Civil Wars* (1984), her novel about a white family living in a black neighborhood in Jackson, Mississippi, in 1979, fifteen years after their intense involvement in the Civil Rights movement.

After the experience at Tougaloo, Brown and Hoffman returned to New Hampshire, where they raised their daughters; Brown also taught during these years at the Bread Loaf Writer's Conference and Goddard College in Vermont, and at Boston University. Because few Jews lived nearby in New Hampshire, Brown remembers feeling "different," "outside," and somehow "special." Hoffman became the center of the small Jewish community that did exist, teaching children Hebrew songs and rituals. In her latest novel, *Before and After* (1992), Brown uses an actual comment made to her husband by a Jewish New Hampshire neighbor to indicate her characters' ambiguous position as a Jewish family in a rural New Hampshire community: "if everything went well, we'd never hear about it [being Jewish]. But if anything ever went wrong . . . " (211). In search of greater diversity and a larger Jewish community for their teenage daughters, Brown and Hoffman moved in 1982 to Houston, where they became affiliated with a synagogue. Since then, Brown has found her increasing engagement with Jewish ritual and thought "enthralling," and is even considering a *bat mitzvah*. She enjoys the religious and cultural observances, including the discipline of observing the Sabbath. She says it helps her remember that she's "not indispensable," but asserts that she views Judaism more as a "religion of actions" for social justice than beliefs (Telephone interview).

Since moving to Houston in 1982, Brown has taught in the Creative Writing Program at the University of Houston, but she and her husband continue to spend their summers in New Hampshire. Her numerous awards include two National Endowment for the Humanities creative writing grants and a Guggenheim Fellowship. In 1984, she was named *Ms.* Woman of the Year for examining important contemporary issues in her fiction.

MAJOR THEMES

The Jewish commitment to social justice has influenced most of Brown's work, which blends a concern for social issues with the daily domestic lives of her characters. Her first book of poems, *Some Deaths in the Delta* (1970), reveals the feelings of individuals caught up in the terrors of the Civil Rights movement in Mississippi and the reflections of a woman who moves back to Brooklyn, New York, after being in Mississippi. Brown's next work, a collection of stories called *Street Games* (1974), portrays the inhabitants of a block in Brooklyn rather than in Mississippi, but the issues remain those of race, class, and gender. These stories, like the poems of *Some Deaths in the Delta*, are filled with suffering, disaster, and the details of daily life—coming home to find a burglar going through one's jewelry, the distress of a hyperactive child, unsuccessful attempts to rehabilitate the neighborhood.

Brown's first novel, *The Autobiography of My Mother* (1976), concentrates on the suffering of one family, Gerda Stein, a seventy-two-year-old civil liberties lawyer who places rationality above all else, and her overly-dependent daughter Renata, who moves back to her mother's house at the age of twenty-nine with her small daughter, Tippy. Because she always wanted independence for her daughter, Gerda never nurtured Renata, who, consequently, feels deprived and angry and now demands the nurturing her mother refuses to give. The novel records the daily stresses in Gerda's and Renata's relationship and the events leading, ultimately, to Tippy's death. The child drowns in a waterfall because her grandmother does not hold her hand as they walk along a trail while on a picnic. Brown suggests with this catastrophic ending that no amount of public success—even for righting wrongs done to strangers, as Gerda has done—can substitute for successful family relationships.

Brown says that *Cora Fry* (1977), a series of poems filled with the carefully observed details of one woman's daily life, was written in direct relationship to *The Autobiography of My Mother*, as a "respite from all that exaggeratedly rational thought" (Interview with Hammond 119). The title character of these connected poems feels isolated even though she has a husband and two children. Brown's exploration of the individuality of her characters and their frequent isolation even in the midst of busy families carries over into her subsequent novels, *Tender Mercies* (1978), *Civil Wars* (1984), and *Before and After* (1992).

One manifestation of Brown's emphasis on individual consciousness is her use of multiple narrators. Each of her novels incorporates the perspectives of more than one character: In *The Autobiography*, she alternates Gerda's and Renata's point of view from chapter to chapter; in *Tender Mercies*, the story of a marriage in the aftermath of a terrible boat accident which left the wife a quadriplegic because of her husband's carelessness, Dan's linear narrative is juxtaposed with the crippled Laura's interior monologues; in *Civil Wars*, the protagonist's perspective is frequently interrupted by excerpts from her niece's diary; and in her most recent novel, *Before and After*, the mother, father, and sister of a teenager accused of murdering his girlfriend take turns telling their versions of the story. Brown explains the "double points of view in all the novels" as her way of illustrating that "we don't see ourselves as others see us . . . there is no single truth about anyone" (Interview with Walker 153).

In each of these novels, Brown uses a particular disaster to subject the families to unusual pressure—a boat accident in *Tender Mercies*, an auto accident that forces an orphaned niece and nephew to move in with the Carll family in *Civil Wars*, and a brutal murder the Reisers' son allegedly commits in *Before and After*. Each trauma affects individual family members differently, and the novels focus attention on the soul-searching and self-examination each character undergoes as a result while also highlighting their intense scrutiny of family members. In all the novels, however, the families survive the various traumas—changed, indeed, but still intact.

The pressures her characters encounter require readjustments—to death, accidents, and changed relationships, surely, but also to political and social ideals gone awry. In an interview with Melissa Walker, Brown reveals her fascination with "the conflict between ideology in a pure form and the messy details of everyday life" (1952). Teddy Carll, of *Civil Wars*, whom Brown says is "in love with his own vision of himself" as a hero of the Civil Rights movement (Interview with Walker 154), now feels diminished in his role as book salesman and ordinary husband and father. Because he lives with an ideal vision not only of himself, but also with how he believes relations between the races should be, he finds it very difficult to accommodate the actual needs of his family for a larger home when those needs necessitate a move away from the black neighborhood that is the only remaining emblem of his ideal self.

When she is questioned about the influence Judaism has had on her fiction, Brown is careful to point out that authors write out of their "whole selves," not just the part that is Jewish or female, for example, so that some of their books may concern Jewishness or issues of concern to women while others may not (Telephone interview). In fact, several of Brown's families are Jewish, but she does not overemphasize their backgrounds. In *The Autobiography of My Mother*, Gerda Stein has a sense of Jewish history, but the book is not about Jewish ideology; *Cora Fry* and *Tender Mercies*, however, have no Jewish characters. Jessie of *Civil Wars* is Jewish, but little attention is paid to her background; only Jessie's feeling of displacement in the South seems a result of her heritage. Brown has said that it would not have been appropriate to emphasize the Jewishness of those who were active in Mississippi because Jews were not in the majority there; far more of the activists, she notes, were ministers' children who had come to put the lessons of their fathers' sermons into action (Telephone interview).

The Jewish heritage of her characters is more important in Brown's latest book. The Reisers of *Before and After* are Jews living in rural New Hampshire, wondering how much they are accepted by their neighbors. Though conscious of their heritage, the Reisers' current "religious" practice consists of special placemats on Friday nights. Their son Jacob had both a *brit* [ritual circumcision] and *bar mitzvah*, but at seventeen, after being accused of murder, he wonders whether his parents pray. Jewish custom does affect the plot of this novel, however. When Ben Reiser is called before the Grand Jury to testify about his son's actions, his own father's example convinces him to remain silent, causing him to spend six months in jail for contempt. Ben is comforted by a rabbi who tells him that he is justified by the Jewish practice of a father's silence on the subject of his son.

One suspects that as Brown becomes more involved in Jewish ritual herself, her characters may reflect a similar increasing commitment to Judaism. The novel on which Brown is currently at work has an historical Jewish content and a concentrated exploration of Jewish life. Under the working title of "The Angel of Forgetfulness," the new book concerns a group of Russian Jews who settle in New Hampshire. A primary difficulty of the book, which Brown confesses has been "in the drawer for a while," is how one can "reconstruct history for people whose history has been destroyed" (telephone interview).

SURVEY OF CRITICISM

Some Deaths in the Delta (1970) has been praised as a collection of generally effective poems of social protest based on Brown's experience in Mississippi. Margaret Wimsatt suggests that they might have been subtitled "The Impact of the Deep South on a Nice Barnard Girl," perhaps reacting to the book's obviously autobiographical persona—a woman from the North observing and attempting to assimilate what she sees in Mississippi. *Street Games* (1974), Brown's collection of stories about people living on one block in Brooklyn, has received mixed reviews. Critics have generally praised Brown's depiction of everyday lives but have disliked the sometimes forced symbolism and the frequent catastrophes. Jean Strouse praises these stories "about class and sex and race" for not being "politically rhetorical or didactic." Strouse notes that they are effective because "Brown is interested not in misery or blame or histrionics, but in everyday life" (40).

The Autobiography of My Mother (1976) has received more extensive critical attention than Brown's other texts, perhaps because of its focus on the mother-daughter relationship. Most critics dislike the novel's unlikable main characters but admire Brown's detailed evocation of the two women. Anatole Broyard's comment is typical, describing Gerda as one who loves principles rather than people, and her daughter as a "parody of every psychoanalytic theory of rebellion, a negative parasite that hates what it feeds on."

Laurie Stone praises the book's humor and its accumulation of facts and details, while Anne Lake Prescott appreciates Brown's subtle portrayal of family patterns. Eve Ottenberg emphasizes the psychological warfare that takes place between Gerda and Renata, who feel a mixture of love and hate for each other. Noting that the title seems to merge two separate identities into one, Ottenberg praises Brown's "ability to crystallize the delicate interconnections of love and identity" (22). Merla Wolk analyzes the mother-daughter relationship in *The Autobiography* as the negative "underside" of Nancy Chodorow's theory that "women, as mothers, produce daughters with mothering capacities and the desire to mother." Brown's novel, Wolk suggests, illustrates the converse—bad mothers also "reproduce themselves cyclically," with each generation's failure to mother blamed on the previous generation's failure. Wolk asserts that "conflicts over separation [of daughter from mother] impinge on the social and political scenes of the novel" (164–65).

Dee Seligman concentrates on the Jewishness of the mother-daughter conflict in *The Autobiography of My Mother*, pointing to Gerda's rejection of Judaism and its stereotypical Jewish mother image—an image Gerda interprets as one of passive victimization. Instead, she takes on the role of the Jewish male, and as a civil liberties lawyer, substitutes the Constitution for the *Tanach*, the Jewish Bible. Because Gerda rejects a maternal role, her "sense of self is narrowed to an incomplete and fragmented woman," (116) and she passes on to Renata the credo that "women are victims who will inevitably suffer if they depend on religion to bring them solace or respite." Seligman suggests that Gerda's own experiences of pain and suffering (and witnessing her mother's suffering) caused her own numbness to the experience of love. Ironically, Gerda recognizes too late the sustaining power of the mother-daughter bond that has strengthened Jewish women even in the midst of pain and suffering (121).

Responses to *Cora Fry* (1977) have been mixed. Rochelle Ratner finds the poems effective because Brown describes a "persona close to herself" and because the poems are subtle. Mary Kinzie, however, brands some of the poems "foolish." Responding to one reviewer's complaint about the poems' interdependence, Brown suggests this quality is the essence of the book. In an interview with Karla Hammond, Brown asserts that "the very point of the book [is] to take a woman's experience and see how it is kaleidoscopic, how every tiny piece of her life can be set against another and made to create the illusion of the whole life. The greatest pleasure of writing a book-length narrative like this . . . is those repetitions" (119).

Tender Mercies (1978) has received positive critical response for its portrayal of Dan's awkwardness and desperation as he tries to deal for the first time with the daily problems associated with his quadriplegic wife Laura and her brilliant monologues that convey what it means to be quadriplegic. Critics have also praised Brown's evocation of the guilt felt by a husband whose carelessness caused his wife's paralysis.

Brown's representation of the tensions of the Carll family in *Civil Wars* (1984) has received similar praise; critics appreciate her skillful blending of racial issues and family traumas. Lynne Sharon Schwartz praises the risks Brown takes in *Civil Wars*: "It dares to be about ideals and the perils awaiting those committed to them, and it dares to dwell on the most quotidian of matters, with critical scenes taking place in the kitchen and the family car. It directly confronts the sorely ambivalent position of a white family enmeshed in the fight for black people's rights."

Nancy Porter discusses *Civil Wars* in the context of an analysis of women's interracial friendships in civil rights novels. Porter concentrates on the relationship between Jessie and her neighbor Andrea, an "idealized super black woman" (259). Porter asserts that Brown takes for granted the possibility that "black and white women of good will and common interests and experience may be friends" (260), but that her idealization of Andrea may signal "white guilt."

The reviews of *Before and After* (1992) have been very positive. It has been called Brown's best book, with a plot line as spellbinding as a mystery novel.

BIBLIOGRAPHY

Works by Rosellen Brown

In addition, short stories appear in *O. Henry Prize Stories* 1972, 1973, 1976 and *Best American Stories* 1975, 1979. Brown's travel writings and her reviews of contemporary fiction and children's books appear frequently in the *New York Times* and in other publications.

Fiction and Poetry

Some Deaths in the Delta and Other Poems. Amherst: University of Massachusetts Press, 1970.
Street Games. New York: Doubleday, 1974.
The Autobiography of My Mother. New York: Doubleday, 1976.
Cora Fry. New York: Norton, 1977.
Tender Mercies. New York: Knopf, 1978.
Civil Wars. New York: Knopf, 1984.
The Rosellen Brown Reader: Selected Poetry and Prose. Hanover, NH: University Press of New England, 1992.
Before and After. New York: Farrar, Straus, Giroux, 1992.

Nonfiction

Additional nonfiction is published in *The Rosellen Brown Reader.*

[et.al.], eds. *The Whole Word Catalogue: Creative Writing Ideas for Elementary and Secondary Schools,* rev. ed. New York: Teachers and Writers Collective, 1972, 1975.
Interview with Karla Hammond. *Chicago Review* 33.3 (Winter 1983):117–25.
Interview with Melissa Walker. *Contemporary Literature* 27.2 (1986):145–59.
"Rosellen Brown." With Mickey Pearlman. *Inter/View: Talks with America's Writing Women.* Eds. Mickey Pearlman and Katherine Usher Henderson. University Press of Kentucky, 1990. 103–110.
Telephone Interview. 29 Sept. 1992.

Works about Rosellen Brown

Broyard, Anatole. "Questioning the Questions." *New York Times* 26 May 1976:37.
Craig, Patricia. "Cripples." *New Statesman* 13 July 1979:62–63.

Crain, Jane Larkin. Rev. of *Street Games*. *Saturday Review/World* (29 June 1974):19.

Epstein, Joseph. "Is Fiction Necessary?" *The Hudson Review* 29.4 (Winter 1976–77): 593–604.

Gornick, Vivian. "The '60's Are Over." *Village Voice* (19 June 1984):47.

Horn, Carole. Rev. of *Tender Mercies*. *Washington Post Book World* 18 November 1978. B6.

Hulbert, Ann. "In Struggle," *New Republic* (7 May 1984):37–40.

Kinzie, Mary. "What Are You Doing Up There in Those Grapes?" *Parnassus* 7 (Fall–Winter 1978):96–116.

Lehmann-Haupt, Christopher. Rev. of *Tender Mercies*. *New York Times* 24 November 1978:C25.

McManus, Jeanne. "Mississippi Breakdown." *Washington Post Book World* 27 May 1984:9ff.

Oates, Joyce Carol. Rev. of *Tender Mercies*. *New York Times Book Review* 10 December 1978.

Ottenberg, Eve. Rev. of *The Autobiography of My Mother*. *Christian Science Monitor* (16 August 1976):22.

Porter, Nancy. "Women's Interracial Friendships and Visions of Community in *Meridian, The Salt Eaters, Civil Wars*, and *Dessa Rose*." *Tradition and the Talents of Women*. Ed. Florence Howe, Urbana: University of Illinois Press, 1991. 251–67.

Prescott, Anne Lake. "Rock-a-Bye Mamas." *Village Voice* (21 June 1976):43.

Ratner, Rochelle. Rev. of *Cora Fry*. *Library Journal* (15 March 1977):713.

Schwartz, Lynne Sharon. "End of a Movement, End of a Marriage." *New York Times Book Review* 6 May 1984:15.

Seligman, Dee. "Jewish Mothers' Stories: Rosellen Brown's *The Autobiography of My Mother*." *Mother Puzzles: Daughters and Mothers in Contemporary American Literature*. Ed. Mickey Pearlman. Westport: Greenwood, 1989. 115–22.

Stone, Laurie. Review of *Autobiography of My Mother*. *New York Times Book Review* 20 June 1976:7.

Strouse, Jean. "Crimeless Victims." *Ms.* 3 (September 1974):40–41.

Wimsatt, Margaret. Rev. of *Some Deaths in the Delta*. *Commonweal* 96 (10 March 1972): 22.

Wolk, Merla. "Uncivil Wars: The Reproduction of Mother-Daughter Conflict and Rosellen Brown's *Autobiography of My Mother*." *American Imago* 45.2 (Summer 1988):163–85.

HORTENSE CALISHER (1911–)

Marcia Littenberg

BIOGRAPHY

Hortense Calisher was born in New York City on December 20, 1911. The daughter of Joseph Henry Calisher, a manufacturer whose family had been established in Richmond, Virginia, since the 1820s, and Hedwig Lichstern Calisher, a German immigrant of the early 1900s. Calisher grew up in a comfortable, middle-class Jewish family, enlivened and extended by frequent visits from relatives and family friends. The often-conflicting values of her paternal Southern roots and her mother's Old World traditions continue to provide Calisher with themes, characters, situations, and questions about Jewish and American identity that she explores in her fiction and autobiographies. Both sides of her family were proudly Jewish, although neither would fully accept the other's ethical or social worth. Add to this ongoing debate a household packed with talkers and storytellers, and it is not surprising that Calisher developed her love of words, a keen interest in the psychology of character, and her characteristic subtle irony.

As Calisher explains in her first autobiographical work, *Herself* (1972), her position as an assimilated, middle-class American Jewish writer excluded her from the *Yiddishkeit* tradition that grew out of the immigrant experience. Instead, Calisher attempted to find her own voice, one that would reflect her own experience and heritage. Calisher found her subject in the self-questioning and conflicts of characters, many of whom are second-, third-, or fourth-generation Jews whose comfortable and seemingly secure social status led to different problems of identity and conscience. Her Jewish American female sensibility is central to Calisher's style, which reflects the complex inner life and social world of her characters.

Calisher graduated from Barnard College in 1932 as a philosophy major. Her first job was as a sales clerk at Macy's; she also worked temporarily as a model before she took a position as a social worker with the Department of Public Welfare from 1933 to 1934. Her job included responsibility for distributing and assessing the need for emergency relief in New York's tenements.

Calisher was married in 1935 to Heaton Bennet Heffelfinger, an engineer. He was, Calisher notes, the only member of his graduating class to get immediate employment. They moved to upstate New York, the setting of many of Calisher's early *New Yorker* stories, which also draw upon her increasing dissatisfaction with suburban domesticity. Calisher had two children, a daughter, Bennet, and a son, Peter, before her marriage to Heffelfinger ended in divorce in 1958.

Calisher began writing stories in 1948, drawing extensively at first on autobiographical material and later writing stories that explore the self- doubts and moral questioning of imagined characters. Many of these early stories appeared first in the *New Yorker*; they were later collected and published in one volume in 1951. Calisher won critical acclaim for this first volume of short stories, *In the Absence of Angels* (1951).

In 1952 and 1955, Calisher received a Guggenheim Fellowship in creative writing. Two works were nominated for the National Book Award, *False Entry*, in 1961, and *Herself*, in 1973. She has also received awards from the National Council of Arts and the American Academy of Arts and Letters.

In 1956–57 Calisher returned to Barnard College as an Adjunct Professor of English, where she taught creative writing and literature. In 1957 she took a position as Visiting Lecturer at University of Iowa, Iowa City. She then taught at Stanford University, where she met and married the writer Curtis Harnack in 1959. She finally returned to New York in 1959–60.

In 1958 Calisher was awarded an American Specialist Grant from the Department of State to lecture in Southeast Asia. Many of her experiences from this tour are recorded in *Herself* (1972). Since 1962 Calisher has taught creative writing and literature at colleges and universities across the country, among them Sarah Lawrence (1962), Brandeis University (1963–64), Columbia University (1968–70; 1972–73), Bennington College (1978), and Brown University (1986). She has been widely acclaimed. In 1980 Calisher received a Litt. D. from Skidmore College. She has been elected president of P.E.N. and the American Academy of Arts and Letters, where she was a member of the Literature Award Committee of the American Academy of Arts and Letters for 1993. Calisher's careful attention to the craft of fiction characterizes her achievement as a writer and her lifelong commitment to teaching and writing.

MAJOR THEMES

The major theme of Calisher's eleven novels, six collections of short stories, and two autobiographical works has been an exploration of what Calisher calls "an aesthetic of conduct," "a sense of form applied to life" (*Herself* 398). Her fiction raises moral questions. What are the rules by which we choose to live our lives? What are the compromises we are willing to make? What are the means by which we can understand our limitations? In the absence of absolute truths, how can we have hope or discover meaning and purpose in our lives?

The characteristic movement of Calisher's stories and novels is toward the characters' growing consciousness of themselves and their limitations. This theme of self-discovery is reflected in both the early stories and later fiction, in which she explores with analytical skill the complexities of human experience and the nuances of individual consciousness. Calisher's characters are observers, listeners, thinkers. They speculate about the meaning of their lives; they search for viable modes of action and belief; they dwell on the question of choice and commitment; they search for love, friendship, empathy. In order to affirm their commitment to one another, they first must learn to accept their solitary selves and find truth in their lives.

All of the stories in Calisher's first collected volume, *In the Absence of Angels* (1951), deal in varying ways with love and hope, although the world they portray is often filled with sorrow, loneliness, and despair. The first story in this collection, "In Greenwich There Are Many Gravelled Walks," is characteristic of Calisher's best work in its structure and theme. This story affirms the possibility of love and hope against all odds. The central character of the story, Peter, the son of an alcoholic mother who must periodically be checked into a sanitorium in Greenwich, Connecticut, the only place in which she feels secure, meets Susan, the daughter of an aging homosexual father and a thrice-married mother, just as Susan's father's latest lover leaps to his death from a fifth-story window after a disagreement. From such an unpromising emotional landscape, Calisher fashions a modern love story, a story of hope wrenched from despair. The young couple move toward an uncertain future at the end of the story, perhaps toward love, having made a conscious choice to survive on their own terms.

Other stories in this first volume, particularly those about the Elkins family, are autobiographical. In these stories, young Hester and her brother Joe, both of whom represent Calisher, also must resist the emotional burdens of their parents and overcome pain and hypocrisy in order to grow in understanding, love, and forgiveness. They, too, are survivors of a new world only by being brave enough to have faith in human potential. In a number of these stories, particularly in "The Middle Drawer" and "Old Stock," Calisher treats the theme of anti-Semitism not only as it defines the attitudes of others toward Jewish characters, but as internalized hatred and denial of one's heritage. Her mother's pride in being able to pass as a Gentile horrifies the adolescent heroine of "Old Stock" and overshadows the more overt prejudice of a good Christian lady. In daring to treat the theme of Jewish self-denial in her 1950 story, Calisher reveals her characteristic fascination with the cost of self-deception and the dangers of unquestioned moral and social values.

Other stories in this volume depict different emotional and moral dilemmas that Calisher's characters must acknowledge and overcome by confronting the truth of their imperfect lives, like the middle-aged, "assimilated" Jew who realizes only at a college reunion that he has been unable to escape anti-Semitism, even in his fondly but imperfectly remembered days as a college athlete. Such characters in the early stories face existential dilemmas but reach beyond their despair toward acceptance of their imperfect lives. The title story affirms the moral importance of self-acceptance. "In the absence of angels and arbiters from a world of light, men and women must take their place.'' This humanistic ethical stance characterizes Calisher's fiction throughout her career and places her as a modernist, not only in form, but in theme as well. The primary focus of Calisher's fiction is on her characters' philosophical and psychological journeys from delusion and despair to qualified hope. The stories resist full closure, bringing the characters instead toward recognition and change.

In Calisher's 1961 novel *False Entry*, the central character, an eminent encyclopedist, has used his learning to obscure the truth of his past. In order to live his own life and not remain merely a listener and recorder of others, he must use his prodigious memory to uncover the truths beneath the lies or false entries of his own past. In this novel, self-acceptance and self-disclosure, treated through a series of geographical and spiritual journeys, serve as secular revelations that transform the character's self and underscore the bravery and mystery of ordinary life, if one can but learn to see.

The collected volume of stories *Tale for the Mirror* (1962) contains a number of brilliant stories that focus on the pathos of life. The themes of this collection are metaphors for loneliness, particularly of aging women. In "The Scream on Fifty-Seventh Street," Mrs. Hazlett moves from self-pity toward an epiphany in which she realizes that her lonely scream in the night unites her with others like herself who share the burden of solitude. In her acceptance of the human condition, she finds a measure of comfort. In "Mrs. Fay Dines on Zebra" and "The Night Club in the Woods," Calisher uses humor to examine the pathos of self-delusion. The compassionate irony of the narrators of these stories reveals that, for all the eccentricities of the central characters, they share a common human desire for hope and love. In the balance she creates between the odd and the ordinary, Calisher underscores both the variety and commonality of human experience even as she returns to the same themes, our sense of isolation and our capacity for self-deception.

Textures of Life (1963) examines problematic relationships, particularly those between the mother of this novel and her daughter, Elizabeth. As in later novels that deal with the compromises one must make in order to grow into adulthood, *Queenie* (1971) and *The Bobby Soxer* (1986), Calisher examines the intricate emotional web that links parent and child. In focusing the generalizational conflict on the daughter's rejection of materialism in *Textures of Life*, Calisher links the personal with the political, thus reflecting the central moral questions that divided the generations during this decade. She is less successful in her comic political novel, *Queenie*, which traces the adventures of a bourgeois, quixotic heroine during the Nixon era largely through her sexual/political adventures.

In *Journal from Ellipsis* (1965), Calisher has written a philosophical fable in the form of a science-fiction story. An intelligent oval, an ellipsoid (Eli), has come to earth to change places with a human and experience variety and mutability. Although a number of social and political themes emerge in this ironic journey, the theme of mutability extends to even the more interesting side issues, such as the hint of an international conspiracy of women against men, which seems to evaporate as the story progresses. A later work, *Mysteries of Motion* (1983), set in the near future, also uses space travel to explore the limitations of contemporary civilization and the necessary compromise between utopian ideals and human imperfection. In this work, as in *Journal from Ellipsis*, the philosophical questions frequently overwhelm the narrative itself.

Two novellas, *The Railway Police* and *The Last Trolley Ride* (1966), represent a return to the narrative strength of the short stories and a progression in Calisher's ability to unite style, narrative form, and theme. The acceptance of human imperfection in *The Railway Police* focuses on the recognition by the central character, a woman who suffers from hereditary baldness, that she does not need the false beauty of her many wigs for selfhood. The central character rejects a society that defines women by superficial standards of beauty and confuses gesture with value. Rejecting the artificial values of society, the central character temporarily enters the world of the dispossessed and homeless whom she has observed. The ending establishes an unstable balance between the character's rebellion and her hope for a more honest existence. Calisher underscores the link between theme and method in this work when she says, "It is entirely possible to be both honest and frivolous, a role that men deny exists, of course, since only women are perfect for it" (56). *The Last Trolley Ride* is a pastoral reminiscence of two male friends. The compromises they make with their hopes and ideals is narrated with gentle nostalgia, the prose sepia-toned, unlike the harsher irony of *The Railway Police*.

Love, marriage, and infidelity in the age of analysis are explored in *On Keeping Women* (1977), which draws more consciously on the psychological and existential questions of being a woman. The theme of this novel is a conscious exploration of female sensibility and sexuality, as the heroine, Lexie, struggles to find the truth of her life, herself, and her marriage. This novel is also about learning to speak as a woman not only to others, but also to oneself. Read in this way, Lexie's resistance to others' definitions, her search for an authentic female language, can be seen as an exploration of feminine consciousness. Although she is not often identified as a feminist writer, Calisher's themes and narrative form, particularly in this novel, explore many of the theoretical and textual issues raised by feminist literary theory.

In *Age* (1987) and in her autobiographical memoir *Kissing Cousins* (1988), Calisher returns to the themes of earlier works, exploring the need for love and hope, the human capacity for forgiveness in a less-than-perfect world. What characterizes these later works, as it does the best of Calisher's writing, is her ability to convey sympathy for ordinary people and to resist the temptation to oversimplify humanity's struggle against lives of quiet desperation. By affirming the value of being human, with its large terrors and smaller consolations, Calisher's fiction addresses the central moral concerns of contemporary life. Her fiction examines the elusive truths of human experience that often escape a less demanding sensibility.

SURVEY OF CRITICISM

Although Calisher's fiction has been reviewed extensively on publication, surprisingly little formal critical attention has been paid to her fiction as a whole. In one exception, an appreciation of Calisher published in *Contemporary Literature* (1965), Emily Hahn identified Calisher's concern with language and the subtle delineation of emotions through word and image as the writer's most significant achievement. She suggests that Calisher's stories and most of the novels are difficult for readers because they demand close attention and intellectual agility. Kathleen Snodgrass provided the most extensive thematic analysis of Calisher's work in her 1987 dissertation "Rites of Passage in the Works of Hortense Calisher." The best general overview of Calisher's life and literary work is by Carolyn Matalene in *American Novelists Since World War II.*

Criticism of Calisher's work is divided between attention to thematic issues and evaluation of form and style. Critics have praised Calisher's fiction for its moral seriousness, verbal intricacy, intense psychological portraits, the complexity of her portrayal of human experience, and her attention to the formal design of the narrative. She has also been criticized for being abstruse, verbose, and too self-consciously literary. She has been compared to Henry James and Flaubert as well as to Proust because of her concern with the craft of fiction, her interest in the subtle evocation of states of mind, and her verbal complexity.

In her review of *The New Yorkers*, Cynthia Ozick suggests that the difficulty of Calisher's fiction stems from her rejection of many of the metaphorical resources of the novel. She compares Calisher's concept of the novel to Nabokov's antinovel. Instead of accepting the mimetic principle that the novel represents reality, Calisher turns the elements of fiction back on themselves. Everything is questioned; everything must be explored anew. Calisher is a modernist rather than a realist in her assumption that meaning emerges as a process of discovering and examining the world and the self. The governing idea of Calisher's fiction, according to Ozick, is "design" rather than plot. The narrative "design" reflects the characters' need to define for themselves the shape and meaning of their lives in a world where everything seems arbitrary or relative. This process does not move in an orderly, linear fashion but loops back on itself, as another question is raised or an easy answer rejected. Calisher's narratives often reflect the movement within the consciousness of individual characters and their relationship to one another. Their complexity of form, syntax, and idea demand the reader's close attention.

Calisher's short stories have received more favorable critical acclaim than the novels. In her preface to *The Collected Stories*, Calisher describes the short story as "an apocalypse served in a very small cup" (ix). The brevity and economy of emotional impact demanded by the short story require a tighter control of the design and language. Reviewing the stories in *Tale for the Mirror*, Granville Hicks concluded that "within her range [Calisher] is beautifully precise and her way with language is exciting" (22), and he noted that he had seldom read stories that gave him more satisfaction. David Boroff also offered qualified praise in his review of *Extreme Magic* (1964), noting that in her best stories, Calisher "sounds rich and complex chords that reverberate lastingly in the mind" (36). Robert Keily noted in the *New York Times Book Review* (1972) that Calisher's fiction often reads like poetry because the language is charged with imagery and there is an intensity of expression (3). R. V. Cassill praised *The Railway Police* (1966) for its "near-perfect synthesis of symbol, language, narrative and theme" (4), calling it a small masterpiece. Virgilia Peterson attributes the success of this work to Calisher's "brilliant manipulation of language, her endlessly apt observation of character and behavior, and the sudden illuminating generalities with which she is not afraid to sprinkle her texts"; however, she cautions that, for many readers, Calisher is "too devious and mysterious" for them to discover what she really means to say (66).

Reviewing *Mysteries of Motion* in the *New York Times Book Review* (1983), Joyce Carol Oates notes that Calisher has written an ambitious, "defiantly risky species of science fiction" that is "primarily a meditation upon the nature of heroism and self-sacrifice in the service of an ideal" (7).

Carolyn Matalene's assertion that Calisher's literary reputation rests primarily on the short stories and novellas is sustained by critical commentary on *The Collected Stories* published in 1975. Anne Tyler, among other reviewers, praised the stories as beautifully crafted, intense, and brilliantly characterized. They alter "our perceptions of the world" (E3). Where they succeed, Calisher's stories achieve a congruence between art and life that Calisher says is her intent.

BIBLIOGRAPHY

Works by Hortense Calisher

"Box of Ginger." *New Yorker* (16 October 1948):31–34. (First published story.)
In the Absence of Angels: Stories. Boston: Little, Brown, 1951; 1963.
False Entry. Boston: Little, Brown, 1961. New York: Weidenfeld, 1988.
Tale for the Mirror: A Novella and Other Stories. Boston: Little, Brown, 1962.
Textures of Life. Boston: Little, Brown, 1963.
Extreme Magic: A Novella and Other Stories. Boston: Little, Brown, 1964.
Journal from Ellipsis. Boston: Little, Brown, 1965.
The Railway Police and *The Last Trolley Ride.* Boston: Little, Brown, 1966.
The New Yorkers. Boston: Little, Brown, 1969; Weidenfeld, 1988.
Queenie. New York: Arbor, 1971; Dell, 1972.
Herself: An Autobiographical Work. New York: Arbor, 1972.
Standard Dreaming. New York: Arbor, 1972, 1983; Dell, 1974.
Eagle Eye. New York: Arbor, 1973; St. Martin's, 1975.
The Collected Stories of Hortense Calisher. New York: Arbor, 1975.
On Keeping Women. New York: Arbor, 1977; Berkley, 1979.
Mysteries of Motion. New York: Doubleday, 1983.
Saratoga, Hot. Garden City, NY: Doubleday, 1985.

The Bobby Soxer. Garden City, NY: Doubleday, 1986.
Age. New York: Weidenfeld, 1987.
Kissing Cousins: A Memory. New York: Weidenfield, 1988.

Works about Hortense Calisher

Boroff, David. "The Saving Remnants of Grace." Rev. of *Extreme Magic: A Novella and Other Stories. Saturday Review* 2 May 1964:36–37.
Cassill, R. V. "Feminine and Masculine." Rev. of *The Railway Police* and *The Last Trolley Ride. New York Times Book Review* 22 May 1966:4–5.
Hahn, Emily. "In Appreciation of Hortense Calisher." *Contemporary Literature* 6.2 (1965):243–49.
Hicks, Granville. "The Quiet Desperation." Rev. of *Tale for the Mirror: A Novella and Other Stories. Saturday Review* 27 Oct. 1962:22.
Keily, Robert. "A Sort of Memoir, a Sort of Novel." Rev. of *Herself and Standard Dreaming. New York Times Book Review* 1 Oct. 1972:3, 20, 22.
Matalene, Carolyn. "Hortense Calisher." *American Novelists Since World War II.* Jeffrey Helterman and Richard Layman. Detroit: Gale, 1978. 75–81.
Oates, Joyce Carol. "The Citizen Courier in Outer Space." Rev. of *Mysteries of Motion. New York Times Book Review* 6 Nov. 1983:7, 26.
Ozick, Cynthia. "Hortense Calisher's Anti-Novel." Rev. of *The New Yorkers. Midstream.* Nov. 1969:77–80.
Peterson, Virgilia. "Mystery Stories." Rev. of *The Railway Police* and *The Last Trolley Ride. Reporter* 17 Nov. 1966:66–67.
Snodgrass, Kathleen. "Rites of Passage in the Works of Hortense Calisher." Diss. University of Delaware, 1987.
———. "Hortense Calisher: A Bibliography, 1948–86." *Bulletin of Bibliography* 45.1 (1988):40–50.
Spacks, Patricia Meyer. Rev. of *Queenie. Hudson Review* 25.1 (1972):163–64.
Tyler, Anne. "Apocalypse in a Teacup." Rev. of *The Collected Stories of Hortense Calisher. Washington Post Book World* 18 Sept. 1977:E3.

KIM CHERNIN (1940–   )

Jerilyn Fisher

BIOGRAPHY

On May 7, 1940, as Rose Chernin went through labor, she was reading a book between contractions: *On the Woman Question*, by Lenin's comrade Clara Zetkin. Ushering Kim into the world with that book by her side, Rose may have hoped to inspire Communist vision and activism in the adult her baby would become; instead, she seems to have unknowingly augured her daughter's commitment to and gift for writing about women.

Born in the Bronx to two fiercely committed Marxists, Kim Chernin was exposed from the start to leftist teachings and impassioned political involvement. As a child, she marched with her mother, helped hand out Party leaflets, sang organizing songs, and overheard weekly Party meetings. Yet the Marxist teachings of Chernin's parents did not result in her later commitment to revolutionary ideologies and activism; rather, she became a poet, a mystic, and an interpreter of women's psychological experiences. These interests and capacities seem to have stemmed from the extended family circle of compelling storytellers.

For young Kim Chernin, one early source of inspiration for writing came from her *shtetl*-born grandmother, Perle, who created Yiddish tales for other women to use in their letters abroad. Chernin was also influenced by her storytelling father, Paul Kusnitz, who liked to recite Pushkin and delighted his daughter with daily "homespun tales." Rose Chernin, another gifted teller of tales, sometimes left Kim bored with her didactic stories "about madness, revolution, the struggle to survive . . . " (*Crossing the Border* 22). Yet from her mother, too, Kim learned to harness and relish the power of the raconteur.

While her mother's work as a Party organizer etched the contours of Kim's childhood, her early life was profoundly touched in a different way when her only sister, Nina, died of Hodgkin's disease. For Kim, the loss was incomprehensible: She and her teenage sister had shared a room until the last unbearable months. Chernin believes that her inevitable struggle with a child's confusion and guilt about Nina's death was prolonged by the family's inability to engage fully in mourning. Thus, confronting and resolving loss becomes a major artistic theme in her work.

Distracted with grief at losing her first-born, Rose Chernin became emotionally inaccessible to four-year-old Kim, the survivor. Trying to eclipse haunting memories of Nina, Rose moved the family to California, where other relatives had settled. There, in a rough central Los Angeles community, Kim attended school. By the time Kim was six, her mother had overcome the paralysis of depression and had resumed full-time work as an organizer for the Party. Then in 1951, Rose Chernin made national headline news when she was arrested for "advocating the overthrow of the government."

What was it like to grow up a child of the Communist Left in the 1950s? Proud of her mother's dedication to the people, Kim also experienced social ostracism at school and lived nervously waiting for daily news about the outcome of her mother's court appearances. From the beginning of Kim's adolescence until she was eighteen years old, she came home from school each day not knowing if her mother would be at home or in jail.

Paradoxically, Kim's youthful Marxist vision was deflated during a summer trip to Moscow after high-school graduation. Returning to Los Angeles, she quarreled with her mother more loudly than before, refuting Marx's ideas as insufficient for revolution. Soon, Kim left home for Berkeley with a calling: She began to identify herself as a poet and a mystic, thus increasing the ideological distance between her and her mother.

In 1958, at age eighteen, Kim married, perhaps in part to reinforce this separation. Two years later, she went with her young husband to Oxford; in 1963, daughter Larissa was born. Within the next several years, the couple returned to America and separated. By this time, Kim had reassessed her feelings about her mother: When she divorced, she changed her name, not back to Kusnitz but to Chernin, the last name of her mother and her mother's mother, Perle. As an adolescent, Larissa would also change her name to Chernin.

Throughout much of her life, Kim Chernin has wrestled with the desire to uphold or rebel against the ideals of her politically heroic, but often dogmatic, mother. These complex feelings about Rose Chernin have fueled not only Kim's writing about her own life, but also her studies of contemporary women's ambivalent responses to their mothers.

When Kim's beloved father died in a car accident in 1967, Kim and Rose began to reconcile their differences, sharing their loss of the man who had always tried to build bridges between them. In fact, *In My Mother's House*, begun a few years after Paul's death, carries out his lifelong desire for peace between mother and daughter. But not until she wrote *Crossing the Border* does Kim Chernin give full voice to cherished memories of him. Most of this autobiographical story takes place in Israel in 1971, where Kim felt strangely drawn to travel. Responding to this mysterious pull, Kim went there to search for memories of her father. She also went hoping to satisfy her secret yearnings for communal Jewish life.

Today, twenty-odd years later, Kim Chernin is particularly moved by her identification as a Jew; she struggles to figure out what it means for a strongly feminist, goddess-loving daughter of Marxists to be a Jewish woman. While Chernin raises challenging questions about where women fit into the traditional observances and stories, she says that being Jewish defines her core self and "requires no external show of itself for [me] to feel it and be held by it"; being Jewish, she continues, "has a kind of archetypal power; depth, vision, inspiration, meaning tend always to be organized for me in Jewish terms" (letter to the author, 8 July 1992).

In 1987, for the Women's Studies/Jewish Studies Convergences Conference at Stanford University, Kim Chernin gave a talk that was published in *Tikkun*. For the first time, she addressed a Jewish audience, speaking of her mother's ambiguous relationship to Judaism and her own thoughts about what it means to be a Jewish woman. Reflecting on that talk, Chernin says, "It was the first time I had heard of myself as a Jewish writer. You can't imagine my pride! No, more than pride. The inexplicable thrill to find out that I really was Jewish! Really!" (letter to the author, 25 July 1992).

After returning to America from Israel in 1972, Chernin married again, and the marriage lasted six years. After the divorce, Kim Chernin and Susan Griffin lived-as-married for four years, residing with their two daughters. Then, in 1985, Chernin went back to Paris, where she renewed the friendship she had begun years before with Renate Stendhal, coauthor of *Sex and Other Sacred Games*. In their private lives, Chernin and Stendhal did meet in Paris; Chernin subsequently wrote an erotic short story about their second encounter, "An American in Paris." Today, they live together in Berkeley.

At present, Kim Chernin sees herself in a "home-bound period . . ." (Letter to the author, 8 July 1988). She writes and works as a psychotherapist in private practice, work for which she was trained psychoanalytically, and then in the interpersonal approach, with Otto Will, a colleague of Frieda Fromm-Reichmann and Harry Stack Sullivan. In 1981, Chernin began counseling as an adjunct to writing: Steadily, her practice has grown to occupy a place of central importance in her life. She counsels patients who suffer with eating and identity disorders as well as those in profound spiritual distress.

In addition to her work as a consultant and a writer, Chernin's attention is absorbed by her life with Renate Stendhal, by her daughter's return to California, and by plans for building/growing projects (both real and metaphoric) in her home and in her garden. Working against her dreamy, reclusive tendency, Kim Chernin feels urgently challenged by desire for involvement in social activism. She lives with the tension between her mystical inclinations and the imperative to work for world change. From this fruitful dialectic bequeathed to her, Chernin tells her tales.

MAJOR THEMES

Reading Kim Chernin's books, one is quickly struck by their thematic unity: Consistently, she writes about the female psyche, mothers, daughters, The Great Mother, food, loss, memory, and storytelling. In recent works, she also explores her sexual relationships, both lesbian and heterosexual ("An American in Paris," *Sex and Other Sacred Games*, and *Crossing the Border*), characterizing women's sexuality as dynamic, potentially creative energy that, when accepted and freed, will deepen our personal and spiritual growth.

Kim Chernin's works span a number of different genres: memoir, fiction, poetry, psychological study, and a psychosociological/religious study of women's search for self. In writing nonfiction, she moves between ideas and compelling narrative accounts, her own and her clients', weaving together intellectual discovery with personal stories. This form, a hallmark of Chernin's literary style, works as an extension of her profoundly feminist perspective in which "the personal" carries great political and cultural importance.

The impact of her sister Nina's death, and other significant losses suffered by her extended family, have prompted Kim to write analytically and imaginatively about women's experience with different kinds of emptiness. In her studies of women's identity and body image, Chernin explores their psychological responses to physical hunger and cravings, connecting that hunger to women's emotional and spiritual emptiness, unnourished by patriarchal traditions. She contends that understanding women's hunger—accepting it as a natural, healthy appetite for more than the scanty life portion women have been fed—can lead to discovery and satisfaction with the forbidden fruit of female knowledge and power. Women lovingly preparing food for (or experiencing interpersonal intensity as they eat with) other women recurs, motif-like, in several books and recurs imagistically in her poetry.

In Chernin's view, the act of eating has become a uniquely meaningful source of memory for women unconsciously seeking union with the original, mother-nourished, infant-self. Seeing food in this way brings Chernin to believe that the modern daughter's struggles with her biological mother can manifest themselves in the daughter's overwhelming appetite: Food can represent to us a symbolic "return" to the powerful mother we once saw, the model with whom we once identified as female and from whom we once hoped to draw our own potential. With *Reinventing Eve*, Kim Chernin explores her understanding that, when biblical Eve compulsively bites what has been forbidden, she is hungering for "the power of the Mother Goddess . . . a deity who embodies the possibilities of female self-development . . . that female creative power all mention of which has been left out of the Genesis story" (xviii). Thus, Chernin uses psychological insight to cast Eve as our courageous, feminist progenitor in her extended revision of this Old Testament story.

Chernin consistently shows that storytelling itself—one way to capture memory—can empower women, in particular, by retrieving and guarding a fragile, woman-centered past. She also has her narrators reflect on the arduous work of the storyteller. Often her narrators/storytellers feel ambivalent about their assigned task: In *In My Mother's House*, the daughter-writer is at first reluctant—but soon, emotionally and artistically committed—to take the story Rose narrates and inscribe it onto the printed page. In the book, daughter-writer Kim understands the responsibility she has in having been "chosen to set these stories down" (18). Likewise, in *The Flame Bearers*, Rae Shadmi understands that, having been so designated by her grandmother, she can no longer resist acting as the sect's storyteller. In *Crossing the Border*, the older-self-as-narrator feels impelled to relate her version of the story about her younger self, the protagonist of the memoir.

Reflecting her family's storytelling tradition, Chernin often uses a narrative structure that centralizes one tale and casts it within an interlocking web of other women's stories. Often she spins her own story into this web. During the latter part of *In My Mother's House*, Kim, who has previously heard the tale of her mother's life, begins to narrate events that occurred to her from the time that Rose Chernin was imprisoned. In *Crossing the Border*, the narrator becomes split in two, and the present-day Kim Chernin takes over the narrative from her thirty-year-old self, the subject of the central plot/story. Through her memoirs, fiction, and the article appearing in *Tikkun*, Chernin reminds us that any story—family, biblical, and newspaper—is subject to multiple interpretations through the teller and the telling. Personal and cultural memories, inevitably subjective, reveal a great deal about the tellers. Through memories and what others learn from them, meanings and images reshape the future.

In *The Flame Bearers*, Chernin shows the value of memory to retrieve the spiritual vision of the past. Challenging women's exclusion in traditional Judaism, Chernin creates the Flame Bearers, a sect of women who are Jewish, yet not traditional observers; when these women read the Holy Book, they reconstruct Old Testament stories to reassert the days before women were excluded from Orthodoxy. Retelling and recording their stories is how the Flame Bearers' traditions survive. In the novel, to hear the Flame Bearers' woman-centered stories is to take responsibility for remembering them. To remember them is to prepare for retelling them to the next generation of women. Through the memory of Chochma, the Great Mother, the story of female power and knowledge lives on.

This symbolic carrying-on of stories and traditions through women in the family becomes another central theme in Kim Chernin's work. *The Flame Bearers* centers on Israel (Rae) Shadmi's gradual acceptance of herself as the sect's next leader. First, she resists this role; slowly she grows into the knowledge that her grandmother's ancient stories have all become "entangled around her very core" ("In the House of the Flame Bearers" 58). Similarly, *In My Mother's House* displays mother-to-daughter bonding between generations of Chernin women, bonding effected through Rose's telling of tales and through daughter Kim's ability to set them down.

At the same time that Chernin emphasizes the passing of traditions, especially from mother to daughter, she is also concerned with the daughter's desire and need to be unlike her mother. Of *In My Mother's House*, Chernin says: "Writing that book I was . . . preoccupied with the struggle to be different from my mother" ("In the House of the Flame Bearers," 56). In fiction, she explores this theme as Rae Shadmi struggles to distance herself from and yet retain the powerful spiritual traditions of her grandmother, matriarch of the Flame Bearers. Psychologically, Chernin examines mother-daughter opposition and attachment in *The Obsession*, *The Hungry Self*, and *Reinventing Eve*.

With her latest memoir, Chernin continues to create narrative form that is provocative, sexually charged, and highly experimental. As a storyteller and a psychologist, Kim Chernin's re-visioning of feminine consciousness expresses women's hunger for personal, sacred truths about their maternal and erotic powers.

SURVEY OF CRITICISM

In light of the multidisciplinary content of her work, it is not surprising that no scholar has yet presented an overview of Kim Chernin's writing. However, Chernin's books have been widely reviewed: Responses most often focus on her experiments with narrative form and her feminist interpretations.

Esther Broner is one who admires Chernin's innovations in form. *In My Mother's House*, Chernin's most reviewed and highly acclaimed book to date, Broner describes as having a "Chaucerian" structure, with its many tales-within-a-tale format. Chernin's narrative structure results, she says, in the readers' experience of intimacy with the characters, as we find ourselves "listening in" on Rose and Kim's private conversations. Similarly, critic Diane McWhorter hails *In My Mother's House* as "ingeniously" structured and "operatic" in construction. Yet McWhorter also expresses frustration with the story's irregularities in chronology and historical context. She contends that the book lacks sufficient social and historical context, suggesting that Chernin avoids the larger world by using narrative ellipses. The effect, according to McWhorter, is to recreate "the claustrophobic environment of her mother's Russian *shtetl*."

Similarly narrated in the fluid shape of a tale within a tale, Chernin's psychological studies have enormous appeal for their accessibility. Most reviewers commend Chernin's ability to make complex thought both readable and intriguing. This achievement, says Susan Wooley, lies partly within Chernin's literary talent for writing with a "liquid" style. Reviewing *The Hungry Self*, Wooley applauds Chernin's ability to create a "stunning word-portrait of women"; at the same time, she concludes that Chernin's impressive writing talents seem to "plug gaps in research," leaving some serious theoretical questions unresolved or undisputed. Anne Llewellyn Barstow, reviewing *Reinventing Eve*, agrees that "Chernin's gifts are poetic and visionary . . . "; after enthusiastically offering this book's praise, Barstow adds that at times the "experiential material and the religious re-visioning do not come together."

What such comments suggest is that reviewing scholars who value her work sometimes take Chernin to task for not going far enough, wishing she could have applied her keen powers of insight to more expansive conclusions, or could have incorporated current feminist research into her books of analysis and personal thought about women's experiences.

Chernin wrote what is perhaps her most unconventional book to date, *Sex and Other Sacred Games*, with Renate Stendhal. In this fictional exchange of letters, an American femme fatale and a European lesbian meet and then write to discuss sexual "truths" concerning passion, attraction, pleasure, honesty, risk-taking, and power. Shana Penn in *The Women's Review of Books*, values the rhetorical substance of the dialogue in which Claire and Alma thoroughly explore the reaches of their respective sexual identities and growing intimacy. A review in *Publishers Weekly*, on the other hand, questions the book's sexual and political assumptions. This novel of heady conversation drew either unmitigated criticism or solid respect, depending on the reviewer's interest in abstract, lengthy, feminist discussion of sexual politics and tolerance for an epistolary structure with only minimal suggestions of plot.

The Flame Bearers, Chernin's only work of pure fantasy to date, deserves special mention. Reviewed as a novel to be "read with delight by those who enjoy good ideological revenge," Anne Roiphe describes *The Flame Bearers* as Jewish, feminist science fiction, celebrating its imaginative, mythical, woman-centered rendering of Hebraic tradition and God-wrestling. While admiring the book's "richness of traditional knowledge that shines on every page," Roiphe wishes that Chernin had resolved women's historical exclusion from Judaism by creating more than "a turning of the tables." That disappointment notwithstanding, Roiphe abundantly praises the book's power and vision, hailing Chernin's playfulness in using kabbalistic imagery and folkore to display the possible incompatibility of modern feminism and mainstream Jewish observance.

Overall, Kim Chernin's work reveals her commitment to understanding women's inner lives and her fascination in exposing memory's truthful fictions, with both personal and political life-story significance. Chernin's latest memoir, *Crossing the Border*, has not been reviewed to date. In it she extends her penchant for crossing boundaries of narrative convention and continues to blend the "surprise and suspense . . . depth and humor" that Roiphe found in *The Flame Bearers*. Chernin intends to write a sequel to *Crossing the Border*.

BIBLIOGRAPHY

Works by Kim Chernin

The Obsession: Reflections on the Tyranny of Slenderness. New York: Harper and Row, 1981.

The Hunger Song. London: Menard Press, 1982.

In My Mother's House: A Daughter's Story. New York: Ticknor and Fields, 1983.

The Hungry Self: Women, Eating and Identity. New York: Times Books, 1985.

"An American in Paris." *Erotic Interludes.* Ed. Lonnie Barbach. New York: Harper and Row, 1986.

The Flame Bearers. New York: Random House, 1986.

Reinventing Eve: Modern Woman in Search of Herself. New York: Times Books, 1987.

"In the House of the Flame Bearers." *Tikkun* July–August 1987:56–59.

Sex and Other Sacred Games, coauthored with Renate Stendahl. New York: Times Books, 1989.

Letter to the author. 8 July 1992.

Letter to the author. 25 July 1992.

Crossing the Border: A Memoir. New York: Ballantine Books, 1994.

Works about Kim Chernin

Barstow, Anne Llewellyn. "Hungering for a Credible Goddess." Rev. of *Reinventing Eve. New York Times Book Review* 3 Jan. 1988:2.

Broner, E. M. "Embraced and Embattled." Rev. of *In My Mother's House. Women's Review of Books* June 1984:3–4.

McWhorter, Diane. Rev. of *In My Mother's House. New York Times Book Review* 21 Aug. 1983:14.

Penn, Shana. "Platonic Dialogue?" Rev. of *Sex and Other Sacred Games. Women's Review of Books* Mar. 1990:28–29.

Roiphe, Anne. "Daughters of the Israelites." Rev. of *The Flame Bearers. New York Times Book Review* 9 Nov. 1986:12.

Rev. of *Sex and Other Sacred Games: Love, Desire, Power and Possession. Publishers Weekly* Apr. 1989:60.

Wooley, Susan C. "Consuming Emotion." Rev. of *The Hungry Self. Women's Review of Books* Apr. 1986:1; 3.

ANDREA DWORKIN (1946–   )

Meryl F. Schwartz

BIOGRAPHY

After describing her personal experiences of sexual assault, prostitution, and wife battery in a letter to the *New York Times*, Andrea Dworkin writes, "My imagination can barely grasp my real life" ("Pornography and the New Puritans"). Indeed, readers' imaginations often resist comprehension of the brutal details of her life, but Dworkin has devoted herself to facing her experience, creating a language to describe it, and developing strategies to fight the social conditions that circumscribe it. Throughout her career as feminist activist, scholar, lecturer, teacher, and writer of fiction, nonfiction, and poetry, Andrea Dworkin has boldly insisted that her audience confront the systemic oppression of women that has so violently manifested itself in her life.

Born in Camden, New Jersey, on September 26, 1946, Dworkin is the grandchild of Russian and Hungarian Jewish emigrés. Her father, Harold, taught high-school science, and her mother, Sylvia, was a secretary. Sylvia was very ill through much of Andrea's childhood, and Harold was often Andrea's primary caregiver. While both parents encouraged her to read, Dworkin's father's encouragement of her intellectual development was particularly influential. Both parents were political liberals who encouraged her to trust her own perceptions and take principled stands. Nonetheless, Dworkin's childhood did not prepare her for the devastating impact that living in a patriarchal society was to have upon her consciousness as well as her body during her adolescence and young adulthood.

First sexually assaulted by a stranger at age nine, Dworkin was subsequently beaten and raped as an adolescent. Though she told her parents of the first assault, she told no one of the second, for she was sure she would not be taken seriously. At the time, she was working for a peace group, where she continually heard jokes about rape. Dworkin found leftist men indifferent at best to women's concerns, and she discovered that male domination of the New Left had the effect of silencing women.

Dworkin majored in literature and minored in philosophy at Bennington College. During her freshman year, in February 1965, she was arrested for taking part in a sit-in to protest the Vietnam War. While incarcerated in New York City's Women's House of Detention, she was brutalized by two prison doctors. Their violent vaginal exam left her bruised and lacerated, causing fifteen days of vaginal bleeding. Describing the impact of this experience, Dworkin writes:

I came out of the Women's House of Detention mute. Speech depends on believing you can make yourself understood: a community of people will recognize the experience in the words you use and they will care. You also have to be able to understand what happened to you enough to convey it to others. I lost speech. I was hurt past what I had words for. (''Pornography and New Puritans'')

In these years before the feminist movement was a visible social presence, Dworkin was only able to describe her experience when the writer Grace Paley convinced her that she would understand. And then, as Dworkin puts it, ''I spoke a lot'' (''Pornography and New Puritans''). Her story was covered by the international press, and a Grand Jury investigated her charges. But while Dworkin was eventually instrumental in closing down the notorious women's jail, neither of the prison doctors was charged with sexual assault or sexual battery, and the Grand Jury concluded that the prison's conditions were acceptable. This was a pivotal moment in Dworkin's life: It was the first time that she spoke publicly against women's systematic victimization, and it was her first lesson in the difficulty of challenging male supremacy in a society whose institutions collaborate in their support of a patriarchal order. In despair after the verdict, she left the country for the island of Crete.

Dworkin returned to America a year later, graduating from college in 1968. Determined to be a writer, a dream she had nourished since childhood, she spent the next several years developing her craft while struggling for economic survival. Living within the counterculture, both in New York City and in Amsterdam, Dworkin saw herself as a tough survivor and sexual libertarian. Like many women who have been sexually traumatized, she traded sex for money, and she suffered repeated encounters with male sexual aggression. During this period she married, and for a few years she suffered repeated beatings and torture at her husband's hands. After several unsuccessful attempts to solicit help from friends, neighbors, doctors, and the police, Dworkin again found herself unable to speak. ''My words didn't seem to mean anything,'' she has written, ''or it was O.K. to torture me'' (''Pornography and New Puritans'').

These repeated experiences of abuse and silencing make Dworkin's career as a prolific writer and public speaker all the more remarkable; her memories of these experiences and the stories of the thousands of women who have trusted her with their histories of sexual abuse serve as constant reminder of the imperative to speak about the violence perpetrated upon women.

Within weeks after leaving her husband, Dworkin began work on *Woman*

Hating (1974), her first book of feminist theory. Unable to place her essays in periodicals, she went on the lecture circuit in the mid-1970s and has since become well known as a powerful speaker. Her speeches are collected in *Our Blood* (1976) and *Letters from a War Zone* (1989).

Although she has published two books of poems,[1] several books of theory, and three volumes of fiction, Dworkin is best known in the United States for her antipornography activism, particularly for her authorship, with Catharine MacKinnon, of a civil-rights ordinance that gives individuals the right to sue for damages caused by pornographers or pornographic artifacts. In the 1980s, versions of this ordinance were passed in Minneapolis and Indianapolis, and it has been considered by numerous additional localities in the United States and abroad.

A controversial public figure, Dworkin is known for her uncompromising opposition to male domination, particularly as it is expressed in violence against women. Dworkin has had to struggle to gain access to the mainstream media, but she has persisted in making herself heard. She has published as widely as possible, appeared on several television shows, testified before government commissions, and spoken at innumerable conferences, college campuses, and "Take Back the Night" marches. She has also taught literature and a course on pornography at the University of Minnesota. Dworkin has attributed her strength and endurance to the nurturant "power and passion" of her love for women (*Our Blood* 73). Currently a resident of New York City, Andrea Dworkin has been a public presence in the United States for nearly two decades, but her writing remains relatively unknown.

MAJOR THEMES

As all of her published writing indicates, Andrea Dworkin is a radical feminist, both in the sense that she seeks a revolutionary transformation of society, and in the sense that she sees male domination of women as the basis for all other systems of domination. The feminist project, as she sees it, includes struggle against imperialism, colonialism, racism, war, poverty, anti-Semitism, and homophobia. But, as she says in an early speech, these are all "forms of social injustice which derive from the patriarchal model of male dominance" (*Our Blood* 61). So while Dworkin has written at length about the ways in which sexism intersects with racism, anti-Semitism, and economic exploitation in the lives of women, she has addressed the Right's hatred of Jews and homosexuals, and has frequently recalled the Holocaust. Her primary concern is always with what she sees as the "root cause," male supremacy (*Our Blood* 96).

In the introduction to *Woman Hating*, Dworkin wrote, "this book is an action, a political action where revolution is the goal" (17). This remains her approach to writing, whether theory or fiction. In either case, she seeks through her subject matter and prose style to effect a revolution in the reader's consciousness. *Woman Hating* inaugurates Dworkin's career-long analysis of the operation and effect of patriarchy. In this text, Dworkin sets out to demonstrate that, throughout human history, misogyny has had a devastating impact on women's lives. She supports her claim by analyzing culture and history, including fairy tales and pornography, as well as the Chinese practice of footbinding and the Inquisition's slaughter of "witches." Arguing that "man" and "woman" are social constructs "inappropriate to human becoming" (174), Dworkin concludes this book with a utopian vision of an egalitarian community based on androgyny. While the rhetorical strategy of *Woman Hating* is more conventional than her later books, this early polemic displays a boldness characteristic of all her work. Eschewing polite language, Dworkin asserts herself without qualification, without sentiment, and without compromise.

As Dworkin's career progressed, she narrowed her focus to writing about sexual violence against women, which she came to see as a crucial vantage point from which to view the myriad-intersecting masculinist institutions and practices. In *Pornography: Men Possessing Women* (1981), she critiques the institution of pornography, and in *Intercourse* (1987), she questions the social meaning of sexual intercourse, an act, she argues, that takes on disturbing features and significance within patriarchal societies. Dworkin's extremely unconventional rhetorical strategy implicitly challenges readers to weave together the different threads of her discussions; she begins these books without exposition, proceeds in a nonlinear fashion, and ends without conventional conclusions. The texts work by immersing the reader in masculinist perceptions of women, often as presented in literature and philosophy as well as pornography, forcing her to confront an extremely violent world view. For example, she begins *Intercourse* with an extended analysis of Tolstoy's life and art. Following a characteristic rhetorical pattern, she entraps the reader within his misogynistic logic while deconstructing its circularity with a savage, ironic wit.

The most rhetorically conventional and accessible presentations of Dworkin's position on pornography can be found in the 1989 introduction to the second edition of *Pornography*, in the speeches collected in *Letters from a War Zone*, and especially in her book on the antipornography ordinance, *Pornography and Civil Rights*, coauthored with Catharine MacKinnon. The latter systematically argues against viewing pornography as a simple exercise of speech, protected by the First Amendment. Dworkin and MacKinnon seek to demonstrate that pornography is a violation of the civil rights of women and thus liable to civil suit under the Fourteenth Amendment. They argue that pornography's pivotal role in the high rate of violent crimes against women justifies privileging the Fourteenth Amendment rights of women over the First Amendment rights of pornographers.

Dworkin also discusses the resistance of women and men to confronting the enormity of women's victimization. In *Right-Wing Women* (1983), she analyzes the perspective of antifeminist women. According to Dworkin, right-wing women understand women's powerlessness in our society. They have chosen to support the program of the Right because they believe it offers them greater safety than feminism. In a 1983 speech, she noted that feminists are often seen as "the bringers of a terrible message." Many women, she writes, "rebel against feminism because [they] think we are the ones insisting that their full human uniqueness cannot be expressed because they are women" (*War Zone* 151). They resist the pain of recognizing that this is a condition imposed by male supremacy, not the feminist movement. Even self-identified feminists resist experiencing the pain that inevitably accompanies feminist activism. In a society that values "consumer-happiness," Dworkin writes, "you are not supposed to feel pain," but in the women's movement, "you feel your own pain, the pain of other women, the pain of sisters whose lives you can barely imagine" (*War Zone* 138). While Dworkin's nonfiction comes out of her own pain and takes an emotional toll on readers, it is in her fiction that she sears readers with the raw agony of sexual victimization.

Dworkin's fictions, including *Ice and Fire* (1987), *Mercy* (1991), and the short stories collected in *the new woman's broken heart* (1980), all draw on autobiographical material. First-person narratives told by women who are survivors of rape and other abuses, these texts confront the reader with detailed descriptions of physical and emotional pain. As in her nonfiction, Dworkin subverts prosaic conventions; her sentences and paragraphs frequently continue for several pages, graphically representing the agonized stream of consciousness of her narrators. Dworkin uses this breathless prose style to immerse the reader in the inexorable brutality of the world she describes, as in this passage from *Mercy*, narrated in the voice of a nine-year-old girl:

I wasn't raped until I was almost ten which is pretty good it seems when I ask around because many have been touched but are afraid to say. I wasn't really raped, I guess, just touched a lot by a strange, dark-haired man who I thought was a space alien because I couldn't tell how many hands he had and people from earth only have two, and I didn't know the word rape, which is just some awful word, so it didn't hurt me because nothing happened. (5)

Here, as elsewhere in her fiction, Dworkin's style and subject matter aim at breaking down the reader's resistance to feeling the pain entailed in feminist consciousness and activism.

In *the new woman's broken heart* and *Mercy*, the Holocaust is a central reference point for narrators who measure the pain they have experienced as women, a pain society refuses to validate, against the unspeakable horrors that immediately preceded their postwar births. The persona bertha schneider, who narrates several of the stories in *the new woman's broken heart*, is a victim of poverty and rape, but she struggles to put her pain in perspective, noting "she wasn't pressed up straight shitting in her pants in a cattle car on the way to Dachau" (17). The burden of the bertha schneider stories and Dworkin's novels is to demonstrate that the conditions of women's lives are also an "atrocity," also a holocaust (17). Like Hitler's targets, women are subject to a systematic program of destruction, and it is both as Jews and as feminists that Dworkin's narrators address familiar questions about victimization, resistance, survival, and faith.

While emphasizing the pain of women's lives, Dworkin's fictions tell stories of women's development in which, particularly in the novels, the narrators achieve an empowering critical consciousness about the social structure that confines them. Toward the conclusion of *Ice and Fire*, the narrator repeatedly tells us, "I have become a feminist, not the fun kind." Indeed, after recognizing that her late 1960s bohemian life has not liberated her from male domination and violence, the narrator turns to a career of feminist research and writing that closely mirrors Dworkin's own career.

Mercy retells some of the experiences described in the earlier fiction, but in the context of a more fully developed and elaborately crafted narrative. The body of the text, in the voice of a character named Andrea, is a relentless recital of the violence perpetrated upon the narrator by specific men as well as by a patriarchal system. As Dworkin is apparently aware, her representations of women's vulnerability can lead readers to distance themselves from the experience of her texts and their overwhelming implications. *Mercy* anticipates this reaction in its prologue and epilogue, narrated by "Not Andrea." This frame is a parodic portrayal of an emotionally remote, liberal academic feminist, whose rejection of Andrea's insistent struggle against misogynistic violence is shown to result from a severe state of denial. In the epilogue, "Not Andrea" asserts that "it is, of course, tiresome to dwell on sexual abuse" (334). She insists that politicizing rape creates a "false consciousness, one of victimization," and she implicitly compares this to "the refusal of Holocaust survivors to affirm the value of the Holocaust itself in their own creative lives" (341). "Not Andrea" enjoys tying and gagging her lover and insists that while she has herself been a victim, "it was a long time ago. I'm not the same girl" (342). Unfortunately, the very extremity of this preemptive strike against resistant readers risks further alienating them. Though Dworkin's uncompromising rage and enormous grief are the sources of her great power as a writer, these qualities have also limited the range of her vision and the size of her audience.

SURVEY OF CRITICISM

Dworkin is considered controversial not only by reader's unsympathetic to the women's movement, but also by feminist critics, activists, and sympathizers. She has been the subject of innumerable interviews and articles, both in the mainstream and the feminist press, although with the exception of the book reviews, most of this coverage has focused on Dworkin's political analysis and activism rather than on her writing.

To date there has been little scholarly attention to Dworkin's writing. The notable exception is Cindy Jenefsky's dissertation, "Confronting Male Power with Integrity: Andrea Dworkin's Rhetoric, Art, and Politics" (1990).[2] Jenefsky's detailed, sympathetic study of Dworkin's nonfictional writings argues that Dworkin's politics can only be understood through analysis of her rhetorical artistry. Jenefsky illuminates the significance of Dworkin's unconventional rhetorical strategies, basing much of her analysis on a lengthy interview she conducted with Dworkin. She finds that Dworkin's craft depends heavily on synecdoche—the use of the part to illuminate the whole. In her review of *Mercy*, Jenefsky extends her analysis to Dworkin's fiction, concluding that this novel "is a work of artistic integrity that, in the manner of Dworkin's body of writing generally, synthesizes form and content, art and politics" (7). Jenefsky is currently completing a book on Dworkin.

Reviews of Dworkin's books have been mixed. The majority of reviewers note the impassioned vigor of her prose while objecting to her uncompromising, radical politics. Where Jenefsky defends Dworkin's synecdochic style, many other critics fault Dworkin for grossly reducing the variety of human experience. Anne Tyler finds the language of *Right Wing Women* "florid—often beautiful, as a matter of fact, very much like a sort of martial poetry," but objects that Dworkin "avoids the particular and makes generalizations so sweeping that the reader blinks and draws back" (35). In her review of *Letters from a War Zone*, Alice Echols criticizes "Dworkin's reluctance to acknowledge women's differences" (6), while Zoe Heller argues that "one doesn't have to think rape is transformative to query whether all men are 'Nazis without uniforms.' " Heller describes *Mercy* as a "mad, bad novel" and insists that "one doesn't have to be a man, rapist, or a self-hating woman to admit as much." Wendy Steiner is more sympathetic, stating that the language in *Mercy* is "lyrical and passionate—a cross between the repetition of the early Gertrude Stein and, ironically, the unfettered flights of Henry Miller." But while she concedes that Dworkin's argument "may be moving," she concludes that it is "also intolerant, simplistic and often just as brutal as what it protests."

Another contentious issue is the fine line Dworkin walks between social constructionism and biological determinism. In her review of *Intercourse* and *Ice and Fire*, Carol Sternhell faults Dworkin for "reducing real (I hope changeable) political arrangements to (unchanging) biological design." Both Jenefsky and Echols argue that this is a misreading of Dworkin but find that Dworkin's elusive style is partly to blame. Echols's review of *Letters from a War Zone* notes that "Dworkin's characterization of male dominance as eternal and unchanging makes social constructionism, in her hands, seem virtually indistinguishable from essentialism" (6).

Several reviewers, including Dickstein, Echols, Steiner, and Sternhell, object to Dworkin's labeling of all those who don't agree with her, including self-identified feminists, as collaborators with male supremacy. Steiner's review of *Mercy* ends with the question, "If all women are either victims or collaborators and all men are rapists, can the cry for mercy fall on any but deaf ears?" (11). Further, in her single-minded focus on women's victimization, Sternhell argues, Dworkin seems to deny any possibility of women's agency. She objects to the implication that women's historical role has been entirely limited to that of passive receiver of masculine abuse. Ellen Willis notes that Dworkin's unremitting focus on women's victimization can undermine her activist agenda. She finds "*Pornography*'s relentless outrage less inspiring than numbing, less a call to arms than a counsel of despair" (9). Significantly, however, many of the reviewers who take exception to Dworkin's representation of social reality praise her eloquent, powerful prose and admire her determination to give voice to the most painful and suppressed truths about women's lives under patriarchal rule. There are also readers who recommend Dworkin without hesitation. Reviewing *Ice and Fire*, Barney Bardsley writes, "Andrea Dworkin is soaking wet with life. She is ice and fire. Read her. Be dangerous."

NOTES

1. Privately printed very early in Dworkin's career, these volumes are not available.
2. See Jenefsky for an extensive bibliography, including published and taped interviews.

BIBLIOGRAPHY

Works by Andrea Dworkin

Books: Fiction and Poetry

Child. Poems published on Crete, 1966.
Morning Hair. [fiction and poetry.] Handprinted by author, 1968.
the new woman's broken heart: short stories. Palo Alto, CA: Frog in the Well, 1980.
Ice and Fire. New York: Weidenfeld and Nicolson, 1987.
Mercy. New York: Four Walls Eight Windows, 1991.

Books: Nonfiction

Woman Hating. New York: E. P. Dutton, 1974.
Our Blood: Prophecies and Discourses on Sexual Politics. New York: Harper and Row, 1976.
Right-Wing Women: The Politics of Domesticated Females. New York: Coward, McCann & Geoghegan/Perigee, 1983.
Intercourse. New York: The Free Press, 1987.
With Catharine A. MacKinnon. *Pornography and Civil Rights: A New Day for Women's Equality.* Minneapolis: Organizing Against Pornography, 1988. Distributed by Southern Sisters, 411 Morris St., Durham, NC 27701.
Letters from a War Zone: Writings 1976–1989. New York: E. P. Dutton, 1989.
Pornography: Men Possessing Women, 2d ed. New York: Perigee, 1989.

Writing for Theater and Film

The Cloister. Dir. Gretchen Langheld. Distributed by the Filmmakers Cooperative, New York, 1967.
A Girl Starts Out. Emma Troupe, New York. April and May, 1978.

Selected Published Speeches, Essays, Contributions to Anthologies, Letters

Marx and Gandhi Were Liberals—Feminism and the 'Radical' Left. Pamphlet, Palo Alto, CA: Frog in the Well, n.d. (Adapted from article originally published in *American Report* [1973]).

"A Prophet of Perversion." Special issue on "Sex, Pornography and Male Rage." *Mother Jones* April 1980:24–29.

"The Way Women Are Used in Pornography Being Produced and Sold Now in the United States." Testimony of Dworkin. Effect of Pornography on Women and Children: Hearings Before the Subcommittee on Juvenile Justice of the Senate Committee on the Judiciary. 98th Congress, 2nd Session, S521–55. September 25, 1984:227–55.

"A Question of Censorship." *Spare Rib* January 1987:44.

"Speak Truth to Power." *New Directions for Women* 16 July 1987:12.

"Resistance." In *Sexual Liberals and the Attack on Feminism*, ed. by Dorchen Leidholdt and Janice Raymond, New York: Pergamon, 1990. 136-39.

"Pornography and the New Puritans: Letters from Andrea Dworkin and Others." Letter. *New York Times* 3 May 1992, sec. 7:15.

Works about Andrea Dworkin

Abel, Katy, "Andrea Dworkin: 'What is Intercourse?' " *Sojourner: The Women's Forum* September 1987:19–20.

Armstrong, Louise. "Dissident for the Duration." *Women's Review of Books* May 1986: 5–7.

Assiter, Alison. *Pornography, Feminism, and the Individual.* London: Pluto, 1989.

Bardsley, Barney. "Close to the Edge of Hell." *Tribune* 18 April 1986:8.

Bart, Pauline. "Unexceptional Violence." *Women's Review of Books* December 1986: 11–13.

Echols, Alice. "Fighting for Feminism." Rev. of *Letters from a War Zone. Women's Review of Books* Jan. 1990:5–6.

Ferguson, Ann. "Pleasure, Power and the Porn Wars." *Women's Review of Books* May 1986:11–13.

Forum: The Feminist Sexuality Debates. Special Issue. *Signs* 10 (1984):106–35.

Heller, Zoe. "Nasties." Rev. of *Mercy* by Andrea Dworkin. *Times Literary Supplement* 5 Oct. 1990:1072.

Jenefsky, Cindy. "Confronting Male Power with Integrity: Andrea Dworkin's Rhetoric, Art, and Politics." Diss. University of Wisconsin, 1990.

———. "To Remember the Pain." *Women's Review of Books* February 1992:6–7.

Merck, Mandy. "Bedroom Horror: The Fatal Attraction of Intercourse." *Feminist Review* 30 (1988):89–103.

Russo, Ann, and Lourdes Torres. "Why Feminists Should Read Andrea Dworkin." *Sojourner: The Women's Forum* June 1990:16–17.

Steiner, Wendy. "Declaring War on Men." Rev. of *Mercy. New York Times* 15 Sept. 1991: sec.7:11.

Sternhell, Carol. "Male and Female, Men and Women." *New York Times* 3 May 1987: sec.7:3.

Tyler, Anne. "The Ladies and the Tiger." *New Republic* 21 Feb. 1983:34–35.

Willis, Ellen. Rev. of *Pornography: Men Possessing Women*, by Andrea Dworkin. *New York Times Book Review* 12 July 1981:9.

EDNA FERBER (1885–1968)

Daniel Walden

BIOGRAPHY

Born August 15, 1885, in Kalamazoo, Michigan, of "mixed" parentage (her father, Jacob Charles, was a first-generation Hungarian-Jewish immigrant; her mother, Julia Neumann, was a second-generation German Jew from Chicago), Edna Ferber at age five moved with her family to Ottumwa, Iowa. During the seven years that her father ran a general store in Ottumwa, Edna experienced for the first time the overt and vicious anti-Semitism that was to influence her for the rest of her life. Reacting understandably to this stressful situation, she withdrew, read omnivorously, and developed her imagination and her critical faculties. Loneliness was an inevitable concomitant of being pointed out as "the other," as reflected in the characterizations in her novels and short stories.

In 1897, after her father's business failed (he was not a good businessman and often had to start over), the family moved to Appleton, Wisconsin. After she graduated from the Appleton High School at seventeen, Ferber took over the family store. Because of strained finances, she then went to work for the *Appleton Daily Crescent*; she was the first female newspaperperson to work for the paper. She had to go to work because her father developed severe eye problems that eventually led to blindness. Despite being aware of her economic need, the townspeople were critical of a woman working as a journalist. Though her life was often difficult, her seriousness led to a better job on the *Milwaukee Journal*. Perhaps because of the added pressures of a big city paper or from the trauma of being separated from her family, she became anemic, had a nervous breakdown, and had to return home (see Reed, Horowitz and Landsman, Uffen, and Gilbert). During this period of her life she sold her first short story, "The Homely Heroine," to *Everybody's Magazine* in 1910 for $50.60. Her first novel, *Dawn O'Hara: The Girl Who Laughed* (written earlier, and saved from the trash by her mother), was published in 1911 by Frederick Stokes.

In 1912, urged by Stokes, Edna Ferber went to New York City. Although her earliest fiction was centered in the Midwest, from 1912, when she attended the

Democratic National Convention in Chicago, her home base was urban New York, out of which she fashioned novels and short stories of the American panorama. She won the Pulitzer Prize in 1925 for *So Big*; by the beginning of the 1930s, in spite of the Great Depression and in part because of it, Ferber's heartfelt stories and novels had established her as one of the major writers of her day. She gained widespread popularity when *Giant* (1952) was made into a movie starring James Dean; she focused public attention on Alaska and in part justified its later drive to statehood with *Ice Palace* (1958), a mediocre novel and film.

In addition to writing fiction, Ferber collaborated on several plays. In 1915, she teamed up with George Hobart to dramatize the Emma McChesney stories, which ran for 151 performances in New York as *Our Mrs. McChesney*. Thereafter, she worked on a number of plays with George S. Kaufman. *Minick* (1924) was based on Ferber's story "Old Man Minick." It was followed by *The Royal Family* (1928), *Dinner at Eight* (1932), *Stage Door* (1936), *The Land Is Bright* (1941), and *Bravo!* (1949). *The Royal Family*, *Dinner at Eight*, and *Stage Door* each had respectable runs on Broadway; the others were less successful.

Influenced by her upbringing in the Midwest, by her relationship with her family, and by her experiences as a Jew and a woman, she was an important writer for some fifty years. When she died on April 17, 1968, at the age of eighty-three, Edna Ferber was world famous.

MAJOR THEMES

Ferber was a well-known short story writer before she became known as a novelist. With a string of short stories, she wrote of typical working people in rooming houses, hotel kitchens, and shoe stores. In the first collection of these stories, *Buttered Side Down* (1912), a pun on the term *schlimazel* as differentiated from "buttered side up," characterizing a *schlemiel*, Ferber introduced us to big city types such as Birdie Callahan, whose face looked like a "huge mistake"; Sophy Epstein, "triumphantly pretty"; Rudy Schlachweiler, the "bush league hero"; Effie Bauer; Gussie Fink; and the "homely heroine" Pearlie Schultz. Inevitably, her people were streetwise, with good values, but they were caught up in the urban problems and conflicts that resulted in loneliness, hunger, and alienation. Ferber, as she often explained in her stories, liked to hang around newsstands, hotels, and restaurants observing people. What she saw and heard was transcribed into her fiction. There is little doubt that Ferber's short stories were escapist, in the sense that her fictional characters escaped into a universe replete with products of pure imagination (Uffen 93).

Probably because of her own familial problems, she was particularly insightful in investigating mother-daughter relationships. This theme emerges strongly in *The Girls* (1921) and *American Beauty* (1931). A generational novel, *The Girls* evoked nostalgia but criticized what Ferber perceived as the Victorian morality of the day. Patterning her poet-protagonist, Jesse Dick, on Carl Sandburg, she let her imagination run rampant (she placed some of Dickens's characters in America) while castigating possessive mothers. *American Beauty*, a novel about the old stock New England Puritans, into which Polish immigrants intruded, was impelled into being by two forces: her sensitivity to social conditions and her reflections upon her relationship with her mother. In the novel, Ferber depicts rather horrifyingly the psychological punishment that a sexually frustrated spinster inflicts on her niece, who nonetheless, recovers her vitality and sexual drive with a farm hand.

In an essay, "Joy of the Job" (1918), Ferber emphasized the importance of work to a human being's individual growth. Rarely taking a day off, she wrote under the assumption that the value of work was in the doing. Ferber's character, Emma McChesney, exemplifies that precept. A salesperson for T. A. Buck's Featherloom Petticoats, a working woman who traveled (a unique situation early in this century), Emma, who ran the store and was the bulwark of her family, embodied the strength of Ferber's own mother. When Ferber wrote about a feisty, youthful, middle-aged divorcee working to support her teenage, probably weak-minded son, she was drawing a picture of a courageous woman essentially in a nontraditional role.

Other novels in which the importance of hard work emerges as a major theme include *Fanny Herself* (1917), *So Big* (1924), and *Show Boat* (1926). Drawn from personal experience, her second novel, *Fanny Herself* again used Molly Brandeis as the mother figure, while, oddly perhaps, the main character (fashioned on herself) was called Fanny, her real sister's name; and a younger brother Theodore was invented. After her mother's premature death from pneumonia, Fanny becomes a successful, hardheaded businesswoman, to the exclusion of her "womanly" side. Only when she has enjoyed the love of a good man, and through her innate sense of integrity, does she gain insight into herself. *So Big* was one of Ferber's greatest literary successes. A teacher and daughter of a gambler, the novel's protagonist, Selina DeJong, marries a stolid Dutch farmer and makes the farm prosper after his death. Disappointed in her son's life choices, DeJong was able to make a life for herself by simple hard work and dedication. Although criticism of *Show Boat* has focused on the theme of miscegenation involving a light-skinned black woman and a white man, the predominant theme, is again, hard work.

In her next novels, *Cimarron* (1930), *Saratoga Trunk* (1941), *Giant* (1952), and *Ice Palace* (1958), Ferber began to explore a new theme: American promise and the sheer power of the region. *Cimarron* dealt with the opening up of the Oklahoma Territory and the discovery of oil. *Saratoga Trunk* was set in Texas, and *Ice Palace* was a plea for Alaskan statehood. In *Giant*, based on extensive research in 1940 and then again in 1950, Texas emerged not as a Southwestern state of the United States, but as a separate kingdom with its own laws, speech, mores; and above all, its apartness, other than geographically from the rest of the nation (*A Kind of Magic* 246, 265–66).

In 1939, Ferber published her first autobiography, *A Peculiar Treasure* (the title comes from Exodus XIX, 5). It had two dedications, the first published, the second in her notes. The published dedication was to Janet Fox and Mina Fox. The second unpublished one is private and fierce: "To Adolph Hitler who made of me a better Jew and a more understanding and tolerant human being, as he has of millions of other Jews, this book is dedicated in loathing and contempt" (Qtd. in Gilbert 291).

A Kind of Magic (1963) was the second half of her autobiography, from 1938 to 1963. Writing as an angry, sick, old woman, she recorded again her early life in Appleton, Wisconsin, her early writings briefly, and dwelt on her war correspondent years, her visits to Buchenwald and Nordhausen, and on the writing of *Giant*, her views on women, her feelings about Israel and New York City, and her continuing and constant love of America. "It is my misfortune to be fascinated by the United States of America," she wrote at one point (*A Kind of Magic* 261). She knew such feelings may be interpreted as overly sentimental, but she excused her affection and love for her country by explaining that she balanced its glories and promises with its imperfections and flaws. "Potentially, it could be the wonder-government of the world, if only it would grow up" (*A Kind of Magic* 261). For this reason she claimed that, from 1921 on, in *The Girls* to *Ice Palace* and after, she had written a succession of novels of protest, loving protest, but protest nonetheless. At the same time, she had never forgotten her ethnic roots, from the high-school years in Appleton, when she sang every Friday night and Saturday morning in the choir at services in Temple Emanuel to her efforts to write, with George S. Kaufman, a play called *Bravo!* in 1948 (a flop) about refugees in New York.

SURVEY OF CRITICISM

Her novels, with the exception of *Show Boat* (1926), were serious social criticism, so she claimed, of lasting literary value (Reed 307). At best, they are didactic but carefully researched panoramic views of the American society from the early nineteenth-through the mid-twentieth century. The novels most lauded by the critics were *So Big* (1924), *Cimarron* (1930), *Saratoga Trunk* (1941), and *Giant* (1952). One senses that the sheer speed with which Ferber forced herself to write contributed, at least in part, to the limited critical success of her several other works. At any rate, book reviews provide the most reliable index of Ferber's critical reception since more serious criticism of her work is scarce.

So Big was undoubtedly Ferber's most praised work. Said Burton Roscoe of the *New York Tribune*, "To Miss Ferber's narrative and descriptive powers I genuflect in homage. Her voice is rich and vital; she sees material objects with penetrating and delightful vision; she has portrayed aspects of Chicago more vividly and with greater distinction than any writer I know." The reviewer for the *New York Times*, L. M. Field, recommended Ferber's novel as a "thoughtful book, clear and strong, dramatic at times, interesting always, clearsighted, sympathetic, a novel to read and remember." Finally, the reviewer for the *Literary*

Review of the New York Evening Post voiced qualified praise, but praise nonetheless, for *So Big* when he said, "With all its flaws and crudities it has the completeness, and finality that grips and exalts and convinces." He even goes so far, later in the review, as to call the novel a "masterpiece."

Cimarron received less enthusiastic, though generally positive, reviews, as well. Harry Hansen, the reviewer for *The World*, was impressed with Ferber's ability to "shape an enormous amount of detail into a flowing narrative." Unable, it seems, to cull enough complimentary adjectives, the reviewer of the *New Statesman* agreed with Hansen's take on the novel: "Its pace, its color, its *panache*, its gallant and defiant courage, its admirable, unapologetic Americanism are all delightful." The *New York Times* reviewer praised the novel as well, for "its splendidly kaleidoscopic view of a young American city coming into existence." Despite the overall kudos for *Cimarron*, Harvey Ferguson of the *New York Herald Tribune Books* adds a dissenting voice. In stark contrast to the reviewer of *The World*, he concluded that Ferber's "immense mass of material is never sufficiently fused and molded by any emotion." As a result, he asserted that the characters came off as unconvincing.

Reviewers seemed especially to appreciate Ferber's uncanny ability to put her finger squarely on the pulse and character of the nation. Of *Saratoga Trunk*, the reviewer for the *Springfield Republican* noted that the novel's "real value lies in its revival of another phase of American growth and national character. This is a glimpse of America in the making." Margaret Wallace of the *New York Times* predicted "skyrocket success for 'Saratoga Trunk,'" and the reviewer for the *New York Herald Tribune Books* appears every bit as enthusiastic when she says, "one closes *Saratoga Trunk* with the feeling of having lived in a rich and exciting world, peopled by fascinating and exciting characters no less real because they are eccentric and romantic." The reviewer also lauds Ferber's "meticulous care with all the details of background and characterization."

Of Ferber's four most important novels, *Giant* probably received the most mixed criticism. John Barkman of the *New York Times* clearly admired Ferber's courage in her frank criticism of Texas. He noted that Texans won't like Ferber much after reading the book, but he also asserted that "*Giant* makes marvelous reading—wealth piled on wealth, wonder on wonder in a stunning, splendiferous pyramid of ostentation." The *Saturday Review* reviewer, William Kittrell, also noted that "*Giant* will be joyfully received in forty-seven states and avidly though angrily read in Texas." On the other side of the critical fence, the reviewers for the *Christian Science Monitor* and *Kirkus* had only negative things to say about the novel (one must wonder whether they were, in fact, from Texas). The *Christian Science Monitor* reviewer argued that "the whole picture seems lacking in perspective" and warned that "the discriminating reader may want to investigate further before deciding upon the book's over-all validity." In agreement, the *Kirkus* reviewer asserted that the novel "reads like broad caricature" and "created frank distaste."

According to Mary Dearborn in a recent treatment, Edna Ferber found in the concept of intermarriage confirmation of the centrality of ethnic female sexuality in American culture. Seduced by the metaphor, aware of the sexual content of the symbolic content of the Pocahontas story, Ferber used the subject often in exploring the multiethnic and multiregional character of American life. *Cimarron* (1929) best typifies Ferber's response to the nexus of American and ethnic identity, in that intermarriage between Cimarron Cravat and Ruby Big Elk was smoothly translated into a classically American middle-class rhetoric, absorbed as an inevitable part of the American way. As Mary Dearborn sums it up, "intermarriage is woven seamlessly into the multi-ethnic fabric of American life, and becomes one of the multitude of unforced, natural, benevolent metaphors for the multi-ethnic American way" (127).

Diane Lichtenstein, however, in a more recent formulation, claims that Ferber, especially in *A Peculiar Treasure*, her first autobiography, remained ambivalent about public declarations of her Jewish identity, although she called herself an "American, a writer, and a Jew." Countering Dearborn, Lichtenstein raises the question of Ferber's response to her gender, observing that "woman" is not included in Ferber's self-description. The point, according to Lichtenstein, is that Ferber was a highly self-conscious author who brought together an American, a Jewish, a female, and a literary sensibility as integral parts of her "regional" formula. Ferber's particular exposure was veiled in the persona of the female pioneer who was an outsider but was ironically transformed from the "other" (the Jew and the woman) into the "one," the insider (130).

BIBLIOGRAPHY

Works by Edna Ferber

Books

Dawn O'Hara: The Girl Who Laughed. New York: Stokes, 1911.
Buttered Side Down. New York: Stokes, 1912.
Roast Beef, Medium: The Business Adventures of Emma McChesney. New York: Stokes, 1913.
Personality Plus: Some Experiences of Emma McChesney and Her Son, Jock. New York: Stokes, 1914.
Emma McChesney & Co. New York: Stokes, 1915.
Fanny Herself. New York: Stokes, 1917.
Cheerful, By Request. Garden City, NY: Doubleday, Page, 1918.
Half Portions. Garden City, NY: Doubleday, Page, 1920.
$1200 a Year, by Ferber and Newman Levy. Garden City, NY: Doubleday, Page, 1920.
The Girls. Garden City, NY and Toronto: Doubleday, Page, 1921.
Gigolo. Garden City, NY: Doubleday, Page, 1922.
"Old Man Minick," and *Minick*, by Ferber and George S. Kaufman. Garden City, NY: Doubleday, Page, 1924.
So Big. Garden City, NY: Doubleday, Page, 1924.

Show Boat. Garden City, NY: Doubleday, Page, 1926.
Mother Knows Best: A Fiction Book. Garden City, NY: Doubleday, Page, 1927.
The Royal Family, by Ferber and Kaufman. Garden City, NY: Doubleday, Doran, 1928.
Cimarron. Garden City, NY: Doubleday, Doran, 1930.
American Beauty. Garden City, NY: Doubleday, Doran, 1931.
Dinner at Eight, by Ferber and Kaufman. Garden City, NY: Doubleday, Doran, 1932.
They Brought Their Women. Garden City, NY: Doubleday, Doran, 1933.
Come and Get It. Garden City, NY: Doubleday, Doran, 1935.
Stage Door, by Ferber and Kaufman. Garden City, NY: Doubleday, Doran, 1936.
Nobody's in Town. Garden City, NY: Doubleday, Doran, 1938.
A Peculiar Treasure. New York: Doubleday, Doran, 1939.
The Land Is Bright, by Ferber and Kaufman. Garden City, NY: Doubleday, Doran, 1941.
No Room at the Inn. Garden City, NY: Doubleday, Doran, 1941.
Saratoga Trunk. Garden City, NY: Doubleday, Doran, 1941.
Great Son. Garden City, NY: Doubleday, Doran, 1945.
One Basket: Thirty-One Short Stories. New York: Simon & Schuster, 1947.
Your Town. Cleveland: World, 1948.
Bravo! by Ferber and Kaufman. New York: Dramatists Play Service, 1949.
Giant. Garden City, NY: Doubleday, 1952.
Ice Palace. Garden City, NY: Doubleday, 1958.
A Kind of Magic. Garden City, NY: Doubleday, 1963.

Selected Plays

Our Mrs. McChesney, by Ferber and George V. Hobart, New York, Lyceum Theatre, 19 October 1915.
Minick, by Ferber and Kaufman, New York, Booth Theatre, 24 September 1924.
The Royal Family, by Ferber and Kaufman, New York, Selwyn Theatre, 28 December 1927.
Dinner at Eight, by Ferber and Kaufman, New York, Music Box Theatre, 22 October 1932.
Stage Door, by Ferber and Kaufman, New York, Music Box Theatre, 22 October 1936.
This Land Is Bright, by Ferber and Kaufman, New York, Music Box Theatre, 28 October 1941.
Bravo! by Ferber and Kaufman, New York, Lyceum Theatre, 11 November 1948.

Papers

The State Historical Society of Wisconsin is the main repository for Edna Ferber's papers.

Works about Edna Ferber

Brenni, V. J., and B. L. Spencer. "Edna Ferber: A Selected Bibliography." *Bulletin of Bibliography* 22 (1958):152–56.
Dearborn, Mary V. *Pocahontas's Daughters: Gender and Ethnicity in American Culture.* New York: Oxford University Press, 1986.
Gilbert, Julie Goldsmith. *Ferber: A Biography.* Garden City, NY: Doubleday, 1978.
Horowitz, Stephen, and Miriam Landsman. "Edna Ferber." *Dictionary of Literary Biography* 28 (1984):58–64.

Lichtenstein, Diane. *Writing Their Nations: The Tradition of Nineteenth Century American Jewish Women Writers.* Indianapolis: Indiana University Press, 1992.

Reed, Paula. "Edna Ferber." *Dictionary of Literary Biography.* 9 (1981):306–12.

Uffen, Ellen Serlen. "Edna Ferber." *Dictionary of Literary Biography* 86 (1989):91–98.

Selected Reviews

SO BIG

Field, L. M. Rev. of *So Big*, by Edna Ferber. *New York Times* 24 February 1924:9.

Roscoe, Burton. Rev. of *So Big*, by Edna Ferber. *New York Tribune* 16 March 1924:19.

Smertenko, J. J. Rev. of *So Big*, by Edna Ferber. *Literary Review of the New York Evening Post.* 1 March 1924:555.

CIMARRON

Rev. of *Cimarron*, by Edna Ferber. *New Statesman* 24 May 1930:217.

Rev. of *Cimarron*, by Edna Ferber. *New York Times* 23 March 1930:4.

Ferguson, Harvey. Rev. of *Cimarron*, by Edna Ferber. *New York Herald Tribune Books* 23 March 1930:7.

Hansen, Harry. Rev. of *Cimarron*, by Edna Ferber. *The World* 20 March 1930:13.

SARATOGA TRUNK

Feld, Rose, Rev. of *Saratoga Trunk*, by Edna Ferber. *New York Herald Tribune Books* 2 November 1941:5.

Rev. of *Saratoga Trunk*, by Edna Ferber. *Springfield Republican* 2 November 1941:7.

Wallace, Margaret. Rev. of *Saratoga Trunk*, by Edna Ferber. *New York Times* 2 November 1941:4.

GIANT

Barkham, John. Rev. of *Giant*, by Edna Ferber. *New York Times* 28 September 1952:4.

Rev. of *Giant*, by Edna Ferber. *Christian Science Monitor* 2 October 1952:6.

Rev. of *Giant*, by Edna Ferber. *Kirkus* 15 July 1952:419.

Kittrell, William. Rev. of *Giant*, by Edna Ferber. *Saturday Review* 27 September 1952: 15.

REBECCA GOLDSTEIN (1950–   )

Sylvia Barack Fishman

BIOGRAPHY

Rebecca Goldstein was born in 1950 in White Plains, New York, into a tradi-tionally observant Jewish family. Her father was a cantor who had emigrated to the United States from Poland, and whose sweetness of nature and dedication to both traditional Judaism and to cantorial music had an enormous impact on Goldstein's life and work. Goldstein attended public elementary school but was enrolled in a rigorously Orthodox girls' *yeshiva* for her high-school years. She earned her bachelor's degree from Barnard College and went on for a Ph.D. in the Philosophy of Science from Princeton University. Goldstein taught philos-ophy at Barnard College for ten years but today devotes herself entirely to writing. She is the winner of a Whiting Writers Award and of an American Council of Learned Societies Grant.

Although Goldstein says she "never intended to become a writer," with the publication of her first novel, *The Mind-Body Problem*, in 1983 and a powerful story about Holocaust survivors, "The Legacy of Raizel Kaidish," in 1985 her career as a writer was firmly launched. She has published three novels and a number of short stories; her collection of largely unpublished stories, *Strange Attractors*, was published by Viking in 1993. She is currently working on a novel about four generations of mothers and daughters, which depicts, among other themes, currents that distance her characters from Judaism only to return them closer to Jewish life. She is a frequent reviewer for the *New York Times* and writes book reviews for other publications. Goldstein is married to a phys-icist and has two daughters. She describes her lifestyle as "traditional" and says she has "close ties to Orthodoxy," although her mixed feelings about Orthodox attitudes are apparent in her fiction as well as conversation.

MAJOR THEMES

Rebecca Goldstein's fiction often explores the mind-body problem, the theme spelled out by the title of her first novel, in ever deeper and more complex literary modes. She demonstrates that people who try to live entirely according to intellectual, rational dictates and to deny the seemingly irrational demands of their physical selves are fundamentally living a lie. Moreover, by rejecting part of themselves, they essentially create within themselves a fifth column, an alienated and unacknowledged aspect of their own being. When Goldstein's characters imagine that they have totally cleansed themselves of whatever they consider undesirable needs and emotions, those very needs and emotions lay in wait, ready to ambush them when they are vulnerable. The more rigorously her characters reject and suppress their own bodily passions and physicality, the more savagely the body reasserts itself eventually.

This tendency to reject aspects of oneself is especially pronounced in female characters in Goldstein's fiction. Thus, in her books, an Orthodox mother rejects her daughter's beauty as being sexually inflammatory and thus religiously problematic; a college professor has nothing but scorn for overtly sexual female students; and an atheistic academic rejects her own female sexuality as an indication of intellectual inferiority. A brilliant young wife fears her own intelligence is an irritant incompatible with domestic peace, and a proper, tightly controlled woman so completely rejects and fears her own lively imagination that she creates a separate identity to embody it.

In Goldstein's novel *The Mind-Body Problem* (1983), the protagonist is a woman both beautiful and brilliant, pulled between Judaism and secularism, and surrounded by individuals who try to convince her that her variety is really inconsistency and is problematic rather than delightful. The character Renee Feuer, pursuing a Ph.D. in Philosophy at Princeton University, is not taken seriously by her professors because she is too pretty to be smart and too smart to be pretty. Her family has been equally unsupportive: Her mother "had greeted each announcement of my educational plans with 'Nu, Renee, is this going to help you find a husband?' so that the consequence of all my academic honors, Phi Beta Kappa, *summa cum laude*, scholarships, fellowships, prizes, was only a deepening sense of guilty failure." When Renee calls to tell her mother that she has become engaged to a world-famous mathematician, her mother uses this happy occasion to strip Renee even further: "You should be very proud, Renee, that such a man should love you. Of course, I know you're not just any girl. Who should know if not me? This is why God gave you such good brains, so that you could make such a man like this love you" (67–70).

But it is not only Renee's Orthodox mother and her atheistic male professors who have trouble dealing with the concept of a beautiful but brainy woman. Her best friend from undergraduate days at Barnard, a fiercely antireligious female physicist named Ava, is convinced she must make herself both androgynous and intentionally ugly to be taken seriously by herself and others as an intellectual, "because feminine is dumb." Ava urges Renee to observe "the women who make their living from their brains," and she will see that they too believe "you just can't be a cunt with intelligence." Although Ava yearningly notes that "it would be an act of feminist heroism, an assertion of true liberation from the chauvinist myth, to wear eyeliner and mascara,'' she admits that she herself will never have the strength to integrate mind and body (216–17).

In Goldstein's fiction, characters can feel isolated not only because they have ambivalent feelings about being women, but also because they have ambivalent feelings about being Jews. Renee Feuer, the protagonist of *The Mind-Body Problem*, grew up in an Orthodox home but moves incrementally away from her religious training during college and then graduate school. Doing undergraduate work at Barnard, she discovers modern Orthodoxy, sexuality, and totally secularized Jews. Later, while she is working on a Ph.D. in Philosophy at Princeton, the scope of her religious antecedents allows her to experience particularly poignant varieties of knowledgeable, spiritual ambivalence. Within Goldstein's fiction, religious environments are depicted unselfconsciously and with a balanced awareness of their strengths and weaknesses.

Although Renee is no longer religiously observant, she is repeatedly drawn to the richness of Orthodox life, both as she remembers it from her parental home and as she observes it in the home of her brother and sister-in-law, a pious young couple living among others of their kind in Lakewood, New Jersey. Renee is troubled by the position of women in Orthodox societies, which often put women into marginal positions. On the other hand, Renee admires and yearns after the spirituality often woven into the texture of Orthodox life.

When Renee abandons religious ritual for the study of philosophy, there is more than a little religious intensity and spiritual searching in her choice. She marries a mathematical genius, and once again her choice is related to a search for definitive spiritual answers. Much to her surprise, she finds that her Jewishly ignorant husband is as sexist—perhaps more so—as her ultra-Orthodox brother. She finds herself increasingly disoriented and spiritually hungry. Chilled by the intolerance for or apathy toward Judaism of her Jewish companions, she feels isolated:

I stared out at the winter-stripped elms and remembered Shabbos at home. I could hear my father's singing, the sweet warm tenor rising up in his love. Beside the secular chatter of the Jewish *goyim* I had surrounded myself with, circumcised by doctors and not knowing what it is to yearn for the coming of the Messiah, sounded insignificant and despicable. But I had despised the religiosity of my past. How could I expect anyone to share my outlook, contradictory as it is? (277)

Thus, Goldstein's protagonist Renee is isolated because she is not simple or simplistically defined; she is simultaneously beautiful and brilliant, intellectual and sensual. She is drawn to the sweetness of traditional Jewish life but repelled by its distorted view of women. But despite Renee's discomfort, she manages not to internalize the destructive categories that a variety of societies would like to impose upon her life. She remains, more or less, an organically integrated personality. In her subsequent fiction, Goldstein depicts characters who have been less successful at holding their internal lives together. Her later female protagonists can only survive by rejecting part of themselves.

Sometimes rejection of an aspect of oneself is passed on to a child in Goldstein's fiction, especially when an earlier trauma has crippled the parent in some way. In a short story, "The Legacy of Raizel Kaidish" (1985), Goldstein brings the traumatic impact of the Holocaust to bear on issues of mother-daughter relationships and the moral education of children. The story portrays a mother who engineers her daughter Rose's personality through the strongest kind of emotional manipulation. She tries to create of her daughter a selfless, dispassionately altruistic saint, all in an effort to expiate her own profound moral failure within the hell of the concentration camps. Rose's childhood is subsumed by her father's sadness at the "quiet blue fury" of her mother's total "goodness." Rose discovers that her mother's rationalistic spirituality is a fraud—a fraud that has divested her of both the carefree joys of childhood and the soul-building conviction of unearned and unshakable parental affection, when dialogue with her mother has become impossible. Only on her deathbed does the mother acknowledge that she has been wrong to sacrifice her daughter's autonomy.

In an essay, "Looking Back on Lot's Wife" (1992), Goldstein spells out her beliefs that "the fullness of human life" demands love that transcends reason or even personal safety. Working from classical rabbinic sources as well as her own interpretations, Goldstein speculates that Lot's wife was turned into a pillar of salt because she was tormented by the knowledge that she was leaving two married daughters behind in Sodom. The safety that lay ahead of her could not compete with love for the children who remained behind her, facing certain and horrible destruction. Suggesting that parents ought to love their children more deeply than they love any ideal, even if such love does not fit into a rational scheme, Goldstein says it is "right for a human life to be subject to contradictions, for a person to love in more than one direction, and sometimes to be torn into pieces because of . . . many loves" (41).

Goldstein expands themes that include the necessary irrationality of love, the Holocaust, and the mind-body problem to include the darkest aspects of human nature in her second novel, *The Late Summer Passion of a Woman of Mind* (1989). Eva Mueller, the protagonist, is a forty-six-year-old German intellectual, a highly popular yet uncompromisingly rigorous university professor who eschews what she sees as the mediocrity of the commoner passions. She believes that most women—including many of her female students—are inextricably bound up in a mediocre, common, and unpleasant physicality: "This girl, whom she could quite easily imagine as attractive to a certain kind of man, represented what Eva herself found most distasteful in womanhood. . . . the members of her own sex for the most part disgusted her. This heaving, viscous pool of feelings and sensations. . . . " (18).

Eva's rejection of her own female sexual impulses is connected in complicated ways to her intellectual disconnection with her once-idolized father and his past involvement with the Nazi movement. Eva distances herself emotionally from her biological father and her own biology. She lives—she thinks—on a purely intellectual level, unsullied by the dark and dangerous impulses over which, she fears, she may have no control. Her only link with the murky world of sexuality is music, which is at once sensual and intellectual. When she is, unexpectedly, swept away by a passionate affair with one of her students, the emotions that come flooding in on her force her to confront, finally, the savagery of which humanity is capable and her own animal nature as well.

Squeamishness about one's own female physical nature, to the point of outright denial, is carried even further in Goldstein's next novel, *The Dark Sister* (1991). Here, her Jewish female protagonist is once again brilliant and talented, but she looks and behaves like an all-mind *golem*. A huge, hulking, reclusive, almost sexless creature, Hedda (head-a?) James has adopted the *nom de plume* Dunkele, Yiddish for "little dark one," her mother's pet name for her. Throughout the book, with interwoven and overlapping novels within the novel, Goldstein explores the phenomenon of women choosing to explore some aspects of their own inner world while denying others.

In prose that suggests in equal measures the influence of Henry James and Cynthia Ozick (who was herself influenced by James), Rebecca Goldstein suggests in *The Dark Sister* that American Jewish women have often come to regard large segments of their own personhood as alien, as other, as "the dark sister" to their more politically correct, acceptable public personae. One of the critical lines of battle facing Jewish feminists has been to free themselves and their sisters of these pervasive negative images that have done much to erode the self-esteem of American Jewish women, as well as their standing in Jewish and non-Jewish society. When American Jews think about the nature and capacity of Jewish women, they are influenced not only by changes in the social, economic, and political realities around them, but also by a lifetime of contact with often negatively portrayed female characters in the books they read, the movies they see, and the television programs they watch.

Goldstein draws the reader into the novel as a collaborator and coconspirator by making the reader a lot more aware of what is motivating Hedda and her literary creations than is Hedda herself. Throughout the novel, Hedda is involved in writing her own novel, a piece in which each of the James siblings—Henry, William, and their sister Alice—are characters. While Hedda is infuriatingly obtuse about herself, huge chunks of her family history, the people she meets, and the motivations of her literary characters, she has previously produced an impressive opus of wildly successful novels, each of which explores a stereotype of the Jewish woman. Rejecting the image of the JAP, the "Jewish American princess," Hedda has produced instead a series of JAWs—the "Jewish angry woman." Their titles and some details of their action enable Goldstein to satirize not only male misogynist stereotypes, but also feminist stereotypes, which are also based in misogyny because they require women to deny aspects of themselves. Each of the protagonists of Hedda's books is a "fierce but beautiful

JAW'' who appeals not only to feminists but also, unaccountably (to Hedda) to ''an untallied number of unregenerate pigs.'' Thus, Hedda's successful books include *Etta, The Rebbe's Daughter!*; *Hanna, The Husband's Whore!*; *Sara, The Savant's Sister!*; *Mona, The Momzer's Mother!*; *Minna, the Messiah's Mother-in-Law!*; *Clara, The Corporate Korva!*; and *Dora, The Doctor's Daughter!* (222).

The novel shows that women can be alienated from their inner selves as Jewish women. Women can also reject themselves if they feel that they are unacceptably intellectual, artistic, scientific, mystical, violent, angry, or non–maternal—any of these pieces of themselves can potentially be viewed as ''other.'' If they acknowledge these pieces of themselves, women sometimes feel like ''monsters,'' as in the poem ''Planetarium'' by Adrienne Rich in which a female astronomer sees a sky full of female monsters. Women have been manipulated by society to reject intrinsic aspects of their personhood, doing irrevocable damage to their own mental health and productivity and self-esteem. In different societies the objectionable—or monstrous—portions of the female psyche change, but the dynamic of creating within oneself a ''dark sister'' remains the same.

SURVEY OF CRITICISM

To date, most criticism of Rebecca Goldstein's works has consisted of book reviews and scattered sections of larger works of criticism of American Jewish fiction. The reviews of her first novel, *The Mind-Body Problem* (1983), were largely positive. Frances Taliaferro wrote admiringly in *Harper's*, ''I know of no other novel of the feminist era that not only anatomizes the dilemma of the intellectual woman in an anti-intellectual woman's thinking.'' Taliaferro felt the novel was much enhanced by ''Rebecca Goldstein's didactic gifts'' and ''pellucid clarity.'' *New York Times* book reviewer Caroline Seebohm praised Goldstein's ''generous sense of humor'' and wrote that the novel is ''clever and funny,'' especially because Goldstein takes the dichotomy between intellectual and emotional aspects of life and ''makes it sparkle.'' A somewhat different approach was taken by Galen Strawson, in the *Times Literary Supplement*, who asserted that ''the *Mind-Body Problem* is lightweight, stylistically routine, and structurally spasmodic,'' and that ''there are moments when a curious didacticism prevails.'' Although faulting the book for ''caricature,'' Strawson concluded that ''in its own flip way, it conveys a real sense of the drama of ideas.''

Goldstein's second novel, *The Late-Summer Passion of a Woman of Mind* (1989), ranged into highly symbolic and more experimental novelistic territory. Michiko Kakutani wrote in the *New York Times* that the symbolism at times is heavy-handed, but that Goldstein's writing achieved by the end ''a pleasing emotional chiaroscuro, a deepening and darkening of ambition.'' More critically, Robert Cohen, also writing in the *New York Times*, faulted the novel for ''predictability'' and asserted that Goldstein ''has been crippled by her own conceptions.'' Cohen felt that the protagonist's shockingly divided sense of the world and herself, combined with her "dearth of common sense and her general slowness on the uptake," have the effect of reinforcing "some of the least imaginative stereotypes that are applied to her profession."

The most mixed reviews were garnered by Goldstein's third and, to date, most literarily ambitious novel, *The Dark Sister* (1991). Angeline Goreau, reviewing the book in the *New York Times*, commented on Goldstein's "complex narrative form," which proceeds through "borrowings and mirrors, parallel plots and possession." She admired Goldstein's explorations of the divisions between "masculine and feminine, self and other, fiction and reality, the corporeal and the fantastic," and was especially impressed with the novel's "send-up of academic feminist theory." However, Goreau saw as a "serious weakness" a weighty "structure of symbols and references constructed around them," which seemed to her more vivid and lifelike than the characters themselves.

New York Times book reviewer Michiko Kakutani, however, lauded *The Dark Sister* and declared that "one has the sense, with this book, of reading a writer who has just discovered the full possibilities of her talent." She noted that Goldstein's "clever, observant and nimble" writing excels in illuminating "the transactions that take place between life and art . . . and how fictional characters can take on a life of their own, eluding the control of their creator even as they lay bare the workings of the unconscious." Kakutani admired Goldstein's ability to simultaneously re-create "the sonorous tones of Henry James," to create "a wicked satire on feminist fiction," and to explore "the relationship between reason and passion, the intellect and the hungry soul," in a mode even more nuanced, rich, and compelling than in her earlier writing.

BIBLIOGRAPHY

Works by Rebecca Goldstein

The Mind-Body Problem. New York: Dell Publishing, 1983.
The Late Summer Passion of a Woman of Mind. New York: Farrar, Straus and Giroux, 1989.
The Dark Sister. New York: Viking Penguin, 1991.
"Rabbinical Eyes—A Story." *Commentary* June 1991:39–51.
"Looking Back at Lot's Wife." *Commentary* September 1992:37–41.
Strange Attractors. New York: Viking, 1993.

Works about Rebecca Goldstein

Robert Cohen, "Roll Over Spinoza." Rev. of *The Late Summer Passion of a Woman of Mind*. *New York Times Book Review* 7 May 1989:28–29.
Angeline Goreau, "She Is Henry James, Only Taller." Rev. of *The Dark Sister*. *New York Times Book Review* 11 August 1991:29.

Michiko Kakutani, "Ah, Comes the Spring and Love Liberates Logic." Rev. of *The Late Summer Passion of a Woman of Mind. New York Times* 18 April 1989:28–29.

———. "From Fierce Feminism to Jamesian Subtlety." Rev. of *The Dark Sister. New York Times* 6 August 1991:C16.

Caroline Seebohm, "Husbands, Lovers and Parents." Rev. of *The Mind-Body Problem. New York Times Book Review* 25 September 1983:14.

Galen Strawson, "Idea-dramas: Rebecca Goldstein." Rev. of *The Mind-Body Problem. Times Literary Supplement* 1 March 1985:227.

Frances Taliaferro, Rev. of *The Mind-Body Problem. Harper's* December 1983:74–75.

ALLEGRA GOODMAN (1967–   )

C. Beth Burch

BIOGRAPHY

Allegra Goodman might be considered a New Yorker because she was born in Brooklyn. She might be considered a Hawaiian because her parents moved to Honolulu, Hawaii, when Allegra was two-and-a-half and because she grew up there. And she might also be considered a Californian because she has lived in Stanford since 1990. But Allegra Goodman is at once all and none of these: She is above all a writer whose cosmopolitan Jewishness informs and infuses her fiction.

Goodman is the child of an academic family. Her father, Lenn Goodman, is a philosopher at the University of Hawaii; Madeleine Goodman, her mother, a human biologist by training, is now an administrator also at the University of Hawaii. Allegra Goodman and her younger sister, Paula, grew up in Honolulu, Hawaii, which has become the setting for many of her stories. Goodman studied at the private Punahou School in Honolulu, then attended Harvard as an undergraduate; there she concentrated on English and philosophy and accrued honors as a John Harvard Scholar, an Elizabeth Carey Agassiz Scholar, and a winner of the Briggs Prize for English. At Harvard, she also met her husband, David Karger, a computer scientist; after her graduation they married, then spent a year in England, where, as a Churchill Fellow, David studied mathematics at Cambridge and she spent her time "just writing."[1] They have a son, Ezra, born in 1992.

By the time she spent that year in England, Goodman was already a published author who had garnered many awards. Her poems had been published in *Bamboo Ridge: Hawaii Literary Quarterly* (1985), *New England Sampler* (1985), *Honolulu Star Bulletin* and *Honolulu Advertiser* (1985), *Harvard Advocate* (1986), and *Mosaic* (1988). She had begun writing the stories that were published in *Total Immersion* when she was seventeen, but she had been preparing to write them all her life, for she always "thought of [her]self as a writer." Her first published story, "Variant Text," appeared in *Commentary* in June 1986, after Marion Magid, the managing editor, "plucked it out of the slush pile." Soon after it was followed by "Wish List," also in *Commentary*, and then out tumbled a cascade of stories in *Commentary* and the *New Yorker*. The publication of *Total Immersion* came in June 1989. In October 1991, Goodman was one of ten writers, including Rebecca Goldstein, Stanley Crouch, and Cynthia Kadohata, who received the Whiting Writers Awards, which was accompanied by a cash prize of $30,000 for each recipient. Goodman is now a Ph.D. student at Stanford studying Renaissance literature, her longtime interest. The history of ideas, poetry, verse plays—all these make the Renaissance "a good place to work" for Goodman, who plans a dual career as a scholar and a fiction writer.

Goodman does not acknowledge any influences, but she admires Shakespeare and Milton, the short stories of Chekhov, Henry James, James Joyce, and Katherine Anne Porter, and the novels of George Eliot. Among more recent writers she is drawn to the work of Cynthia Ozick, Eudora Welty, Tillie Olsen, and Saul Bellow, all of whose work she believes to be very different from hers. For Goodman, each story writes itself anew. When she prepares to write a story, she "sits down and thinks about what [she has] to write rather than [about] other people's work."

Does Allegra Goodman think of herself as a Jewish writer? Labeling herself "traditional, somewhere between Conservative and Orthodox," she believes that, in many ways, she is a Jewish writer because many of the topics and people she writes about are Jewish. Jewishness has provided her with rich material: a community and a culture to write about a literary tradition that includes both scriptural and theological traditions. Goodman is keenly interested in religion, and this interest often manifests itself directly in her work. In "Onionskin," one of her favorite stories, she draws explicitly on Psalms and liturgical phrases, but the Jewish presence is everywhere in her work, from the intonation of her characters' speech to their family relationships and the very themes undergirding the fiction.

MAJOR THEMES

Most of Goodman's stories take place in Hawaii—surely an atypical Jewish milieu. Readers have perhaps grown inured to acculturation tales from Brooklyn and Boston, but Goodman's characters wearing muu-muus at Yom Kippur and spreading cream cheese on whole wheat bagels from Hawaiian Bagel remind us anew of the protean nature of Jewish culture, always changing yet always remaining the same, a drama with a boilerplate plot and a wide cast of alternating actors.

Goodman's characters include malcontents in the congregation as well as more earnest questors who evince the serious ideological tensions within Judaism. In "The Succession," for example, Rabbi Everett Siegel of Martin Buber Temple, Honolulu, struggles in relinquishing leadership of his congregation to the younger Rabbi Leibowitz, who is very good with the young people of the congregation, but unfortunately, Siegel thinks, unable to comfort mourners properly. In ''And Also Much Cattle,'' an ultra-Orthodox family newly arrived to Hawaii builds its own synagogue, a louvered room at the back of their house, complete with separate seating for the women—in the section of the room where the air from the fan doesn't reach. ''Fait'' is Goodman's only story without a Jewish protagonist—but Ginnie, its main character, does have a Jewish boyfriend, Noam, and this story reveals something of Jewish culture by virtue of its explication of a contrasting Christian culture. Ginnie returns to Hawaii from school at Berkeley to attend her sister's wedding and discovers that her education and removal from her family have totally alienated her from their culture and values; the presence of Noam, a figure from her life at Berkeley and a Jew in their fundamentalist Christian household, merely emphasizes her displacement. The name ''Fait'' in the title refers to a pidgin abridgment of *Faith*, the name of a character in a local nightclub act, as Ginnie explains to Noam in a lecture on local color—and in this story it is Ginnie's Christian faith that is foreshortened.

In other stories, Goodman presents us with other searchers, frequently female, whose quests for meaning are half-serious, half-comedic, a curious and ironic mix. ''Onionskin'' is an epistolary story in which a ''mature'' student, Sharon, writes the story of her life and tribulations in a long letter to her former professor at the University of Hawaii, Dr. Friedell. Sharon appends an almost incidental plea that Friedell accept her letter as the final paper for the course, a class on religion, because it ''basically summarizes [her] current views and independent research of religions'' while ''touching on Augustine briefly'' (''Onionskin,'' 35). In the story ''Total Immersion,'' an inadvertent questor, Sandra Lefkowitz, who planned to enter the diplomatic service, instead marries and stays in Hawaii, where she finds herself teaching French at Oahu Prep School. Sandra's notion of teaching conflicts with that of the head of the French Department, who reminds the teachers, Sandra included, that oral survival skills are the focus of the curriculum: ''total immersion in what we're after. Context will come. The fine points will come'' (247). Sandra resists this French acculturation: She just wants her students to know verbs. Her struggle with her students' total immersion is emblematic of conflicts within the Jewish community, and hers is an unresolved but somehow humorous struggle. Goodman's work does not suggest solutions; rather, it offers accommodation and an intimation of redemption. In ''Wish List'' and ''The Wedding of Henry Markowitz,'' Henry Markowitz, lover of small and beautiful objects, reaches for the exquisite that exists beyond the quotidian—and never quite finds it. He is left searching for some kind of transcendence, unlike his brother Ed Markowitz, a straight-ahead and egocentric academic. The Markowitz brothers' idiosyncrasies balance neatly, negate one another, and a family equilibrium is thereby maintained. In Goodman's universe, visions and realities don't collide: they simply grow into one another and become indivisible, each an inextricable part of a seamless whole.

Goodman overlays her portraits of Jewish life with unmistakable satire. She is a Jewish Jane Austen with an edge, producing wry, intimate scenes and small landscapes. Her prose, frequently laced with unexplained words from Hebrew and Yiddish, is tight, controlled, yet rich, evocative, and dense with detail, like a tightly woven fine tapestry. Her "England stories" are especially lapidary and comical. In "Variant Text," the literary scholar turned househusband, Cecil, struggles to rein in all the members of his and his wife's family. He must fix the old folks' breakfast oatmeal, keep an eye on the crazy poet sister-in-law Clare, and mind his children, who are enrolled in the local Jewish day school, the *gan*. Cecil is an agnostic, but he loves Jewish law. The story addresses his difficulties in acknowledging variant texts in all their manifestations—even though, ironically, his life is a variation of a traditional male text. "Clare," a companion story, focuses on Cecil's sister-in-law, Clare Cahen, who thinks she is wanted by the police in Germany and the nuns in Spain, both of whom "want her words" and "pick at her brain" ("Clare" 213). Clare writes poems, which are published by another American living in England, Henry Markowitz, who also appears in "The Wedding of Henry Markowitz," "Wish List," and "Young People." Henry, an Anglophile American expatriate, manages a Laura Ashley store, publishes fine books of literature, and embodies the conflict of cultures so prevalent in Goodman's work—and so is an ideal candidate for her sly and subtle wit.

What gives all of Goodman's stories coherence is the bittersweet experience of Jewish life; it is the lever of her fiction. *Tzuris* (troubles) and *mazel* (luck) compete for attention in the stories. Jewishness informs her created cosmos; it is the engine that drives life and experience. Her characters, male and female alike, struggle with the realities of being Jewish, but her female characters seem to hold it in an easier embrace; her male characters want to scrutinize it, debate, use, and manipulate it. The aging Rose Markowitz in "Oral History" may not remember specific details of her life from one interview to the next, but she has survived, and she has the wisdom of someone at peace with who she is—and who she has been as well. Sharon, the protagonist of "Onionskin," just wants to "put everything on the line for religion" and have her "big questions" answered (29), but her professor keeps getting lost in the details, much to Sharon's frustration. In fact, almost everyone Sharon encounters in her quest for answers is mired in materialism, reality, or "the negative," and she alone searches for "the stars" (35).

A keen observer, Goodman sifts and catalogues Jewish experience in Hawaii, England, and California and manages to wed them all. Every story increases the number of connections and widens the screen on which the settings converge. Characters duck out of one story and emerge in others. Rose Markowitz, interview subject in "Oral History," is the mother of the aging groom in "The Wedding of Henry Markowitz." Ed Markowitz, Henry's brother, appears in "Wish List" and also in "The Wedding of Henry Markowitz." This sense of a reconvening story underscores the reader's feeling of absorption—if you will, immersion—in a peculiarly exotic yet at the same time familiar and comfortable

Jewish world. The notion of immersion operates in more than one way and for the reader as well as for the characters. Immersion is, as Sanford Pinsker has written, that possibility of imminent engulfment in something unfamiliar, and by extension, something disquieting. In the story "Total Immersion," immersion is literally the intense acculturation of students to a "foreign" environment. But Goodman's immersion may also refer to the astronomical phenomenon where one celestial body obscures or shadows another. Thus immersion can describe the struggle for light, clarity, vision, and even for ascendancy—as Ed Markowitz competes with not only his brother, but also with the other Wantage scholars for intellectual capital ("Wish List"). Immersion may also allude to the profound absorption that many of Goodman's characters seek. Sharon in "Onionskin," Henry Markowitz, Rabbi Siegel in "The Succession," Sandra Lefkowitz in "Total Immersion": These characters are among the seekers. They have not achieved total immersion yet; after all, there are con men in the congregation, recalcitrant French students, real terrorists who don't follow rules, and a constant stream of *pilpul*. There is, however, the possibility of finding the ineffable and the possibility of redemption, both personal and theological—and this is what Goodman holds before us.

SURVEY OF CRITICISM

Goodman's collection of stories, *Total Immersion*, was widely reviewed by well-known critics, who often responded with surprise at her skill, given her youth; virtually all reviewers marvel at her being only twenty-one when *Total Immersion* was published. Sanford Pinsker laments that even the word *precocious* seems inadequate to describe her talent: He calls the satire in her stories "deliciously satiric" ("Jews, Jewish Traditions" 8). Faye Moskowitz also notes the satire in Goodman's work but sees that her stories reflect current tensions in the Jewish community (7). Sylvia Rothchild agrees that Goodman's stories are about familiar Jewish issues: "struggles between generations, problems with rabbis, styles of fund raising, progressive Orthodox day school conflicts, and the never-ending struggle between tradition and acculturation" (16). She notes the constant use of displacement and alienation as a theme. This alienation provokes spiritual searching, as Francine Prose writes in a review of *Total Immersion*. Prose sees many of the characters as spiritual questors trying to find a "balance between tradition and change" (20).

Fault-finding in the reviews is rare, but two reviewers do indicate weaknesses. In an otherwise favorable review, Sherie Posesorski suggests that Goodman's stories are shallow: "Ms. Goodman is young, and her stories lack depth of feeling." Posesorski thinks that Goodman overuses present-tense narration and is ultimately "unable to sustain her narrative" (Posesorski n.p.). Randi Hacker's very short notice of *Total Immersion* in the *New York Times Book Review* was decidedly unfriendly: Hacker claims that Goodman's characters express themselves "too academically to elicit much sympathy" (26).

Goodman has earned notice in some major critical pieces. In a front-page essay in the *New York Times Book Review* on Jewish American writers, Ted Solotaroff argues that the future of American Jewish writing lies "in the keeping" of writers like Allegra Goodman, writers with roots in the observant community but who are caught up in the intersections of "Judaism and modernity under the impact of feminism, the sexual revolution, and the Holocaust" (1). Goodman's story "Variant Text" was anthologized in *Writing Our Way Home: Contemporary Stories by American Jewish Writers*, and Mark Krupnick singles out the story in his review of the collection. Krupnick likes "Variant Text" because its "character and situation depart from the conventions of Jewish American fiction." He suggests that Goodman's satirical target, the "progressive wing of the religiously Orthodox," is a sharp new focus (14).

The major critical discussion of Goodman's work is Sanford Pinsker's article, "Satire, Social Realism, and Moral Seriousness: The Case of Allegra Goodman," published in *Studies in American Jewish Literature*. Pinsker asserts that Goodman's work is demonstrable proof of the vitality of Jewish American fiction and that she is writing toward a "compassion wise beyond her years" (184). He points out that her writing incarnates the requisite "moral edge" and "special angle of vision" that Theodore Solotaroff believes defines Jewish-American fiction. Pinsker places Goodman in the tradition of satire and social realism: Her targets are political correctness, exaggerated moral seriousness, the inflated and conflated academic, and all sorts of stereotypical Jewish personalities that become, in her hands, not only exposed but somehow transmogrified to beings less stereotypical, more human. For Goodman, he says, a Jewish wedding is an occasion rich with satiric opportunity, as are congregational relationships, synagogue business, and power struggles between rabbis. As Pinsker indicates, though, Goodman takes religious ideas and religious practice seriously: "In her stories Jewishness is not merely an occasion for the mounting up of sociological detail, but rather it is a reckoning of how widely differing constituencies define, and act, on religious matters" (192). What amuses and intrigues Pinsker most, however, seems to be the note of irony, that hint of a fine balance going vaguely askew in Goodman's work. For him "total immersion" is "that prospect of being swamped—of a total immersion into the unfamiliar" (193) always looming as a possibility. Pinsker considers Goodman one of the very important new voices in American Jewish literature.

NOTE

1. All quotations are from telephone interview, 12 March 1992, unless noted otherwise.

BIBLIOGRAPHY

Works by Allegra Goodman

Total Immersion. New York: Harper and Row, 1989.
"Onionskin." *New Yorker* 1 April 1991:29–35.

"The Wedding of Henry Markowitz," *New Yorker* 13 Jan. 1992:26–36.
"Fantasy Rose." *New Yorker* 16 Nov. 1992:108–19.
"Mosquitoes." *New Yorker* 9 Aug. 1993:68–80.

Works about Allegra Goodman

Dukore, Margaret Mitchell. "Local Details Used to Good Effect." Rev. of *Total Immersion. Honolulu Star-Bulletin & Advertiser* 17 Sept. 1989:G-6.

Fein, Esther B. "Ten Writers Win $30,000 Whiting Awards." *New York Times* 25 Oct. 1991:C29.

Kendall, Elaine. "Bagels and Leis: An Ethnic Potpourri of Odd Couples." Rev. of *Total Immersion. Los Angeles Times* 27 July 1989:9.

Krupnick, Mark. "New Writers, Old Stories." Rev. of *Writing Our Way Home: Contemporary Stories by American Jewish Writers.* Ed. Ted Solotaroff and Nessa Rapoport. *Forward Books* 6 Nov. 1992:14.

Magida, Arthur J. "Who Will Be the Next Philip Roth?" *Baltimore Jewish Times* 4 Jan. 1991:36ff.

Moskowitz, Faye. Rev. of *Useful Gifts*, by Carole L. Glickfield and *Total Immersion. Lilith* 14.4 (1989):6–7.

Pinsker, Sanford. "Jews, Jewish Traditions, and the Disarming Individual Artist." Rev. of *Total Immersion. The Forward* 8 Dec. 1989:8.

———. "Satire, Social Realism, and Moral Seriousness: The Case of Allegra Goodman." *Studies in American Jewish Literature* 11.2 (1992):182–94.

Posesorski, Sherie. "Goodman's First Collection Reveals Her Natural Talent." Rev. of *Total Immersion. Baltimore Sun* 16 August 1989:n.p.

Prose, Francine. "Going Up to the Torah for an Aloha." Rev. of *Total Immersion. Newsday* 20 May 1989:20–21.

Rothchild, Sylvia. Rev. of *Total Immersion. Jewish Advocate* July 1989:16.

Solotaroff, Ted. "American Jewish Writers: On Edge Once More." *New York Times Book Review* 18 December 1988:1.

"Surprise Award for Surprising Young Writer." *Honolulu Advertiser* 4 November 1991: B5.

JOANNE (GOLDENBERG) GREENBERG (1933–)

Barbara Pitlick Lovenheim

BIOGRAPHY

Joanne Greenberg was born in Brooklyn, New York, on September 24, 1933. Her fiction is strongly autobiographical, with a specific basis in her past, her experiences, her religion, and her family life. Greenberg's teenage years are recounted in her novel, *I Never Promised You a Rose Garden* (1964), written under the pseudonym Hannah Green in order to protect her young sons from the knowledge that she had been institutionalized as a teenager. The book's protagonist, Deborah Blau, is fighting against a severe mental illness in which she escapes into a fantasy world called the Kingdom of Yr, an appealing and horrifying place. Deborah's struggle with her own demons and the traditional expectations of her middle-class, Jewish family reflect Greenberg's youth in Brooklyn with her parents Julius and Rosalie Goldenberg.

She was eventually able to overcome her mental disorder and attended American University, where she received a B.A. degree. She married Albert Greenberg on September 4, 1955, and they have two children, David and Alan. Albert Greenberg, a vocational rehabilitation counselor, provided the model for the tough but sensitive Ralph Oakland in *The Monday Voices* (1965). Greenberg lives with her family in Golden, Colorado, and uses that area of the country as the setting for many of her novels: *The Far Side of Victory*, *Founder's Praise*, *Simple Gifts*. She evokes the lovely scenery and vast open spaces that still exist in that part of America.

Joanne Greenberg writes both novels and short fiction. She has worked as a teacher's aide in a rural school, teaching etymology to sixth-graders. She has also been a member of a fire-fighting and emergency-rescue team, which gave her insights for the creation of her character Grace Dowben, a middle-aged, Jewish woman who is a member of such a team in the novel *A Season of Delight* (1981).

MAJOR THEMES

Joanne Greenberg's novels show her concern with the concept of forgiveness, the sense of being an outsider, and the idea of faith. Greenberg's connection with the idea of forgiveness is the ability to forgive oneself as well as others; this is forcefully stated in her novel *The Far Side of Victory* (1983). Eric Arnold Gordon is responsible for a fatal car accident that kills a family, except for the mother, Helen, whom he marries. Years later, Eric and Helen have their own family and she and the children are involved in a car accident that kills them all. Eric is afraid that Helen has set up this accident as retribution for the previous accident that killed her first family. He starts to unravel what took place before the second accident by reading his wife Helen's journal and eventually forgives Helen (who was driving the car) and himself. He had made an agreement with himself to work out his guilt, an agreement that extended to his family, his job, and his community. As he reads his wife's diary, he comes to terms with the two car accidents and his role in both of them.

Simple Gifts (1986) is also about forgiveness. The Fleuris family lives on a run-down ranch in Colorado and, in order to survive hard times, opens the ranch to visitors who come for a working vacation. The family members are also involved in several illegal activities: killing deer out of season, making and selling moonshine, and keeping a herd of Texas longhorns. The climax comes on the Fourth of July, when the Fleurises are caught by the government and forced to confess to their crimes. Their illegal activities are forgiven by the people who come to the ranch on vacation; the visitors have a direct effect on the Fleuris family as the guests integrate in various ways into ranch life and the Fleurises change their guests as well. Despite the fact that the Fleurises are in trouble with the IRS for their activities, Greenberg conveys that what the family did was necessary for survival.

Many of Greenberg's novels are centered on the idea of the outcast, which is viewed from several different perspectives. Greenberg's first novel, *The King's Persons* (1963), deals explicitly with the Jew as an outcast in society. This story takes place in England in 1182, after the exile of the French Jews to York. The king gave the York Jews special protection and their community flourished. When the book begins, however, Christian hatred is on the rise because economic decline is blamed on the Jews. The armies of the Crusades are forming, and Christians are told not to associate with Jews. Greenberg depicts the changing situation through the fortunes of two wealthy Jewish families who live in large houses in the Jewish section at the end of Northstreet. Hatred explodes when a monk, Brother Lewis, decides he is the savior and must rid the world of Jews. He leads those who feel downtrodden and oppressed against the Jews, a convenient scapegoat, and sets fire to Northstreet. This historical novel mirrors a cyclical hatred for Jews that has always resulted in violence and death. The doubting and sensitive Abram, son of one of the wealthy families, survives. He has experienced alienation and will continue to be an outcast, but hope and freedom are kept alive with the knowledge of the sacrifices entailed to maintain them.

Daniel Sanborn, in the book *Age of Consent* (1987), is a man who never feels that he is part of the society in which he lives. Daniel is the adopted son of a wealthy New York City Jewish family. He is taken from his biological family in Jerusalem and moves to his new family in Manhattan, where he feels isolated and lonely. Sanborn earns his medical degree and works as a plastic surgeon in the wilds of South America and Africa, repairing facial injuries of those who have suffered in war and natural disasters. He wanders from place to place, not feeling part of any society, driven to help others since he cannot help himself.

Greenberg expands on the idea of the outcast with her sensitive portrayal of the handicapped. In *Of Such Small Differences* (1988), Greenberg explores what life is like for the twenty-five-year-old deaf/blind John Moon. His experiences of being deaf and blind are transformed into art (his writing), so he can be understood and not pitied. Instead of being victimized by his condition, he is empowered by it. Greenberg explores this issue further through Abel and Janet Ryders, a deaf couple in *In This Sign* (1970). Abel does not surrender to his disability but learns all he can about the world and his job in a print shop. While he fights for acceptance and success, his wife gives in to frustration and despair. Also focusing on the handicapped, the short story collection, *Rites of Passage* (1966), includes people who are deaf, epileptic, insane, and people who are marginalized yet who find ways to survive.

Greenberg explores individual faith in her novel *Founder's Praise* (1976), the story of the Bisset family during and after the Depression and the establishment of a new religion, The Apostles of the Spirit of the Lord. This faith is a personal experience that each man and woman must discover individually. Edgar Bisset, the founder, represents the confrontation of the individual with himself, expressed in terms of spirituality and faith but not in ritual. In Greenberg's perception, the balance between faith and skepticism can make a religion viable for each person. She further investigates the interrelationship between faith and skepticism in her novel *A Season of Delight* (1981).

Grace Dowben, a middle-aged, Jewish woman who is the protagonist of *A Season of Delight*, struggles to define herself within the context of Jewish life in America. Her son and daughter have renounced Judaism, and she fears that Judaism will disappear. Grace's hope for the future of Judaism is revitalized through her friendship with a young man named Ben Sloan who works with her on a volunteer ambulance team in the small town of Gilboa, Pennsylvania. Ben turns to Grace to teach him about the Jewish tradition, and she shares with him the history, culture, and spirituality that she is unable to give to her own children.

In her short story "Certain Distant Suns," from the collection *High Crimes and Misdemeanors*, Greenberg probes the individual's connection with faith. The protagonist, Aunt Bessie, stops believing in God three weeks before her turn to prepare the Passover Seder. She is told by an Hasidic spirit, which appears on her unplugged television screen, that God needs man as much as man needs God, so she must do her part and believe again. Aunt Bessie wants God to fight for her belief, but the rabbi on the television tells her that she is the one who must fight to believe. The ambivalence that Aunt Bessie feels about religion is an integral part of this story and suggests Greenberg's own spiritual searching. When she was asked about her Jewishness by Susan Koppelman in a recent interview, Greenberg commented:

I am not an Orthodox Jew; I am a paradox Jew. . . . Judaism is very important to me— I would say vital. But our candles are not lit at the exact moment of sundown, and we do Havdalah in the evening rather than at sundown. . . . The essence of Shabbat is that the clamor stops for us—all of the running, being summoned, having to show up on time, driving we would have to do, answering the telephone. The fact that this is true hints that I am very observant. On the other hand, my spotty participation would mean that I am not. That is what a paradox Jew is—I have lots of questions, but my questions are all within a Jewish context and framework. (33)

Greenberg's notion of "paradox Jew" permeates her writing, which reveals a strong Jewish tradition intersecting with the American way of life.

SURVEY OF CRITICISM

Although Greenberg has written eleven novels and four short story collections, no full-length book discusses her work. The critical articles that do exist are either interviews of the author or reviews of her work right after publication. The critics have praised her work, but she has not gained widespread popularity. She is described as "a charming writer, who writes about our current social problems without being doctrinaire or propagandistic or stuffy" (Morse, 681). Greenberg is also an author who is able to write with ease about many different subjects. "Her extraordinary reach is one of several proofs of a distinguished talent" (Rogers 39). Reviewers also remark on her well-written, readable, and knowledgeable stories that contain "moments of sensibility and minor revelation ensconced in often elegant, little narratives" (Stern 39).

Greenberg is best known for her books about people who are disabled either mentally or physically. "Joanne Greenberg has made a career of describing the troubles that beset the handicapped" (*New Republic* 31). She is sensitive to the internal warfare that is part of each person's struggle but does not try to sensationalize or sentimentalize these problems. "Joanne Greenberg's stories concern special cases, strangers in a crowd, people cut off by loneliness and misunderstanding" (Howes 9). She connects with these people in an intimate way that forces the reader to enter into the character's experience. She raises "an authoritative voice claiming human status and human understanding for neglected pockets of experience, buried lives, half-forgotten isolates who live, too often, on the fringes of our inattention" (Howes 9).

Greenberg's treatment of religion has also intrigued reviewers. In the novel

Founder's Praise, Greenberg "never indulges in cheap mockery or cynical patronizing of the religious impulse" (Frakes 28–30). Critics note the spiritual quest in this work and in *A Season of Delight*, where Grace Dowben teaches Ben the Jewish rituals and the delights of Judaism. Greenberg's "sense of responsibility for the perpetuation of [the Jewish] people runs as the unbroken theme of her life" (Wisse 86).

The novels and short stories are "full of the moral concern and magical twists we have come to associate with Greenberg's best works" (Pinsker 512).

BIBLIOGRAPHY

Works by Joanne Greenberg

Summering. New York: Holt, Rinehart, and Winston, 1961.
The King's Persons. New York: Holt, Rinehart, and Winston, 1963.
I Never Promised You a Rose Garden. New York: Holt, Rinehart, and Winston, 1964.
The Monday Voices. New York: Holt, Rinehart, and Winston, 1965.
Rites of Passage. New York: Holt, Rinehart, and Winston, 1966.
A Cry of Silence. New York: Hearst Corporation, 1967.
In This Sign. New York: Holt, Rinehart, and Winston, 1970.
Founder's Praise. New York: Holt, Rinehart, and Winston, 1976.
High Crimes and Misdemeanors. New York: Holt, Rinehart, and Winston, 1977.
A Season of Delight. New York: Holt, Rinehart, and Winston, 1981.
The Far Side of Victory. New York: Holt, Rinehart, and Winston, 1983.
Simple Gifts. New York: Henry Holt and Company, 1986.
Age of Consent. New York: Henry Holt and Company, 1987.
Of Such Small Differences. New York: Henry Holt and Company, 1988.
"Interview with Joanne Greenberg." S. Steinberg, *Publishers Weekly* 23 September 1988:50–51.
With the Snow Queen. New York: Arcade, 1991.
"Belles Lettres Interview." With Susan Koppelman, *Belles Lettres* 8.4 (Summer 1993): 32–36.

Works about Joanne Greenberg

Borghi, Liana. "Joanne Greenberg: Lo spazio del tempo." Fink, Guido, and Morisco, Gabriella, Eds. *Il recupero del test: Aspetti della letteratura ebraico-americana*. Bologna: Univ. Ed. Bologna, 1988.
Brophy, Brigid. "An Yri Story." *New Stateman*. 14 August 1964:221–22.
"Calling Mad Mad." *Times Literary Supplement*. 13 August 1964:721.
Cassill, R. V. "A Locked Ward, A Desperate Search for Reality." *New York Times Book Review*. 3 May 1964:36.
Davies, R. R. "In This Sign" *New Statesman*. 3 September 1971:308.
"Fire and Sword." *Times Literary Supplement*. 5 July 1963:497.
Frakes, James. "Founder's Praise." *New York Review of Books*. 13 October 1976:28, 30.

Frankel, Haskel. "Alone in the Kingdom of Yr." *Saturday Review*. 18 July 1964:40.

Garber, Meg. "A Season of Delight." *ALAN Review*, 10.2, (1983):27.

Gravel, George. "The King's Person." *Best Sellers*. 1 March 1963:442.

Gray, Paul. "Stony Parables." *Time*. 21 January 1980:89.

Howes, Victor. "Fiction: Speaking for the Stranger." *Christian Science Monitor*. 9 August 1972:9.

Maguire, Gregory. "The Far Side of Victory." *The Horn Book Magazine*. December 1983:739–41.

McBroom, Gerry. "High Crimes and Misdemeanors." *ALAN Review*, 7.3 (Spring 1980): 19.

Morse, J. Mitchell. "Summering." *The Hudson Review*. 9.4, (1966–67):681.

Oates, Joyce Carol. "The Need to Communicate." *Washington Post*. 19 March 1972:3.

Pinsker, Sanford. "High Crimes and Misdemeanors." *Studies in Short Fiction*. 17.4 (Fall 1980):511–13.

"Pogram in Yorkshire." *Time*. 29 March 1963: M23–M24.

Rogers, W. G. "Broken Lives Remade." *New York Times Book Review*. 11 July 1965: 38–39.

Sale, Roger. "Whom Can You Trust?" *New York Review of Books*. 4 May 1972:3–4, 6.

Small, Robert. "The Far Side of Victory." *ALAN Review*, 11.1, (Fall, 1983):31.

Stern, Daniel. "Tales Told Out of Time." *Saturday Review*. 10 September 1966:63–64.

"The Silent World." *Times Literary Supplement*. 15 October 1971:1291.

Williams, John. "Joanne Greenberg." *Denver Quarterly*. 20.3 (1986):96–102.

Williamson, Norma. "A Season of Delight." *National Review*. 15 October 1982:1297.

Wisse, Ruth. "Rediscovering Judaism." *Commentary*. May 1982:84–87.

Wolfe, Kary, and Wolfe, Gary. "Metaphors of Madness: Popular Psychological Narratives." *Journal of Popular Culture*. 19.7, (1976):895–907.

Wolitzer, Hilma. "Fables of Identity, Parables of Passion." *Washington Post*. 2 March 1980:14.

LILLIAN HELLMAN (1906–1984)

Bruce Henderson

BIOGRAPHY

In her second memoir, *Pentimento*, Lillian Hellman recalls an argument between her mother and father over whether Lillian or her father had been considered "the sweetest-smelling baby in New Orleans" (*Three* 456–57). Her father accused her mother of stealing the epithet, which he claimed was used to describe him, and giving it to Lillian. This incident suggests the difficulty of separating fact from fiction in Hellman's biography.

Lillian Hellman was born in New Orleans in 1906, to Max and Julia (Newhouse) Hellman, both German American Jews. The Newhouses were a wealthy family who served as models for the rapacious Hubbards in *The Little Foxes*. The Hellmans lived in New Orleans until 1911, when Lillian was six, and when Max Hellman's shoe business failed the family moved to New York City. Lillian and her parents divided their time between the two cities until she was sixteen. Max Hellman's two sisters, Jenny and Hannah, ran a boardinghouse in New Orleans, and the family stayed with them while they were in the South.

Hellman attended New York University, and in 1924, went to work for the publishing house of Boni and Liveright. She married the writer Arthur Kober in 1925; Kober was offered a job as scriptwriter in Hollywood, and the couple moved there in 1930. Hellman worked as a script-reader and later as a screenwriter for Samuel Goldwyn. The marriage ended in divorce, though Hellman and Kober remained friends.

In 1930, Hellman met the mystery writer, former Pinkerton agent Dashiell Hammett, with whom she had a thirty-year relationship. She and Hammett were lovers, confidants, and coworkers. Hammett was her most important adviser and was the center of her emotional and romantic life. The relationship was a stormy one, with periods of silence, anger, and jealousy; both pursued other affairs at various times.

During the late 1920s and 1930s, Hellman traveled to Europe; these travels helped her develop a political consciousness. A 1937 trip, including stops in

Spain and Moscow, the former to observe the Spanish Revolutionary War, the latter to attend a theatre festival, provided the backdrop for the material Hellman memorialized in ''Julia.'' Critics, historians, and biographers continue to disagree about the veracity of Hellman's account of her involvement in anti-Nazi activities in Europe during this period, and about whether Hellman actually knew the woman she named ''Julia,'' the underground fighter and doctor.

Concurrent with Hellman's growing political consciousness was her development as a playwright. Her first produced play was *The Children's Hour* (1934). This play, whose use of lesbianism caused extraordinary controversy, was based on an actual Scottish case in which two schoolteachers were accused by a child of having a lesbian relationship. Hellman shifted the scene of the play to America and altered many details of the case. Perhaps the greatest single resulting controversy revolved around the refusal of the Board of Directors to award the Pulitzer Prize to the play despite the recommendation of the Drama Jury. Most critics believed Hellman's play was denied the Pulitzer because of the presence of lesbianism in its plot. Hellman adapted her play, omitting the lesbianism, for Sam Goldwyn, under the title *These Three* (1936). *The Children's Hour* was followed by the commercial and artistic failure *Days to Come* (1936). Next was Hellman's most popular play, *The Little Foxes* (1939), in which she first chronicled the machinations of the Hubbards, a Southern family based in part on her mother's relatives. Seven years later, Hellman returned to the Hubbards, depicting their earlier years in *Another Part of the Forest* (1946). In the meantime, Hellman turned her attention to World War II in her next two plays, *Watch on the Rhine* (1941) and *The Searching Wind* (1944), as well as in her screenplay *The North Star* (1943), a pro-Soviet film.

Hellman was blacklisted in 1948, as the beginnings of McCarthyism swept the Hollywood movie industry. Undaunted, Hellman continued to be productive in the New York theatre, focusing most of her attention on adaptation or direction. Her adaptations included Emmanuel Robles's *Montserrat* in 1949, Jean Anouilh's *The Lark* (1955), and the libretto for Leonard Bernstein's operetta *Candide* (1956); she directed *Montserrat* and a revival of *The Children's Hour*. This period also included Marc Blitzstein's opera *Regina*, based on *The Little Foxes*. In 1951, working through some of the family material about her father's relatives, Hellman wrote what she and a number of critics consider her finest play, *The Autumn Garden*.

In 1952, Hellman was called to testify before the House Un-American Activities Committee (HUAC). In a letter dated May 19, 1952, and addressed to John S. Wood, chairman of that committee, Hellman declined to testify, not because of her own fears of self-incrimination, but because she did not wish to inform, as had Elia Kazan and others, on her friends and acquaintances. This letter became a central text in the creation of the Hellman ethos, both in Hellman's own memoirs and in the writings of essayists and biographers.

In 1960, she wrote her last original play, *Toys in the Attic*, where she finally described her father's family in her story of two spinster sisters, their brother, and his young bride. The play won the New York Drama Critics Award (as had *Watch on the Rhine* almost twenty years earlier), but once again it was denied the Pulitzer Prize. The following year, Hammett died after an agonizing battle with emphysema. Hellman was to write no more original plays, only adapting Burt Blechman's novel *How Much?* as *My Mother, My Father and Me*, which closed quickly.

No longer a major force in the creation of new plays, Hellman shifted into her second literary career, as memoirest. In 1969, *An Unfinished Woman*, the first of her memoirs, was published, and won the National Book Award. *Pentimento*, the second volume, was published in 1973, and *Scoundrel Time* in 1976. The last two volumes became the source of a controversy that was to follow Hellman to (and beyond) the grave. Several critics took issue both with the "Julia" section of *Pentimento* and with Hellman's version of history in *Scoundrel Time*. Writers such as Martha Gelhorn pointed out historical inaccuracies and impossibilities in "Julia"; others, such as Diana Trilling (whose book was blocked by Hellman's publisher, initiated much of the debate) and Irving Howe took issue with Hellman's revisionist view of her own involvement in pro-Stalinist activities and in her conduct during the HUAC hearings. The debate came to a head with Mary McCarthy's appearance on the "Dick Cavett Show" in 1980, during which she called Hellman a liar. Hellman subsequently sued McCarthy; the suit ended only with Hellman's death on June 30, 1984.

MAJOR THEMES

The thematic thread that runs from *The Children's Hour*, the earliest of Hellman's plays, through the memoirs is a consideration of moral questions individuals face in their lives and actions, a theme that ties her to such masters of dramatic realism as Ibsen and Chekhov. Hellman's vision of morality revolved around two recurring issues: first, the nature and meaning of truth; second, the nature and meaning of action. In the universe of Hellman's plays, the telling of truth becomes the central, morally implicated act, even when it leads to suicide, violence, or death; truth itself, unaccompanied by considered action, lacks moral weight. Critics have identified Addie's speech in *The Little Foxes* as a key to Hellman's view of the moral polarities of her world; Addie, the middle-aged black servant, a surrogate mother to Regina's daughter Alexandra, says, "Well, there are people who eat the earth and eat all the people on it like in the Bible with the Locusts. And other people who stand around and watch them eat it. ... Sometimes I think it ain't right to stand and watch them do it" (*Collected Plays* 188). The questions Hellman poses, in this play and throughout her writings, are how to know the truth and how to choose to live—and whether these two questions are irreconcilable.

The significance of truth in Hellman's dramatic writings is seen most vividly in her first produced play, *The Children's Hour*. What is truth in the world of this play: that Mary Tilford, the fourteen-year-old accuser, lies about what she heard or saw? that Martha Dobie does have erotic feelings for Karen Wright? that these feelings are irrelevant to the woman's moral worth? Is truth a universal state, or is it much more protean and socially constructed, changing as the pressures of history and individual lives change? Hellman continues to develop such complex issues in other plays.

Truth becomes a central concern in the memoirs as well, as Hellman self-consciously reflects on the process of memory as an unreliable source of factual truth. It is fair to say that the theme of truth becomes even more complicated in the minds of critics, because Hellman's dramatic works and public statements held her own view of truth as an absolute value. The most dramatic moments in the memoirs revolve around actions in which the telling or withholding of truth determines artistic or intellectual life or death: her deceiving the Germans in the "Julia" episode in *Pentimento*, her own action toward the HUAC in *Scoundrel Time*, and the honesty of her relationship with Hammett over thirty years.

In addition to the overarching themes of truth and moral action, Hellman also explores a number of other themes. The role of money is central to most of her plays: the financial burdens placed on Karen and Martha as a result of the trial in *The Children's Hour*; the capitalist strike-breaking in *Days to Come*; the machinations of the Hubbards over money; the violence engendered by Julian's money in *Toys in the Attic*. While Hellman is less interested in drama as propaganda than were some of her leftist contemporaries, there is always an undercurrent of Marxist critique in her plays.

Hellman is also concerned with the South. The two Hubbard plays are clearly her most Southern in theme and setting, depicting a family that represents the deterioration of the Old South and the morally suspect origins of the New South. Hellman's last two plays, *The Autumn Garden* and *Toys in the Attic*, take her even closer to her roots as a Southerner: The former takes place at a summer resort on the Gulf, and the latter moves into Hellman's home town of New Orleans, as she rewrites the lives of her parents, her aunts, and herself. Throughout the plays, the oppressed position of blacks is often present, perhaps in part a result of Hellman's relationship with Sophronia Mason, the black nurse with whom she formed a deep emotional bond in childhood.

While Hellman constantly used her experience as a Southerner (albeit a transplanted one) in her writings, she had less to say about feminist issues and even less to say about Jewish issues. Women certainly figure importantly in both her plays and memoirs. For example, the Hubbard plays feature extraordinary characterizations of women, from the charming monster Regina to the painfully poignant Birdie to the surprisingly spirited young Alexandra, not made of "sugar-water" as her mother is surprised to learn. In all of Hellman's plays, the women are complex figures, often the strongest characters in the play. It is possible to read Regina's evil, not as an inherent, essential part of her being, but as a product of the restrictions of gender roles in the antebellum South (as well as a product of a dysfunctional family, in which the father-daughter relationship borders on the incestuous).

Significantly, Hellman's first memoir is titled *An Unfinished Woman*, in which she explores what it means to be a woman in personal and social ways. The memoir is not overtly programmatic in its feminism; rather, it presents the complexities of Hellman's individualistic experience of being a woman in the twentieth century. She describes her experiences as one of a handful of commercially successful women playwrights, as well as her experiences as caretaker for both Hammett and her friend, the writer Dorothy Parker. She devotes entire chapters of *Pentimento* to such important women in her life as "Julia" and her cousin Bethe, both of whom provide examples, if not necessarily models, of womanhood for her.

Her Jewishness is perhaps the most problematic and the least-discussed aspect of her identity. In none of her original plays is Jewish identity, Jewish culture, or Jewish religion central. Only her final play, *My Mother, My Father, and Me*, an adaptation of the Burt Blechman novel has a Jewish focus. Thematically, it works through the consciousness of a young man coming to adulthood in the late 1950s and early 1960s, with social satire of such popular movements as the Beat Generation and the popularization of Freudian analysis. In particular, Hellman focuses on the figure of the Jewish mother, Rona Halpern, a middle-class social climber, desperate to acquire all the material and cultural trappings of those better off economically than she. That she is a humorous figure rather than an avaricious one suggests the difference between this play and such earlier works as *The Little Foxes*. In addition, Hellman moves away from the "well-made play" to some of the elements of Theater of the Absurd, such as exaggerated characterizations and more abrupt shifting of scenes.

In her memoirs, Hellman confronts her own Jewish background more fully, stating that she was not even conscious of being Jewish until her encounter with National Socialism in Germany in 1929. She recalled being approached by two youths on a bus, inviting her to join a National Socialist group, "no dues for foreigners if they had no Jewish connections" (*Three* 64). In interviews, she suggested that being a Southern Jew was different from being a Northern Jew, that Southern culture tended to discourage Jews from emphasizing their heritage or from practicing Jewish religion openly. For example, many Jewish families left New Orleans during Mardi Gras to minimize their sense of exclusion from the ceremonies and balls that were open only to white Christians. Even in "Julia," Hellman's memoir of her odyssey through Nazi Germany to help the underground, Jewishness is almost totally absent; indeed, Jews are mentioned only as one of a number of groups of people suffering at the hands of the Nazis. Hellman chose not to spell out what it might have meant for her as a Jewish woman to help the underground.

If one asks why Hellman did not write in important ways about her Jewishness, the simple but probably clearest answer might be that it was overshadowed by other aspects of her identity. Clearly, her time in New Orleans marked her more profoundly as a Southerner; and her gender marked her in ways more immediately relevant to her professional and private life. To be a woman in playwriting, an occupation traditionally dominated by men, meant confronting sexism head on. But, from all accounts, Jewish practices were not stressed by either side of her family, nor does Hellman record prejudice as a result of being a Jew or celebration as a result of being included in Jewish culture or heritage. It is not exactly that she "passed" as a non-Jew; rather, she made no claims for the importance of Jewishness until interviews late in life when she stated that she was grateful to be a Jew and would not want to be otherwise. Little in her writing suggests reasons for that sentiment or acknowledgment of what it means to be a Jew, other than to share a history. For Hellman, perhaps that history was enough to create an identity.

SURVEY OF CRITICISM

From the start, Hellman's dramas received high praise, though rarely without qualification. *The Children's Hour* was clearly the play of the 1934–35 season, and not simply because of the taboo subject of lesbianism. Critics praised the writer's courage in attacking "difficult" subjects and in asking morally complex questions. Most critics praised the generally taut dramaturgy of the play, some harkening back to Ibsen's problem plays, others to the nineteenth-century French master of the well-made play, Eugene Scribe. Many critics, even those generally well-disposed to the play, found fault with its ending, seeing it as either drawn-out or melodramatic.

Hellman's characterizations often received praise, though that praise was typically linked to specific performers, such as Tallulah Bankhead's Regina in *The Little Foxes*, Patricia Neal's younger version of the same character in *Another Part of the Forest*, and Paul Lukas's Kurt Muller in *Watch on the Rhine*. Critics often cited Hellman's ability to create an ensemble of characters, as in the Hubbards plays, *The Autumn Garden* and *Toys in the Attic*.

Hellman's handling of themes or ideas left her open to attack. Her most supportive critics saw in her work a seriousness of purpose and an execution of the interplay of ideas that made her a worthy successor to Ibsen at his best. Other commentators, particularly those of the 1950s and later (both reviewers of the plays in their original or revived productions and contemporary scholars) take issue either with reductionism in Hellman's moral positions or with lack of consistency. Nonetheless, Hellman received consistently positive reviews for her plays, with the decided exception of *Days to Come*. Even a play that today seems rather weak, like the propagandistic *The Searching Wind*, initially received considerable praise for its technical skill and seriousness.

Her translations and adaptations were a different matter. In some cases, Hellman was criticized for transforming the original source too much, not allowing the original voice of the primary author to come through; this charge was made particularly with the first three translations/adaptations.

As might be expected, the criticism in the popular media of Hellman's autobiographical writings tends to be more personal and more controversial. Critics often made little attempt to separate judgments of texts from judgments of the woman's life or character. Reviews of *An Unfinished Woman*, which won the National Book Award, were generally favorable. The majority of critics, including many who confessed to not liking Hellman's plays, found the memoirs fascinating reading, literate, and intelligent. Other critics, either hoping for a more linear or inclusive autobiography or suspicious of what the elliptical style might be hiding, found *An Unfinished Woman* disappointing precisely because it seemed unfinished.

It was with the publication of *Pentimento* and *Scoundrel Time* that the critical controversy caught fire. The "Julia" section of *Pentimento* began the debate, with Martha Gelhorn and others questioning Hellman's veracity. Gelhorn exposed several instances in which Hellman was either duplicitous or possessed of an extremely faulty memory. Others accused Hellman of plagiarizing the life of Dr. Muriel Gardiner, an Englishwoman whose own life paralleled Julia's in many specific ways. Though Gardiner herself declined to make formal accusations, the truth of "Julia" continues to remain in question.

Scoundrel Time was at least as much a source of controversy for such critics as Irving Howe and Hilton Kramer. Hellman was accused of distorting and misinterpreting what happened during the McCarthy hearings and of waffling on her own sympathies to Communism. The controversy over her memoirs climaxed in the famous feud with Mary McCarthy. At the same time, there was a revival of interest in Hellman's life and work, and something of a cult of celebrity grew around her.

Initially, there was a handful of book-length monographs on her plays, most notably those by scholars such as Richard Moody and Katherine Lederer. Most of these books surveyed Hellman's dramaturgy, examining plot construction and themes, and asking questions about the tensions between tragedy and melodrama in her work. There are also essays containing analyses of this type, including Jacob Adler's important work in establishing links between Hellman and Ibsen and Chekhov (Estrin 31–42; 43–49). Other book-length studies of Hellman are biographies, ranging from Peter Feibleman's adulatory memoir of her last years to more objective studies of her life, such as Carol E. Rollyson's and William Wright's biographies.

While Hellman has consistently been included in surveys of twentieth-century American drama, she has received much less attention than such contemporaries as Williams, Miller, and O'Neill, perhaps because she has been considered less important and perhaps because of her gender. Feminist scholars, among others interested in gender issues, have begun to look at Hellman in more depth. The memoirs have received considerable attention, perhaps because the question of autobiography has become such a complex one for critics following postmodern and deconstructionist lines. A number of such critics, Timothy Dow Adams perhaps most notable among them, have tried to exonerate Hellman of charges of dishonesty by invoking a postmodern approach to autobiography as a literary genre situated between fiction and truth, in which the autobiographer is as much an inventor as a documenter of reality. If the notion of a stable, physical author is in question, then so is the necessity of absolute fidelity to historical event. Grossman has put it most eloquently, saying "[Hellman's] need for a coherent aesthetic and moral vision went against the expectations of documentary veracity inherent in her chosen form": The artist as formalist/fabulist was in conflict with the audience's need for absolutes of historical truth.

One other critical essay merits specific mention, as it addresses the concerns of this volume, and that is Bonnie Lyons's discussion of Hellman as "Jewish nun" (a term coined by Hellman's father). Lyons argues against Hellman as Jewish writer, although she concedes that that term is finally undefinable in simple or universal terms. Nonetheless, Lyons argues, not only does Hellman omit virtually any mention of Jewish issues in either her dramatic or autobiographical writings, but her world view is "non-Jewish" or even "anti-Jewish," in Lyons's terms. Hellman, she suggests, was always most interested in the role of the individual in the world; Jewish culture and Judaism, Lyons argues, center around the opposite—the greater good of the group, even at the expense of the individual. While Lyons's claims for this particular world view as either inclusively or specifically Jewish are clearly open to debate, Lyons rejects the assumption that because Hellman was born a Jew, she should be classified as a "Jewish writer."

BIBLIOGRAPHY

Works by Lillian Hellman

Drama

The Dear Queen, with Louis Kronenberger. Unpublished play. 1932.
The Collected Plays. Boston: Little, Brown, 1972. (Contains all of the original plays and adaptations, other than *The Dear Queen.*) Contents:

The Children's Hour (1934).

Days to Come (1936).

The Little Foxes (1939).

Watch on the Rhine (1941).

The Searching Wind (1944).

Another Part of the Forest (1946, 1947).

Montserrat (1949, 1950).

The Autumn Garden (1951).

The Lark (1955, 1956).

Candide (1957).

Toys in the Attic (1959).

My Mother, My Father and Me (1963).

(Note: Dates are copyright dates for the works, not production dates.)

Memoirs

Three. Introduction by Richard Poirier. Boston: Little, Brown, 1979. Contents:

An Unfinished Woman (1969).

Pentimento (1973).

Scoundrel Time (1976).

Maybe: A Story. Boston: Little, Brown, 1980.

Other

Eating Together, with Peter Feibleman. Boston: Little, Brown, 1984.
Conversations with Lillian Hellman. Ed. Jackson R. Bryer. Jackson: University Press of Mississippi, 1986.

Works about Lillian Hellman

Adams, Timothy Dow. *Telling Lies in Modern American Autobiography.* Chapel Hill: University of North Carolina University Press, 1990.

Austin, Gayle. "The Exchange of Women and Male Homosocial Desire in Arthur Miller's *Death of a Salesman* and Lillian Hellman's *Another Part of the Forest.*" *Feminist Rereadings of Modern American Drama.* Ed. June Schlueter. Rutherford, NJ: Fairleigh Dickinson University Press, 1989. 59-66.

Bills, Steven H. *Lillian Hellman: An Annotated Bibliography.* New York: Garland, 1979.

Brown, Maurice F. "Autobiography and Memory: The Case of Lillian Hellman." *Biography: An Interdisciplinary Quarterly* 9 (1985):1–11.

Chinoy, Helen Kritch, and Linda Walsh Jenkins, eds. *Women in American Theatre.* Revised and expanded. New York: Beech Tree Books, 1987.

Curtin, Kaier. *"We Can Always Call Them Bulgarians": The Emergence of Lesbians and Gay Men on the American Stage.* Boston: Alyson, 1987.

Dick, Bernard F. *Hellman in Hollywood.* Rutherford, NJ: Fairleigh Dickinson University Press, 1982.

Estrin, Mark W., ed. *Critical Essays on Lillian Hellman.* Boston: G. K. Hall, 1989.

Falk, Doris V. *Lillian Hellman.* New York: Ungar, 1978.

Feibleman, Peter S. *Lilly: Reminiscences of Lillian Hellman.* New York: Morrow, 1988.

Friedman, Sharon. "Feminism as Theme in Twentieth Century American Women's Drama." *American Studies* 25.1 (1984):69–89.

Georgoudaki, Ekaterini. "Women in Lillian Hellman's Plays, 1930–1950." *Women and War: The Changing Status of American Women from the 1930s to the 1950s.* Ed. Marian Diedrich and Dorothea Fischer–Hornung, New York: Berg, 1990. 69-86.

Gillin, Edward. " 'Julia' and Julia's Son." *Modern Language Studies* 19.2 (1989):3–11.

Goodman, Charlotte. "The Fox's Cubs: Lillian Hellman, Arthur Miller, and Tennessee Williams." *Modern American Drama: The Female Canon.* Ed. June Schlueter. Rutherford, NJ: Fairleigh Dickinson University Press, 1990. 130-42.

Grossman, Anita Susan. "Art Versus Truth in Autobiography: The Case of Lillian Hellman." *CLIO: A Journal of Literature, History, and the Philosophy of History* 14 (1985):289–308.

Holditch, W. Kenneth. "Another Part of the Country: Lillian Hellman as Southern Playwright." *The Southern Quarterly* 25.3 (1987):11–35.

Holmin, Lorena Rose. *The Dramatic Works of Lillian Hellman*. Uppsala, Sweden: [s.n.], 1973.

Lederer, Katherine. *Lillian Hellman*. Boston: Twayne, 1979.

Lyons, Bonnie. "Lillian Hellman: 'The First Jewish Nun of Prytania Street.'" *From Hester Street to Hollywood: The Jewish-American Stage and Screen*. Ed. Sarah Blacher Cohen. Bloomington: Indiana University Press, 1983.

Moody, Richard. *Lillian Hellman, Playwright*. New York: Pegasus, 1972.

Newman, Robert P. *The Cold War Romance of Lillian Hellman and John Melby*. Chapel Hill: University of North Carolina Press, 1989.

Patraka, Vivian M. "Lillian Hellman's *Watch on the Rhine*: Realism, Gender, and Historical Crisis." *Modern Drama* 32 (1989):128–45.

Riordan, Mary Marguerite. *Lillian Hellman: A Bibliography, 1926–1978*. Metuchen, NJ: Scarecrow, 1980.

Rollyson, Carl E. *Lillian Hellman: Her Legend and Her Legacy*. New York: St. Martin's Press, 1988.

Wright, William. *Lillian Hellman: The Image, the Woman*. New York: Simon and Schuster, 1986.

BETTE HOWLAND (1937–   )

Babette Inglehart

BIOGRAPHY

Bette Howland was born on January 28, 1937, in Chicago, to Sam Sotonoff, a factory worker, and Jessie Berger Sotonoff. She grew up on the West Side of Chicago, around Roosevelt and Crawford, a neighborhood of working-class Jews. After two years at Marshall High School, she won a scholarship to the University of Chicago, which, under the Hutchins program, had attracted intellectually precocious students to its atmosphere of high culture and independent learning. After she graduated at eighteen, in 1955, she attended law school at the university. She soon dropped out to get married and to see her husband, Howard Howland (now a prominent neurobiologist), through graduate school. They were divorced in 1962.

Howland had to support two young sons (Frank, born in 1958, and Jacob, born in 1959) at a time when single mothers were not given much in the way of support services, so she worked at various part-time jobs, including editorial assistant and librarian. Meanwhile, she had enrolled as a student at the Committee on Social Thought of the University of Chicago, in order to work with Saul Bellow; her dissertation is still unwritten. When her sons enrolled at Harvard and Swarthmore, she moved East, and has since led a peripatetic life, residing in New England, the Northwest, and New Mexico. Now the grandmother of five, her sons both college professors (of Economics and Philosophy), she lives in central Pennsylvania. In 1993 she accepted a one-semester appointment as Professor of Literature at the University of Chicago and the Committee on Social Thought which she still calls her ''true home'' (Letter to the author, 2 Oct. 1992).

Howland's writing career began in the early years of her marriage. Her first short stories were accepted before she was twenty and were published for the next few years in little magazines such as *Epoch*, *The Quarterly Review of Literature*, and *The Noble Savage*. She did not resume publishing her work again until her children were in high school.

Howland's major literary forms have remained the short story, the novella, and the autobiographical sketch. Her first book, *W-3*, recounts life in a psychiatric ward. While it is based on a personal experience, the work is closest in form to a documentary, a detached chronicle of daily life in the ward.

Blue in Chicago (1978) is a collection of six stories with interlocking themes and characters, most of them Jewish. Again, the question of genre arises. Howland says she had thought of calling it a "chronicle of city life" (Letter to the author, 1992). It was reviewed as a novel, a memoir, a collection of short stories, and in each case, very favorably. Beginning with a wedding in the family and ending with a funeral, using throughout the controlling images of the decay of the city and human old age, *Blue in Chicago* examines the remnants of our institutions, public and private.

Things to Come and Go (1983) was a collection of three long stories, apparently unrelated, again, all of them set in Chicago. Howland says she thought of the three, respectively, as a story of the 1950s, the 1960s, and the 1970s (letter to the author 2 Oct. 1992). Some critics went further, adroitly recognizing that these were three stages in the life of a woman. A Jewish family is again at the center of this collection.

German Lessons (forthcoming) is a collection of two short novels, *Lehrzeit* and *The Landlady*. One, narrated by a young runaway apprentice (*Lehrzeit*, literally "learning-time" or apprenticeship), is set in Germany and Holland in 1908–09; the other, also set in Germany, which Howland calls a "sort of ghost story," belongs to the mid-1960s.

She has contributed short stories, critical essays, and numerous reviews to newspapers and magazines and has been the recipient of fellowships and grants from the Rockefeller Foundation, the Marsden Foundation, the Guggenheim Foundation, and the MacArthur Foundation.

MAJOR THEMES

The powerful themes of Bette Howland's work weave in and out of her stories, memoirs, and novellas. Always, there is the strong and unique voice observing, commenting on, and describing with keen eye and compassionate heart the troubles of her own life and the lives of those she shares: a family, a community, a city, and the modern world they mutually, if often fragilely, inhabit.

The themes are introduced somewhat indirectly in *W-3*, where the main emphasis is on a psychiatric ward and the isolation and loneliness of the patients as they try to cope with their situations; Howland's watchful eye records every detail. Here, as in her subsequent work, her sharp wit and ironic detachment temper and control the urge to reveal personal troubles or probe personal problems. The camera is pointed at the other occupants of the ward—the doctors and staff, the machinery of the hospital itself—and the observing "I" misses very little. And although she reveals only a few details of the circumstances that brought her to "W-3," not far off we detect the worried family, the two young children she is responsible for, and the decaying urban milieu that make up her day-to-day life, all of which will appear and reappear throughout the next two volumes.

Her interest in the politics of a teaching hospital, institutional life, and the power struggles between patients and staff adds a sociological dimension to what might have been a purely personal memoir.

Howland's major themes in her next two volumes (*Blue in Chicago* and *Things to Come and Go*) are so interwoven and interdependent that the reader feels privy to a world of intimate detail and observation that becomes remarkably familiar and moving. Characters emerge and reemerge, old wounds are opened time and again, old neighborhoods are revisited, family scenes are reenacted in many ways and on a variety of occasions—from weddings to funerals, from endless car rides filled with bickering relatives to heartbreaking hospital rooms filled with impending death and recognition of abiding connections.

The focus of each story is a Jewish woman, at various stages of her life— from adolescence to midlife—an observer of her own life, her family relationships, her errors and regrets, her pride and unwillingness to be sucked into the dynamics of a difficult milieu. Many of these family issues remain unresolved. Thus, the theme of family conflict is omnipresent—the large Jewish family and its discontents and feuds: the working-class family of immigrant background, its habits of wrangling, bad manners, and sloppy grammar, resentments about intermarriage and outsiders. Within this theme is imbedded a mother-daughter conflict (the mother judgmental, demanding, emotionally distant, disappointed in her daughter; the daughter equally distant, impatient, and unwilling "to be" her mother). The father-daughter relationship is a more gentle one, as his strength diminishes with illness and old age. The power of the parents over the daughter, despite their growing weakness and helplessness, is revisited in several stories. The impending or realized deaths of grandparents, parents, the constant coming to terms with their aging, and, ultimately, a partial or conditional acknowledgment of the ties of love and connection that exist, despite disappointments and bitterness on both sides, give strong emotional richness to this theme.

The theme of family conflict also takes on a class dimension in Howland's stories as the "intellectual," college-bred daughter finds herself at odds with the values of her working-class family, a theme that has its roots in early twentieth-century immigrant literature. The strong bonds that keep the family clinging together in destructive and repetitive patterns and the "dissonance" that emerges between the generations of this Jewish family is in the forefront of such stories as "Blue in Chicago," "Birds of a Feather," and "The Life You Gave Me" but is also apparent throughout her work.

Closely associated with the theme of family conflict is that of the terrors of old age. As the illnesses, old age, and death of the older generation accelerate, Howland turns her camera again and again on the misery and terror of old age in the city: She also looks at Florida, where those with the means can attempt to escape the ravages of aging. Above all, Howland laments the isolation of the elderly, cut off and under attack, in the decaying neighborhoods of Chicago, often deserted by family members or grudgingly taken in when there is no other alternative. These themes figure prominently in "Golden Age," "The Old Wheeze," "26th and California," and "Public Facilities." In this last story, those who have no place else to go gather at the neighborhood library for companionship and warmth, as the narrator bemoans their situation: "Let us speak frankly. Where are people to go? People, I mean, who have no place to go. There are no clean well-lighted places" (72–73). This sense of despair is what propels the young narrator and her children to seek refuge in "the country" and to find that "safe place" that continues to be elusive in her "makeshift life."

"Public Facilities" brings together three major themes of Howland's work: the autobiographical story of a young, single mother, working at a series of part-time and unsatisfying jobs (this one at a library), trying to find a safe place and a life that fits together; the vulnerability and terrors of old age; and the third major theme, that serves as the background of all of these, the city as threat and as paradigm of the conflicts and brutalities of human existence. She locates a number of her stories in Chicago's Hyde Park, Uptown, or other areas in which racial tensions, high crime rates, and the perception of danger define the everyday lives of the inhabitants. Focusing particularly on the women in the lead story, "Blue in Chicago," she describes them as "a passive population under siege." No wonder her protagonist is always on the move, trying to escape the city, the family conflicts, the loneliness of her condition. And in a similar way, the elderly are "cut off, under attack, no retreat" in an aging and decrepit city landscape, bereft of comfort.

For all of these pained and frightened, yet struggling human beings, the cry that resounds through Howland's work is the dream of escape and perhaps of reconciliation: "So where is it, then? Where is the rightful life that is awaiting us? Where is that undiscovered territory? Where the air is clear and consciences are clean. How do we get there? How do we cut our path through this wilderness? How do we run up our flags and stake our claims? The tyranny, the tyranny of these dreams of peace and quiet" ("To the Country" 66).

SURVEY OF CRITICISM

Howland's canon, though relatively small, has been widely reviewed and, generally, in the most positive terms. Her first book-length work, *W-3* (1974), was enthusiastically reviewed in a variety of magazines and newspapers including the *New York Times*, the *New York Times Book Review*, *Commentary*, the *Chicago Tribune*, the *New Republic*, *The New Leader*, *The National Observer*, and the *Village Voice*, as well as in several smaller publications.

Critical agreement about this documentary of life in a psychiatric ward recognized her avoidance of the common fallacies of diatribe or inspirational saga of madness and cure, as well as the lack of self-pity and sentimentality. Critics concurred that the narrative was a compelling one, in large part due to powerful and evocative writing and to the writer's intense powers of observation. Howland's style received high praise from the critics: terms such as "toughness, wit, matter-of-factness, candidness, and bluntness" recur in many of the reviews, always in a positive way.

Critics also are intrigued by her stance in this work as a participant-observer, her unusual angle of vision, her ability to distance herself from her own suffering and to focus her critical eye on the institution and its staff as well as the other patients. Although a few of the critics (notably Barbara Smith in the *National Observer* and Kathleen Moloney in the *Chicago Tribune*) seem somewhat unsettled by what Smith calls her "eerily dispassionate voice" (27) and by her reluctance to recount her own story of recovery, most critics applaud her ability to be objective but not detached from the suffering around her and within herself. "Those hoping for the pornography of personal trouble will be disappointed" (22), according to reviewer Sara Sanborn in the *New Republic*.

Blue in Chicago (1978), Howland's collection of six stories of Jewish middle-class life in the Chicago of her childhood and young womanhood, was also very favorably reviewed. Major reviews appeared in the *New York Times Book Review*, the *New Republic*, *The Nation*, the *Chicago Tribune*, and the *New York Times*, with somewhat briefer reviews in the *New Yorker*, *Ms.* magazine, and *Booklist*.

Again, almost all critics admired her style, use of language, power of observation and evocation, honesty, precision, and self-questioning. They agreed that her style is blunt, spare, often startling, unflinchingly honest, self-questioning, and passionate. Commentary on her tone and stance toward the material of these stories highlighted its anger, pain, absence of sentimentality, stubborn pride, and lack of despair, on the one hand; and, on the other hand, its insight, compassion, pity, and, above all, the complex vision of her family, herself, and the city in which these dramas are played out.

All critics agreed on the power of her subjects: the decay of the city, the breakdown of the Jewish family, the horrors of old age, the sense of isolation and lack of relatedness that permeates the lives of her characters.

The only major lack of agreement centers on the question of genre: These range in the reviews from "autobiographical sketches" to "novel or memoir" to "short stories" to "autobiographical stories" to "essay/short stories" to "carefully documented record of personal experience [whose] method and texture are those of fiction" to "largely autobiographical essays." This confusion, if such it is, did not, however, detract from appreciation of the quality of the work, the voice unlike any other, the unforgettable people she gives us, the unflinchingly honest and painful evocation of a city and a family in late stages of deterioration.

Things to Come and Go (1983), Howland's collection of three long stories, all set in Chicago, was not as widely reviewed as were the two previous works, but there were major reviews in the *New York Times Book Review*, the *New*

Republic, Ms. magazine, and the *Chicago Tribune*, with shorter reviews in at least four other publications.

Somewhat predictably, each of the three major critics had a different preference among the three. Once again, however, the reviewers remarked quite favorably about Howland's fierce honesty, her unsparing specifics, her lean and direct style, her powers of precise observation and knife-sharp details.

Once again, as well, the major disagreement was about the narrative voice. Ann Hulbert in the *New Republic* found the young narrator of "Birds of a Feather" "an unsettling observer" (38) who rarely records the depths of her own reaction; while Johanna Kaplan in the *New York Times Book Review* described the same narrator as an ideal observer, sharp-eyed, and "mercilessly acute" (13).

Kaplan lauds Howland as a writer of unusual talent, power, and intelligence, possessed of an original voice, an incisive mind, and an uncompromised lyrical vision, capable of writing "descriptive passages of stunning power and beauty" (29). Yet she concludes, somewhat paradoxically, that "Bette Howland hasn't yet fully found her fictional voice" (29).

The critics agree that the stories excel in their depiction of the estrangements and cruelties within families; the terrible loneliness of the urban dweller; the fear and vulnerability of the elderly; and the fragmentation of daily life. They assert Howland's skill, power, and honesty in addressing these painful themes. Similarly, most critics comment on Howland's remarkable talent for rendering "place"—Chicago—a city in danger of crumbling and the residents who reflect this fragility in their lives of separateness and solitariness.

BIBLIOGRAPHY

Works by Bette Howland

Fiction

"Julia." *Quarterly Review of Literature*, 4, 1958:274–81.
"Sam Katz." *Epoch*, 2, 1958:105–16.
"Aronesti." *Noble Savage*, no. 5, 1962:102–15.
W-3. New York: Viking Press, 1974.
Blue in Chicago. New York: Harper and Row, 1978.
Things to Come and Go. New York: Knopf, 1983.
Letter to author 2 October 1992.
German Lessons. Forthcoming.

Works about Bette Howland

W-3

Bell, Pearl K. "Suffering and Survival." *New Leader* 14 Oct. 1974:17.
Broyard, Anatole. "As Told to the Coughing Machine." *New York Times* 2 Sept. 1974: 13.
Kaplan, Johanna. "View From the Ward." *Commentary* Feb. 1975:91–94.
Moloney, Kathleen. "The Value of Meaninglessness: Notes from a Psycho Ward." *Chicago Tribune* 25 Aug. 1974, Sec. 7:3.
Rabinowitz, Dorothy. "W-3." *New York Times Book Review* 6 Oct. 1974:22.
Sanborn, Sara. "Life in the Snake Pit." *New Republic* 21 Sept. 1974:22–23.
Smith, Barbara. "Dispassionate 'W-3' Recalls Life in the Ward." *National Observer* 21 Sept. 1974:27.
Supree, Burt. "W-3." *Village Voice* 3 Oct. 1974:38.
"W-3." *Booklist* 1 Sept. 1974:9.
"W-3." *Kirkus Review* 1 June 1974:612.
"W-3." *Publisher's Weekly* 15 July 1974:111.

Blue in Chicago

Bell, Pearl K. "Urban Anxieties." *New York Times Book Review* 19 Feb. 1978:9, 37.
"Blue in Chicago." *Booklist* 15 Dec. 1977:660.
"Blue in Chicago." *Book World* 19 Feb. 1978:E5.
"Blue in Chicago." *Kirkus Review* 1 Nov. 1977:1158.
"Blue in Chicago." *Ms.* July 1978:32.
"Briefly Noted." *New Yorker* 24 April 1978:161.
Garrett, George. "Coming Out of Left Field, The Short Story Today." *Sewanee Review* July 1978:461.
Jefferson, Margo. "Makeshift Lives." *Newsweek* 27 March 1978:94–95.
Lawson, Steve. "Blues and the Concrete Truth." *The Nation* 18 March 1978:310–11.
Lehmann-Haupt, Christopher. "Blue in Chicago." *New York Times* 2 March 1978:26.
Milton, Edith. "Blue in Chicago." *New Republic* 8 July 1978:40–41.
Petrakis, Harry Mark. "Two Images of Chicago drawn from memory and fantasy." *Chicago Tribune* 5 Feb. 1978, Sec. 7:1.
Singer, Eleanor. "Blue in Chicago." *Library Journal* 15 Feb. 1978:455.

Things to Come and Go: Three Stories

Freeman, Suzanne. "A Gift for Telling Moments: Two Story Collections." *Ms.* April 1983:34.
Hulbert, Ann. "The Country and the City." *New Republic* 7 March 1983:37–38.
Kaplan, Johanna. "Dry-Eyed Observer of City Lives." *New York Times Book Review* 20 March 1983:13.
Rodgers, Bernard. "Bette Howland: Poetic Impressions of an Outsider." *Chicago Tribune* 20 March 1983:1, 5.
Soete, M. "Things to Come and Go: Three Stories." *Library Journal* 1 Mar. 1983:517.
"Things to Come and Go." *Booklist* 1 March 1983:861.
"Things to Come and Go: Three Stories." *Kirkus Review* 1 Jan. 1983:22.

FANNIE HURST (1889–1968)

Carol Batker

BIOGRAPHY

Although she wrote about ordinary and underprivileged people throughout her career, Fannie Hurst was not one of them. Reputedly the highest-paid short-story writer of her time, Hurst published eighteen novels, most of them best-sellers, and hundreds of short stories. Popular magazines vied for exclusive publication rights, offering her unprecedented sums of money. Twenty-eight films were adapted from her work, with the movie rights selling for as much as $100,000 during the Depression. She wrote for and broadcast on the radio and had her own television talk show, "It's a Problem." By the thirties, an enormously popular Fannie Hurst had become a household name. Socially, she moved among luminaries. She stayed occasionally at the White House with her friend Eleanor Roosevelt, dined with Charles Lindbergh, lunched with Albert Einstein, interviewed Trotsky, and rehearsed a nervous Mary Pickford for a joint appearance at Madison Square Garden.

Despite her affluence and high connections, Fannie Hurst was known for her solidarity with the underprivileged, who were not only the subject of her writing, but also the focus of her liberal politics. She met Eleanor Roosevelt by advocating improved working conditions for domestic laborers and was later appointed chair of the Committee on Workman's Compensation for Household Employees. Hurst supported the public-health work of Lillian Wald and advocated birth control as well as the rights of homosexuals. She argued for equal pay for equal work, belonged to antiwar organizations, and urged African Americans to use their votes to make political change. Fighting on behalf of Eastern European Jews in the 1920s, Hurst continued to work for Jewish causes as she raised money for refugees in the 1940s and actively supported the state of Israel. As a writer, Hurst was famous for her sojourns into the working class for story material. She managed to obtain brief engagements as a sales clerk, waitress, and factory worker. She also frequented Ellis Island, the New York settlement houses, and once sailed to Europe in steerage to get to know "the unhyphenate Smiths and Joneses" of America (*Anatomy* 138).

From early on, Hurst's life and work was characterized by the disquiet she felt as a member of a privileged class passionately interested in those less privileged than herself. She was born into the German Jewish middle-class family of Rose Koppel and Samuel Hurst in Hamilton, Ohio, in 1889. She grew up in St. Louis where her father owned a shoe factory. Her only sibling, Edna, died of diphtheria at age four. The daughter of doting parents, Hurst as a child was secure, beloved, and restless. Intellectually curious and an avid reader, she describes the conventional life-style of her parents as limited:

> They were my people. They were my scrutiny. They were my world and already they were my vast unhappiness. . . . How could I cry out to Papa, who awed me: I love it here, but I don't like it here. It's warm and nice being with you and Mama, but I have no one to talk to. (*Anatomy* 26)

Uneasy with the dictates of convention, Hurst argued her disapproving but indulgent parents into financing her education and literary endeavors. At her request, they removed her from an elite girls school and placed her in a public high school. As early as age fourteen, Hurst began submitting her writing for publication. Even at this early stage, her fascination with working-class subjects was evident in a graduation speech she wrote but never presented, entitled "All the Little Human Ants":

> It was not to be about an event in history or a character analysis of Thomas Jefferson or the story of the Statue of Liberty and our debt to France. I preferred to write a paper about people who were not in history. People. The people in the streets and in little houses who were thick as ants and got stepped on like ants. (*Anatomy* 77)

In 1905, she convinced her parents to postpone indefinitely any serious consideration of her marriage while she attended Washington University. Hurst eventually did marry Jacques S. Danielson in 1914. Keeping their marriage secret, they lived in separate apartments and pursued their own careers for five years. Hurst's first publication, a character sketch of a woman frying her supper, appeared in *Reedy's Mirror* while she was in college. This well-respected St. Louis journal was edited by Marion Reedy, who was to become a long-time friend and advisor to Hurst and who also encouraged Kate Chopin. Hurst also wrote and acted in a one-act play at a local St. Louis theater.

After her graduation from college in 1909. Hurst convinced her parents to send her to New York to further a literary career that had just begun to show potential. Her parents reluctantly financed the move in 1910 so Hurst could be closer to publishers and could observe life "the way Dickens did. Roaming the highways and byways of—life—I mean the big city—standing on its bridges the way he did in London—watching the world" (*Anatomy* 115). Hurst received over thirty rejections from *The Saturday Evening Post* before the magazine bought "Power and Horse Power" in 1912 for $300, launching her career. She sold more than fifty works in the following decade. Publishers competed for the rights to her stories, and she became one of the highest-paid writers of her time.

Although Hurst's literary career was enormously successful, in her autobiography she represents herself apart from the most prestigious literary circles of the day. Hurst claimed that she

> was happier in the surging swarms. The lusty life of the heterogeneous city seemed to flow over and into me. The bluish dead-faced murals of people with the unseeing stares, sitting in rows in subways, were more eloquent, it seemed to me, than the processed epigrams of the wits of the Round Table could ever be. (*Anatomy* 226)

In spite of her professed outsider status, Hurst knew many of the most prominent authors of her time, including Willa Cather, Theodore Dreiser, F. Scott Fitzgerald, Sinclair Lewis, Dorothy Parker, Rebecca West, and Edna St. Vincent Millay. She was also a good friend of Carl Van Vechten's and employed Zora Neale Hurston as her secretary and chauffeur. Hurst continued to write into the 1960s, but her popularity and literary status diminished from World War II on. She wrote her last novel, *Fool Be Still*, in 1964 and died in 1968. Once at the center of the literary establishment, Fannie Hurst has been moved to the margins and is best known today through the movie adaptations of her work.

MAJOR THEMES

Concerned with power and privilege, Fannie Hurst wrote social fiction in the naturalist tradition. She focused primarily on gender politics, exploring domesticity, motherhood, the hazards and rewards of women's work outside the home, and sexuality. Historically, Hurst's preoccupation with domesticity and labor was not only the product of increased employment opportunities for women at the time, but also of her observations of working-class immigrant women, many of whom were longtime participants in the work force. Hurst's fiction explores the inequities women faced as wage laborers. It also highlights the ways in which women's domestic positions are socially constructed. While many of Hurst's characters aspire to a middle-class domestic ideal, as "leisured" wives and mothers, her fiction often represents middle-class homes as the site of women's exploitation and sexual repression. In her autobiography, Hurst expresses her ambivalence toward gender politics. She writes, "I find myself classified as a writer largely concerned with women. The impeachment is soft, but it irks." A few lines later, however, she argues that "the unexplored continent of the female creative mind is an exciting frontier that remains to be crashed" (*Anatomy* 354, 355). Much of Hurst's fiction attempts this exploration.

Adapted into two popular films, *Imitation of Life* is probably Hurst's best-known novel. Published in 1933, the novel simultaneously endorses women's roles as wife and mother and critiques middle-class domesticity as stifling for women. It is the story of Bea Pullman, who enters the work force as a single mother and makes a fortune. Set free from a conventional and sexually repressed marriage, Bea transforms her husband's maple sugar sideline into a chain of pancake houses which simulate the domestic setting of a home in urban environments:

soft light, amber atmosphere of indoor security, which, however fleeting, was respite from the duress of that strife and stone and steel out there; the something she yearned to create was akin to the kennel warmth and brightness she so passionately wanted to pour around herself and little family in the house on Arctic Avenue. (127)

In an interesting reversal, Bea acquires money and power in a male-dominated business world by selling domesticity. That her fortune is built upon her own exploitation of an African American woman is examined below. Although the novel celebrates the success of a businesswoman, by the end of the novel, Hurst represents Bea's career as merely an imitation of the more meaningful domestic life of wife and mother she has forfeited. However, the parallel between Bea's dual roles of homemaker and restaurateur does not simply reinforce women's positions in the home; rather, it serves to critique both institutions. In her marriage, Bea devotes herself to husband and child. Her work, which she finds ultimately dissatisfying, makes the same demands of her, in that she works to provide for her child and to make a temporary home for wayfaring men. The critique of Bea's career as having repressed her own desires is a critique of her domestic role as well.

Similarly, in *Lummox*, Hurst's favorite novel, Bertha's role as a wage earner parallels her role as a mother figure. The novel examines the exploitation of Bertha, a domestic worker, by her middle-class employers. It is the story of a domestic worker who puts her own child up for adoption and moves from home to home, laboring to earn her living. Bertha's nurturing labor is central to the families she serves. While Bertha's working-class status proves a barrier to her own mothering and the fulfillment of her desires, her representation as both exploited laborer and nurturer forces a reevaluation of middle-class domesticity as well as the institution of motherhood.

Back Street examines the exploitative relationship between a mistress and her married lover. For approximately twenty years, Ray Schmidt is the mistress of Walter Saxel, a successful German Jewish banker. The juxtaposition of Walter's "legitimate" and "illegitimate" homes serves to question them both. Ironically, by assuming the role of a married woman, Ray facilitates her own ruin. Her increasingly domestic role precipitates her growing social isolation and financial dependence on Walter. Ray gives up her job and withdraws from other social interaction even as she coaches Walter to succeed in his own business affairs. She cooks for and serves him without ever asserting her own needs. Paradoxically, while Ray's sexual liaison with Walter is the legal basis for her dispossession, it is her domestic disempowerment, not her sexual mores, that leads to her destitution at the end of the novel. Ray's relationship with Walter is sexually satisfying, but within a domestic framework, it is fundamentally exploitative. While Hurst's characters long for middle-class domesticity, Hurst does not simply endorse this position for women. Rather, she examines how women, serving others, are exploited and profoundly disempowered within and outside of the family.

Hurst's gender politics are constituted by problematic representations of race and class as well. Thematizing interracial relations, Hurst all too often resorts to racist stereotypes in her characterizations. In *Imitation of Life*, for example, Bea succeeds in business by exploiting the labor of an African American woman, Delilah. While Bea becomes a millionaire businesswoman, Delilah's labor goes unrewarded and unacknowledged throughout the text. Bea makes a fortune by trafficking in domesticity, and Delilah embodies that domesticity. Delilah's face is stamped upon the candy, syrup, and promotion for each restaurant. She can signify domesticity in the restaurant because her role as wage laborer in the restaurant and in the home are coextensive. Just as Delilah's domestic labor enables Bea to leave the house, her position as cook enables Bea to leave the restaurant for executive offices. *Imitation of Life* is illustrative of the extent to which racial politics inform class and gender politics in Hurst's fiction.

SURVEY OF CRITICISM

The contemporary criticism of Fannie Hurst's work is primarily concerned with biography. Articles by Cynthia Ann Brandimarte (1987) and Susan Koppelman (1987) are important sources of information on Hurst's family, education, and career. Gay Wilentz's (1986) article in the *Library Chronicle of the University of Texas* addresses Hurst's relationship with Zora Neale Hurston as well as Hurst's attitudes toward race and her own ethnicity.

In their textual analysis, various critics highlight Hurst's concern for the discrimination women suffer as workers. Critics also applaud Hurst for creating strong women in spite of the difficulties they face in a hostile environment. For instance, Alice Childress (1989) argues in her introduction to *Lummox* that Hurst's women live "according to the dictates of [their] free mind[s], regardless of opposition" (ix). At the same time, readers are critical of Hurst for creating passive victims of abuse and of her inability to create working women who stand alone without the nagging desire for a man. Diane Lichtenstein's (1988) article in *Studies in American Jewish Literature* argues that "few if any, of Hurst's female characters are alone out of choice, and even fewer feel happy when they are alone" (35). A collection of film criticism, *Imitation of Life: Douglas Sirk, Director* (1991), edited by Lucy Fischer, is also very useful. While the films do not reproduce the novel—the 1959 version differs quite dramatically from the novel—the similarities in racial and sexual politics as well as plot structure make this criticism suggestive. Lucy Fischer's "Three Way Mirror: *Imitation of Life*" is particularly helpful in its analysis of motherhood, as is

Sandy Flitterman-Lewis's reading of Peola as transgressor in her *"Imitation(s) of Life*: The Black Woman's Double Determination as Troubling 'Other.' "

Like earlier readers, contemporary critics also focus on Hurst's racial politics. Wilentz (1986) discusses the critical reception *Imitation of Life* received in the African American community at the time: "black critics were appalled by the book and the stereotypic portrayal of Delilah, the warm-hearted, all-forgiving mammy who made such delicious pancakes" (38). Langston Hughes wrote a one-act parody entitled "Limitations of Life," reversing Bea and Delilah's roles. Sterling Brown (1969), in *The Negro in American Fiction and Negro Poetry and Drama*, argued:

It is no wonder that, longing to be stable, Peola "passes" and marries on the other side. Delilah, with a "rambunctious capacity for devotion," is a contented slave, brought up to date, worshipful of her white Miss Honey Bea, to whom her drudgery has brought wealth. The statement is clear: Black Negroes contented with serving and worshipping whites; mixed Negroes, disoriented, aspiring, and therefore, tragic. Alas the poor mulatto! (Etd. in Wilentz 39)

Lichtenstein (1988) and Wilentz (1986) also argue that Hurst "was simultaneously embarrassed by and proud of being a Jew" (Lichtenstein 26). While Wilentz perceives instances of anti-Semitism in Hurst's work, Lichtenstein argues that Hurst's treatment of intermarriage is better than that of most of her predecessors. She claims that *Family* "leaves us not with a happy ending, but with doubts and questions about what it means to be a Jewish woman living in a non-Jewish America" (30).

Susan Koppelman (1987) explains the decline of the once-popular Fannie Hurst as "parallel[ing] the decline in the economy and the rise of anti-Semitism and xenophobia that corrupted the United States on the edge of World War II" (504). However, as Koppelman suggests, Hurst's fiction may once more be coming of age, inviting analysis from a wide variety of scholarly fields, including Jewish studies, women's studies, film studies, studies of popular culture, and labor history.

BIBLIOGRAPHY

Works by Fannie Hurst

Just Around the Corner. New York: Harper, 1914.
Every Soul Has Its Song. New York: Harper, 1916.
Gaslight Sonatas. New York: Harper, 1918.
Humoresque. New York: Harper, 1919.
Star Dust: The Story of an American Girl. New York: Harper, 1921.
The Vertical City. New York: Harper, 1922.
Lummox. New York: Harper, 1923.
Appassionata. New York: Knopf, 1926.

Song of Life. New York: Knopf, 1927.
A President Is Born. New York: Harper, 1928.
Five and Ten. New York: Harper, 1929.
Procession. New York: Harper, 1929.
Back Street. New York: Cosmopolitan Book Corporation, 1931.
Imitation of Life. New York: Harper, 1933.
Anitra's Dance. New York: Harper, 1934.
Hallelujah. New York: Harper, 1934.
No Food with My Meals. New York: Harper, 1935.
Great Laughter. New York: Harper, 1936.
We Are Ten. New York: Harper, 1937.
Lonely Parade. New York: Harper, 1942.
The Hands of Veronica. New York: Harper, 1947.
Anywoman. New York: Harper, 1950.
The Man with One Head. London: Cape, 1953.
Anatomy of Me: A Wonderer in Search of Herself. Garden City, NY: Doubleday, 1958.
Family! Garden City, NY: Doubleday, 1960.
God Must Be Sad. Garden City, NY: Doubleday, 1961.
Fool Be Still. Garden City, NY: Doubleday, 1964.

Works about Fannie Hurst

Antler, Joyce. "Introduction." *America and I.* Boston: Beacon Press, 1990. 1–24.
Brandimarte, Cynthia. "Fannie Hurst: A Missouri Girl Makes Good." *Missouri Historical Review*, April 1987: 275–95.
———. "Fannie Hurst and Her Fiction: Prescriptions for America's Working Women." Ph.D. diss. University of Texas at Austin, 1980. 317.
Brown, Sterling. *The Negro in American Fiction and Negro Poetry and Drama.* New York: Arno Press, 1969. 144–45.
Burke, Virginia. "Zora Neale Hurston and Fannie Hurst as They Saw Each Other." *College Language Association Journal*, June 1977: 435–47.
Childress, Alice. "Introduction." *Lummox.* Fannie Hurst. New York: New American Library, 1989. v–xiii.
Currier, Susan. *Dictionary of Literary Biography: American Short-Story Writers, 1910– 1945.* Ed. Bobby Ellen Kimbel. Detroit, MI: Gale Research Inc., 1989. 151–58.
Dague, Elizabeth. "Images of Work, Glimpses of Professionalism in Selected Nineteenth- and Twentieth-Century Novels." *Frontiers* 5.1: 50–55.
Fischer, Lucy, ed. *Imitation of Life,* New Brunswick, NJ: Rutgers University Press, 1991. 346.
Frederick, Antoinette. "Fannie Hurst." *Notable American Women.* Eds. Barbara Sicherman, Carol Hurd Green, et al. Cambridge: Belknap Press of Harvard University Press, 1980. 359–61.
Koppelman, Susan. "The Education of Fannie Hurst." *Women's Studies International Forum* 10 (1987) 503–16.
Lichtenstein, Diane Marilyn. "Fannie Hurst and Her Nineteenth-Century Predecessors." *Studies in American Jewish Literature* 7 (Spring 1988): 26–39.
———. "On Whose Native Ground? Nineteenth-Century Myths of American Woman-

hood and Jewish Women Writers.'' Ph.D. diss., University of Pennsylvania, 1985. 260.

Shaughnessy, Mary Rose. *Myths About Love and Woman: The Fiction of Fannie Hurst.* New York: Gordon, 1979.

Uffen, Ellen Serlen. ''Fannie Hurst.'' *American Women Writers.* Eds. Lina Mainiero and Langdon Lynne Faust. 2nd ed. 4 vols. New York: Frederick Ungar, 1982.

Wilentz, Gay. ''White Patron and Black Artist: The Correspondence of Fannie Hurst and Zora Neale Hurston.'' *Library Chronicle of the University of Texas* 35 (1986) 20–43.

JOYCE (GLASSMAN) JOHNSON (1935–   )

Blossom Steinberg Kirschenbaum

BIOGRAPHY

Joyce Glassman, after early childhood in Bay Ridge and Kew Gardens, New York, grew up in the milieu of neighborhood stores and fine apartment buildings near Columbia University. Her paternal grandparents had moved from Riga, Latvia, to England, and from there her father had immigrated to New York City after World War I. He worked for the same tobacco company for thirty-five years. Her mother, born Rosalind Ross in New York City, was the daughter of shopkeepers from Warsaw.

Ambitious for their only child, the Glassmans encouraged Joyce's artistic inclinations. At age ten she acted with the Broadway company of *I Remember Mama*, while attending Professional Children's School. Her piano lessons included theory and composition, and her mother copyrighted some juvenile musical scores. Joyce had guitar lessons too. During 1947 to 1951 she was enrolled at academically select Hunter College High School. Her work appeared in the literary magazine along with pieces by schoolmates Audre Lorde and Diane di Prima. In her thirteenth year, she started venturing downtown on weekends to the fountain in Washington Square Park, where folksingers gathered in what she has called "a cameraderie of loneliness."

Glassman attended Barnard College (1951–55), scene of her first novel, *Come and Join the Dance* (1962), which was published when she was twenty-six. Through fictional stand-in Susan Levitt, Glassman used this novel to explore her own sense of being an outsider vis-à-vis others who "did not see the world as a magnificent party to which they had not been invited" (32).

Working at jobs in publishing and taking courses at the New School for Social Research, she lived in the bohemian New York style reflected in such stories as "The Fall of Texas" and "Launching Day, 1962." Along with the heady freedom of grungy tenements and urban anonymity, of dissolving social barriers, hedonistic sexuality, and flowering of the beat counterculture, her stories capture also the dark side of the 1950s: especially abuse of drugs, failure of responsible parenting, and terror of atomic apocalypse.

While she worked at Farrar, Straus, and Cudahy, early in 1957, on a blind date arranged by Allen Ginsberg, Joyce at age twenty-one met thirty-four-year-old Jack Kerouac; for two years or so she was his girl friend, subordinating her creativity to his needs. In 1962, she married abstract expressionist painter James Johnson, who was killed in a motorcycle accident a year later. This marriage inspired the novel *In the Night Cafe* (1989). In 1965, Johnson married British painter Peter Pinchbeck, by whom she had a son, Daniel. That marriage ended in divorce.

A second novel, *Bad Connections* (1978), received wider critical attention than did *Come and Join the Dance*. Molly, the protagonist, is also autobiographically based; a magazine editor, she opts for divorce and brings up her son alone, much like the author. Johnson had been supporting herself by editorial positions at William Morrow and Co. (1965–67), The Dial Press (1967–69), and McGraw-Hill (1969–77). She would go on to become executive editor at Dial, part of Doubleday (1977–85); senior editor at Atlantic Monthly Press (1985–86); and contributing editor at *Vanity Fair* (1986–88).

Johnson's memoir *Minor Characters* (1983), in which she elaborates on her sheltered adolescence as well as on beat society, the affair with Kerouac, the careers of contemporaries, and the death of her father, won the National Book Critics Circle Award in 1983, the same year she got the John Gardner Memorial Fellowship of the Bread Loaf Writers Conference. The book pays tribute to the author's best friend at Barnard, Elise Cowen, who committed suicide at age twenty-eight. As critic Laurie Stone noted, ''Johnson's outrage about the waste of women's lives is by far the strongest emotion in her book.''

From 1985 to the present, Johnson has been teaching at Columbia University as adjunct professor of Creative Writing, and at the 92nd Street Y and Bread Loaf, with visiting appointments at American University, SUNY-Purchase, Bennington College, and Warren Wilson College in Swanannoa, North Carolina. She was one of two first-prize winners in the 1987 O. Henry Awards for ''In the Children's Wing,'' which has been anthologized in *The Bread Loaf Anthology of Contemporary American Short Stories* and in *The Human Experience*, a collection of Soviet and American writing. The story is incorporated in her third novel, *In the Night Cafe* (1989), set in New York in the early 1960s, which explores the theme of the abandoned child. The novel was a Book-of-the-Month Club and Quality Paperback Book Club choice.

A nonfiction work that followed, *What Lisa Knew: The Truths and Lies of the Steinberg Case* (1990), details the background and much-publicized trial of Joel Steinberg, a lawyer who abused his illegally adopted little daughter until she died. Johnson expends no pity on Steinberg's abused but complicit companion Hedda Nussbaum; she sees the two adults as ''Nazis; Lisa was the Jew'' (Interview, 18 January 1993).

After the trial Johnson traveled to Prague and then attended a writers' conference in Moscow. She published articles about these trips and continues to publish short fiction, articles, and book reviews. She serves on the Board of Governors for the New York State Foundation on the Arts (1991–94) and was awarded a National Endowment for the Arts Fellowship for 1992. She writes in her apartment on West End Avenue and in a cabin in Vermont.

"It's possible," Johnson recently reflected, "that if my family had had a more authentic relationship to Judaism,. . . . I might have been drawn to it. . . . My family was very afraid of being Jews in the 1940s. They really wanted to assimilate. My mother couldn't always distinguish kitsch from culture, but she wanted refinement. Many people went through denatured rituals. They didn't light candles but you had to be home for Passover" (Interview, 15 August 1992).

Currently, Johnson is writing about her maternal grandmother, a merchant's daughter from Warsaw, who in an arranged marriage wed Talmudic scholar–poet Samuel, descended from an eminent rabbinical family. Joyce Johnson has been told that in the United States he found he was an anachronism. His wife kept having children; he worked in a factory. After a hand injury incapacitated him, he gassed himself to death. Joyce Johnson's mother was five years old at the time. When Joyce was sixteen, she found out the manner of his death when her grandmother died. Joyce has been given to understand that her own literary talent comes from "that side of the family." Patently, it is not an easy legacy.

Joyce Johnson's mother is elderly now, and to avoid giving pain, the daughter advises against reading her books: "I only do it for the money, Mother," she has fibbed. Her future projects include an article on a child-actress for the entertainment section of the *Sunday New York Times*; for *The New Yorker*, an article about a forensic psychiatrist; and a novel about a mother-daughter relationship over four decades (Telephone interview, 17 January 1993).

MAJOR THEMES

In fiction and memoir Johnson recreates the Sexual Revolution (her capitals, in *Bad Connections*) and the artistic and literary ferment of the bohemian 1950s and counterculture 1960s, from an evolving feminist perspective. Her first novel dramatizes rejection of parental constraints. Protagonist Susan Levitt, a student at Barnard College, is more intent on losing her virginity than on graduating. She substitutes campus rituals (class sing, class luncheon) for those of family, politics, or religion. Her rebellion involves postponing adult life by deferring graduation. To preserve her own authenticity, while she is breaking loose, she reflects:

You always had to lie a little and each time you lied a little piece of you was eaten away. And you lied to protect yourself, too. They had a way of rushing in upon you if you ever let them think they knew what you were feeling. You had to protect yourself from their greed. They wanted all your secrets; they wanted terrible scenes where everyone wept and forgave one another. At the same time, they wanted you to preserve their innocence. They wanted that most of all. (122)

Pressured to conform, please, and placate. Susan learns to survive by being both loving and cruel—and by leading a double life.

The memoir *Minor Characters* (1983) shows Johnson living out her concept of liberation, leaving the parental home "on Independence Day, 1955—a day I'd chosen not for its symbolism but because it was the first day of a long weekend" (101). A year later she had an illegal and, therefore, secret abortion. Johnson describes how by day she dressed properly for typing in a Midtown office, but at night she frequented Greenwich Village's Cedar Bar and took Dexamils and worked on her novel: "Everyone on the East Side was taking dexies. One prescription serviced half a dozen people" (249). The same concept of liberation informs her novels.

Bad Connections (1978) about marriage, adultery, and divorce—and the concept of liberation as financial independence from a husband—has another theme, too: addiction. Magazine editor Molly, the author's persona, is raising a son and thinks she has an independent life, but she repeatedly entangles herself in painful relationships with men. Her lover Conrad, a radical and self-indulgent lawyer, is unreliable from the start. Throughout the book he avoids commitment and remains involved with another woman. The Sexual Revolution against "bourgie" values occurs in a moral vacuum, while "social diseases" reach epidemic proportions—and are seen by Molly as "a form of communication" (82)! A second lover, though kind, cannot merge lovemaking with intimacy. An earlier dream of Conrad's wedding to her rival—"a Jewish wedding complete with canopy, chopped liver, and the traditional glass that was to be broken by the groom" (143)—contrasts with what Molly feels she has always been too faithful to: "the illusion of others" (247), not any values legitimately her own. During the act of intercourse, "Finally, she thinks, she understands addiction" (255). She flees, preferring honor and wholeness to addictive erotic passion.

Maternal care and the needs of children are concerns of the later books. The crying baby left unattended in "The Fall of Texas" has been succeeded in *In the Night Cafe* by the abandoned son listening intently for clues about his father—and, finally, by the fully developed relationship between Joanna and Nicky, as separately and together, mother and son grapple with private pain and the suffering of others. Joanna becomes a strong, caring, responsible adult rising to the challenge of nurturing children, even one who is disturbed and dangerous. The theme of the neglected or abused child is made resonant in *What Lisa Knew*. Johnson's authorial voice makes the child a claimant on our conscience.

While Jewish identity is not a central concern, aspects of Judaism occasionally enter Johnson's fiction. In *Bad Connections*, when Molly observes a group of Chasidic Jewish women on a bus, she remarks, "With all their rules and their wigs, their obliviousness to the passage of time and the price they must have paid for it, they at least had the advantage of moral clarity" (179). In contrast, Molly suffers in a moral vacuum. But if Judaism offers moral certainty, it is also seen as a liability. In *In the Night Cafe* the father of a painter from Phoenix "hated artists and said New York was full of Jewish Communists and queers . . . the kinds of people he didn't want his son to meet'' (137). To assert Jewishness in some contexts is to court trouble.

SURVEY OF CRITICISM

As the entry about Joyce Johnson in *Contemporary Literary Criticism* notes, her fiction ''often focuses on the external and intrinsic causes of the social repression of women during the late 1950s and the difficulties experienced by female protagonists attempting to abandon subservient roles'' (283). Though *Come and Join the Dance* (1962) received little critical acknowledgment beyond its precocity, *Bad Connections* (1978) was generally praised. Seymour Krim noted its bleak climate and ''brave self-sufficiency and poise'' (10). Its narration, according to Bruce Woods, ''shuffles between the first and third person. This is initially confusing, but does, perhaps, offer a greater perspective upon the happenings depicted'' (36). Unlike Woods, who did not like Molly, the narrator-protagonist Ellen Willis found that ''Molly's intelligence and self-deprecating irony make her both interesting and likable. Her tenacity in pursuit of what she wants has, even at its most misguided, a certain saving violence; she is not pathetic; she doesn't whine'' (86). Novelist Helen Yglesias finds the book ''controlled, smooth, deftly written'' but ''dispiriting'' (87). For Hermione Lee, on the other hand, it is ''lively and poignant enough,'' but still ''something of a disappointment'' (36).

Minor Characters has been unanimously praised. Calling the book ''hauntingly, delicately written,'' Anne Tyler notes, ''catlike pounces upon exactly the right detail, the single sight or smell or sound that could bring a whole era flooding back into memory'' (6). Beyond its success as autobiographical narrative, it corrects perceptions of cultural history. As Laurie Stone says, ''Johnson revitalizes the '50s confessional because her writing says as much about the past as about Joyce Johnson'' (10). Seymour Krim, too, sees Johnson as ''handing over to us the safe-deposit box that contains the lost, precious scrolls of the New York '50s'' (10). ''Never again,'' wrote Robbin Schiff, ''can I comfortably reconcile the lure of that time with what I now know of its boy-clubbiness and the silences of its women'' (36). Media critic Todd Gitlin concurs, in his *The Sixties: Years of Hope, Days of Rage* (1987); his 1983 review notes that *Minor Characters* is ''memorable for evoking the losses that grown boys have inflicted on women in the name of manhood'' (665). Most critics, however, still discuss the beat collectivity as male. Lee Bartlett's 1981 anthology *The Beats: Essays in Criticism* does not list Joyce Glassman or Joyce Johnson in its index; Fred W. McDarrah's 1985 *Kerouac and Friends* makes only a single reference in the caption to a photo of ''Heddie Jones (coeditor of *Yugen* with husband Le Roi Jones) and Joyce Glassman (later Johnson) at Artist's Club, March 10, 1960.'' Herbert Gold, in his 1993 *Bohemia: Where Art, Angst, Love, and Strong Coffee Meet*, notes: ''The band of leather women ignored the ex-girlfriends of Jack

Kerouac, even the ones who had written books. Book-writing girlfriends weren't their thing'' (234).

Phillip Lopate praises *In the Night Cafe* as ''a vivid romance'' with ''a gift for social history'' that ''sails on its first-person narration: a fiercely believable, testifying voice that is pungent, close to the bone, stinging with candor.'' He sees the evolution of Joanna, rather than their Big Love, as what the novel ''triumphantly conveys.'' By critical consensus, ''The Children's Wing'' (penultimate section of *In the Night Cafe*), ''simple, spare, plain,'' as William Abrahams says, and ''engendering a kind of urban poetry'' (xii), is Johnson's finest achievement to date as a writer.

BIBLIOGRAPHY

Works by Joyce (Glassman) Johnson

Fiction

Come and Join the Dance. New York: Atheneum, 1962.
Bad Connections. New York: G. P. Putnam, 1978.
''The Fall of Texas.'' *The New Yorker.* 11 Nov. 1985: 40–42.
''In the Children's Wing.'' *Harper's.* July 1986: 66–69.
''Launching Day, 1962.'' *The New Yorker.* 13 April 1987: 30–35.
In the Night Cafe. New York: E. P. Dutton, 1989.

Selected Nonfiction

Minor Characters (memoir). Boston: Houghton Mifflin, 1983.
What Lisa Knew: The Truths and Lies of the Steinberg Case. New York: G. P. Putnam, 1990.
''Worlds Apart.'' *New York Times Magazine.* 18 Nov., 1990: 54ff.

Interviews

''Beat Generation Survivor.'' Interview with Jim Seavor. *Providence (R.I.) Evening Bulletin* 9 March 1984: C–4.
Telephone interviews, 15 August 1992, 31 December 1992, and 17 January 1993.
Personal interview, New York City, 18 January 1993.

Works about Joyce (Glassman) Johnson

Abrahams, William. ''Introduction.'' *Prize Stories 1987: O. Henry Awards.* Garden City, NY: Doubleday & Co., 1987. ix–xiii.
Atlas, John. Rev. of *Minor Characters. The Atlantic.* Feb. 1983: 100–01.
Campbell, James. ''Camp Follower.'' Rev. of *Minor Characters. Times Literary Supplement.* 3 June 1983: 576.
Chasin, Helen. ''The Girl in the Boy Gang.'' Rev. of *Minor Characters. New York Times Book Review.* 16 January 1983: 9.

Gitlin, Todd. "Where the Boys Aren't." Rev. of *Minor Characters. The Nation.* 28 May 1983: 663–65.

Gold, Herbert. *Bohemia: Where Art, Angst, Love, and Strong Coffee Meet.* New York: Simon and Schuster, 1993.

"Joyce Johnson." *Contemporary Literary Criticism.* (58): 283–93.

Krim, Seymour. "Beats and Bit Players." Rev. of *Minor Characters. Washington Post Book World.* 6 Feb. 1983: 3, 10.

Lee, Hermione. "Backwoods Messiah." Rev. of *Bad Connections. The Observer.* 19 August 1979: 36.

Lopate, Phillip. "Bohemia Died, but Life Went On." Rev. of *In the Night Cafe. New York Times Book Review.* 30 April 1989: 11.

Maynard, Joyce. "Love after Death." Rev. of *In the Night Cafe. Mademoiselle.* May 1989: 92–94.

Prince, Peter. "Boy Gang." Rev. of *Minor Characters. London Review of Books.* 19 Jan.–1 Feb. 1984: 23.

Schiff, Robbin. Rev. of *Minor Characters. Ms.* March 1983: 36.

Steinberg, Sybil. Rev. of *In the Night Cafe. Publishers Weekly.* 27 Jan. 1989: 454.

Stone, Laurie. "Memoirs Are Made of This." Rev. of *Minor Characters. VLS,* 19 April 1983: 8–11.

Tyler, Anne. "Painting with Words." Rev. of *In the Night Cafe. Chicago Tribune—Books.* 16 April 1989: 6–7.

Willis, Ellen. "The Trouble Is Not Just with Molly's Men." Rev. of *Bad Connections. Village Voice.* 3 July 1978: 86.

Woods, Bruce. Rev. of *Bad Connections. West Coast Review of Books.* July 1978: 36.

Yglesias, Helen. "News from the Sisterhood." Rev. of *Bad Connections. Harper's.* August 1978: 86–88.

ERICA JONG (1942–   )

Bruce Henderson

BIOGRAPHY

The fiction and poetry of Erica Jong feel so autobiographical, even confessional, that it is a temptation to read them merely as documents of her life. Her own comments on this tendency are complex, somewhat contradictory: In one interview, she will caution the reader against too literal a reading of the fiction as a rendition of her life; in another interview, she will admit, with a kind of guilty pleasure, that she did make mischief with events taken from her personal history. Clearly, there is a correspondence between Jong's fictional creations and her own self or repertoire of selves; the poetry is more openly in the lyric mode, in which autobiography and fiction are often blurred.

Erica Jong was born Erica Mann to Eda Mirsky Mann and Seymour Mann on March 26, 1942. Her mother was a ceramics designer and her father a businessman. In addition, her maternal grandfather was a painter, a factor that also plays itself out both in the fiction and the poetry: That both mother and grandfather were artists had a great influence on Jong's earliest ambition, which was to be a painter.

Jong attended the High School of Music and Art in New York City, graduated from Barnard College in 1963, and entered a program of graduate studies in English Literature at Columbia. She received a Master's degree in Eighteenth-Century Literature from Columbia in 1965 and began doctoral studies in the same department. She abandoned graduate studies when she realized that they were interfering with what was becoming her most important professional priority: writing poetry and fiction. She supported herself by teaching at such New York City institutions as the City University of New York, Manhattan Community College, and the YM-YWCA Poetry Center.

Jong has married four times and has been divorced three. These marriages and divorces show up in lyrical and fictionalized forms in her poetry and novels. Her first marriage was to Michael Werthman, a Columbia student. Her second husband, Allan Jong, a Chinese American child psychiatrist, provided the inspiration for Bennett Wing in *Fear of Flying*; the episodes set in Heidelburg (also the source of a number of her early poems) correspond to the period of their life when Allan Jong was stationed in the military in Germany and Erica Jong taught in the University of Maryland Overseas program. Her third marriage was to Jonathan Fast, who is "transformed" into Josh Ace, the writer/younger man in *How to Save Your Own Life* and in *Parachutes & Kisses*. Her marriage to Fast produced Jong's one daughter, Molly Miranda Jong-Fast.

Her career has consisted of an alternation of volumes of poetry and fiction. When she is asked which is primary in her life, Jong always describes the poetry as that which made her a writer and as the primary center of her artistry. Read in tandem, the poetry and the fiction, at some level, produce a supertext of Jong's life. Indeed, throughout the volumes, she mixes genres, including poems and quotes from her own poems and others', and moving into prose-poetry (often expressionistic or hallucinatory in quality) in some of the poems.

MAJOR THEMES

The central theme of Jong's writings, both her poetry and her fiction, is the journey toward liberation, toward openness to experience—what in Jungian terms might be viewed as the processes of individuation and integration. For Jong and for her heroines, this process is an episodic, ongoing one, in which identity and experience are always negotiated through the personal, aesthetic, and historical texts of family, erotic relationships, and intellectual traditions. While Jong stresses the role of physical and psychological experience in depicting these journeys, she is keenly aware of the political dimensions of being a woman: The feminist dictum that the personal is the political is always present, whether in the foreground or the background in Jong's writing.

Jong began as a poet, and, while she is less celebrated for poetry than for fiction, the early poetry in particular suggests the directions in which Jong would develop. Her poetry moves between a demonstration of her knowledge of English lyric tradition, her sisterhood with twentieth-century women writers (particularly the confessional poets), and her development of a voice through which to present her own autobiographical experiences. Her grand theme is the woman as subject of her own physical, emotional, and intellectual experience: Like Plath and Sexton, Jong not only used poetry to describe the phenomenology of women's lives, but, like Adrienne Rich, she used poetry to argue for the value of such experience. Much of the poetry in her first several volumes might be classified as "public poetry," rhetorical, almost oratorical in its sense of occasion and audience. Poems like "Bitter Pills for the Dark Ladies" and "Alcestis on the Poetry Circuit" are devoted to the tragic heroines of women's letters: The latter poem is subtitled, "In Memoriam Marina Tsvetayeva, Anna Wickham, Sylvia Plath, Shakespeare's Sister, Etc., Etc.," referring to the woman–artist as suicide. The "Etc., Etc.," in particular suggests something of Jong's voice and tone: There is a slangy breeziness to it; at the same time, it suggests the anger and bleakness of a history of cultures that must destroy the independent voice of the woman writer. She is aware of her culpability within the critical tradition that romanticizes, trivializes, or simply ignores the traditions of such writers, as in her poem "The Critics," which she subtitles "For Everyone who writes about Sylvia Plath, including me."

At the same time, much of Jong's poetry is intensely personal (not to say that the public poems do not possess a passion of their own). Jong moves between the lyric and dramatic modes, sometimes cutting so close to the bone and working through images that, while accessible to the reader, seem so grounded in a private realm of experience, one assumes they are based in autobiographical experience. "Mother," for example, is a poem written in extremely short, tense free-verse lines, in which the speaker (one assumes it is Jong from the specificity of the details, which match her own life) parallels Plath's "Daddy," excoriating the female parent this time for the inability of the two women to remain connected or to communicate. Yet the poem is finally warmer and more conciliatory than Plath's, as Jong concludes the poem with an understanding of the way in which her mother's life and her own are mutually implicated in painful (and joyful) ways beyond their own control. Similarly, both "Sexual Soup" and "Colder" reflect on failed relationships with men; yet, for all the pain and anger pervading both poems, there is also an understanding of the emptiness of the man's experience, the ways in which he too has been robbed by the social forces that make it virtually impossible for him to escape his own death of the heart. "Penis Envy," one of the poems found in the section of *Loveroot* titled "In the Penile Colony," shows Jong able to imagine what it might be like to be a man desiring and constructing the female body. She does so with generosity and without condescension.

Within both the public and the personal matrices of Jong's poetry, there is also another side—both playful and allusive—building in thought and sentiment, if not in form or diction, on Jong's expertise in the eighteenth century. Thus, while her poetry is almost always technically free verse, sometimes of a very loose and conversational kind, she also often uses the repetitive figures of anaphora and refrain, for both comic and didactic effect. A poem like "Seventeen Warnings in Search of a Feminist Poem" uses the rhetorical form of the catalogue to comment with irony on the paradoxes within feminism's views of men, both those men sympathetic to and those antagonist toward feminism. "The Eggplant Epithalamion" takes as its jumping-off point a comment by archeologist Iris Love about the centrality of the eggplant to everyday life in Turkey; Jong moves from this to a series of pastiches of Turkish verse forms, in which she weds the fecund, feminine image of the eggplant to observations on marriage. Both Jong's themes and stylistic techniques demonstrate considerable innovation and intellect. Jong's early poetry stands as a considerable achievement in its own right and at the same time suggests the theme on which she will elaborate in her novels: the woman "at the edge of the body," to borrow the title of one of her volumes of poetry—the artist negotiating personal and cultural spaces between her own experience and the pressures of a patriarchal society. Both the pleasures and difficulties of living in the female body are present in the poems: They achieve something not unlike the concept of *l'écriture feminine* developed by French feminists, translated either as "feminine writing" or "writing the woman." Jong asserts herself as subject, writing her own "texts" of selfhood.

For Jong, to be a woman means to be an artist, whether the artistic creation is a child, a novel, or a painting. Isadora Wing, who comes as close to an alter ego as any character in Jong's fiction, begins as a frustrated, somewhat isolated figure, in some ways a construction of the many psychiatrists whose convention in Vienna is the site of the crisis in *Fear of Flying*. While Isadora develops as a literary artist, in *How to Save Your Own Life* and *Parachutes & Kisses*, she struggles to integrate her authentic love for her daughter with the competing demands of her career as writer and her always optimistic, always doomed-to-fail relationships with men. In Jong's world, it seems easier to integrate the maternal and the artistic: The erotic and the wifely are far more difficult sets of relationships to reconcile.

The nexus of body, mind, heart, and soul is omnipresent in Jong's poetry and fiction. The poetry is filled with images of corporeality and juxtaposes the sensuous and the spiritual: The "Fruit and Vegetable" poems (particularly "The Eggplant Epithalamion" in *Half-Lives*) are her finest meditations on the connection between the physical and metaphysical. Yet body is not always something to be trusted, particularly in the fiction. Jong celebrates female sexuality. Indeed, it is the explicitness of the language and scenes she describes that so upset a number of her early critics. She reclaims the erotic life for the American middle-class woman. At the same time, there always seems to be a cost: Emotional and political heartbreak is the inevitable result. The "zipless fuck," to use her most famous phrase, remains more an ideal than a reality: For Jong, virtually any sexual encounter, whether with men or women, is fraught with meaning, overdetermined by history, society, and emotion. Still, the pain and the recounting of it do not erase the *jouissance* of the moment.

Along with the erotic, the life of the intellect provides another set of relationships that Jong explores throughout her works. Critics have noted that there are so many references to other writers in her works that, at times, they seem simply to be a display of random knowledge rather than an intertextual web of allusions. Clearly important to Jong is using knowledge, engaging in dialogue with other minds of the past and present, particularly as she situates herself as a woman intellectual and artist. Part of Isadora Wing's journey to self is an understanding of the traditions in which she works, out of which her own style grows. *Serenissima*, her "novel of Venice," is a reworking of Shakespeare's problematic *The Merchant of Venice*. In the novel, Jong presents Jessica, a modern American movie star, who, while in Venice for a film festival, travels back to Renaissance Venice, as another Jessica, Shylock's daughter. She encounters William Shakespeare as he lives through a set of events that parallel both the language and action of his play. While Jong alludes to the anti-Semitism of Shakespeare's play, she emphasizes more the conflicted yet extraordinarily moving father-daughter relationship between Shylock and Jessica.

Perhaps Jong's most ambitious attempt to incorporate all her themes of womanhood is *Fanny*, a pastiche of the eighteenth-century English picaresque novel. Here Jong not only takes on the major figures in that field, Defoe, Richardson, and Fielding, but also has her heroine engage in physical and intellectual intercourse with such other luminaries as Swift, Pope, and John Cleland, author of *Fanny Hill*, from whose novel Jong takes the first name for her heroine. Jong, through her intelligent and finally virtuous heroine Fanny, reclaims tales of piracy, debauchery, and romance. Jong builds on her knowledge of eighteenth-century literature and society to create a text that both speaks out of that age yet also speaks to and in our own. As with her previous novels, the role of woman as subject and object in a male-dominated society becomes the central issue, with woman triumphing as author of her own life literally and figuratively. The erotic life again plays a prominent role, particularly as Jong revises motifs of "seduction and betrayal," to use Elizabeth Hardwick's phrase, in which women figure as commodities for men. The novel also explores both utopian and dystopian themes, in which Fanny and the other rogues—including thieves, murderers, prostitutes, and pirates—form an alternative, if imperfect, family.

While Jewishness is not as central a theme in her writings as is gender, it is always present and fuels both images and experiences in many of the novels. Isadora is aware of her own position as a Jew, both in her stay in Germany in *Fear of Flying* and in her trip to Baba Yar in *Parachutes & Kisses*. Her Jewishness is part of her allure for Adrian Goodlove, the impotent British psychiatrist with whom she sets out on her journey in *Fear of Flying*. Yet even as she seduces and is seduced by Goodlove, Isadora is uncomfortably aware of his anti-Semitism when he professes fascination with Jewish women. For Isadora, her Jewishness always involves a complex web of history, culture, and family. She is aware of the exoticism it holds for her Gentile lovers, and she responds ambivalently: On the one hand, she enjoys the power it gives her over them; on the other hand, it reduces her once again to an object, a stereotyped "other" that does not wholly represent her.

Most importantly, Isadora's Jewishness characterizes her family, particularly her relationships with her parents and her sisters in these novels. In one of the most moving scenes in her later fiction, Isadora delivers the eulogy for her grandfather in *Parachutes & Kisses*. She participates in a traditional Jewish ritual, yet also brings her own unique, iconoclastic perspective to it: The eulogy she delivers does not attempt to maintain a ceremonial moment; it is to celebrate the sometimes gritty individualism of the grandfather she loved. It is a eulogy of an artist by an artist rather than a fulfillment of ritual obligation.

SURVEY OF CRITICISM

The criticism of Jong's writings divides into two major categories: a large number of popular reviews of her work and fewer scholarly essays. As a rule,

Jong fared better in the early part of her career: Reviewers typically loved or hated her work, though many were able to praise what was strong while identifying weaknesses at the same time. Whatever the stripe of the review, it typically spoke to the liveliness and controversial nature of her voice and themes.

Jong's first two volumes of poetry, published before *Fear of Flying*, provoked excitement and praise from such reviewers as Chad Walsh and Linda Pastan, both accomplished poets themselves, as well as from scholar Helen Vendler. Reviewers praised her wit, passion, and humor, pointing to the originality of her images in *Fruits and Vegetables* and to her successful, if somewhat predictable, use of formal repetition within a free-verse system. Alicia Ostriker, writing later, but summarizing general critical sentiment about Jong's poetry, suggests that her strength lies in her self-conscious humor and the poems work "less successfully when she attempts to make narcissism look sublime rather than ridiculous" (107).

If Jong's profile was that of the somewhat brainy, sexually uninhibited "Barnard girl," this image was intensified with the publication of *Fear of Flying*. Notable critics and novelists took sides in their evaluation of Jong's first foray into the life of her alter ego, Isadora Wing. Particularly interesting were the positions of male critics, many of whom were also novelists. Those who praised the book, almost to the point of adulation, were Henry Miller, whose *Tropic of Cancer* may be seen as one predecessor of Jong's own erotic narrative, and John Updike, who compared Jong to Chaucer, saying, "the Wife of Bath, were she young and gorgeous, neurotic and Jewish, urban and contemporary, might have written this" (411). On the other side was Paul Theroux, whose scabrous review was quoted at length in Jong's own essay on responses to *Fear of Flying* in *Here Comes*, calling it a "crappy novel, misusing vulgarity to the point where it becomes foolish" (qtd. in *Here Comes* 274). Female reviewers, even when they identified stylistic and thematic excesses, were more taken with the novel because of its representation of women's erotic, intellectual, and emotional lives.

As a result of its polarized reviews, *Fear of Flying* became a critical cause célèbre and a bookseller's dream. While the remainder of Jong's works have continued to sell well, popular reviews have become consistently more negative. Because of Jong's celebrity, many of the reviews suggest, the self-consciousness that was present in the first three books and that was reasonably intriguing has become obsessive and uninteresting. *How to Save Your Own Life*, the second of the Isadora books, suffered from "sophomore slump" and also from the dangers inherent in focusing a book on the travails of a writer who has had a controversial, if commercially successful, book: In general, reviewers felt that Jong did not develop either her characters, especially Isadora Wing herself, or her themes in new ways in this second book. The same is true with the other two Isadora books, *Parachutes & Kisses* and *Any Woman's Blues*.

Much the same charge has been made against her poetry. According to most of the reviews, the mixture of erudition and eroticism for which the first two books of poems were praised turns into self-satisfied cleverness and coyness in later volumes. Even her specialty books, such as *Witches*, a profusely illustrated coffee-table book on women's spiritual connection to "magick" through the ages, are viewed as a kind of easy going feminism. Her one "children's book for adults," *Megan's Book of Divorce*, received a savage review from the *School Library Journal*, which saw no use in it for either children or adults.

Fanny was an exception. Even those critics who were predisposed to dislike anything Jong published had to admit that, whatever its many flaws, *Fanny* was a genuine and generally successful attempt to rethink the picaresque eighteenth-century novel. *Serenissima*, however, was deemed less successful. A number of critics pointed out Jong's preciousness in having William Shakespeare utter his own most-quoted lines as everyday conversation as a consistent flaw in the book's dialogue; they also found the Renaissance not as good a fit for her style or sensibility as was eighteenth-century England.

Jong has received much less scholarly attention than many of her contemporaries, perhaps as a result of the later works, which call into question her credibility as a serious artist. Even her poetry has been neglected. Those critics who have written about her poetry have typically done so in surveys of her career as a whole rather than in studies focused on the poetry or on specific poems. Carol Simpson Stern, one critic who has written exclusively about Jong's poetry, praises her "Pantagruelian word play" (438), suggesting that "Jong has a quality her mentors lack—her exuberant, affectionate, frolicking humor" (439).

The scholarship on Jong, sparse as it is, has focused on two major areas: *Fear of Flying* as a novel of personal and sexual liberation, and *Fanny* as pastiche, picaresque, and novel of development. Mary Anne Ferguson sees in *Fear of Flying* a reworking of the myth of Psyche, emphasizing Jong's treatment of the value of maternal aid, of the "witch-mother" as positive figure. James Mandrell situates *Fanny* in the contemporary "feminine picaresque" tradition, tying Fanny, with her outlaw sexuality, to such lesbian heroines as Rita Mae Brown's Molly in *Rubyfruit Jungle*. Robert Butler, also writing of Jong and the picaresque tradition, considers *Fear of Flying* as a narrative of "open journeying," the liberation of the self from social constraints, a search for rootlessness that Butler sees at the heart of American literature from its earliest days to the present.

The handful of other scholarly essays are, in general, curios, such as Francis Baumli's anti-intellectual, misogynist diatribe, holding Jong responsible somehow for male responses to feminism in general, and Kelsie Harder's odd and somewhat incoherent piece on naming in *Fear of Flying*. Finally, Marie Ann Clabe, in her essay "Fanny Hackabout-Jones: Roman juif?" [Fanny Hackabout-Jones: a Jewish novel?] attempts to argue for that novel as part of a Jewish tradition in fiction, despite the absence of Jewish characters or explicitly Jewish themes. Clabe asserts that certain themes or motifs in the novel mark it as Jewish: wandering and rootlessness, victimization and persecution, pastiche and humor (particularly what Clabe sees as *schlemiel* and *chutzpah* humor), and the Witch as Other.

A systematic treatment of Jewishness in Jong's writings remains to be written. One wonders if Jong would receive more scholarly attention if she had stopped writing poetry after the first two volumes and had written only *Fear of Flying* and *Fanny*, novels that might make claims to "seriousness" in canonical ways, building as they do on traditional, favored forms (*bildungsroman*, and *picaresque*).

BIBLIOGRAPHY

Works by Erica Jong

Poetry

Fruits and Vegetables. New York: Holt, Rinehart, and Winston, 1971.
Half-Lives. New York: Holt, Rinehart, and Winston, 1973.
Loveroot. New York: Holt, Rinehart, and Winston, 1975.
Here Comes and Other Poems. New York: New American Library, 1975.
At the Edge of the Body. New York: Holt, Rinehart, and Winston, 1979.
Ordinary Miracles. New York: New American Library, 1983.
Becoming Light. New York: Harper & Row, 1991.

Fiction

Fear of Flying. New York: Holt, Rinehart, and Winston, 1973.
How to Save Your Own Life. New York: Holt, Rinehart, and Winston, 1977.
Fanny: Being the True History of the Adventures of Fanny Hackabout- Jones. New York: New American Library, 1980.
Parachutes & Kisses. New York: New American Library, 1984.
Serenissima: A Novel of Venice. Boston: Houghton Mifflin, 1987.
Any Woman's Blues. New York: Harper & Row, 1990.

Other

Witches. New York: Harry A. Abrams, 1981.
Megan's Books of Divorce: A Kid's Book for Adults. New York: New American Library, 1984.
"Interview." *Contemporary Authors.* With Jean W. Ross. Eds. Harry May and James G. Lesniak. New Revision Series. Vol. 26. Detroit: Gale, 1989.
The Devil at Large: Erica Jong on Henry Miller. New York: Turtle Bay Books, 1993.

Works about Erica Jong

Baumli, Francis. "Erica Jong Revisited (Or) No Wonder We Men Had Trouble Understanding Feminism." *University of Dayton Review* 17.3 (1985–86): 91–95.
Butler, Robert J. "The Woman Writer as American Picaro: Open Journeying in Erica Jong's *Fear of Flying.*" *The Centennial Review* 31 (1987): 308–29.

Clabe, Marie Anne. *"Fanny Hackabout-Jones*: Roman juif?'' *Caliban* 25 (1988): 77–85.

"Erica Jong.'' *Current Biography.* New York: Wilson, 1975.

"Erica Jong.'' *The Feminist Companion to Literature in English.* Eds. Virginia Blair, Patricia Clements, and Isobel Grundy. New Haven: Yale University Press, 1990.

Ferguson, Mary Anne. "The Female Novel of Development and the Myth of Psyche.'' *The Denver Quarterly* 17.4 (1983): 58–74.

Gordon, Lois. "Erica Jong.'' *Contemporary Novelists*, 4th ed. Ed. D. L. Kirkpatrick. New York: St. Martin's, 1986.

Harder, Kelsie B. "The Masculine Imperative: Naming by Gael Greene and Erica Jong.'' *Literary Onomastics Studies* 11 (1984): 147–63.

Mandrell, James. "Questions of Genre and Gender: Contemporary American Versions of the Feminine Picaresque.'' *Novel: A Forum on Fiction* 20 (1987): 149–70.

Ostriker, Alicia Suskin. *Stealing the Language: The Emergence of Women's Poetry in America.* Boston: Beacon, 1986.

Shepherd, Kenneth R. "Erica Jong.'' *Contemporary Authors.* Eds. Harry May and James G. Lesniak. New Revision Series. Vol. 26. Detroit: Gale, 1989.

Stern, Carol Simpson. "Erica Jong.'' *Contemporary Poets*, 4th ed. Eds. James Vinson and D. L. Kirkpatrick. New York: St. Martin's, 1986.

Toth, Emily. "Erica Jong.'' *Twentieth-Century American-Jewish Fiction Writers.* Ed. Daniel Walden. Volume 28 of *Dictionary of Literary Biography*, 28 volumes. Detroit: Gale, 1984.

Updike, John. "Jong Love.'' *Picked-Up Pieces.* New York: Knopf, 1975. 411–15.

JOHANNA KAPLAN (1942–   )

Evelyn M. Avery

BIOGRAPHY

Author of *Other People's Lives* (1975), an acclaimed collection of short stories, and *O My America!* (1980), an award-winning novel, Johanna Kaplan explores the lives of urban Jews, the impact of the Old World on the New World, the distance between generations and the tensions that separate men and women.

Born and raised in New York City, Kaplan is very familiar with the city that frequently serves as a setting in her fiction. A graduate of Manhattan's High School of Music and Art, Kaplan attended the University of Wisconsin for two years, and when her mother became ill, she returned to New York. In 1964, she received a B.A. from New York University and two years later earned a Master's degree in Special Education from Teacher's College, Columbia University. With her training, Kaplan became a teacher of emotionally disturbed children in Mount Sinai Hospital's Psychiatry Department, a position she has held since 1968. At the same time, she has continued to write, review books for the *New York Times* and *Commentary*, and give presentations at colleges and at the 92nd Street Y in New York City. A recipient of grants from New York State and the National Endowment for the Arts, Kaplan has taught at the noted Bread Loaf Writer's Conference in Vermont.

To some extent, Kaplan's fiction reflects her parents' urban Jewish background as well as her own. Raised on the Lower East Side, her father, Max Kaplan, devoted himself to teaching remedial students in Harlem. Her mother, Ruth Duker Kaplan, a teenage immigrant from Poland, was active in Labor Zionism and involved her daughter in *Habonim*, a Jewish youth movement that emphasized fellowship and good works, values reflected in Kaplan's fiction.

MAJOR THEMES

Kaplan's first work, *Other People's Lives*, includes a novella and five short stories whose eccentric characters, urban settings, colorful conversations, and unpredictable turn of events characterize the author's distinctive viewpoint and style. She is not ideological or polemical, focusing primarily on her characters' behavior and their treatment of each other. A realist, Kaplan portrays her characters as flawed but deserving of sympathy.

In "Sickness," for example, measles-ridden Miriam caustically reflects on her mother's fears, the gossipy neighbors, dour Dr. Lichtblau, and Jewish suffering. Lonely and confined to bed, Miriam imagines pogroms in Russia and problems in Palestine, but her gloom is somewhat dispelled when she views the setting sun, "a thick orange globe, [which] floats in the sky like a bumpy Jaffa orange, a streaky golden desert, the land of Israel itself" (131). The overall effect combines despair and hope, the haunted European past, contemporary Israeli struggles, and the possibility of a fruitful Jewish future.

In "Baby-Sitting," a delightful parody of the self-important "artist," Ted Marshak is all posture; he is a blueprint for the pretentious Ezra Slavin whom Kaplan skewers in her novel *O My America!*. Based on an actual experience, Kaplan satirizes Ted and his wife Sunny, vain bohemian types who neglect their children, "Sasha" and "Pietro." Disgusted by the naked children and slovenly home, the narrator realizes that talent and decency do not always exist in the same person.

In "Other People's Lives," Kaplan contrasts self-centered, insensitive characters with the rare, generous individual. Abandoned by her financially strapped, divorced parents, emotionally disturbed Louise Well cannot remain in a private asylum and is placed in Maria Tobey's home. As a middle-aged immigrant ballerina whose dancer husband is dying of Hodgkin's disease, Maria must provide for herself and her seven-year-old son, Matthew. The boarding arrangement is mutually beneficial, both financially and emotionally. Maria, a survivor, juggles household details, hospital visits, her son's needs, and the new lodger's requirements.

In contrast to her petty neighbors in the Upper West Side apartment house, Maria retains her simplicity and honesty, her concern for other people's lives. Refusing to live extravagantly and exploit her connections, she is an island of sanity in a sea of irresponsible New Yorkers. From Maria, the depressed Louise learns that her future could "change, be different" (106). Despite her trials, Maria is a model of strength to her friends, a source of faith based on her view that "history . . . did not [necessarily] determine the future, sealing it up" (106). At the end, looking into the mirror, Louise realizes it could only tell her the past, not the future, which she could shape herself.

The balance between painful circumstances and promising prospects, between despairing and hopeful characters so evident in Kaplan's short stories, characterizes *O My America!* (1980), her satire on Jewish "gurus" who shed their ethnic accents and mannerisms and become American cult figures. Through extended flashbacks, the novel traces Ezra Slavin's meteoric career as the prophetic voice of America's rebellious intellectuals and flower children. Preaching honesty and decency, he flourishes on duplicity and adulation. While his public image seems principled and compassionate, his private behavior is ambitious and cruel. In his lifetime, Ez tyrannizes three wives and several children, turning his teenage daughter Frenchy into a mindless street person, desperate for her father's attention. Similarly, his twenty-four-year-old son Nicky courts danger, riding the rapids and roaming India in a futile attempt to impress his father. Only Slavin's oldest child, Merry, is sensitive and mature enough to care for herself and sustain the family. Even Ezra turns to her when he is especially vulnerable.

While the other children embrace the hedonistic 1960s, Merry, a serious young woman, is drawn to traditional values imparted by her paternal grandmother and an immigrant cousin, Joe Sender, a repository of family memories. It is Joe who acquaints Merry with her dead mother, Pearl Milgrim, an attractive Polish Zionist, whom Ezra rejects as too parochial, too Jewish, and ultimately too threatening to his position as the American intellectual.

Ultimately, *O My America!* is an epic journey through the tumultuous 1960s, but it is also a portrait of a Jewish guru who sought to save society and ended by leading his followers astray. At its conclusion, the novel returns to its beginning, with Ezra having suffered a fatal coronary, an attack consistent with his high-pressure, volatile life. The funeral reflects the two faces of Ezra Slavin. While the groupies, phony philosophers, and ex-wives step forth to sing his virtues, his perceptive children, Merry Slavin and Jonathan Spivak, reject the "messiah" but demonstrate their love for Ezra. After all the saccharine tributes, the undeserved praise, Jonathan dashes to the stage and quickly recites the *Kaddish*, the mourner's prayer, in Hebrew. As onlookers express shock and embarrassment at the "barbaric" custom, Jonathan fulfills his duty as a Jewish son and acknowledges the roots of his assimilated father. Joined briefly by Ira Slavin, a distant cousin, Merry recalls her father as a Gatsby type who had bet "all his money on [his] idea of America. . . . and nearly gambled it away" (286).

In *O My America!* Kaplan tackles the problems of assimilation, of 1960s values, and of a self-styled messiah who cannot save himself. Though acknowledging the novel's Jewishness, she believes that "art transcends ethnicity" (personal interview) 16 July 1992, and *O My America!* speaks to all readers. In her recently completed novel, tentatively titled "Music of the Cities," Kaplan departs from Jewish themes. Although two of the characters, Joel Wisotsky and his first wife, Rona Auslander, are Jewish, the novel includes Gentiles such as Holly Treadwell, Joel's second wife. A novel of manners, it depicts New York City in the 1980s, where strangers live together and the concept of family assumes new meaning. The embryo for "Music of the Cities" first appeared as a short story in *Commentary* (May 1986).

SURVEY OF CRITICISM

Calling Kaplan "one of our most talented new Jewish writers," Sam Girgus, in *The New Covenant: Jewish Writers and the American Idea*, compares *O My*

America! to Norman Mailer's *The Armies of the Night*, since the protagonists are interpreters of America, "comparable to such intellectuals as Paul Goodman and Alfred Kazin" (7). In "O My *Mishpocha*!" Evelyn Avery describes Kaplan as "vividly affirm[ing] the importance of traditional values, of an immigrant past for the transient superficial present" (52).

Generally, reviews of Kaplan's fiction have been quite positive. In the *New Leader* Pearl Bell credits *Other People's Lives* with a "sharp but affectionate eye for ultra-liberal hypocrites and upwardly mobile families" (18). Similarly, Dorothy Rabinowitz praises Kaplan's "impeccable ear [and] memorable portraits" (36). In her review of *O My America!*, Alice Adams compares the novel to E. L. Doctorow's *The Book of Daniel*, which is more ambitious but similar in "social, political . . . , and historic [insights]" (14). Both her stories and a "remarkable first novel" (Bell, 73) have earned Kaplan recognition. In addition to receiving good reviews, *Other People's Lives* won the Jewish Book Award for fiction in 1976. Five years later, *O My America!* won the Edward Lewis Wallant Award, the Kenneth B. Smilen/Present Tense Literary Award, and the Jewish Book Award for fiction.

BIBLIOGRAPHY

Works by Johanna Kaplan

Fiction

Other People's Lives. New York: Alfred A. Knopf, 1975.
O My America! New York: Harper & Row, 1980.
"Music of the Cities," recently completed.

Works about Johanna Kaplan

Adams, Alice. Rev. of *O My America!*. *New York Times Book Review*, 13 January 1980.
Avery, Evelyn. "O My *Mishpocha!* Some Jewish Women Writers from Antin to Kaplan View the Family." *Studies in Jewish Literature* 5 (1986) 52–53.
Bell, Pearl. Rev. of *Other People's Lives*, *New Leader* 9 June 1975: 18.
Girgus, Sam. *The New Covenant: Jewish Writers and the American Idea.* Chapel Hill: University of North Carolina Press, 1984. 6–7.
Personal interview. 16 July 1992.
Rabinowitz, Dorothy. Rev. of *Other People's Lives*. *Saturday Review* 17 May 1975: 35–36.
Shaw, Peter. "Johanna Kaplan." *Twentieth Century American-Jewish Fiction Writers*. Ed. Daniel Walden. Detroit: Gale, 1984. Vol. 28 of *Dictionary of Literary Biography*. 28 vols.

ILONA KARMEL (1925–   )

Sara R. Horowitz

BIOGRAPHY

Ilona Karmel was born in Cracow in 1925 to Hirsch and Mita (née Rosenbaum) Karmel. While her grandparents were ultra-Orthodox Gerer Hasidim, Karmel describes her father as "transitional," bridging the modern and the religious worlds.[1] She recalls that the family took pride in Poland and that her mother "had me down as a future prime minister" (qtd. in Nichols). Her aunts and uncles—professionals and Bundists—were even more "liberated" Jews; some no longer kept kosher nor observed the Sabbath. Yet, Karmel recalls, her extended family remained close, tolerating with little internal tension this variance in traditional religious practice. People "accommodated one another." The German invasion of Poland and the subsequent murder of that country's Jewish population overturned young Ilona's life, destroying the community she had known.

She cherishes particularly vivid images from her childhood—for example, the beggar seated at the head of the *Seder* table on Passover. She tells of a Hasidic uncle whose store was used as a front to issue false papers and other illegal but life-saving documents during the war. He turned down opportunities to flee and, instead, accompanied his family into the ghetto. There, one Friday night, on the eve of an announced transport (a Nazi euphemism for deportation to a concentration camp), his mother worried that she would sin on the day of her death. To comfort her, he set a white table cloth, challah, sang *zemirot*, telling her it was sinful not to celebrate the Sabbath. Like most of Karmel's relatives, her uncle and his mother perished in the Nazi genocide. Such memories of the Jewish past, with their marked contrast to the more brutal memories of Nazi actions, serve as a touchstone to "real dignity and morality and spirituality."

After the Nazi invasion of Poland, the Jews of Cracow were forced into a crowded ghetto, subjected to hard labor, meager food rations, random shootings, and the threat of transport. In 1942, Ilona, her sister, and her mother were interned in Plaszow, the first of three labor camps in which they would live. A year later, they were taken to Starzysko Kamienna, a camp whose conditions were far worse. The name means "complaint of stone—a prophetic name," Karmel explains. Brutal conditions quickly killed off the older and weaker women; some women worked with picric acid—a chemical used in the production of explosives—whose toxic effects turned their hair and skin yellow and eventually killed them. In 1944, the three Karmel women were taken to the labor camp near Leipzig. Karmel remembers this as "paradise after Starzysko"—a "good camp" where there was "almost enough to eat." To preserve their sanity in the camps, Ilona and Henia wrote poetry on the back of pilfered work sheets. A collection of these Polish poems were published in New York as *Spiew za Drutami* [Song Behind the Wire] (1947); several were later translated into Yiddish.

Karmel credits her mother's alertness, intelligence, and devotion to her daughters with keeping Ilona and Henia alive and together. "My mother always knew what to do." When Ilona was hospitalized with typhus in 1942, her mother—knowing that Jewish patients were often executed—stole her out of the hospital. Another time, Ilona's mother hid her daughters under a mattress during a camp selection (a Nazi euphemism for choosing murder victims), enabling them to escape death. Karmel makes use of this incident in *An Estate of Memory*. Both Ilona and Henia survived the war.

In the final days of the infamous death marches at the end of the war, a vehicle crushed both of Ilona's legs. She was taken to a German hospital, where "the kindness of the Germans" who tended her left her "confused." The same Germans capable of creating the death camps now treated her with compassion. This experience shaped the way she views human behavior. In an early interview in the United States, a reporter expressed surprise at Karmel's "remarkably unbitter" attitude toward the Germans. Karmel reflected, "People are not evil. They are just weak. And I saw Poles as well as French and Russians who collaborated with the enemy. You can't hate every one if you are to go on living" (qtd. in Hutchens).

After the war, Karmel tried to make sense of the catastrophe that destroyed the Jews of Europe and the enigma of good and evil, reflections that form the basis for her writing. Like many survivors, Karmel eschews the term "Holocaust," which "mythologizes and institutionalizes" the brutal events of World War II. "Holocaust" contains the idea of sacrifice, implying that the Jews chose their fate. She and her friends refer simply to "the war."

Karmel spent two years in a Swedish hospital recuperating from her injuries. There, she learned Swedish, studied English by correspondence with Cambridge University, and wrote her first story in English, about a labor camp. Her first novel, *Stephania* (1953), was based on "a girl I knew in the hospital" (Nichols). In 1948, Karmel immigrated to the United States, joining Henia and her husband. She enrolled at Hunter College, where she wrote "Fru Holm," which won the *Mademoiselle* magazine college fiction contest in 1950. Karmel transferred to Radcliffe College to study creative writing with Archibald MacLeish, under whose tutelage she produced *Stephania*. She attributes her ability to write in English to MacLeish's "unlimited faith in me." In 1952, she graduated from Radcliffe a Phi Beta Kappa, four short years after her arrival in this country. The next year saw the publication of her first novel, written in a language only recently acquired. Her sister, Henia Karmel-Wolfe, also published two novels. Ten years of intensive and exhausting work went into the writing of *An Estate of Memory* (1969, reissued by Feminist Press in 1986), one of the few fictional narratives set entirely within a concentration camp.

At present, Karmel is a senior lecturer at the Massachusetts Institute of Technology, where she teaches creative writing. She has developed lasting friendships with many of her students. She is married to Francis Zucker, a physicist who came to the United States from Germany with his parents in 1938. The couple lives in Belmont, Massachusetts.

In addition to MacLeish, Karmel has learned from many writers, including Shakespeare and Tolstoy (Hutchens). She feels a strong affinity with Samuel Beckett—"I trust every line"—whose life and work were profoundly influenced by his role in the Maquis during World War II. Karmel dislikes literary realism which falsifies the self: Even when characters think and feel, we view them externally, "with thoughts piped in." Karmel is interested in how postmodern thinkers reconfigure the idea of the self, the inexpressible and the unknowable. Karmel also esteems the writing of the Jewish German literary critic Walter Benjamin, who perished during the war. Through Benjamin she discovered the ground-breaking work of his friend Gershom Scholem. Both writers speak to her concerns about theology and spirituality. Although early in her life Karmel questioned her family's way of conceptualizing God, she acknowledges, "We're not finished, Her and me."

According to Karmel, the destruction of the Jews of Europe has deeply depleted Jewish spiritual life. "We are lean, and we shouldn't pretend we are fat," she cautions. "We should not mistake our ethnic customs for our intuition for the divine" and "not think customs are the same as the faith of the past." Karmel remembers the community of her childhood as one saturated with spiritual meaning, but "the faith I witnessed" survives only in diminished form. In Karmel's view, the Nazi genocide does not pose a problem for Jewish theology, which has always absorbed the existence of unjust suffering. Rather, Christian theology must grapple with its long history of anti-Semitism and anti-Judaism in light of the destruction of European Jewry. Although she is not a traditionally observant Jew, Karmel feels deeply connected to Jewish texts, such as Midrash. For Karmel, the "god of prayer"—the god of our imagination—represents what we want, interposing a false barrier to an encounter with the real, transcendent God.

In her writing and thinking, Karmel values honesty. "If we lie to ourselves we lose those rare moments of grace and purity we live for."

MAJOR THEMES

An ever-narrowing world of physical confinement—and the freedoms and limitations possible within such settings—characterizes all of Ilona Karmel's fiction. Whether in a hospital for the handicapped, an old-age home, or a concentration camp, Karmel's characters fight for physical and psychological survival. Within these contexts, Karmel considers the fluidity of the human subject, the possibility of moral choices, the complexity of human relations, the limitations of language. Karmel writes with an unsentimental lucidity that borders on harshness as the characters in her works sometimes flee from and sometimes embrace the honest clarity necessary for survival *in extremis.*

In "Fru Holm" (1950), an early short story, Karmel explores the fragility of human connections and the price of isolation. Set in a Stockholm "convalescent home"—a euphemism for old-age home—the story charts the rapid physical and emotional decline of the robust Fru [Mrs.] Holm, placed in the home against her will by a daughter who was bothered by the inconvenience of an aging mother. As the energetic Fru Holm deteriorates in the presence of "spinsters, old and lonely, and widows, equally old and lonely" (293), she finds less and less to say in response to her daughter's dutiful phone calls. The distance of her daily walks shortens until she rarely leaves her room. Only the weekly visits of her little grandchildren—symbolizing the life force and human connectedness—restore her. The daughter lies to her mother and to herself, pretending that the home offers Fru Holm companionship, leisure, and amusement. Finally, the daughter blames her children. "Grandma needs rest. . . . You kids make so much noise" (294). A bond develops between Fru Holm and one of the aides in the home, who sees in Fru Holm's loneliness the person she herself might become: aging, abandoned, fearful of death but still vital. Annalisa serves as witness to the relationship between mother and daughter. After Fru Holm dies of a sudden stroke—really of a broken heart—Annalisa pronounces judgment on the daughter.

In this story, Karmel introduces themes she will develop in later writing: conflicting needs and competition for limited resources that pit family or friends against one another, situations that strip a person of the sense of self and meaning. Karmel also explores the power shift that occurs when parent and child reverse roles, a recurrent aspect of Holocaust writing.

Like "Fru Holm," *Stephania* (1953) takes place in enforced confinement with arbitrarily selected companions. Room Five, Ward Two, in a Swedish hospital for the severely handicapped comprises the claustrophobic setting of three women: Thura Svenson, a shy teenager making little progress in overcoming the effects of polio; Maria Nilsson, a petty, self-pitying woman in her late thirties whose multiple leg fractures resist healing; and Stephania Ackermann, an aloof, articulate survivor of the Nazi genocide determined to straighten her deformed spine. The novel explores the precarious interactions among these three unsuited companions, the relationship of each to her own memory, and the struggle of each with her own infirmity.

In *Stephania*, Karmel probes the way people struggle to define themselves and to make moral choices. The predicaments of the three hospital roommates throw into sharp relief the ways in which one's body imposes limitations on, but does not wholly define, oneself. Stephania's hunchback—exacerbated by the harsh wartime conditions and by Nazi brutality—makes her a stranger to herself. "Here something happens to your body, and you just sit back and watch and can't do a thing about it. It's as if your body were not yours at all, as if someone else was telling it what to do" (48). She pits her will against her body, although the series of physicians she consults hold out little hope. Stephania berates her companions for giving in to their disabilities, blaming Fröken [Miss] Nilsson's self-indulgence for the obesity that imperils the fragile bones of her injured leg. When Thura struggles vainly to move her paralyzed fingers, Stephania tells her "it is your fault Thura. Whose if not yours? . . . You've talked yourself into believing that you can't do it" (243).

The tension between self-determination and destiny, as acted out on one's physical being, serves as analogy to the tension between responsibility and limits in making moral choices. Truthfulness constitutes the necessary precondition for all meaningful actions. Any acceptance we come to on the basis of lies or self-delusion will not fortify us. Stephania scorns Fröken Nilsson, who comforts herself with a fabricated past. Stephania's harsh but honest words keep her companions from self-indulgence, helping them overcome their impediments. Thura moves her fingers, Fröken Nilsson loses weight, and both are eventually released from the hospital.

Stephania harbors a memory whose moral implications weigh on her far more heavily than do self-pity and overindulgence. She reproaches herself for the death of her parents, both murdered by the Nazi genocidal machinery. With what has come to be termed "survivor guilt," she blames herself for abandoning her father, grown increasingly helpless as conditions worsened. Stephania confesses her guilty memory in the hope that her companions will condemn her. Instead, made wise by their own struggles against intractable circumstances, they point out the limitations to moral responsibility, not unlike those of physical self-determination. Stephania could no more save her father than she could undo her hunchback or Thura's paralysis.

If, at best, one can win only a provisional victory over suffering, what meaning does life have? Rather than asserting a grand plan that justifies human existence, the novel indicates that human connection of itself is meaningful. Out of despair, Stephania begins helping other patients and finds that this soothes her. She tells Thura that "if we could, can mean so much to each other, we two and then Fröken Nilsson too, then that shows something; it must. It means that it was not just senseless, that year in here, not just doing nothing, but there was something. . . " (352).

The window by Stephania's bedside reminds her that clinical routine, medical crises, and hospital personalities increasingly define the parameters of life for the hospitalized women. The seemingly unbridgeable gulf between the infirm and the healthy serves as a metaphor for the difficulties survivors face when they attempt to communicate their experiences to those not affected by the Nazi genocide. When Stephania tells her Swedish roommates that her father was shot because he was a Jew, they cannot comprehend it.

In *An Estate of Memory*, Karmel takes up the challenge of writing about the concentration camps. One of the few novels set entirely (except for a brief epilogue) within the boundaries of a camp, *Estate* depicts the way Jewish women lived and died under Nazi atrocity. Karmel examines the social structures that developed among women—hierarchies based upon physical and emotional stamina, access to needed resources, and assigned work. The women form "makeshift camp families—women, young girls, whom loneliness unaccustomed and sudden had brought together" (7). Within these surrogate families, they help one another endure.

Estate focuses on the members of one such "family": Tola Ohrenstein, sole survivor of a wealthy family, aloof, smart, and resourceful; Barbara Grünbaum, a large, generous, "saintly," woman who had once been mistress of the estate of the book's title; Aurelia Katz, an obsequious, whiny, dependent woman, "a professional victim" who "knew how to exploit her helplessness to the hilt" (138); and Alinka, a quiet teenager, loyal to Aurelia. Katz and Alinka initially present themselves as mother and daughter. Later it becomes clear that they met "in the grave"—literally, they survived a mass murder and burial. Karmel's narrative follows the interaction of four women whom circumstances place together in a Nazi slave labor camp. The concentration camp is a crucible in which each woman is pared down to her essence; every act and every choice is intensified *in extremis*. Through their different responses, Karmel explores the self, memory, morality, and survival.

"The self," Karmel once remarked, "is more fluid than Western thought has imagined." The style and structure of *An Estate of Memory* build on shifting perspectives, alternations of internal and external views of the characters, closeness to and distance from the human subject. These multiple perspectives make apparent the inner shifts and discontinuities that comprise the self, emphasized by the extreme situation. Designed to dehumanize its victims before killing them, the Nazi camp stripped its victims of many of the conventional earmarks of identity.

Displaced from community and family, stripped of social status and possessions, forced to live in filth, the women in Karmel's novel watch themselves do, say, and eat things they once thought unimaginable. At times this erosion of self feels more dangerous than the physical hardships. Barbara relinquishes her disguise as a Polish non-Jew and the relative privilege it confers because she "hungered for the sound of her name, longed to hear it spoken and to speak of herself. . . " (84). Barbara and Tola connect initially because Tola recognizes her as the mistress of the mansion where her family briefly hid. This connection reminds each of who she had been.

As each woman holds fast to the self she once was, she also recognizes the instability of that self. At particular moments, characters see themselves as they have become, either by catching sight of their reflection in a glass or by learning how others perceive them. They sense an inner discontinuity. In moments of lucidity—rare for some, more frequent for others—the women realize they contain contradictions: kindness and cruelty, fear and courage, selfishness and altruism. When Barbara struggles with the realization she has wronged Tola, she reflects, "someone. . . . had been wrong. . . . 'Someone,' not 'I'. . . . Because to say 'I' would have been a travesty of truth; because it was not she who had once done wrong to Tola, only an intruder, a brazen creature with whom Barbara could feel no kinship, no bond" (350). Karmel elsewhere recollects how some women committed "spiritual suicide" when extreme circumstances forced them to go against their natural compassion. Such conditions make one appear "monstrous from the outside and destroy the self."

Memory not only connects the women to their life before the war, it offers a promise of return and restitution. But Nazi atrocity creates a rupture with the past. For Tola, the world outside of the camp grows unreal. Her parents "had simply never existed; she had always been alone—this camp, this bunk her only home, the only greeting of her mornings the hoarse 'All up!' " (40). Barbara's memories of her husband, her manor, her servants, are most vivid, perhaps because she alone did not witness the death of those closest to her. The four women hitch their hopes for survival to Barbara's memories, dreaming themselves back and ahead into a group reunion with her husband at her home. This estate of memory fortifies the women. As the present blocks out remembrances of the past, Barbara's memory of her husband fades; she imagines only her surrogate family on the estate.

Linked to the sense of self and to memories of normal life is the women's concern about morality. The extreme situation intensifies the importance of all actions; each minute decision has life-and-death consequences and tremendous ethical implications. Forced to choose among hideous actions to ensure survival, Tola contemplates her own moral deterioration. "Two kinds of evil, she felt, were at work here. The first came from outside: once localized, once enclosed within huge helmeted figures, it grew ubiquitous here, lurking in hunger, in typhus and the bitter dust. The other evil was new. It came from within" (121). Fighting to retain moral agency, the women forge a code of behavior: act on behalf of the group's survival. To struggle for "us" rather than solely for oneself constitutes altruism rather than selfishness. Barbara gives up the safety of her Polish disguise so that "she would not spend this war like a parasite, helping no one, thinking of nothing but saving her own skin" (84); Tola does things that the other women find distasteful or frightening—peddling extra clothes or soup, for example—and shares the life-preserving proceeds, so that she may be "called not 'enterprising,' not 'clever,' but simply 'good' " (253).

This simple but difficult code unravels in the complexities of camp life. The novel's opening establishes the conflict between self and others, by depicting the way that the Nazis deliberately pit individual against group welfare. Any escape from the labor camp would result in random retaliation. On the one hand, to protect the others, one should not escape; on the other hand, as Tola reflects, "whoever had the chance to save himself also had the right" (6). In any case, whatever one chooses, one plays into genocidal practices. As the novel progresses, Tola begins to question the group ethic. "What is it? Anything done for someone else is a sacrifice, a noble deed; but try to do the same thing for yourself and the sacrifice becomes a disgrace. Why? I too am someone; I've no contract for survival, I too am afraid" (342).

The novel poses Tola's "selfishness" against Barbara's altruism. While Tola serves as *Anweiserin* (work supervisor) in a munitions factory, a position in which she must perform morally compromised acts, Barbara works in the infirmary barracks. But even Barbara's "goodness" unravels; the romantic "idea of a sacrifice" which guides her behavior cannot withstand the extraordinary pressures of atrocity. She frenetically beats the sick women in her care, and she comes to recognize that her own distaste for the "dirty" chores that Tola performs for her played a role in Tola's subsequent choices.

Although the characters judge themselves harshly—a sign that they have not abandoned moral consciousness—the reader is prevented from doing so by the conditions depicted in the novel. The unsentimentalized tone of the novel makes clear that what counts most is truthfulness, the ability of the characters and the narrative as a whole to look unflinchingly at what is.

The most intense focus of group purpose centers on the women's decision to help Aurelia Katz through her secret pregnancy. At great personal risk, the other three provide for her from their own inadequate ration, cover for her at work sites, deliver her baby in secret, and arrange to smuggle it from the camp to the safety of Barbara's estate. The survival of Aurelia Katz's baby girl symbolizes the triumph of the life force over the machinery of death. "So the child, carried like a parcel out of the camp, kept growing, until it was big enough to take upon itself the burden of their longing for a proof, for the sign that out 'in the Freedom' they still mattered" (277).

At the same time, this symbolic victory is undercut by a counter narrative, the story of another baby born in the camp and left to starve upon doctor's orders: "The child should be laid in cotton wool . . . the child should not be fed anything, not even water" (255). Women feed that infant sugar water, which only prolongs its agony—a kindness which becomes a cruelty. This brutal story, part of the oral history transmitted among the women at the camp, serves as a touchstone to Nazi cruelty.

The chasm between normal life and atrocity is exemplified by the differences in what pregnancy connotes in the camps and in memory. Rather than an occasion for joy, pregnancy threatens the mother's life. Barbara remembers "her longing for a child" (166) before the war. But Aurelia's baby is "a tormentor who sucked her strength, snatched every crumb away'' (242). Like other Jews, the fetus exists under a death sentence to which the women have become numbed. ''Back at home a woman had gone mad because her child had perished in a fire. . . . And here each had lost her all in something a thousandfold worse than a fire, yet they just chatted and primped themselves'' (146).

Karmel's writing reverses the conventional war narrative wherein heroic men protect endangered women. Men are portrayed most frequently as weak and passive, becoming wholly reliant upon women for survival as conditions worsen. In moments of crisis—and Karmel's narratives depict an enchainment of such moments—men regress to a childlike dependence which threatens everyone's survival. In ''Fru Holm,'' the daughter cannot invite her mother to live with her because her husband ''is opposed to it'' (302). Stephania remembers her father helpless with fear in face of an impending roundup. Pathetically seeking the reassurances of a vanished domesticity, he asks his wife, ''Myrele, what should I put on?'' (*Stephania* 270), just as Aurelia Katz's husband asks, on the eve of his death, ''Aurelia, should I shave tomorrow?'' (*Estate* 160).

Although loved by their wives and daughters, men weigh upon them. Stephania's brother-in-law cannot hold down a job. His wife supports them and also cares for their infant, as her husband lolls about their apartment demoralized. In *Estate*, Barbara's husband fails his professional examinations, and his infertility leaves the couple childless. A few men come through in important ways for the women in Karmel's narratives. But the harsh circumstances of life severely circumscribe what these men can accomplish.

With survival comes the obligation to remember. The ''estate of memory'' transmutes into the remembrances which will constitute testimony. Already in the camps the narrator recognizes that the transmission of testimony will be difficult. ''Everything was a legend among them, the eyewitnesses gone, the stories they had left behind blurred by much repeating'' (234). In the epilogue, Barbara's servant reluctantly gathers these stories, absorbs them, and mourns.

SURVEY OF CRITICISM

With the publication of her earliest works in English, Ilona Karmel was recognized as a gifted writer of keen intellect and psychological insight. Particularly noteworthy to most early reviewers was her ''remarkable'' ability to navigate complex and emotionally demanding material in a language only recently learned. Virgilia Peterson noted, ''Not only has she mastered the English cadence; she has mastered the meaning of experience itself'' (1).

In an early review, Peterson praised Karmel's first novel, *Stephania*, for its power and lack of sentimentality, not ''the usual raw, still-bleeding account written before scar tissue has begun to cover the suffering'' (1). In a later retrospective essay on Karmel's work, Ruth Angress places *Stephania* ''in the tradition of the great modern prison books.'' For although the novel takes place in a hospital, with a medical staff genuinely committed to helping the patients heal, the physical encumbrances the women endure and the "enforced community" of the ward room imprison them. The novel thus shares the concern of all prison novels, which are "always about freedom, which they define by its absence."

An Estate of Memory is considered Karmel's masterpiece, a powerful psychological portrayal of life in a concentration camp. At the time of its publication, reviewers compared it to Solzhenitsyn in subject and Hemingway in style. Elizabeth Janeway calls it "a very good book," praising its double achievement. Karmel's novel makes accessible to readers an experience radically different from their own, presenting "life in the prison camps . . . as plausible, possible human experience" (1). At the same time, the novel universalizes an aspect of that experience, so that readers may learn from it something relevant to their own lives. "Salvation is an inner process that keeps alive the ability to find, even in camp, some of the human connection, some quality of spirit, some willingness to participate in life" (38).

In her critical analysis, Sidra Ezrahi places *An Estate of Memory* in the context of what she terms "survivor-novels." Comprised mostly of writing by women, this subgenre of Holocaust literature links the narrative of survival with biology (often childbirth). Survivor novels focus on the ways in which survivors resisted utter victimization by holding on to the ability to make moral choices. Ezrahi calls *Estate* "a monumental story of the struggle for survival" (70). The concerted effort to save Aurelia's baby "is perhaps the most moving account of the temptation, the devotions, the sacrifices, and the breakdowns in the fragile network of group survival in concentration camp literature" (70). The baby's survival "affirms both the normal life cycle and faith in the future" (87).

Ezrahi discusses Karmel's exploration of good and evil within the concentration camp setting. Karmel places her characters in "the borderline situation which would test the limits of their humanity" (79). Some, like Tola, falter morally, as "a prostitution of self for the sake of the group crosses the line of altruism into Darwinian survivalism" (77). Ezrahi sees Tola as "just one of those thousands who, when the time came, and the need, did not have the courage to give their all"; Barbara, on the other hand, represents "the archetype of the 'human' survivor" made resilient by her powerful prewar memories. Ezrahi stresses the possibility Karmel presents for inner resistance to Nazi atrocity. "The key to human survival, as it is represented here, lies in maintaining one's identity and humanity . . . even when there are no chances of changing or in any way altering the dire conditions in which one is condemned to live" (86). In Karmel's novel, "the imagination provides a retreat from and a defiance of reality" (217).

Ruth Angress praises Karmel's complex treatment of Nazi atrocity as "the best antidote against . . . simplification" (445). She sees the book as "a psychological novel . . . [which] asks us to follow shifts of perception and misperception in circumstances we ourselves have not fully grasped" (447). According to Angress, Karmel has written a feminist novel which looks closely at women's unique ways of surviving physically, psychologically, and morally. In that light, *Estate* is "largely about friendship, about women bonding." Like Ezrahi, Angress focuses on the protagonists' inner resistance to their brutal circumstances. As women do elsewhere, the prisoners "cling to relationships that stand out more sharply in a life where selfishness would seem to be identical with self-preservation" (446). The key to survival lies in the "basic assumption . . . that human beings live by bonding and not in isolation." But in looking after the welfare of others, the women in Karmel's novel are not merely altruistic; rather, the women act "out of the psychological need not to be alone and the willingness to make great physical sacrifices for the sake of warding off isolation." In helping one another, each woman helps herself, solidifying her "moral self-definition" (447).

Karmel's writing has not garnered "the readership it deserves" (446), conjectures Angress, because of "the complex of prejudices and preconceptions" (445) that have long existed against Holocaust fiction—that it is too gory, too sentimental, too literary, too commercialized. In addition, until recently, women's Holocaust texts have received little critical attention, compared to works by men (Horowitz, "Memory and Testimony"). Marlene Heinemann mentions *Estate* in connection with "the thematic importance of childbirth" in women's memoirs (26), while Sara Horowitz touches on the theme of muteness in connection to Tola's refusal to speak ("Linguistic Displacement" 76).

Not surprisingly, critics focus on the relationship between Karmel's life and writing. Peterson asserts that *Stephania* is "undoubtedly in part autobiographical," since, like the protagonist, Karmel herself spent two years in a Swedish hospital recovering from war injuries. Janeway, too, explains that the novel was "based on her hospital ordeal" and that *An Estate of Memory* "comes straight from those barbed-wire compounds, and her fight for survival, vis-à-vis the SS" (38). Karmel posits a more complicated relationship between lived experience, observation, memory, and the transmuting of all of these into fictional narrative.

NOTE

1. Unless otherwise indicated, all quotations are based on an interview with Ilona Karmel.

BIBLIOGRAPHY

Works by Ilona Karmel

Spiew za Drutami [Song Behind the Wire]. With Henryka Karmel-Wolfe. New York: Polish Jewish Press, 1947.
"Fru Holm," in *Mademoiselle* (August 1950): 203ff.
Stephania. Boston: Houghton Mifflin, 1953.

An Estate of Memory. New York: Feminist Press, 1986.
Personal interview, 13 September 1992.

Works about Ilona Karmel

Angress, Ruth K. "Afterword." *An Estate of Memory.* New York: Feminist Press, 1986, pp. 445–57.

Ezrahi, Sidra DeKoven. *By Words Alone: The Holocaust in Literature.* Chicago: University of Chicago Press, 1980, pp. 67–95.

Heinemann, Marlene E. *Gender and Destiny: Women Writers and the Holocaust.* Westport, CT: Greenwood Press, 1986.

Hook, Stuart. "Poor Girls," *Listener.* 6 August 1970: 187.

Horowitz, Sara R. "Linguistic Displacement in Fictional Responses to the Holocaust." Diss. Brandeis University, 1985. Ann Arbor: University of Michigan, 1985.

———. "Memory and Testimony in Women's Holocaust Memoirs," in *Jewish Women in Literary Perspective*, ed. Judith Baskin. Detroit: Wayne State University Press, forthcoming 1994.

Hutchens, John K. "On an Author." *New York Herald Tribune* (April 12, 1953): 2.

Janeway, Elizabeth. Rev. of *An Estate of Memory*, *New York Times Book Review* (September 21, 1969): 1ff.

"Literature: Ilona Karmel." *Mademoiselle* (January 1954): 83.

Nichols, Lewis. "Talk with Ilona Karmel," *New York Times Book Review* (March 29, 1951): 2.

Peterson, Virgilia. "To a Yellow-Walled Room in a Stockholm Hospital Came Stephania," Rev. of *Stephania*. *New York Herald Tribune* (March 29, 1953): 1ff.

SHIRLEY KAUFMAN (1923–   )

Devon Miller-Duggan

BIOGRAPHY

Shirley Kaufman was born in 1923, in the generation of American poets that includes Denise Levertov, James Wright, Adrienne Rich, and Allen Ginsberg. Profoundly diverse, that generation's free-verse poets share interests in the political and surreal poetry of Lorca and Neruda, and in the use of poetry to explore the truths of their lives. Also like many in her generation, Kaufman claims Pound and Williams as important influences on the style and structure of her poetry and partly credits Rilke for her own belief in the poem as an act of discovery ("Exile" 16).

Kaufman's parents were Polish Jews from the Vilna area who emigrated to the United States before World War I. It was her mother who encouraged her writing, buying Kaufman a leather-bound blank book when she was seven. Kaufman continued to write throughout her childhood and adolescence and stopped only after her graduation from UCLA in 1944. While Kaufman lost no immediate family members to the Holocaust, members of her extended family perished. Kaufman was involved in the Zionist movement in the United States and in the rescue and resettlement of survivors, working for the American Zionist Youth Commission in New York during 1945–46. While not a specifically religious Jew, she is strongly conscious of her Jewishness and the long, deep history that being Jewish carries with it ("Interview" 12).

Married to her first husband, Bernard Kaufman, in 1946, Shirley Kaufman had three daughters with him. When a broken hip kept her bedridden for the better part of a year, Kaufman spent her time reading the then new beat poets and existential philosophers. Inspired by her year of intense reading, she started writing again after the birth of her third daughter and enrolled in evening classes in creative writing. Twenty-three years after she earned her Bachelor's degree, Kaufman received her Master's degree in Creative Writing from San Francisco State University. Her first book of poetry, *The Floor Keeps Turning* (1970), won the International Poetry Forum United States Award. Her second book, *Gold*

Country, followed in 1973. That year she was divorced and remarried to Hillel M. Daleski, professor of literature at Hebrew University.

Drawn by history and identity, Shirley Kaufman had visited Israel several times before moving there with her second husband in 1973. While biblical women appear fairly frequently in her poetry, Kaufman's knowledge of the Bible was largely gained from reading the King James translation; she has continued to study Hebrew since moving to Israel and now reads the Bible in Hebrew.

Since moving to Israel, Kaufman has published three more books of her own poetry: *Looking at Henry Moore's Elephant Skull Etchings in Jerusalem During the War* (1977), *From One Life to Another* (1979), and *Claims* (1984). Working with native Hebrew and Dutch speakers, she has translated work by Abba Kovner (*My Little Sister* [1971], *A Canopy in the Desert* [1973], *My Little Sister and Selected Poems* [1986]), by Amir Gilboa (*The Light of Lost Suns*, 1979), and by Judith Herzberg (*But What*, 1988). Her work continues to appear in major American journals, and a sixth book of poems, *Rivers of Salt*, was published in the spring of 1993. In 1991, Kaufman received the Poetry Society of America's Shelley Memorial Award, given annually in recognition of "genius and need." She also teaches Creative Writing to Israelis writing in English. She has spoken of feeling marginalized in Israel by virtue of being neither a native nor a fluent Hebrew speaker, so that ultimately she seems to have exchanged one subtle foreignness (Jewish American) for another one less subtle (American Israeli). What is remarkable is the grace with which she inhabits each of these margins.

MAJOR THEMES

Kaufman's mixed chorus of artistic ancestors seems to have suggested a number of the themes that recur in her work. Her poetry explores the tensions inherent in the relatively easy security of American life. The intersection of histories the American Jew embodies and the concern with finding a secure way to be both Jewish and American, to embody the European Jewish and biblical pasts and the American present, invest and enrich many of her poems. Many of her poems profound hungers—the hunger for stability in the physical and historical worlds, the hunger for some sense of control over her life, and the hunger for love.

Some of these themes have more to do with being an educated American woman in the twentieth century than with being Jewish—those that concern the unresolved angers of family life, with divorce and remarriage, and with the search for a secure personal identity separate from that of mother, daughter, or wife. To the extent that Kaufman writes about these themes, she writes in the mainstream of American women poets in this century. Beyond these, Kaufman explores issues new to the pre-World War II discourse of American Jewishness. These are the themes and issues of dual citizenship and mixed allegiances that the State of Israel introduces into the conversation of Jewishness. The uniqueness of Kaufman's poetry lies in her ability to harmonize the concerns of American feminism and Israeli identity into a strong and supple poetic voice.

The unreliable floor in the title of Kaufman's first book, *The Floor Keeps Turning* (1970), is the controlling metaphor for the entire book. If the floors, the grounds on which the poems' speakers stand, are unreliable, then they are dependably so, since no single ground is sufficient to support the poem's speakers. When, in the first poem in the book and the first of Kaufman's biblical poems, Lot's wife looks back, she is clearly right to do so. She is leaving her life, and she needs to witness her separation from that life in order to know who she is: "Not to be curious . . . But to be only who she was / apart from them" ("His Wife," *Floor* 3). When she worries her lips until she tastes salt, we know that it is not just the salt of the pillar that she is becoming, but the salt of her own blood. In Kaufman's version, it is not Lot's wife's stubbornness or foolishness that turns her into a pillar of salt, but her need to be separate from "them"—her family and her former neighbors are equally implicated—so that the first poem of the first book addresses the problem of belonging neither to the old country nor to those with whom one flees.

Other poems use aboriginal images to explore the same themes. "Turtles" talks about the collection of shells from living turtles by the natives of Chagos. The poem pictures the turtles' survival for "more / than a hundred / years" (*Floor* 4). Kaufman depicts the turtles grieving in their new, thin skins for the entire hundred years, so that the poem offers the turtles as a metaphor for people ripped from their shells and surviving, but never truly letting go of their old shells, old houses, old selves. "Casualties" opens on an apparently ordinary and ordered breakfast scene, except that the bread gets toasted "still frozen" and burns, the dead "stare out of their numbers / every day," the speaker sits under the table "where it's safe," there are Indians on the lawn putting war paint on their faces, and the speaker's daughter can speak the Indians' language (*Floor* 5). To cope with the dead, the Indians, and her disconcerting daughter, the speaker can only recite her ancestors' names. The poem ends with the speaker commenting blankly that she has "nothing / to go with the jam," and it seems likely that the jam is both fruit preserves and the cultural traffic jam with which she is confronted daily.

Throughout the rest of the book, the grounds shift from under the speakers' feet and then re-form, only to shift again. No normal source of stability holds still—not in the unconnected but mirrored morning rituals of "Neighbors"; not in the breaking, broken, and stable family relationships of the second section; not in the crumbling sand of "Lately"; and not in the "never enough / time to exceed / the flesh" of "Poems for the End of the World" (*Floor* 54). But the shifting becomes increasingly Jewish in its sense of being "bunched between miracles and fear," as though the speakers in the poems were constantly aware of the threat of expulsion or abuse at the same time that they believe in the imminence of salvation. Even though the places the poems inhabit include

Watts, Mycenae, Florence, and New York, the admonition / prayer that titles "Keep Moving" seems to be answered by the question of the fifth section, "Where is there left to go?"

Gold Country (1973), Kaufman's second book, opens with a number of poems about loss—loss of love, loss of voice, loss of power, of pride, of truth, of memory. Each of the ten strophes of "After the Voices" begins with an aphorism from Antonio Porchia about endings, sadness, and uncertainty, and the poems themselves are a set of fugues on the danger and impossibility of a breaking relationship. The great losses in this second book are of seeing and knowing. Many of the poems deal with the dissolution of Kaufman's first marriage, and the failure of the marriage makes it impossible for the poem's speaker to trust what she sees, hears, and knows. Without the ability to trust what she learns, she is robbed of even the unreliable grounds of her first book—family dissolves, history wavers, nationality shifts.

Gold Country is also a book about places. Woodstock, Amherst, Stonehenge, San Francisco, Moscow, Seattle, and San Diego all figure in poems of transition and loss, but the book's major geographical location is Israel. Jerusalem is the speaker's destination, but it is a singularly elusive destination. The mythic worm that split the rocks for Solomon's temple and the tattooed survivors of the death camps exist together in the city, confused and afraid. The living past and present of Jerusalem confuse and frighten anyone who submits herself to the city's strange discipline of sensual and historical excess.

The book closes with "For Joan at Eilat," a poem about date farming, the difficulties of irrigation, and most importantly, wading in the Red Sea. Of the "warm water / near the edge of the desert" the speaker says that you "wade in it / as far as you can go" (*Gold* 79). It is not so much that Israel either solves or resolves any of the thematic dissolutions of *Gold Country* as that it is as far as the speaker can go—an end without closure. The waters in which we stand neither part for us nor pursue us, they simply permit us to stand there, up to our ankles in biblical history and contemporary dislocation.

Kaufman's third book, *From One Life to Another*, again takes up the themes of loss and dislocation. But loss itself is not always negative. The book opens with a poem about mating horseshoe crabs, "giddy" in the moonlight and air, but intending, always, to go back to the sea, and dreaming of solo movement ("Horseshoe Crabs," *Life* 3). Poems like "Come Back" examine the rush of the world from "where it ought to be" by speaking of the sudden disorder of divorce (*Life* 18). Poems that come later in the book, such as "Letting Go," talk about the rediscovery of sexuality and pride. "Divorce" begins by talking about the fragility of everything—"even a diamond / breaks / with one hard blow"—but ends by figuring the process of divorce itself as water and the speaker's hands as a boat (*Life* 32). The major theme of this book is healing and recovery, but it does not offer them as pleasant functions. Recovery and certainty are, in Kaufman's poems, earned by facing the horror in the world and embracing both its natures. In *Looking at Henry Moore's Elephant Skull Etch-*

ings in Jerusalem During the War Kaufman writes about Jerusalem, war, art, and acceptance, seeing it all as both extinct and alive, monstrous and shining (*Life* 49).

Knowing and seeing become certain, if not reliable, in Kaufman's fourth collection of poems, *Claims* (1984). This may be the most explicitly titled among her books. It focuses ultimately on the claims we may and must make on family and history and place. In this book, laying claim to emotional and geographical territories allows us to keep going long enough to find the few comforts the world permits to people who are paying real attention to it. A new home and a richly loving second marriage, the one a source of complexity and the other a source of simplicity, are the comforts *Claims* records. These are not comforts that make life easy, but they do permit acceptance of both the past and the future.

The past with which Kaufman makes a kind of peace contains both her own family's history and the turbulent history of Israel. The tolerable future is the one in "Levitation" that is already here and "already regrets what hasn't begun to happen" (*Claims* 77). The book's opening poem, "Jacaranda," declares that "our lives are sagging with miracles / ready to fail us" (*Claims* 1). Kaufman treats all of the book's subjects as though they were miracles, seeing the miraculous in subjects ranging from the bride-faces of newly sheared sheep to the romantic memories of a dying aunt, each of them brutal and lovely in precisely sufficient measure. Such seeing is a very real kindness, one that she says, in "Spring," is the single "thing / we're ready for" (*Claims* 59).

The characters in Shirley Kaufman's poems span traditions and histories—Adam, Lot's wife, Leah, Sarah and Hagar, Rabbi Yochanan ben Zakkai, the Bedouin, Giotto, Brunelleschi, and the Cossacks. They span continents—a U.N. compound in the Israeli desert, Brest Litovsk, Seattle, and the International Harp Contest at the Jerusalem YMCA. In "The Dome" (*Claims* 23), the speaker stands in the Dome of the Rock in Jerusalem (the site of Solomon's destroyed Temple and Mohammed's Christ-like ascension), thinking about the architectural miracle of Brunelleschi's Duomo in Florence, watching Muslim pilgrims and Jewish and Gentile tourists. The first two words of the poem might encompass, if such a thing were possible, all the multiple themes of Kaufman's poems: "Stressed essentials."

SURVEY OF CRITICISM

Criticism of Shirley Kaufman's poetry is confined to reviews of her books. In his review of her first book, *The Floor Keeps Turning*, Ronald Hayman anticipates much of what will be said about each of her subsequent books when he praises her "elegant, glassy structures" and admires the control with which her poems "tremble on the brink of the surreal" (76). He also comments on the "stabilizing influence" of the Jewish tradition in Kaufman's poetry. J. J. McGann, reviewing *Gold Country*, speaks of her poems as "intimate, concrete, and quietly revealing,'' calling them the products of a clearly ''reflective mind'' (44). Ruth Nevo, reviewing *From One Life to Another*, speaks of Kaufman's ''eloquent economy,'' ''finely strung consciousness,'' and ''purity of diction'' as she comments on the power with which Kaufman's poems explore many levels of absence (10ff). And John Felstiner, reviewing *Claims*, talks about the tensions between nature and history and the search for integrity that occupy the poems in her most recent book. Felstiner's review typifies critical opinion on Shirley Kaufman's poetry. He, like her other reviewers, acknowledges the delicacy and strength of Kaufman's poems, the tact and bravery she brings to reporting the objects of her unblinking gaze, and the affection with which she greets the complicated world her poems inhabit and chronicle.

BIBLIOGRAPHY

Works by Shirley Kaufman

Poetry

The Floor Keeps Turning. Pittsburgh: University of Pittsburgh Press, 1970.
Gold Country. Pittsburgh: University of Pittsburgh Press, 1973.
Looking at Henry Moore's Elephant Skull Etchings in Jerusalem During the War. Unicorn Press, 1977.
From One Life to Another. Pittsburgh: University of Pittsburgh Press, 1979.
Claims. New York: Sheep Meadow Press, 1984.
Rivers of Salt. Port Townsend, Washington: Copper Canyon, 1993.

Nonfiction

''Charles Reznikoff, 1894–1975: An Appreciation.'' *Midstream* 22 (1976): 38.
''The Obvious and the Hidden: Some Thoughts About 'Disasters.' '' *Ironwood* (Fall 1985): 152–58.

Translations

My Little Sister in *Abba Kovner and Nelly Sachs: Selected Poems*. Edited by Stephen Spender. New York: Penguin Books, 1971.
A Canopy in the Desert: Selected Poems of Abba Kovner. Translated with Ruth Adler and Nurit Orchan. University of Pittsburgh Press, 1973.
The Light of Lost Suns: Selected Poems of Amir Gilboa. New York: Persea Press, 1979.
''Answers to Questions on 'Potato Pie.' '' *Field*. (Spring 1984): 18–28.
Kovner, Abba. *My Little Sister and Selected Poems*. Oberlin, Ohio: Field Translation Series, 1986.
Herzberg, Judith. *But What: Selected Poems*. Translated by Shirley Kaufman and Judith Herzberg. Oberlin, Ohio: Field Translation Series, 1988.

Interviews

''An Interview With Shirley Kaufman.'' With Anna Sujatha Mathai. *The Indian Literary Review* (Oct. 1986): 3–12.

"The Poem Wants to Look Forward." Interview. With Vivian Eden. *The Jerusalem Post Magazine* 16 June 1989: 10–12.
"Always an Exile." Interview. With Grace Shulman. *The Women's Review of Books* (July 1991): 16–17.

Works about Shirley Kaufman

Cotter, J. F. Rev. of *Gold Country*. *Choice* April 1974: 259.
Felstiner, John. Rev. of *Claims*. *Tikkun* 1986: 107–08.
Hayman, Ronald. Rev. of *The Floor Keeps Turning*. *Encounter* Dec. 1970: 76.
Langendorf, Adele. Rev. of *Claims*. *San Francisco Chronicle* 21 July 1985.
Marvin, P. H. Rev. of *The Floor Keeps Turning*. *Library Journal* Jan. 1970: 164.
McGann, J. J. Rev. of *Gold Country*. *Poetry* Oct. 1974: 44.
Nevo, Ruth. Rev. of *From One Life to Another*. *The Jerusalem Post Magazine* 21 Sept., 1979. 10ff.
Pastan, Linda. Rev. of *Gold Country*. *Library Journal* Sept. 1973: 2446.

IRENA KLEPFISZ (1941–   )

Ronit Lentin

BIOGRAPHY

Irena Klepfisz was born in Warsaw, Poland. Her father, Michal Klepfisz, was a Bund activist, a member of the Jewish Fighters Organization, and a participant in the Warsaw Ghetto uprising. Fair and blue-eyed, her father was able to smuggle Klepfisz and her mother, Rose, in early 1943 to the Aryan side. Her blue-eyed mother, able to "pass," got a job as a maid in a Polish family and Klepfisz was placed in a Catholic orphanage. On April 20, 1943, her father, with a group of resisters, was trapped in an attic, where he killed a German but was immediately killed himself. When the ghetto was destroyed, her father's grave became part of the rubble. Most of her family died in Treblinka. Klepfisz and her mother were hidden by Polish peasants, and after the war, in 1946, they emigrated to Sweden. In 1949, they moved to the United States. Initially, Rose Klepfisz made a living as a seamstress.

By the time Klepfisz was eight, she spoke four languages: Polish, Swedish, English at the New York City public schools, and Yiddish in the Bronx Workmen's Circle Yiddishe Shule No. 3, where she was given a Socialist and Yiddish education so that she would be "ready to master/even more languages for the sake of survival" ("'67 Remembered" *A Few Words in the Mother Tongue* 232).

Irena graduated with honors in Yiddish and English from City College (CCNY) but still felt an outsider in America. In 1963, she started studying at the University of Chicago where she received an M.A. and, in 1970, a Ph.D. in English Literature. Between 1969 and 1973 Klepfisz had a full-time teaching job as an assistant professor of English in New York City. When she was laid off, she fell back on office work, which she did intermittently during the next two decades. She has also taught Yiddish, women's studies, and creative writing.

Klepfisz started publishing poetry and prose in the early 1970s. In 1975 Out and Out Books published *Periods of Stress*. *Keeper of Accounts* was published in 1982 by Persephone Press. In 1985, the London-based Onlywomen Press published *Different Enclosures,* which included selections from *Periods of Stress, Keeper of Accounts,* and a long short story, "The Journal of Rachel Robotnik." In 1990, Eighth Mountain Press published her poetry collection *A Few Words in the Mother Tongue: Poems Selected and New (1971–1990)* and a collection of prose, *Dreams of an Insomniac: Jewish Feminist Essays, Speeches, and Diatribes (1976–1990).* In September 1990, her play *Bread and Candy: Songs of the Holocaust* was produced at the New York City Jewish Museum and in 1991 was published in *Bridges* magazine. Klepfisz was a founder of *Conditions,* a feminist/lesbian magazine, the coeditor of *The Tribe of Dina: A Jewish Women's Anthology,* and currently serves as a contributing editor of *Sinister Wisdom* and as consultant on Yiddish language and literature for *Bridges: A Journal for Jewish Feminists and Our Friends.* In 1988, she became cofounder of The Jewish Women's Committee to End the Occupation of the West Bank and Gaza, and in 1990 she was appointed Executive Director of New Jewish Agenda.

Her feminism informed her Jewish consciousness and, encouraged by feminist models, she started incorporating Yiddish into her poetry and is keen to establish a dialogue with a Yiddish/Jewish past that would include women.

In 1983, she returned to Poland with her mother. At that time her mother was the archivist of the American Joint Distribution Committee, for the fortieth anniversary of the Warsaw Ghetto uprising. She now lives in Brooklyn and her deep commitment to the lesbian and feminist movements, to Yiddish and *yidishkayt* [Yiddish culture], to the Jewish community, and to radical politics, including a peaceful solution in the Middle East, has become as important to her as her writing. For Klepfisz, writing and doing are linked, both constituting a refusal to remain passive in the face of oppression.

MAJOR THEMES

Irena Klepfisz's life and work has been informed, above all, by being a child Holocaust survivor. "As a child, I was old with terror and the brutality, the haphazardness of survival," she says in "Resisting and Surviving America" (*Dreams of an Insomniac* 61).

The main questions Irena Klepfisz poses in the two strands of her writing, poetry and prose, are what it means to grow up as a Jew in the United States after the Holocaust; and what it means to be a Jewish woman and writer—poor, single, childless, lesbian—in America and in a Jewish community of survivors who see their hope for meaning in a new generation of Jewish children.

As a child survivor, she had to grapple with an absent father, "hero and betrayer/legend and deserter" ("The Widow and Daughter," *A Few Words,* 38), whose absence becomes enormous presence. Her absent father is as much an influence as her "heroic, desperate, determined" mother (Glazer 223), but Michal Klepfisz's absent body, absent grave, haunt his daughter so much that she feared at various stages of her writing life that her Holocaust poetry dwarfed anything else she had written.

In his death, Michal Klepfisz had committed his daughter, who "at one time expected/to live/not survive" ("The Widow and Daughter," *A Few Words* 35), to mere survival. But survival for Klepfisz, who engages her readers in a dialogue in the Midrashic tradition as interpreter and rememberer, is multilayered.

Holocaust motifs tend to dominate. Klepfisz's Holocaust poems chart the experiences of women and depict, especially in *"Bashert"* [inevitable, predestined], not only survival, but also what happens after survival. Survival is also about daily battle. Klepfisz writes about doing paid work, counting pennies, "keeping accounts," in order to eat, pay the rent, love, and especially write: "A block of uninterrupted time—unencumbered by a job or financial anxiety—is critical to every form of creativity and rarely available to most of us, especially to those of us who are out of the mainstream" ("Persephone," *Keeper of Accounts* 91).

Despite the two very definite strands of writing—theory and poetry—similar themes recur in both. Klepfisz has written both poetry and prose about this daily tight-rope act: The story "The Journal of Rachel Robotnik," Polish for "worker" (*Different Enclosures* 59–87), details the minutiae of how a book of stories "came to be." The essay "The Distances Between Us: Feminism, Consciousness and the Girls at the Office" (*Dreams of an Insomniac* 15–49), the sets of poems "Contexts" (*A Few Words* 131–37), and "Work Sonnets with Notes and a Monologue about a Dialogue" (138–53) tell, among other things, of her work experiences as coworker to Gentile women who operate Xerox machines and pound keyboards and who show clear understanding of the patriarchal structure of their lives.

When she talks about survival, Klepfisz speaks not only of bag ladies and the homeless, but of ourselves. No longer will any of us be able to claim "I didn't hear a thing. How could I have known? I wasn't in the forest and the trees didn't make a sound" ("Rhythm & Jews").

Klepfisz's political beliefs, her (Jewish) pursuit of justice, in recent years especially against the Israeli occupation, features in her essays but also in her poetry. Her communal work has helped to displace the nightmare image of herself as bag lady, seen by most as a "species apart"; nonetheless, Klepfisz returns to this image in "From the Monkey House and Other Cages" poems (*A Few Words* 109–28), where she represents herself as the ultimate outsider, the Jew, the lesbian, the survivor.

Klepfisz's work searchlights relentlessly the "distances" of class, but also of geography—Poland—New York—Israel—always, despite the pain the distances imply, aiming to make us believe that bridges are a possibility. To Klepfisz, writing, as a process of interpretation and recovery, of asking fundamental questions about the uses of history rather than simply of self-expression, is one means of survival.

Survival is also the trajectory from Holocaust to contemporary America, from Holocaust to (Israeli) occupation. *A Few Words in the Mother Tongue* begins, emblematically, with "Searching for My Father's Body" and ends with "East Jerusalem, 1987: *Bet Shalom* (House of Peace)," dedicated to "a Palestinian woman who I am afraid to name." Yet Klepfisz's theoretical work is an attempt to de-emblematize her own history and the history of the Jews.

She interweaves contradictory identities that some may see as imcompatible: working-class woman and poet, lesbian and ardent Jew, Holocaust survivor and defender of Palestinian rights.

Her work reflects her multi-layered exile, that of the lesbian/feminist threatened in America and of the Jew threatened by the elusive anti-Semitism within the feminist movement, which is "either the anti-Semitism of omission or one which trivializes the Jewish experience and Jewish oppression" (*Dreams of an Insomniac* 54). There are other contradictions: As a lesbian/feminist she is an outsider in the Jewish community, but as a Jew in a Christian, anti-Semitic America, "the Jewish community is, and will always remain, my community" (*Dreams* 67). To be a lesbian in our culture, to be a lesbian/feminist among mainstream Jews, to be a Jew in WASP America, demands new resources of survival.

Thematically, outsiderness figures prominently in all her work. She confronts head on her multiple exile on America's "inhospitable soil" but refuses to remain a child survivor forever: "I don't want to bury myself in dreams or myths. I don't want to go back and I don't want to mourn forever. It's not what I survived for" ("Bread and Candy: Songs of the Holocaust" 38). Her poems to women lovers are as direct and as revealing as her Holocaust poetry. This is poetry probing "with a questioning scrutiny what happens in bed, in relationship...always there is compassion for both self and other" (Rich 24).

Just as the Jewish content had informed her feminism, it was the *bavegung* [the (feminist) movement] that helped her to return to Jewish themes, abandoned temporarily prior to the invitation to contribute to *Nice Jewish Girls: A Lesbian Anthology* (1982). Her upbringing as a secular, Socialist Jew and the resulting vision of an inclusive, multiethnic, multidimensional Jewish community have further pushed her toward the edge, this time toward reclaiming the secular Jewish culture that had thrived in the forties. Secular Judaism, to Klepfisz, provides a means of building a Jewish identity outside of fighting anti-Semitism, becoming a Zionist, or assimilating.

The Holocaust robbed her not only of her father, but also of Yiddish, the *mame-loshn* [mother tongue] that in her work as translator of women Yiddish writers, as teacher of Yiddish, and, ultimately, as writer of bilingual poetry, she is helping to keep alive. In "Fradel Schtok," the introduction of Yiddish crystalizes the Klepfisz paradigm: "Think of it: *heym* and *home* the meaning/the same of course exactly/but the shift in vowel was the ocean/in which I drowned" (*A Few Words* 228).

Klepfisz has always wrestled with language. She first struggled to master high-school composition in English class, and, later, in college, to "match style to form." Eventually, she chose her own fragmented, nonlinear approach, combining poetry and prose in her poetry; and journal entries, statements, and memoirs in her essays, because "form and content are determined by our spiritual and material circumstances" (*Dreams of an Insomniac* xiii).

Finally, she wrestles with the dichotomy between language and silence, typical of many post-Holocaust artists from Celan to Lanzmann, delicately balancing the inability to tell with the duty to tell. Another silence, stemming from her sense that people were "tired of hearing about what Jews feel," hid her "extreme pain, frustration, and rage with Jews and non-Jews alike" at the Holocaust having been "commercialized, metaphored out of reality, glamorized and severed from the historical fact" (*Dreams of an Insomniac* 63–64). Her poems, sparse, with words far apart from each other, are "as much about speaking as about silence . . . silence had become and remains a central theme in my writing" (*Dreams of an Insomniac* 168). But silence equals death, she affirms in *Rhythm + Jews,* and Irena Klepfisz's personal and historical struggle is, ultimately, for much more than mere survival.

SURVEY OF CRITICISM

There is a growing body of scholarship about Irena Klepfisz's work. Her poetry is universally praised; her theoretical writing is addressed mostly by critics who laud her "moral and artistic integrity" (Beck xvii), though some take issue with her ideas.

Miriyam Glazer views Klepfisz's poetry as "a poetry of the viscera, the heart, the mind, and the soul . . . a political poetry whose ideology is shaped by the magma of lived experience," as a poetry "rare in this country" (Glazer 227). Her "proud, uncompromising, and profoundly resonant voice" (Glazer 226) is employed to chart women's experiences, to evoke the lost language through her "magnificently wrought bilingualism" (229). Klepfisz's poetry is so powerful, Glazer says, not only because it bridges the vast gap between what was and what is now, between the Yiddish *kholm* and the American "dream," but also because it moves to the now, speaking of present-day American experiences of ethnic minorities and caged enclosures.

In a chapter devoted to the poetry of Adrienne Rich and Irena Klepfisz, Jan Montefiore acknowledges Klepfisz's strategy of rooting her poetry in history rather than in myth. Klepfisz's poetry does not insist on a feminist significance, but, Montefiore says, "this is apparent nonetheless in the way that the poet simply takes for granted that the lives and experiences of women are important" (Montefiore, 94). In fact, "Irena Klepfisz draws one so successfully into her visions of lives destroyed . . . that it is easy not to notice that all the people in her poem ["*Bashert*"] are women" (Montefiore 93).

James McCorkle writes that Klepfisz's poetry expresses the poet's responsibility to bear witness and at the same time resist emblematizing recent Jewish history. Klepfisz's work, McCorkle says, rejects Adorno's claim that "there can be no real history after such an event." Her poetry, he writes, "takes on the fundamental task of retrieving a whole language—the east European Yiddish—and drawing it into relation to her new language—American English'' (McCorkle 183).

Adrienne Rich's introduction to *A Few Words in the Mother Tongue: Poems Selected and New (1971–1990)* praises Klepfisz's poetry as an important part of an unassimilated cultural re-creation. Klepfisz's early poems on women in the Holocaust ''floodlight a neglected dimension of the genocide: the survival strategies, the visceral responses, of women'' (Rich 19). In *''Bashert,''* ''a poem unlike any other I can think of in American, including Jewish-American, poetry . . . Klepfisz has written one of the great 'borderland' poems'' (Rich 19–20).

While Judy Keiner is unequivocal in her praise of Klepfisz's poetry and lauds her prose because it evokes like nothing else the ''might-have-been experience'' (37), she, nonetheless, argues with Klepfisz on three scores. First, she objects to Klepfisz's all-inclusive vision of the Jewish community: ''I'm sure Klepfisz *would* reject Jews for Jesus . . . '' (Keiner 39). Second, she questions Klepfisz's silence about the Yiddish, alive and spoken by large Jewish communities in Israel, the United States, Britain, and the Netherlands. Is she silent because these communities are strictly Orthodox and therefore homophobic? Keiner asks. Third, Keiner questions Klepfisz's silence on the ordinary lives of Israelis and on the writings by Israelis such as Joshua Sobol and David Grossman on the Holocaust.

The chapter on Irena Klepfisz in my own unpublished master's thesis ''Twice an Outsider: A Study of the Dual Exile of Three Jewish American Women Writers'' concentrates on her multilayered exile as child survivor, as Jew, and as woman in contemporary America.

Evelyn Torton Beck's introduction to *Dreams of an Insomniac: Jewish Feminist Essays, Speeches and Diatribes* speaks of the integrity and ability to bring together that which is Jewish, lesbian, feminist in Klepfisz's prose, and it presents her as an opponent of anti-Semitism, compulsory motherhood, commercialization of the Holocaust, and Israeli occupation of the West Bank and Gaza Strip.

Ellen Stone admires Klepfisz's poetry, but remains uncomfortable with her insistence on ''negative'' secularism in her prose writing, wondering whether this secularism is as exclusive as the rigidities it reacts against. Stone feels bombarded by Klepfisz's call to heal a wounded and unfinished world: Klepfisz's politics, she writes, becomes something to live up to, an obligation.

BIBLIOGRAPHY

Works by Irena Klepfisz

Poetry

Periods of Stress. New York: Out and Out Books, 1975.
Keeper of Accounts. Watertown, MA: Persephone Press, 1982.

Different Enclosures. London: Onlywomen Press, 1985.
A Few Words in the Mother Tongue: Poems Selected and New (1971–1990). Portland, OR: Eighth Mountain Press, 1990.

Nonfiction

"Anti-Semitism in the Lesbian/Feminist Movement." *Nice Jewish Girls: A Lesbian Anthology.* Edited by Evelyn Torton Beck. Trumansburg, NY: Crossing Press, 1982. 45–51.
"From Perspectives on the Second World War." *Nice Jewish Girls,* 99.
"Resisting and Surviving America." *Nice Jewish Girls.* 100–08.
The Tribe of Dina: A Jewish Women's Anthology. With Melanie Kaye/Kantrowitz. Boston: Beacon, 1989.
Dreams of an Insomniac: Jewish Feminist Essays, Speeches and Diatribes (1976–1990). Portland, OR: Eighth Mountain Press, 1990.
"The Politics of Snails." *The American Voice* (Winter 1991): 67–71.
"Rhythm + Jews." Liner notes for the record of *Klezmatics,* 1991.

Drama

"Bread and Candy: Songs of the Holocaust." *Bridges* (Fall 1991): 13–43.

Works about Irena Klepfisz

Altman, Meryl. "Uneasy Understandings." Rev. of *A Few Words in the Mother Tongue.* *Women's Review of Books,* (October 1990): 16–18.
Beck, Evelyn Torton. Introduction. *Dreams of an Insomniac: Jewish Feminist Essays, Speeches and Diatribes (1976–1990).* Portland, OR: Eighth Mountain Press, 1990. xvii–xxix.
Blackford, Anne. "Klepfisz Poems Penetrate Historic Guilt." Rev. of *Keeper of Accounts. Motheroot Journal* (Fall 1984): 8.
Borghi, Liana. "Irena Klepfisz: Accounts of Self-Enclosure." *Rivista di Studi Anglo-Americani* 9 (1993): 167–77.
Epstein, Rachel. Rev. of *Dreams of an Insomniac. Outlook* (April 1991): 16.
Felman, Jyl Lynn. "The Search for a Place to Call Home." Rev. of *Dreams of an Insomniac. Lambada Book Reports*: 15–17.
Frieden, Ken. "A Daughter of the Mother Tongue." Rev. of *A Few Words* and *Dreams of an Insomniac. Forward* Sept 13 1991: 9–10.
Glast, Liz. "Irena Klepfisz Brings Yiddish to Lesbian Writing." *The Advocate* 18 Dec. 1990: 77.
Glazer, Miriyam. Rev. of *A Few Words. Studies in American Jewish Literature* 11.12 (Fall 1992): 226–32.
Hochman, Andree. "Looking Back, Reaching Forward." *Just Out.* April 1989.
Keiner, Judy. "Paradox Regained? The Writings of Irena Klepfisz." *Jewish Quarterly* 39 (Fall 1992): 37–40.
Lehrer, Chaia, "A Powerful Awareness." Rev. of *Dreams of an Insomniac. New Directions for Women,* Sept/Oct 1991.
Lentin, Ronit. "Surviving and Resisting America: The Use of Language as Gendered Subversion in the Work of American Jewish Poet Irena Klepfisz." *Teanga—the Irish Yearbook for Applied Linguistics* 12 (Fall 1992): 61–72.
Loewenstein, Andrea F. "A Life in the Balance." Rev. of *Keeper of Accounts. The Women's Review of Books,* (August 1984): 10–11.

McCorkle, James, "Contemporary Poets and History." *The Kenyon Review* (Winter 1992): 177–83.

Milner, Jenney. "Nourishing Difference, Bridging Distances." Rev. of *Dreams of an Insomniac. Sojourner* (September 1991): 39–40.

Montefiore, Jan. "Communities of Women: Adrienne Rich and Irena Klepfisz." *Feminism and Poetry: Language, Experience, Identity in Women's Writing*. Ed. Ian Montefiore. (London: Pandora, 1987): 85–96.

Penn, Shana, "The Reclamation of *Yidishkayt*." Rev. of *Dreams of an Insomniac. The Women's Review of Books*. (July 1991): 45–46.

Piercy, Marge. Rev. of *Keeper of Accounts. American Book Review*. (Sept 1983): 11.

Rich, Adrienne. Introduction. *A Few Words in the Mother Tongue: Poems Selected and New (1971–1990)*, 13–25. Portland, OR: Eighth Mountain Press, (1990).

Silberg, Richard. "New and Noted." *Poetry Flash*. (January 1991): 20.

Stone, Ellen. "Darkness Is the Incubator." Rev. of *Dreams of an Insomniac* and *A Few Words. Bridges* 2 (Spring 1991): 122–29.

EDITH KONECKY (1922–   )

Merla Wolk

BIOGRAPHY

When you ask Edith Konecky about her life, she replies, "it's all in the fiction"—a connection suggested in the name of the heroine of her first novel, *Allegra Maud Goldman.* Henry Wadsworth Longfellow's poem "The Children's Hour" may be the source for the exotic name of her heroine, one that establishes Allegra's kinship with her author.

> From my study I see in the lamplight,
> Descending the broad hall stair,
> Grave Alice, and laughing Allegra,
> And Edith with the golden hair.

Edith Konecky was born in Brooklyn in 1922, and like Allegra and Rachel Levin—the heroine of her other novel, *A Place at the Table* (also an autobiographical fiction)—the daughter of a dress manufacturer. She became a writer in circumstances similar to those she creates for Allegra. Konecky submitted a short story to a contest when she was still in high school, for which she was paid a penny a word, perhaps impressing her father as Allegra did hers, not so much by the writing ["What do I know about poems?" was Allegra's father's dismissive remark (172)], but by the financial reward. Educated at New York University and Columbia, for twenty years she lived the life of a suburban housewife, raising two sons. During her years in suburbia and later at the Mac-Dowell Colony, Yaddo, and Banff, she has been writing fiction and has served as a critical reader for the writing of others. In 1992, Konecky was a New York Foundation for the Arts Fellow. She presently lives in New York City and is at work on a new novel.

Although she is not a religious Jew, Edith Konecky, as her fiction indicates, has a strong Jewish identification. Religious practices, says Konecky, made her "a feminist before [she] even had a word for it." Identifying herself as more a cultural than religious Jew, she sums up her experience as the odd mixture of "ignorance and indifference common to the upwardly mobile first generation American-born Jews, our parents" (Letter to the author, 24 October 1992). Whatever connection Konecky had to traditional Judaism came, as it did for her heroine Allegra, through her grandmother who lived with her family when Edith was a child, and who left a legacy of Jewish cooking, superstition, and humor.

MAJOR THEMES

How to get from "It's a girl"—the first words of Edith Konecky's 1976 novel, *Allegra Maud Goldman*—to "you're a person"— the final words—constitutes Konecky's major concern in this and her other novel, *A Place at the Table* (1989). Allegra is born into a world in which the common question— "What are you going to be when you grow up"—has already been answered for females: "you'll grow up and marry some nice man and have children" (65). Her parents and teachers feel perfectly convinced that any other answer, whether it be Allegra's smart-alecky "a gentleman farmer" or her more reasonable "supreme court justice" are equally comical. Assistance toward her real aspiration to be a writer—in the form of a typewriter—comes only because her father thinks it the first step in her "training for a secretarial career" and the means to earning "her first dollar" (91). What makes Konecky's presentation of these familiar circumstances so fresh is the distinctive voice of her artist/ heroines—particularly the highly intelligent, profoundly imaginative, and unusually sensitive Allegra, and her grown-up version, Rachel Levin. The humor, honesty, and insight with which Konecky invests these characters infuse these circumstances with originality and vitality. Although Konecky has written several fine short stories, her two autobiographical novels represent her most significant work. In *Allegra Maud Goldman,* she chronicles the life of the Jewish female artist-in-the-making, confronting and affronted by the crass, materialistic values of her upper-middle-class family living in Brooklyn in the 1930s and, in *A Place at the Table,* the artist as mother and lover, still looking with wonder and trepidation at "why we write and why we live" (198) and at being female in twentieth-century America.

Being female undergoes sea changes from *Allegra Maud Goldman* to *A Place at the Table,* providing quite different socially constructed models. In part, those changes represent the dramatic restructuring of society's expectations for women from the time of the first novel, the 1930s—when Allegra goes from four to about fourteen—to the time of the second, the 1980s, when Rachel approaches her sixtieth year. In part, they represent the inevitable altering of perception that comes with maturing. In the early novel, Allegra's wit and youthful promise allow us to read the traumas—the nervous breakdown, the terror of death and fear of sexuality, the emotionally absent mother and the terrifying father—as richly portrayed circumstances that for all their injurious potential will not seriously impede the development of this brave, smart little girl. One can envision an equally brave, smart adult, ego intact, goals achieved. In the latter novel, however, a sadder, wiser estimation of the possible informs the humor. With Rachel, we have a much keener understanding of the consequences of having been the "small and frightened and helpless [child], . . . the child terrified of that abominable, noisy giant, [her] father" (195).

Female identity in Konecky's fiction emerges essentially from the tension between her protagonists' innate artistic sensibilities and their familial and cultural inheritance. Combining a romantic faith in individualism with shrewd realistic analysis, Konecky implies a definition of free will that could be stated as *what one can do with what one's given*. In *Allegra Maud Goldman*, she explores the boundaries of individual control when Allegra decides to run away from home but then returns, recognizing that she can't escape her family because "They were [her] fate. They were who [she] was" (45). Konecky continues to question how far free will extends when Allegra asks her mother why her father, "a self-made man" couldn't, as long as he was at it, have made "himself nicer" (39). We leave Allegra still asking these existential questions and find Rachel supplying answers shaped by experience and maturity. When the older woman— who shares all of Allegra's biography except her name—thinks about her emotionally primitive, verbally cruel father, she realizes that what thwarted his ability to make himself nicer was the fact that he, too, had parents whose difficult psychology narrowed his choices. The inheritance he had to work against included an ineffectual but kind father and a stingy, strident, "virago" (153) of a mother. Rachel comes to find her father as pitiable as he is objectionable: "he had to fight and claw his way into the only kind of manhood and survival he could forge for himself" (152).

Konecky indicates that not only the tyrant of a father suffers the restrictions of his familial and cultural influences. Even the self-aware, psychologically savvy Allegra/Rachel can break through some barriers but not others. Konecky roots the adult woman's (Rachel's) need to maneuver herself in her relationships into positions of control in her young self's (Allegra's) insensitive treatment by those in control of her life. This same causal relationship can be seen in Rachel's propensity for choosing lovers who—like her parents—betray, disappoint, or reject her. With these details, Konecky acknowledges the unwilling eroticism of early modes of interaction, thus confirming an uncomfortable truth of human motivation that no matter how self-destructive, it is not uncommon to find even what is painfully familiar (the familial) attractive. Despite her satiric attack on those who fail Allegra and Rachel, causing them pain, Konecky does not show her heroines to be self-pitying, and the texts support the compassionate judgment that finally we are all victims of victims.

In negotiating the obstacle course from girlhood to personhood, Konecky's heroines inherit from their mothers a very limited range of adaptations to the socially prescribed female role. In both Allegra's mother and her maternal grandmother, Konecky presents women who have achieved their respective generation's standard of a successful woman. Her mother, bowing to her own parents' conception of what's good for her, marries a seemingly "bashful" young man, expected to bend to her "strong will." Immediately transformed after marriage, he becomes tyrannic and she subdued. In this bargain, she gains material comforts, a nervous stomach, and a shallow existence devoted to Mah-Jongg, shopping, and gossiping with friends. He gets license to run roughshod over his family while she placates him, "selling out her own child for the sake of peace" (37). Allegra's beloved, Old World grandmother gives and finds joy in her domesticity, but at sixty, a widow, she remarries to avoid becoming one of the "shipwrecks" Allegra, in her first published poem, envisions as the destiny of a woman alone. Neither option—submissive wife nor *balabusteh* [fine housekeeper]—engages Allegra's mind or her abilities. To follow her mother would mean marrying a man like her father. To follow her grandmother means to call upon domestic skills that she doesn't have or want. Konecky demonstrates a wonderfully comic rendering of Allegra's failed efforts in home economics classes, classes that highlight learning "toast" and how to light ovens: " 'If they're preparing us to be housewives and mothers,' [Allegra's friend] Melanie says, 'why don't they teach us something really useful like sexual intercourse' " (94).

In *A Place at the Table,* Rachel Levin and her friends, eager to create their own model of female success, experience the difficulties of their expanded options. The echo of Virginia Woolf's *A Room of One's Own* in Konecky's title locates the conflict her aspiring writers experience in a tradition of female writers. Competing ambitions—Freud's twin necessities for a meaningful life, love and work—require balancing. Love, for many of these women, means marriage, but only one finds it there; and no doubt significantly, she makes no attempt to balance it with work. Konecky presents Rachel's long-time friend, Rebecca, as a self-described "creative appreciator," an imaginative woman whose ideas only develop responsively—"I don't think it or say it until someone else has said something I can *react* to" (61).

For Rachel and her writer friends, whose artistic aspirations go beyond this subordinate, essentially passive, role, success in intimate relationships is far more elusive. Rachel herself—writer, wife, mother, grandmother, friend, love of both men and women—constantly searches for ways to enjoy at once her lover and her art. What she finds is at best a see-saw relationship between the two. When in love, she suffers writers' block. And, conversely, as one of her friends says when Rachel tells of her breakup with her lover, Lisa, "if you're not loving, you must be writing." Through Rachel's writer friends, Konecky examines other choices, other destinies: writing for money, giving up writing, giving up. Despite the diversity in Konecky's carefully drawn characters, these aspiring women share a propensity for anxiety, an unwilling attraction to victimhood, and an impaired sense of self.

Attempting to understand the contrary forces that complicate loving and working for women, Rachel repeatedly questions what constitutes adult, intimate love. Alternately, she identifies "possession" (113, 131), abuse, jealousy, illusion—something "done with trick mirrors" (154), and forms of self-love, in which the real object is one's self loving and the real pleasure, one's own feelings (4, 55, 157–58). Rachel comes to a sad conclusion that can be applied to most of the women in Konecky's fiction: that in seeking a love partner, "nobody is ever good enough when you can't love yourself properly" (158). Konecky leaves the impression, however, that writers have the opportunity to repair their failure through their work. Writing fiction, after all, legitimizes the use of "trick mirrors." At novel's end, Rachel has broken with her lover and has begun a new book about a couple, Art and Barbara; his name suggests a successful merger of creative work and love that can occur at least in the imagination.

For Konecky's heroines, becoming a person depends not only on the peculiarities of being female in a society that privileges males ["In the beginning is the sex," Konecky writes in *Allegra Maud Goldman* (1)], but on the exigencies of being Jewish. In the same novel, Konecky sees these influences—more cultural than religious, more habit than belief—as both "heavy" and "rich" (1). Being Jewish contextualizes the materialism of Max Goldman/Mr. Levin, locating their values in the experience of being outside a system, sons of immigrants, growing up poor and poorly educated—conditions that prompt this characteristic judgment: In the value system of Max Goldman, "If she's so smart, . . . why isn't she rich" (54). Being Jewish provides a framework for making sense of the questionable ethics of Uncle Julius in Konecky's short story "Eric and Max and Julius and Ethics": "where . . . I come from . . . they didn't have much in the line of ethics. Pogroms they had. Dogs attacking us they had" (161). And although in this story, Eric, like Rachel and Allegra, has neither pogrom nor gas chamber as his immediate experience, Konecky suggests that understanding what influenced those who influenced oneself is a necessary element in the search for personal identity. Each of the successors to this ambiguous legacy (Allegra, Rachel, Eric) acknowledges that for all their coarseness, people like Max and Julius project a certain vigor and directness that makes others colorless in comparison.

The richness that Konecky's protagonists find in being Jewish comes from an "ethnic tone" that speaks of love and humor and the delights of Allegra's grandmother's special *kreplach* (8), a religion no less "devout" for being primarily "domestic" (90). But for all her loving rendering of these ethnic pleasures, Konecky places greater emphasis on the "heaviness"—the burdens—of being Jewish. She sees these burdens in the demands of barely explicable superstitions—Allegra's grandmother slaps her when she gets her period, "something to do with evil spirits and being dirty" (162), and in patriarchal Judaism's reinforcement of the misogyny of the American culture: "Even when it came to God, [Allegra reflects] alas, the women's place was in the kitchen" (90). And she finds the burdens when the experience of being Jewish compounds the liabilities of being female, providing another focus in *A Place at the Table* for Rachel's masochism. Just as this masochism represents an incorporation of society's devaluing of women, the frequency with which Rachel finds anti-

Semitism in her lovers, her friends, even her daughter-in-law, suggests an incorporation of the social evaluation of Jews: what one of Rachel's lovers calls a "learned masochism."

For the most part, Konecky refigures the themes of her novels in her shorter fiction. The protagonists, like Allegra and Rachel, fear death, puzzle over sexual identity, and question life's disappointments and absurdities. In several of these stories, the action turns around the protagonists' nervous breakdowns and the failure of presumably more stable figures to provide meaningful help. In "The Power," (1963), "Past Sorrows and Coming Attractions" (1993), and "The Hour" (unpublished), the sufferers find in doctors and parents only a reflection of their own anguish, their own limitations. A few characteristics, however, distinguish the shorter fiction from the novels: the near absence of her customary humor to lighten the serious concerns; more Gentile protagonists and environments; the frequent use of third-person narration rather than the first person of the novels. All of these choices suggest some distancing from the autobiographical connections so evident in the longer fiction. And while the protagonists display the same precocity as the novels' heroines, that gift (and curse) takes a new form in two of the stories, one early, one late. The fourteen-year-old Prudence has the disturbing ability to see into the future in "The Power" (1963), where she not only can see what others can't, but believes her wishes have the capacity to destroy the neglectful mother. Thirty years later, in "Past Sorrows and Coming Attractions," Brenda has similar visions, but without the accompanying destructive desires. She emerges from her breakdown, recognizing her mother as more another victim than a victimizer and imagining herself—using the metaphor of movie previews signaled in the title—blessed with choice; she envisions the option to select which "coming attractions" she likes.

Despite the high quality of her stories, Konecky's novels remain her most exciting achievement. In them she writes of the ordinary experiences of life in her extraordinary voice. With wit and irony she celebrates contradiction and ambiguity. Working economically in *Allegra Maud Goldman,* Konecky presents what on one level is a series of very funny—at times painfully so—scenarios about growing up Jewish and female in a particular time and place. Konecky's humor is so sharp, so delightful, that the temptation to quote Allegra at every turn is almost irresistible. On another level, however, Konecky offers the reader a symbolically condensed canvas in which small details in what seems a series of anecdotes about growing up imply expansive versions of the conflicts attendant on suffering and survival.

In *A Place at the Table,* again in what seems a loosely constructed plot, she links scenes built around questions about being and becoming. Here, instead of wresting a self out of the difficult challenges of childhood and adolescence, her subject is accommodating the inevitable losses of aging. Here, her heroine battles the predominantly female "diseases" of masochism and breast cancer, figures out how to assert a self and not be selfish, and finally recognizes that fears of dying are really fears of living. In the end, Konecky posits an ideal, particularly for Rachel, of rejoicing in modest achievements. Confronting her "*doppleganger,*" the-genius-turned-bag-lady Deirdre, who represents for her "that fate worse than death" (193), Rachel finds that what compels one to live and work with pleasure is simply being "interested" (198). Konecky concludes that life is a "feast," even though some of what's served may make one ill and some don't find a "place at the table." She presents this vision through an ironic, self-deprecating, unsentimental Jewish humor that can both recognize and mask the dark forces within.

SURVEY OF CRITICISM

There is little critical material on Konecky's work. The newly reissued *Allegra Maud Goldman* (1987) includes an introduction by Tillie Olsen, who sees the novel as "one of the few books that prove to be a timeless delight for all ages" (ix). She cites its "charm" and "wit," its re-creation of "the limited, limiting, and material-minded Jewish family," seeing it as "a marvel of creation, firmly set in her particularity, her pre-*bas mitzvah,* pre-Jewish feminism, pre-having-a-destiny-other-than-marriage, time"(x). Bella Brodzki writes the afterword for this same edition, locating the novel in the tradition of the *kuntsler-roman,* seeing it as a "coming-of-age" story that provides a "significant variation on the theme" (125). For Brodzki, the "clash of cultural values, alternating by generations, as is often the case in *nouveau riche* immigrant families," is one of the "major themes of the book" (177). Other commentary on *Allegra* can be found in book reviews. Alix Kates Shulman provides a glowing review, which, like all commentaries on Konecky, applauds the marvelous humor. Martin Levin calls it a novel whose "wit and humor prove that childhood is no joke."

Critical material on *A Place at the Table* is also in book reviews. Stacey D'Erasme calls Rachel "a wisecracking Mrs. Dalloway" and asserts that Allegra lives, with wit and the spirit of adventure intact in the figure of sixty-year-old Rachel Levin. Barbara Fisher Williamson calls the novel "warm, witty" and "poignant and sage."

BIBLIOGRAPHY

Works by Edith Konecky

"The Sound of Comedy," *Esquire* (January 1961): 53–56.
"Turn Your Back and Walk." *Best College Writing.* New York: Random House, 1961. 97–108.
"Charity." *Kenyon Review* 25 (1963): 81–90.
"The Breakdown." *Story Magazine* (July-Aug. 1963): 40.
"The Power," *The Massachusetts Review* 4 (1963): 651–70.

"The End of the Wedding." *Best American Short Stories of 1964*. Ed. Martha Foley and David Burnet. Boston: Houghton Mifflin, 1964. 173–90.

"The Passion of Magda Wickwire." *Saturday Evening Post* (31 July 1965): 58–60.

"The Box," *Virginia Quarterly* 46 (1970): 624–28.

"Ralph." *Cosmopolitan* (Oct. 1970): 204–05.

"Love and Friendship." *Cosmopolitan* (Dec. 1971): 202–09.

"Death in New Rochelle." *Cosmopolitan* Sept. 1973: 206–13.

"Lessons," *Virginia Quarterly* 52 (1976): 79–90.

"Eric & Max & Julius & Ethics." *From Mt. San Angelo*. London and Toronto: Associated University Presses, 1984. 145–62.

Allegra Maud Goldman. 1976. Rpt. New York: The Feminist Press, 1990.

A Place at the Table. 1989. Rpt. New York: Ballantine Books, 1990.

"The Place." *America and I: Short Stories by American Jewish Women Writers*. Ed. Joyce Antler. Boston: Beacon Press, 1990. 209–16.

Letter to the author. 24 Oct. 1992.

"Past Sorrows and Coming Attractions." *Women on Women II*. New York: NAL, 1993.

"The Hour," unpublished story.

Works about Edith Konecky

Brodzki, Bella. Afterword. *Allegra Maud Goldman*. New York: The Feminist Press, 1990. 175–87.

Cuseo, Allan A. *Homosexual Characters in YA Novels: A Literary Analysis, 1969–82*. Metuchen, NJ: Scarecrow Press, Inc., 1992.

D'Erasme, Stacey. Rev. of *A Place at the Table*. *Village Voice* 19 Sept. 1989: 55.

Jacobs, Barbara. Rev. of *Allegra Maud Goldman*. *Booklist*, 73 (1976): 526.

Levin, Martin. Rev. of *Allegra Maud Goldman*. *New York Times Book Review*, 19 Dec. 1976: 22.

Olsen, Tillie. Introduction. *Allegra Maud Goldman*. New York: The Feminist Press, 1990. ix–xi.

Shulman, Alix Kates. "A Me Grows in Brooklyn." Rev. of *Allegra Maud Goldman*. *Ms* 5 April 1977: 37.

Williamson, Barbara Fisher. Rev. of *A Place at the Table*. *New York Times Book Review* 4 June 1989: 22.

MAXINE KUMIN (1925–)

Deborah Lambert Brown

BIOGRAPHY

Maxine Kumin was born in Germantown in Philadelphia, in 1925, the fourth child and only daughter of Peter and Doll (Simon) Winokur. Her father was a pawnbroker; her mother, one of eleven children, had hoped to be a concert pianist. Kumin describes her childhood as one of "wondrous confusions": A Jewish child, she attended the convent school next door for three years, and nuns taught her "anxiety about [her] immortal soul" (*To Make a Prairie* 12). Kumin also records that she was aware of being a safe American teenager during World War II when her father's relatives were sent to gas chambers and concentration camps by Nazis; and that a German woman was her caretaker until she was seven or eight years old.

After graduating from high school in Elkins Park, Pennsylvania, she earned a B.A. in History and Literature at Radcliffe College in 1946 and an M.A. there two years later. She married Victor Kumin in 1946 and had three children.

When her youngest child entered kindergarten, Kumin began her teaching career with a part-time position at Tufts University. Since then she has taught on a short-term basis as a visiting fellow or poet-in-residence at many colleges and universities, among them the University of Massachusetts (1973), Columbia University (1975), Brandeis University (1975), Princeton University (1977, 1979, 1981–82), and Massachusetts Institute of Technology (1984). She also served as a member of the staff at the Bread Loaf Writer's Conference for six seasons.

At the age of eight Kumin wrote her first poem. Its subject was the death of a newborn pup. She continued writing poetry until she was discouraged by an instructor in college who wrote on a sheaf of poems, "Say it with flowers, but for God's sake, don't try to write poems" (*To Make a Prairie* 18). Although Kumin gave up writing for six years after that, she returned to poetry in 1956 when, unhappy as a housewife, she joined a workshop led by John Holmes at the Boston Center for Adult Education. Other members of the workshop were

Sam Albert, George Starbuck, and Anne Sexton. John Holmes became Kumin's "Christian academic Daddy," while Anne Sexton became her intimate friend and poetic ally. Living in the same Boston suburb, Kumin and Sexton installed second phone lines in their homes so that they could discuss drafts and revisions throughout the day. They also collaborated on four books for children. In a recent poem, one of a number Kumin has written grieving for Sexton's death in 1975, she refers to Sexton as the sister she never had ("October, Yellowstone Park").

Kumin moved to Warner, New Hampshire, in the 1970s, to a farm that had been the family's summer home. The farm rests on a wooded hillside at the end of a dirt road. The chores of her farm life—raising horses, tending her vegetable garden, collecting sap for maple syrup—are the raw material for some of her poems. However, she often steps out of her private farm life to give lectures, interviews, and poetry readings.

Kumin has received many awards, honors, and honorary degrees. These include the Lowell Mason Palmer Award, 1960; National Endowment for the Arts grant, 1966; National Council on the Arts and Humanities Fellow, 1967–68; William Marion Reedy Award, 1968; Eunice Tietjens Memorial Prize, Poetry, 1972; Pulitzer Prize for Poetry, 1973, for *Up Country*; Borestone Mountain Award, 1976; Radcliffe College Alumnae Recognition Award, 1978; an American Academy and Institute of Arts and Letters Award, 1980, for excellence in literature; and an Academy of American Poets Fellowship, 1986. Kumin was Consultant in Poetry to the Library of Congress in 1981–82 and was appointed Poet Laureate of the State of New Hampshire in 1989. She received the Sarah Josepha Hale Award in 1992. Her honorary degrees include doctorates of humane letters from Centre College, 1976; Davis and Elkins College, 1977; Regis College, 1979; New England College, 1982; Claremont Graduate School, 1983; and University of New Hampshire, 1984.

MAJOR THEMES

Maxine Kumin's writing stays close to her experiences. She writes of being a daughter and a granddaughter, a mother, a Jewish American woman, and a farmer on a hilly farm in New Hampshire. Her first volume, *Halfway* (1961), published when she was thirty-five, introduces characteristic themes and attitudes. The title poem tells us that she grew up in a house halfway up a hill and between a convent and a madhouse where she heard "plain song and bedlam" in the yard and could not distinguish priest from doctor or the kind nuns from the suffering insane. The poem's conclusion expresses a characteristic stance: Responsive to the nuns, she is nevertheless skeptical of judgments and classification, finding only partial truths in most of the world's wisdom. In "400 Meter Free Style," also from *Halfway,* the swimmer has "schooled out all extravagance," a description, too, of Kumin's poems, which are clear and controlled.

Beginning with this first book, Kumin has written a "history of loss" ("September 22nd"). In "Nightmare," she is unable to comfort her young daughter and suffers the separation that began with the "first cell that divided." The family, as well as the tenderness, loyalty, and loss we feel as members of families, has continued to be one of Kumin's primary themes. She affirms her connection to Rosenberg the tailor, her great-grandfather who settled in Virginia; through him, to her origins in Polish-Jewish Europe ("For My Great-Grandfather: "A Message Long Overdue""); and to her grandson as they play Monopoly in Chavannes and she realizes that his task will be "to usher us out" ("A Game of Monopoly in Chavannes").

Always highly conscious of her own obsessions, Kumin has dubbed as "tribal poems" those poems that define her web of connections; her tribe includes chosen friends and mentors as well as her family. In "Marianne, My Mother and Me," Kumin traces the differing experiences of her mother and the poet Marianne Moore, born in the same year, claiming them both as "shapers of [her] alphabet." Among Kumin's chosen, Anne Sexton is foremost. In many poems she mourns the loss of her close friend and collaborator. In "How It Is," she wears Sexton's jacket a month after her death and knows she "will be years gathering up [our] words." In "Splitting Wood at Six Above" the poet is angry, abandoned: "I'm still/talking to you. . . "

Many of Kumin's family poems express a longing for children who have grown up and moved away. In one of her frequently anthologized poems, "Making the Jam Without You," she mourns a daughter's absence while comforting herself with a fantasy of her daughter's romantic happiness, making bread and jam with a man she loves. Kumin's use of "jam" here is an example of her gift for using the domestic act or object as a resonant symbolic image. In "The Absent Ones," she grieves over her mother's preparation for dying and her children's growing independence, which leaves her alone to "braid up the absent ones like onions."

Another of Kumin's central themes is her vision of nature and the place of humans in the natural world. She celebrates the fecundity of nature, as the "strut of the season," which brings her "almost bliss" ("Strut"). She invites a moose into her backyard, addressing the animal familiarly as "my wild thing" ("My Elusive Guest"). And in "Going to Jerusalem," she praises horses for halting a battle. When crusaders' stallions encountered the Turks' Arabian mares, they created "chaotic bliss" on the Eastern front.

Kumin has a variety of tones at her command and frequently uses wit to make her points. "You Are in Bear Country," a "found" poem inspired by advice in a pamphlet published by the Canadian Minister of the Environment, presents assorted methods for dealing with the bear one may encounter on a hike. Kumin's concluding stanza invites us to "Come on in": death by bear is preferable to death by bomb.

Kumin's many animal poems (thirty-three in *Nurture* alone) do not reflect sentimental attachment to them or to her chosen role of caretaker. Her focus on animals tells us rather that she sees people and animals as living together, sharing the earth's resources, undergoing the same biological processes of mating, birthing, and dying while experiencing the same urgent desire to protect the young and satisfy individual hungers. In the "Amanda" poems, written to her mare, a "sensible strawberry roan," Amanda becomes an alter ego. In "Thinking of Death and Dogfood," Kumin compares their eventual fates: Amanda will go to Alpo or Gaines while she herself expects to become a "pint of potash" used to sweeten the soil. With a characteristically light touch, she makes the similarity of their fates as obvious as the absence of her hope for transcendence. Yet we are all part of "how it goes on" ("How It Goes On").

Kumin came to this central theme at least as early as *The Nightmare Factory* (1970). In "The Presence" in that volume, she acknowledges the place in nature of humans, one of many voracious groups. Like the raccoon, porcupine, and fox, the speaker of the poem also preys, takes, and uses; here, crossing a snowy field, she wears snowshoes woven from the sinews of creatures "that went before" her. "The Vealers" describes the way calves are separated from their mothers, penned so as not to develop muscle, then slaughtered after ten weeks and returned, wrapped in plastic, perfectly un-muscled flesh that "we will eat."

Her portraits of animals and humans have darkened with time. The suffering we inflict is beyond what is justified by our need for survival. Increasingly, she convicts us of cruelty to others, especially to animals, and of a heedless destruction of the environment. Rarely, she says in "Sunday in March," do we simply observe. In this poem she celebrates the rare moment of watching a bear with friends, the bear being one creature they "let be." More often now, her poems depict the ways we do not let creatures be. In "Thoughts on Saving the Manatee," "Repent," and "Homage to Binsey Poplars," all from *Nurture* (1989), she deplores the ways humans abuse the planet, making the lives of other species intolerable or impossible.

Her vision is fundamentally tragic. Nature, and the human life that is part of it, is a "catchment of sorrows," doomed by time and mortality, abetted by human evil and stupidity ("Catchment"). But Kumin is not primarily a doomsayer. She writes as a survivor, a caretaker, a spokeswoman. At times she stands in awe of the persistence of individuals, including her own ability to withstand losses and to go on. In "Distance," she mourns aging and the androgyny that comes with age and that foreshadows death. Nevertheless, Kumin's vision is predominantly maternal, saving, committed to preservation.

One critic, she says in the opening poem of *Nurture,* has complained that she has an "overabundance of maternal genes." She acknowledges the rightness of his remark, having already made the point that the need to save both people and animals comes from the same source and is seamless.

In her latest volume, *Looking for Luck* (1992), Kumin brings the themes of her earlier work to their fullest expression. Her tone is assured, even stern with conviction. In the introductory poem "Credo," she claims to believe in magic, but she defines magic naturalistically, as a gift for seeing that our lives are connected to the lives of animals and to the earth itself. The language of "Credo" is religious and expresses a sacramental relation to mundane activity. "Progress" celebrates survival and the victory that can be won through endurance. The theme is elaborated through the piling up of diverse examples of persistence: Bunyan's pilgrim, ants, a doomed Indian horse, and a kind of fish, the Hiroshima carp; and, finally, the Japanese people, to whom Hiroshima means this fish and a baseball team, not just death. In "Hay," a six-page poem from *Looking for Luck* (1992), she surveys an "all but obsolete small scene above the river." Hired men cut timothy and brome on her farm; an ancient baler shapes four-foot cubes that are hoisted, fifty-two per load, onto an old truck that takes them to the barn. Watching the haying and later, "trundling hay in her own barn," Kumin remembers an idyllic summer as a child when she boarded at a dairy farm. She learned to milk and to love her "black and white ladies." The barn was "radiant with sun-dried manna," it was a "paradise with dusty sun motes toes" where she felt an "ancient hunger in [her] throat." The poem is an ecstatic elegy to a childhood moment and to one part of a vanishing way of life; most of all, it is an exploration of her own deep "allegiance to the land," an allegiance that continues to enrich her poetry.

In addition to her ten volumes of poetry, Kumin has published four novels, a collection of short stories, twenty-two children's books, and two collections of essays and interviews. Her fiction explores family relationships, especially the lives of women in their roles as daughter, mother, wife, and friend. Her fiction tends to develop the themes of her poetry in unexpected ways. In *The Passions of Uxport,* one character obsessively collects and buries the dead animals he finds along the roadside. In *The Abduction,* a woman who works for an educational program for ghetto children comes to love a black child and then kidnaps him. Kumin's essays and interviews offer insights into her views on the theory and practice of writing poetry, as well as moments of autobiography and richly-specific accounts of farm life.

SURVEY OF CRITICISM

Maxine Kumin's work has now been published for more than thirty years, and in that time, critics have been increasingly impressed by the skill, range, and depth of her poetry. According to many, she began as a good poet who, against the odds, has grown and developed. From the beginning, critics appreciated her clear, precise descriptions. Of her early poems John Ciardi wrote: "She teaches me, by example to use my own eyes. When she looks at something I have seen, she makes me see it better. When she looks at something I do not know, I therefore trust her." Joyce Carol Oates described *Up Country,* Kumin's Pulitzer Prize-winning volume, as "dramatic and visionary, but above all convincing," while reviewer Ralph Mills notes feeling steeped in the "actualities of soil, pond, trees, beans, local topography. . . ." Other critics have consistently admired her ear for patterned sounds; her ability to use traditional forms such as the sonnet in contemporary ways; her control over strong emotions; and, most of all, her consistent high intelligence.

The flaws that critics have observed concern aspects of her use of language and, occasionally, her tone. Some have said that her use of language is utilitarian rather than exciting or experimental. Dona Gioia, for example, misses a "joy in language for its own sake" (225).

These criticisms have diminished over the years. Kumin's work has deepened in tone and has become richer and freer in language as experience has changed her. One of the pleasures of reading Kumin, for some critics, has been seeing the evolution of her work. Fellow poet Philip Booth has observed that Kumin has "outrun the limitations of her generation" by "trusting those elements of [her] work which are most strongly individual," among them the ability to combine a "Frostian delight in metaphor with Marianne Moore's insistence on being a "literalist of the imagination" (18). Reviewer Julie Stone Peters believes that Kumin's encounters with "Time and Death" have "allowed her to see beyond a world redeemed by the regenerative powers of nature into a world darkened by the unyielding passage of time. . . " (223).

Recent feminist critics have offered another perspective on Kumin's work. By writers such as Alicia Ostriker, she is described as an apostle of a gynocentric, nurturing ethic and her poems viewed as the embodiment of women's values. According to Ostriker, Kumin's poetry reveals a "reimagining of the sacred" (197). Kumin has separated spirituality from traditional theology and embedded it in the body. Reversing the traditional assumption of our separation from nature, Kumin depicts our biological lives as connecting us to the living world beyond the human. Kumin's humor, incomprehensible to some readers, Ostriker interprets as a "comedic confirmation of earthliness." Currently, Maxine Kumin's work is receiving serious attention and appreciation as the ethic of caring for animals and the environment, as well as for our own tribes, becomes more widely respected.

BIBLIOGRAPHY

Works by Maxine Kumin

Poetry

Halfway. New York: Holt, Rinehart, and Winston, 1961.
The Privilege. New York: Harper & Row, 1965.
The Nightmare Factory. New York: Harper & Row, 1970.
Up Country: Poems of New England, with Drawings by Barbara Swan. New York: Harper & Row, 1972.
House, Bridge, Fountain, Gate. New York: Viking Press, 1975.
The Retrieval System. New York: Viking Press, 1978.
Our Ground Time Here Will Be Brief: New and Selected Poems. New York: Viking Press, 1982.

Closing the Ring: Selected Poems. Lewisburg, PA: The Press of Appletree Alley, Bucknell University, 1984.
The Long Approach. New York: Viking Press, 1985.
Nurture: Poems. New York: Viking Press, 1989.
Looking for Luck: Poems. New York: Norton, 1992.

Novels

Through Dooms of Love. New York: Harper & Row, 1965.
The Passions of Uxport. New York: Harper & Row, 1968.
The Abduction. New York: Harper & Row, 1971.
The Designated Heir. New York: Viking Press, 1974.

Juvenile

Sebastian and the Dragon. New York: Putnam, 1960.
Spring Things. New York: Putnam, 1961.
A Summer Story. New York: Putnam, 1961.
Follow the Fall. New York: Putnam, 1961.
A Winter Friend. New York: Putnam, 1961.
Mittens in May. New York: Putnam, 1962.
No One Writes a Letter to the Snail. New York: Putnam, 1962.
(With Anne Sexton). *Eggs of Things*. New York: Putnam, 1963.
Archibald the Traveling Poodle. New York: Putnam, 1963.
(With Sexton). *More Eggs of Things*. New York: Putnam, 1964.
Speedy Digs Downside Up. New York: Putnam, 1964.
The Beach Before Breakfast. New York: Putnam, 1964.
Paul Bunyan. New York: Putnam, 1966.
Faraway Farm. New York: Putnam, 1967.
The Wonderful Babies of 1809 and Other Years. New York: Putnam, 1968.
When Grandmother Was Young. New York: Putnam, 1969.
When Mother Was Young. New York: Putnam, 1970.
When Great-Grandmother Was Young. New York: Putnam, 1971.
(With Sexton). *Joey and the Birthday Present*. New York: McGraw- Hill, 1971.
(With Sexton). *The Wizard's Tears*. New York: McGraw-Hill, 1975.
What Color Is Caesar? New York: McGraw-Hill, 1978.
The Microscope. New York: Harper & Row, 1984.

Short Stories

Why Can't We Live Together Like Civilized Human Beings. New York: Viking Press, 1982.

Essays

To Make a Prairie: Essays on Poets, Poetry, and Country Living. Ann Arbor: University of Michigan Press, 1979.
In Deep: Country Essays. New York: Viking Press, 1987.

Works about Maxine Kumin

Booth, Philip, "Maxine Kumin's Survival." *The American Poetry Review* (Nov.-Dec. 1978): 18–19.

Gioia, Dana, Rev. of *Our Ground Time Here Will Be Brief. The Hudson Review* 35.4 (Winter, 1982–83): 652–53.

Gordon, David. J. "Some Recent Novels: Styles of Martyrdom." *The Yale Review* (October, 1968): 112–26.

Harris, Peter, "Poetry Chronicle" *The Virginia Quarterly Review* 67 (Summer, 1991): 454–77.

Mills, Ralph J. Jr., "Poetry in Review." *Parnassus,* (Spring-Summer 1972): 222–23.

Oates, Joyce Carol. Rev. of *Up Country: Poems of New England. New York Times Book Review* (Nov. 1972): sec. 7:7.

Ostriker, Alicia. *Stealing the Language,* Beacon Press, 1986.

Peter, Julie Stone, "Sprinting Toward the Finish Line," *Village Voice* 37.29 (20 July 1982): 39.

EMMA LAZARUS (1849–1887)

Diane Lichtenstein

BIOGRAPHY

Emma Lazarus was born into a wealthy American Jewish family on July 22, 1849. Her mother, Esther Nathan, was of German Jewish descent, and her father, Moses, of Sephardic descent. Emma grew up with three older sisters, two younger sisters, and one younger brother. Educated by private tutors, she studied mythology, music, American poetry, European literature, as well as German, French, and Italian. Moses Lazarus, a successful sugar merchant, provided his family with material comforts in their New York and Newport, Rhode Island, homes. He supported his daughter's writing financially as well as emotionally; in 1866, when Emma was only seventeen, he had *Poems and Translations Written Between the Ages of Fourteen and Sixteen* printed ''for private circulation'' (Emma dedicated the volume ''To My Father'').

Between the appearance of this volume and her death at thirty-eight on November 19, 1887, Lazarus cultivated a conscious identity as a writer. More than any other American Jewish woman of the nineteenth century, she established her own literary credentials in the world of American letters. She was able to accomplish this in part because of her economic and social privilege: She never had to work, to marry, or to take responsibility for family members. She could and did dedicate herself fully to her writing.

Early in her career, Lazarus turned to Ralph Waldo Emerson as a mentor. The two probably met soon after the appearance of her *Poems and Translations* (1866); Lazarus visited the Emersons in Concord in 1876; they continued corresponding until Emerson's death in 1882. During the early years of their relationship, Lazarus sought and received Emerson's approval. Later, after he omitted her work from his anthology of poetry, *Parnassus* (1874), she viewed him less idealistically. Lazarus also corresponded with several other influential American writers and thinkers of the time, including John Burroughs, E. Clarence Stedman, Thomas Wentworth Higginson, John Hay, and William James.

Lazarus spent most of her life in New York. She did, however, make two trips to Europe. During the first of these, May to September 1883, she met Robert Browning and William Morris as well as British Jewish leaders. In May of 1885 she began a two-year journey that took her to Holland, Italy, England, and France. She returned to New York in September 1887, just two months before she died.

During the productive period of the mid-1870s to the mid-1880s, Lazarus published extensively. The most notable works from this period include *Alide: An Episode in Goethe's Life* (novel), *The Spagnoletto* (drama), "The Eleventh Hour" (story), *Poems and Ballads of Heinrich Heine* (translations), "American Literature" (essay), *Songs of a Semite* (poems), "By the Waters of Babylon," a group of "little poems in prose," "The New Colossus" (for the Statue of Liberty's pedestal fund), an essay on Heinrich Heine, and a sonnet on the occasion of Emerson's death.

Lazarus's Jewish identity has been the subject of debate, primarily because of the apparent sudden interest she began to show in that identity in the early 1880s. Before that period, she perceived herself as "loyal" to her "race" but "somewhat apart from [her] people" (Schappes, *Letters* 21), despite the fact that her family belonged to the Sephardic Shearith Israel Synagogue in New York and that she wrote at least one poem early in her career on a Jewish topic ("In the Jewish Synagogue at Newport," 1867). Some biographers suggest that it was the Russian *pogroms* which motivated Lazarus to write more openly about Jewish issues, to publish more frequently in Jewish periodicals such as *The American Hebrew,* to work with Eastern European Jewish immigrants at Ward's Island, and to help establish Jewish agricultural communities as well as the Hebrew Technical Institute.

MAJOR THEMES

Lazarus wrote poems on a wide variety of topics such as nature ("Long Island Sound," "A June Night," "Niagara"), "epochs" (including "Youth," "Grief," and "Work"), and contemporary issues ("Poverty and Progress" and "Sunrise"—an elegy for James Garfield). She also translated poems, not only by Heinrich Heine, but also by Victor Hugo, Petrarch, and a number of Medieval Spanish and Portuguese Jews, including Solomon Ben Judah Gabirol and Abul Hassan Judah Ben Ha-Levi. The subjects of her essays range from notable people such as Heinrich Heine and Ralph Waldo Emerson to "A Day in Surrey with William Morris" and to Jewish issues. The topics she returned to most often in her poetry, essays, and fiction include Jewish identity, America, womanhood, and art.

Jewish Identity

Although Lazarus was always conscious of herself as a Jew, the early 1880s marked her growing commitment to a public Jewish identity. Three essays in

Century, a mainstream American magazine, demonstrate that growth. In the first of these essays, "Was the Earl of Beaconsfield a Representative Jew?" (April 1882), Lazarus offered an equivocal portrait of Benjamin Disraeli; "representative," she claimed, meant embodying the best as well as the worst of Jewish traits. The two essays that followed were less apologetic. In "Russian Christianity vs. Modern Judaism" (May 1882), Lazarus included a personal plea for an accurate understanding of Russian Jews and their situation. And in "The Jewish Problem" (February 1883), she openly observed that Jews who are always in the minority "seem fated to excite the antagonism of their fellow-countrymen" (602). She also offered a solution: the founding of a state in Palestine for Jews by Jews. Because of proposals such as this, as well as similar proposals in "An Epistle to the Hebrews" and in several of her poems, Lazarus is credited with being an early Zionist.

In those "Epistles," a series of fifteen "letters" that appeared in *The American Hebrew* between November 1882 and February 1883, she not only suggested that Eastern European Jews settle in Palestine, but she also reminded assimilated Jews of their privileged status as well as their vulnerability in America. Throughout the series, Lazarus emphasized the need for Jews to understand their history in order not to be misled by anti-Semitic generalizations. Written in the early 1880s, these "Epistles" reveal Lazarus in the process of convincing herself as well as her readers of the need for open Jewish self-identification and solidarity.

Lazarus's growing confidence in her Jewish identity is evident in *Songs of a Semite,* a volume of poetry published by *The American Hebrew* in 1882. The title of the volume and the publisher were both public proclamations that Lazarus wanted to be identified as a Jewish poet. Many of the poems in the collection reveal Lazarus in the role of warrior, prepared to use her pen in the battle against anti-Semitic non-Jews and complacent Jews. In "The Banner of the Jew," for example, she called upon "Israel" to "recall" the "glorious Maccabean rage," and she reminded readers that "With Moses' law and David's lyre" Israel would remain strong.

America

For this self-conscious writer, the meaning of "American" was often perceived through a literary lens. In an early poem, "How Long!" (*Admetus*), for example, Lazarus expressed frustration with America, particularly because of its insecurity about its literature; it is time, she wrote, for America to protect itself against British "songs" that cannot accurately or honestly express America's uniqueness. In a similar vein, she used her 1881 essay "American Literature" (*The Critic*) to defend American literature against the charge that America had no literary tradition and that America's poets had left no mark.

Lazarus also explored her American identity via an American Jewish path. A self-identified American writer on the one hand, and an increasingly outspoken

Jew on the other, Lazarus could not ignore either national identity: She had to cultivate each to its fullest. Particularly in the 1880s, Lazarus spoke in a voice that established her as an American, as well as a Jewish, writer. "The New Colossus" (1883), Lazarus's best-known contribution to American literature and culture, exemplifies this integration through its implicit metamorphosis of "homeless...wretched refuse" into American citizens who bring new vitality to their adopted nation. Lazarus's contributions to *Century* magazine also demonstrate a method by which Lazarus synthesized her American and Jewish identities. "Was the Earl of Beaconsfield a Representative Jew?" appeared in April 1882, "Russian Christianity vs. Modern Judaism" in May, and "Emerson's Personality," a eulogy for the dean of American letters, appeared in July. To regular readers of the magazine, Lazarus would have been known as an essayist concerned with Jewish issues as well as American literature.

Womanhood

Lazarus exhibited very little conflict about stepping onto the "public stage" of authorship. In fact, she knew with surprising certainty that she deserved recognition as an American author. At the same time, she understood that, because she was a woman, she would encounter obstacles in pursuing a literary career, as her sonnet "Echoes" acknowledges: "Late-born and woman-souled I dare not hope,/ The freshness of the elder lays, the might/ Of manly, modern passion shall alight/ Upon my Muse's lips." The speaker of the poem, who recognizes that she is at a disadvantage because she cannot share with men the common literary subject of wars' "dangers, wounds, and triumphs," turns her own experiences into assets, valorizing the female poet's "elf music" and "echoes." Through this speaker, Lazarus implied that women artists must compromise in order to be heard at all. Lazarus again expressed frustration with limited expectations and privileges in another sonnet, entitled "Sympathy." Unlike "Echoes," however, "Sympathy" describes personal rather than literary limitations.

Art

Lazarus's two works of fiction, *Alide: An Episode in Goethe's Life* (1874) and "The Eleventh Hour" (*Scribner's* 1878), articulate the author's views on art. *Alide,* based on Goethe's own autobiographical writings that chronicle a love affair between the young writer and a country woman Fredericka Brion (Alide Duroc in the novel), reaches its bittersweet climax when the lovers part; both presumably understand and accept that Fredericka is not Goethe's spiritual or intellectual equal. Lazarus developed Goethe as a "great" man whose "simplest action [is] fresh and original" and who "shed[s] a peculiar glory upon whatever claims [his] regard" (153). In this portrait, Goethe is the "great" artist who had the right and ability to break earthly bonds in order to find the fulfillment of his artistic capacities.

"The Eleventh Hour" traces the alienation and bewilderment of a young Romanian artist, Sergius Azoff, who has left his European home to experience American liberty. Sergius is disappointed not only by the seeming sham of American freedom, but also by the state of art in this young nation. Another character in the story explains, " 'America is a country where art and beauty must and will thrive, though in the present transition-period of upheaval and reconstruction, it is impossible to discern what forms they will assume' " (256). Through a passage such as this one, Lazarus urged American artists to be patient, and, more subtly but more importantly, to cultivate America's unique artistic expression.

SURVEY OF CRITICISM

Throughout her publishing life, Lazarus received consistently positive, if not unqualified, accolades. By the last decade of her life—the late 1870s and 1880s—she was known to other American writers and to the American reading public, as the frequency with which her name appears in widely read magazines such as *Lippincott's* and *Century* suggests. The praise her poetry received also implies acceptance by the American literary world. The following lines from *Lippincott's* 1871 review of *Admetus* exemplify this praise: "There is very much to commend and very little to condemn" in the volume. The poems "exhibit careful study, intelligent and conscientious labor, vigor of thought and diction, and a superiority to all the artifices by which popularity is sought and sometimes gained." Even the criticism is tempered: The author will gain more poetic power when "emotions and sympathies deeper and stronger than the contemplation of heroic ideals can awaken shall give ardor and inspiration to her verse" (527).

Lazarus's work also garnered praise from European writers, including Ivan Turgenev who, in 1874, wrote that *Alide* "is very sincere and very poetical at the same time." He also told Lazarus that "an author, who writes as you do— is not a 'pupil in art' any more; he is not far from being a master himself" (letter, 2 September 1874, in Rusk 17).

Such rhetoric was not atypical during Lazarus's life. And even after her death, the woman and the work continued to elicit favorable "reviews," as is evident in *The American Hebrew's* December 9, 1887, "Emma Lazarus Memorial Number." John Hay, for example, noted that Lazarus's death "is not only a deep affliction to those of her own race and kindred; it is an irreparable loss to American literature . . . her place is already secure among our best writers. . . " (70). The prominent philanthropist Cyrus L. Sulzberger expressed the common Jewish sentiment in the "Memorial Number": "no words of praise can be too great for one who . . . voluntarily returns to the old household, publicly proclaiming herself one of its members, and bringing to it . . . the pen of a prophet to arouse the moral sense of Jew and Gentile. It was an act of heroism on the part of Emma Lazarus, performed at a cost she alone could know—thus to put herself at the head of a cause which was so unpopular in the general world'' (79).

Not all American Jews were happy with Lazarus's ''cause,'' particularly in its Zionist form. Abram S. Isaacs, for example, the influential editor of *The Jewish Messenger,* claimed in a public response to Lazarus's ''The Jewish Problem,'' ''It is unwise to advocate a separate nationality for the Jews at a time when anti-Semites are creating the impression that Jews can never be patriots, but are only Palestinians, Semites, Orientals'' (156).

Despite the attention Lazarus received during her life, she did not find a permanent place in readers' minds. Indeed, only twenty-five years after her death, Warwick James Price described Emma Lazarus, Emily Dickinson, and Amy Levy as ''Three Forgotten Poetesses'' who had all achieved real and noteworthy work but who each left ''a large possibility unfulfilled'' (*The Forum* 376). Since the 1940s, scholars have studied Lazarus's relationships with contemporary authors, her divided loyalties to America and Judaism, the origins and genesis of her Jewish identity, and, most recently, her gendered sensibilities and experiences. In 1986, the year of the Statue of Liberty's centennial celebration, Lazarus received attention as the author of ''The New Colossus.'' Although Lazarus does not appear as regularly in anthologies as does Walt Whitman or Emily Dickinson, she has earned a respected place in American literary history in part because of her contribution to the ideology which the Statue of Liberty represents, but also because of her unique voice which, in its blending of Jewish and American strains, speaks creatively to that ideology.

BIBLIOGRAPHY

Works by Emma Lazarus

Poems and Translations

Poems and Translations. Written Between the Ages of Fourteen and Sixteen. New York: H. O. Houghton, 1866.

Admetus and Other Poems. New York: Hurd and Houghton, 1871.

Poems and Ballads of Heinrich Heine. New York: R. Worthington, 1881.

Songs of a Semite: The Dance to Death and Other Poems. New York: The American Hebrew, 1882.

Untitled poem for the opening of the Concord School of Philosophy on July 23, 1884, included in ''Emerson and the Concord School.'' *The Critic* OS 5, no. 31 (1884): 55.

Poems of Emma Lazarus, I and II. Boston: Houghton Mifflin, 1889.

Emma Lazarus: Selections from her Poetry and Prose. Ed. Morris Schappes. New York: Cooperative Book League, Jewish-American Section, International Workers Order, 1944.

Manuscript notebook of poems at American Jewish Historical Society, Waltham, MA.

Fiction

Alide: An Episode in Goethe's Life. Philadelphia: J. B. Lippincott, 1874.
"The Eleventh Hour." *Scribner's* 16 (1878): 242–56.

Essays and Letters

"American Literature." *The Critic* OS 1, no. 12 (1881): 164.
"Henry Wadsworth Longfellow." *American Hebrew* 11 (1882): 98–99.
"Was the Earl of Beaconsfield a Representative Jew?" *Century* 23 (1882): 939–42.
"Russian Christianity vs. Modern Judaism." *Century* 24 (1882): 48–56.
"Emerson's Personality." *Century* 24 (1882): 454–66.
"The Jewish Problem." *Century* 25 (1883): 602–11.
"The Poet Heine." *Century* 29 (1884): 210–17.
"A Day in Surrey with William Morris." *Century* 32 (1886): 388–97.
An Epistle to the Hebrews. New York: Federation of American Zionists, 1900.
Letters of Emma Lazarus. Ed. Morris Schappes. New York: New York Public Library,
    1949.

Works about Emma Lazarus

Rev. of *Admetus and Other Poems*. *Lippincott's* 8 (1871): 526–27.
Rev. of *Alide: An Episode in Goethe's Life*. *Lippincott's* 13 (1874): 774–75.
American Hebrew, "Memorial Number" (9 December 1887).
Angoff, Charles, *Emma Lazarus: Poet, Jewish Activist, Pioneer Activist*. New York:
    Jewish Historical Society of New York, 1979.
"A Problematic Champion." *Jewish Messenger* (26 January 1883): 4.
Baym, Max. "A Neglected Translator of Italian Poetry: Emma Lazarus." *Italica* 21
    (1945): 175–85.
———. "Emma Lazarus and Emerson." *Publications of the American Jewish Historical
    Society* 38 (1948–49): 261–87.
Catalogue of the Pedestal Fund Art Loan Exhibition at the National Academy of Design.
    1 December 1883.
Cohen, Mary. "Emma Lazarus: Woman; Poet; Patriot." *Poet-lore* 5 (1893): 320–31.
Cohen, Rachel. "Emma Lazarus." *Reform Advocate*, (24 September 1927): 184–89.
Cowan, Philip. "Emma Lazarus." *Autobiographies of American Jews*. Philadelphia: Jew-
    ish Publication Society of America (1965): 26–37.
Eulogy. *The Critic*, n.s. 8 (1887): 293–95.
Frank, Murray. "Emma Lazarus: Symbol of Liberty." *Chicago Jewish Forum* (1948):
    251–56.
Harap, Louis. *The Image of the Jew in American Literature*. Philadelphia: Jewish Pub-
    lication Society of America, 1974.
Hurwitz, Samuel J. "Emma Lazarus." *Notable American Women*. Cambridge: Belknap
    Press of Harvard University Press, 1971.
Isaacs, Abram S. "Will the Jews Return to Palestine?" *Century* 26 (1883): 156–57.
Jacob, H. E. *The World of Emma Lazarus*. New York: Schocken, 1949.
Kramer, Aaron. "The Link Between Heinrich Heine and Emma Lazarus." *Publications
    of American Jewish Historical Society* 45 (1955–56): 248–57.

Lazarus, Josephine. "Emma Lazarus." *Century* 36 (1888): 875–84. (Unsigned.)

Lichtenstein, Diane. "Words and Worlds: Emma Lazarus's Conflicting Citizenships." *Tulsa Studies in Women and Literature* 6 (1987): 247–63.

———. *Writing Their Nations: The Tradition of Nineteenth-Century American Jewish Women Writers*. Bloomington: Indiana University Press, 1992.

Lyons, Joseph. "In Two Divided Streams." *Midstream* 7 (1961): 78–85.

Merriam, Eve. *Emma Lazarus: Woman with a Torch*. New York: Citadel Press, 1956.

Monteiro, George. "Heine in America: The Efforts of Emma Lazarus and John Hay." *Turn-of-the-Century Women* 2 (1985): 51–55.

Mordell, Albert. "The One Hundredth Birthday of Emma Lazarus." *Jewish Book Annual* 7 (1948–49): 79–88.

———. "Some Final Words on Emma Lazarus." *Publications of the American Jewish Historical Society* 39 (1949–50): 321–27.

———. "Some Neglected Phases of Emma Lazarus' Genius." *Jewish Forum* 32 (1949): 181–82, 187.

Pauli, Hertha. "The Statue of Liberty Finds Its Poet." *Commentary* 1 (1945): 56–64.

Price, James Warwick. "Three Forgotten Poetesses." *The Forum* 47 (1912): 361–76.

Ruchames, Louis. "New Light on the Religious Development of Emma Lazarus." *Publications of the American Jewish Historical Society* 42 (1952–53): 83–88.

Rusk, Ralph L. *Letters to Emma Lazarus in the Columbia University Library*. New York: Columbia University Press, 1939.

Rev. of *Songs of a Semite. Century*, n.s. 3 (1883): 471–72.

Sulzberger, Cyrus L. "Emma Lazarus as a Jew." *American Hebrew* 33 (1887): 79.

Vogel, Dan. *Emma Lazarus*. Boston: Twayne, 1980.

Zeiger, Arthur. "Emma Lazarus: A Critical Study." Diss. New York University, 1951.

RHODA LERMAN (1936–   )

Claire R. Satlof

BIOGRAPHY

Rhoda Lerman, née Sniderman, was born in Far Rockaway, New York, January 18, 1936, one of a pair of twin sisters. She spent her childhood there and in New Britain, Connecticut, until the age of thirteen, when, after her father's death, the family moved to Miami, Florida. Lerman studied geology at the University of Miami until her advisor told her she would not be able to accompany male students (or the male advisor) on field trips. After graduating with a degree in English, she married Robert Lerman, a Naval officer, and traveled abroad with him for several years, as his career demanded. The Lermans eventually settled near Syracuse, New York. They have three children. Lerman currently has four Newfoundlands that she shows and breeds.

Lerman's attachment to Judaism and the Jewish community reflects equally her awareness of her marginal status in the community because of her gender and her conviction that the Jew must be spiritually attached to God. Raised in an observant family, although with a formal Jewish education limited to Sunday School, Lerman recalls, " 'I won a writing contest about why I was a Jew, but I never really had a sense that I belonged in Judaism because I was a girl. It was clear early on that there was no equality; that there was no place for my soul' " (Chayat 5). As an adult, her experiences were similar. In a speech she helped her nephew write for his Bar Mitzvah, she wrote, " 'Judaism is a chain between father and son, linked by woman.' When the rabbi crossed out 'linked by woman,' that was it. I'd had it'' (Brzowsky 42).

Even with these feelings of exile from organized religion, Lerman has always considered herself a spiritual person, deeply interested in religion. She explains, " 'I've always led a mystical life. There's a constant awareness in my day that every act is both profane and sacred' " (Chayat 8). However, modern Judaism could not produce a religious home for yet a second reason: " 'No one was talking about illumination and transcendence' " (Chayat 5). Then, about eight years ago, Lerman met a Chassidic rabbi who moved her to a formal study of Judaism and whose own family history prompted her to write *God's Ear*.

Since then, she has studied not only with this rabbi, a well-known and universally respected man she prefers not to name in print, but also with Rabbi Meir Fund and a student of Professor Joseph Dan, professor of Kabbalah at Hebrew University (Brzowsky 42). Nonetheless, Lerman is not certain how Jewish women can reconcile their Jewish spiritual needs with their gender. Judaism that has not been made Protestant/American is only available through Orthodoxy, she claims, yet the strictures there are so confining and have such terrible costs for women that we are forced back into modern Judaism "where there is no soul" (Interview with author, 25 June 1991). However, she has not given up on the possibility of transforming modern Judaism—or Orthodoxy—as the endings of her explicitly Jewish books confirm. Both her life and her fiction emphasize that changed perceptions lead to changed lives. After all her experiences, she still confidently says, " 'Ultimately, I am as deeply Jewish as a person can be' " (Brzowsky 42).

Lerman has taught at various universities, including the University of Colorado at Boulder and Syracuse University (where she taught writing and parapsychology). She was an NEA Distinguished Professor of English at Hartwick College and held the Edward H. Butler Chair in English literature at SUNY Buffalo. In addition, she has written several screenplays, including *Soul of Iron* and *First Lady of the World,* both produced by Norman Lear and starring Jean Stapleton. As a member of Lindisfarne (the scientific and religion consortium), she has participated in a number of conferences on topics such as planetary culture and conscious evolution. Lerman is also a founding member of Val-Kill, Inc., the foundation responsible for preserving Eleanor Roosevelt's home; and she was formerly the manager of a rock band.

MAJOR THEMES

Lerman's novels are on widely disparate subjects. She has written an almost-ignored novel about the reincarnation of the goddess Ishtar in the body of a suburban Jewish housewife, a best-seller on the pitfalls of finding the right husband, a fictional autobiography of Eleanor Roosevelt, a *sui generis* volume about a woman who transforms herself into a cow, and a lovingly rendered portrait of a reluctant Chassidic rabbi who must learn to circumcise his heart by confronting the spiritual condition of Jewish women. In these works, Lerman covers issues of religion, sex, language, identity, and power, but all her books focus on the possibility of transcendence. In varying contexts, Lerman considers those boundaries and dichotomies established by religious and/or secular tradition and explores the potential for transforming them into a vision of organic unity. While that vision may exist only on the level of narrative, Lerman firmly believes in the power of the word correctly used to create new realities.

Call Me Ishtar offers the most explicit account of the problems that result from traditional Jewish divisions of male and female, with their firmly, if artificially, designated realms of sacred and profane, spiritual and physical. In a wildly imaginative account of the goddess Ishtar's return, Lerman restores the source of ritual and textual power to women, who can heal the rifts imposed by male authority and so end the exclusion of Jewish women from any real religious or social power. In a prologue that self-consciously merges the conventionally discrete categories of sacred and secular text, the goddess/narrator explains her mission:

> What am I doing here? It is very simple. Your world is a mess . . . If your philosophers insist the world is a dichotomy tell them that two plus two don't make four unless something brings them together. The connection has been lost. But I'm back. Don't worry . . . I am one and my name is one and there shall be no one before me. (xi–xii)

Ishtar is a particularly appropriate figure to use since her domain was cast as domestic. Goddess of fertility and eros, she hardly qualified for Jewish patriarchal spiritually, since these traits epitomize the profane physical world. However, a second prologue goes on to expand the "ordinary" role of housewife into a clearly prophetic one. Echoing and recontextualizing Zechariah (and Jeremiah before him), Lerman writes,

> And she spread it before me and it was written within and without this roll of a book. A roll of a book was therein, and there was written lamentations, mourning and woe.
> "Moreover," she said unto me, "Son of Man, eat that thou findest; eat this roll and go speak unto the House of Israel."
> So I opened my mouth and she caused me to eat that roll. And she said unto me, "Son of Man, cause thy belly to eat. Fill thy bowels with this roll that I give thee."
> Then I did eat it; and it was in my mouth as honey for sweetness.

Not only is this book a domestic "product," it is a sexual one as well since all language is erotic when properly understood: " 'Cunt . . . is from the Sumerian cunnus and means burden . . . All cookies,' she went on patiently into the night, 'are cognate, as are bread, bagels, and language' " (36).

With the recognition that we have misunderstood secular language comes the realization that we have misunderstood ritual as well. In one of the novel's most provocative scenes, Lerman emphasizes a constant theme—Judaism's need to acknowledge its debt to feminine power. As Ishtar appears at a Bar Mitzvah to sexually initiate the young man, she catalogues the true source of Jewish ritual trappings such as the Torah cover, *tephillin,* and *tallit* in a female-oriented pre-Biblical/mythic sexuality, not in male-oriented Jewish law. The ceremony over, she instructs the initiate, " 'Go now and read the Torah to your people. Someday, for your sons, there will be new laws' " (205), and these will end the exile of the feminine.

God's Ear, Lerman's most recent book, acts as a companion to *Ishtar,* continuing related themes on a more mellow note. Here, Lerman makes even clearer that a secure and authentic Jewish future can only be the result of a new vision of the Jewish world that hears the feminine voice and recognizes and includes the feminine nature. Lerman does *not* simply want women to be included in the male ritual world; she wants men *and* women to acknowledge the root presence of the female in a previously unacceptable way. To the end, she uses a man as her central figure and voice in *God's Ear*. Also, in contrast to *Ishtar, God's Ear* provides a loving view of traditional Judaism with all its essential flaws. The flaws, however, become her theme.

While *Ishtar* retells and recasts Bible stories, *God's Ear* plays more conventionally with the role of language and text as it tells the story of Yussel Fetner, descendant of generations of saintly rabbis, who refuses to circumcise his heart and cleave to God. Instead, Yussel happily sells life insurance until his father dies and finds he will be allowed into heaven only if Yussel agrees to fulfill his destiny. To do so, however, requires that Yussel feel the pain of others, see others as fully human, and accept the task of ministering to their needs. Accomplishing this task, even with the help of the dead rabbi's stories, parables, and lectures, is formidable since it involves removing the obstructions (hence, "circumcising") from his eyes, ears, and heart—and forfeiting a very large income.

Lerman's answer to the familiar love of material objects characterizing Yussel's present life is not a simple return to traditional Jewish spiritual values, as her intriguing use of "uncircumcised heart" suggests. While the term is a biblical one (see, for example, Ezekial 44:1,9; Jeremiah 6:10; or Jeremiah 9:25), the post-Freudian reader senses sexual echoes that correctly lead to the book's religious innovation. To see "the angel behind every blade of grass" whispering, " 'Grow, darling, grow' " (280), as his father did, Yussel must forge a new text, with his saintly father's encouragement, that depends on first seeing the feminine as intrinsically Jewish and intrinsically powerful.

As a youth, Yussel had refused to marry a woman his own size because, he later realizes, he had felt he could not control her. Her "big healthy generous" good looks (18) intimidated him, recalling the traditional male aversion to the physicality of the menstruating, arousing, child-bearing female nature. As a mature adult still unable to face female sexuality—and, by extension, his own—Yussel sends the "succulent" Flower Child, his father's second wife, out of his house after his father's death. This act inadvertently sets in motion the events that cause her death. When Yussel meets Lillywhite, though, a woman he lusts for overwhelmingly, his father insists in a vision that she is "intentional" from God, to help him find his way. Completely obsessed with her, Yussel sees her as an emblem of Judaism even as he tries to deny the recognition. "She had the pale white skin redheads have, with little blue veins, hot blue eyes. Yussel thought of the Shabbas candle burning, the white shoulders of the candles, the blue flame, the hot blue center of her eyes, the flaming face of Sabbath" (152).

Working through his feelings, again with the help of a thousand-year-old dynastic voice behind him, Yussel finally comes to see that feminine power and sexuality have always pervaded Judaism, despite male denial and exclusion:

It's a man's religion, isn't it? We're supposed to love Hashem [God] the way we love a woman . . . the Shabbas [Sabbath] Bride. Why does a new Torah get married under the chupa [canopy]? Because the Torah is a woman . . . You take off her dress, you take off her jewels, you spread her legs, you read her, you know her . . .

Women can't read Torah. They can't welcome the Sabbath Bride, they can't be part of a *minyan* . . . they can't say Kaddish for their parents. They can't carry the Torah at Simhas Torah . . .

What are Jewish women supposed to do? Make a religion out of housework and raising kids? (218)

Eventually, as Yussel transcends his former uncircumcised heart, his resulting view of Judaism transcends the circumcised one embodied in traditional texts. Early on, Rabbi Fetner says, " 'I was once so dumb. I thought because I knew all the letters, I understood the alphabet' " (157–58). At book's end, he explains that he now realizes the Torah contains but one word, " 'The name of God . . . the blueprint for creation. But until men give it sound, it means nothing . . . it waits like yeast, someone should come along and give it a new shape . . . The shapes from our past . . . maybe they don't fit into our time" (291–92). Acknowledging his father's words, Yussel teaches Lillywhite first the Hebrew alphabet, then the Kaddish (traditionally forbidden to women), so she can recite it for her father. As she does so, "The universe held its breath" (306) and the figures of the storied past rise up to embrace him. " 'I think it's time to make up some new stories,' " Lillywhite—and Lerman—concludes (309).

The books written between *Ishtar* and *God's Ear* are not explicitly on Jewish topics, but they display the same playfulness with boundaries and explore similar issues of perception, identity, and power. *The Girl That He Marries,* Lerman's second book, was written to make money (and it did) but even in a comic potboiler, she strikes a serious note. Stephanie, intent on making herself over into the girl Richard (a "nice" Jewish boy) will marry, sees the quest as a mythic reenactment. Contemplating a famous tapestry in the Cloisters, Stephanie sees Richard as the Unicorn who is programmed to lay his head in the lap of a virgin. If he is programmed, Stephanie reasons, perhaps she is too, and she tries to consider her refashionings as discovery of her own "programming." The end result is a woman unidentifiable to herself who forfeits all of her sexual being—and her vision of the phallic Unicorn—before realizing that she has forfeited even more by trying to become the girl Richard wants to see. "Trade off the worship of God for the worship of man and what do you get? You get a jug-eared neurotic, a fake, an illusion, a cheat. Tell Plato his stupid cave's empty. Because now, now, I have nothing to believe in' " (213).

Eleanor, a fictional autobiography of Eleanor Roosevelt, covers the years from 1918, when Eleanor discovers FDR's affair with Lucy Mercer, to the summer of 1921, when he contracts polio. During these three years, she begins to discover the need for her own voice, and, in fact, the book is most notable for its vividly rendered self-discovery motif. The central metaphor is the alchemical change of lead, which Henry Adams tells Eleanor is "her" metal, to silver. Misunderstanding him at first, Eleanor hears only continued depression (and repression) in the words, " 'Yes, you are lead . . . metallic seeds, then planted by the planets in you to become precious metals' " (30). Consequently, she sees herself weighted down by familial duty and the belief "that a woman can only be happy by being useful to others" (290). Happiness for oneself, self-gratification, are to be avoided, as is seen when FDR discovers Eleanor has tied three-year-old Anna's hands to keep her from masturbating. She says, " 'No one in my family has been happy unless they were insane' " (40). Gradually, as she lets herself become involved in causes she cares about, she shapes a life of her own, finally finding the strength to say, in response to praise for producing beautiful children, " 'I am not beautiful yet and I have not been brought into the world yet. I haven't made myself yet and I don't want to die unmade' " (266–67). At book's end, when FDR has become "heavy as lead" from the polio, Eleanor, ironically, is freed. Adams's prophecy is about to be realized, that, " 'After great forest fires . . . the silver runs from the blackened forest . . . in shining streams' " (30). His condition for this prediction has begun to come about as we, with our historical hindsight, can see: " 'You'll change history, little lady, only if you can change yourself' " (31).

The Book of the Night, a generic anomaly, attempts total synthesis of sexuality and spirituality, religion and science, history and eternity, animal and human. The story is of a young girl raised near a monastic community built in the twelfth and twentieth centuries. Her father initiates her into all mysteries except sexual ones. Disguised as a boy when she reaches puberty, Celeste must face her feminine sexual nature when she and the new Abbot have sexual relations and fall in love. To avoid permanent exile and/or death at the hands of the monks, who are afraid of all sexual power, Celeste transforms herself into a white, cow, and most of the book centers around the nature and significance of her transformation. The striking language games in the novel point to Lerman's thesis of organicism:

"Zeus, Deus, juice, Jews, Yid, Druid, druse, Methuselah, Medea, Madua, Medusa, Madonna," I recited.

"Do you hear . . . in the roots? Listen. The root is the Hebrew 'why,' *Medusa*. Why, a God's name. Why. That is the question. . . "

"Gaballa, Kabbalah, Kadush, Cabosh, Caboose," I recited. (29)

The "why" becomes intermingled with the search for "how," as Celeste learns to follow her father's instructions ["You must make your own lists" (32)] in her attempt to change back into human form. As Celeste is attacked, she hears her dead father's voice, " 'Sing, Celeste, one note!' " (285) and, striking that note, she realizes she can "Invent the future" (284) through sheer force of will.

SURVEY OF CRITICISM

While Lerman's novels have been favorably reviewed and have sold well, the critical response is strikingly limited. As early as 1975, *The Jewish Woman in America,* one of the pioneering volumes on Jewish feminism, had identified *Ishtar* as being on the cutting edge of Jewish feminist fiction. Baum, Hyman, and Michel distinguish it from such books as Gail Parent's *Sheila Levine Is Dead and Living in New York* and Alix Kate Shulman's *Memoirs of an Ex-Prom Queen.* They characterize these books as light-hearted rebellion against the Jewish Princess syndrome or Sue Kaufman's *Diary of a Mad Housewife* and Anne Roiphe's *Up the Sandbox,* which, again, serve as early protests, but "in which oppression is recognized but neither confronted directly nor transcended" (258). In contrast, they present *Call Me Ishtar* as a "recognizably Jewish attempt to reinvent and reinvigorate a *sui generis* female culture. . . . " (258). In addition, when it was first published, *Ishtar* was reviewed in the *New York Times Book Review,* which called the "anti-Mosaic mosaic" a real "find" (Rosenstein 46), and in *Ms.,* which titled the review "A Magnificent Possession" (Dickstein 37). Despite these reviews and a popular reception that prompted a second hardcover publication with a second publisher, the book seems almost an underground classic. The Jung Society, at its request, held the reception for the novel's second publication, and an early article on the development of Jewish feminist fiction as an identifiable canon used *Ishtar* as a proof text (Satlof 186–206), but the book has otherwise been almost ignored in print.

There are two possible reasons: (1) feminism and religion do not go together in some minds and (2) the book is threatening because it invokes real feminine power. The resulting readings reveal how these two issues have often determined the critical view. For example, while the *Times* reviewer clearly liked the book, she minimizes its importance by reassuring us that "it cannot be called feminist fiction. First and least importantly because Earth Mothers, however powerful, are hardly what the age demands. . . . And because the attitudes toward sexuality here are contradictory in the extreme . . . " (46). If the *Times* review does not see sexual power, the *Ms.* review refuses to acknowledge spiritual power and concludes that behind the book's fun and games is the "sad knowledge that women have no real power" (37). The one male writing on the book claims that American women in the 1970s are not sufficiently oppressed to be the stuff of great literature. Writing in *Partisan Review,* Thomas R. Edwards explains, "Virginia Woolf once remarked that 'when a woman speaks to women she should have something very unpleasant up her sleeve.'. . . Rhoda Lerman finally doesn't . . . " (472).

The Girl That He Marries, an intentionally more accessible work, met with the same unmixed praise as other witty New York Jewish social satires. With advance praise from much-publicized writers Gloria Steinem and Susan Brownmiller, the book was compared to *Fear of Flying* and praised for "outstripping Philip Roth in his own milieu" (Nelson 10). In addition to detailed discussions of "at what price women entrap their men" (Abeel 35) or the importance of Stephanie's final realization that "I'd prefer the Big O" to an engagement ring and a charge account at Bloomingdale's, reviewers also note the message of feminine solidarity in the implicit attack on women's poor treatment of women (O'Reilly 111; Abeel 35). Lerman's evolving comic prose style is also singled out: "Like her characters, Lerman's language plays games," notes Abeel in the *Voice* (35), while Nelson proclaims in the *Times* that "author Rhoda Lerman here 'hulls [Alexander Portnoy] from the belly button like an overripe strawberry' to prove that writing well is the best revenge" (10).

Eleanor was Lerman's first book to receive serious, widespread recognition, partly because of Lerman's access to Eleanor's friends and family members (the book was written at the urging of Eleanor's grandson Curtis), and partly because of its integration of fact and fiction in a hybrid genre that was under much examination at the time of publication. In general, the response to the novel has been extremely positive, and its popular reception led to its publication as a Book-of-the-Month Club featured selection. Overall critical response can be characterized by two reviewers' summations of the book as "a meticulously researched, beautifully written novel that brings Eleanor Roosevelt to life" (Wood 1) and as a "narrative that captures its subject with discretion, compassion, and honesty" (Wickenden 46). Much of the praise centers on the author's writing: "Eleanor's struggle are admirable because Lerman does such a good job of inventing them. . . . The *our de force* is . . . in the strength of Rhoda Lerman's imagining, her careful integration of research and reportage into a fictional document" (Mernit 8).

The most interesting discussions, however, center around the connection between fiction and history. Several critics recall that "history in its first sense is narrative" (Taliaferro 98) and point out the interconnections between genres: "Fiction illuminates character; biography shapes history into some coherent path" (Mernit 8). However, E. L. Doctorow, in a *New York Times* article on *Eleanor* and other "mixed" genre books, most closely suggests the underlying source of Lerman's fascination with generic synthesis and boundary issues in *Eleanor*: "In an age that celebrates facts, the writer who begins to break down the line between fact and fiction represents the authority and perception of the individual mind" (Kakutani 28).

The fictionality of the text, the use of a created first-person narrator, and the self-scrutinizing stream of consciousness presenting the woman rather than the myth disturb other critics. *The West Coast Review of Books* reviewer "finds little to justify the book," since its "prose is stilted and formal, and the entire account is written in first person" (D.H.R. 23). Similarly, a reviewer for the English *Ham and High* complains that the novel "isn't one thing or the other" (Tucker 59). More pointedly, she writes that *Eleanor* is "shot" with "self-indulgent women's libbish writing about pregnancy and childbearing which probably reflects author, not subject" (59).

The criticism of *The Book of the Night* reflects the novel's ambitious goals.

The *New York Times* review classifies it as a "collage of *Yentl, The Empire Strikes Back, Dr. Doolittle,* and the *Gnostic Gospels*" (Miner 27), for example, which provides an idea of its range. Diane Bauerle's evaluation of the novel best characterizes its critical reception: Lerman's "eccentric and sometimes fascinating tapestry" and her "impressive" scholarship sometimes "overwhelm her story. . . . While in the end I found the whole to be intriguing, I was still missing many answers" (Bauerle 17). Science fiction fans have been the most sympathetic readers. (The paperback edition was published in Great Britain by the Women's Press in its science fiction series.) For example, *The Book of the Night* is a featured work in an essay on feminist science fiction whose author notes that Celeste is one of the few *women* characters to attempt any kind of transcendental understanding through metamorphosis (Tuttle 97–108).

God's Ear is the book that has finally brought Lerman recognition in the Jewish world. Reviewed widely in the secular press (from the *New York Times* to the *Los Angeles Times* to the *Annsiton* (AL) *Star*), the book was also reviewed by major and more specialized Jewish publications. Named a Book of the Year by the Jewish Book Council and nominated for Hadassah's Ribalow Prize, the novel is part of the Jewish Theological Seminary's small fiction collection. The *New York Times* review begins by promoting Lerman to the ranks "of generations of Jewish fabulists—Stanley Elkin, Cynthia Ozick, Bernard Malamud, Sholem Aleichem, Isaac Babel . . ." (Singer 6). Most reviews include substantial quotations to convey the language and tone. "Hers is a unique voice—wildly funny, achingly spiritual, profoundly Jewish and feminist at the same time," concludes the *Times* review (6). Even the few reviews that find flaws in the narrative generally find much to praise, although the *Christian Science Monitor* reviewer, labelling the novel "overlong, overbearing, and overdetermined," complains of "humor" about the Holocaust in several of the book's parables (Rubin 13). A few reviewers wonder if readers must be Jewish to appreciate the book. The review in the *West Coast Review of Books* begins with the statement that the novel is "of obvious limited appeal" and concludes that it is, "in the end, quite irrelevant" to the general public (27). This question seems answered by a clearly non-Jewish reviewer's appreciation of and praise for the novel in the Madras, India *Express*: While noting that its "profoundly" Jewish idiom may pose difficulties for some readers, the reviewer continues, "But Rhoda Lerman is a writer of compelling talent who steers away from obscurities, making the narrative readable. She can be wildly funny and solemn too" (Joseph 11).

What is most consistent and notable about the critical response is that critics treat the novel's goals seriously and with respect. The *Chicago Tribune* review (widely syndicated) calls it "a hymn of praise to God authored by a woman" concluding that "we need to grow holier in each generation" (Grossman 3). Sanford Pinsker finds a "religious epiphany" at the end ("kvetching"); and the *Washington Times* reviewer designates Lerman as "the next great American

Jewish writer'' for a generation of readers who are serious about their Jewishness (Fenyvesi 8). Lerman's current status in the Jewish American literary realm
is formally classified by Pinsker in the 1991 *Jewish Book Annual,* a volume that
puts a communal stamp of approval on books of Jewish interest. Using Lerman
as one of three examples, Pinsker argues against Irving Howe's claim that there
is not enough identifiably Jewish in American culture to continue the tradition
of authentic American Jewish writing. In so doing, Pinsker firmly establishes
Rhoda Lerman as a member of the canon of Jewish American literature that
holds onto the past while imagining the future (6–20).

BIBLIOGRAPHY

Works by Rhoda Lerman

Call Me Ishtar. 1973. Republished, New York: Holt, Rinehart, and Winston 1977.
The Girl That He Marries. New York: Holt, Rinehart, and Winston, 1976.
Eleanor: A Novel New York: Holt, Rinehart, and Winston, 1979.
The Book of the Night. 1984. London: The Woman's Press Ltd.—Namara Group,
    1986.
God's Ear. New York: Holt, Rinehart, and Winston, 1989.
Interview with author, 25 June 1991.

Works about Rhoda Lerman

In addition, I am grateful to Alexandra Eyle for access to her unpublished interview
    with Rhoda Lerman.
Abeel, Erica. ''Laughing, Sort of, All the Way.'' Rev. of *The Girl That He Marries. The
    Village Voice* 19 July 1976: 35.
Bauerle, Diane K. ''An Eccentric, Sometimes Fascinating and Obscure Tapestry.'' Rev.
    of *The Book of the Night. Fantasy Review* 8.1:17.
Baum, Charlotte, Paula Hyman, and Sonya Michel. *The Jewish Woman in America* 1975.
    NY: Plume-New American Library, 1977.
Blank, Barbara Trainin. Rev. of *God's Ear. Na'amat Woman* May–June 1989: 20.
Bloom, Kathryn Ruth. ''God, Lost and Found.'' Rev. of *God's Ear. Hadassah Magazine*
    June–July 1989: 36–37.
Brzowsky, Sara. ''The Price of Freedom.'' Rev. of *God's Ear. The Jewish Week, Inc.*
    (NY) 26 May 1989: 42.
Chayat, Sherry. ''Mining Judaism's Rich Lode of Spirituality.'' Rev. of *God's Ear. The
    Jewish Observer* (Syracuse) 25 Jan. 1990: 5ff.
D.H.R. Rev. of *Eleanor: A Novel. The West Coast Review of Books* May 1979: 23.
Dickstein, Lore. ''A Magnificent Possession.'' Rev. of *God's Ear. Ms.* Jan. 1974: 37–
    38.
Eder, Richard. ''Rabbi Redux: An Unorthodox Tale.'' Rev. of *God's Ear. The Los An-
    geles Times Book Review* 30 Apr. 1989: 3.
Edwards, Thomas R. ''Women Beware Women.'' Rev. of *Call Me Ishtar,* by Rhoda

Lerman; *Small Changes,* by Marge Piercy; and *Advancing Paul Newman,* by Eleanor Bergstein. *Partisan Review* Sept. 1974: 469–76.

Evans, Nancy. Rev. of *Eleanor: A Novel. Glamour* Apr. 1979: 94ff.

Fenyvesi, Charles. "Buoyant Jewish Yarn Recounts Southwest Exodus." Rev. of *God's Ear.* The *Washington Times* 10 Apr. 1989, Sec. E: 8.

Grossman, Ron. "A Rabbinical Romp Ample in Hilarity." Rev. of *God's Ear.* The *Chicago Tribune* 26 Apr. 1989, Sec. 5: 3.

Grumbach, Doris. "Four Compelling Novels about the Lives of the Young." *The Chronicle of Higher Education* 16 Apr. 1979: R12–R13.

Jacobs, Naomi. "Raising the Dead: Fiction Biographies." *The Character of Truth.* Ed. Naomi Jacobs. Cross Currents: Modern Criticism Ser. 3. Carbondale: Southern Illinois University Press, 1990.

Joseph, Jailboy. "Deliver Us Son from Gehenna, Amen!"' Rev. of *God's Ear. Madras Express* (India) 27 Nov. 1989: 11.

Kakutani, Michiko. "Do Fact and Fiction Mix?" The *New York Times Book Review* 27 Jan. 1980: 3ff.

Maloff, Saul. "History Used and Abused." Rev. of *Eleanor: A Novel.* The *New York Times Book Review* 27 Jan. 1980: 3ff.

Mernit, Susan. Rev. of *Eleanor: A Novel.* The *American Book Review* Feb. 1980: 8ff.

Miner, Valerie. Rev. of *The Book of the Night.* The *New York Times Book Review* 28 Oct. 1984: 27.

Nelson, Alix. Rev. of *The Girl That He Marries.* The *New York Times Book Review* 8 Aug. 1976: 10–11.

O'Reilly, Jane. "Always Believe the Woman Ahead of You." Rev. of *The Girl That He Marries. Ms.* Aug. 1976: 111.

Pinsker, Sanford. "Kvetching on the Way to the Promised Land." Rev. of *God's Ear. Philadelphia Inquirer* 16 Apr. 1989, Sec. J: 4.

———. "New Voices and the Contemporary Jewish-American Novel." *Jewish Book Annual.* Ed. Jacob Kabakoff. NY: Jewish Book Council, 1991. 6–20.

Rev. of *God's Ear.* Rhoda Lerman. *West Coast Review of Books* June 1989: 27.

Rosenstein, Harriet. "Supernatural Housewife, Sexual Subversive." Rev. of *Call Me Ishtar. New York Times Book Review* 25 Nov. 1973: 46.

Rubin, Merle. "Good Novels Need More Than a Clever Idea." Rev. of *God's Ear. Christian Science Monitor* 17 July 1989: 13.

Satlof, Claire R. "History, Fiction, and the Tradition: Creating a Jewish Feminist Poetic." *On Being a Jewish Feminist: A Reader.* Ed. Susannah Heschel. NY: Schocken Books, 1983. 186–207.

Schneider, Susan Weidman. Rev. of *God's Ear. Lilith* 14. 3: 8.

Shapiro, Susan. "Static on a Direct Line to God." Rev. of *God's Ear. Newsday* 30 Apr. 1989: 22.

Singer, Brett. "The Calling of Yussel Fetner." Rev. of *God's Ear. New York Times Book Review;* 2 July 1989: 6.

Taliaferro, Frances. "History Enhanced." Rev. of *Eleanor: A Novel. Harper's* June 1979: 94ff.

Tucker, Eve. Rev. of *God's Ear. Ham and High* 28 Mar. 1980: 59.

Tuttle, Lisa. "Pets and Monsters: Metamorphoses in Recent Science Fiction." *Where No Man Has Gone Before: Women and Science Fiction.* Ed. Lucie Armitt. London: Routledge, 1991. 97–108.

Wickenden, Dorothy. Rev. of *Eleanor: A Novel. New Republic* 4 August 1979: 46.

Wood, Susan. "Portrait of a President Lady." Rev. of *Eleanor: A Novel. Washington Post Book World* 3 June 1979: 1 ff.

KAREN MALPEDE (1945–   )

Cindy Rosenthal

BIOGRAPHY

Karen Malpede was born in Witchita Falls, Texas, on June 29, 1945. The timing of her birth became significant for Malpede, because it was synchronous with the dropping of the atom bombs on Japan and the ending of World War II in Europe. Pacifism, and especially women's connection with this movement, has been a driving force throughout Malpede's life and work.[1]

Her sense of herself as a "displaced" Jewish woman originated during her girlhood in Chicago, where her family moved six months after her birth. Raised as an assimilated, secular Jew in a predominantly Presbyterian suburb, Malpede's experience of "not fitting in" was intensified by the conflict between her parents' families. Her mother, Doris Jane Liebschutz, came from an upper-middle-class Jewish family that opposed the class difference more than the religious difference between Doris and her husband. Karen's father, Joseph Malpede, came from a working-class Italian Catholic family that was vehemently anti-Semitic. Malpede and her twin brother, John, felt pressure to pass as non-Jews among their neighbors. Malpede, small and dark like her father's side of the family, usually had a more difficult time with this than did her tall, fair-haired twin. However, Malpede recalls that when her brother's friends realized he was Jewish, they stopped speaking to him.

When Malpede's mother was pregnant with Karen and John, she dreamt she was going to give birth to a poet. Malpede reports (with a chuckle) that her mother envisioned her son, John, in the poet role. [John Malpede is currently a performance artist in Los Angeles, known for his provocative work with homeless people.] Malpede's mother's casting of her male child as the poet may have been in response to her husband's fierce opposition to her own creative endeavors as an actress and radio performer. Joseph Malpede could not reconcile her theatrical activities with his image of the proper Italian wife.

Despite her mother's dream of a poet son, Karen Malpede always knew she wanted to be a writer. She came to write plays via "a circuitous route." On the way to playwriting, she envisioned herself first as a novelist, then as a journalist. Malpede explains that the shift to journalism was not sparked by desire but because when she reached high-school age, she had a diminishing sense of self, an experience she shares with many women of her generation who had few female role models to follow. With the example of her unfulfilled mother before her, and because of the dearth of literary female figures in high school and college curriculums of the day, journalism seemed an infinitely safer, more manageable option. Witnessing her father's wrath toward his wife because of her work, Malpede steered away from theatre as a girl. Yet, their mother's interests clearly had an impact on both Malpede children, as did their father's passionate nature, fiery temper, and his love of Italian operatic music.

As an undergraduate at the University of Wisconsin, Malpede met Jewish students from New York and, for the first time, found a community of kindred spirits with whom she felt at home. During her years in Madison (1963–67) she attended her first antiwar protest; as an English major and a drama minor, she frequently wrote reviews for the college "free press." Her father died when she was a sophomore. The difficulty of this time for Malpede was intensified by her unresolved feelings toward her father, an emotional tearing apart and coming together conveyed in her first play, *A Lament for Three Women* (1974), and in her 1987 work, *Us*.

Malpede's encounter with Irish literature during her undergraduate years, and particularly with the work of Yeats and Lady Gregory, the first woman playwright she studied, had a great impact on her. She was enamored of the "notion of the Abbey Theatre, as a social/political/poetic force" that employed myth and had the power to "create a community, create poetry and . . . have an effect on the culture of [one's] time."

In the graduate program in theatre criticism at Columbia University (1969–71), Malpede garnered a reputation for being a "political thinker . . . a radical." Her thesis on the Theatre Union, an important left-wing theatre of the 1930s, became her first published work, *People's Theatre in Amerika* (1972).

When Malpede wrote her first play, *A Lament for Three Women,* she was in "a very positive space," supported by Joe Chaikin as a member of the select group of critics and theatre artists Chaikin had invited to participate in a workshop, following the dissolution of the Open Theatre. A summer production of *Lament* introduced her work to Ned Ryerson, who became the major private patron of the New Cycle Theatre in Brooklyn (1976–80), which Malpede cofounded with producer/director, Burl Hash. Malpede's and Hash's daughter, Carrie Sophia, was born in 1980.

At the New Cycle Theatre, Malpede was interested in achieving the nexus of political/poetic activism that she had found so inspiring in the work of the Abbey Theatre. She also sought the relative privacy of working in a theatre outside of Manhattan and the control that having her own theatre afforded her. She readily admits that the knowledge of how one builds a career as a playwright was not "part of [her] vocabulary. It still isn't really." Remarkably, New Cycle existed as a free theatre; hence, it had a diverse, atypical audience consisting of neighborhood families, activists, and artists. Even more unusual for a small theatre of its kind, New Cycle paid its actors.

Concurrent with her residency as playwright/producer at New Cycle, Malpede regularly met with an extraordinary group of women writers and artists that was called the Woman's Salon. Uncommon women such as Dorothy Dinnerstein, Grace Paley, Irene Fornes, Adrienne Rich, and Kate Millet convened at Erika Duncan's Westbeth apartment for readings organized by Malpede and two other women. Dinnerstein and others, like Judith Malina, producer/director/actor with the Living Theatre, were Malpede's close friends and feminist role models. According to Malpede, "a number of us began to take ourselves seriously." It was in this setting that Malpede premiered her second play, *Rebeccah.*

In 1983, Malpede published a popular, esteemed feminist anthology: *Women in Theatre: Compassion and Hope.* The volume was motivated by the dearth of material on and by women who had made significant contributions to the theatre, specifically to what Malpede describes as the feminist aesthetic of "compassion and hope." Drawing on her widespread knowledge of theatre history, Malpede selected lesser-known texts by women theatre artists whose work spans the centuries as well as the countries of the world. Malpede's political thrust throughout this volume is also clear—the sense of "hope" these women foster with their work is vital for survival in a world Malpede sees spinning toward nuclear disaster.

In the anthology's acknowledgments, Malpede declares her special interest in reaching an audience of young theatre students. In addition to her work as a dramatist, Malpede has developed an ongoing relationship with college students, as guest lecturer at Smith College (1983–87), and as adjunct (1987–90) and assistant professor of theatre (1991 to the present) at New York University.

Malpede's most recent work, *Blue Heaven,* opened September 17, 1992, at Theatre for the New City in Manhattan. *Blue Heaven* concerns the response of an American performance artist and her urban community to the brutality of the Persian Gulf War.

MAJOR THEMES

"Feminism released me to write plays," declares Malpede, for whom feminism was a natural extension/expansion of her long-time involvement in the peace movement. "If one was to pursue non-violence, the next logical place to pursue it was in gender issues." Malpede explains, "The feminist movement was a totally transformative experience . . . the sense that my story mattered, that I had a story that could be read in a universal way."

Malpede's first play, *A Lament for Three Women,* is about the death of her father. It deals with three women mourning the death of a man, the death of a culture, the onslaught of the plague (cancer or AIDS, says Malpede). The trio of female voices in the hospital waiting room (they belong to women with Old

Testament names: Naomi, Ruth, and Rachel) brings forth a metaphoric birth of feminism. The incantations of three women together, evoking the mystical/life-changing power of the witches in *Macbeth,* is a pattern repeated later in *The End of War,* Malpede's play about revolutionary Russia. *Lament* resonates as a Jewish play for Malpede in the choice of character names and in the powerful presence of the old woman in the play, a Jew, who mourns and finally transcends the death of her son, the central figure in her life.

Jewish characters frequently take center stage in Malpede's work. Her second play, *Rebeccah,* is the tragic tale of a Jewish woman's journey. Forced to suffocate her infant son during a pogrom in Eastern Europe, Rebeccah then immigrates to America and loses her only daughter in the Triangle Shirtwaist Factory fire in New York City. Finally, quite mad, she becomes one of the city's lost souls, a homeless woman, a gatherer of found objects. Ultimately, she founds a shanty town, a community for the homeless.

The homeless or displaced woman is a recurring image for Malpede, evocative of her own place as woman playwright in what remains a very male world. Malpede's sense of herself as a "pagan Jew," an outsider in the Jewish community, is another aspect of her "otherness." As a writer, she feels the language she writes in is not her own. The tone of what she does is much more Mediterranean—Malpede describes this as "hotter"—than American.

Malpede's choice has been to create plays that are intensely political, as well as poetic. Her language and imagery challenge her audiences with the startling combination of visual, rhythmic lushness layered with gritty sequences of physical and sexual violence. One example of Malpede's unique style is a monologue in scene six of *The End of War* delivered by a woman who describes the brutal rape and murder of her young daughter. This scene and others in Malpede's plays are especially provocative because of the collision of visceral imagery and poetic language. These kinds of disturbing dichotomies separate Malpede's *ouevre* from mainstream commercial theatre.

Malpede herself acknowledges the rift between her work and the contemporary avant garde, although she believes her work shares many of the values of avant garde theatre. A significant difference between Malpede and auteurs like Robert Wilson, Richard Foreman, and Elizabeth LeCompte is Malpede's interest in character and character development. Contrary to the current wave of postmodern performance theory, which explodes the notion of a unified self, Malpede says she is "very interested in the individual person and how she/he relates to other individuals." Relationships between men and women, women and women, and the struggle/journey of humans toward personally/politically responsible action is at the heart of most of Malpede's texts, beginning with the three women in *Lament,* and most recently in Malpede's characters Aria, Herbie, and Dee in *Blue Heaven.* For Malpede, a "movement toward wholeness in character" signifies "the movement toward a healthier community." At the center of her work, the symbol of this healthy community is frequently a circle of women, supporting, working, living together, creating/evolving a new way of being in the world.

Following the Brechtian concept of "making new," Malpede seeks to create "a new dramatic action." She explains, "I try not to kill characters off . . . I want to do it another way—without the death of Pentheus, the death of Hamlet." In her introduction to *Women in Theatre,* Malpede describes the dynamic "pull together, toward intimacy" as being as potent as the patriarchal "drive toward dominance" (13). "Battle," she writes, "is not the essential life-experience; birth, death, rebirth, and nurture are" (12).

One of her most successful plays, *Sappho and Aphrodite* (two productions in New York, 1983–84; one in Cleveland, 1989; one in London, 1987) is an excellent example of Malpede's feminist strategies in action. Based on the poetry of the sixth-century Greek poet, Malpede's play is populated only by women, whose lives intertwine in Sappho's school/community. In Malpede's view of Sappho's world, women sing, dance, and freely show their feelings for one another; ritual reawakens creativity and strengthens the bonds between them.

"When we did *Sappho and Aphrodite* I used the word 'vulva' in the text: 'the vulva-like waves of the sea.' A man came running back afterwards and grabbed the actress who had said vulva and said: 'you can't say that word on stage. That's not writing.' It really had never occurred to me that one couldn't say the word vulva on stage." The maternal figure of Sappho in Malpede's play was problematic for some, because, according to Malpede, "people wanted to see an image of Sappho that was perfect. But Lois Weaver [the director] and I weren't interested in perfect—we were interested in the Sappho that changes and grows." Malpede adds, "I don't set out with the intention to deeply disturb people."

Us, an exploration of child abuse and incest, also juxtaposes pregnancy, birth, and maternity with images of graphic violence. Malpede's intention was to provide the audience with "a kind of raw, confessional, autobiographical experience." The play's family violence provoked negative response from some critics and spectators. Malpede remarks, "Male playwrights are respected for making people uncomfortable. Women are not. And of course we make people feel uncomfortable in a different way." She explains, "*Us* came out of the same moment as performance art. I'm always trying to see what will revitalize the theatre—what will make the theatre work again. I feel every play of mine reinvents the theatre, trying to get it to work, trying to get it to matter." She feels her next play, *Better People* (1990), is an extension of this project—a collision of "scientific language and dream language." She recalls, "I wanted to give a lot of information and it became funny because the material is so horrific." Billed as "the first play on the controversial subject of genetic engineering," *Better People* is another amazonian effort on Malpede's part to tackle explosive material in a lively, fantastical/poetical fashion.

The mother/artist in *Blue Heaven,* Aria, is another of Malpede's women who "belongs nowhere." Like Malpede, she was born of a mixed marriage. Aria is half-Israeli, half-Palestinian, an incarnation of the Middle East conflict Malpede is deeply concerned about: "I can identify in a great part with the displacement of the Palestinians," says Malpede. Aria, like Sappho and other Malpede female figures, is caught in the good mother/bad mother bind. Malpede claims that a society so concerned with "family values" sees only a good mother or a bad mother—nothing in between. Malpede believes Aria is a good mother, even though she must leave her child for a time in order to make a documentary film in Iraq.

Malpede's purpose in writing *Blue Heaven* was "to capture the moment." She asserts, "I don't want to forget it. It's interesting because everyone else wants to forget it." Malpede is referring to the United States participation in and response to the Persian Gulf War. Originally titled *Going to Iraq,* Malpede changed the title to *Blue Heaven* just before going into rehearsal for the September 1992 production. She explains,

Going to Iraq is about a question of empathy. What was so shocking to me about the war and what I was trying in my own small way to counter with the play is that empathy seemed to be absolutely forbidden. We were not supposed to feel anything for the people we were killing—nothing. And my feeling is if you can't have empathy for others then you also can't have compassion for yourself. That in a sense, is what Aria learns when the play ends. . . . This is very Jewish—and Mediterranean. The more that one's feelings come out and can be expressed, the more real chance there is for communication, love of community, caring for the world, valuing of human life.

Achieving a global community committed to human survival through empathy, intimacy, and nonviolence, and invoking "memories of mothering" that invite her audience to join in the "dance of life" (*Women in Theatre,* 12–13) are the missions of playwright/activist Karen Malpede.

SURVEY OF CRITICISM

Karen Malpede is a self-acknowledged "bad girl of the American theatre." She admits, "I actually pay very little attention to the critics which doesn't mean I don't suffer because of them. I suffer a lot. Plenty. Enough. . . . My ability to get grants and to fund my work has been really hurt by the critical reception of it."

A survey of the criticism of her produced plays is very mixed and, at times, contradictory. Malpede's combination of the political, personal, and the poetical has been perceived as a disturbing, even a perverse, union by some critics. Though many find fault with her use of poetic language, the lushness and lyricism of her writing also earn Malpede the most praise. Compare these views of *Sappho and Aphrodite:* Jan Stuart complains: "Problems develop in the realization of Malpede's language strategy. She has attempted to weave Sappho's verses through dialogue of her own devising, which is compatible with Sappho's lyric style rather than mimetic. This tangle of ancient poetry and quasi-archaic language is fraught with thorns'' (55). Barbara Krasnoff felt differently: "semipoetic dialogue, in unskilled hands, easily becomes stale and ridiculous. In this case, however, the prose only reinforces an impression of having entered a somewhat different, more mystical universe'' (13). *Sappho* is Malpede's most critically acclaimed play. Dance critic Jennifer Dunning wrote: "Miss Malpede has created a fluid and sophisticated weave of drama, movement and music that incorporates the poetry as ingeniously as it makes use of the small-scaled stage space in the Wonderhorse Theatre'' (62).

Writing about *The End of War,* Rosette Lamont calls Malpede "the creator of an oneiric, mythic theater where 'people speak as if in dreams.' . . . The language she brings to the stage is strong and resonant . . . Nor does she fear tackling large subjects, painting frescoes; for she interweaves history, politics, folk culture, myth, and religion'' (5).

Critics have found fault with the ideological center of Malpede's plays. Her writing was labeled didactic and she was strongly criticized for oversimplifying feminist concerns in *Rebeccah* (Munk and Marranca); Malpede was also accused of confusing or losing her audience by overcomplicating her language (Patterson 12) and her imagery (Dace, Wetzsteon). By contrast, the visual and physical aspects of her productions are usually singled out with high praise (Dace, Massa, Haye).

Us and *Better People* stimulated energetic debates in the press. Most critics responded negatively to Malpede's language in *Us* (Goodman, Dace, Hart, Wetzsteon). For example, Dace comments, "*Us* is written . . . in a poetic, or heightened prose, which is risky, sometimes ineffective, lyricism or rage, but often also ludicrous, prompting audience titters just when we're supposed to be moved'' (22). Critics found Malpede's gender reversals in the first two scenes to be difficult to follow: "In attempting to convey ambiguity and paradox, Malpede too often falls into confusion and contradiction . . . using cross-dressing not to extend gender traits to their essences but to reduce them to their caricatures'' (Wetzsteon 87). Wetzsteon and Dace found Malpede's characters to be an awkward melding of individuals and archetypes; they also found the situations cliché.

Critics Kris Oser and Sharon Mazer declared *Better People* to be intellectually challenging. Oser called it "shocking, funny, tight and richly original . . . a dazzling offspring that has caught the attention of scientists as well as theater goers'' (6). Robert Massa disagreed with Malpede's antigenetic engineering argument and commented: "A play warning us about the loss of humanity should have more humanity. The cartoonishness and cant don't pause for a moment of honest feeling; the script is so loaded with ideology that much of the humor is stiff'' (82). Rosette Lamont counters in her letter to the *Village Voice*: "Malpede has created an Aristophanic farce . . . grounded in up-to-date facts about reconstructive ecology, medicine, ethology . . . This solid structure . . . constitute[s] the skeleton of the play; its flesh ripples with laughter'' (6).

While some critics have complained that Malpede's work "take[s] itself too seriously" (Evett 10F), reviewer Rachel Koenig, on the other hand, notes the impact and implication of that seriousness, writing that Malpede "joins the radical theatre artists—Genet, Brecht, Gertrude Stein . . . and others—whose tradition she has mapped out, and now extends" (15).

NOTE

1. This entry on Karen Malpede was written following an interview with the playwright on May 22, 1992. All statements by the playwright, unless otherwise noted, are quoted from this interview.

BIBLIOGRAPHY

Works by Karen Malpede

Published Plays

A Lament for Three Women. A Century of Plays by American Women. Ed. Rachel France. New York: Richards Rosen Press, 1979.
A Monster Has Stolen the Sun and Other Plays. Marlboro, VT: Marlboro Press, 1987.
Better People. Angles of Power. Eds. Susan Hawthorne and Renata Klein. Melbourne, Australia: Spinifex, 1991.
Us. Women on the Verge. Ed. Rosette C. Lamont. New York: Applause, 1992.

Nonfiction

People's Theatre in Amerika. New York: Drama Books, 1972.
Three Works by the Open Theatre. New York: Drama Books, 1974.
Women in Theatre: Compassion and Hope. New York: Limelight, 1983.
Introduction. *A Monster Has Stolen the Sun. The Dream Book: An Anthology of 'Writings by Italian-American Women.* Ed. Helen Barolini. New York: Schocken, 1985. 84–92.
Interview with Rachel Koenig. *Interviews with Contemporary Women Playwrights.* Eds. Kathleen Betsko and Rachel Koenig. New York: William Morrow, 1987. 259–73.

Works about Karen Malpede

Chinoy, Helen Krich, and Linda Walsh Jenkins. "Rebeccah Rehearsal Notes" in *Women in American Theatre.* New York: Theatre Communications Group, 1981. 308–10.
Orenstein, Gloria. "Karen Malpede." *Notable Women in the American Theatre.* Eds. Alice M. Robinson, Vera Mowry Roverts, and Milly S. Varanger. Westport, CT: Greenwood, 1989. 581–84.

Reviews

Dace, Tish. "*Us* vs. Them." Rev. of *Us*. Theatre for the New City. *New York Native* (25 June 1988): 22.

Dunning, Jennifer. Rev. of *Sappho and Aphrodite*. *New York Times* (23 Oct. 1983): 62.

Evett, Marianne. Rev. of *Sappho and Aphrodite*. *The Plain Dealer* (14 June 1989): 10F.

Goodman, Walter. "Discontented Passion." Rev. of *Us*. Theatre for the New City. *New York Times* (28 Dec. 1987): C21.

Haye, Bethany. "Celtic Furies." Rev. of *A Monster Has Stolen the Sun*. Church of St. Ann. *Soho Weekly News* (25 Feb. 1981): 26.

Koenig, Rachel. "Revolutions on Stage." Rev. of *A Monster Has Stolen the Sun and Other Plays*. *The Women's Review of Books* (Oct. 1987): 13–15.

Krasnoff, Barbara. "New Cycle *Sappho and Aphrodite* Not Meant for Women Only." *Prospect Press* (13 Oct. 1983): 13, 16.

Lamont, Rosette C. Rev. of *The End of War*. The Arts at St. Ann's. *Other Stages* (3 June 1982): 5.

———. Letter in response to review of Robert Massa. *Village Voice* (27 Feb. 1990): 4, 6.

Marranca, Bonnie. Rev. of *Rebeccah*. Playwrights Horizons. *Soho Weekly News* (16 Dec. 1976): 29.

Massa, Robert. Rev. of *A Monster Has Stolen the Sun, Part One*. New Cycle. *Village Voice* (11 Mar. 1981): 82.

———. "The Origin of the Specious." Rev. of *Better People*. Theater for the New City. *Village Voice* (13 Feb. 1990): 102.

Mazer, Sharon. Rev. of *Better People*. Theatre for the New City. *Theatre Journal* (Oct. 1990): 369–70.

Munk, Erika. "Ring Out the Awful." Rev. of *Rebeccah*. Playwrights Horizons. *Village Voice* (10 Jan. 1977): 79.

Oser, Kris. "Genetic Engineering Can Be Fun." Rev. of *Better People*. *New York Law Journal* (16 February 1990): 6.

Patterson, John. "*Making Peace: A Fantasy* Stays Earthbound." All Crafts Center Theatre. *Villager* (4 Oct. 1979): 12.

Stuart, Jan. "Even Sappho Gets the Blues." Rev. of *Sappho and Aphrodite*. *New York Native* (7 Nov. 1983): 55.

Wetzsteon, Ross. "The Ploys of Sex." Rev. of *Us*. Theatre for the New City. *Village Voice* (5 Jan. 1988): 87.

EMILY MANN (1952–)

Ellen Schiff

BIOGRAPHY

Born in Boston on April 12, 1952, Emily Mann is the younger daughter of Sylvia Blut Mann, a reading specialist, and Arthur Mann, an American history professor. Though her Jewish upbringing did not emphasize religion, Mann attended Sunday School. As a teenager, she furthered her Jewish education and was confirmed in a Reform temple. As a mother, Emily is proud that her son, Nicholas, born in 1983, is going to Hebrew school to prepare for his *Bar Mitzvah*.[1]

In 1966, Arthur Mann joined the faculty of the University of Chicago and Emily enrolled at the University's Laboratory High School. The major directions her career would take were determined by her adolescence in Chicago, the eye of the political storm of the 1960s, and matriculating at an experimental school where the most interesting people were engaged either in politics or theatre. Mann was drawn to both, along with the visual arts, literature, and music.

All of her interests merged in the theatre. The magic of the stage had struck Mann as a child. She recalls the specific moment: At a Second Avenue production of Anski's Yiddish classic, she "heard the dybbuk speak through the girl in the white dress." At Radcliffe, where she earned the B.A. in French and English literature in 1974, Mann was heavily involved in theatrical activities. A member of the Board of the Harvard Drama Club, she moved quickly from acting to directing.

Following graduation, she traveled in Europe with a friend. The trip engendered Mann's first play. Before they left for Poland to seek their family origins, the Americans visited a Holocaust survivor in London. Mann set down the intrepid seventy-four-year-old woman's harrowing account almost verbatim in *Annulla Allen: Autobiography of a Survivor (A Monologue)* (1977). In the 1985 revision, *Annulla, An Autobiography,* Mann adds a dimension to the subtitle, inserting herself as an unseen voice that "needed to go to someone else's relative to understand my own history because by this time my only living relative of that generation was my grandmother . . . and she had almost no way to communicate complex ideas'' (6).

Upon her return from Europe, Mann entered the graduate theatre program at the University of Minnesota, from which she received the M.F.A. in 1976; she simultaneously held a directing fellowship at the Guthrie Theatre in Minneapolis. Mann made her professional directing debut at the Guthrie 2; in 1977, she directed the original *Annulla Allen: Autobiography* there. Mann later directed the play for National Public Radio's drama series, Earplay. *Annulla, An Autobiography* premiered in 1985 at The Repertory Theatre in St. Louis; Mann directed the 1988 Off-Off Broadway production.

Mann's second play, *Still Life*, whose 1980 premiere she directed at Chicago's Goodman Theatre, intertwines three perspectives on the violence generated in American society by the passions of the Vietnam era. Mounted at New York's American Place Theatre in 1981, the play won four Obies. *Still Life* grew from an unusual genesis. Though the horrors of war recalled in *Annulla* and Mann's own antiwar sentiments were still vivid in her mind, she reluctantly agreed to listen to a Vietnam veteran recount his experiences. His horrifying testimony stunned her; when she heard the radically conflicting responses to him of the two women in his life, she knew she had the makings of a play. *Still Life,* which also won the Fringe First Award at the 1984 Edinburgh Festival, distills 140 hours of taped interviews into a ninety-minute script.

After a five-year residency at the Guthrie, during which she became the first woman to direct on its main stage (*The Glass Menagerie* 1979), Mann became a resident director at the Brooklyn Academy of Music in 1981. The same year she married actor Gerry Bamman; the marriage has since ended in divorce.

In 1982, San Francisco's Eureka Theatre commissioned a play from Mann. Eureka's location and the commitment to political theatre it shared with Mann yielded a natural subject: the trial of Dan White for the assassination of Mayor George Moscone and City Supervisor Harvey Milk. Aided by a Guggenheim Fellowship, Mann spent eighteen months in research and interviews. *Execution of Justice,* which incorporates actual records of the trial, premiered in 1984 at the Actors Theatre of Louisville, the cowinner of that institution's 1984 Great American Play Contest. Mann made her Broadway debut as playwright and director with the 1986 New York production of *Execution,* which received a Drama Desk nomination for Outstanding New Play. The work's other honors include the Helen Hayes Award, the Bay Area Theatre Critics Award, the HBO/USA Award, and the 1986 Women's Committee of the Dramatists Guild Award for ''dramatizing issues of conscience.''

Throughout the 1980s, Mann staged plays at leading theatres across the country, including the Mark Taper Forum, La Jolla Playhouse, Actors Theatre of Louisville, and the Hartford Stage Company. In addition to her work in the ''legitimate'' theatre, she has written three screenplays: *Naked: One Couple's Intimate Journey Through Infertility* (1985), based on the book by Jo Giese Brown; *Fanny Kelly* (1985); and *You Strike a Woman, You Strike a Rock: The*

Story of Winnie Mandela (1990), for a feature film by Camille Cosby and Judith James. NBC Theatre has commissioned Mann to write a filmscript about the Greensboro Massacre.

In 1989, Mann accepted the artistic directorship of the McCarter Theatre in Princeton, New Jersey. "I'd been turning down offers to run theaters for quite a while because I want to remain an artist," she told an interviewer. However, she saw that such a position would allow her to "develop a body of work consistently, in one place" (Scasserra 19). The 1990–91 season at McCarter included a production of *Betsey Brown,* the rhythm and blues opera on which Mann collaborated at the invitation of its originator, Ntozake Shange and jazz trumpeter-composer Baikida Carroll. Mann's adaptation of Strindberg's *Miss Julie* was staged at McCarter in January 1993.

With the notable exception of Annulla and her own projected persona in the 1985 revision of that play, Mann's work is devoid of explicitly Jewish characters and situations. Nonetheless, her insistent liberalism and humanitarianism bespeak her grounding in Jewish ethics. Her concern for the vulnerable and the striving extends from her screenplay about Winnie Mandela to the infertile would-be parents in *Naked.* She notes that it was altogether fitting that her first play be about surviving the Holocaust, believing that her understanding of prejudice and her resistance to oppression are based in her Jewishness. From the same source comes the understanding of humanity that enables her to direct successfully. She told an interviewer,

I can't separate who I am from who I am as a Jew because I think it absolutely informs who I am as a human being on the planet, and who I am as a writer. . . . It even informs who I am running an institution like this [the McCarter Theatre], which is serving a large community and challenging it and stimulating people to think about the human condition. (Cohen 23)

A member of the New Dramatists Workshop for play development (1984– 91), Mann served on the Theatre Communications Group Board from 1983–87 and as its vice-president from 1984–86. She is a lecturer in the Council of the Humanities and the Program in Theatre and Dance at Princeton University. In October 1992 she traveled to Moscow under a cultural exchange program sponsored by the U.S. Information Agency to unite members of the Moscow Art Theatre with their American counterparts. Her honors include the Rosamund Gilder Award from the New Drama Forum for outstanding creative achievement in theatre (1983), a McKnight Fellowship (1985), a Bush Fellowship (1986), NEA grants (1984, 1986), and a Creative Artists Public Service grant (1985).

MAJOR THEMES

Annulla Allen: Autobiography of a Survivor, which Mann wrote and directed in her twenties, announced not only her principal concerns, but also her chief occupations, which are inseparable from them. Directing was to become as significant a form of expression as playwriting. *Annulla* also established Mann's dramatic mode, what she calls "theatre of testimony." The recognition of the dramatic potential inherent in documentary material first struck her while reading transcripts of interviews with Holocaust survivors that her father did for the American Jewish Committee's oral history project.

All Mann's plays are distinguished by her dedication to social responsibility. This commitment is manifest in her unrelenting focus on political and social issues. *Annulla* represents the strategies by which an inventive woman who had rescued her husband from Dachau rebuilds life as a survivor, a widow—and an aspiring playwright with a message about world peace built on matriarchy. *Still Life* explores the climate of the Vietnam War: the return to a troubled society of a veteran obsessed with the rage, guilt, and physical pleasure stimulated by his acts as a Marine; the adversity of his beset wife, vainly seeking the securities of a pre-60s America; and the situation of his independent-minded mistress, disturbed by nothing because she has become unshockable. *Execution of Justice* deals with homophobia and the pervertibility of justice. It depicts a community where radically changing values have bred confusion and intolerance. The work throws into question the very definitions of law and order. It also demonstrates the dearth of ethics in media coverage of the news. The screenplay *Fanny Kelly* deals with the plights of the U.S. Cavalry, sworn to enforce this country's merciless Indian policies, and of the Sioux, its savage victims.

Having chosen such subjects, Mann handles them with an even-handedness that has become a signature of her "theatre of testimony." She provides contrasting perceptions that compel spectators to draw their own inferences. While the veteran's mistress in *Still Life* styles him as the gentlest man she has ever met, his battered wife is terrified of him. The barbarous cruelty of the Indians trying to preserve their lands in *Fanny Kelly* is matched by that of soldiers in the service of their country. *Execution of Justice* uses as a repeating motif the sympathy-evoking sound of the high heels of the assassin's wife running to meet him in a cathedral after he had confessed his crimes. In presenting multiple perspectives on the issues they dramatize, Mann's plays typically cause theatregoers to reevaluate attitudes and reconsider opinions.

Mann's concept of theatre as a thought-provoking forum shapes her presentational style—docudrama that makes a jury of its audiences. The trio in *Still Life* sit behind a table addressing the auditorium, as if they were giving testimony. Mann specifies in an author's note that "these people have no sentimentality about their experiences and the producers of this play must not either" (DPS 7). Judgments and the emotions they arouse must come from theatregoers. Toward that end, *Execution of Justice,* a busy courtroom drama, incorporates documentary slides, recorded sounds, and a film clip. Mann aims to present a vast amount of data as objectively as possible, but also to show how information is acquired. The point is furthered by using television cameras to record onstage events, immediately projecting them so as to demonstrate the results of reducing people and events to the scope and style of the electronic screen.

Mann's penchant for turning factual events into compelling theatre is facilitated by her skill in transforming real-life people's actual words into effective dialogue. She is well served by her musical education (she plays three instruments), which sensitized her to the rhythms and poetry of ordinary speech, and by the kind of attention to language that results in double entendres like *Still Life,* and *Execution of Justice.* Her musical training also informs the structure of her plays, which characteristically orchestrate polyphany and counterpoint.

Mann does not shy away from depicting the violence rooted in the political, social, and historical issues she dramatizes, often using visuals to do so. However, her interest is not in the abusive acts themselves, but on their effects on their victims. This is especially evident in *Still Life,* where Mann consciously set out to reject the prevailing association of eroticism with violence between the sexes (Betsko and Koenig 285).

Mann attributes the femininism that constitutes yet another theme in her work to her ability to listen. Women, she points out, talk to one another about the "traumatic, devastating events in their lives." She adds that "most of what I know about human experience comes from listening" (Betsko and Koenig 281). Hence, the dominant point of view in several of the plays is that of a woman. As Annulla recounts her Holocaust experiences, she is cooking for her invalid sister whose demands on Annulla's time keep her from working on the play she is writing. The argument of her manuscript, which lies strewn haphazardly about, is that if women ruled the world, evil would disappear. But first, women have to start to think. The point is clear: Women have been too distracted (perhaps even fulfilled) by more traditional concerns to do intensive, constructive thinking even when, like Annulla, they have the intelligence and the experience to make notable contributions.

The gruesome events of *Fanny Kelly* are viewed through its eponymous heroine's eyes. Fanny sees that the apparently limitless capacity for bloodshed of both Indians and whites washes out any meaningful distinctions between them. Fanny's despair is heightened by her bonding with the Indian woman who saves her life and her love for the Sioux child thrust into her care, apparently as a painful reminder of Fanny's own scalped daughter.

In *Betsey Brown,* the perspective is that of the title character who, coming of age, looks to disparate role models. Her mother is a "modern" woman who, despite her genuine concern that her daughters be educated to realize their potential, abandons her family to pursue her own intellectual needs. In sharp contrast is the Browns' housekeeper, a woman who sings gospel songs with exquisite conviction and knows how to please men and console crying children. It is consistent with Mann's personal and professional philosophy that she collaborated with Shange on a work whose feminist concerns are treated in the context of the Civil Rights movement. Speaking at a conference on New Directions in American Theatre in 1990, Mann observed that, as more women are empowered to run theatres, audiences are going to hear very different voices. *Betsey Brown,* designed to shatter the cliché of the black musical and produced during Mann's first year at McCarter, illustrates the point forcefully.

SURVEY OF CRITICISM

In a *New York Times* interview that preceded the Broadway run of *Execution of Justice,* Mann reiterated her commitment to drama of social significance and her dedication to writing ''intelligent plays for intelligent people'' (Bennetts 4). Predictably, critical response to her plays, almost all of it to date in the press, is rarely dispassionate.

The majority of reviews of *Still Life* incorporate the words ''powerful,'' ''moving,'' or ''harrowing.'' One reviewer compared watching the play to facing three guns randomly and repeatedly shooting at the audience (Kocan). Several commentators had more personalized responses, the most extreme being Michael Feingold, calling *Still Life* ''a jagged and arresting chunk of dramatic shrapnel that is now lodged permanently in my brain.'' Feingold's imagery is literalized in the observations of a brain specialist. She was reminded by the play's structure of the way the brain functions in recalling traumatic memories, thus capturing the experience of both its characters and its author (Betsko and Koenig 281).

''Powerful'' was echoed by reviewers of *Still Life*'s European premiere at the Edinburgh Festival (McMillan, Fowler). The play's uncommon exploration of the consequences for women of the Vietnam era was emphasized by Barbara Bannon, reviewing the Salt Lake Acting Company's production, and by Lawrence Christon, who, seeing the Mark Taper staging, distinguished the play from other Vietnam drama for its depiction of the ''alarming discord'' the war sowed between the sexes.

When Christon asked about the appropriateness of a thirty-year-old playwright tackling the subject of Vietnam, Mann recalled the days of rage she experienced in Chicago, adding, ''The war continues to be part of me. It changed my way of looking at myself and my country.'' Nevertheless, Mann's youth and, doubtless, gender made her vulnerable to vituperation in the New York press where some critics, clearly disturbed by *Still Life*'s message, attacked the messenger (Betsko and Koenig 459). Most intemperate was John Simon, who apostrophized, ''O my dear, liberal, radical, feminist, juvenile Emily Mann!'', charging ''nostalgia for the sixties,'' and ''bourgeois radicalism'' (Simon, ''Various Ways''). Even New York's less traditional papers found fault. *Variety* wondered why the play's male protagonist was not in analysis and faulted the ninety-minute work for being ''too long and too depressing for popular taste'' (Humm); *The Soho News* called it ''bleakly static, strangely numbing despite its awesome power to move'' (Gerard).

The incongruity between the New York reviews and all others, where there is clear consensus of the brilliant success of *Still Life,* reveals less about the play than about profound differences in the criteria and expectations by which theatre is assessed in this country. Those differences are manifest in the reception of *Execution of Justice*. After winning acclaim on eight major regional stages, *Execution* came to Broadway, directed by Mann herself, to close after only twelve performances.

This time, however, critics focused on the work and the production, and they found some merit in both. The *Best Plays* yearbook designated *Execution* one of the year's Ten Best, though coeditor Jeffrey Sweet felt that Mann's direction did not serve her script effectively. Though *Variety*'s Humm warned that the play would repel "escapist-oriented" Broadway audiences, he hailed the arrival on the commercial stage of a play "on a pressing contemporary issue." That welcome was seconded by *Women's Wear Daily,* which signaled the production as "validat[ing] any Broadway season with an insightful seriousness of purpose" (Cohen). Although Douglas Watt and Clive Barnes were discomfited, Barnes, along with Edwin Wilson, took the play seriously enough to question whether Mann had gone wide of her subject by focusing on the trial rather than on the emotional climate surrounding the crime and the sentencing (Cohen, Watt, Barnes, Wilson, *NY Critics Reviews*). The *New York Times*'s Mel Gussow proved one of *Execution*'s most loyal followers (having seen both the Louisville and Arena productions); he saluted its exploration of "contemporary moral values and the criminal justice system."

Two observations dominate the reviews of *Execution*'s regional productions. First is appreciation of the vast proportions of the play which, despite its "documentary coolness," moved audiences deeply and provoked thought (Hawley, Weiner, Steel). The second is evidence of the work's local impact and pertinence. In St. Paul, the play was the subject of a major legal symposium (Hawley 14A). *The Houston Chronicle* signaled the Alley production's relevance to an approaching mayoral election in a city riven by a recent referendum conspicuously involving gays (Holmes 1). Unlike Barnes and Wilson in New York, "out-of-town" reviewers saw at the center of *Execution* not the Dan White trial, but the trial of "the meaning of justice and politics in contemporary America," as the *San Francisco Chronicle* put it (Weiner).

While full-length studies of Mann have not yet been written, she and her work are the subject of several essays. There are two excellent, wide-ranging interviews. With Betsko and Koenig, Mann discusses her goals in playwriting and her views of the currents shaping the theatre. David Savran's article focuses more intensively on Mann's contribution to the American stage of "a new political sophistication" (146–47). *Execution of Justice* is considered as exemplary of the new sophistication with which American Jewish playwrights are treating issues of morality and justice (Schiff, "From Black"). The press responded generously when Mann became artistic director at McCarter. Much of this coverage was carried in publications (New Brunswick *Home News,* Trenton *Times, New Jersey Goodlife*) difficult to track down in libraries, but available from the McCarter Theatre (91 University Place, Princeton, NJ 08540).

NOTE

1. Much of the biographical information in this essay was supplied by Emily Mann in a phone interview, November 11, 1992.

BIBLIOGRAPHY

Works by Emily Mann

Still Life. New Plays USA 1. Ed. James Leverett. New York: Theatre Communications Group, 1982; New York: Dramatists Play Service, 1982.
Nights and Days. Paris: *Avant-Scene* July 1984.
Annula, An Autobiography. New York: Plays in Progress-Theatre Communications Group, 1985. Rpt. as *Anulla. Plays from the Contemporary American Jewish Repertoire*. Ed. Ellen Schiff. New York: NAL, forthcoming.
Execution of Justice. New Plays USA 3. Ed. James Leverett and M. Elizabeth Osborn. New York: Theatre Communications Group, 1986; *American Theatre* Nov. 1985, pull-out section.
———, and Ntozake Shange. *Betsey Brown* (excerpts). *Studies in American Drama, 1945-Present* 4 (1989).

Interviews

"Emily Mann." *Interviews with Contemporary Women Playwrights*. With Kathleen Betsko and Rachel Koenig. New York: Quill-Beech Tree, 1987. 274–87.
"Emily Mann." *In Their Own Words: Contemporary American Playwrights*. With David Savran. New York: Theatre Communications Group, 1988.
Emily Mann. Telephone interview. 11 Nov. 1992.

Works about Emily Mann

Cohen, Sonya Freeman. "Emily Mann: The 'Jewish Visionary' Behind Princeton's McCarter Theatre." *Jewish Post* 28 Nov. 1991: 23.
Kilkelly, Ann Gavere. "Emily Mann." *Notable Women in American Theatre*. Ed. Alice M. Robinson, Vera Mowry Roberts and Milly S. Barranger, Westport, CT.: Greenwood, 1989. 584–87.
Scasserra, Michael P. "A New Voice at McCarter." *New Jersey Goodlife* Sept. 1991. 18–19.
Schiff, Ellen. "Emily Mann." *Contemporary Dramatists*. Ed. Daniel Kirkpatrick, 4th ed. London: St. James, 1989. 342–43. (5th ed., ed. Kate Berney. Forthcoming 416-18).

Selected Articles and Reviews of Mann's Plays

(NB: In instances where page numbers are not supplied, the citation is to photocopied reviews obtainable from George Lane, William Morris Agency, 1350 Avenue of the Americas, New York, NY 10019.)

Bannon, Barbara. "Under Siege." Rev. of *Still Life. Utah Holiday*. May 1984.

Bennetts, Leslie. "When Reality Takes to the Stage." *New York Times* 9 Mar. 1986, sec. 2: 1ff.

Brown, Joe. "Injustice and 'Justice' for All." Rev. of *Execution of Justice. Washington Post* 17 May 1985.

Christon, Lawrence, " 'Still Life' With Echoes of 'Nam.' " Rev. of *Still Life. Los Angeles Times* 23 May 1982.

Revs. of *Execution of Justice. New York Theatre Critics Reviews* 19 March 1986: 348–53.

Feingold, Michael. "Home Fronts." Rev. of *Still Life. Village Voice* 22 Feb. 1981: 75.

Fowler, John. "Harrowing View of One Man's Nightmare." Rev. of *Still Life. Glasgow* [Scotland] *Herald* 21 Aug. 1984.

Gerard, Jeremy. "Threnody." Rev. of *Still Life. The Soho News* 25 Feb. 1981: 26.

Gussow, Mel. "Testimony of a Survivor." Rev. of *Annulla, An Autobiography. New York Times* 2 Nov. 1988: C23.

Hawley, David. "Breathtaking Size, Acting Turn Guthrie Play Into Epic." Rev. of *Execution of Justice. St. Paul Pioneer Press Dispatch* 20 Oct. 1985: A13–14.

Holmes, Ann. "Alley's 'Justice' Powerfully Staged." Rev. of *Execution of Justice. Houston Chronicle* 12 Oct. 1985: 1ff.

Humm. "Still Life." Rev. of *Still Life. Variety* 4 Mar. 1981.

———. "Execution of Justice." Rev. of *Execution of Justice. Variety* 14 Mar. 1986.

Kocan, Rick. " 'Still Life' Probes Pain of Three Lives." Rev. of *Still Life. Chicago Sun Times* 27 Oct. 1980: 49ff.

McMillan, Joyce. "Fringe Round-up." Rev. of *Still Life. Guardian* [London and Manchester] 13 Aug. 1984.

Parks, Suzan-Lori. "In Search of 'Betsey Brown.' " *American Theatre* Apr. 1991: 20–24.

Rich, Frank. "Stage: 'Still Life' by Emily Mann at American Place." Rev. of *Still Life. The New York Times* 20 Feb. 1981: C3.

Schiff, Ellen. "From Black and White to Red and Pink: Political Themes on the American Jewish Stage." *Studies in American Jewish Literature* 8 (1989): 66–76.

Simon, John. "Various Ways to Lose Your Head." Rev. of *Still Life. New York* 2 March 1981: 52.

———. "Court and Courtroom." Rev. of *Execution of Justice. New York* 24 March 1986: 96.

Stasio, Marilyn. " 'Still Life' a Moving and Harrowing Drama." Rev. of *Still Life. New York Post* 20 Feb. 1981.

Steele, Mike. "Guthrie's Play's Power Comes from History." Rev. of *Execution of Justice. Minneapolis Star and Tribune* 21 Oct. 1985.

Weiner, Bernard. "Compelling Dan White Docu-drama." Rev. of *Execution of Justice. San Francisco Chronicle* 7 July 1985, 42ff.

DAPHNE MERKIN (1954–   )

Carolyn Ariella Sofia

BIOGRAPHY

That "sadness flows under the skin of things, like blood" is the message Daphne Merkin gleans from her reading of *Ecclesiastes,* for a collection of essays by contemporary writers on the Jewish Bible. One can say as much for her recollections about her childhood.

The fourth of six closely spaced children born to a well-to-do German Jewish Orthodox couple who had emigrated to the United States, Merkin was raised in Manhattan and sent to Jewish day schools. Recalling that spiritual impulses at home were sometimes "buried under layers of German formality and propriety," she describes her childhood attitude toward the day-to-day observance of Orthodox law as "an admixture of resentment and a not wholly unappreciative compliance" (Telephone interview). The resentment may have stemmed from a perceived marginality based on gender: Although she was sent to study Talmud-Torah like her three brothers, she recalls that while they got the chance to showcase their knowledge publicly at the time of their Bar Mitzvahs, her twelfth-year rite of passage consisted simply of a family outing to a local kosher restaurant.

An emotionally sensitive child, Merkin chafed under the authoritarian character of her parents and developed a tendency toward depression at an early age. Hospitalized for two weeks of psychiatric observation at age eight because of a belief that she was being "hounded" by family and friends, she was sent home and continued individual therapy on an out-patient basis.

In 1975 Merkin graduated *magna cum laude* from Barnard College and was awarded departmental honors in English as well as the school's prize for poetry. During the following year she worked briefly as an assistant at both the *New York Review of Books* and at the *New Yorker.* Deciding to return to school in 1976, she enrolled in a graduate program at Columbia University to study literature. She remained there until 1978 but she left before being awarded a degree. During her time at Columbia, Merkin published her first literary criticism in *Commentary* and *The New Leader,* as well as her first fiction in *Mademoiselle* and *Encounter.* Named *The New Leader*'s lead fiction critic in 1978, she left several years later to join the editorial staff at *McCall's* and to work on her own fiction.

Asked in a telephone interview which author she considered the most influential on her development, Merkin readily cited V. S. Pritchett because of a "certain kind of limpidness" in his writing and because, like her, he has combined careers as a fiction writer and as a literary critic. Running a close second was Walker Percy, whose 1961 novel, *The Moviegoer,* is one Merkin wishes she "had written herself," both for its use of language and for its inclusion of her twin obsessions, fiction and movies.

Always interested in the movies, Merkin first had the opportunity to publish criticism on the subject at Barnard when she served as movie critic for a student publication. Her movie reviews have since appeared in diverse places, including *Film Comment, Premiere,* and *The New Leader.*

Enchantment, her debut novel, aroused more fanfare than the typical first novel in part because of the wealth of literary friends Merkin accumulated as she moved in and around the publishing world. Her fiction-writing abilities were brought to the attention of publisher William Jovanovich by critic Diana Trilling, who showed him one of Merkin's short stories. Jovanovich invited Merkin to lunch and ended up offering her a $20,000 advance to complete a manuscript that would become a semiautobiographical novel about a girl growing up in a wealthy, modern Orthodox, German Jewish family in Manhattan. Subsequently, he hired Merkin as a senior editor.

Currently a contributing editor at the *Partisan Review,* Merkin lives in New York City with her husband, Michael Brod, a stockbroker, and their three-year-old daughter, Zoë. Using the events of her personal life as a springboard to matters of cultural criticism, she often writes personal essays for the *New York Times* and other publications. But a new novel is underway and Hannah Lehmann, the protagonist of *Enchantment,* will be making a second appearance. As the narrator of *The Discovery of Sex,* Lehmann will be relating the story of a woman in publishing who is sexually obsessed with a lawyer.

MAJOR THEMES

Thwarted love, not for a man, but for a mother, lies at the heart of *Enchantment* and the nexus of memory and identity forms another persistent trope. Hannah Lehmann, the twenty-six-year-old narrator, shares her recollections of growing up in a family remarkably similar to Merkin's own: the well-off Lehmann clan is German Jewish Orthodox, lives on Manhattan's Upper East Side, includes six closely spaced children, and has one daughter apparently more sensitive than the others.

Written in the tone of a memoir, the novel traces no distinct plot, but it relies instead on the vagaries of memory to order its scenes. Linked vignettes shape it into a series of prose snapshots highlighting the Lehmann family's emotional history. The ordering and meaning of the scenes belong to Hannah, but she realizes by the novel's end that family histories may be more constructed than factual: "Even my brother's memories don't match mine," she thinks, recalling that he cites a different litany of facts and perceptions concerning remembered childhood events.

What Hannah therefore wants, and cannot seem to find, is someone to agree with her vision of the past, someone to share her recollections completely: "I would love to find someone whose memories matched mine, little hurt for little hurt." The reader is positioned to be the active, sympathetic listener, and what Hannah especially wants confirmed is the part her mother played (and continues to play) in her emotional life.

Love is not a strong enough word to describe the attachment Hannah feels for her mother. It is an implacable need, a driving force: "It is a mystery to me, the waves of emotion I keep breaking against her," she says. "I am a Woodpecker, and my mother is a tree. Love. Hate. Emotions keep slipping off the end of my mind, to be followed by wholly different ones. Hate. Love. Which will do to wear her bark away? And who is torturing whom?" At its center Hannah's problem is that she cannot accept her psychiatrist's interpretation that the solution to her obsession lies within herself, that her mother has no real power over her anymore, other than what Hannah grants her. Unable to give up the desire to be totally, unconditionally loved, she relives scenes of desperate longing. Close to the novel's end, she is still recalling a time when, trying repeatedly to attract her mother's attention and to succeed in getting her to confess her failings as a mother, Hannah drove herself as far as self-mutilation, marking her wrists with a pair of her mother's nail scissors and deliberately pointing out the cuts in case they should escape detection.

The father is virtually absent in this book; Mr. Lehmann is reduced to a kind of stranger who just happened to marry Hannah's mother. The relationship between mother and child remains the preeminent dyad, especially for its ability to serve as a paradigm for future relationships. Thus, the troubling aspect of Hannah's relationship with her mother broadens and becomes sexualized by the novel's close when she forms a masochistic attachment to a man determined, alternately, to love and humiliate her.

Merkin's novel-in-progress, *The Discovery of Sex,* will focus on similar themes of love and obsession. According to Merkin, however, questions about Jewish identity may be explored more fully since one of the book's male characters will undergo a spiritual conversion and consider significantly increasing his level of Jewish ritual observance.

SURVEY OF CRITICISM

Enchantment was well received by reviewers, all of them appearing sensitive to the tangle and intensity of childhood emotions portrayed in the story.

For Janet Hadda it is a ''deeply female'' work because of the way Merkin portrays the ''doubt and frustration of dawning womanhood.'' The obsessive quality of the attachment Hannah Lehmann has for her mother causes Patricia Hampl to redefine Hannah's enchantment for her female parent as a kind of thralldom, a state of emotional bondage from which the twenty-six-year-old protagonist is unable to free herself or her reader. Katherine Bucknell likewise sees a coerced role for the reader, this time as someone who is expected to join Hannah in finger-pointing accusation at her family.

Unlike Hampl or Bucknell, John Gross does not find the closed world that Hannah inhabits claustrophobic. And where Mrs. Lehmann is portrayed by Hampl as a woman who ''seems not unfeeling, but possessed of a peasant faith, an airy confidence in life's habit of righting itself,'' and not as a woman arbitrarily cruel enough to merit the position of villain in her daughter's mind, Gross concentrates on what he considers an accurate perception by Hannah of her mother's ''coolly punitive approach'' to child raising, so much so that the daughter, as a child, fantasized that her mother had once been an officer in a concentration camp.

Like Gross, Rochelle Ratner also finds that the buildup of minute details, the television trivia that resurrects the zeitgeist of the 1950s, for instance, helps intensify the portrait of Hannah's family life.

BIBLIOGRAPHY

Works by Daphne Merkin

''Why Potok is Popular.'' *Commentary* Feb. 1976: 73–75.

''Looking Back.'' *Commentary* July 1977: 63–65.

Enchantment. San Diego: Harcourt Brace Jovanovich, 1986. An excerpt from the novel-in-progress appeared originally in the *New Yorker* 2 April 1984: 42–46.

''The Plight of Reading: In Search of the New Fiction.'' *Partisan Review* 51–52:4–1. 1984–85: 739–50.

''All About Mommie Damnedest.'' *Film Comment* Nov.-Dec. 1985: 38–40.

''Ecclesiastes: A Reading Out-of-Season.'' *Congregation: Contemporary Writers Read the Jewish Bible*. Ed. David Rosenberg, San Diego: Harcourt Brace Jovanovich, 1987. 393–405.

''Dreaming of Hitler: From the Postwar Generation, a Memoir of Self-Hatred.'' *Esquire* August 1989: 75–83. Rpt. in *Testimony: Contemporary Writers Make the Holocaust Personal*. Ed. David Rosenberg, New York: Random House, 1989. 13–34.

''Ready, Willing and Wary.'' *New York Times Magazine* 16 July 1989: 12–14.

''Prince Charming Comes Back.'' *New York Times Magazine* 15 July 1990: 18–20.

''Now Voyeur.'' *Premiere* Winter 1991: 108.

''Court Your Losses.'' *New York Times Magazine* 5 May 1991: 22–24.

''Are These Women Bullies?'' *New York Times Magazine* 21 July 1991: 17.

''Name that Decade.'' *New York Times* 25 May 1992: 14.

Telephone interview 17, Sept. 1992.

Works about Daphne Merkin

"Between Issues." *The New Leader* 8 Sept. 1986: 2.

Bucknell, Katherine. *Times Literary Supplement* 14 August 1987: 873.

Cieri, Carol des Lauriers. Rev. of *Enchantment*. *The Christian Science Monitor* (Eastern edition) 29 Sept. 1986: 22.

Gross, John. Rev. of *Enchantment*. *New York Times* 8 Sept. 1986, sec. C: 19.

Hadda, Janet. Rev. of *Enchantment*. *Los Angeles Times Book Review* 14 Sept. 1986: 2ff.

Hampl, Patricia. Rev. of *Enchantment*. *New York Times Book Review* 5 Oct. 1986: 7.

Ratner, Rochelle. Rev. of *Enchantment*. *Library Journal* August 1986: 171.

Tyre, Peg. "By the Books." *New York*. 22 Sept. 1986: 38.

ROBIN MORGAN (1941–   )

Elizabeth Q. Sullivan

BIOGRAPHY

Robin Evonne Morgan was born January 29, 1941, in Lake Worth, Florida, to a mother already divorced from Robin's father. She grew up in Mount Vernon, New York. Faith Berkeley Morgan's ambitions and the young Robin's own considerable talents led to child stardom in her role of Dagmar in the television series "I Remember Mama," which aired in the mid-fifties. She graduated with honors from the Wetter School in 1956, and, as her career necessitated, she was taught by private tutors from 1956–59. From 1956–59 she attended Columbia as a non-matriculated student. She married the writer Kenneth Pitchford on September 19, 1962, and was divorced fifteen years later. They have one son, Blake Ariel Morgan-Pitchford, born in 1969 (Basel 305). Morgan worked as a freelance editor from 1961–69, also devoting substantial energy to her political activism, her domestic responsibilities, and her own writing.

The hardship involved in juggling these often-conflicting roles is described in "Letters from a Marriage," an early chapter of her book *Going Too Far: The Personal Chronicle of a Feminist.* Calling these years a period "before any feminist consciousness had touched [her] life" (21), she mentions the undue pressures to be the perfect wife, mother, and housewife. Reaction to the stress of these years was an obvious impetus to her eventual feminist activism, feminist writings, and her poetry.

Involvement with the political activities of the New Left during this period also spurred her feminism. In *The Demon Lover: The Sexuality of Terrorism,* she describes an intense moment of self-recognition when, as a member of Congress of Racial Equality (CORE) and other groups that often met together, including the Students for a Democratic Society, Revolutionary Youth Movement, and the Weathermen, she refused to plant a bomb in the women's room of an office building without a warning call. As she herself suggests, her pregnancy at this time may have influenced her rejection of violence, yet just as important was her growing understanding of the subservient role these avowedly revolutionary groups forced women to play as "birds" or "chicks" (233). Her cofounding of the group *Witch* (Women's International Terrorist Conspiracy from Hell) in 1968 is a key event in Morgan's public role as a feminist and, as she puts it, a more "life-affirming politics" (242). Significant women's liberation activities and political writings continued in the late sixties and early seventies. Among these were the 1968 Atlantic City protest against the Miss America Contest; the hexing of Wall Street on Halloween of the same year, among other WITCH activities; and the protest against the papal encyclical on abortion. *Sisterhood Is Powerful,* the best-selling anthology of the women's liberation movement, which Morgan edited, appeared in 1970.

Her retreat from the Radical Left also marked a new flourishing artistically, for terrorist tactics implied for her a deep cynicism about words and communication. "The very tools which were my best offering to the politics of my own generation were often regarded with contempt," Morgan writes (*Going* xi). She speaks also of the shift in style and subject matter, occasioned by knowledge of sexism within language, that feminist consciousness allowed her (*Going* xi). Her book of poems, *Monster,* came out in 1972. For the years 1964–70, she lists "writer" as her sole occupation (Basel 305), though of course she was doing much more. Her identification of herself as a writer indicates wholehearted commitment to her craft.

In 1972, she served as Visiting Chair and Guest Professor of Women's Studies at New College, Sarasota, Florida. Here she learned "the sexist hypocrisy of academia first hand" (*Going* 194). The administration reneged on its promise that she would be teaching only women in her women's studies course and otherwise restricted her autonomy. She therefore returned to editing, writing, and political activism, serving as an editor and writer for the World *Ms.* magazine (1984–87). Aside from her work on *Ms.,* she has also published in over one hundred magazines and journals.

Morgan's experience extending feminism to global dimensions is described in *The Demon Lover,* most dramatically by her visit to the Palestinian refugee camps of the Gaza Strip in 1986. She sees the camps, and the subjugation of women within them by their own subjugated husbands, as the "normalization of terrorism" (242). Her descriptions of encounters with these women and their families are harrowing, and she herself suffered miserably from dysentery.

Subsequent to these travels, Morgan has continued an active life as a writer and editor, bringing out a novel, *Dry Your Smile,* in 1987, and a book of selected and new poems in 1990, *Upstairs in the Garden.* She tried academia again in 1987, serving at Rutgers University as Distinguished Visiting Scholar and Lecturer, in the Center for Critical Analysis of Contemporary Culture. In that year, she also participated in the UN Convention in Brazil to End All Forms of Discrimination Against Women. In 1990, she assumed the editorship of the new *Ms.,* which she re-started as an independent women's magazine without advertising and its often stifling influence upon editorial freedom. She heads or participates in several feminist organizations, including The New York Women's

Center, which she founded in 1969; The Women's Law Center; Feminist Self-Help clinics; Battered Women's Refuge; Women's Institute Freedom Press; National Alliance of Rape Crisis Centers; and The Sisterhood Is Global Institute, a think tank that she helped found in 1984. She is an honorary member of the Pan-Arab Feminist Solidarity Association and Israeli Feminists Against Occupation. She has received the Front Page Award for Journalism, a writer-in-residence grant from Yaddo, and Ford Foundation grants in 1982, 1983, and 1984. In 1992, she published another book, one that recapitulates the highlights of her total career to date as a feminist, *The Word of a Woman: Feminist Dispatches 1968–1992*. She also has a novel in progress, *The Tenth Power.* Morgan lives in Manhattan and has described herself as "apostately Jewish" (*Going* 3), listing "Wiccean atheist" as her religion (Basel 305).

MAJOR THEMES

Though she is well known as a voice of feminist anger, the title of Morgan's first published volume of poetry, *Monster,* is not in any simple way descriptive of the persona she presents in the poems. (As she suggests in the title poem, the word appears to have come to her when her son caught sight of her pubic hair and exclaimed, "Monster!" (82; rept.) in *Upstairs* 38). Yet the word does appropriately describe the true proportions of the rift between the sexes and the horror of stereotyping, which, even in this early book, Morgan sees as taking a terrible toll on men as well as women. She writes in the title poem, "I hate not men, but what it is men do in this culture" (82; rept. in *Upstairs* 39). Nevertheless, Morgan also senses a struggle of monstrous proportions as men will not give up without a fight their "power to hold power" (83; rept. in *Upstairs* 39). A major theme of this early volume is the male sex as the enemy. She worries even about her baby lying in his crib, "White. Male. American./Potentially the most powerful deadly creature/of the species" (81; rept. in *Upstairs* 37). But the monster is also the woman who gives birth to men and who is therefore paradoxically capable of bringing forth the revolution between the sexes. Polarities of viewpoint thus characterize this and later volumes of Morgan's poems.

"Monster" moves from a child's more or less benign Sesame Street view of the monster to a sense of the complex issues involved in the battle between the sexes; the speaker becomes a monster created by sexism who cannot be stopped. Important subthemes in this poem become major in other poems in the volume: her support of the non-macho, sensitive male; the hatred of war and genocide, the subject of the villanelle, "Dachau"; the importance of the mother/nurturer role; and the mutual struggle by men and women to effect a revolution between the sexes, as she poignantly and humorously expresses it in "Quotations from Charwoman Me." Other poems in the collection are very angry in tone. In the acerbic "Arraignment," she visits an imagined castration/murder upon Ted Hughes for his sins against women and poetry.

The terrible anger that she sometimes felt toward men as individuals and in groups, however, could not be mitigated for Morgan merely by turning to women instead. In "Lesbian Poem," she takes up the subject of lesbian love only to show it as an important subtheme of female fulfillment, connected to one's own self-love, which finds its truest expression in relationships between individuals overcoming sociopolitical pressures. The poem is set up in a three-sectioned Hegelian pattern of thesis, antithesis, and synthesis, which allows for a prismatic turning of the topic for viewing from different angles and reconciliation of seemingly divergent views. The first section, the "Thetic," deplores the male historians who tried to pass off Joan of Arc's lesbianism as mere girlhood friendship; the second, or "Antithetic," derides the eroticism of Sappho with its reduction of women to sex objects; and the third, or "Synthetic" part, dedicated to Katherine Phillips, "the first *feminist* poet in English who wrote of loving women" (73; rept. in *Upstairs* 30), tries to free not only lesbians from the narrow heterosexually dictated roles, but also all women to love themselves. The speaker's derision of Sappho in the middle section alludes to the Greek poet's references to "honeyed skin,/ and supple legs/ breasts like pears,/ and a smell of the goddamned sea," and climaxes with the line, "Get off my back, Sappho, / I never liked that position/ anyway" (73; rept. in *Upstairs* 30). Morgan is not just rejecting possible erotic objectification of women within lesbianism; she is also refusing to give the prurient reader details about lesbian sex and thus deny what is "concrete, specific, individual" about relations between women (72; rept. in *Upstairs* 29). The lesbian relationships in the poem "Two Women," from *Upstairs in the Garden* and the novel *Dry Your Smile,* are affirmed because they are based on the spontaneous attraction between individuals that transcends politics.

In *Lady of the Beasts,* her next volume of poetry (1976), the process of creating a replacement for the dominant patriarchal society is more fully apparent though problematical. The frequently praised poem, "The Network of the Imaginary Mother," represents the speaker's efforts to recover and make use of her personal past, including her relationship to her mother, who ultimately dies of Parkinson's disease; her relationship with other women, and a significant particular woman, which itself reiterates the mother/daughter relationship; her bond with her child, who in the poem, as in her life, is male; and most important, her relationship to herself, which all the others have helped realize. The life that the speaker envisions and recovers in this five-sectioned poem is continually linked to historical and social context. Thus, when she writes about her child and her hopes for him, she makes wishes for all children, though not without underscoring the horrible conditions most children in our world face daily, such as war, starvation, and addiction to drugs. She asserts: "You shall be disinherited of all these legacies./ And in their place,/ and in your footprints,/ tendrils green with possibility will tremble/ awake" (*Lady of the Beasts* 81–82; rept. in *Upstairs* 86). Yet as if to underscore the terrible odds against this wish of life and growth coming true, every section but the last ends with a list of the names of women who were put to horrible tortures and deaths as so-called witches.

In the last section of ''Network,'' Morgan reworks traditional religious symbols, liturgies, and doctrines (Christian, Hindu, Wicca, Egyptian, and Greek) prepared for in the earlier sections, which represent the integration of the speaker's arisen self and which celebrate her connection with past and future. Female procreative and nurturing powers become the means not just of her own, but of the world's redemption; mother's milk is ''substituted'' for wine, suggesting at the same time that historically it's the other way around: Holy Communion is the male appropriation of what were originally female powers. Like this poem, many others in the volume *Lady of the Beasts* deal with the restoration of women to their archetypal mythic roles, ascribing to them their rightful power at each stage of life: virgin, mother, or crone.

The autobiographical material of ''Network'' ties it to Morgan's autobiographical novel, *Dry Your Smile,* which is dominated by the Demeter/Persephone pattern of connection to the mother, departure from her, and return, and also celebrates the finding of an independent self partly through involvement with others, especially husband, child, and female lover (often presented as simply love for one's female self).

In Morgan's work, the growth of the self is intimately tied to her political activity and to her sense of women's suffering, not only historically, but globally as well. Her latest volume, *Upstairs in the Garden,* while evidencing a wide range of theme, subject, and use of form, is powerfully eloquent on this subject of the bond among all women, created in part by their shared oppression by men or male-dominated society, but it also goes much deeper. ''Arbitrary Bread'' is a plea for women to regain the power taken by men and to stop disguising reality for them. It cleverly phrases the all-too-common conventional situation:

Men make impressions, arbitrary decisions, names for themselves, wars, profits, laws, reputations, deals, fortunes, threats, enemies, promises, tracks.

Women make do, ends meet, babies, way, clothing, breakfast and dinner and supper, quilts, homes, apologies, baskets, beds, light of it, room. (235)

The poem contains vignettes of both Winnie Mandela, beside her burned-down house, and Marion Todd, a ''shy'' Nebraskan woman who, holding a handful of wheat, parked herself in front of a train bearing nuclear materials, and, just shy of being flattened after the train stopped two feet in front of her, was hauled off to jail. It ends with an imperative that women make ''mischief, a difference, a miracle, ready'' and prays ''Give us this day/ our arbitrary bread'' (239). The freedom to experience self-actualization goes hand-in-hand with the freedom to act politically in the world without threat of cruel reprisal.

Robin Morgan writes eloquent poetry on a number of subjects, not just those that are overtly feminist. Some of the poems are responses to paintings, by Van Gogh and Bosch among others, the implicit theme being the growth of the artist through encounters with other artists' work. She parodies John Donne and

Shakespeare (this with a feminist twist, as in "Ten Sonnets to the Light Lady"). Her witty parody of Richard Lovelace's "To Lucasta," entitled "Going to the Wars," implies that the real battlefield is work and life. She flees the "vagary/ of . . . silk breasts/ and brain erotic" and taunts the vacuity of the love Lovelace had left (for the ill-conceived purpose of actual warfare) with the final lines: "I cannot love you just a little/ without loving living less" (205). As in "Lesbian Poem," the point is a disdain for the interference of empty romanticism with true fulfillment of the self in the battle of life.

The title poem for this collection, "Upstairs in the Garden," illustrates the interrelated themes of world harmony and self-fulfillment. The garden is the one on the rooftop of her apartment building in Manhattan, making it a sort of upstart androgynous fertility symbol. "The top of anything is just the base for something else," she tells us, noting that her guests watch the view of "other buildings," but she watches the garden itself. She thinks herself "eccentric" for tilling it. It is hard work, and technically the garden isn't even her own, but the landlord's. (She hints that she's a kind of sharecropper, but points out that she's had worse jobs.) Yet the garden, persisting in the polluted air, is a wonderful symbol of the potential of life, its surprises, and of Morgan's own creativity and connection to life.

SURVEY OF CRITICISM

There is no full-length critical study on the poetry of Robin Morgan, although her work has attracted the attention of serious critics from the beginning of her career to the present. The reviews are generally mixed, but from the publication of *Monster* to her latest volume, *Upstairs in the Garden,* reviewers show growing appreciation of Morgan's craft.

David Lehmann finds that *Monster* "cannot withstand the extra-literary demands its author places on it." It fails, he says, "to take an active cognizance of the problem . . . of the conflicting exigencies of politics and literature (174)." He faults "Arraignment" for the murder/castration scenario I have mentioned above, yet he praises individual poems like "Dachau" and "The Invisible Woman" for channeling anger into the restraint of traditional poetic forms. May Swenson says the genitalia scene from the title poem, "Monster," is "a snatch [she] liked" (26) and like Lehmann, praises "The Invisible Woman" and some of the sonnets. She complains, however, that "The main body of [Morgan's] book consists of sprawling manifestoes, diatribes, polemical essays and editorials, laments, and excoriations—too much that is deliberately formless" (26).

Adrienne Rich, however, describes Morgan more sympathetically as a poet of "considerable means. There is a savage elegance, a richness of vocabulary, a thrust and steely polish." She sees the final section of the book as "stripped down, almost asceticized, in language . . . frankly militant, didactic and functional," implying that Morgan intentionally sacrifices form and other poetic conventions to write a "powerful, challenging book" (294).

Reviews of *Lady of the Beasts* are generally enthusiastic. Jay Parini notes that the volume surpasses *Monster* and asserts that Morgan will "soon be regarded as one of our first ranking poets." He praises "Network of the Imaginary Mother," especially its final sequence "Voices from Six Tapestries," which "reaches beyond politics into an ecstatic vision of 'birth, initiation, consummation, repose, and death' " (Review of *Lady* 303). Alicia Ostriker, while noting some lapses into "*West Side Story* star-crossed by C. G. Jung," celebrates her ability to combine "comedy and strong rhetoric" and perform successfully in a "middle style" (158).

Depth Perception draws further praise from Parini: Morgan has, he argues, departed further from "unassimilated feminism" and has "gradually absorbed its ideas and concerns into an eloquent and forceful lyricism" (*Times Literary Supplement*). Sheila Coghill notes the way Morgan "evokes, expands, and transforms archetypal imagery" (1982). Still another reviewer remarks, "an assured and engaging voice that need not be strident to be persuasive" (*Booklist*).

Dry Your Smile, Morgan's first novel, has been called "poignant but frustrating," complicated more than elucidated by its many perspectives, created by a fictional strategy of setting a novel within the novel and a number of diaries commenting on the action. Still, according to Alida Becker, the book takes on "marvelous vividness and strength" when politics and philosophizing are not too much at the fore (16). One review of the children's book, *The Mer-Child,* also find politics obtrusive and sees Morgan outperformed in the genre by Randall Jarrell.

Morgan's latest volume of poetry, *Upstairs in the Garden: Poems Selected and New 1968–1988,* is lauded by Christine Stenstrom as a "generous collection" that proves "that politically informed poetry can stir the spirit as well as the conscience." There is a "hard-hitting incantatory expansiveness" in the longer poems, and they "successfully wed feminist rhetoric with vivid imagery and a sensitivity to the music of language" (99). Remarks Catherine R. Stimpson, "A large audience will welcome them" (back cover).

BIBLIOGRAPHY

Works by Robin Morgan

Poetry

Monster: Poems. New York: Random House, 1972.
Lady of the Beasts: Poems. New York: Random House, 1976.
Death Benefits: Poems. Copper Canyon Press, 1981.
Depth Perception: New Poems and a Masque. New York: Anchor/Doubleday, 1982.
Upstairs in the Garden: Poems Selected and New: 1968–1988. New York: Norton, 1990.

Fiction

Dry Your Smile. Garden City, NY: Doubleday, 1987.
The Tenth Power: A Novel. Work-in-progress.

Nonfiction Books

Sisterhood Is Powerful: An Anthology of Writings from the Women's Liberation Movement (ed.). New York: Random House (Vintage), 1970.

The New Women: A Motive Anthology on Women's Liberation. (ed., with Charlotte Bunch-Weeks and Joanne Cooke). New York: Bobbs-Merrill, 1970.

Going Too Far: The Personal Chronicle of a Feminist. New York: Random House, 1977.

The Anatomy of Freedom: Feminism, Physics, and Global Politics. Garden City, NY: Doubleday/Anchor, 1982.

Sisterhood Is Global: The International Women's Movement Anthology (ed.). Garden City, NY: Doubleday Anchor. 1985.

The Demon Lover: On the Sexuality of Terrorism. New York: Norton, 1989.

The Word of a Woman: Feminist Dispatches 1968–1992. New York: Norton, 1992.

Other

"Our Creations Are in the First Place Ourselves" (in two cassettes). Iowa State University of Science and Technology, 1974.

(With Jesse Spicer Zerner) *The Mer-Child: A Legend for Children and Other Adults.* CUNY: The Feminist Press, 1992.

Works about Robin Morgan

Basel, Marilyn K. "Robin Morgan." *Comtemporary Authors: New Revision Series* 29: 305–07.

Becker, Alida, Rev. of *Dry Your Smile. New York Times Book Review* 27 Sept. 1987: 16.

Coghill, Sheila. Rev. of *Depth Perception: New Poems and a Masque. Library Journal* 1982: 1329.

Ostriker, Alicia. "Drought and Flood." Revs. of *Sphere: The Form of a Motion,* by A. R. Ammons; *Lady of the Beasts,* by Robin Morgan; and *Ginkgo,* by Felix Pollak. *Partisan Review* 10 Jan. 1980: 153–61.

Parini, Jay. Rev. of *Lady of the Beasts* (one of several poetry volumes reviewed in same review). *Poetry* Aug. 1977: 301–03.

———. Rev. of *Depth Perception: New Poems and a Masque. Times Literary Supplement* 12 Nov. 1982: 125.

Rev. of *Depth Perception. Booklist* July 1982: 1415.

Rev. of *Depth Perception. Publishers Weekly* 9 Apr. 1982: 49.

Rev. of *The Mer-Child: A Legend for Children and Other Adults,* by Robin Morgan and Jesse Spicer Zerner. *Publishers Weekly* 22 Nov. 1991: 57.

Rich, Adrienne. "Voices in the Wilderness." Rev. of *Monster. Washington Post Book World* 31 Dec. 1972: 3.

"Robin Morgan." *Who's Who of American Women,* 17th ed. 1991–1992.

Stenstrom, Christine. Rev. of *Upstairs in the Garden. Library Journal* July 1990: 99.

Stuttaford, Genevieve. Rev. of *Upstairs in the Garden: Poems Selected and New, 1968–1988. Publishers Weekly* 1 June 1990: 53.

Swenson, May. Rev. of *Monster. New York Times Book Review* 19 Nov. 1972: 7, 26.

LESLÉA NEWMAN (1955–   )

Annie Dawid

BIOGRAPHY

Born in 1955 in Brooklyn, New York, to working-class parents, Lesléa Newman says of her origins: "I come from a long line of immigrants who came to America not by choice. I don't know what would have happened to my writing if there hadn't been raging anti-Semitism" (Koplow 8A).

Newman's life as a writer is inextricably linked to politics, and she dates her coming-of-age to her exposure to feminism in her late twenties. "I started reading feminist literature and asked myself where I had been my whole life" ("I Have a Lot to Say" 1).

Geographically, Newman grew up on Long Island, New York; she then lived in Burlington, Vermont, where she received her Bachelor of Science degree in Education from the University of Vermont in 1977. For several years she roamed the northeastern United States, Israel, and Europe, working at a variety of jobs. Eventually she attended the Naropa Institute in Boulder, Colorado, where she studied poetry with Allen Ginsberg and Anne Waldman and received a certificate in Poetics in 1980. At twenty-seven, she came out as a lesbian, discovered the fiction writer inside her, and newly embraced her Judaism. During a workshop with writer Grace Paley she produced her first story, "A Letter to Harvey Milk." She credits Paley with giving her "permission to write in Yinglish. I didn't know you were allowed to " (Interview 19 Apr. 1992).

Although Newman had described herself as "very staunchly a poet"—she had two poems in *Seventeen* as a teenager—she took to prose immediately. "One day I was writing and the image of a piece of garlic bread just came into my mind, and it was attached to a hand and the hand was attached to a character's arm" (Koplow 7A). Her first novel, *Good Enough to Eat,* had its genesis in a short story that kept growing; she finished the book in six months.

By this time Newman had returned East: first, to Boston for another stint at graduate school; then to New York; and, finally, permanently, to Northampton, Massachusetts, where she now lives and works as a full-time writer and teacher, conducting a series of writing workshops for women, "Write From the Heart." Traveling often to give readings and workshops, Newman is in demand as a lesbian writer, a Jewish writer, a writer whose work often touches on crucial women's issues—including incest and eating disorders—and as a writer who speaks from outside mainstream publishing.

Newman assumes that her books are not reviewed in the *New York Times Book Review* because of homophobia. "A lesbian has to work twice as hard as a straight woman to get her work into the mainstream," she says (Interview 19 Apr. 1992). Other barriers arise in the Jewish and gay communities. "I feel divided constantly. In gay communities I'm too Jewish, and in Jewish communities I'm too gay" (Interview 19 Apr. 1992). She worries that the multi-cultural climate does not seem to include Judaism. However, her 1992 novel, *In Every Laugh a Tear,* is, according to Newman, "very Jewish, very lesbian." While she experiments with writing without Jewish content, her work inevitably turns toward Jewish themes. She finds this both a weakness and a strength. When she gets far from Judaism, she finds she is not writing "in her own language" (Interview 19 Apr. 1992), which leads her away from the solidly Jewish and Yiddish voice that permeates her best work. Quoting Irena Klepfisz, Newman says, "Language is our only homeland" (Koplow 8A). For Newman, the voice of her Yiddish-speaking grandmother shapes both style and content. "I remember how hard I worked not to talk like my grandmother, and I feel like that's a big loss. When I hear Yiddish I get all choked up" (Koplow 8A).

But Newman is now branching out, writing stories where "not all the characters are Jewish lesbians" (Interview 19 Apr. 1992). Her plans include more children's books with Jewish and gay themes, a young adult novel, and nonfiction works based on her writing workshops.

MAJOR THEMES

Instead of asking what Newman writes about, one might better ask: What doesn't she write about? In her poems, short stories, novels, plays, and children's books, Newman covers a range of material that does not easily lend itself to neat categorization. In fact, her most successful work combines personal, political, Jewish, sexuality related, feminist, and other concerns. Sometimes it is difficult to separate out homophobia from anti-Semitism.

Jewish Identity

Newman's work is marked by the use of Hebrew and Yiddish, as well as a liberal discussion of the Jewish predilection for culinary delights. (Most of her books are accompanied by glossaries to aid the uninitiated.) "Shabbos," the second poem in *Love Me Like You Mean It,* begins with the preparation of the Sabbath meal: "I arrive at your door with a bag/full of *challah,* candles, candlesticks,/apples, honey. . . . '*Shabbos* to go,' I announce." The second half of the poem speaks of the shared history of two lesbians whose grandmothers fled pogroms in neighboring towns in Russia. These young women find each other in Western Massachusetts, another foreign land, and "grow/to love each other as fiercely/and as passionately as their grandmothers'/will for survival" (5).

In her prose, Newman often writes of the intersection between Jewish history and contemporary Jewish issues. "A Letter to Harvey Milk" charts the story of an old man, Harry, originally from Russia, now living out his widower's life in San Francisco. He attends a creative writing course taught by a Jewish lesbian, Barbara, who wants to learn more about her people's history. Her family has disowned her and will tell her no stories. "Believe me," says Harry, "life in the *shtetl* is nothing worth knowing about. Hunger and more hunger. Better off we're here in America, the past is the past" (33). But Barbara is hungry for knowledge, and she presses Harry to reveal his secrets. In his journal, Harry writes of his friend, Izzie, a Holocaust survivor, who announces to Harry he has seen a person wearing a pink triangle, as homosexuals were forced to do in the camps. Izzie then confesses a secret love he shared with a young man in the camps after Izzie's wife and family were killed. The man was beaten to death for not giving Izzie's name to the guards, and Izzie has kept this story to himself since the camps. After revealing the story, Izzie weeps and sleeps in Harry's arms and, not long afterward, dies peacefully. Harry's stories of anti-Semitism are not confined to the Old World. In San Francisco, Harry's friend, the gay politician Harvey Milk, is assassinated in yet another tragedy of Jewish homosexuality:

In the old country, I saw things you shouldn't know from, things you couldn't imagine one person could do to another. But here in America, a man climbs through the window, kills the Mayor of San Francisco, kills Harvey Milk, and a couple years later he's walking around on the street? This I never thought I'd see in my whole life. But from a country that kills the Rosenbergs, I should expect something different? (34)

In "The Gift," a chronological account of a girl growing up Jewish in a gentile world, we witness the phenomenon of the self-hating Jew. Rachel's very Jewish physical appearance aggrieves her all through childhood and adolescence. She tries desperately to unkink her curls, slim down her hips, and bleach her hair blonde with sunlight. She is surrounded by female family members with "nose jobs." As she comes into an understanding of her own Jewish identity, she finds herself with a non-Jewish girlfriend who cannot understand Rachel's anger when the lover complains that she is "a little Jew-ed out" after so many *Seders* ("A Letter to Harvey Milk" 23). Later, she splits with a Jewish lover after the other woman goes to a Christmas party on the first night of Chanuka. Being both a Jew and a lesbian makes Rachel very lonely. "Being alive is lonely," she reminds herself (27). The story ends with Rachel and a new Jewish lover, Aviva, singing the "*Shema*" together in a synagogue as the two lesbians find community and support in a return to their religious heritage.

Lesbian Identity

"Three years ago I came out as a lesbian/and came home/to my Jewishness./ All of a sudden Yiddish sprang from my lips/like leaves from a barren tree" ("Passover Poem," *Love Me Like You Mean It* 74). Inevitably, we find homosexuality in Newman's characters linked to their Jewish identities. The lesbian in "A Letter to Harvey Milk" says of her attempt to speak with her parents: "I tried to explain I couldn't help being gay, like I couldn't help being a Jew, but that they didn't want to hear" (39).

Homophobia, like anti-Semitism, is a cause that Newman's characters take on again and again, bravely, though not always successfully, even when the homophobia exists within Jewish contexts. In her story "The Word Problem" (*Secrets*), the protagonist's parents fail to invite her lover of ten years to her brother's wedding. Unlike the parents in "A Letter to Harvey Milk," who disown their daughter for her homosexuality, these parents prefer to pretend their daughter's lesbianism does not exist. The word problem of the title is the "L-word," whose presence in any conversation turns talk into warfare. "Ma," says Patty in a telephone call in which she tries to rectify the wedding invitation problem, "I know it's hard, but you've got to accept the fact that I am a lesbian." Her mother's response: "Don't you dare use that word with me" (187). Patty's retort to her mother's admonishment is "Lesbian, lesbian, lesbian" (187).

The language of lesbian sexuality, rare in mainstream literature, also is expressed in Newman's poetry. In Part IV of her most recent collection, *Sweet Dark Places,* Newman offers twenty love poems, freely celebrating sex between women. In "Signs of Love," she uses the vocabulary of street signs for a humorous take on women's bodies. "Enter Here/Merge/Bump/Slippery When Wet/No Exit/Stay in Lane" (90). And in "How I Want You," the speaker adds to the list of ways she wants her lover: "I want you the way only a woman/ can want another woman/with lips smiling arms open/cheeks blushing knees shaking/cunt throbbing heart pounding" (81).

While Newman celebrates lesbianism, she also reminds us of the problems lesbians face in a homophobic world. In "August Night," a lesbian's house is set afire by a gang of young men. "Supreme Sodomy" explores the impact of the High Court's ruling on sodomy as the decision makes its way into the bedroom of the lesbian speaker. The gay parents—male and female—in Newman's books for children must aid their children in overcoming the prejudice they inevitably face at school and on the street. On Gay Pride Day, Gloria (*Gloria Goes to Gay Pride*) sees a solemn nuclear family with their sign, "Gays Go Home." She learns for the first time that her two mamas, her pet dog,

Butterscotch, and she are not, in fact, the happy family she believed them to be, at least not beyond their politically progressive small world.

Eating Disorders

Newman's first book of prose, *Good Enough to Eat,* deals with eating disorders in young women, a theme present in nearly every volume—no matter what the genre—of Newman's work. Eventually, the protagonist evolves from a self-hating, bulimic heterosexual to a lesbian learning to accept her body and herself. Anorexics, bulimics, and compulsive eaters inflict endless pain upon their bodies and psyches for not living up to the American feminine ideal. In her non-fiction book, *Some Body to Love,* Newman says to her readers: "This book is for any woman who wishes or who has wished that her body was a different shape or size, and if you were brought up in the United States of America in the twentieth century, that probably means you" (4). She calls eating disorders eating "dis-eases," "to describe the condition of a woman not being at ease with herself" (8). The book contains numerous writing exercises designed to help women resolve their obsession with food and its attendant self-hatred. She offers autobiographical details from which we learn that Newman's eating disorders controlled her entire life—as they do many women's—until she did extensive therapy and feminist reading in her early thirties. With the end of her eating disorder came a new surge of creativity in her writing (eleven books) and the surfacing of memories of child abuse.

Sexual Abuse

"Rage," a seventeen-page poem chronicling the effects of sexual abuse, begins: "I saw the best women of my generation destroyed/by incest" (*Sweet Dark Places* 7). What follows is a catalogue of ills that links female self-destructive behavior and childhood sexual abuse. Newman describes the way some male adults destroy a female child's trust, sense of self, sense of wholeness, and ability to love. In this poem, she praises the heroism of Dr. Elizabeth Morgan, who went to jail rather than hand her daughter over to her husband who allegedly abused her. Newman also addresses the abuser in this poem as well, wishing upon him the horrible life of the abused. That section ends with: "I want you to feel all this rage/and not know what to do with it" (21).

Other Political Themes

Newman's work, particularly her poetry, addresses topics of the day, especially when they involve women. In "That Woman Is Drumming," Newman looks at the history of racism faced by women of color in the United States. In "Central Park Jogger," she imagines the very ordinary day preceding the violent gang rape of a woman out for an after-work run to relieve the stress of an urban, fast-track, lonely life.

SURVEY OF CRITICISM

Depending upon the source of the reviews of her work (whether Jewish-oriented, gay, mainstream), Newman's critical reception has evoked a variety of responses. At least one Jewish reviewer complains that Newman "does not successfully convey what it is she feels about being Jewish" (Kinberg 42). Meanwhile, mainstream publications have trouble with her very Jewish language. "The work's immediate and genuine poignancy is sometimes marred by Newman's insistence on sprinkling Yiddish terms and speech patterns throughout the dialogue" (Rev. of *A Letter to Harvey Milk, Publisher's Weekly,* 88). And, in an interesting conflation of gay and Jewish responses, Judy Greenspan, reviewing *A Letter to Harvey Milk* in *Lambda Rising Book Report* writes: "Even the most assimilated Jew (like myself) can't help but be moved and reminded by the warmth and vitality of the stories. Newman's style, while differing from story to story, contains a self-consciousness that is distinctly and ethically Jewish."

Interestingly, her children's books have received the most media exposure. Reviewers from *Newsweek* to *The Bulletin of the Center for Children's Books* agree that, as there are now approximately seven million children of gay parents in the United States, books such as *Heather Has Two Mommies* serve a growing need. The *Library Journal,* for example, noted: "As more lesbian couples are choosing to have children through alternative insemination, this book is an important addition to library collections serving both conventional and alternative families" (1354).

BIBLIOGRAPHY

Works by Lesléa Newman

Novels

Good Enough to Eat. Ithaca, NY: Firebrand Books, 1986.
In Every Laugh a Tear. Norwich, VT: New Victoria Publishers, 1992.

Short Story Collections

A Letter to Harvey Milk. Ithaca, NY: Firebrand Books, 1988.
Secrets. Norwich, VT: New Victoria Publishers, 1990.

Poetry

Just Looking for My Shoes. Seattle: Back Door Press, 1980.
Love Me Like You Mean It. Santa Cruz, CA: HerBooks, 1987.

Bubbe Meisehs by Shayneh Maidelehs: An Anthology of Poetry by Jewish Granddaughters About Our Grandmothers. Santa Cruz, CA: HerBooks, 1989.
Sweet Dark Places. Santa Cruz, CA: HerBooks, 1991.

Nonfiction

Some Body to Love: A Guide to Loving the Body You Have. Chicago: Third Side Press, 1991.

Children's Books

Heather Has Two Mommies. Boston: Alyson Publications, 1990.
Gloria Goes to Gay Pride. Boston: Alyson Publications, 1991.
Belinda's Bouquet. Boston: Alyson Publications, 1991.

Films

A Letter to Harvey Milk. Produced and directed by Yariv Kohn, York University, Canada, 1990.

Plays

After All We've Been Through. Durham, NC: Women in Performance, April, 1989; Portland, OR: Portland, Women's Theatre Co., April, 1989; Lexington, KY: Between the Acts, February, 1990; Springfield, IL: The Writers Barbeque, 1991.
Rage. Gay Performances Company, New York, 1991.

Articles

"Writing as Self-Discovery," *The Writer,* January 1988, 9.
"I Have a Lot to Say—All Women Do," *Mama Bears' News & Notes,* March 1990, 1.
Telephone interview. Annie, 19 April 1992.

Works about Lesléa Newman

Becker, Robin. "Arguing with Each Other, God, Governments, and Torah." *Sojourner,* August 1990, 12B–13B.
Berry, Henry. Rev. of *Love Me Like You Mean It. The Small Press Book Review,* July/ August 1988, 4.
"Daddy Is Out of the Closet." *Newsweek,* 7 January 1991, 60.
Fensome, Helen. "Sickening for Something." *Times Literary Supplement,* 13–19 November 1987, 1249a.
Geduldig, Lisa. "Interweaving Histories." *Bay Area Reporter,* August 1991, 24–25.
Rev. of *Good Enough to Eat. off our backs,* October, 1987.
Green, Allison. "Revelations." *Bay Windows,* November 8–November 14, 1990.
Greenspan, Judy. Rev. of *A Letter to Harvey Milk. Lambda Rising Book Report.*
Rev. of *Heather Has Two Mommies. The Bulletin of the Center for Children's Books* February 1990, 144.
Rev. of *Heather Has Two Mommies. Library Journal,* 1 March 1990, 1354.
Rev. of *Heather Has Two Mommies. Small Press Book Review,* July 1990, 20.

Jurgens, Jane. Rev. of *Secrets: Short Stories. Gay and Lesbian Taskforce Newsletter,* 3.1-2, Fall 1990/Winter 1991: 13.

Kinberg, Clare. ''Come Out, Come Out, Wherever You Are!'' *Genesis* 2: Autumn 1988, 41–42.

Koplow, Gail. ''Lesléa Newman: Writing from the Heart.'' *Sojourner,* August 1989: 7–8A.

Rev. of *A Letter to Harvey Milk. Publishers Weekly,* 20 May 1988, 86–88.

Pfeifer, Deborah. ''A Garden of Readerly Delights.'' *Bay Area Reporter,* 11 October 1990, 45.

Stato, Joanne. Rev. of *Gloria Goes to Gay Pride. off our backs,* July 1991: 21–22.

Sturgis, Susanna J. ''One Step at a Time.'' *Women's Review of Books,* May 1987: 13–14.

Tilchen, Maida. ''Internal Imperatives of a Charming Addict.'' *Gay Community News Book Review,* February 1987: 15–21.

In addition to the above, Newman's stories and poems have appeared in numerous magazines and anthologies. Magazines include: *Seventeen, Lilith, Common Lives, Sojourner, Outlook, Sinister Wisdom, The James White Review.* Anthologies include: *America and I* (Boston: Beacon Press, 1990); *Women on Women* (New York: New American Library, 1990); *Lesbian Love Stories* (vols I and II) Freedom, CA: Crossing Press, 1989, 1991); *Bushfire* (Boston: Alyson Publications, 1991).

TILLIE OLSEN (1912–   )

Kay Hoyle Nelson

BIOGRAPHY

In a 1991 talk at the Jewish Community Center in Omaha, Tillie Lerner Olsen traced her heritage back to her parents' involvement in the failed 1905 Russian revolution when Samuel Lerner's sentence to Siberia was averted by Ida's daring rescue. She brought several women wearing extra clothing to the jail so that Samuel could dress as a woman and escape without detection. His subsequent departure from his family produced an equally difficult break. Unable to bend to his father's insistence on adherence to the old Jewish Orthodoxy, Samuel left, refusing to kiss the proffered *mezuza*. Olsen concluded this part of her history with the lesson her father later drew: "I did not know then what I know now, that I could have kissed it with my lips and my heart and I would not be betraying any of my principles, only living up to them because they are really about trying to make a world in which we can love and not be cruel" (Wade 29).

The young Tillie Lerner grew up, daughter to the avowed Socialists who made their separate ways to New York City then settled in Nebraska, where Samuel was employed variously as a farmer, packing house worker, and house painter while Ida raised their six children. Olsen's *Yiddishkeit* developed as her family took part in the Socialist heritage and political organizations of secular Jews. From her father, who served as secretary of the Nebraska Socialist Party, she learned the value of activism; from her mother, who briefly attended an Omaha night school for reading and writing, she learned the importance of education. Although stuttering limited her early speech, Tillie listened attentively to those who visited her home—Socialist orators, immigrant and African American neighbors, packing house workers, even cowboys. With a social conscience came a lifelong love of language. She read voraciously and in high school she began to write. During those formative years she grew up with literature about the working class. When she discovered an April 1861 issue of *Atlantic Monthly* with Rebecca Harding Davis's unsigned story *Life in the Iron Mills*, Olsen found the first art outside of Socialist literature that revealed the possibility of speaking for the working class.

In 1929, after the eleventh grade, Olsen's formal education ended. She embarked on a decades-long, low-income employment odyssey. Like so many of her contemporaries in the 1930s, she joined the Young Communist League for its anti-Nazi posture, its promises of community for the common worker, its activity against hunger and joblessness, and its perspectives on national and international issues. In Kansas City, she helped in organizing packing house workers and, by the end of 1931, was jailed. A year later, she moved to Minnesota to recover from the pleurisy she had contracted in jail; there, pregnant with her first daughter, Karla, she began writing. In 1933, she relocated to California, where she balanced family, activism, and writing. During the 1934 San Francisco Maritime strike and its "Bloody Thursday," she worked behind the scenes, mimeographing and typing. During that year, she published two social-protest poems, the first chapter of *Yonnondio*, and two articles. Impressed Random House editors located the writer who had been jailed again and offered her a monthly stipend for succeeding novel chapters. Planning to accept, the young mother sent her daughter to stay with relatives; she worked on drafts of chapters but did not publish.

During the later 1930s and into the 1940s, she began living with Jack Olsen, and her family grew to four daughters. In that era of internationalism, her energies centered on efforts to keep World War II from happening (personal interview 30 Dec. 1991). She worked at various jobs, helped with the PTA and women's issues; she wrote several columns for *People's World*, but there was no time for other writing. The Cold War and the McCarthy era brought economic hardship: Jack's record as an open Communist Party member barred his warehouse employment, and Tillie's jobs lasted only until FBI agents met with her employers. But by the mid-1950s, freed somewhat from a mother's persistent worries about young children, Tillie Olsen began to write again.

In 1962, four exceptional stories were collected in *Tell Me a Riddle*. During this decade and the next, the working-class woman writer earned academic and literary awards, and she began university teaching. In 1974, she published the unfinished novel *Yonnondio: From the Thirties*. The American Academy and National Institute of Arts and Letters recognized her distinguished contribution to American literature. Universities began conferring honorary degrees. Her interest in women's literary heritage led her to reissue the Davis work along with her own extensive commentary; she developed the first women's studies reading list. In 1978, various works about the relationship of circumstances and creativity were collected in *Silences*. International acclaim flowed from England and Norway; honor at home came in a "Tillie Olsen Day" in San Francisco and in a Tillie Olsen Week at a five-college symposium in the Illinois-Iowa Quad Cities. Although the years were marred by the death of Jack Olsen, the 1980s and early 1990s were filled with travel, lectures, readings, writing, and tributes to marginalized working women—all activities that enhanced her place in American letters as a feminist and advocate for the working class.

MAJOR THEMES

The 1934 poems and fiction show a young writer steeped in working-class issues and determined to re-educate her audience. A reader's letter to *New Masses* protesting sweatshops in San Antonio provided the details for the first poem, "I Want You Women Up North to Know." Relying on the sensitivity of women to material conditions, seeing a common ground in their sewing tasks, and trusting readers to change if informed, Tillie Lerner stitches together the power of upper-middle-class women buying the children's dresses in northern department stores with the labor of Mexican American women sewing those garments. The second poem, "There Is a Lesson," widens the range of concern as it argues against the Nazi takeover in Austria that cleared the streets, brought fear and repression, and kept from their schooling the children who are the hope, promise, and potential of a nation. But Olsen's signature emerges in the first fiction that makes the plight of the working class the experience of its women. With many voices as foils for that of the young Mazie, "The Iron Throat" tells a disrupting tale of a 1920s American heartland rife with a physical and spiritual exploitation of land and worker.

The reportage of that year cultivates the art of testimony. In "Thousand-Dollar Vagrant," the nineteen-year-old speaks out. She indicts a system that incarcerates those, like herself, who would alleviate social inequity and human misery. In "The Strike," she initiates the twin themes of a working-class confinement and its imminent revolt. Using the seagoing and longshore response to the ouster of waterfront unions as a backdrop, she recounts the dilemma for the activist who is torn between the desire to participate and the need to report, the paradox for the artist who is astonished by the irony of violent clash and the necessity of an ordered and orderly representation. The article concludes with the image of a pregnant woman left behind on a street corner in the aftermath of violence, standing rigid and impassioned against the sky, collecting events into memory and promising soon to revolt again. This image depicts the writer's posture as well.

While the vision rooted in the Communist Old Left ties Olsen to the later Socialist and feminist movements, the voice connects her with an American poetic tradition singing out against imperialism, war, and slavery (personal interview 20 Dec. 1991). The title of the novel, started in the early 1930s and worked on until mid-decade, then put aside to be rediscovered and published forty years later, alludes to Whitman's "Yonnondio," which laments a world that survives only in sounds like the Iroquois word. *Yonnondio: From the Thirties* also laments the "unlimned" and ties this early novel with her later discussions in *Silences*, but it challenges as well. The powerful myth of a prosperous American westward expansion is deflated as the story tracks the

Holbrook family from Wyoming coal mine to Dakota tenant farm to Nebraska slaughter house, each employment castigating the oppressive capitalist system. The women who may lack full understanding, power, and voice nevertheless evidence an attentiveness, aspiration, and energy—in the young daughter, Mazie, awakened by the whistle that sounds death in the deep mines; in the mother, Anna, bowing to the needs of her husband and his abuse yet remaining sensitive to the dreams and potential of their children and believing that education will improve their lives; in the baby, Bess, pounding into the kitchen table a statement of her incipient worth. This theme of survival reappears years later in "Requa," another first chapter for a planned longer fiction. Almost a companion piece, it follows an orphaned boy in the Pacific Northwest coming to his potential under the care of a ministering uncle.

Olsen's most celebrated stories, however, are collected in *Tell Me a Riddle*. The first story, "I Stand Here Ironing," frequently anthologized and often taught, captures within a moment of reverie a mother who, while she stands and irons a dress, also attempts to iron out the complexity of motherhood and the intricacies of the mother-child relationship. Asked by an unknown speaker to talk about her eldest daughter, Emily, she recalls two lives so interwoven that she cannot speak of one without the other, cannot relate individual circumstances without the economic, social, and psychological deprivations that shape and misshape. The history of the nineteen-year-old mother deserted by a man who cannot bear their poverty becomes the story of her daughter left daily by a mother who had to work as a waitress to keep their lives intact. It becomes a story of tellings—of Emily, first as a baby enchanted by light, color, texture, and sound; then in childhood, scarred by her social circumstances as well as by childhood chicken pox; later, as a school girl with crushes rejected; finally, with siblings, relationships full of rivalries and love. It ends with the nineteen-year-old girl's successful high-school pantomimes as a parallel to her mother's history-making gestures. This articulation of social and cultural conditions, suggested by gesture, frees Olsen to highlight broader questions of human relationships—the ability to comprehend, articulate, or influence.

These same provocative motifs reappear in the second story, "Hey Sailor, What Ship?" The drunken sailor Whitey stumbles out of a stinking Frisco tavern, unable to recall where his pay has gone. He seems to reach safe harbor, only within his own thoughts of days on ship or in the thoughtfulness of his old friends Lennie and Helen who take him in, feed him, and minister to his sickness, loneliness, and isolation. Yet he attains the stature of a hero because he can understand, speak, and move a listener. For the family, and the children, particularly, he revives the idealism of Jose Rizal, hero of the Philippines, as he recites "El Ultimo Adiós." For Olsen, words such as those she first heard in 1949 from a small Filipino seaman enable us to "learn from living lips" (personal interview 30 Dec. 1991). Impassioned words startle and precipitate change. In the third story, "O Yes," Olsen dramatizes the vitality in language which fascinates her. Carrie, a young white girl, attends the baptism of her young, black friend Parry and nearly succumbs in the sea-surging of the congregational voice. Later at home, the young witness listens to her family's analysis of the events at the church, equally confounded by their ordered discourse and rational explanation of the differences between segregated communities. This stunning contrast proposes, for young girl and reader alike, a new measure of the human spirit, one taken by its vocal dimensions.

↓   The fourth and most admired story, "Tell Me a Riddle," with its subtitle from a Socialist hymn "These Things Shall Be," comes as a retrospective of the activist-writer committed to speaking and listening. Speech moves into the center with the colorful Yiddish sounds, with an old Jewish couple planning retirement and arguing—he calling her "Mrs. Word Miser," she thinking him a "babbler." Twentieth-century communication blocks are parodied in her hearing aid turned off in protest of his too-loud television. This story of the loss of sympathetic and empathetic hearing works like a *midrash* as Eva and David replay the Edenic Fall into discord. After years of marriage, with the wellspring of their earlier revolutionary Russian idealism nearly buried, they approach life alone together. Their roles have shifted once more, as he looks forward to play at his lodge's Haven and she turns silent, obstinate, solitary, shutting out even the grandchildren. Then, with discovery of the old woman's cancer comes their odyssey across the country and a revisiting of the change in values. In their children's home, they find offspring who barely know that early history of struggle; in a retirement community, they meet old comrades who rarely recall their momentous feats. This journey moves Eva into introspection and reenvisioning. On her deathbed, she begins to sing. Within the refrains of a haunting song of that revolution live the memories of a girlhood in her native Russia, her fight against her father's prohibition against reading, and her countrymen's proscription against dreaming. She sings into the source of meaning, and the song takes her back, and her husband also.

In *Silences*, Olsen embarks on a literary odyssey and performs a similar reclamation. In this collection of works about barriers to artistic productivity, she delves past the dailiness of the human condition in order to locate the creative strength driven beneath a flood of activity; she seeks, by this educative process, to release the waiting creative and idealistic impulse that valiantly struggles to survive. Another Eva, she moves back through the years of silence to that time of her own inspiration in the work and life of Rebecca Harding Davis; she sings of that earlier writer's survival and her own, prompting listeners to undertake a comparable journey.

SURVEY OF CRITICISM

From her earliest work, Olsen has been singled out as a writer with exceptional talent. In a 1934 review of new fiction, Robert Cantwell said of "The Iron Throat," "the imagery, the metaphors distilled out of common speech, are startling in their brilliance" (297). Fifty years later, readers of *Tell Me a Riddle* cite anew the poetic sensitivity cultivated through meticulous writing and re-writing. Finding the clarity reminiscent of a Thornton Wilder or a Dylan Tho-mas, William Van O'Connor praises those voices that ameliorate her anguished worlds. Linda Park-Fuller, who has used *Yonnondio* as performance art, suggests that the multivocality enriches and energizes the social issues. Constance Coiner, however, looks beyond aesthetic and ideological virtuosity. Using Bakhtinian theory to elucidate the style in *Tell Me a Riddle*, she uncovers modes of dis-course that not only envigorate the writer's text, but that actually draw the readers into a complicity. This political end, she contends, links her analysis with Elizabeth Meese's assessment of the style in *Silences*. By arguing that Olsen's prose induces reader collaboration, critics establish the theoretical ori-entation of her art. But always Olsen has insisted that she depends on the reader to fill in the gaps in her text. By giving the reader freedom to create within the literary frame, to produce as well as respond, this writer steps to the forefront of our ways of thinking about communication.

Although for some readers, Olsen's fragmented and idiosyncratic narratives seem a violation of artist tenets, for others, they offer the epitome of stunning insight. These competing views, shaped in part by twentieth-century debates over the intersection of aesthetics and politics in art, come into sharp relief with evaluations of *Silences*. Looking for traditional development, support, and unity in art, Joyce Carol Oates complains of a lack of explanation, verification, co-herence. At the same time, however, Margaret Atwood praises the innovative form as "reminiscent of a biblical messenger, sole survivor of a relentless and obliterating catastrophe, a witness" (27).

A longtime admirer, Robert Coles reckons her appeal in a writing that not only entertains and enlivens but "upholds." Elaine Orr concurs, suggesting a feminist spirituality. As a harbinger of hope, the fiction engages every manner of critic, the professional and neophyte as well. Linda Kirschner notes how high-school students quickly grasp circumstances that affect the young Emily in "I Stand Here Ironing"; Naomi Jacobs hears college students, mothers themselves, identify the intersection of motherhood, racism, and poverty in "O Yes."

Particularly among women, this sensitivity to the complexities of women's lives has raised Olsen to the stature of an icon, a position she repeatedly resists. Joanne S. Frye supplies one rationale for adulation when she explains that "I Stand Here Ironing" re-establishes and returns to women the creative metaphor of motherhood. Economic and psychological paradigms crossed with the mother-daughter situation lure fewer compliments than the wider-ranging im-plications for human relationships. Helen Pike Bauer sees as more compelling a mother's fear that her daughter will learn and live the patterns that she herself models. Judith Gardiner probes an authorial ambivalence: She contends that Olsen's pairing of grandmother and granddaughter in the deathbed scene at the conclusion of *Tell Me a Riddle* allows her to recognize but circumvent a latent twentieth-century matrophobia.

With an uncanny ability to detect emerging issues, Olsen brings together disparate disciplines. Readers from sociology, psychology, and health care look for insights in her models of human behavior. With expertise in literature and medicine, Joanne Trautmann Banks cares less about illness as a metaphor for twentieth-century experience in *Tell Me a Riddle* than its actual ability to foster a new relationship between the body and spirit. Critics concentrating on the 1930s, the working class, the Communist Party, and the American Midwest find a mother lode in *Yonnondio: From the Thirties.* While a feminist like Catharine Stimpson might quarrel with the idealism that precludes a realistic model for action, others shift the inquiry to the rise of a working-class woman writer. Thus, Erika Duncan concentrates on Olsen's early life as instrumental to writing and activism, and Deborah Rosenfelt, anxious to establish a link between the Old Left of the 1930s and contemporary feminist culture, draws on unpublished letters and journals and the political context.

Because Olsen remains steadfast in opening wider perspectives and because she prefers to think in terms of universality rather than ethnicity, she is not widely recognized for her Jewish heritage. Nevertheless, she has eloquently traced her *Yiddishkeit.* Naomi Rubin interviewed Olsen on that period when her parents left the Russian ghetto and joined the Bund—that first Jewish Socialist Party that exacted a critical sorting—a clinging to knowledge, a discarding of tribal superstitions. This sorting may have become the model for Olsen's own persistent sifting of the past. With that generation of her parents, Olsen shares a fundamental belief in the human potential, the urgency of action against hatred and injustice, a sense of a life larger than the individual, and the simple joys of people coming together. Yet her own Jewish experience has been quite distinct from that of her parents. Linda Ray Pratt explores the unique features of her midwestern American heritage and Jewish background; and while mapping out the early working-class family life in Omaha, she simultaneously lays the groundwork for autobiographical studies. Other critics have tested strengths of these cultural ties. The ideology of the radical humanism and socialism that shapes Olsen's thinking has been examined by John Clayton, and Helge Normann Nilsen has explained how an insistence on potential and human perfectibility fits the radical movement. In focusing on the specific tradition that depicts the Jewish mother, Jacqueline Mintz situates Olsen between Anzia Yezierska and Susan Fromberg Schaeffer, but Bonnie Lyons undertakes a broader identification, one that ties political and social ideals, an emphasis on the mother-child relationship, the deep physical, emotional, intellectual, and spiritual hunger, and the poignant voice.

By these accounts and her own as well—witnessed in her Socialist convictions and in the actions she takes to keep those ideals from fading; confirmed in her commitment to language as the primary shaper—Tillie Olsen participates as an essential member of the community of Jewish American women writers.

BIBLIOGRAPHY

Works by Tillie Olsen

Poetry

"I Want You Women Up North to Know." *Partisan* 1 (Mar. 1934): 4.
"There Is a Lesson." *Partisan* 1 (Apr. 1934): 4.

Fiction

"The Iron Throat." *Partisan Review* 1.2 (Apr.-May 1934): 3–9.
Tell Me a Riddle. 1961. Rpt. New York: Delta, 1989.
Yonnondio: From the Thirties. 1974. Rpt. Delta, 1981.
"Requa" *Iowa Review* 1 (Summer 1970): 54–74.

Selected Nonfiction

"The Strike." *Partisan Review* 1 (Sept.-Oct. 1934): 3–9.
"Thousand Dollar Vagrant." *New Republic* 29 (Aug. 1934): 67–69.
"Dream Vision." *Mother to Daughter: Daughter to Mother: Mothers on Mothering: A Daybook and Reader,* Selected and Shaped by Tillie Olsen. Old Westbury, NY: Feminist, 1984. 261-64.
Silences. 1978. Rpt. New York: Delta, 1989.
Personal interview. 30 Dec. 1991.

Audiotapes

Tillie Olsen: A Profile. All Things Considered. National Public Radio. AT-800303.01/ 01-C 1980. 29 min.
Tillie Olsen Interview with Kay Bonetti. American Audio Prose Library AAPL 1132. 1981. 51 min.

Works about Tillie Olsen

Atwood, Margaret. "Obstacle Course." Rev. of *Silences. New York Times Book Review* (30 July 1978): 1ff.
Banks, Joanne Trautmann. "Death Labors." *Literature and Medicine* 9 (1990): 162–71.
Bauer, Helen Pike. " 'A child of anxious, not proud, love': Mother and Daughter in Tillie Olsen's 'I Stand Here Ironing.' " *Mother Puzzles: Daughters and Mothers in Contemporary American Literature.* Ed. Mickey Pearlman, Westport, CT: Greenwood, 1989. 35-39.
Burkom, Selma, and Margaret Williams. "De-Riddling Tillie Olsen's Writings." *San Jose Studies* 2 (Feb. 1976): 64–83.
Cantwell, Robert. "The Little Magazines." Rev. of "The Iron Throat." *New Republic* (25 July 1934): 295–97.
Clayton, John. "Grace Paley and Tillie Olsen: Radical Jewish Humanists." *Response: A Contemporary Jewish Review* 46 (1984): 37–52.
Coiner, Constance. " 'No One's Private Ground': A Bakhtinian Reading of Tillie Olsen's *Tell Me a Riddle.*" *Feminist Studies* 18.2 (Summer 1992): 257–81.

Coles, Robert. "Reconsideration." Rev. of *Tell Me a Riddle*. *New Republic* (6 Dec. 1975): 29–39.

Duncan, Erika. "Coming of Age in the Thirties: A Portrait of Tillie Olsen." *Book Forum* 6.2 (1982): 207–22.

Frye, Joanne S. " 'I Stand Here Ironing': Motherhood as Experience and Metaphor." *Studies in Short Fiction* 18.3 (Summer 1981): 287–92.

Gardiner, Judith Kegan. "A Wake for Mother: The Maternal Deathbed in Women's Fiction." *Feminist Studies* 4 (June 1978): 146–65.

Gelfant, Blanche K. "After Long Silence: Tillie Olsen's 'Requa.' " *Studies in American Fiction* 12.1 (Spring 1984): 61–69.

Jacobs, N[aomi] M. "Olsen's 'O Yes': Alva's Vision as Childbirth Account." *Notes on Contemporary Literature* 16.1 (Jan. 1986): 7–8.

Kamel, Rose. "Riddles and Silences: Tillie Olsen's Autobiographical Fiction." *Aggravating the Conscience: Jewish-American Literary Mothers in the Promised Land*, New York: Peter Lang, 1988. 81-114.

Kirschner, Linda Heinlein. "I Stand Here Ironing." *English Journal* 65 (Jan. 1976): 58–59.

Lyons, Bonnie. "Tillie Olsen: The Writer as a Jewish Woman." *Studies in American Jewish Literature* 5 (1986): 89–102.

Martin, Abigail. *Tillie Olsen*. Boise State University Western Writers Series 65. Boise, ID: State University, 1984.

Meese, Elizabeth A. "Deconstructing the Sexual Politic: Virginia Woolf and Tillie Olsen." *Crossing the Double-Cross: The Practice of Feminist Criticism*, Chapel Hill: University of North Carolina Press, 1986. 89-113.

Mintz, Jacqueline A. "The Myth of the Jewish Mother in Three Jewish, American, Female Writers. *Centennial Review* 22 (1978): 346–55.

Nelson, Kay Hoyle, and Nancy Huse. *The Critical Response to Tillie Olsen*. Westport, CT: Greenwood, [1993].

Nilsen, Helge Normann. "Tillie Olsens's [sic] 'Tell Me a Riddle': The Political Theme." *Etudes Anglaises: Grande-Bretagne, Etats-Unis* 37.2 (Apr.-June 1984): 163–69.

Oates, Joyce Carol. Rev. of *Silences*. *New Republic* (29 July 1978): 32–34.

O'Connor, William Van. "The Short Stories of Tillie Olsen." *Studies in Short Fiction* 1 (Fall 1963): 21–25.

Orr, Elaine Neil. *Tillie Olsen and a Feminist Spiritual Vision*. Jackson, MS: University Press of Mississippi, 1987.

Park-Fuller, Linda. "Voices: Bakhtin's Heteroglossia and Polyphony, and the Performance of Narrative Literature." *Literature in Performance: A Journal of Literary and Performing Art* 7.1 (Nov. 1986): 1–12.

Pearlman, Mickey, and Abby H. P. Werlock. *Tillie Olsen*. Boston: Twayne, 1991.

Pratt, Linda Ray. "Tillie Olsen's Omaha Heritage: A History Becomes Literature." *Memories of the Jewish Midwest* 5 (Fall 1989): 1–16.

Rosenfelt, Deborah. "From the Thirties: Tillie Olsen and the Radical Tradition." *Feminist Studies* 7.3 (Fall 1981): 370–406.

Rubin, Naomi. "A Riddle of History for the Future." *Sojourner* (June 1983): 3–4ff.

Stimpson, Catharine R. "Tillie Olsen: Witness as Servant." *Polit: A Journal for Literature and Politics* 1.2 (Fall 1977): 1–12.

Tillie Olsen Week: The Writer and Society. Symposium sponsored by St. Ambrose College, Davenport, IA; Augustana College, Rock Island, IL; Marycrest College,

Davenport, IA: Scott Community College, Bettendorf, IA; Black Hawk College, Moline, IL. 21–26 Mar. 1983. Proceedings published by The Visiting Artist Series of Davenport, Iowa, include critical essays.

Wade, Gerald. "Mari Sandoz Award Recipient Tillie Olsen Speaks from the Heart." *Omaha World-Herald* 5 Nov. 1991, sunrise ed: 29.

ALICIA OSTRIKER (1937–   )

Maeera Y. Shreiber

BIOGRAPHY

Alicia Suskind Ostriker was born in New York City on November 11, 1937. Now the mother of three grown children, she resides with her husband, Joseph Ostriker, in Princeton, New Jersey. Ostriker's father was an employee of the New York City Commission of Park Services; her mother was a folk-dance instructor. Ostriker received little in the way of a formal Jewish education. In a recent autobiographical essay, Ostriker describes herself as a "third generation Jewish atheist socialist raised to believe that religion was the opiate of the people" ("Back to the Garden" 24). Although she received her bachelor's degree from Brandeis University and served briefly as an editor for a newsletter issued by the B'nai B'rith Youth Organization, Ostriker did not, until recently, claim affiliation with any Jewish institution.

After receiving her Ph.D. in English Literature from the University of Wisconsin in 1964, she joined the faculty of Rutgers University, where she is now a full professor in the Department of English. She has been the recipient of numerous awards and fellowships, including grants from the Guggenheim and Rockefeller foundations, the National Endowment for the Arts, and the American Association of University Women. Ostriker is currently a board member of The Poetry Society of America and creative editor of the journal *Feminist Studies*. Long recognized for her literary scholarship, first in Blake studies and then in women's poetry, Ostriker has recently begun to make Judaism a focus of critical and pedagogical as well as creative concerns. She has just completed a collection of feminist essays on biblical hermeneutics, *Unwritten Volume: Rethinking the Bible*, and has written review essays of such works as Judith Plaskow's *Standing Again at Sinai* and Harold Bloom's interpretation of the *Book of J*. Ostriker has taught graduate seminars on "The Bible and the Feminist Imagination" and workshops at the Havurah Institute on women's *midrash*. Ostriker is currently composing a "revisionist *midrash*"—poetic reinterpretations of biblical material from a feminist perspective. Many poems from this collection, entitled *The Nakedness of the Fathers: Biblical Visions and Revisions*, have appeared in such diverse journals as *Tikkun, Kenyon Review*, and the *New Yorker*. In an effort to remedy a self-proclaimed ignorance of Hebrew texts, Ostriker has begun to study Hebrew formally at the Jewish Theological Seminary. Her commitment to study should not, however, indicate her desire to align herself with normative Judaism. On the contrary, Ostriker is intent on shoring up her own transgressive practice. As she puts it, "It is easy to be an atheist, but it is not a light thing to be a heretic" ("Back to the Garden" 12).

MAJOR THEMES

Alicia Ostriker has long been recognized for her poetry and for her scholarship as an important voice in American letters. Her poetry in particular constitutes a profound exploration of what it means to write as a woman. Beginning with *The Mother Child Papers* (1980), her concern with questions of sexual identity has led to an increasing awareness of the need to challenge long-standing assumptions about women's writing as occupied exclusively with private matters—affairs of the heart rather than the world. In *The Mother Child Papers*, Ostriker tracks the complex psychic interplay between the joy and ambivalence she experiences with the birth of her first son and the abhorrence she feels as witness to the violence of the Vietnam War. The resistance to simple divisions between private and public matters leads to such powerful expressions as the poem "The War of Men and Women" (*The Imaginary Lover* 1982). Bombarded by daily news reports of the violence men have wracked upon the world, the poet finds it nearly impossible to comfort a friend mourning the end of his marriage: "Forgive me/ You are crying/ I like to see men cry" (83).

This sustained inquiry into the links between personal identity and political obligation informs Ostriker's relatively recent turn to explicitly Jewish concerns. Before 1987, only a few poems suggest that questions of Jewish identity will become central to her aesthetic vision. In the opening section of *A Dream of Springtime* (1979), Judaism is treated largely within the framework of family relations. Like a taste for pickled herring, Judaism is an old-fashioned habit belonging to that generation of immigrant relatives who speak in "anxious syllables." The poet remembers, "*Shayne Maydel* was me," invoking the Yiddish phrase in such a way as to mark the distance that separates her from those "Armies of aging Jews, soaking up sun/ As if it were Talmud . . . " ("Benny and Becky in Farockaway," *Dream* 9). Ostriker sustains this distance in a later work, "Poem Beginning With a Line from Fitzgerald/Hemingway," where she addresses the lessons of the Holocaust by focusing on the heroism of righteous Gentiles. Her identification with the profound courage of Raoul Wallenberg, a "righteous Gentile," is at once characteristic of her ability to represent the familiar in an unfamiliar light and reflects her professed disassociation from Judaism that is a consequence of a secular upbringing and a feminist sensibility.

Because Judaism plays a relatively minor role in Ostriker's early poetry, her current interest in the Hebrew Bible may strike readers as unanticipated. But Ostriker is an extremely thoroughgoing artist who works both by intuition and by induction. Early models for her visionary poetics include Allen Ginsberg, Walt Whitman, and William Blake, whose work has occupied a good deal of Ostriker's critical attention. (She has published a book-length study of Blake and an annotated edition of his collected poems.) Like Blake, Ostriker is a religious poet in the sense that she is compelled by questions of ultimate being. And, like Blake, whom Ostriker celebrates as a ''true poet . . . a partisan of energy, rebellion and desire'' (''Dancing at the Devil's Party'' 580), she is driven to challenge the dominant view of theology that takes divine authority to be unassailable and absolute. Like her poetic mentor, Ostriker is not known for piety.

As much as Ostriker's current interest in Jewish texts can be linked to her early passion for the radical energy of Blake, it must also be understood within the context of her extensive work on women poets, particularly those who are engaged in what Ostriker describes as ''revisionist myth-making.'' In the last chapter of her landmark study, *Stealing the Language: The Emergence of Women's Poetry in America* (1986), Ostriker discusses how contemporary women poets take on mythic personae in the interest of interrogating the past, as well as in imagining social change. Such is Ostriker's own strategy in *Green Age* (1989), her most recent collection. In a poem ironically entitled ''The Bride,'' Ostriker depicts Jerusalem in her familiar guise as a once-beautiful woman now abandoned and bereft. Instead of a dream of redemption, the poem is dominated by a chorus of street cats who cruelly transform the classical vow ''If I forget thee O Jerusalem'' into a bitter chant: ''Forget even the fleshy mothers/ Sarah and Hagar/ Praying, shopping, cooking . . . '' (*Green Age* 44). In a subsequent poem, ''Meditation in Seven Days,'' we learn that the poet's commitment to classical biblical and Hebraic texts entails more than twisting familiar images to lodge a political critique. She begins by confronting the paradox posed by a religion where identity is a maternal legacy but where authority belongs to a violent paternal deity. Rather than dwell exclusively on those aspects of the tradition that view woman as ''a defilement and a temptation'' or a more affirmative image of the feminine as fecund and redemptive, Ostriker lays out the range of conflicting images asking, ''What can I possess/ But the history that possesses me . . . '' (*Green Age* 55). The question is central to her understanding of the relation between Judaism and feminism as a matter of mutual implication. She considers both the difference Judaism makes to her understanding of feminine, as well as the difference feminism makes to her experience of Judaism.

The Nakedness of the Fathers: Biblical Visions and Revisions constitutes Ostriker's most sustained effort to interrogate the Hebrew Bible from a feminist perspective. In its structure, the ''revisionist *midrash*,'' as Ostriker calls it, reflects the influence of both Judaic and non-Judaic texts. In her analysis of twentieth-century women poets and revisionist mythology, Ostriker pays particular attention to several long poems that inspire her own aesthetics. Like H. D. in

her epic "Helen in Egypt," Ostriker gives voice to quasi-historical female figures who have been largely inaudible. In the spirit of Susan Griffin's encyclopedic poem *Woman and Nature*, Ostriker takes on a variety of personae, male
as well as female, from Isaac to the Queen of Sheba. And in the spirit of Anne
Sexton's *Transformations*, Ostriker adopts a heretical approach to culturally re-
vered stories, using colloquial, often comic, language to counter any charges of
sentimentality to which she might be liable.

As much as Ostriker's book owes to these secular texts, its inclusion of prose
and verse reflects a special debt to the generic diversity of biblical narrative.
One must note, however, that *The Fathers* cannot be described as "revisionary"
in the sense of seeking to replace or correct the precursor text. Rather, it constitutes an act of reading or, to use Ostriker's own central metaphor, an act of
wrestling with the Hebrew Bible. In this respect her work is aligned with the
current trend in biblical scholarship that stresses the inherently fractured, dis-
continuous nature of scripture. But to view *The Fathers* solely as an imaginative
synthesis of feminist, biblical, and literary criticism would mean eliding its explicitly spiritual objectives. Unlike readers such as Harold Bloom who dismiss
normative Judaism on the grounds that it is all part of a "rabbinic fantasy"
("The Book of J" 43), Ostriker finds that the literary as opposed to the strictly
historical account of the Bible indeed animates the possibility of a passionate
engagement with tradition.

Divided into five parts, *The Nakedness of the Fathers* suggestively invokes
the five books of Moses. But Ostriker departs from biblical chronology, gathering stories according to her own sense of their interrelated meanings. In the
opening section, "Entering the Tents," Ostriker explores the attachment and
ambivalence characteristic of her relationship to scripture. Shuttling between
personal memories and expository meditations, Ostriker asserts an indelible connection to Jewish tradition, even as she is enraged by the marginal position to
which she, as a woman, has been assigned. From the outset, Ostriker foregrounds her interest in the Bible as a text central to her sense of self. For this
reason, the section devoted to stories of origins, "As in Myth . . . ," begins not
with the creation of the world, but with the creation of humanity. "The Garden"
playfully counters the typical focus on exile and loss, proposing that the story
of Eden be read as an account of the pleasures as well as the pains attendant
upon the acquisition of identity—a process imaginatively staged as a consequence of the interplay between Divine Presence and Absence.

Although many poems are spoken by the lyric "I," *The Nakedness of the
Fathers* is filled with numerous other voices, including those of Abraham and
Isaac. The latter is figured as a stand-up comic in a bitter-sweet portrait entitled
"Laughter." To those feminist readers who would question the attention paid
to those patriarchs Ostriker replies, "I *am* my fathers as much as I *am* my
mothers" ("Back to the Garden" 24). In the sequence devoted to "The Wrestling of Jacob: Man of Touch," a retelling of the biblical narrative is intertwined
with a contemporary story of the poet's own invention. The latter does not so

much update the ancient text as interpret it. In the contemporary version of the tale, a mother is conspicuously excluded from the final agon between a young man and his father, who must wrestle to dissipate the cold silence engulfing them. The exclusion comments powerfully on the biblical account of Jacob at Peniel, where the maternal figure is altogether absent.

Ostriker's book concludes on a prophetic note with a section entitled "The Return of the Mothers." The sequence owes something to the recent scholarship of such feminist theologians and biblical theorists as Judith Plaskow and Ilana Pardes, who seek to recover a long-repressed history of feminine representations of the godhead. After a wrenching explication on the anger of Job's wife, which Ostriker claims has yet to be fully voiced, the work takes a sharp-witted turn with "Intensive Care." The scene is initially somber as we are presented with what seems to be a deathwatch at the bedside of God. But the mood quickly changes as two women reporters (named Olivia and Chloe in tribute to the would-be lovers in Virginia Woolf's *A Room of One's Own*) speculate laughingly that the paternal deity isn't in danger of dying; he is only pregnant. The imagined transformation concludes with a suite of three prayers "To the Shekinah," sung in the future tense:

We believe that you live
Though you delay   We believe that you will certainly come

Thus in the spirit of the redemptive Jeremiah, Alicia Ostriker tempts her auditors with songs of possibility.

SURVEY OF CRITICISM

Most of the critical attention paid to Alicia Ostriker's work focuses on her literary scholarship. Her 1983 volume, *Writing Like a Woman*, which appeared as part of the series *Poets on Poetry*, was lauded by Robert McDowell for its historical acuity and careful rhetorical analysis of Adrienne Rich, Anne Sexton, and Sylvia Plath. Her subsequent book, *Stealing the Language: The Emergence of Women's Poetry in America*, has been the subject of some controversy. Reviewed widely in academic journals such as *Signs, Contemporary Literature*, and *Georgia Review, Stealing the Language* has provoked both high praise and strident critiques. Some reviewers such as Cheryl Walker and Wendy Martin proclaimed *Stealing the Language* to be a landmark study in the then-burgeoning field of feminist aesthetics. The study was praised particularly for its encyclopedic overview of contemporary women poets, many of whom had previously gone unnoticed. Other readers, most notably Bonnie Costello and Mary Karr, questioned the conspicuous absence of experimental writers in Ostriker's account of contemporary poetry. They also took issue with the emphasis placed on the idea of female identity as the driving concern of women poets in America. Costello's review led to a thoughtful and lively exchange between Ostriker and her critics which was published in the pages of *Contemporary Literature* (Spring and Fall 1989). These remarks on the field of women's poetry provide Ostriker's readers with further opportunity to understand her interest in gender as a category of analysis which addresses poetry in light of its social and political concerns.

In contrast to her scholarly work, Alicia Ostriker's poetry has not received extensive analysis. Her two most recent collections, *Imaginary Lover* and *Green Age*, have received favorable notices in such journals as *Virginia Quarterly* and *Canadian Literature*. Both volumes of verse have been recognized for their candor and deeply ethical concerns. Although Ostriker's poetry has yet to be discussed specifically in light of its Jewish themes and concerns, it is worth noting that works such as "Poem Beginning . . . ," a Holocaust poem, and "Meditation in Seven Days" have been singled out by critic Judith McCombs as particularly moving examples of Ostriker's own brand of visionary poetics (202–04).

BIBLIOGRAPHY

Works by Alicia Ostriker

Poetry

Once More Out of Darkness and Other Poems. Berkeley, CA: Berkeley Poet's Cooperative, 1974.
A Dream of Springtime: Poems 1970–78. New York: Smith Horizon Press, 1979.
A Woman Under the Surface: Poems and Prose Poems. Princeton: Princeton University Press, 1982.
Stealing the Language: The Emergence of Women's Poetry in America. Boston: Beacon, 1986.
The Imaginary Lover. Pittsburgh: Pittsburgh University Press, 1989.
Green Age. Pittsburgh: Pittsburgh University Press, 1989.
The Nakedness of the Fathers (forthcoming). Poems to be included in *The Nakedness of the Fathers* have appeared as follows:
    "The Story of Noah," "The Story of Joshua." *Lilith* (Fall 1989): 10–14.
    "Cain and Abel: A Question in Ethics." "The Cave." *Ontario Review* 30 (Spring 1990): 11–13.
    "The Passion of Sarah." "The Opinion of Hagar." *Tikkun* (September 1990): 52–53.

Critical and Scholarly Works

Writing Like a Woman. Ann Arbor: University of Michigan Press, 1983.
Stealing the Language: The Emergence of Women's Poetry in America. Boston: Beacon Press, 1986.
"Job: or, the Imagination of Justice." *Iowa Review* 10 (Fall 1986): 87–92.
"Dancing at the Devil's Party: Some Notes on Politics and Poetry." *Critical Inquiry* 13 (1987): 579–96.

"The Garden." *Michigan Quarterly Review* 27 (1988): 388–94.
"Intensive Care." *Santa Monica Review* 1 (1988): 30–36.
"The Bible and Feminist Imagination." *American Writing Programs Newsletter* 6 (1988): 10–15.
"Entering the Tents" *Feminist Studies* (1989): 24–32.
"The Wisdom of Solomon." *Kenyon Review* 12.2 (1990): 149–55.
"Back to the Garden: Reading the Bible as a Feminist." *Reconfiguring Jewish Identity*, ed. Shelley Fisher Fishkin. University of Wisconsin Press: Forthcoming.
Unwritten Volume: Re–thinking the Bible. Cambridge: Basil Blackwell, 1993.

Works about Alicia Ostriker

Bromley, Anne. Rev. of *Stealing the Language: The Emergence of Women's Poetry in America. The Georgia Review* (Fall 1987): 630–33.
Costello, Bonnie. Rev. of *Writing Like a Woman. Contemporary Literature* 29.2 (1988): 304–10.
Rev. of *Green Age. Virginia Quarterly* 66 (1990): 65.
Karr, Mary. "Sexual Politics." *Poetry* (1987): 294–303.
Martin, Wendy. Rev. of *Stealing the Language: The Emergence of Women's Poetry in America. America Literature* (October 1987): 474–67.
McCombs, Judith. "Territory." *Canadian Literature* (Spring 1989): 202–04.
Walker, Cheryl. Rev. of *Stealing the Language: The Emergence of Women's Poetry in America, Signs* (Fall 1988): 110–14.

CYNTHIA OZICK (1928–   )

S. Lillian Kremer

BIOGRAPHY

Cynthia Ozick, one of the most prolific and universally acclaimed figures in contemporary Jewish American literature, was born in New York City in 1928 to Russian Jewish immigrants, William and Celia Regelson Ozick. After she graduated from Hunter High School, a secondary school for intellectually gifted young women, Ozick attended New York University, where she was elected to Phi Beta Kappa and graduated *cum laude*; she completed a Master of Arts degree at Ohio State University, Ozick and her husband, attorney Bernard Hallote, live in New Rochelle and are parents of a daughter, Rachel, who is an archeologist.

Jewishness was impressed upon Ozick by her family members' commitment to Jewish life and by the anti-Semitism she experienced in her public school and her neighborhood, where she was reprimanded for refusing to sing Christmas carols and frequently accused of being a Christ-killer. In an evocative autobiographical essay, ''A Drugstore in Winter,'' the closing work of *Art & Ardor*, Ozick reveals much about her warm family environment. Her father was a Talmudic rationalist and devotee of Yiddish literature who also knew Latin and German, a father who, Ozick observes, wrote ''beautiful Hebrew paragraphs'' (304); her mother was an avid reader who painted and wrote. Ozick herself read voraciously, ranging from the classics to Nancy Drew books. In addition to parental influence, Ozick also credits her maternal uncle, the reputed Hebrew poet, Abraham Regelson, with paving the way in the family for her literary intentions. Although Ozick attended a school for religious instruction, the Judaic erudition that is evident in her work is the product of adult, intensive, independent study of such thinkers as Leo Baeck, Martin Buber, Franz Rosenzweig, Heinrich Graetz, and Hermann Cohen.

Ozick's master's thesis, ''Parable in the Late Novels of Henry James,'' suggests the literary influence that dominated her early writing career. She labored for seven years writing a long philosophical novel, *Mercy, Pity, Peace, and Love*, which she eventually abandoned. Intense, independent study of Judaic sources during the period of writing her first published novel, *Trust*, accounts for Ozick's literary metamorphosis and her commitment to writing fiction deeply rooted in Jewish texts, ethics, and history. Diane Cole quotes Ozick's characterization of her literary conversion from Hellenism to Hebraism while writing *Trust*: "I began as an American novelist and ended as a Jewish novelist. I Judaized myself as I wrote it" (214).

Ozick has translated Yiddish poetry and writes across the genres, producing novels, novellas, short stories, poetry, essays, and, most recently, a play. Translations of her work have been published in Sweden, Finland, Germany, France, Spain, Italy, and Israel. Although recognition was slow to arrive, Ozick is now widely acclaimed by critics; she has received numerous awards, including a Guggenheim, a National Endowment for the Arts Fellowship, the Edward Lewis Wallant Award, the Strauss Living Award from the American Academy and Institute of Arts and Letters, and the Jewish Book Council Award. Five of her stories have been selected for republication in *Best American Short Stories* and three have won first prize in the O. Henry Prize Stories competition. She has been nominated for the National Book Award and the PEN/Faulkner Award. As the preponderance of criticism affirms, Ozick is clearly perceived as a powerful cultural force, a stylist and intellect of major significance.

MAJOR THEMES

The moral, aesthetic, and intellectual tension at the heart of Ozick's fiction reflects her desire to embody Jewish ideas in fictional form. In "America: Toward Yavneh," reprinted under the title "Toward a New Yiddish" in *Art & Ardor*, Ozick advocated creation of an indigenous American Jewish literature, "centrally Jewish in its concerns" and "liturgical in nature," not a "didactic or prescriptive" literature. She felt that it should be "*aggadic*," that is, based on traditional Jewish interpretive narrative, "utterly freed to invention, discourse, parable, experiment, enlightenment, profundity, humanity" (174–75). Ozick exhorts American Jewish writers to preserve Judaic culture and to make New Yiddish, a creative union between Yiddish and English, its medium to "pour not merely the Jewish sensibility, but the Jewish vision, into the vessel of English" (175). Among Ozick's most significant recurrent and intersecting themes are the Hellenic-Hebraic dichotomy, the Judaic principles of *tikkun*, *t'shuva*, and the relevance of Jewish texts and history to Jewish American writing.

Western civilization's Greek/Hebrew dichotomy—with its oppositions of fate and free will, aestheticism and moral seriousness, the gods of nature and the God of history—constitutes one of the central thematic and stylistic tensions of the Ozick canon. Her first published novel, *Trust*, portrays the identity quest of an unnamed recent college graduate who confronts the Hebraic, Christian, and Hellenic values represented by her mother's three husbands. The initial section, "America," introduces the contradictory social and political influences in the narrator's life. Each of the remaining sections takes its title from a place-name associated with a principal character. "Europe" develops Enoch's Jewish historicism; "Brighton," William's Calvinist constraint and Mammonism; and "Duneacres," Tilbeck's sensual paganism. The two central forces vying for the quester's loyalty are those of Nicholas Tilbeck, "a male muse," an elusive quintessential pagan, unfettered by divine or human law, and Enoch Vand, the Mosaic foil to Tilbeck's Pan, the incarnation of alternative Jewish American perspectives: from assimilationist Socialist and liberal political affiliations to Jewish renewal. Although the novel's time frame suggests the diminution of Vand's influence, it remains the dominant moral and intellectual force of the novel. Even "Duneacres," ostensibly devoted to Tilbeck's paganism, ends with a coda introducing a dissenting Hebraic analytic voice supplanting the seductive appeal of the Hellenic influence.

The conflicting lure of Hellenism and Hebraism reappears in several shorter narratives, pitting monotheistic Judaism against the temptations of nature and art and the Christian sensibility. In "The Pagan Rabbi," Ozick creates a fantasy, elaborating an epigraph from *The Ethics of the Fathers*, a traditional rabbinic text that advocates concentration on and dedication to monotheistic worship and study. A rabbi, forced to choose between Jewish and pagan values, seizes upon Nature as god. In the shape of a studious old Jew indifferent to the glories of nature, the rabbi's soul denounces his excursion into paganism as contrary to his essential character, that of the observant and scholarly Jew. Convinced that he has erred irrevocably, the rabbi commits suicide, hanging himself with the aid of the soul's prayer shawl. "Levitation," another fantasy, insists upon the distinctions between Jewish and Gentile sensibilities, a recurrent theme of the canon. A Christian convert to Judaism, Lucy Feingold, can imagine suffering only in Christological terms, an instinctive reversion to her Christian origins. Unsympathetic to testimony of Holocaust persecution and bereft of imagination, Lucy envisions multitudes of Crucifixions as images of protracted Holocaust suffering rather than as multitudes of emaciated corpses that a historically knowledgeable Jew would envision. During her epiphany, as she remains earthbound while the fiction's Jews levitate, Lucy realizes that response to the Holocaust as an orienting event distinguishes authentic Jews from de-Judaized Jews and Gentiles. Furthermore, Ozick's attribution of the italicized "They" for Lucy's reference to the levitating Jews emphasizes the perceived chasm that exists between historically attuned Jews and herself. Another separation based on the monotheistic/pagan dichotomy is suggested in Lucy's vision of herself and her children, without Jewish husband and father, in a park celebrating nature, a restatement of Ozick's earlier divergence of monotheism and pagan nature worship. Hellenic-Hebraic polarization reemerges in "Usurpation," through a creative writer's transgression of the second commandment by her idolatrous worship of art. The protagonist, a writer lusting for stories, confronts the dilemma of espousing Apollo or God, selects Apollo, and infringes upon the divine province of creation. Writing in the "Preface" to *Bloodshed and Three*

Novellas, Ozick explains that "Usurpation" is an "invention directed against inventing—the point being that the story-making faculty itself can be a corridor to the corruptions and abominations of idol-worship, of the adoration of magical event" (11). Pitting Pan against Moses or, in this case, Saul Tchernikhovsky, who tried to find a bridge between the pagan Apollo and the Jewish God against S. Y. Agnon, the Hebrew monotheistic voice, Ozick cautions against the "religion of Art." In Ozick's fantasy pantheon of the poets, both Tchernikhovsky and Agnon live on, but while Agnon who articulates the story's credo: "All that is not law is levity" (144, 177) receives worldly and other-worldly rewards, Tchernikhovsky, who abandoned traditional strictures for the freedom of paganism, suffers the rewards of idolatry in the form of anti-Semitic barbs. This story reaffirms Ozick's support for centrally liturgical Jewish writing professed in "Toward a New Yiddish."

Contention and reconciliation between the artist and the monotheistic sensibility animate Ozick's critical essays as well as her fiction. In "Literature as Idol: Harold Bloom," she rebukes Bloom for treating the poem as literary idol. In "Innovation and Redemption: What Literature Means," she argues against the theory of art for art's sake, literature that is merely self-referential, which she judges as amoral. Instead, Ozick advocates a Judaic literature, writing advancing the theme of freedom to change one's life, the energy of creative renewal, the sense that we are morally responsible. Implicit in this Hebraic literature, according to Ozick, is the fluid, changing possibilities of humankind in opposition to the Hellenic fated or static view of life. Ozick condemns as idolatrous the position of writers who insist that literature is solely about the language from which it is fashioned. Instead, Ozick promotes literature that interprets and decodes the world for humanity. Her essay "The Riddle of the Ordinary" proposes a reconciliation between the creative imagination and monotheism, noting that being an observant Jew is similar to being a writer, for each involves noticing and sanctifying the ordinary that is part of God's creation. "Bialik's Hint" heals the rupture more completely through the Yiddish and Hebrew writer's conciliatory vision of *Aggadah*, the story-telling faculty of the Talmud, with *Halachah*, Judaic law. As Bialik contends that Jewish lore and Jewish law are neither separate nor separable and that the lore leads to the law, so Ozick sees in the Talmud's dual structure justification for imagination to express humanity's creative potential for self-directed change. Finally, during a 1987 *Paris Review* interview with Tom Teicholz, Ozick reverses her long-standing equation of image-making and idolatry, her insistence that the artist's creation competes with God's sovereignty and therefore transgresses the monotheistic code. Her new position is based on recognition of subtle distinctions and consideration that

the idol-making capacity of the imagination is its lower form, and that one cannot be a monotheist without putting the imagination under the greatest pressure of all. To imagine the unimaginable is the highest use of the imagination . . . only a very strong imagination can rise to the idea of a non-corporeal God. (167)

Text-centeredness, as Harold Bloom points out in *Agon*, is the essence of Jewish learning. So, too, text-centeredness is the hallmark of Ozick's narrative method. A master of Jewish sources, Ozick reinforces structural and thematic balance and unity by juxtaposing traditional Judaic writings with her own tales. In the classic *midrashic* mode [creating new narratives to comment on older texts] Ozick affirms and enlarges the Judaic literary and ethical legacy.

Judaism's ethical imperatives, manifested as repairing the world through good deeds and spiritual return, are among the most important elements in Ozick's fiction. Representative are the Puttermesser stories which reverberate with these principles and exemplify the writer's organic integration of Jewish text and myth to convey contemporary moral quest. The repair theme appears in the lawyer's activism on behalf of Soviet Jews, her interest in political reform, and her dream of bettering the world, values she associates with the Eastern European Jewish societies for her ancestors.

Central to Ruth Puttermesser's character is her passion for Jewish values and texts, her recognition that learning Hebrew is an essential assertion of Jewish identity, that knowledge of the language is indispensable to a Jewish world view. Through the study of Hebrew texts, she discerns a civilization, a value system, a distinctive culture, and she forges a link to the history of the Jews. Just as "The Pagan Rabbi" is a *midrash* on an idea from *The Ethics of the Fathers*, so the social satire "Puttermesser and Xanthippe" is derived from and extends the folktale of the *golem*, a figure constructed in the form of a human being and endowed with life to do its creator's bidding. Ozick's narrative borrows its twelve-part structure from the pattern of construction and destruction of the *golem* employed in Gershom Scholem's "The Idea of the *Golem*." It is this essay that Ruth has been studying while growing disheartened by the corruption and mediocrity of city government. Obsessed with reform, she inadvertently performs the rituals described in Scholem's essay. From houseplant soil, she creates Xanthippe, breathes life into her, and charges her to repair a flawed city. Following the commandment of Deuteronomy, "Justice, justice shalt thou pursue," Puttermesser's *golem*, like Rabbi Loew's creature who presided over the civil reforms of late sixteenth-century Prague, implements a "Plan for the Resurrection, Reformation, Reinvigoration and Redemption" of New York City and helps Puttermesser ascend to the mayoralty. Ozick's metamorphosis of the legendary character incorporates a gender change and endows the *golem* with sexual and procreative desires. Like the legendary figure who eventually acts destructively despite its creator's intent, Xanthippe eventually rejects her redemptive charge and destroys both Puttermesser's political career and the new order in the city. While Xanthippe's disorder and doom adhere to traditional myth, Ozick adds the predicament of idolatry to her version. Ruth recognizes that her plan for urban reform has become her idol in violation of the uncompromising commandment against idolatry. As with the literary idolater in "Usurpation," participation in the mystery of creation has led Ruth to worship her own artifact. Destruction of the *golem* is Puttermesser's only option.

Another example of Ozick's use of the repentance/spiritual return theme appears in "Bloodshed," a tale of a secular Jew's spiritual odyssey to a Hasidic colony. The narrative includes a synagogue prayer and a study session that focus on Torah readings concerning the ancient rites of *Yom Kippur* sacrifice and atonement that lead to the quester's spiritual awakening and return. The story plumbs the ancient ritual of sacrifice in juxtaposition with aggression unleashed by modern technological societies. As an assimilationist, suffering the modern crisis of faith, Bleilip becomes the subject of a Hasidic exemplum in an interior tale whose commentary reveals theological and human implications of the Holocaust. The Hasidic *rebbe*, a Buchenwald survivor, counters the nihilism of the alienated American Jew by helping him discover the values of collective memory, tradition, and communal responsibility. As a believer in the individual's power to change and reform, the survivor-rebbe leads the skeptic to spiritual renewal by helping him understand that the believer and doubter are often one. Acknowledging his belief in God despite Holocaust history, the skeptic metamorphoses, freely accepting the identity he had earlier misappropriated, "A Jew. Like yourselves. One of you" (67). Having arrived at the Hasidic colony in scorn to deprecate his cousin's conversion, Bleilip now concludes his visit in praise. The story ends with Bleilip's recognition that he had unconsciously come "for a glimpse of the effect of the rebbe. Of influences" (72) and his realization that "The day . . . felt full of miracles" (72).

Reflective of Ozick's commitment to a literature "centrally Jewish in its concerns" is her incorporation of Jewish history and her treatment of the Holocaust, the orienting event of the twentieth century. The Holocaust theme recurs throughout the Ozick canon, each work examining a different historic or psychological aspect of the Holocaust experience or exploring another artistic strategy for transmitting its significance. Indirect treatment of ghetto and concentration camp through survivor memory and meditation on the psychological, political, and theological implications of the Holocaust are manifest in much of Ozick's writing. Atrocities leading to political meditation and religious renewal are documented in *Trust*, concentration camp deprivation and degradation are dramatically presented in "The Shawl," and the Warsaw ghetto is recalled in "Rosa." The extraordinarily direct and compact rendition of the concentration camp universe in "The Shawl," the sole instance in which Ozick sets her narrative in the camps, contrasts sharply with the indirect development of Holocaust themes in her other works.

Indirection is seen by many commentators as the appropriate path for a writer who has herself not experienced the world of the ghettos and concentration camps. The approach resonates through Ozick's fiction. In "A Mercenary," she examines the psychological and political effects of a survivor's assimilation of Nazi anti-Semitic propaganda, and in "A Suitcase," she dramatizes a confrontation between an American Jew and a German immigrant on the matter of Holocaust denial. Through the memory and obsessions associated with survivor syndrome, Ozick charts the moral and ethical collapse of European civilization and the incessant postwar trauma of Holocaust victims in *The Cannibal Galaxy* and "Rosa," published in 1983. In the novel, she juxtaposes three literary devices to render Nazi brutality: symbolic evocation of *Kristallnacht* book burnings; a historically accurate account of the July 1942 roundup of Parisian Jews; and an allusively mythic rendition of that event. Survivor memory and nightmare convey the ruthless arrest of Parisian Jews and their inhumane incarceration in the Vil d'Hiv before deportation to Drancy. Ozick's description compares the French gendarmes and police recruits, official representatives of a state that boasts liberty, fraternity, and equality, with primitive barbarians of mythology, as they herd Jews to the sports arena. In "Rosa," the survivor's letters to a dead daughter spur recollection of the hardships endured in occupied Poland and in the Warsaw Ghetto. Indirection is again employed by Ozick in *The Messiah of Stockholm* as she explores a child survivor's adult search for his real and spiritual father, a search conducted among the manuscripts of a famous writer, Bruno Schulz. The imagined work, *The Messiah*, symbolizing the lost accomplishments of artists, intellectuals, and scientists murdered by the Nazis, is the subject of a literary critic's fantasy and quest.

Redemptive theme and Holocaust subject intersect in *Trust* and "Envy; or, Yiddish in America." A recorder of Holocaust history and the novel's moral register, Enoch Vand adopts the judaic belief in man's restorative task in history. Beyond his compulsion to bear witness, Vand seeks to reinvigorate the Jewish people and to rebuild Judaism. He commits himself to the traditional Jewish life of prayer and study. Guided by a Holocaust survivor, he learns Hebrew to read the Bible in its original language, and studies *The Ethics of the Fathers* and the Talmud. Echoing his creator's self-description in "Toward a New Yiddish," he studies the classic Jewish texts to know "what it is to *think* as a Jew" (157, Ozick's italics). By insisting on bearing witness to the Holocaust and affirming his commitment to Judaism, Vand embraces the task of finding meaning and purpose through the historic event. In "Envy," Ozick addresses the tragic cultural loss of Yiddish language and literature, and, by implication, the preservation of Jewish history, in light of the Holocaust. Her narrative examines the plight of a language whose primary constituency has been murdered in the Holocaust, a language virtually abandoned by acculturated American Jews. To redeem Yiddish from the Holocaust ashes, the Yiddish protagonist-poet seeks a translator. His reproach of writers of "Jewish extraction" who are ignorant of the great body of Jewish texts, writers unlettered in the ancestral culture, echoes the criticism Ozick has levelled at her colleagues. That Yiddish contains Jewish history is axiomatic in Edelshtein's proclamation "whoever forgets Yiddish courts amnesia of history" (74). The moral imperative to remember one's history is associated in the protagonist's mind, as it appears to be in the author's, with the need to preserve one's language.

Ozick's literary treatment of Jewish history affirms her belief, recorded in *Response*, that "History for the Jews, is not simply what has happened, it is a judgment on what has happened" (92) and her pronouncement in the "Preface" to *Bloodshed and Three Novellas* "that stories ought to judge and interpret the world" (4). Confounding the Nazi goal to extinguish Jewish civilization and that of universalists to negate the significance of the culturally particular, Ozick honors Jewish culture and contributes to its vibrancy. Her writing is characterized by the values she identifies in "Toward a New Yiddish," writing that expresses Jewish moral values, is "centrally Jewish in its concerns," "liturgical in nature," speaks with a communal voice, and is distinguished by a "sacral imagination" (175). Cynthia Ozick writes about Judaism and Jewish history, infusing the postmodernist narrative with the values of religious, historic, and cultural Judaism.

SURVEY OF CRITICISM

Writing by women has been traditionally devalued in male-dominated critical discourse. Ozick's novels, short stories, and essays are an important exception. Critics concur that Judaism is the dominant force in Ozick's work, that Judaic thought, identity, and history are her major thematic concerns. Unanimity is evident in the critical identification of her themes and subjects: idolatry and creative writing, paganism and Western culture, Jewish history and themes, and literary influence. There is wide critical acclaim for her stylistic virtuosity, intellectual rigor, and imaginative range. Representative of the praise Ozick receives as a stylist is the assessment of A. Alvarez who views her writing as "intricate and immaculate." He praises her "ear and precision and gift for the disturbing image . . . combined with the storyteller's sense of timing and flow, the effortless shift between the colloquial and the allusive" (22). Hardly a critic writes of Ozick without paying tribute to the lyricism of her prose, the richness of her imagery and imagination, the range and brilliance of her intelligence, and her moral authority. Detractors, few in number, temper their praise by charging her with polemicism, occasional overwriting, and obscurity. Although the most lavish praise is for her fiction, Ozick is also heralded as a masterful literary critic and essayist. Of the many essays she has published on religious, cultural, political, and literary topics, a small portion have been collected in *Art & Ardor* and in *Metaphor & Memory*. It is largely these works that are the subject of critical commentary. Ozick's poetry has appeared in a number of journals but has not been collected. Her translations of Yiddish verse appear in *A Treasury of Yiddish Poetry*, edited by Irving Howe and Eliezer Greenberg, *Voices from the Yiddish: Essays, Memoirs, Diaries*, edited by Howe and Greenberg, and *The Penguin Book of Yiddish Verse*, edited by Howe and Ruth Wisse. Aside from Joseph Lowin's brief analysis, Ozick's poetry has received virtually no critical attention.

Four book-length critical studies of Ozick's work have been published. The first is *Modern Critical Views: Cynthia Ozick*, nineteen essays edited by Harold Bloom. These selections range from brief reviews and studies of single texts to examination of recurrent motifs in the fiction to 1983. The most important essays of the volume are the introduction by Bloom addressing Ozick's artistic and polemic writings and arguing that when they clash, the reader ought to trust the tale rather than the teller; the reprints of Victor Strandberg's insightful study of the early fiction, and Ruth Wisse's identification of Ozick as the leader of the new American Jewish writing. The first critical study by a single author is Sanford Pinsker's *The Uncompromising Fictions of Cynthia Ozick*, a brief chronological survey emphasizing Ozick's redirection of American Jewish fiction by stressing its essential Jewishness. Liberally interspersed with quotations from the fiction and essays, Pinsker writes in celebration of Ozick's sharp intellect, prose style, and her commitment to treating Jewish history and ideas in her early and middle periods. The most extensive analysis of Ozick's narrative style and Judaic influences is Joseph Lowin's *Cynthia Ozick*, a study of the Jewish influences and *midrashic* narrative mode. Lowin elucidates representative fiction through *The Messiah of Stockholm* and, unlike other critics, explicates some of Ozick's poetry. Thoroughly versed in the Jewish textual tradition, Lowin offers a formalist and thematic assessment and explication of Ozick's Jewish aesthetics within the cultural/religious context. Lawrence Friedman's *Understanding Cynthia Ozick* is a lucid overview to the author's career and ideas, a guide to the literary, philosophic, and cultural influences on her work. Pinsker and Friedman illuminate the fiction through extensive reference to the essays. Critics who devote substantive chapters to Ozick in their critical studies of American Holocaust literature are Alan Berger in *Crisis and Covenant: The Holocaust in American Jewish Fiction*, which addresses the theological and religious modes of the writing, and S. Lillian Kremer in *Witness Through the Imagination: Jewish American Holocaust Literature*, which focuses on critical analysis of Ozick's Holocaust themes and stylistic strategies. Sarah Blacher Cohen treats Ozick briefly in a chapter on "The Jewish Literary Comediennes" in *Comic Relief: Humor in Contemporary American Literature*. Ellen Pifer considers Ozick's Orthodox vision as the element setting her narrative techniques apart from those of her postmodernist contemporaries in an essay titled "Invention and Orthodoxy" that appears in *Contemporary American Women Writers*, and Sanford Pinsker devotes a chapter to Ozick as the writer whose fiction "has radically changed the way we define Jewish-American writing, and, . . . the way Jewish-American writing defines itself" (138) in *Jewish-American Fiction: 1917–1987*.

Two journals have devoted special issues to Ozick's work. *Texas Studies in Literature and Language: A Journal of the Humanities* 25.2 (Summer 1983) contains Victor Strandberg's long essay, "The Art of Cynthia Ozick," a study of Ozick's early fiction. *Studies in American Jewish Literature* 6 (Fall 1987) sheds extensive critical light on the canon through the later fiction and includes a lengthy bibliographic essay.

Forthcoming is an interview in *Salmagundi* and books by Sarah Blacher Cohen, Victor Strandberg, and Elaine M. Kauvar. Cohen's book, *From Levity to Liturgy: The Fiction of Cynthia Ozick*, argues that liturgy and levity are not discreet entities but often undercut or reinforce each other and analyzes the intertwining of both dimensions. Elaine Kauvar's work, *Cynthia Ozick's Fiction: Tradition and Invention*, focuses on Ozick as a feminist both influenced by the patriarchal tradition and in conflict with it and her recurrent themes: the battle between Hebraism and Hellenism, the lure of paganism and the dangers of idolatry, the implications and consequences of assimilation, and the perplexities of the artist and the dangers of art. Victor Strandberg's work, which is as yet untitled, will be organized around three major areas: The Matrix of Art, focusing on Ozick's intellectual, cultural, and aesthetic bearings; Readings, an analysis of each of her major writings in fiction through the spring of 1992; and Judgment, an overview of the criticism and Strandberg's own assessment.

BIBLIOGRAPHY

Works by Cynthia Ozick

Trust. New York: New American Library, 1966.
The Pagan Rabbi and Other Stories. New York: Alfred A. Knopf, 1971.
Bloodshed and Three Novellas. New York: Alfred A. Knopf, 1976.
Levitation: Five Fictions. New York: Alfred A. Knopf, 1982.
The Cannibal Galaxy. New York: Alfred A. Knopf, 1983.
Art & Ardor. New York: Alfred A. Knopf, 1983.
The Messiah of Stockholm. New York: Alfred A. Knopf, 1987.
Metaphor & Memory. New York: Alfred A. Knopf, 1989.
The Shawl. New York: Alfred A. Knopf, 1989.

Interviews

Cynthia Ozick. With Kay Bonetti. American Audio Prose Library, n.d.
"Trust the Teller." With Edward Grossman. *Jerusalem Post Magazine*, 19 September 1986, 6–7.
"*PW* Interviews Cynthia Ozick." With Peggy Kaganoff. *Publishers Weekly* 27 March 1987, 33–34.
"An Interview with Cynthia Ozick." With Elaine M. Kauvar. *Contemporary Literature* 26.4 (Winter, 1985): 375–401.
"The Rich Visions of Cynthia Ozick." With Eve Ottenberg. *New York Times Magazine* 10 April 1983: 47, 62–66.
An interview with Cynthia Ozick. With Catharine Rainwater and William J. Scheick. *Texas Studies in Literature and Language* 25 (Summer 1983): 255–65.
With Tom Teicholz. *Paris Review* (1987) no. 102.

Works about Cynthia Ozick

Books

Bloom, Harold. Ed. *Modern Critical Views: Cynthia Ozick.* New York: Chelsea House, 1986.

Cohen, Sarah Blacher. *From Levity to Liturgy: The Fiction of Cynthia Ozick*. Bloomington: Indiana University Press, 1993.

Friedman, Lawrence S. *Understanding Cynthia Ozick*. Columbia: University of South
Carolina Press, 1991.

Kauvar, Elaine M. *Cynthia Ozick's Fiction: Tradition and Invention*. Bloomington: Indiana University Press, 1993.

Lowin, Joseph. *Cynthia Ozick*. Boston: Twayne Publishers, 1988.

Pinsker, Sanford. *The Uncompromising Fictions of Cynthia Ozick*. Columbia: University
of Missouri Press, 1987.

Articles and Book Chapters

Alexander, Edward. "Cynthia Ozick and the Idols of the Tribe." *Midstream* January
1984: 54–55.

———. "The Holocaust in American Jewish Fiction: A Slow Awakening." *The Resonance of Dust: Essays of Holocaust Literature and Jewish Fate*, . Columbus:
Ohio State University Press, 1979. 138-41.

Alvarez, A. "Flushed with Ideas." Rev. of *Levitation: Five Fictions*. *New York Review
of Books* 13 May 1982: 22.

Bell, Pearl K. "New Jewish Voices." *Commentary* June 1981: 62–66.

Berger, Alan. *Crisis and Covenant: The Holocaust in American Jewish Fiction*, Albany:
State University of New York Press, 1985. 49-59, 120-37.

Bernstein, Richard. "On Being Nice or Rotten in Writing." *New York Times* 3 October
1989: 14.

Burstein, Janet Handler. "Cynthia Ozick and Transgressions of Art." *American Literature: A Journal of Literary History, Criticism, and Bibliography* March 1987:
85–101.

Chenoweth, Mary J. "Bibliographical Essay: Cynthia Ozick." *Studies in American Jewish Literature* 6 (Fall 1987): 145–63.

Chertok, Chaim. "Ozick's Hoofprints." *Yiddish* (1987): 5–12.

Cohen, Joseph. 'Shots': A Case History of the Conflict Between Relativity Theory and
the Newtonian Absolutes." *Studies in American Jewish Literature* 6 (Fall 1987):
96–104.

Cohen, Sarah Blacher. "Cynthia Ozick and her New Yiddish Golem." *Studies in American Jewish Literature* 6 (Fall 1987): 105–10.

———. "The Jewish Literary Comediennes." *Comic Relief: Humor in Contemporary
American Literature*. Ed. Sarah Blacher Cohen, 172–86. Urbana: University of
Illinois Press, 1978.

Cole, Diane. "Cynthia Ozick." *Twentieth-Century American-Jewish Fiction Writers.
Dictionary of Literary Biography*, 28 vols. Vol. 28 edited by Daniel Walden,
1984. Detroit: Gale Research Co., 1978–1991. 213-25.

———. "I Want to Do Jewish Dreaming." *Present Tense* 10 (Summer 1982): 54–57.

———. "The Uncollected Autobiography of Cynthia Ozick." *Studies in American Jewish Literature* 6 (Fall 1987): 5–12.

Criswell, Jeanne Sallade. "Cynthia Ozick and Grace Paley: Diverse Visions in Jewish
and Women's Literature." *Since Flannery O'Connor: Essays on the Contemporary American Short Story*. Eds. Loren Logsdon and Charles W. Mayer, Macomb,
IL: Western Illinois University, 1987. 93-100.

Currier, Susan, and Daniel Cahill. "A Bibliography of Writings by Cynthia Ozick."
Contemporary American Women Writers: Narrative Strategies. 109-15. Eds.

Catherine Rainwater and William Scheick. Lexington: University Press of Kentucky, 1985.

———. "Cynthia Ozick." *Dictionary of Literary Biography, Yearbook 1982*, Detroit: Gale Research Co., 1983. 325–33.

Elias, Amy J. "Puttermesser and Pygmalion." *Studies in American Jewish Literature* 6 (Fall 1987): 64–74.

Epstein, Joseph. "Cynthia Ozick, Jewish Writer." *Commentary* Mar. 1984: 64–69.

Farr, Cecilia Konchar. " 'Lust for a Story' Cynthia Ozick's 'Usurpation' as Fabulation." *Studies in American Jewish Literature* 6 (Fall 1987): 88–95.

Finkelstein, Norman. "The Struggle for Historicity in the Fiction of Cynthia Ozick." *Lit: Literature Interpretation Theory* May 1990: 291–302.

Fisch, Harold. "Introducing Cynthia Ozick." *Response* 22 (1974): 27–34.

Fishman, Sylvia Barack. "Imagining Ourselves: Cynthia Ozick's *The Messiah of Stockholm.*" *Studies in American Jewish Literature* 9 (Spring 1990): 84–92.

Gertel, Elliot B. "Cynthia Ozick and the 'Jewish' Short Story." *Midstream* December 1983: 43–47.

Gitenstein, Barbara R. "The Temptation of Apollo and the Loss of Yiddish in Cynthia Ozick's Fiction." *Studies in American Jewish Literature* 3 (1983): 194–201.

Harap, Louis. "The Religious Art of Cynthia Ozick." *Judaism* 33 (1984): 353–63.

Kauvar, Elaine M. "American Jewish Writers and the Breakup of Old Faiths." *Contemporary Literature* 30.3 (Fall 1989): 452–61.

———. "Courier for the Past: Cynthia Ozick and Photography." *Studies in American Jewish Literature* 6 (Fall 1987): 129–44.

———. "Cynthia Ozick's Book of Creation: *Puttermesser and Xanthippe.*" *Contemporary Literature* 26.1 (1985): 40–54.

———. "The Dread of Moloch: Idolatry as Metaphor in Cynthia Ozick's Fiction." *Studies in American Jewish Literature* 6 (Fall 1987): 111–28.

Knopp, Josephine Z. "The Jewish Stories of Cynthia Ozick." *Studies in American Jewish Literature* 1 (1975): 31–38.

Kremer, S. Lillian. "The Dybbuk of All the Lost Dead: Cynthia Ozick's Holocaust Fiction." *Witness Through the Imagination: Jewish American Holocaust Literature*, Detroit: Wayne State University Press, 1989. 218-78.

———. "Holocaust-Wrought Women: Portraits by Four American Writers." *Studies in American Jewish Literature* 11.2 (Fall 1992): 150–61.

———. "Post-Alienation: Recent Directions in Jewish American Literature." *Contemporary Literature.* In press.

———. "The Splendor Spreads Wide: *Trust* and Cynthia Ozick's *Aggadic* Voice." *Studies in American Jewish Literature* 6 (Fall 1987): 24–43.

Lowin, Joseph. "Cynthia Ozick and the Jewish Fantastic." *Identity and Ethos.* Ed. Mark H. Gelber, Bern: Peter Lang, 1986. 311-23.

———. "Cynthia Ozick's Mimesis." *Jewish Book Annual* 42 (1984–85): 79–90.

———. "Cynthia Ozick: Rewriting Herself: The Road from 'The Shawl' to 'Rosa.' " *Since Flannery O'Connor: Essays on the Contemporary American Short Story.* Ed. Loren Logsdon and Charles W. Mayer, Macomb, IL: Western Illinois University Press, 1987. 101-12.

Lyons, Bonnie. "Cynthia Ozick as a Jewish Writer." *Studies in American Jewish Literature* 6 (Fall 1987): 13–23.

Martin, Margo. "The Theme of Survival in Cynthia Ozick's 'The Shawl.' *RE: Artes Liberales* 14.1 (Fall-Spring 1988): 31–36.

Mort, Jo-ann. "Cynthia Ozick and the Future of American Jewish Literature." *Jewish Frontier* January 1985: 20–21, 26.

Pifer, Ellen. "Cynthia Ozick/Invention and Orthodoxy," *Contemporary American Women Writers: Narrative Strategies.* Eds. Catherine Rainwater and William J. Scheick, Lexington, KY: University Press of Kentucky, 1985.

Pinsker, Sanford. "Astrophysics, Assimilation, and Cynthia Ozick's *The Cannibal Galaxy.*" *Studies in American Jewish Literature* 6 (Fall 1987): 75–87.

———. "Jewish American Literature's Lost-and-Found Department: How Philip Roth and Cynthia Ozick Reimagine Their Significant Dead." *Modern Fiction Studies* 35.2 (Summer 1989): 223–35.

———. "New Directions," *Jewish-American Fiction*, New York: Twayne Publishers, 1992. 137-52.

Redmon, Anne. "New Fiction by Oates and Ozick." *Michigan Quarterly Review* 27.1 (Winter 1988): 203–13.

Rosenberg, Ruth. "Covenanted to the Law." *MELUS: The Journal of the Society for the Study of the Multi-Ethnic Literature of the United States* 9 (1982): 39–44.

Rosenfeld, Alvin H. "Cynthia Ozick: Fiction and the Jewish Idea." *Midstream* August–September 1977: 76–81.

Rovit, Earl. "The Two Languages of Cynthia Ozick." *Studies in American Jewish Literature* 8 (Spring 1989): 34–49.

Rush, Jeffrey. "Talking to Trees: Address as Metaphor in 'The Pagan Rabbi.' " *Studies in American Jewish Literature* 6 (Fall 1987): 44–52.

Sokoloff, Naomi B. "Interpretation: Cynthia Ozick's *Cannibal Galaxy.*" *Prooftexts* 6.3 (1986): 239–57.

Strandberg, Victor. "The Art of Cynthia Ozick." *Texas Studies in Literature and Language* 25 (1983): 266–312.

Uffen, Ellen Serlen. "The Levity of Cynthia Ozick." *Studies in American Jewish Literature* 6 (Fall 1987): 53–63.

Walden, Daniel. "The World of Cynthia Ozick: An Introduction." *Studies in American Jewish Literature* 6 (Fall 1987): 1–4.

Weiner, Deborah Heiligman. "Cynthia Ozick, Pagan vs. Jew (1966–1976)." *Studies in American Jewish Literature* 3 (1983): 179–83.

Wilner, Arlene. "The Jewish-American Woman as Artist: Cynthia Ozick and the Paleface Tradition." *College Literature* 20.2 (June 1993): 119–32.

Wisse, Ruth. "American Jewish Writing, Act II." *Commentary* June 1976: 40–45.

GRACE PALEY (1922–   )

Victoria Aarons

BIOGRAPHY

For Grace Paley, all storytellers are story hearers: "When I say a story hearer, that doesn't mean that you just listen to people tell stories. Sometimes you really are extracting them from people. You say, Well, what happened?" (interview with Lidoff 4). The child of Socialist Russian Jewish immigrants, Grace Paley grew up in the Bronx, among stories told by her parents, her aunts, and her grandmother, as well as stories she heard on the street, and the stories of friends and neighbors who would sit on stoops telling of their lives and of the lives of their families. Paley openly acknowledges the importance of this urban setting for her fiction, both in terms of dramatic setting and the texture and resonance of the voices of her characters: "Whatever I say comes from what I hear. It comes from the speech of my city. But that has to go through my American-Jewish ear" (interview with Hulley 19). The languages of her home were English, Russian, and Yiddish, languages that resonate with highly particular characters, lives, and histories, public and communal voices. Paley grew up in the rich texture of these voices, individuated voices that later informed and punctuated her fiction. As the narrator in her short story "Debts" reveals: "It was possible that I did owe something to my own family and the families of my friends. That is, to tell their stories as simply as possible, in order, you might say, to save a few lives" (*Enormous Changes* 10).

Paley was born December 11, 1922, to Isaac and Manya Goodside, the youngest child by a number of years (a sister was fourteen years older; a brother, sixteen years older). She grew up in a household peopled by adults: her parents, her father's mother, her aunt, and her siblings. She describes herself as a much-loved and well-treated youngest child who, during her early years, was encouraged to succeed. Her parents had already married by the time they came to America at the age of twenty, and they were among that generation of upwardly mobile Jews whose experience in America began on the Lower East Side, where they had their first two children and where the women—Paley's mother and aunts—put her father through school. The women worked in shops in the garment district, and Paley's mother was also a touch-up brush worker, since photography had been a family trade in Russia. Like so many immigrant Jews of the time, her family ascended to the middle class and moved to the Bronx, where her father, by that time a physician, ironically learned more Yiddish from his patients than he knew from his earlier years in Russia.

So Paley herself was a child of the middle class, while her brother and sister were children of the working class. Paley was reared against the backdrop of Russian Jewry, of stories of pogroms, revolution, Zionism, Socialism, immigration, and upward mobility. Paley grew up with a rearward view of the Depression and a forward view of impending war: "My generation really grew up at a very scary time. . . . The Second World War was coming, the Spanish Civil War was happening when I was in high school. Mussolini had invaded Ethiopia . . . Hitler was coming inch by inch" (interview with Silesky, 105).

Grace Paley attended Hunter College, NYU, and Merchants and Bankers Business and Secretarial School (1938–44), and at nineteen she married cameraman and filmmaker Jess Paley (divorced, 1971), then a soldier in the Army. From 1942–44, Paley lived in U.S. Army camps among other women whose husbands were soldiers. In the army camps, Paley acquired what she called a kind of feminine consciousness: "I won't say feminist consciousness, because I didn't know enough, but a certain female or feminine or woman's consciousness . . . .Just feeling that I was a part of this bunch of women, that our lives were common and important" (interview with Lidoff 6–7). She became drawn to the lives of women and children, women with whom she shared an active and involved daily community. In the Army camps, Paley was drawn to the individual and collective voices of women that would come to populate her fiction.

The mother of two children, Nora (born, 1949) and Danny (born, 1951), Paley has always been interested in the lives and stories of women, and most of her fiction, narrated by women, addresses the concerns of women, women dealing, more often than not by themselves, with children: women in neighborhoods, at playgrounds, at PTA meetings, women talking, recounting their lives, fighting the same quotidian battles. Paley has defined herself as "a Jewish woman, and . . . a feminist. I take those facts very seriously" (Telephone interview 22 Nov. 1991). Paley's dedication to politics, her commitment to feminism and to a shared community, all seem connected to a Jewish world view. Her early life was influenced by politics, by political discussions in her home. And while her family were atheists, with the exception of her grandmother, whom she would walk to the Orthodox synagogue, her father and mother were, as she puts it, "very Jewish-identified" (interview with Satz 483). Paley's Jewish background, which she has described as "a social tradition of the Jewish family of very deep charity toward others . . . of helping other people, of sympathy, of empathy . . . and a strong social consciousness" (interview with Satz 483), would appear to be the catalyst for her commitment to community, to a kind of ongoing struggle to oppose oppression and to bring about change.

Paley's earliest politics were municipal. During the sixties, she became actively involved in antiwar demonstrations; her first arrest took place at a demonstration at an Armed Forces Day parade in 1966. Paley has devoted herself to political activism, to speaking out against oppression and tyranny, and her interest in politics has framed her life, from her earliest recollections of family politics to her own political advocacy: In 1969, she visited North Vietnam; in 1972, she traveled to Chile during the Allende government; in 1973, she was a delegate of the War Resisters League to World Peace Congress in Moscow; in 1980–81, Paley helped organize the Women's Pentagon Action.

Paley began writing poetry, but she found that the short story lent itself best to the expression of the ordinary lives of women—their relationships with men, with other women, and with children. Although Paley had been writing poetry since her early years, she did not begin writing stories until she was in her thirties. Her first published story, "Goodbye and Good Luck," was not published until 1956, and her first book of stories, *The Little Disturbances of Man*, was published in 1959. In 1961, Paley received a Guggenheim Fellowship, and, in the same year, she began teaching at Sarah Lawrence College, where she has taught until recently. (Paley also has held teaching positions at City College, Columbia, and Syracuse.) In 1970, Paley received the American Academy and Institute of Arts and Letters Award in Literature, and in 1980, was elected a member of the American Academy and Institute of Arts and Letters. Her second collection of short stories, *Enormous Changes at the Last Minute*, was published in 1974; her third collection, *Later the Same Day*, was published in 1985. Paley has had stories selected for and included in the O. Henry Prize Stories and in *Best American Short Stories*. In 1987, Paley was named a National Endowment for the Arts Senior Fellow and the first New York State Author and the first winner of the Edith Wharton Citation of Merit for Fiction Writers. In addition to her short story collections, Paley is also the author of two collections of poetry, *Leaning Forward* (1985) and *Long Walks and Intimate Talks* (1991).

Paley, married since 1972 to the writer Robert Nichols, currently lives half the year in New York and half the year in Vermont, where she continues to write and be involved in community activities and political concerns.

MAJOR THEMES

Storytelling, for Grace Paley, functions as both primary theme and form in her short fiction. Her stories are at once about telling stories as much as they structure themselves around the act of storytelling. Storytelling for Paley is both metaphor—it comes to represent the ways in which characters envision and invent themselves—and major structural device—shaping the texture and controlling the ironic unfolding of textual space. More often than not, Paley's stories are told in the first person, by narrators who are characters themselves, who tell their own stories, stories that record, question, and validate their own lives and the lives of their families and friends. Paley's characters reveal storytelling as a purposeful, even defiant, act of self-individuation, as her character in "The Loudest Voice" unswervingly and characteristically asserts: "I expected to be heard. My voice was certainly the loudest" (*The Little Disturbances of Man* 63). For Paley, storytelling is essentially an act of remembering, of bearing witness, of saving lives through memory, an intrinsic characteristic of Jewish fiction and ideology. It is this saving power of storytelling that motivates Paley's short fiction and that demonstrates the importance for her of the life-affirming force of memory.

Thus, storytelling, for Paley's characters, is both a private and a collective enterprise. For in telling stories they define themselves, but they do so in relation to a wider community; talk, in fact, both frames and forms communities and individual identities. Paley's characters seldom see themselves in isolation. Rather, the defining nature of talk serves as a bridge to connect them to others in their self-made communities: neighborhoods, playgrounds, meetings, old-age homes, all places of ordinary living. As one character reveals to another: "I like your paragraphs better than your sentences." What he likes is the duration of talk, the continuous voice, the very rhythm of language, both self-defining and embracing. Talking, for Paley's characters, is both the means and the measure of forming alliances, part of the dance, a couple of awkward, critical steps from theory to practice ("Listening," in *Later the Same Day* 205). Paley's characters are not autonomous; they are rarely defined separately from communities, from their connections and obligations to others. They, like Paley herself, are committed to community, to a kind of collective perseverance and vigilance that Paley treats with critical discernment, with sympathetic humor, and with ironic reverence.

The language of Paley's fiction is, not surprisingly, an urban tongue, the language of the streets—simple, colloquial, abbreviated, and recognizable. The urban landscape of Paley's childhood contributed significantly to her own world view, and it becomes the dramatic backdrop of her fiction. Her characters' sensibilities are urban, revealing a sense of shared lives, shared battles, and an acute awareness of other people that locates itself in the very language of expression. Very simply, like her characters themselves, the language of her fiction is ordinary. It is an "insider's" language, shared by neighbors, by friends and relatives, by those committed to similar ideologies and to shared memories. Replete with linguistic shortcuts, dramatic expletives, and rhetorical questions, the language of these characters moves with a momentum of its own, a characteristic literary simulation of orality that contributes to the fluidity of Paley's prose, to her economical, almost minimalist style.

Most notably, however, in Paley's fiction, women do the talking. Paley's women are defined by their resilience and by their ironic, good-humored, and understated self-analysis. Her fiction chronicles the lives of women, women who participate in everyday situations that provide the basis of their friendship: women who have raised and have lost children, women who struggle in intimate relationships with men, women who battle municipal politics, women who gather at PTA meetings, on playgrounds, in each other's apartments. They are all products of an urban environment that allows for a limited kind of shared privacy, one often expressed in the ways in which women talk to one another and perpetuate and justify their lives through stories. Friendships among women are valued in Paley's works. Such relationships, defined through ongoing talk, can be restorative and life-affirming. The narrator in the short story "Friends," for instance, discloses, with characteristic good-natured self-irony, what is for her the healing power of dialogue: "Luckily, I learned recently how to get out of that deep well of melancholy. . . . You grab at roots of the littlest future, sometimes just stubs of conversation" (*Later the Same Day* 83).

Two central, thematic concerns that grow out of Paley's emphasis on community and storytelling are feminism and Judaism. In fact, her fiction reveals an interesting intersection of Judaism and feminism, the attempt to form an ethos that both accounts for and accommodates their inherent contradictions. We find in her corpus of stories a conscious refashioning of Judaism through the lens of feminism, the confrontation changing each. Paley's recurring narrator, Faith, refers to "an old discussion about feminism and Judaism," by affirming the following: "Actually, on the prism of isms, both of those do have to be looked at together once in a while" ("Friends" in *Later the Same Day* 81). The prism metaphor here suggests that the one is refracted through and in the other. Judaism and feminism join in Paley's works as ideological points of departure for shared embattlements, located in issues of marginalization, oppression, activism, and collective and generational memory.

And we now come full circle to the life-giving properties of storytelling revealed through the metafictional qualities of Paley's work. When, for example, a character, a friend of the narrator in the story "Listening" finds herself absented from her friend's stories, she asserts herself with unabashed outrage at what she considers a denial of herself:

Why don't you tell my story? You've told everybody's story but mine. I don't even mean my whole story, that's my job. You probably can't. But I mean you've just omitted me from the other stories and I was there. . . . Where is *my* life? . . . it's really strange, why have you left me out of everybody's life? (*Later the Same Day* 210)

This passage illustrates the central concerns of Paley's work and focuses on what is for her the essential thematic and structural crux of her work: the emphasis on character. For Paley, plot is subservient to character, to the ways in which people define and invent themselves. As a result, Paley's stories elucidate a self-reflexive relation between invention and reality, nowhere more markedly displayed than in her famous story "A Conversation with My Father." The story itself is about the construction of stories, the making of fictions. Asked by her father to write a "simple story . . . the kind de Maupassant wrote, or Chekhov . . . .Just recognizable people and then write down what happened to them next" (*Enormous Changes at the Last Minute* 161), the narrator makes claim to her own powers of invention. Her disinclination to write such a story is bred from her aversion to "plot, the absolute line between two points which I've always despised. Not for literary reasons, but because it takes all hope away. Everyone, real or invented, deserves the open destiny of life" (161–62). Character, not plot, makes stories real, because it creates empathy and identification. Through the open-endedness of her stories, Paley, like her narrators, develops a kind of ideology of character, of character-in-the-making, character that is malleable, that defies tragic closure.

In this attention to the development of character through dialogue, Paley strikes one as indelibly a Jewish writer. The invention of self, for Paley, depends largely upon identifying with a community in which individuals feel an abiding and perhaps consanguineous affinity. It is a community wherein characters identify with one another, not because they desire to emulate the qualities and actions of others, but because they recognize themselves in one another. Necessarily, then, Paley's characters are unremarkable, ordinary people who view the world from their well-defined neighborhoods and communities. In their ordinariness, however, such characters achieve a unique and most remarkable stature. They do so through their perseverance, their struggle to survive, and their willing commitment to others. They are framed, bracketed by history, by a shared past and by the mythology of the outsider characteristic to the Jewish protagonist since the fiction of Sholom Aleichem. This mythology produces at once a source of security to redefine and of alienation to overcome.

Thus, Paley's fiction has earned a place in the tradition of Jewish fiction begun by the late-nineteenth-century/early-twentieth-century Eastern European Yiddish writers, who formed a written tradition of Jewish storytelling. The complexion of Paley's fiction shares with this tradition the following characteristics: the recording of personal histories; an orality suggestive of an insider's sense of intimacy and shared language; a fluidity of dialogue through which a multiplicity of perspectives is established; humorously ironic self-exposure; a subtle understated recognition of the necessity for the humorous within the tragic; dramatized narrators, whose relation to the writer is intentionally self-reflexive; ambiguous nuances of character and motivation; the embracing of ordinary people, the *kleine menshele*; abrupt disjunctions and ironic resolutions; and the continual reinvention of the self. It's a tradition determined by multiple levels of storytelling, by a commitment to bearing witness, and by the reaffirmation of a shared language of memory. Finally, one wants to say this of Paley: One can only tell stories; but that telling is everything.

SURVEY OF CRITICISM

Although uniformly well reviewed, Grace Paley's work has only recently received widespread critical acclaim. While her first two stories published in *Accent*, "Goodbye and Good Luck" (1956) and "The Contest" (1958), attracted considerable attention—she "emerged as an overnight cult figure"

(Isaacs, *Grace Paley* 153)—her readership was constituted by a rather small group. Some general publicity has followed her political involvements in protests and demonstrations. Criticism of Paley's work, however, did not really materialize with any regularity until the 1970s, not surprisingly at the time of the women's movement, when Paley was embraced by feminists; it is only in recent years that critics have addressed her fiction in academic journals. Since then, scholars have conducted numerous interviews with Paley, and a substantial number of scholarly articles have appeared in journals and edited volumes. Those who write about Paley uniformly praise her narrative technique, her realism, and her ironically humorous voice. In general, criticism of Paley's work falls into the following categories: women's fiction, ethnic literature, short story as genre, comic form, communal fictions, and regional-urban color.

Critics who regard Paley as a writer of women's fiction view her work primarily in terms of the feminist concerns in her work and see Paley as an astute chronicler of women's experiences, with a keen ear for their speaking voices. Thelma Shinn, for example, in *Radiant Daughters: Fictional American Women*, argues that "Paley presents an American subculture which . . . operates along the lines of a matrilineal culture" (162–63). Those who regard Paley as first and foremost a feminist writer often address the feminine communities established in her work and the ways in which Paley creates strong, durable, tenacious women who speak out for the rights of women and whose dialogue suggests unbreakable ties and friendships among women, women who share common interests, struggles, and language.

Paley's fiction has also received attention as ethnic literature. Articles have appeared in *Studies in American Jewish Literature* and *Journal of Ethnic Studies*, for example, and entries on and references to Paley have been included in volumes devoted to contemporary Jewish writers. Bonnie Lyons has viewed Paley within the tradition of Jewish literature, especially in terms of a fundamental *Yiddishkeit* in the construction of her dialogue and characters. As Lyons puts it:

The world of *Yiddishkeit* and Yiddish literature is pervasively social, oriented toward the group rather than any one soul. . . . *Dos kleine menshele*, the little person, with all his imperfections and foibles, is accepted and embraced. . . . The ordinary person struggling with his everyday problems is the core of Yiddish literature; the heroic individual and sharply climactic plot are conspicuously absent. (31)

As a Jewish writer, Paley is often seen as re-creating an oral Jewish voice in fiction, in her ordinary characters, who, with considerable fluidity and intimacy, tell their stories to internal addressees or to readers with whom they assume a unique familiarity. Along these lines, Ruth Wisse, in *The Schlemiel as Modern Hero*, makes reference to Paley's storytellers as reminiscent of the monologue tradition in Jewish literature.

The structure and texture of the short story as genre is, most notably, Paley's forte, and writers such as Philip Roth have applauded her for her bold and impassioned style, "a language of new and rich emotional subtleties, with a kind of back-handed grace and irony all its own" (231). Scholars who consider Paley a skillful craftsperson of the short story speak to the oral qualities of her written dialogue, the ironic narrative twists, abrupt closures, and the taut, frank style that characterizes the rapid-fire movement of her work. Paley's inventive layering of stories, fictions within fictions, balanced by her commitment to a minimalist, economical style, becomes the focal point for criticism that sees her work as an innovative combination of the traditional and the postmodern.

When critics speak of Paley's humor, they do so in terms of her optimism, her "hopeful view of human nature and her cheerful acceptance of human limitations" (Sorkin 145). The humor in Paley's works, never far removed from a recognition of tragic potential, is achieved not only through the urbanized voices of her characters, but also through the ironic unfolding and the often abrupt, open-ended, and realistic nature of the narratives. Humor, for Paley's characters, is the essential perspective by which they maintain their balance, their self-knowledge, and their willingness to embrace communities of their own making.

BIBLIOGRAPHY

Works by Grace Paley

Short Story Collections

The Little Disturbances of Man. New York: Doubleday, 1959.
Enormous Changes at the Last Minute. New York: Farrar, Straus & Giroux, 1974.
Later the Same Day. New York: Farrar, Straus & Giroux, 1985.

Poetry

Leaning Forward. Penobscot, ME: Granite Press, 1985.
Long Walks and Intimate Talks. New York: Feminist Press, 1991.

Interviews

"Conversation with Grace Paley." With Leonard Michaels. *Threepenny Review* 3 (1980):
    4–6.
"Clearing Her Throat: An Interview with Grace Paley." With Joan Lidoff. *Shenandoah*
    32.3 (1981): 3–26.
Interview with Kathleen Hulley. *Delta* May 1982: 19–40.
"Grace Paley: A Conversation." With Barry Silesky, Robin Hemley, and Sharon Sol-
    witz. *Another Chicago Magazine* 14 (1985): 100–14.
"A Conversation with Grace Paley." With Peter Marchant and Mary Elsie Robertson.
    Massachusetts Review 26 (1985): 606–14.
"Looking at Disparities: An Interview with Grace Paley." With Martha Satz. *Southwest
    Review* 72 (1987): 478–89.
Telephone interview, 22 November 1991.

Works about Grace Paley

Aarons, Victoria. "The Outsider Within: Women in Contemporary Jewish-American Fiction." *Contemporary Literature* 28.3 (Fall 1987): 378–93.

———. "A Perfect Marginality: Public and Private Telling in the Stories of Grace Paley." *Studies in Short Fiction* 27.1 (Winter 1990): 35–43.

———. "Talking Lives: Storytelling and Renewal in Grace Paley's Short Fiction." *Studies in American Jewish Literature* 9.1 (Spring 1990): 20–35.

Arcana, Judith. *Cultural Dreamer: Grace Paley's Life Stories.* Urbana: University of Illinois Press, 1993.

Baba, Minako. "Faith Darwin as Writer-Heroine: A Study of Grace Paley's Short Stories." *Studies in American Jewish Literature* 7.1 (Spring 1988): 40–54.

Clayton, John. "Grace Paley and Tillie Olsen: Radical Jewish Humanists." *Response* 46 (1984): 37–52.

Coppula, Kathleen A. "Not for Literary Reasons: The Fiction of Grace Paley." *Mid-American Review* 7.1 (1986): 63–72.

Crawford, John W. "Archetypal Patterns in Grace Paley's Runner." *Notes on Contemporary Literature* 11.4 (1981): 10–12.

Criswell, Jeanne S. "Cynthia Ozick and Grace Paley: Diverse Visions in Jewish and Women's Literature." *Since Flannery O'Connor: Essays on the Contemporary American Short Story.* Eds. Loren Logsdon and Charles W. Mayer. Macomb, IL: Western Illinois University, 1987. 93–100.

DeKoven, Marianne. "Mrs. Hegel-Shtein's Tears." *Partisan Review* 48.2 (1981): 217–23.

Eckstein, Barbara. "Grace Paley's Community: Gradual Epiphanies in the Meantime." *Politics and the Muse: Studies in the Politics of Recent American Literature.* Ed. Adam J. Sorkin. Bowling Green, Ohio: Popular, 1989. 124–41.

Halfmann, Ulrich, and Philipp Gerlach. "Grace Paley: A Bibliography." *Tulsa Studies in Women's Literature* 8.2 (Fall 1989): 339–54.

Hulley, Kathleen. "Introduction: Grace Paley's Resistant Form." *Delta* May 1982: 3–18.

Isaacs, Neil D. "Fiction Night at the Comedy Club." *New England Review and Bread Loaf Quarterly* 11.3 (Spring 1989): 305–19.

———. *Grace Paley: A Study of the Short Fiction.* Boston: Twayne, 1990.

Kamel, Rose. "To Aggravate the Conscience: Grace Paley's Loud Voice." *Journal of Ethnic Studies* 11.3 (1989): 305–19.

Klinkowitz, Jerome. "Grace Paley: The Sociology of Metafiction." *Delta* May 1982: 81–85.

Lyons, Bonnie. "Grace Paley's Jewish Miniatures." *Studies in American Jewish Literature* 8.1 (Spring 1989): 26–33.

Malin, Irving. "The Verve of Grace Paley." *Genesis West* 2 (1963): 73–78.

Mandel, Dena. "Keeping Up with Faith: Grace Paley's Sturdy American Jewess." *Studies in American Jewish Literature* 3 (1983): 85–98.

Meier, Joyce. "The Subversion of the Father in the Tales of Grace Paley." *Delta* May 1982: 115–27.

Neff, D. S. "Extraordinary Means: Healers and Healing in a Conversation with My Father." *Literature and Medicine* 2 (1983): 118–24.

Perry, Ruth. "Grace Paley." *Women Writers Talking.* Ed. Janet Todd. New York: Holmes & Meier, 1983.

Roth, Philip. "Writing American Fiction." *Commentary* 31 (March 1961): 223–33.

Schleifer, Ronald. "Grace Paley: Chaste Compactness." *Contemporary American Women Writers: Narrative Strategies.* Eds. Catherine Rainwater and William J. Scheick. Lexington: University Press of Kentucky, 1985. 30–49.

Shinn, Thelma. *Radiant Daughters: Fictional American Women.* Westport, CT: Greenwood, 1986.

Sorkin, Adam. "What Are We, Animals?: Grace Paley's World of Talk and Laughter." *Studies in American Jewish Literature* 2.1 (1982): 144–54.

Taylor, Jacqueline. "Documenting Performance Knowledge: Two Narrative Techniques in Grace Paley's Fiction." *Southern Speech Communication Journal* 53.1 (Fall 1987): 65–79.

———. "Grace Paley on Storytelling and Story Hearing." *Literature in Performance.* April 1987: 46–58.

Wisse, Ruth. *The Schlemiel as Modern Hero.* Chicago: University of Chicago, 1971.

LINDA PASTAN (1932–   )

Gerda S. Norvig

BIOGRAPHY

Born in New York City in 1932, Linda Pastan grew up as the only surviving child of Jacob L. and Bess Schwartz Olenik (an older brother, Peter, died in infancy). Her father, a surgeon, had offices in the Bronx apartment building where the family lived until Pastan was a teenager. Both parents came from Eastern European Jewish stock, but their Jewishness was cultural rather than religious: In their daily lives they professed an uncompromising, rationalist atheism. Nevertheless, the forms and domestic details of Pastan's upbringing were saturated with the looks, smells, sounds, and generational expectations of Old World Jewry, refashioned in typical New York style by grandparents still carrying memories of the life of the *shtetl*.

From the first through the twelfth grade, Pastan attended the Fieldston School in Riverdale, New York, a self-styled progressive, private prep school where other assimilated Jews from upper-middle-class families also sent their talented children. Fieldston's affiliation with the Ethical Culture Society—a nonsectarian, humanist organization for free-thinking Jews—had its effect on the curriculum and moral atmosphere of the school. Even in the lower grades, for example, there was a required course called "Ethics" in which tales of Greek gods and heroes were told as moral paradigms meant to be questioned. Pastan's adoption of these myths as her own personal reservoir of archetypal stories is evident in her treatment of the many "heroes in disguise" that people her poems and essays.

From Fieldston, Pastan went on to Radcliffe College, where she studied literature and wrote poetry, winning *Mademoiselle*'s Dylan Thomas Award in her senior year from a field of competitors that included Sylvia Plath. She took her B.A. in English in 1954. She had met and married Ira Pastan a year earlier, and the couple lived in the Boston area until 1958, while Ira went to medical school and Linda earned both a Library Science degree at Simmons College and a 1957 M.A. in English at Brandeis University. During the latter part of this period, and through the next decade when the family moved to Maryland, Pastan tried playing the exclusive role of the fifties housewife and mother—she bore three children, immersed herself in domestic life, and wrote little or no poetry. In the late sixties, however, determined to break the unhappy cycle of creative isolation, she began systematically to produce a steady stream of poetry that appeared in some of the best journals and magazines in the nation. By the time her first poetry collection came out in 1971, she had published approximately one hundred poems and was working on the staff of the journal *Voyages*.

The seventies proved to be a time of both consolidation and exploration for Pastan the poet. She produced four more books of poetry, including two currently out-of-print chapbooks and a maverick British collection, *Selected Poems of Linda Pastan*; she won a fellowship from the National Endowment for the Arts; she was presented with the Di Castagnola Award by the Poetry Society of America for *The Five Stages of Grief*; and she began her long career as a teacher and a reader at the annual Bread Loaf Writers' Conference where she still works on the faculty each August. Readings at universities and other public venues across the country became a regular part of her professional schedule from this period onward.

In the 1980s, with her children grown and living away from home, Pastan's productivity and concomitant renown increased markedly—but not without a struggle as she sought to find her proper place in a new domestic structure that held as many losses as freedoms. The most profound influence of these years was the separate deaths of her parents that bracketed the decade. But the dispersal of the children, along with the experience of her own near-fatal automobile accident, also had a serious impact, moving Pastan to reevaluate twin imperatives of her life: a desire for the merger and even dissolution of bounded identities versus a respect for the integrity of the self. Traveling with her husband to his professional conferences in Europe, Scandanavia, and the Orient gave her the opportunity to explore the odd coupling of likenesses and differences from a new perspective that increased her sense of the world as contingent on the power of personal perception. These themes, of course, appear in Pastan's poetry, which she continued to publish widely in periodicals, winnowing the best out of many hundreds of such magazine poems for her next six collections: two more chapbooks and four major books. The last three books received institutional recognition and acclaim, with *PM/AM* garnering an American Book Award nomination, *Fraction of Darkness* winning the Maurice English Award, and *The Imperfect Paradise* securing both a nomination for the Los Angeles Book Prize and *Poetry* magazine's Bess Hokin Award. The eighties also brought her a Maryland Arts Council Fellowship.

Recently, Pastan has undertaken a few new career moves. In 1991, in addition to seeing the publication of her latest poetry collection, *Heroes in Disguise*, she accepted the post-laureateship of Maryland and, in that capacity, has traveled the state giving lectures and readings to a variety of audiences. During 1992, she also served as a judge of the National Book Award for Poetry and she, herself, received *Prairie Schooner*'s Virginia Faulkner Award for excellence in writing both poetry and an essay, "Washing My Hands of the Ink." Though she and her husband enjoy socializing with a large circle of friends who are poets, doctors, artists, and so on, they work to preserve sufficient time for introspection and for solitary creative endeavors. They still maintain their home in Maryland and their summer house on Nantucket, affected by the alternate landscapes of woods and shore in ways that continue to be lovingly chronicled, celebrated, and elegized in Pastan's work.

MAJOR THEMES

It is easy enough to catalog the characteristic motifs of Linda Pastan's poetry, since her work is obsessive in its eternal return to the themes and imagery of family relationships, domestic spaces, the processes of aging, the writer's life, and the cyclical transformations of the natural world. Such a list, however, reveals almost nothing about the power of Pastan's idiom. Pastan herself has tried to deflect the undue critical focus that has been placed on the so-called quotidian content of her poems by noting that her selection of topics is not so much deliberate as circumstantial:

Any poet can write about absolutely anything. My subjects . . . just happen to be what my life is full of. It's full of children, and we live in the woods so it's full of trees. Whatever is at hand I write about. If we should move and my life should change entirely, I would choose very different subjects. ("Whatever Is At Hand" 145)

But if the subjects at hand are not the key to Pastan's poetic individuality, what is? Some may point to her metaphoric style; others will single out her poetry's exploration of the abject—a stance frequently held by the female speakers of Pastan's verse; and still others will cite as fundamental the stoic moral vision her poems so often project.

More striking than any of these elements of Pastan's poetry, however, is the unspoken metaphysics of ambivalence that comes through in her work. Each poem seems to create a liminal zone, its speaker often hovering on the threshold of commitment to the unknown, resisting the loss entailed in choices that inevitably "curv[e] towards something,/ away from something else" ("Prologue," *Waiting* 3). Ambivalence expresses itself, too, in the way the outlook of so many Pastan poems straddles the ideologies of romanticism and postmodernism. Thus, belief in a redemptive vision, or in a providential imaginative design underlying the structure and content of any particular poem, is almost always invoked and then countered by pictures of experience unravelling into fragments that are themselves often elegized as the evocative traces of a vanished coherence. In *"Dreams"* (*Waiting* 7) we find an example of this kind of displacement and the metaphysical ambivalence it depends on, for here

Dreams are the only
afterlife we know;
the place where the children
we were
rock in the arms of the children
we have become

They are as many as leaves
in their migrations,
as birds whose deaths we learn of
by the single feather
left behind: a clue
a particle of sleep

caught in the eye.
They are as irretrievable as sand . . .

This speaker's referential universe is without a theodicy. It is a world made tender by repetition (the twice-told children), by plethora (the uncountable leaves), by residue (the feather, the sleep-in-the-waking-eye), by the overwhelming sense of the irretrievability of latent realities. But is it romantic nostalgia for original wholeness or the postmodern sense of pure supplementarity that gets the upper hand here? In Pastan's work, it is always, deliberately, and importantly hard to tell.

Pastan, then, is a poet who stubbornly refuses to resolve competing evocations of order versus entropy, elation versus depression, safety versus danger, merger versus individuation, permanence versus loss. In "All We Have to Go By" (*Heroes* 65), a poem from her latest volume that seems to echo "Dreams," these double themes abound:

As if I had dreamed the snow
into falling,
I wake to a world
blanked out
in its particulars,
nearly erased.

This is the silence
of absolute whiteness—the mute
birds nowhere
in sight, the car
and animal tracks
filled in,

all boundaries,
as in love,
ambiguous.
Sometimes all we have

to go by
is the weather:

a message
the snow writes
in invisible ink,
what the sky means
by its litmus
colors.

In traditional aesthetic terms, we can see Pastan's speaker struggling here to take a position toward the romantic sublime. The snow's sheer power to obliterate distinctions through its "absolute whiteness" evokes a feeling of alienation in which threats of psychic dissolution and the loss of language commingle. That alienation is only made stronger by the speaker's sense that erasure of the world's "particulars" is self-created ("as if . . . dreamed"). Yet the dread that might be expected to flow from such an insight is immediately stanched by the speaker's association of the "blanked out" environment with love. At that point, the poem's sublime contours fade, and the wintery scene becomes charged with a libidinal subtext that writes itself "in invisible ink." Thus, the world remains mysterious, but the terrors of its erasures and transformative mysteries have been leavened by a kind of ecofeminist, eroticized vision of a shared system of beneficial turns and returns.

The erotic component of Pastan's work, virtually ignored by critics despite its pervasiveness, functions at every level to vitalize and complicate what to many has seemed a poetics of timidity and quietism. Sometimes this eroticism is overt, surfacing thematically in love poems or poems about the body; sometimes it is implied by metaphors that hold subtle sexual connotations; sometimes it inheres in the sensuous quality of Pastan's language or in her sudden perceptions of the material world as ablaze with libidinal vigor; and sometimes it seems to be an element of the very structure of her work—the way images relate to one another, linking up like bodies in an embrace or caressing and stroking each other, as it were, across lines on the page or across a sequence of poems in a single volume.

Often the erotic image flares up as a direct reference to heat or fire, burning or smoldering, or to the penetrating force of sunlight. In "Eclipse," for example, we feel a sensual shock at the phallic magic of a sun that suddenly "like a swallowed sword/ comes blazing back" after being effaced by the moon (*Aspects* 54). And the same image, domesticated, retains its sexual suggestiveness at the close of "I Am Learning to Abandon the World," where a dog-like sun comforts the speaker for her losses as it "lays its warm muzzle on [her] lap" (*PM/AM* 18). One might think that depressive poems like this last one would prove inhospitable ground for images of such sensual intimacy. But in the economy of Pastan's ambivalent universe, the opposite is true: Melancholia or abject resignation seems actually to depend upon a strong undertow of erotic sensibility. This notion is thematized in "Meditation by the Stove":

> I have banked the fires
> of my body
> into a small but steady blaze,
> here in the kitchen
> where the dough has a life of its own,
> breathing under its damp cloth . . . (*Waiting* 33)

Here the speaker claims her resignation to domesticity as a deliberate strategy, yet the poem reads as a lament for forsaken pleasures that have become displaced onto the orgasmic transformations of the rising dough. Since "passion happens like an accident," the speaker fantasizes that she "could let the dough spill over the rim/ of the bowl, neglecting to punch it down"; and even though she does not allow this metonymic climax to occur, its erotic potential tempers her depression.

Even in such clinically depressive poems like "Final" (*Five Stages* 42), where life is imagined as a potentially failed exam that is plagued by blanks, errors, and dull repetitions, the poetic persona flashes on a scene of sensual excitement as she recalls how "once when I brushed my hair/ sparks flew out/ igniting/ more than I intended."

In this way, creating more sparks and doing more than her speakers consciously intend is the norm for Pastan's poetry. At the start of her career, she chose formal structures that channeled the surplus of excitement through strings of associated images flowing from a controling metaphor. Occasionally, the synapses connecting these metaphoric strains became overloaded, the effects forced. A case in point is "Prognosis" (*Perfect Circle* 53), where the medical trope implicit in the title is relentlessly overworked, pushing itself awkwardly on the moon, imaged implausibly in the final lines as "starched and impersonal/ as a nurse's cap."

But as Pastan's voice develops, her handling of metaphoric transformations becomes more natural. Like the chameleon she describes in "Camouflage" (*Perfect Circle* 36), who effortlessly "turns from simile/ to metaphor and back to lizard," the figurations of most of her later poems display their own processes with grace and with a sure sense of their relevance to both the material and the imaginal world. Partly this effect of seamlessness arises from the poet's increasingly elegiac sense of the narrowing boundary between life and death. Many of Pastan's most moving poems are about the real and anticipated losses of grandparents, parents, children, herself. In these pieces, fidelity to the stark reality of bodily decay and to the emotional rhythms that surround the experience of human endings boosts both the clarity and power of Pastan's idiom. Spare and direct, the tone of works like "Duet for One Voice" (*Fraction* 58) exudes an urgent authority.

I sit at your side
watching the tides of consciousness
move in and out, watching
the nurses, their caps
like so many white gulls circling
the bed. The window
grows slowly dark,
and light again,
and dark. The clock
tells the same old stories.
Last week you said, now
you'll have to learn
to sew for yourself.
If the thread is boredom,
the needle is grief.
I sit here learning.

Already in poems like "Go Gentle" (*Aspects* 6), about the death of the speaker's father, and later in the many lyrics that celebrate or mourn absent members of the family circle, a pressing narrative line leads to a decided expansion of expressivity that overleaps the clipped artifice of less successful poems based mainly on the elaboration of sometimes tortured conceits.

But it is not only the discipline of death or the threat of departure that draws from Pastan such poetic eloquence. Her work reaches its high point in poems demanding other sorts of restrictions as well. For instance, verses that engage the formulae of mythic tales, such as the sequence titled "Rereading *The Odyssey* in Middle Age," or the run of poems that revision the story of Adam and Eve in *The Imperfect Paradise* (21–33; 69–80), seem to possess a greater freedom and a complexity than many pieces untied to such entrenched sources. Similarly, Pastan's poems about paintings or other art objects (and there are an increasing number of these in her later work) call on a mimetic focus and a descriptive inventiveness often richer than what we get in poems paving metaphoric pathways through mapped events in the natural world. Finally, whenever Pastan places on herself the duty of following conventional poetic forms (she has written sonnets, sestinas, a pantoum) the extreme ease, power, and originality with which she meets the challenge of reinvigorating these genres takes her work to a new level. One wonders why these traditional structures are so rarely used. Perhaps Pastan feels a loss in them of the very metaphysics of ambivalence that elsewhere fuels her gift and her writerly impetus to "drown/ in the loosed wave of language" ("Soundings," *Aspects* 32) in a way that keeps her liminally situated between perceptions of utter abandon and utter abandonment.

SURVEY OF CRITICISM

With only four exceptions (Jellema 1969, Franklin 1980 and 1981, Pastan and Rubin 1989), published discussion of Pastan's work has been limited to either dust-jacket blurbs by fellow poets, newspaper reviews of her individual books, or poetry-journal essays in which Pastan is one of several writers being critiqued.

In all these critical sources, the quality of Pastan's poetry most frequently noted is its dedication to themes of dailiness and the ordinary. Some commentators, like Maxine Kumin who sees in Pastan's work "a mature, intelligent, domestic voice" that is "sharp but humorous, observant but forgiving" (back cover of *Five Stages*), praise this dedication. These are critics who value the "self-consciously female" dimension of Pastan's "luminous" verse and who see her charting afresh the mythic territory of domestic . . . female spaces" (Gilbert 152, 153). Others find the poet's "low-key" role of "chronicler of the quotididan" cloying, timid, or "self-indulgent" (Seidman 33, 34)—and even admirers sometimes balk at an occasional tendency to "suburban narrowness" (Gilbert 154), especially in poems whose allegedly "flippant" tone make one critic "wince" (Stitt, "Violence" 930, "Stages" 209) with what another calls their "sham cuteness" (Gilbert 155).

Often allied to the issue of this poetry's seemingly narrow purview are two other factors: Pastan's largely minimalist style and the quietistic, sometimes resigned sensibility that voices it. Janet Bloom deplores the way so many of the speakers in Pastan's first book "seem to have given up or in" in poems that court "some frozen balance or tepid impasse" (131), while H. Susskind remarks that in her latest volume Pastan's "similes are quiet truisms" that contain "few fireworks, no explosions, and no surprises" (4355). For the most part, however, critics see a power in the "quietness, clarity and depth of feeling" that make Pastan "an ideal poet for those who cannot bear the solipsism of so much modern verse" (*Washington Post*, back cover of *Heroes*). Hugh Seidman may complain that "her poetry takes few overt risks" (33), but Kenneth Pitchford and Joseph Garrison vehemently disagree, seeing her early work as "an exercise in courage" that bravely lays bare "the feeling of utter helplessness" (Garrison 92). Sandra Gilbert's somewhat deflating phrase for the deliberate modesty of verse like Pastan's is "poetry . . . gone on a diet" (149), but she nevertheless regards the best of Pastan's poems as sustained by powerful images of "tempered intensity" and by skillful "clauses [that] are as balanced as they are bare" (156).

Stylistic features that are universally admired include, first of all, clarity and accessibility. Janet Bloom, for example, observes that her syntactical rhythms are "easy, strong and direct" (131). Yet this ease, this contemporary approximation of Wordworth's metrical use of "the language really spoken by men," draws some adverse criticism, too. Robert Shaw, for instance, finds that Pastan's "unpretentious" discourse set in "two- or three-stress" lines imitating colloquial speech patterns can get monotonous (39–40). Yet her formal deftness and her "sure sense of her craft" is lauded by poets such as William Stafford and Mona Van Duyn (both on the back cover of *Five Stages*). Even a fairly grudging critic like H. Susskind respects the way Pastan's poems are "welded in dependable forms" (4355).

Fewer critics than might be expected speak much about what to her is the key ingredient of her poetic imagination: her use of imagery (Pastan and Rubin 140–41). Kenneth Pitchford is the boldest in his claim that the images in her poems are intellectually challenging as well as emotionally evocative in that they so often probe the very "nature of metaphor and language" (108). But it is Roderick Jellema who best puts his finger on the dynamic and "effortless way in which image and association dilate, flow, and contract as they casually discover themselves in new and startling combinations" like crystals (74). Bruce Bennet finds such agons of transformation "disturbing" (44), but Ben Howard praises the way each image presses toward the "exact and exacting trope" (347), while Frederick Smock and others note how the arrangement of poems within a single volume can set up sequential "resonances" among metaphors "that grow deeper and richer as the reader progresses" (Smock 12).

The last topic in Pastan's work that is often scrutinized by critics is the question of her poetic persona. Many assume, with Joseph Lipardi, that her poems voice her own "real" identity in a confessional manner that "record[s] ordeals overcome" by the author (203). This leads such readers to assume a troubled marriage or a bout of clinical depression or any number of other imaginary events. But as the poet herself remarked to Stan Rubin, "I have always thought that the poetic 'I' is more like a fraternal than an identical twin" (Pastan and Rubin 149), a comment that gently rebukes the literalists who regard her work as simply and wholly autobiographical.

BIBLIOGRAPHY

Works by Linda Pastan

Poetry

A Perfect Circle of Sun. Chicago: Swallow, 1971.
Aspects of Eve. New York: Liveright, 1975.
On the Way to the Zoo. Washington and San Francisco: Dryad, 1975.
The Five Stages of Grief. New York: Norton, 1978.
Selected Poems of Linda Pastan. London: John Murray, 1979.
Even as We Sleep. Athens, Georgia: Croissant, 1980.
Setting the Table. Washington and San Francisco: Dryad, 1980.
Waiting for My Life. New York: Norton, 1981.
PM/AM: New and Selected Poems. New York: Norton, 1982.
A Fraction of Darkness. New York: Norton, 1985.
The Imperfect Paradise. New York: Norton, 1988.
Heroes in Disguise. New York: Norton, 1991.

Essays

"Roots." *American Poets in 1976.* Ed. William Heyen. Indianapolis: Bobbs, 1976. 212–23.

" 'Whatever Is at Hand:' A Conversation with Linda Pastan.'' Interview with Stan Sanvel
Rubin. *The Post Confessionals: Conversations with American Poets of the Eight-
ies*. Ed. Earl G. Ingersoll, Judith Kitchen, and Stan Sanvel Rubin. Rutherford:
Fairleigh Dickinson University Press, 1989. 135–49.

''Penelope: The Sequel.'' *The Bread Loaf Anthology of Contemporary Essays*. Ed. Robert
Pack and Jay Pirini. Hanover: University Press of New England, 1989. 273–91.

''Writing About Writing.'' *Writers on Writing: A Bread Loaf Anthology*. Hanover: University Press of New England, 1991. 207–20.

''Washing My Hands of the Ink.'' *Prairie Schooner* (Winter 1991): 32–42.

''Yesterday's Noise. The Poetry of Childhood Memory.'' *The Writer* Oct. 1992:15–18.

Works about Linda Pastan

Bennet, Bruce. ''All Sides of the Transitory.'' *New York Times Book Review* 18 September 1988: 42ff.

Bloom, Janet. ''A Plea for Proper Boldness.'' *Parnassus: Poetry in Review* 1 (Fall/Winter
1972): 130–34.

Coen, Kathy S. ''Poetry.'' *Washington Post Book World* 22 December 1991: 11.

Franklin V, Benjamin. ''Linda Pastan.'' *Dictionary of Literary Biography*. Vol. 5, pt. 2.
American Poets Since World War II. Ed. Donald J. Greiner, Detroit: Gale Research Company, 1980. 158–63.

———. ''Theme and Structure in Linda Pastan's Poetry.'' *Poet Lore* 75 (Winter 1981):
234–42.

Garrison, Joseph. ''Heart and Soul: Two Poets.'' *Shenandoah* 24.4 (Summer 1973): 90–
93.

Gilbert, Sandra M. ''The Melody of the Quotidian.'' *Parnassus: Poetry in Review* 11
(Spring/Summer 1983): 147–67.

Howard, Ben. ''Short Reviews.'' *Poetry* 154 (September 1989): 345–47.

Jacobsen, Josephine. ''*The Five Stages of Grief* by Linda Pastan.'' *Washington Post Book
World* 21 May 1978: 4ff.

Jellema, Roderick. ''The Poetry of Linda Pastan.'' *Voyages* 2 (Spring 1969): 73–74.

Lipardi, Joseph A. ''Pastan, Linda. *A Fraction of Darkness.*'' *Library Journal* 110 (September 1985): 203.

McClatchy, J. D. ''Short Reviews.'' *Poetry* 140 (September 1982): 346–53.

Pitchford, Kenneth. ''Metaphor as Illness: A Meditation on Recent Poetry.'' *New England Review* 1 (1978): 96–119.

Pressley, Sue Anne. ''Messenger of a Muse.'' *Washington Post* 27 March 1991: D1ff.

Seidman, Hugh. ''Word Play.'' *New York Times Book Review* 20 February 1983: 6ff.

Shaw, Robert. ''Short Reviews.'' *Poetry* 148 (April 1986): 36–43.

Smock, Frederick. ''A New Note.'' *American Book Review* 12 (March/April 1990): 26.

Stitt, Peter. ''Violence, Imagery and Introspection.'' *Georgia Review* 33 (Winter 1979):
927–32.

———. ''Stages of Reality: The Mind/Body Problem in Contemporary Poetry.'' *Georgia
Review* 37 (Spring 1983): 201–10.

Susskind, H. ''Pastan, Linda. *Heroes in Disguise: Poems.*'' *Choice* 29 (April 1992):
4355.

Whitman, Ruth. ''Pastan, Linda. *The Imperfect Paradise: Poems.*'' *Choice* 26 (November
1988): 492.

MARGE PIERCY (1936–)

Jaye Berman Montresor

BIOGRAPHY

Marge Piercy was born in 1936 in Detroit, Michigan, and grew up in a working-class neighborhood. She left Detroit at seventeen with a scholarship to attend college, and she received an A.B. from the University of Michigan and an M.A. from Northwestern University. After leaving Detroit, she lived mainly in big cities—Chicago, New York, San Francisco, and Boston—until health problems made it necessary for her to move to the country. Since 1971, she has lived on Cape Cod in Massachusetts.

Piercy says she began writing at fifteen, when for the first time, she had the privacy of her own room. Her earliest literary influences were Shelley and Keats, but she found her imagination constricted by rhyme in her youthful imitative efforts. It was after she had read Walt Whitman in her teens that she produced what she considers her first real poems, for she discovered in Whitman "a confirmation of earlier rhythms from Jewish liturgy and the Torah and the Psalms," rhythms that came more naturally to her than those she had learned in school ("How I Came to Walt Whitman and Found Myself" 99). Her discovery of Allen Ginsberg's poetry in 1959 reinforced her awakened sense that "to write authentically from yourself, no matter how queer or outside the mainstream society seemed to regard you, was inherently valuable if you wrote well" ("Whitman" 99). Piercy also cites another original American voice, Emily Dickinson, as an important influence on her as a developing writer. Piercy credits, too, her Jewish grandmother and mother as instrumental to her development as a novelist and poet: "My grandmother was a great storyteller. She and my mother told many of the same stories, but always the stories came out differently. My mother made me a poet" ("Autobiography" 267).

Piercy has lived a life of political engagement since her involvement with radical groups—civil rights, antiwar, SDS—of the 1960s, and she has been a champion of the women's movement since 1969. Among her writings relevant to these movements are the essays and stories which have appeared in *Off Our*

Backs, The Bold New Women, Sisterhood Is Powerful, Defiance, and *Paths of Resistance*, and she continues to contribute regularly to *Ms.* magazine. There is also a pronounced domestic side to Piercy reflected in her attachment to her cats, her kitchen and garden, her husband, and their home in Wellfleet, Massachusetts.

Piercy's father was not Jewish, and she did not go to Hebrew school, yet Judaism was always something special to her, something she says she "wanted more of" (Henderson 77). She was raised as a Jew by her mother and grandmother, and she always felt closer to this maternal, Jewish side of her family. Although she writes in a poem, "The ram's horn sounding," that being both woman and Jew is a contradiction. She has worked for feminism within Judaism since the 1980s through her poetic contributions to the Reconstructionist prayer book *Hadesh Yameinu: A Siddur for Shabbat and Festivals* (some of which, like the above poem, are collected in *Available Light*). Piercy's three husbands have all been Jewish, for she has said that she was determined not to repeat her mother's mistake of a mixed marriage: "I felt a mixed marriage was more than I personally could handle. Marrying a man is mixed enough" ("Autobiography" 272).

Although she has never been a full-time university professional, Piercy has given readings and conducted workshops at well over two hundred fifty institutions around the world. She has also been in residence at many campuses, among them the University of Kansas, Ohio State University, the University of Cincinnati, as well as numerous writers' conferences in the United States and abroad. Additionally, she has held the Butler Chair of Letters at the State University of New York at Buffalo and been the DeRoy Distinguished Visiting Professor at the University of Michigan. Her awards include two Borestone Mountain Poetry Awards, a fellowship from the Literature Program of the National Endowment for the Arts, and the Literature Award from the (Massachusetts) Governor's Commission on the Status of Women. She is also a recipient of the Sheaffer-PEN/New England Award for Literary Excellence and the Arthur C. Clarke Award for Best Science Fiction Novel Published in the United Kingdom. Piercy also received an Honorary Doctor of Letters degree from Bridgwater State College.

She currently lives with her third husband, writer Ira Wood, in Wellfleet, Massachusetts, where she continues to be active in politics on Judaism.

MAJOR THEMES

Marge Piercy's writing reflects her commitment to radical politics, ecofeminism, and Reconstructionist Judaism, all of which tie together for her, as the title of her most autobiographical novel, *Braided Lives*, suggests. The common denominator to these three aspects of her life is change. The goal of her political vision is a radical transformation of the self, the family, and larger social structures that would eliminate sexism, racism, class distinctions, crime, and poverty. Piercy's eco-feminism holds that the profit motive inherent in male power and the mechanistic view of science held by men are responsible for the exploitation of nature and women. She, therefore, seeks a changed world view that recognizes the seamless interdependence of women and men, earth and its human inhabitants. Reconstructionist Judaism, similarly predicated on change, insists on Judaism's flexible response to a changing world.

Piercy makes explicit the connection between her political, feminist, and spiritual goals when, in her introduction to the woman's poetry anthology *Early Ripening*, she identifies her conception of political revolution with a feminism that "rests on that sense of the self not apart from nature, not above, not instrumental, but on an awareness of being part of the whole, which is holy." For Piercy, this holiness is similarly inherent in Jewish ritual practice, which in its cyclical, seasonal celebrations reveals a deep connection to the ordering rhythms of nature. In describing herself as "passionately interested in the female lunar side of Judaism," Piercy makes a further connection between eco-feminism and Judaism, since Jewish rituals are practiced according to a lunar calendar, and the female menstrual cycle ("Autobiography" 268). The importance of the intimate connection between the moon and women for Piercy, is evidenced by her titling one of her poetry collections *The Moon Is Always Female*. It is thus through their organic ties to nature that Piercy's understanding of political revolution, feminism, and Judaism must be understood.

Poetry, in Piercy's view, is also a braiding together of separate strands, a fusing of her woman's body, brains, and emotions. Her poems are accessible to the ordinary reader and tend to be more autobiographical than her fiction; they record a consciousness in process, continually seeking and finding new ways "to be of use" (as one of her poetry collections is titled). Piercy writes in a loosely organic, as opposed to a tightly structured, form. She finds subject matter for her poems in such everyday occurrences and objects as gardening and cats, as well as love, sex, and relationships in all their variety. Her imagery is most often taken from the natural world, as in "To be of use" where she praises hard-working people "who pull like water buffalo, with massive patience." Awareness of her natural surroundings introduced a new element to her poetry after her move to the Cape, and over the past two decades Piercy has celebrated "a sense of myself as part of the landscape and part of the web of living beings. . . . I not only write a lot about gardening, about the land and sea, the marshes, the tidal creeks, the piney woods, but whatever I am writing about, this place imbues my imagery" ("Autobiography" *To Be of Use* 278).

Some of her poems whimsically address her life as a writer, like "The poet dreams of a nice warm motel" and "The new novel" (which wants to eat her up). A number take a more didactic approach in addressing political concerns, as in "Rape Poem," which compares being raped to a number of other violent acts, like "being pushed down a flight of cement steps." Piercy's liturgical poems celebrate *Shekinah*, the indwelling spirit or female aspect of God. This spirit animates all created things, as Piercy tells us in "The garden as synagogue" (the last section of her tri-partite poem, "Le Sacre du Printemps"). Whether Piercy is praising the sabbath ("Wellfleet Sabbath") or the seasons ("Le Sacre du Printemps," "Summer mourning"), her liturgical poems are deeply connected to her passion for political freedom and her reverence for nature.

By contrast to the Whitmanesque celebration of Piercy's ever-evolving Self, the elaborate character studies of women in her novels—women who very often resemble Piercy in their feisty intelligence, pronounced sensuality, and strong Jewish identity—indicate whom she might have become as a result of altered circumstances or different choices. But for differences in race and class, for example, she might be as powerless a victim of the System as is Connie in *Woman on the Edge of Time* (whom Piercy has noted is based largely on her mother). Given Piercy's involvement with radical movements, it may simply be luck that saved her from becoming, like the title character in *Vida*, an SDS fugitive. And but for accidents of time and place, Piercy might have been any one of the number of Jewish women confronting the horrors of World War II in *Gone to Soldiers*.

Piercy has written that marrying her first husband (a French Jew whose family fled to Switzerland during the war) was a way of identifying with Holocaust survival. *Gone to Soldiers* can also be seen as an exercise in identification, for Piercy does not offer explanations of the Holocaust so much as opportunities to experience it through her richly developed characters, many of whom are women paradoxically mobilized into growth by the destructive event of war. Jacqueline Levy-Monot, for example, is an anti-Semitic French Jew who becomes a courageous worker for the Jewish underground; Bernice Coates is an American who escapes her domineering father to become a bomber pilot; Louise Kahan is an American romance writer who becomes a war correspondent. Rather than focusing exclusively on male soldiers and battlefields as do most novels about World War II, Piercy brings an awareness to her readers that "actual war involves the slaughter mostly of civilian populations and the death of a great many children, women, old people, cats, dogs, horses, cattle, birds—the whole attendant ecology of a place" ("What Rides the Wind" 59). Piercy does not shirk from presenting us with the hideousness of concentration camps and the Polish death march, but neither does she fail to include affirmative events like the love and friendship that develop during the war. Jacqueline's sister Naomi's pregnancy and departure for Eretz Yisroel end the novel on a symbolic note of rebirth for the Jewish people, a reflection of Piercy's essential optimism, her belief "in people's enormous ability to open up, to give, to grow, to shine and stretch and make incredible beauty in the world we inherit and often abuse" ("What Rides the Wind" 61).

Piercy's political struggles are premised on a visionary utopianism, a belief in harmonious, egalitarian communities that foster the individual, creative spirit of each of its members. This ideal is apparent in the tribal community of *Dance the Eagle to Sleep*, the Mattapoisett village in *Woman on the Edge of Time*, and the women's commune in *Small Changes*, all of which propose a superior alternative to the traditional nuclear family. Such social arrangements are always threatened in her fiction, however, by outside forces, as in *Summer People*, where the utopian *menage à trois* is disrupted by outsiders from the surrounding community.

Because it is situated in the future, science fiction is best suited to the creation of utopian worlds, as Piercy discovered in *Woman on the Edge of Time*, and her interest in the genre remains evident in the cyberpunk setting of her latest novel, *He, She, and It*. Cyberpunk, a subgenre of science fiction spawned by William Gibson's 1984 novel *Neuromancer* and Ridley Scott's 1982 film *Blade Runner*, typically depicts a near-future dystopia where present social and technological trends have been taken to a dehumanizing extreme. Like Piercy herself, who uses highly sophisticated computer technology to produce her revolutionary writing, cyberpunk is grounded in a subversive belief that technology can be liberated from its makers and used to oppose the establishment.

In Piercy's computer-mediated twenty-first century, people live under domes as the result of an ecological disaster and plug into computers through sockets in their foreheads. And here, Piercy has most imaginatively braided together the three main strands of her identity. The future dystopia that her Jewish, female protagonist finds herself in is one very much informed by the Jewish past that precedes Piercy, specifically the mysticism of the Kabbalah and the medieval legends of the golem. The parallel between the twenty-first cyborg and the sixteenth-century golem creates a fascinating subtext which allows Piercy to explore familiar themes in her fiction—sexual and family relationships, Jewish identity, political radicalism, alternative societies—with a twist that raises new ethical questions about machines that feel as well as think.

SURVEY OF CRITICISM

Of these three strands that are the substance of Piercy's identity and the subject of her writing—radical politics, eco-feminism, and Reconstructionist Judaism—the last has not been addressed in the existing literary criticism despite the preponderance of Jewish characters and themes in her fiction and poetry. For the most part, critical attention has focused almost exclusively to date on the feminist utopia depicted in Piercy's most popular novel, *Woman on the Edge of Time*. Not surprisingly, given its subject—a woman's struggle to retain her autonomy in the male-dominated present and her concomitant introduction to a radically egalitarian future—most of the criticism on this novel has been written by women using an approach grounded in feminist theory. Critics such as Chris Ferns, Libby Falk Jones, and Carol Farley Kessler have enthusiastically praised the twenty-second century depicted in the novel as one that can alter women's dreams and allow "this leap into our own futures" (Jones 125), yet at the same time noting troublesome aspects of the Mattapoisett community, such as taking away women's procreative privileges.

Although her books sell well, more mainstream criticism has treated Piercy less kindly. Many critics have taken exception to the political rhetoric which is pervasive in Piercy's novels. While Piercy views plot as emanating from character in her fiction, critics often see things differently; for example, Jeanne McManus in her review of *Fly Away Home* complains that "politics sometimes takes precedence over characterization" (4). Critics have also been alienated by Piercy's harsh depictions of male characters who serve as convenient scapegoats for the problems of her highly sympathetic female characters. Another fault that has been found in Piercy's fiction is its old-fashioned form. As Pearl K. Bell wrote in her *Commentary* review of *Vida*: "Though she presents herself as a revolutionary . . . her novels are surprisingly conventional. In conception and style, in the grim determination of her didactic intentions, her work is reminiscent of the radical-proletarian fiction of the 1930s, in which the message outweighed the manner of its telling." Bell's criticism notwithstanding, *Vida* and *Gone to Soldiers* are Piercy's only novels of the last twenty years that have been positively reviewed in the *New York Times Book Review*, a situation that Piercy attributes to the unpopularity of her political views in post-Watergate America. Moreover, Piercy considers her real audience those whose views are not determined by the elitist world of New York critics. The straightforward, realistic prose of even her most fantastic fiction communicates itself to the kind of reader Piercy wants to reach, ordinary women and men endeavoring "to be of use."

Perhaps as a result of the more personal voice and less overt political rhetoric in most of her poems, critics tend to view Piercy more favorably as a poet than as a novelist. The directness and honesty of her poetic voice as well as her often brilliant metaphors (as in the self-mutilation of "The Friend" and "Barbie Doll") contribute to the agreement among most critics that Piercy is an important and gifted poet.

BIBLIOGRAPHY

Works by Marge Piercy

Novels

Breaking Camp. Middletown, CT: Wesleyan UP, 1968.
Going Down Fast. New York: Trident Press, 1969.
Dance the Eagle to Sleep. Garden City, NY: Doubleday, 1970.
Small Changes. Garden City, NY: Doubleday, 1973.
Woman on the Edge of Time. New York: Knopf, 1976.
The High Cost of Living. New York: Harper & Row, 1978.
Vida. New York: Summit, 1979.
Braided Lives. New York: Summit, 1982.
Fly Away Home. New York: Summit, 1984.

Gone to Soldiers. New York: Summit, 1987.
Summer People. New York: Summit, 1989.
He, She, and It. New York: Knopf, 1991.
The Longings of Women. (Forthcoming).

Poetry

Hard Loving. Middletown, CT: Wesleyan UP, 1969.
4-telling. With Bob Hershon, Emmet Jarrett, and Dick Lourie. Trumansburg, NY: New
   Books, 1971.
To Be of Use. Garden City, NY: Doubleday, 1973.
Living in the Open. New York: Alfred A. Knopf, 1976.
The Twelve-Spoked Wheel Flashing. New York: Knopf, 1978.
The Moon Is Always Female. New York: Knopf, 1980.
Circles on the Water. New York: Knopf, 1982.
Stone, Paper, Knife. New York: Knopf, 1983.
My Mother's Body. New York: Knopf, 1985.
Available Light. New York: Knopf, 1988.
The Earth Shines Secretly: A Book of Days. Cambridge, MA: Zoland, 1990.
Mars and Her Children. New York: Knopf, 1992.

Play

The Last White Class: A Play About Neighborhood Terror. With Ira Wood. Trumansburg,
   NY: Crossing Press, 1979.

Selected Non-Fiction

Parti-Colored Blocks for a Quilt. Ann Arbor: University of Michigan Press, 1982.
''Autobiography.'' *Contemporary Authors Autobiography Series.* Ed. Dedria Bryfonski.
   Detroit: Gale Research Co., 1984. 1: 267–81.
''Introduction.'' *Early Ripening: American Women's Poetry Now* [anthology]. Ed. Marge
   Piercy. Winchester, MA: Pandora P, 1987.
''What Rides the Wind.'' *Tikkun* 4 (March/April 1989): 58–62.
''Marge Piercy'' [Interview]. Inter/View: Talks with American Writing Women, 1990.
   A Voice of One's Own: Conversations with America's Writing Women. Ed.
   Mickey Pearlman and Katharine Usher Henderson. Boston: Houghton Mifflin,
   1990. 76–85.
''How I Came to Walt Whitman and Found Myself.'' *Massachusetts Review* 33 (Spring
   1992): 98–100.

Selected Works about Marge Piercy

Abbott, Philip. ''Are Three Generations of Radicals Enough? Self-Critique in the Novels
   of Tess Slesinger, Mary McCarthy, and Marge Piercy.'' *Review of Politics* 53
   (Fall 1991): 602–26.
DuPlessis, Rachel Blau. ''The Feminist Apologues of Lessing, Piercy, and Russ.'' *Fron-
   tiers* 4 (Spring 1979): 1–8.
Ferns, Chris. ''Dreams of Freedom: Ideology and Narrative Structure in the Utopian

Fictions of Marge Piercy and Ursula LeGuin. *English Studies in Canada* (December 1988): 453–66.

Hansen, Elaine Tuttle. "The Double Narrative Structure of *Small Changes.*" *Contemporary American Women Writers.* Ed. Catherine Rainwater and William Scheick. Lexington: University of Kentucky Press, 1985. 209–223.

————— and William J. Scheik. "A Bibliography and Writings by Marge Piercy. *Contemporary American Women Writers.* 224–28.

Jones, Libby Falk. "Gilman, Bradley, Piercy, and the Evolving Rhetoric of Feminist Utopias." *Feminism, Utopia, and Narrative.* Ed. Libby Falk Jones and Sarah Webster Goodwin. Knoxville: University of Tennessee Press, 1900. 116–29.

Kessler, Carol Farley. "*Woman on the Edge of Time*: A Novel 'To Be of Use.' " *Extrapolation* 28 (Winter 1987): 310–18.

Khouri, Nadia. "The Dialectics of Power: Utopia in the Science Fiction of LeGuin, Jeury, and Piercy." *Science-Fiction Studies* 7 (1980): 49–60.

Kress, Susan. "In and Out of Time: The Form of Marge Piercy's Novels." *Future Females: A Critical Anthology.* Ed. Marleen S. Barr. Bowling Green, Ohio: Bowling Green State University Popular Press, 1981. 109–22.

McManus, Jeanne. "Eating Well Is the Best Revenge." Rev. of *Fly Away Home. Washington Post Book World* 19 February 1984: 4.

Moylan, Thomas P. "History and Utopia in Marge Piercy's *Woman on the Edge of Time.*" *Science Fiction Dialogues.* Ed. Gary Wolfe. Chicago: Academy Chicago, 1982. 133–40.

Nowik, Nan. "Mixing Art and Politics: The Writings of Adrienne Rich, Marge Piercy, and Alice Walker." *Centennial Review* 30 (Spring 1986): 208–18.

Wynne, Edith. "Imagery of Association in the Poetry of Marge Piercy." *Publications of the Missouri Philological Association* 10 (1985): 57–63.

FRANCINE PROSE (1947–   )

Rena Potok

BIOGRAPHY

Francine Prose was born on April 1, 1947, in Brooklyn, New York, to physicians Jessie Rubin Prose and Philip Prose. She received her elementary and high-school education at the Brooklyn Friends School, and in 1968 received her B.A. in English from Radcliffe College in Cambridge, Massachusetts. The following year she earned her M.A., also in English, from Harvard University. On September 24, 1976, she married sculptor Howard Michels. The author of eight highly acclaimed novels and numerous short stories, Prose has lived in Arizona, North Carolina, San Francisco, and Bombay. Her stories and articles have appeared in the *New Yorker*, the *Atlantic Monthly*, the *Village Voice*, and *Vogue*.

Prose began writing as a child, but it was not until a trip to Bombay in 1971 that she began to take her writing seriously. During a ten-month stay in that city, she spent much of her time in the Bombay University Library, which, she says, ''probably hadn't been updated in fifty years.'' She immersed herself in the works of nineteenth-century writers Dickens, Dostoevsky, Proust, and Tolstoy and soon became interested in exploring the art of storytelling. She wrote *Judah the Pious* during that year and later gave it to a former college professor, who passed it on to an editor at Atheneum. The novel was published in 1973. Prose was twenty-five.

Well-regarded for her representations of the quirky side of human experience, the fusion of the everyday and the supernatural, Prose has received numerous awards and honors for her novels and short fiction. In 1973, she was awarded the Jewish Book Council Award for *Judah the Pious*; in 1975, the MLLE. Award from *Mademoiselle*; and in 1984, the Edgar Lewis Wallant Award from the Hartford Jewish Community Center for *Hungry Hearts*. In 1989, she received a Fulbright Fellowship for travel to the former Yugoslavia, followed by a Guggenheim Foundation writing grant in 1991.

Francine Prose taught Creative Writing at Harvard from 1971 to 1972 and was a visiting lecturer in Fiction at the University of Arizona, in Tucson, from

1982–84. In the summer of 1984, she was an instructor at the Bread Loaf Writers' Workshop in Vermont. She is a former faculty member of the Master of Fine Arts Program for Writers at Warren Wilson College and has taught writing at Sarah Lawrence, the University of Utah, and the Iowa Writers' Workshop. Although she no longer teaches full time, Prose conducts occasional writing workshops at the New York State Writers' Conference, and at Bread Loaf.

In addition to writing fiction, Prose frequently contributes profiles, "think pieces," travel essays, and reviews to *Mademoiselle, Gentleman's Quarterly,* the *New York Times Magazine,* and the *New York Times Book Review.* Here, she writes of the roles contemporary fathers take in rearing their children, literary sexual stereotypes of boys, women's conflicts of career and home, and the social patterns of high-school girls. Lighter essays address topics such as food intake, evening gowns, and hubris, or what she calls "male ventriloquism" in a humorous look at men's silencing of women's speech. She is also the author of a children's book of bible stories and the cotranslator of two works of fiction by Polish writer Ida Fink.

Prose's latest novel, *Hunters and Gatherers,* is scheduled for release by Farrar, Straus, and Giroux in 1994. It is a novel about a group of women and contains no male characters, because Prose "wanted to see how women interact when there are no men around." A new collection of short stories, titled *The Peaceable Kingdom* was published in 1993, also by Farrar, Straus. A film version of her novel *Household Saints* has been completed and was also released, by Fine Line Productions, in September of 1993. The film was written and directed by Nancy Savoca, director of the acclaimed film *Dogfight* and stars Tracy Ullman, Lily Taylor, Judith Malina, and Vincent Dolmofio. Prose is currently at work on a new novel. She lives in upstate New York with her husband and their two sons.

MAJOR THEMES

Intersections between the magical and the real adorn the pages of Francine Prose's fiction. Her novels raise questions about the nature of art and language, human character and relationships, reality and illusion. Her characters are actors, tabloid writers, a quadroon psychic, and a mysterious storytelling rabbi. They are people who live on the fringe, individuals who dwell on the margins of society.

Prose's writing is separable into four major periods: The novels of the 1970s are characterized by the strong presence of fantasy and magic. These tales, steeped in and often based on history, have the quality of legend. Their characters are mythical, their settings exotic, mysterious, and foreign. *Judah the Pious* is a Hasidic fairy tale set in Poland sometime in the past two or three hundred years; *The Glorious Ones* is the dream-framed legend of a troupe of sixteenth-century Italian commedia dell'arte players; *Marie Laveau* tells the life history of a New Orleans psychic healer from the nineteenth century; and *Animal*

Magnetism is a medical fantasy about hypnosis and transcendentalism set among the textile factories of nineteenth-century New England.

In the novels of the early 1980s, fantasy is no longer isolated from, but is woven into, the fabric of everyday life. *Household Saints* interweaves legend into the daily experiences of a butcher and his strange family; *Hungry Hearts* is a stage memoir that locates magic in the marriage and early career of a Yiddish theatre star; and in *Bigfoot Dreams*, reality collides with storytelling when the invention of a tabloid writer is revealed as an accidental truth. The characters who populate these narratives are less exotic than their predecessors, and more ethnic—they are Jews or Italians, all from New York, all living in the twentieth century.

Between 1987 and 1992, Prose published only short stories, which represent a more pessimistic and realistic attitude toward her fictional subjects. And with the publication of *Primitive People*, Prose appears to be developing the present stage of her writing as one characterized by none of the hopefulness of her earlier works. Moved out of New York City and into its countrified suburbs, this latest novel is a tale of stolen childhood and divorce, nanny problems, racial tensions, infidelity, and asexuality.

One of the major themes woven throughout Prose's fiction is that of story-telling. Rabbi Eliezer of Rimanov, Flaminio Scala and his commedia dell'arte players, the actors of the Yiddish Art Theater—all are master storytellers who entrance their listeners with their tales of magic, intrigue, and romance. Prose is interested in exploring multiple layers of narrative fiction; hers are stories within stories within stories. They are replete with the tricks of the teller: stories are told, then retracted, retold, then revealed as a ruse, a lie, a detour on the path to the real story, or perhaps merely a final diversion. Prose, as narrator or authorial voice, places herself in the role of Homer's Penelope, weaving and unweaving a tapestry while her listeners gather night after night to hear each narrative rebirth, mutation, mystical reincarnation.

Magic and fantasy are perhaps the most dominant and recurring themes in Prose's novels. In the early ones in particular, she knits together the fantastic and the marvelous with the utterly mundane. Characters like Zinnia Turner in *Animal Magnetism* are ordinary people flung into extraordinary circumstances where they discover hidden psychic powers. In *Judah the Pious*, Rabbi Eliezer of Rimanov travels to the king of Poland to reinstate Jewish burial rituals and tells him a fantastic tale of spirits, forest creatures, and mysterious women who share oddly similar physical traits. Reality and illusion are merged in Prose's texts, conflating the everyday with the illusory. Reading her novels is reading beyond the mundane into the realm of the unknown, the realm of magic realism.

Dreams function in Prose's novels as conduits into the realm of fantasy and the supernatural. Rather than a place distinct from the waking state, they are the space between dreaming and waking, between reality and illusion, the space where reality loses its hard edges. Dreams in her narratives are the only realm where truth is spoken, where trickery is no longer necessary or relevant. Dreams in *The Glorious Ones* reveal the voices of the dead, speaking to the living, unburdening themselves of the pain of their lives and of their existence in death. In *Marie Laveau*, dreams are the realm of revelation, a companion to the mirrors where Marie sees visions of the past, present, and future. In *Bigfoot Dreams*, they are a place of escape, where myth becomes reality and monsters are gracious hosts and loyal companions.

Although Judaism is not a central theme in Prose's works, it is a clear influence on it. Her narratives are frequently populated by Jewish characters and often make use of Jewish mysticism and literature: Dinah's and Benno's troubles in *Hungry Hearts* are brought on in part by his dabbling in Kabbalah, and *Judah the Pious*, which mimics the traditional form of the Hasidic folktale, appears to be based loosely on the sixteenth-century *The Book of the Kuzari* by Rabbi Judah HaLevi. The Jewish communal experience of oppression and the ability to use language and intellect to overcome it lie at the center of several of Prose's texts as well.

Often the writer focuses on women, their attempts to grapple with the burdens and responsibilities of the everyday, and their escape to the world of fantasy, mysticism, and mythology. Faced with social, familial, sexual, and economic burdens, these women are single mothers, sickly factory workers, struggling wives, or famous stage stars and healers. These women, while often exhausted, nonetheless display inexhaustibly creative methods of coping with loneliness, unhappiness, and the skepticism of others—who are usually parents, colleagues, and former husbands or lovers. They all cross the line between the mundane and the marvelous, mingling the banal with the fantastic in an effort to breach the gap between the two and bring meaning to their lives.

Marriage, divorce, and infidelity are constant themes in Prose's narratives. At times, marriage represents secret bonds shared between people; more often, it represents the failure of human relationships and proof of the impossibility of human intimacy. Marriage and divorce function in many of Prose's plots as an assault on the human condition, especially that of her female characters. The challenge and failure of marital relations are often located, in her texts, with unfaithful husbands who are unable to find comfort and security in the context of a marriage and a shared home.

The period of the late 1980s and early 1990s was, for Prose, one of increased production in the art of the short story. During that period, she wrote and published numerous stories in both literary journals and popular magazines, beginning with the publication, in 1988, of the collection *Women and Children First*. Her stories deal with marriages that have dissolved, relationships that have crumbled, and careers that have turned uninspiring. In these writings, women often find themselves psychically and physically more connected to their children than to the men with whom they conceived them. The majority of the characters in Prose's short fiction are people in their thirties and forties who are experiencing tremendous disillusionment with their lives. If her novels are filmic narratives, then her stories are like snapshots: snatched moments from the fragmented lives of people who look stunned at being caught in the act of trying to put back the pieces of their broken reality.

With her latest published novel, *Primitive People*, Prose turns her focus away from the fusion of magic and realism. This novel is harshly lodged in reality, in a cold portrayal of American decadence. In the world of Hudson Landing, language is used as a weapon, relationships crumble and fall to infidelity, intimacy has become extinct, and children are used as bargaining chips and protectors of adult secrets in the lethal games of deception and betrayal that adults play with each other.

Prose's narrative style has been compared to that of Chaucer and Isak Dinesen, and it has been described as evocative of the magic realism of Hasidic folktales. It is a sparse and relatively undecorative style, one that contrasts with, and so sets off, the fantastic elements in the content of the writing. Francine Prose is a master storyteller who skillfully establishes and maintains a balance between the colorfulness of the characters and events in her tales and the clever manner of their telling.

SURVEY OF CRITICISM

Francine Prose's impressive canon has been reviewed extensively in the *New York Times*; the *New York Times Book Review*; the *Yale, Hudson,* and *Sewanee* reviews; and several popular magazines such as *New York* and *Newsweek*. The critical response to her writing has been, for the most part, favorable. Her first novel, *Judah the Pious*, is praised as ''an unusually impressive effort, especially for a first novel, notably successful in tone and over-all finish, full of sudden delights and mocking humor'' (Lask 29). One critic places it in the tradition of Chaucer's ''The Pardoner's Tale'' and Isak Dinesen's *Seven Gothic Tales* (Lask 29), two others place it in the genre of *Candide* and *Rasselas* (Cruttwell and Westburg 421). Critics are especially impressed by Prose's ability to navigate between the real and the fantastic and by her Russian-doll style of revealing a story within a story within a story in a folk-legend style.

Her second novel, *The Glorious Ones*, received more mixed reviews. Pearl K. Bell in *The New Leader* and Patricia Meyer Spacks in *The Hudson Review* find the story entertaining but the novel as a whole disappointing, calling it ''an exercise in esoterica'' (Bell 18) and ''a one-gimmick book'' (Spacks 94). But Margo Jefferson praises its language, in *Newsweek*, for being ''rich and graceful, heightened by history and legend'' (90).

Prose's novels of the early to mid-1980s are given a great deal of critical attention, most notably in the *New York Times* and the *New York Times Book Review*. Most critics are impressed with her gothic imagination and exotic style and with her skill as a storyteller who continually addresses the conflicting claims of the ordinary and the extraordinary. They agree that, in her novels, Prose creates worlds whose dimensions are flexible and whose boundaries are fluid. Thomas Lask calls *Marie Laveau* ''an intriguing exploration of that area between dreaming and waking'' (C22), and Gary Davenport, in *The Sewanee Review*, notes favorably the struggle between life and art unfolding in the pages of *Hungry Hearts*.

Critics respond strongly to the evocation of legend in Prose's writing, to the formula of a questor on a journey to find the ultimate meaning of his or her life. Randolph Hogan finds in *Household Saints* elements of what he calls the modern-day legend (37), and Jerome Charyn writes of *Hungry Hearts* that it has ''the force of parable, the clear clean line of prose without adornment'' (10). *Bigfoot Dreams* is described as a book about questors, one that lays out a view of the world as ''a place peopled with unlikely characters and animated by improbable, even fantastic, events'' (Kakutani 12). While Susan Allen Toth claims that the plot of *Bigfoot Dreams* is too crowded and the ending unbelievable (9), Michiko Kakutani likes the idiosyncratic combination of characters and ''precise, psychological descriptions with quirky humor and a kooky, slightly larger-than-life feel for New York City—its subways and its streets, its crazies and its weirdos, its noise and heat and distractions'' (12).

Women and Children First, Prose's only published collection of short stories to date, was reviewed favorably by Stephen McCauley in the *New York Times Book Review*. What distinguishes Prose's stories from others, he says, is her ''strong, distinctive voice; her acerbic humor . . . her bold pursuit of the bizarre that lurks beneath the surface of the mundane . . . and her unsparing, though not unkind, insight into the subtleties of character and the nuances of relationships'' (6). McCauley is impressed with the tension, the Hitchcock-like edginess in these stories, and with the ''double-edged shrewdness'' (6) of the characters, which brings a poignancy and sadness to the collection.

Reviews of *Primitive People*, Prose's most recent published novel, note the increased pessimism in her approach to her subject matter. Critics read the representation of American society in this book as one of a corrupt and decadent place, a wasteland of shopping, betrayal, and meaningless conversation. And several comment on the irony located in Prose's depiction of the characters that populate this landscape. David Plante, in the *Yale Review*, calls this a novel about ''American weirdos and their Haitian nanny'' (103), pointing out that the America of this novel is a place where ''the primitive is not ritualized and has no social meaning, but exists as much here as anywhere and simply isolates people in meaningless horror'' (104). Michael Dorris praises the novel's humor and irony and notes that, ultimately, it is about ''a society in shambles . . . a culture in sharp decline where complications build upon complications and no clear or positive resolution is in sight'' (10). And Rhoda Koenig calls *Primitive People* ''a portrait of American decadence'' (92), with characters who seem to have crawled out of a Charles Addams cartoon and are ''untethered to even the simplest anchors of family, religion, morality, sexual normalcy, or good manners'' (92).

Most of the critics agree that Prose's writings intrigue because of her skill as a storyteller and her ability to weave together in the most imaginative ways elements of the mundane and the supernatural. They laud her depiction of the fluctuations of interpersonal relationships and her clear, sharp development of characters and of the turmoil that they call everyday life.

BIBLIOGRAPHY

Works by Francine Prose

The Glorious Ones. New York: Atheneum, 1974.
Stories from Our Living Past. Jules Harlow, ed. New Jersey: Behrman, 1974.
Marie Laveau. New York: Berkley Publishing, 1977.
Animal Magnetism. New York: G. P. Putnam's Sons, 1978.
Household Saints. New York: St. Martin's Press, 1981.
Hungry Hearts. New York: Pantheon Books, 1983.
"The Arrival of Eve." *Gates to the New City: A Treasury of Modern Jewish Tales*. Ed. Howard Schwartz, New York: Avon, 1983. 118–9.
Bigfoot Dreams. New York: Pantheon Books, 1986.
Judah the Pious. 1973. Boston: G. K. Hall, 1986.
"Tangerine Dreams." *Redbook* 170 (Dec. 1987): 52.
Women and Children First. New York: Pantheon Books, 1988.
"Imaginary Problems." *Antaeus* 62 (Spring 1989): 78–88.
"Amazing." *TriQuarterly* 76 (Fall 1989): 48–59.
"Rubber Life." *North American Review* 276 (June 1991): 44–49.
"Good Guy, Bad Guy." *Antioch Review* 49 (Fall 1991): 538–50.
Primitive People. New York: Farrar, Straus, and Giroux, 1992.
"Cauliflower Heads." *Michigan Quarterly Review* 31 (Winter 1992): 80–95.
"Talking Dog." *Yale Review* 80.1 and 2 (April 1992): 150–64.
"Small Miracles." *Redbook* 180 (Dec. 1992): 70.
A Peaceable Kingdom. New York: Farrar, Straus, and Giroux, 1993.

Interviews

"Francine Prose." With Mickey Pearlman. *Inter/View: Talks with America's Writing Women*. Eds. Mickey Pearlman and Katherine Usher Henderson. Lexington, KY: University Press of Kentucky, 1990. 88–94.
"PW Interviews: Francine Prose." With John F. Baker. *Publishers Weekly* (13 April 1992): 38–39.

Translations

With Madeleine Levine. Ida Fink, *A Scrap of Time and Other Stories*. Translated by Madeleine Levine and Francine Prose. New York: Pantheon Books, 1988.
With Johanna Weschler. Ida Fink, *The Journey*. Translated by Johanna Weschler and Francine Prose. New York: Farrar, Straus, and Giroux, 1992.

Works about Francine Prose

Bell, Pearl K. "The Artist as Hero." *New Leader* (4 April 1974): 17.
Caplan, Brina. "The Jewish Stanislavsky." *Nation* 236.16 (23 April 1983): 518–19.

Charyn, Jerome. "A Dybbuk on Stage." *New York Times Book Review* (6 March 1983): 10.

Cruttwell, Patrick, and Faith Westburg. Rev. of *Judah the Pious. Hudson Review* 26.2 (Summer 1973): 421.

Davenport, Gary. "The Two Worlds of Contemporary American Fiction." *Sewanee Review* 92.1 (Winter 1984): 128–36.

Dorris, Michael. Rev. of *Primitive People. New York Times Book Review* (5 April 1992): 9–10.

Evans, Nancy H. "Francine Prose." *Contemporary Authors* 112: 402–03.

Hogan, Randolph. "The Butcher Won a Wife." *New York Times Book Review* (12 July 1981): 12, 37.

Jefferson, Margo. Rev. of *Judah the Pious. Newsweek* (18 Feb. 1974): 94.

Kakutani, Michiko. "Stranger Than Fiction." *New York Times* (12 April 1986): 12.

Koenig, Rhoda. Rev. of *Primitive People. New York* (6 April 1992): 92.

Lask, Thomas. "The Sage and the Gentleman." New York Times (17 Feb. 1973): 29.

———. "Tale of a Noble Blackmailer." *New York Times* (15 Sept. 1977): C22.

Mano, D. Keith. "Rev. of *Judah the Pious. New York Times Book Review* (25 Feb. 1973): 2–3.

McCauley, Stephen. Rev. of *Women and Children First. New York Times Book Review* (27 March 1988): 6.

Plante, David. Rev. of *Primitive People. Yale Review* 80.4 (Oct. 1992): 103–04.

Spacks, Patricia Meyer. Rev. of *The Glorious Ones. Hudson Review* (Summer 1974): 293–94.

Toth, Susan Allen. "Psychic Sued for Telling Truth." *New York Times Book Review* (25 May 1986): 8–9.

NESSA RAPOPORT (1953–   )

Sharon Deykin Baris

BIOGRAPHY

Nessa Rapoport was born in Toronto, Canada, in 1953, where she spent the formative years of childhood, schooling, and university. Her family's commitment to Jewish tradition, culture, and the Hebrew language was a central influence in her life, as was the education she received in a Jewish day school. The Rapoport family history of learning and commentary—among the most prominent rabbinic lineages tracing back to the fifteenth century—had its impact on her, according to Rapoport; but equally important was her mother's love of Hebrew literature and her maternal grandmother's integration of Jewish observance with intellectual pursuits.

From Rapoport's earliest recollections, she was fascinated by language—both Hebrew and English—and wanted to be a writer. After she graduated from the University of Toronto in 1974, she moved to New York City, where she did graduate work in English literature and began to write fiction. She published several stories in Canada and America. "The Woman Who Lost Her Names," in particular, attracted favorable attention and became the title story of a collection of Jewish women's writing (1980). Soon after, another of her stories, "Katy," won the "*Chatelaine* Annual Fiction Competition" award (1982). Her first novel, *Preparing for Sabbath*, appeared in 1981, was reprinted by Bantam Books in 1982, and was reissued by Biblio Press in 1988, demonstrating a growing interest in her work. Rapoport, meanwhile, became a senior editor at Bantam Books, where until 1990 she edited the autobiographies of Jimmy Carter, Lee Iacocca, and Geraldine Ferarro, among other best-sellers.

She recently completed a book of prose poems and her second novel. With Ted Solotaroff, she edited an anthology of contemporary, Jewish American short stories, *Writing Our Way Home* (1992), which has drawn wide praise. At work on her third novel, she writes and lectures frequently on Jewish feminism and culture. She lives in New York City with her husband, who is an artist, and their children.

MAJOR THEMES

In Nessa Rapoport's best-known short story, "The Woman Who Lost Her Names," the central figure faces a challenge that is repeated throughout Rapoport's writings: A young woman measures the limits and potential of her agency in ever-widening arenas of self-definition. If names are the language by which a person establishes a relation to the world, then the struggle for a name of one's own invokes questions of what it means to be known as a child, daughter, woman, poet, Jew, wife, and mother. Such questions demonstrate a basic dynamic in Rapoport's works, as claims of spiritual insight and individual authority are enacted in several specific contexts, each extending or reshaping the implications of those claims. It is the tension between personal desires and larger frameworks—presented in religious, historical, social, or gendered dimensions—that characteristically shapes Rapoport's narrative structures and informs their content.

Such structuring can be, as in "The Woman Who Lost Her Names," a series of variations upon the theme of confrontations invoked by naming and being named, in a meditation upon the difficulties of hearing a Jewish woman's terms—in this case, her poetic voice. A young woman who is originally given the name Sarah might implicitly have been endowed with a sense of her own significance, since God chose that name for the originary biblical matriarch. But this modern Sarah discovers, instead, that her name and her life are drastically altered by the impinging effects of past and present events. Not only is she fondly known as Sarele at home, she is also called Josephine, Sally, and, later, Yosefah, as conditions require, thus indicating the instability of her identity in repeated familial, communal, and social redefinitions. But it is a presumption concerning gender, as she discovers upon her marriage, that most painfully threatens to transform her status as autonomous individual and poet into a position of mere supplementarity. For the literal meaning of Yosefah, which her husband now renames her, in Hebrew is "addition(al)"; this name seems especially ironic just when he declares that he derives his poetic sources from her very words, telling her he has "transplanted them into his work" (233). Worse still, another connection between her diminished authority or lost authorship and the rapacious overtones of her husband's behavior emerges in his subsequent insistence upon choosing a name for their daughter. His choice is Dina, a name that would echo and "respect" Dinsha, the recently deceased mother of this young wife (235–36). She instead recalls the biblical Dina as a violated figure: "You want a daughter named for a rape," she heatedly retorts (235). "Respect" for a genuine female Jewish heritage is at stake in their confrontation. Desiring to speak out in her own voice, she chooses Ayelet Hashachar (in Hebrew indicating "morning light") for their daughter, thus dramatically signaling her dawning sense of her important place in a historic Jewish continuum. It is childbirth itself that rejoins this woman's physical and metaphoric links to the world. At the story's end she awaits the naming ceremony in the synagogue, to discover whether or not her husband—and all the others, herself perhaps included—can acknowledge her powerful claims.

Rapoport's use of formal juxtapositions in another story is one of stark contrasts: between the silken materiality, yet odd unreality, of the lingerie department in a Fifth Avenue store and the historic, yet idealistic, intensity felt by a friend in Israel; between the penthouse loft of a lovers' tryst and the dark cells of some distant land's captivity. Poised in growing awareness of her partial relation to each of these contrasted realities, a woman considers the contexts of her future destiny in a story that is paradoxically titled "Great Men." Or Rapoport's oppositions can be less extreme: exploring forms of similarity, difference, and overlapping loyalties in another story, she tests even gender boundaries, as the narrator tells of her intense love for her friend Katy, of that love's entanglements during a developing relationship between Katy and the man with whom the narrator is involved, and the painful recognitions that follow ("Katy"). In another short fiction, the conflict of grand ideals and petty emotions among a gathering of friends with intertwined histories is staged in the semiprivacy of a bunk in summer camp or in the midst of a congregation during religious services. This story's perspectives are antithetically traced into two texts excerpted from *Ms.* magazine articles about the particulars of "girdles, stockings, hairpins" (or their absence) and from the weekly Torah portion's detailed concern with "a breastplate, an ephod . . . a turban, and a girdle; they shall make holy garments. . . . " This story's familiar but nevertheless troubling scenes thus become the spiritual and social testing-ground for a thoughtful young Jewish American woman in understanding her relation to others ("Community"). But always, in Rapoport, the process of self-discovery is both heightened and measured by the persistent evocations of contrasting or conflicting public and interior frameworks.

The principle of setting boundaries, especially spiritual and religious ones, is an essential project of Rapoport's essays and her fiction. Such delimitation is perhaps most emphatic in her first novel, *Preparing for Sabbath*. For while it is true (as critics on the novel's cover have noted) that this novel conveys a "radiance of yearning" and a sense of spiritual awakening in an "impassioned" narrative, this work is characterized, as Rosellen Brown in her Introduction observes, by a strong sense of the "balance of constraints." Contending yearnings and constraints are enacted in the plot's dramatic unfolding; they are also built into its structures: its seven-part chapter divisions, as well as less evident configurations present in patterns of repetition, contrasting styles, and intertextual echoes.

The seven numbers of the chapter headings (redoubled in Hebrew numbers for alternate chapters) in a novel whose title refers to the seventh day, or Sabbath, serve to indicate the novel's primary contrast. Although a young woman's life story is being worked out according to her childish wishes, adolescent encounters, later personal triumphs and disappointments typical of so many novels of development, the appearance of this overarching numerology implies the sense of a Creator or creation that looms above her story (literally overhead in each successive chapter heading) as an essential consideration. The number seven also appears in more fleeting forms to suggest other significations. The novel begins with the story of seven-year-old Judith, determined to order her life just as she will order new scattered belongings or her unruly hair. But some years later, when her boyfriend, Ori, points out the constellation Orion with its configuration of "seven stars for seven sisters," she sees more complicated suggestions in this "wonderful" sign—of relationships with her own sisters or bondings with friends as well as with Ori (76).

Still later, in a stroll around Jerusalem, Judith views the seven hills that surround the city—whether as natural fact or symbolic identification is not made clear—just before an erotic love scene near that setting. Elsewhere in Jerusalem she admires a family heirloom of a seven-branched candelabrum representing, she is told, the days of the week; but for her, it is the beauty of the artifact or its very inheritance that seems most striking, and so when Judith hears lectures about the seven mystic spheres of creation, she understands that through them "divine life and created life may meet and join" (271). This is a discovery whose meaning she herself repeats when she names the gates of Jerusalem, one by one, but leaves the last, or seventh, unnamed (like the novel's final unwritten and unnumbered imagined section) as a sign that "this gateless gate" leads toward a path "between earth and heaven" (280). These many sevens taken together become Rapoport's exposition of the plenitude of the world's meanings. The sheer variety, however, becomes her demonstration of the impossibility of their totally definitive explication.

Rapoport often uses patterns of doubling, as if to emphasize the presence of a particular feature or some points of resemblance. But such doubling, at the same time, serves to deny particularity or rather to show, in a postmodern way, only shades of endlessly possible differentiations. Thus, the alternation of Hebrew and English chapter numbering—One, then *Alef*—foregrounds the use of doubling; doing so, it both serves as a marker of separate spheres and yet challenges such theoretical separations. Just as Judith's earliest desire is for childish control, expressed in the novel's humorously stylized diction that is reminiscent of the schoolgirl language of *The Prime of Miss Jean Brody*, so, too, Rapoport's early chapters suggest a simplistic ordering. English and Hebrew, or material and spiritual, mundane and historical realms seem to be simply and charmingly held apart. Chapters One, Two, and Three recount the colorful events of birthday parties, friends' visits, and the romances of adolescent girls in summer camp. In *Alef*, the historical weight of the Rafael family tradition unfolds; in *Bet*, Bobba's intellectual and religious realm is explored; and in *Gimel*, Judith meets her great-aunt Chenya in Jerusalem and visits the Wall. But later as Judith's deeper emotions break out in lyrical expressions, these chapter divisions more noticeably are disrupted as well.

These breaks appear at first in tentative ways, as Judith criticizes her mother's Judaism in Chapter Gimel and notes other kinds of Jewish or other religious practices. More significantly, the distinct realms of these chapters collapse at the book's numerical center, *Dalet*, which begins expectantly with the word ''America.'' Judith and Ori traverse the nation's landscape, as if in search of transcendental meanings. In fact, she experiences her hitch-hiking journey as an alternation of Whitmanesque celebrations and alienating confrontations with people and geography. In the next chapter, her father takes his family on sabbatical leave (a seven figure now emptied of spiritual significance) to England, where Judith meets non-Jewish James. Then the family travels to Israel, and Judith revisits Chenya. There, in Israel—amid unstable numerical orders and faltering presumptions about religion and identity—Judith reconsiders her non-Jewish boyfriend and weighs many less clear differentiations, leading even to the ''thin line between life and unlife'' (207).

As she relates the world's options to her developing perspectives, Judith hears from Chenya that there are ''choices, there are always choices'' (211). The doublings suggested throughout this novel test such tenuous lines and choices—in contrasting friendships, differing religious practices, even recurrent musical references. Most tellingly, a close resemblance between Ori and his sister Jessie underscores the blurring of gender preferences in Judith's relationships with them, leading her to appreciate her double allegiance to friend and to lover as a difficult but necessary enactment of plural bondings. So, too, the repetition of Rafael family features—on Chenya's face, for example—causes Judith to weigh both her historic links and her particular characteristics as a Rafael herself. She eventually contradicts even beloved Chenya to ponder, ''Why is it that Rafaels are unable to consider that you could have both [rituals and feelings of God's presence]?'' (204)

Rapoport's novel thus becomes a modern spiritual *Bildungsroman* of a Jewish girl who not only is born Jewish, but who chooses carefully and in ever more challenging contexts to define her spiritual sources and practices. After chapter distinctions of the novel are undone, and when Judith has reconsidered with Chenya their shared inheritance and their differing personal observances, Judith, in her wider recognition of many possibilities, surpasses even Chenya's wisdom along the way. Having done so, Judith remains a while longer in Israel to celebrate her symbolic personal and historic independence day. She then can return to England, where she rejects James but continues to make choices that, in England as in Israel, will express her own Jewish dreams, realities, traditions. Her decisions, indeed, comprise her unfolding Jewish history.

In some respects, Rapaport's rendition of Judith's story participates in the literary traditions of romantic feminine novels. More specifically, *Preparing for Sabbath* resembles *Jane Eyre* in its repeated physical and romantic successes, leading, like Jane's ''gradations of glory,'' to Judith's remarkable spiritual ascents. Both heroines begin as outsiders in the schoolroom and then become thin and gawky adolescents; like Jane, who grows in physical and social stature, so Judith eventually gets to note her own beauty in her mirror and in others' approving glances. Judith's prophetic claim into the darkness of her camp bunk that "[s]he would win; she knew that" (77) is repeatedly fulfilled, in intense friendship with Jesse, Rachel, Sharon, and in passionate relation to Ori, Gabriel, and James. If she behaves badly toward friends and family, yet she—like Jane—may seem to reach a pinnacle of personal and saintly achievement. For Judith is finally told (in Jerusalem, by her friend, role-model, and teacher) in ultimate tribute: "You are a *tsadeket*" (279). While his term "*tsadeket*" traditionally conveys the sense of a righteous woman, the presence of many doublings within *Preparing for Sabbath* undoes such a single or single-minded evaluation. The novel's persistent comparisons and distinctions undercut any totalizations of Judith, even as the man who says this has meanwhile been critiqued—in two years' contrasting Seder scenes—so that his model and her triumphs become further matter for thoughtful question.

Rapoport's narrative, like Judith's life story, is a criss-crossing of delineations until it becomes, as Judith puts it near the end, a "grid" of God's law and the "fire of my passion" (280). The texture of Rapoport's prose is expressive of many such alternative yet interwoven possibilities. A seven-year-old's charmingly crisp style of thought at home and school is transformed into the sensual language of a young woman's love scenes years later in Jerusalem; her narcissistic adolescent musings on her undeveloped body while gazing in a mirror or daydreaming on a dock at Bobba's become more integrated poetic, natural, and bodily descriptions:

Red, orange and yellow spheres, hills of fruit offerings patterned the earth. People were going up with empty arms and returning laden . . . Judith saw the girls cleaning, partnering their mop sticks in a funny domestic dance . . . they stripped off their work shirts to vests and finished the mopping with bare arms and legs . . . (276)

The device of such interweavings—of simple and lyric discourse, or of perspectives, or of differing definitions—fascinates Rapoport. She works toward that effect, not as a case of given alternatives, but as an ongoing process or action. We can note such a sense of continuing enactment in the gerund verb form of her title *Preparing for Sabbath*, of her story "Selling Out," or of her coauthored television screen play "Saying Kaddish"; such process is implicit in other titles that are suggestive of ceaseless dynamics—"Generation," "Community," and her forthcoming novel, *The Perfection of the World*.

Rapoport's evocation of biblical echoes throughout her works is thus appropriate to a writer so engaged by unfolding spiritual histories and a heightened sense of intertextuality. Her use of traditional sources does not consist of particular and knowing references to discrete lines or scenes. Declaring in an essay on "Text, Language, and the Hope of Redemption" that her aim is that of "drawing on the past without enshrining it in nostalgia or proscription" (43), she focuses, rather, upon textual suggestions that both comment on and subvert a reader's expectations. Her latest novel, *The Perfection of the World*, is written in five parts that parallel the five megillot: Esther, Ecclesiastes, Lamentations,

Ruth, and Song of Songs. Neither a translation nor a retelling, Rapoport's fictional rendition inverts, alters, or otherwise restates the obvious features of these megillot. At the end of its third section, *How the City*, for example, it is the male Ishai who declares to the Ruth figure, "Where you go, I will go"; and in the following *Isa* section, that phrase is restated by Gali, the Naomi figure, who more colloquially puts it to the Ruth-like Isa: "If you don't mind . . . perhaps you'll follow me. Go where I go and do as I do." Later, when Gali sits at the kitchen table, it is she who, in an inversion of gender expectations, is likened to an "ancient judge at the city gate" as a colorful reminder, not of the biblical elders' role, but of Naomi's own spiritual power and stature. In these and other cases, then, the author is working both to acknowledge the underlying impetus of the Bible's stories or traditional songs of love and redemption and to recast them within new conditions.

Rapoport began writing as a poet, winning early recognition in university awards; she has recently written a volume of prose poems, *A Women's Book of Grieving* (forthcoming). Many of its prose poems explicate an individual's pain or grieving; others are more abstract meditations. They are not, she says, specifically Jewish in content, but they draw "strongly on liturgical meter." Taken together, they convey a characteristic sense of the personal and spiritual testings that for Rapoport are sustaining.

SURVEY OF CRITICISM

Criticism of Rapoport's writing often partakes of the dynamic of comparisons and contrasts evident in her own works. Irene Pompea asserts, "What Mary Gordon in her first novel does for the Catholic girl growing up, Nessa Rapoport does in a brilliant novel about Judith Rafael, growing up in a Jewish Family" (50); William Helmreich places it in the genre of "books about growing up Jewish [that] have long occupied a prominent place in Jewish literature," and adds her name to a list that includes Abraham Cahan and Philip Roth (20). Alison Carb goes so far as to claim that Rapoport not only resembles Cynthia Ozick, but her "extremely sensual style" is also "somewhat reminiscent of Marcel Proust" (20).

More probable similarities are noted in Miriyam Glazer's overview of Jewish women's literature that groups Rapoport with Tova Reich and Anne Roiphe to describe a "new spirituality" as they "delve into religious Judaism to understand women's experiences" (7). Ted Solotaroff foresees that the "interesting Jewish bargain or edge in American fiction will be more and more in the keeping of writers like Cynthia Ozick, the late Arthur A. Cohen, and Tova Reich, or younger ones like Nessa Rapoport, Daphne Merkin and Allegra Goodman, who are anchored in the present-day observant Jewish community . . . " (33). Sylvia Barack Fishman's review essay of American Jewish fiction since 1960 discusses a trend toward inwardness and, in this light, links Rapoport, Daphne Merkin, and Allegra Goodman, as well as Tova Reich, Anne Roiphe, and others. An essay by Sara R. Horowitz provides the fullest literary comment to date on

Rapoport's *Preparing for Sabbath*; it does so in the context of surveying the dilemma facing four women writers "who want both spiritual meaning and political empowerment." Horowitz says of Roiphe, Goodman, Vanessa Ochs, and Rapoport, that while "they promise no easy answers," these writers do envision "transformative possibilities for women, for men, for Judaism."

Aside from these comparatist references, criticism has focused primarily on *Preparing for Sabbath*, noting what Howard Schwartz calls the "honest ring" of Jewish spiritual experience and "some of the most authentic perceptions of childhood and adolescence I have encountered" (4B). Lawrence Epstein admires her "finely-detailed account of a young woman's journey into maturity." Another review notes her description of "the joy ... in ... ceremonies and traditions," although that anonymous reviewer feels she "occasionally goes overboard with historical detail" (*Flare*, July 1981). This sense of overinvestment in detail provides the basis for one unsympathetic review by Pearl Bell, which recognizes Rapoport's "copiously informative chronicle" but faults her for being too "doggedly faithful" and for lacking any "principle at work" (65–66). But other critics have pointed to principles shaping the details and more: Alison Carb sees a pattern of contrasts in the "many voices" of Judith, "at once dissonant and harmonious," that make this novel a form of prayer (20); and Susan Willens notes how Rapoport "expands the customary story of a Jewish girlhood" so as to explore diverse aspects and geographic spaces in a "search for faith [that] shapes a powerful novel" (32).

Rapoport has been consistently lauded for her writing's "high seriousness" (Willens 32), "Jewish spirituality" (Glazer 7), and its portrayal of the "conflicting demands of youthful passion and spirituality" (Fishman 39). William Helmreich calls her novel "an elegant love story that is not focused on a single individual but, instead, is an expression of the writer's way of looking at life" (20).

The anthology *Writing Our Way Home: Contemporary Stories by American Jewish Writers*, edited by Rapoport and Ted Solotaroff, has drawn considerable praise as "an important event" that Sanford Pinsker says will "help to shape the discussion of Jewish American fiction for the next decades." Evelyn Toynton notes its "quite surprising emotional liveliness" (52), and Hillel Halkin sees its stories of "lives of complete assimilation" as well as an equal number "completely at home in the world of modern Orthodoxy" as proof of American Jewry's ability to maintain its "unique literary voice" (45).

BIBLIOGRAPHY

Works by Nessa Rapoport

Stories

"Community," *Shefa Quarterly* 1 (Autumn 1977): 17–27.
"Selling Out," *Response* XII (Summer 1979): 19–30.

"Katy," *Chatelaine* Oct. 1982: 118, 180–88.
"Generation," *Shefa Quarterly* Sept. 1978. Rpt. in *Gates of the New City: A Treasury of Modern Jewish Tales*. Ed. Howard Schwartz, New York: Avon, 1983. 126.
"Great Men," *Forward* 10 May 1991: 19–20.
"The Woman Who Lost Her Names," *Lilith* 6 (1979): 31–33. Rpt. in *The Woman Who Lost Her Names: Selected Writings of American-Jewish Women*. Ed. Julia Wolf Mazow, New York: Harper & Row, 1980. 229–36. Rpt. in *Writing Our Way Home: Contemporary Stories by American Jewish Writers*. Ed. Ted Solotaroff and Nessa Rapoport. New York: Schocken Books, 1992. 229–36.

Novels

Preparing for Sabbath. 1981; Rpt. Sunnyside, NY: Biblio Press, 1988.
The Perfection of the World. Forthcoming. Part IV appears as *Isa* in *Reading Ruth: Women's Encounters with the Hebrew Bible*. Ed. Judith Kates and Gail Reimer. New York: Ballantine Books, forthcoming.

Prose Poems

A Woman's Book of Grieving. New York: William Morrow & Co., forthcoming.

Essays

"Summoned to the Feast." Introd. *Writing Our Way Home: Contemporary Stories by American Jewish Writers*. Ed. Ted Solotaroff and Nessa Rapoport. New York: Schocken Books, 1992. xxvii–xxx.
"A Dream of Community." *Hadassah Magazine* Jan. 1993: 16–19.
"Text, Language, and the Hope of Redemption." *The Writer in the Jewish Community*. Rutherford, NJ: Fairleigh Dickinson University Press, 1993. 41–44.

Works about Nessa Rapoport

Bell, Pearl K. "New Jewish Voices." *Commentary* June 1981: 62–66.
Brown, Rosellen. "Introduction" to *Preparing for Sabbath*. Sunnyside, NY, Biblio Press, 1988.
Carb, Alison B. "Poignant Portrait." Rev. of *Preparing for Sabbath. Jewish Frontier*. Oct. 1981: 19–20.
Epstein, Lawrence J. Rev. of *Preparing for Sabbath*. "Ten Best Jewish Books of 5741." *Seven Arts*. 1981.
Fishman, Sylvia Barack. "American Jewish Fiction Turns Inward, 1960–1990." *American Jewish Year Book*. Eds. David Singer and Ruth Seldin. Philadelphia: Jewish Publication Society, 1991: 35–69.
Glazer, Miriyam. "A Red Ribbon, A Flame: The New Jewish-American Women's Literature." *Direction*. Fall 1990: 4–7.
Halkin, Hillel. "Where There's Life There's Fiction." Rev. of *Writing Our Way Home. The Jerusalem Report*. 19 Nov. 1992: 45.
Helmreich, William. "Portrait of a Young Jewish Woman and 1960s Alternative Judaism." Rev. of *Preparing for Sabbath. Congress Monthly*. Nov. 1981: 20.
Horowitz, Sara R. "Portnoy's Sister–Whose Complaining?: The Figuring of Orthodox

Judaism in Contemporary Jewish-American Women's Writing.'' *The Jewish Book Annual* Vol. 51 Ed. Jacob Kabakoff. 1994: 26–41.

Pinsker, Sanford. Rev. of *Writing Our Way Home. Jewish Exponent.* 29 Jan. 1993.

Pompea, Irene N. Rev. of *Preparing for Sabbath. Best Sellers* Spring 1981: 50.

Rothchild, Sylvia. Rev. of *Preparing for Sabbath: The Jewish Advocate* 21 May 1981.

Schwartz, Howard. ''An Odyssey in Israel.'' Rev. of *Preparing for Sabbath. St. Louis Post-Dispatch.* 7 June 1981: 4B.

Solotaroff, Ted. ''American-Jewish Writers: On Edge Once More'' *New York Times Book Review* 18 Dec. 1988: 1, 31–33.

Toynton, Evelyn. ''American Stories,'' *Commentary.* March 1993: 49–53.

Willens, Susan P. Rev. of *Preparing for Sabbath. Belles Lettres,* 1989, p. 32.

TOVA REICH (1942–   )

Blossom Steinberg Kirschenbaum

BIOGRAPHY

Tova Rachel Reich was born December 24, 1942, in Liberty, New York, to Moshe and Miriam Weiss, each descended from a long line of rabbis. Her father spent his early years in the town of Oscwiecim, Poland (later known as Auschwitz); he arrived in the United States just before World War II. An Orthodox rabbi, he now lives in Israel. Tova Reich's three brothers are also rabbis. English, Hebrew, and Yiddish were spoken at home, and "the house was filled with books, newspapers, and magazines in all three of those languages" (letter to the author, 27 October 1992). Until twelfth grade Reich studied at yeshivot; she adds, "I continue to study—and to use for my writing—such texts as the Torah, Prophets, Megillot, Mishna, Talmud, Cabalistic writing, Hassidic literature, Midrashic, Agaddic, rabbinic works, Jewish books old and new." By age eleven she had already decided that she was a writer.

Reich attended Brooklyn College of City University of New York (B.A., 1964) and New York University (M.A., 1965). On June 10, 1965, she married Walter Reich, psychiatrist and Senior Scholar at the Woodrow Wilson Center and the author of books and articles on Soviet psychiatry, Middle East issues, and other topics. Their children are Daniel Salo, David Emil, and Rebecca Zohar.

Tova Reich has taught in the English departments of Southern Connecticut State College in New Haven (1972–73), American University, Washington, D.C. (1974–77), and as Visiting Writer in the Master of Fine Arts Program at the University of Maryland (1991–92, 1994). An NEA Creative Writing Fellowship supported her writing during 1984–85. Her second novel, *Master of the Return*, received the Edward Lewis Wallant Award. She has traveled extensively throughout Europe and has been to Israel many times for visits of varying duration. Her home is in Chevy Chase, Maryland.

MAJOR THEMES

Balancing five millenia of Hebraism against mere centuries of American history, Tova Reich presents sardonic views of what Gertrude Stein called "the making of Americans." In her stories, Americans are made through child-rearing practices at home and at school or acculturation of new immigrants, or reproductive politics, or enforced compliance with American law, or confirmation of American identity through adventures abroad. Reich shows parents with the highest motives and the wackiest foibles blundering to control their young, who must survive and mature through their own painful experiences. Hazards abound, violence hovers, extinction threatens, and yet despite human vice and inanity, life goes on. The narrative voice variously sports with, challenges, resists, withdraws from, or aligns itself with a more ancient and comprehensive history that provides a critical context for the American characters.

A major theme in her work is the Jewish American woman's need to emancipate herself from both controlling father and seductive lover, to achieve her own womanly identity. Thus, in *Mara* (1978) Rabbi Lieb tries to prevent his spirited, nubile daughter's marriage to a wily eighteen-year-old Middle Easterner, but he fails, despite (and because of) all his schemes, bribes, threats, and lies. Instead, Mara cleaves to devious, duplicitous Sudah, who tells her, "You must needs to get free from your father, . . . for the good of growing up" (15). Rabbi Lieb insists that everything his daughter has belongs to him because he paid for it; so, though he provides, he does not give; from that standpoint, Mara has little to lose. And Sudah is charming; Mara says, "When he was put away for hashish, even the judge got to like him" (28). Both father and husband are exploiters. Rabbi Lieb, a capitalist, never visits his properties but, in effect, loots them; Mara knows her father is "a wise guy and a bandit" (204). Sudah is only more uninhibited, freer from cant, in socialistically treating the world's goods as booty. But Sudah gives what her father cannot: amusement, pleasure, and joy. After the attendant at the ritual bath assures her, "You will have a successful marriage if you keep the laws of family purity," Sudah, posing as the cleaning woman in the *mikvah*, locks himself in with her: "Let's fuck" (53). Passion and risk win out. With many options but little guidance, Mara eludes parental control at home as she did in the less savory quarters of Jerusalem and Tel Aviv. Episodes are punctuated by her sitting naked in front of her typewriter clattering out installments of *How I Lost My Virginity*; thus, she claims autonomy both as woman and as author. Neither father nor husband remains faithful. The rabbi, who protests dedication and cites Torah, is a thief; his travel to Switzerland has coincided with the disappearance of nearly a million dollars. Sudah departs to follow his celibate Buddhistic soul path. Mara sees the resemblance between these quite different rogues. Separate from both, inhabiting an island cave—tattered, bruised, and insolvent—she is finally on her own, apart from community, an American individualist, a woman free of entangling roles.

Her integrity consists in having rejected domination, experienced love, and accepted its consequences. She, too, has a soul path to follow.

In her second novel, *Master of the Return* (1988), Reich shows women as wives and devout mothers caring for children and each other independently of men, while fathers are busy with pilgrimages, computers, numerology, fighting, and other affairs. In the book's closing image, crippled Ivriya watches as her three-year-old son Akiva eats bread and honey and drinks milk; she is doing her own and her people's work. Her husband, whose journal details his conversion from hippie to Bratslaver Hasid and his craving for holiness, has found no better way to support her than to go off on abortive pilgrimages to Uman. Like other families in Reich's fiction, Akiva's family appears dysfunctional. Yet the children find love anyway, miraculously escape disaster, endure some measure of suffering, and usually survive misguided parental neglect or zeal.

Destructive zeal and the perversion in a mother's trying to live through her child are shown with gleeful horror in "Gifted and Talented." The narrator, a podiatrist's wife determined to guarantee her only child's future, has his intelligence tested while he is still in diapers. The boy is programmed through special schools and given every kind of "enrichment." The process systematically ruins his childhood. This fanatically controlling mother—obtuse, mechanical, savage, and insane—is herself out of control as she propels him in a gruelling and fatal race. At the story's end, the child is poised for a fall from which his mother will not be able to save him. If *Mara* shows the ineffectuality of parental remoteness, bombast, bribery, threat, and the lack of true guidance, this story shows a middle-class American child deprived and threatened precisely because he is compliant, advantaged, and supervised.

An unlovely, ailing, sloppy, and yet nurturing mother appears in "The Death of Leah Levavi." The narrator tells of a woman twenty years her senior, fat and jolly, frankly mean, terribly depressed, who was her roommate at Sunnyside, a "nut house," and with whom she kept in touch for two decades. "Terminally depressed people are very hard to live with. I should know; I've been living with myself for forty years now," says the narrator (52). She learned how from Leah; as she says, "Leah Levavi's attitude toward me was always protectively maternal" (52). Damaged early, Leah lived out "the eccentric and self-destructive protest of a conventional woman." At the same time, even sharp-tongued and cancer-ridden, she inspired love from her husband, son, and the friend who finds her "in a strange and sorrowful way, heroic" (55).

Varieties of spiritual journey and redemption are other Reich themes. In *Mara*, while Rabbi Lieb professes piety, he flounders hypocritically between Hebraic righteousness and American greed. His wife gorges on food and hungers for more, insatiable because she cannot find spiritual sustenance or love. Amoral Sudah, in becoming a celibate Buddhist, abandons his wife, his people, and traditional faith but ironically realizes Rabbi Lieb's belief that the ideal life is devoted to religious study.

The meaning of spirituality is also questioned in *Master of the Return*, where the Hasidic fathers are preoccupied with mystical redemption, often to the exclusion of earning a livelihood. The protagonist of the novel, Shmuel Himmelhoch (his name means "Heaven-high"), attempts to reach Uman in order to be relieved of nocturnal emissions. He yearns to redeem mistakes and failures by submitting to transcendent powers and following sanctified rules. Though army bulldozers level the sect's headquarters, and though his mother-in-law comments acerbly, "Name one decent, responsible thing he ever did in his entire rotten career" (46), the novel does not discredit his aspirations.

Even crazy Leah in "The Death of Leah Levavi" earns love and respect as she follows her soul path. After reciting the prayers, she dies on Yom Kippur, between afternoon and *Neilah* services, repentant and apparently forgiven.

The most bizarre spiritual journeys, however, occur in the eery "Mengele in Jerusalem." The narrator, a Holocaust survivor who has prospered in America, feels emotionally dead. He learns of a "spiritual spa" at the table of Reb Mendele in Jerusalem. There, he witnesses the ritual drinking of the prune juice to the greater glory of the bowels, rendered with homely exegetical detail in a characteristic Reichian parody of Hasidic ritual that concludes "Ya ba ba, ya ba ba, ya ba bum" (67). Among the converts in an alley, the narrator recognizes Reb Mengele, the sadistic concentration camp doctor. The reader, following the story as it is told to "smug" and unsurprised Krystina, the narrator's consort, is left to ponder this encounter between anti-Semitic Jew and Jew-obsessed persecutor turned Hasid. The deracinated, unhappy narrator of this story, trumped by his torturer, refuses the redemption he cannot buy. As for the unpunished Mengele figure, his conversion remains suspect since there is no evidence that he has confessed or tries to make reparation, and it is not clear for what purpose he has returned.

Reich's fiction also explores the meaning of Israel for American Jews. In *Mara*, Israel functions as a conveniently remote campus to which parents, without having to deal directly with the active sexuality of their daughter, can consign her for further coursework and finding a Jewish spouse. As Reich shows, there are no guarantees, not even when Mara's conventional sister is sent as ambassador to save Mara from herself. Israel is also where American Jews are surprised and even outmaneuvered by other Jews whose Old World is not Europe.

In *Master of the Return*, Israel is an ancient landscape with thousands rather than hundreds of years of acknowledged habitation, the terrain where a Jew's mythos, history, ideals, and daily life may fuse, however perilously and ludicrously. For refugees, Israel provides haven and alternative. Thus in *Master of the Return*, Ivriya, who once performed naked like Lady Godiva, now watches over her son: "For the sake of this milk and this honey, you must speak no ill of the land, and of its inhabitants say no unkind word" (240). In "Mengele in Jerusalem," Israel is the terrain where former enemies meet again. In "Moscow Night in New York," the terrain is the homeland generally not preferred or reluctantly declined. In "The Hostage," it is disputed territory because of which every Jew, whether Zionist or not, has enemies.

Israel, like the United States, is a nation of immigrants and hence a multiethnic society, a laboratory for working out national and ethnic bigotries. Both nations are involved in the story "Solidarity," where Rabbi Ozer, an American who has visited Israel and whose own wife is Middle Eastern, proves too ready to trust another Middle Eastern Jew. Overcompensating for possible bias, Ozer misses clues and fails to heed advice, with drastic consequences within his own congregation. Even in its diversity, Israel complicates Diaspora, however—as illustrated in "Moscow Night in New York," where Kagan, twice hospitalized as crazy in Russia, now feted "like some prize Russian bear" (71) in the United States, would rather be in Israel—but his wife is Gentile.

"Gertrude Stein" (1982), though not about the eponymous author of *The Making of Americans* and *The Geographical History of America*, shares her preoccupation with the American character as shaped by American history and institutions—that is, with the making of Americans. Reich's story probes hostility between desperate whites and vengeful blacks, simultaneously needing and disdaining each other, and simultaneously breeding. Blacks are shown as waxing powerful in number and dangerous in consciousness of sustained wrongs. Events of "some years ago" unfold in Washington, where the title character, as only child and motherless daughter, works as a typist for the Office of Education. She passes out drunk at a party given by the embassy of "a now defunct African country" (46). A strange black man takes car keys from her purse, carries her over the threshold, drives her home, rapes and robs her, and also steals the signpost bearing her father's name. This harsh travesty of a wedding is followed by mockery of bureaucratic integrationist policies: "A black in every family, that's our motto" (49). When Gertrude's menstrual period is late, she seeks an abortion. But when she reveals that the "perpetrator was of Negro persuasion" (52), she is thrown out by Footstool, the abortionist's assistant, who explains that they kill white, not black, babies. Gertrude then becomes her father's patient. He performs a clinically detailed procedure but finds no signs of pregnancy. "Oh Mama, Mama," Gertrude cries, "when will it be over?" To which he replies, "You can get up. The baby is out. It's all over" (53).

In this story, Reich replays Stein's famous dictum as "a rape is a rape is a rape." Gertrude has to infer the rape and much else, overhearing without seeing what Footstool does behind her and unable to take charge of but forced to suffer invasion within her own womb. Verbal and imagistic techniques discomfort a reader with regard to "race" in America, domination and revenge, and the politics of reproductive control. The story also parodies Christian myth. The embassy invitation that "seemed to drop from nowhere" (46), when it came from a black hand in a winged sleeve, is like a bad-joke Annunciation. Gertrude's tormented cry to her mother and her father's use of a dry sponge, harshly parody the Passion of Jesus complete with the giving up, in a sense, of the ghost.

The "making of Americans" as updating of the immigrant experience with its attendant dislocations occurs in "Moscow Night in New York" (1979), where a dinner party brings together an "émigré elite," eight persons "among whom there must already be ten books in various stages, . . . three about the Gulag alone" (67). The "Moscow night" of *borscht* [Russian beet-soup], high culture, and soul-baring that Irina, the hostess, has arranged is soon undercut when the next course is hot dogs and hamburgers. One guest's new patriotism approaches nativist exclusionism; he maintains that "it would be catastrophic for 'our country' " to let in Mexicans and Vietnamese. Doubly a minority, as Jews and as Russians, the small circle individuates rather than coheres; nostalgia counts for less than opportunity. The exiled actress who works at Bloomingdale's can go "where everybody ends up—Radio Liberty" (68). Afterwards, Irina's husband finds her weeping at the kitchen sink because New York cannot provide the "true Russian night" she had wanted. Her guests, not having shared her hopes, need not share disappointments; for Marius, freely drinking vodka, the night had been "Chekhovian, rather than Gogolian" (71), and Pavel, unhappily recognizing a "true Russian night," mourns, "what had once been theirs only in art." What the groups has in common is that things fall apart.

Cohesion of Jews in the Diaspora is the problem in "Solidarity" (1984). An Orthodox American congregation, guided by Rabbi Ozer, rallies to a Middle Eastern Jews named Saadia Rachamim, who has been accused of a crime but protests his innocence. Several conflicts converge: the Orthodox defensiveness against Conservative and Reform factions as well as against Gentiles; national and ethnic bigotry among Jews and overcompensation for it; presence of criminal elements among a people enjoined to be a beacon unto others; the urge to give the benefit of the doubt without denying the sort of evidence on which stereotypes are based—that is, the impulse to trust while fearing betrayal. Rabbi Ozer's misplaced trust results from high-minded failure to imagine evil and from insufficient heed to his wife's cautions. He confounds "solidarity" with "uniformity," as though oneness of a people implied identical individual purpose, interest, and feeling. When his myopic idealism has brought trauma to an already bereaved member of his congregation, the rabbi is forced to violate the Sabbath and call for help from local police.

"The Hostage" (1980) represents a further exploration of the theme of the naive American abroad introduced in *Mara*. The protagonist, accountant Herbie Mitnick, is any Jew, a modest struggling *mensch* at risk just by being alive. At the same time, he is an ordinary good-hearted American, taken hostage when he gets in the way of a terrorist raid. Asked is he a "Zionist agent and provocateur," "No," Herbie replies, "I'm a Jew." So innocent and amiable that his captors think him a superspy, he is first mauled and indoctrinated and later released as irrelevant to their plans. His wife says, when he telephones, "Oh, go on, Herbie. You're a hostage like I'm a hostage" (83) and instructs him to pick up a pizza on the way home. In effect, the story points out, we are all hostages.

A common thread in all the fiction is that things are not what they seem. Nazi-like behavior occurs in Reich's stories where least expected, for instance, in a mother's ruthless determination to make a child "succeed," in the brutal tactics of the rescue squad that tackles Leah Levavi, in the barbarities of arranging an abortion. In "Gertrude Stein," the motherless daughter at the mercy of a masked and clinically detached white doctor is a frightening image, not rendered more reassuring because the doctor is her father. Love blooms unexpectedly, too, as between a crippled woman and a desperate Hasid, or between two women in a madhouse, or between two women close as sisters who "even shared the same pair of eyeglasses; their vision was distorted in exactly the same way" (*Master* 53). Identity is putative and metamorphic. In *Master of the Return*, Sora Katz of Mea Shearim was formerly Pam Buck of Macon, Georgia, and Rebbetzin Bruriah Lurie of Uman House was Barbara Horowitz of Brooklyn. Life teems with possibilities for chicanery and also for new growth.

SURVEY OF CRITICISM

Mara is called "a bitter, black comedy," by A. C. Kempf, noting that the name "Mara" in Hebrew means "bitter." Kempf states that the novel "explores the emptiness of ritual divorced from ethics." Jerome Charyn terms *Mara* "startling, playful and irreverent," adding, "It has none of the pieties one would expect in a book cluttered with wedding canopies, crocheted skullcaps, ritual baths, and the Hebrew bill of divorcement called the *get*. . . . 'Mara' is a fine, poignant first novel, but if Tova Reich had given us more of Leon and less of Sudah and his friends, 'Mara' would have been an extraordinary book." J. N. Baker admired "a series of splendidly crafted set pieces," but felt that the novel did not quite jell, though "Reich's voice is nonetheless a striking one: she has a gift for outrageous, hard-edged comedy that Evelyn Waugh might have appreciated."

Molly Abramowitz highly recommends *Master of the Return*: "Described with affection and great insight, the riotous adventures of these sincere but sometimes misguided penitents easily mix the supernatural with human events. Reich pinpoints absurdity and self-righteousness beautifully. . . . An arresting contemporary treatment of Jewish spirituality and renewal." Benjamin DeMott described the novel as "an ambush—a wildly funny story that becomes mysteriously touching and ponderable before the end." Noting the farcical situations, he adds, "The steadying presence of history in the story also counts for something. . . . And so, too, does the recurrence of feelings that, although extreme in their expression, are normative at their core." He praises Reich's "astringent" manner and "cool, unillusioned eye," concluding, "Tova Reich is a marvelously enigmatic original, and there are effects in her book that are beyond casual summoning, secrets reason can't reach"(94).

Hugh Nissenson praises the way the author "dramatizes her complex theme: that the immemorial Jewish quest for absolute purity is crazy." As he says,

"Almost everyone in 'Master of the Return' is a fanatic of one kind or another. Jews, Arabs, Moslems, Christians, even agnostics and atheists, are possessed by their respective beliefs, which emanate from the land itself. . . . Israel is a state of mind . . . . The past is the present among the wadis, on the sacred mountains, and in the holy city of Jerusalem. It drives everyone nuts." He sees life triumphant over demands of the absolute: "In the end, Tova Reich's comic vision gives the last word to life, not death; her novel becomes a rapturous celebration of the maternal principle."

Elie Wiesel sees Rabbi Nachman in *Master of the Return* as "the celebration of the Hasidic imagination" (8), focusing on his gift for storytelling, anguish, and way of fighting anguish, his oscillating between despair and ecstasy. Like Sanford Pinsker, Wiesel notes that an understanding of this great-grandson of the Baal Shem-Tov is prerequisite to savoring Reich's novel: "She has found here a subject worthy of her talent. The language is rich and poetic, and often penetrated with humor. . . . The scatter-brained, bizarre characters, disgusted by earthly life, search for a way to make it pure." Wiesel continues, "the most incredible events unfold completely naturally," and "we are taken by the rhythm of the language and by the imagination of the storyteller." He concludes, "Tova Reich has given us a gift smiling: How can we not thank her for it?" (8). Pinsker adds that the Bratslav Rabbi also made a difficult pilgrimage, to Israel, and that the novel "refers to specific Nac
hman tales" and 'reduplicates their essential rhythms" (12). He lauds Reich for "pouring old obsessions into new technological bottles," (13) thereby not only calling attention to their vitality, but also reinvigorating Jewish American fiction. Ellen Serlen Uffen, making a similar point, notes the figure of "Ivriya's mother, Dr. Frieda Mendelssohn, a huge comic character who storms in and out of the book and her daughter's marriage, resenting the Chassidic life" (162–63)—a comment that links Reich's perspectives on religion with those on family relations, in fiction that is "actually *about* Jewishness and Judaism" (162).

BIBLIOGRAPHY

Works by Tova Reich

Novels

Mara, New York: Farrar, Straus, Giroux, 1978.
Master of the Return. San Diego, New York, London: Harcourt Brace Jovanovich, 1988.
Birth Wish, Unpublished.
The Beginning of the Redemption (tentative title of work in progress).

Uncollected Stories

"Moscow Night in New York," *Commentary*. December 1979: 67–71.
"The Hostage." *Harper's*. April 1980: 81-84.
"Gertrude Stein." *Harper's*. August 1982: 46–53.

"Solidarity." *Atlantic Monthly.* January 1984: 70–80.
"The Death of Leah Levavi." *Moment.* December 1984: 52–55.
"Gifted and Talented." *Commentary.* July 1985: 56–61.
"Bring Us to Uman." *Moment.* July/August 1985: 35–46.
"Mengele in Jerusalem." *Harper's.* June 1986: 64–68.

Selected Nonfiction

"Boat People Then and Now." *ADL Bulletin.* 36 (1979): 6–7.
"My Mother, My Muse." "Hers" (column), *New York Times Magazine.* 6 November 1988: 30.
Letter to the author, 27 October 1992.

Works about Tova Reich

Abramowitz, Molly. Rev. of *Master of the Return. Library Journal.* 15 April 1988: 96.
Baker, J. N. Rev. of *Mara. Newsweek.* 21 August 1978: 71.
Bell, P. K. Rev. of *Mara. Commentary.* September 1978: 70.
Berman, Paul. Rev. of *Mara. Harper's.* August 1978: 89.
Charyn, Jerome. Rev. of *Mara. New York Times Book Review.* 11 June 1978: 12.
DeMott, Benjamin. Rev. of *Master of the Return. Atlantic.* May 1988: 92–94.
Jonas, Gerald. Rev. of *Master of the Return. Present Tense.* Nov./Dec. 1988: 59.
Kempf, A. C. Rev. of *Mara. Library Journal.* July 1978: 1437.
Lyons, Bonnie. Rev. of *Mara. Congress Monthly.* January 1979: 18–19.
Nissenson, Hugh. Rev. of *Master of the Return. New York Times Book Review.* 29 May 1988: 10.
Pinsker, Sanford. "New Voices and the Contemporary Jewish-American Novel." *Jewish Book Annual.* Edited by Jacob Kabakoff, New York: Jewish Book Council, 1991. 6-20.
Steinberg, Sybil. Rev. of *Master of the Return. Publishers Weekly.* 26 Feb. 1988: 182.
Uffen, Ellen Serlen. *Strands of the Cable: The Place of the Past in Jewish American Women's Writing.* New York: Peter Lang Publishing, 1992. 162-163.
Wiesel, Elie. Rev. of *Master of the Return. The New Leader.* 16 May 1988: 7–8.

ADRIENNE RICH (1929–   )

Karen Alkalay-Gut

BIOGRAPHY

Because Adrienne Rich repeatedly refers to her life in her work, and returns to critical events and situations in her life as touchstones of her development, her chronological biography is particularly intriguing. Rich has been careful, whenever possible, to keep certain aspects of her life private while publicizing and politicizing others, and this selective poetic use of relationships, events, and people, characteristic of her view of the self as political and representative, makes biographical delineation a political issue as well. A survey of her life, then, is also a chart of her poetic evolution, of her ongoing struggle to change the strategies by which we view the world.

Rich was born on May 16, 1929, in Baltimore, Maryland, to a Jewish father (which would, she notes in an article entitled "Split at the Root," define her as Jewish by the Nazis but not by the Jews) and a "Southern Protestant" mother (*Blood* 102). Rich has perceived this as a crucial paradoxical situation: Had she been born in Europe, she would have been counted as a *"Mischling, first degree"* (*Blood* 104) and would have been included in the Final Solution. But according to Jewish law, which acknowledges a Jewish mother as the link with Judaism, she would not be considered Jewish. This complex state in which she would be condemned to death for belonging to a religion that denies any alliance or responsibility for her was dealt with by denial insofar as her education was concerned. Rich was raised in an intellectual, deistic atmosphere and was not given the feeling of being typically one thing or the other (and of this division she speaks in various texts, such as her essay "Split at the Root" in *Blood* and the poem "Sources" in *Your Native Land* 7). However, the demands made upon her were greater than those of either religion. Her father's immigrant status and his consequent desire to excel (an early poem, "By No Means Native," deals with this aspect of her father without mentioning his Jewishness) drove him to drive his daughter to succeed within the traditional conventions of society. Educated at home in her early years, by her mother but under the tutelage of her father, Rich was inculcated with a drive for perfection and a respect for the Anglo-American literary legacy, coupled with an individual need to rebel against absolute authority, that has continued to direct both her life and her poetry. In her early twenties, two events contemporary with her graduation from Radcliffe College illustrate this: First, her first book of poems, *A Change of World* (1951), was published in the prestigious Yale Series of Younger Poets, earning her the envy of Sylvia Plath and the admiration of many contemporaries. The praise of W. H. Auden, who introduced these tightly controlled yet closely original-voiced poems, centered on her modesty and willingness to oblige her (poetic) elders by writing in the accepted traditional manner. Second, she married an older Jewish man, Alfred Conrad (1953), an economist at Harvard University, in an act of both rebellion and concession to her father. For although her father refused to attend the wedding or speak with her afterward, she was, she later acknowledged, marrying her father's image: "The one both like and unlike you, who explained you to me for years . . ." ("Sources," *Your Native Land* 19). Accepted warmly into her husband's family, she soon began to raise children, and by the age of thirty, was already mother to three sons (David, 1955; Paul, 1957; Jacob, 1959): "I often felt that to be a Jewish woman, a Jewish mother, was to be perceived in the Jewish family as an entirely physical being, a producer and nourisher of children" ("Split at the Root," *Blood* 117). This immersion in the roles of mother and docile Jewish wife had its effects, and Rich describes herself as feeling " . . . rebellious, moody, defensive, unable to sort out what was Jewish from what was simply motherhood or female destiny" (*Blood* 117).

It was this experience of motherhood that radicalized her, Rich notes, although it was the experience of being a Jewish daughter that seems to have been the original root for this. She learned to generalize from her father's sense of absolute authority over her, and saw him after his death, as "the face of patriarchy . . . the principle you embodied" (*Your Native Land* 9).

Despite her intense family identification at this time, Rich managed to develop a poetic career and continued to win awards—including the Guggenheim in 1960, the Bollingen in 1962, and the Amy Lowell Travelling Fellowship in 1962–63.

In 1966 Rich and her family moved to New York, where she became involved in the issues of school integration, the protests against the war in Vietnam, and soon after in the feminist movement; she encountered personal traumas with which she continues to wrestle in her work: The death of her father in 1968 was followed by the suicide of her estranged husband in 1970. During this time she became more involved in academe, teaching at Columbia University, City College of New York, Brandeis University, Douglass College, and Cornell University.

Rich's role in the women's movement increased in the decade of the seventies as she searched in her poetry for paths that had not yet been forged. Both in her life and in her work Rich was endeavoring to work out her own now-unscripted life and the concept of the lives of women the world round. Accepting the National Book Award in 1974 for *Diving into the Wreck*, she emphasized her identity with women all over who had not been given the opportunity to speak. Her public identification as a lesbian in 1975 (when she published two poems in an anthology entitled *Amazon Poetry*, New York: Out & Out Books, 9), was also an attempt to pursue the goal of allowing women their own direction in their lives.

In addition to the many significant books of poetry she was writing during this period, Rich coedited *Sinister Wisdom* from 1980–84 and in her poetry and prose endeavored to encourage women to write. Since 1985 Rich has lived in California, teaching at various institutions, helping to edit *Bridges: A Journal for Jewish Feminists and Our Friends*, and continuing to write—influenced both by the landscape of California and the perspective the distance offers upon her past.

Rich was awarded the 1991 Common Wealth Award in Literature, the most recent in a long series that includes an American Academy Award (1961), Shelley Memorial Award (1955), National Book Award (1974), Fund for Human Dignity Award (1981), and numerous honorary doctorates.

MAJOR THEMES

Most important to an understanding of Rich is to be aware of the significance of commitment in her work and life. In a time when so much of poetry has become "fence-sitting / raised to the level of an esthetic ideal" (as John Ashbery puts it), Rich stands as a leader in the opposite movement. Her poetry is of involvement, energy, engagement, communication, and the necessity for change—an intellectually and emotionally discovered change. The figure of the poet as she represents it is responsible for the world and has an obligation to nurture its development. The poet also writes from a total physical involvement—many of her images center upon physical sensations and, later, their political and theoretical implications.

An overview of the subjects and concerns of Adrienne Rich's poetry and prose reveals an inspiring range and level of commitment. Rarely does Rich descend to the trivial or banal; the subjects Rich has written about have all been overwhelmingly central to the lives of all human beings, often with her own life as illustration and embodiment of the issues. And despite the great range of interests, there is a constant drive for intellectual and moral development that characterizes her work. Because this development is inclusive—incorporating earlier approaches and attitudes rather than denying them—it is useful to follow Rich's themes chronologically.

Even in her "modest" and deferential first book, *A Change of World*, there are the themes of rebellion against oppressive authority, the necessity and difficulty of human communication, and the need to rise beyond the bordered vision allotted to the individual by circumstance and education. But there is also a sense of constraint and limitation, of a small individual—a woman—in an overwhelming and authoritative world and the necessity of compromising the individual in the face of greater powers.

Although in her early poems there seems to be an attempt to write poetry that is universal and eternal, from *Snapshots of a Daughter-in-Law* (1967), Rich has been dating her poems, indicating that each poem is in part a product of its time and that it may develop into something later that will be more true for that time.

Snapshots of a Daughter-in-Law marks Rich's clear if not open rebellion with the system—the patriarchal establishment, which permits women's identities and connections—as the title suggests—only through the central male. The style is also less conventional, in accordance with the new "snapshot" method that perceives the old formal systems as unable to reflect a disconnected, nonlinear, female reality.

The conviction, registered in her own poetic as well as biographical commitment—that equality has to be universal, that the denial of opportunities is criminal, that persecution and discrimination of any sort is inhuman—is one that has been maintained throughout her life, but becomes marked first in this period.

Leaflets (1969) asserts the necessity of political, personal, and poetic integration. "I want to choose words that even you/ would have to be changed by" ("Implosions"). This book, like *Necessities of Life* (1966) and *Snapshots*, focuses on the lack of communication in personal and political life, centralizing poetry as a means of finding language, of altering the situation.

The Will to Change (1971) reasserts the politicization of this personal move—the fact that the individual life cannot be changed without an awareness of its context—but it is in *Diving into the Wreck* (1973) that Rich's full feminist power is released. In the title poem of this volume, Rich creates the persona of a woman on an underwater quest for naked identity, looking for the identity of woman that has not been determined by the destructive and destroyed patriarchal society. It is this "androgynous," impersonal yet individual woman who represents in many ways the embodiment of the search for new ways of living. This concept of the necessity for female community (particularly in the face of the failure of the male-dominated world) emerges even more strongly in her prose volume *Of Woman Born: Motherhood as Experience and Institution* (1976), in which she examines male control over the processes of women's bodies and envisions a transformation in the future in which women will give birth to and nurture a creative, cooperative human world. *The Dream of a Common Language: Poems 1974–1977* emphasizes these themes while also elevating the lesbian love that helped to transform her life to a political and personal ideal. Throughout this and subsequent books that discuss and illustrate women's love, there is the opposition between the safe, loving, enclosed spaces that women create for themselves and others, and the anarchic, destructive, dangerous world outside—determined by mankind. Even in her most erotic poetry, this political message is clear—women do not struggle to glorify themselves by conquering or acquiring the other, but endeavor to create equal relationships that allow for open communication, support, and mutual progress. The fundamental difference in approach must be the basis for political change.

In her poetry, especially her more mature poetry, Rich attempts to create and to open the possibilities for dialogue. This is perhaps one of the reasons why such extreme reactions have been elicited by her work—it does not allow a passive and/or indifferent reader/partner. This concern is also apparent in her themes and techniques: Aware that she may be misrepresenting the speech of others, she tries whenever possible to allow others to speak for themselves and to point out her own limitations in her struggle for objectivity. "It's not enough/ using your words to damn you," she writes to Ellen Glasgow after quoting her and revealing her limited attitude toward her slave, *"they could have been my own"* ("Education of a Novelist," *Time's Power*, 40). Writing an analysis of her subject's thoughts in *Time's Power*, she registers her subject's protest when she looks over Rich's shoulder and reads the current page of poetry: *"It's all about you,"* the subject complains, *"None of this/ tells my story"* ("Sleep-walking Next to Death" 19).

Dialogues with herself are also prevalent. Constant reevaluations of political, social, historical, and individual roles and situations permeate her works. She begins "North American Time," for example, with the observation that when she perceives her dreams becoming "politically correct . . . then I begin to wonder" (*Your Native Land* 33).

Most recently other themes have become more salient in Rich's work, particularly her concern with her relationship with Judaism—with being a responsible, Jewish woman. Questions of Judaism and for Judaism permeate *Your Native Land, Your Life* (1986), *Blood, Bread, and Poetry: Selected Prose 1979–1985*, *Time's Power: Poems 1985–1988*, and *An Atlas of a Difficult World: Poems 1988–1991*. Rich's own changing attitude toward Jews and her Jewishness is mixed with her attempts to understand the complexities of the changing political situation in Israel, the many significances and effects of the Holocaust, the psychology and sociology of assimilation, and the intricacies and relevance of the rituals of religion. A poem that integrates these issues is "Eastern War Time" (*Atlas* 35–44), in which recent Jewish history is fused into Rich's personal history.

Throughout her work, there is the sense of a continuing struggle, and Rich takes care to indicate that whatever answers she has given are tentative, preliminary, and will not end with the finale of the poet. The last poem of the most recent book, "Final Notations" (*Atlas* 57), is written not only in the second person (for direct and intimate communication), but in the future tense, and it describes an ongoing and all-encompassing yet undetermined struggle.

SURVEY OF CRITICISM

There is little doubt that Rich is considered one of the most significant poets in the United States today, both because of her popularity and her influence. To the major American poets Rich is a font of discovery and direction. Erica Jong, Sharon Olds, W. S. Merwin, and many other poets choose Rich as the starting point of their own poems. Academic research concerning Rich is less clearly unified in its praise, in part because of her demands for engagement.

Lauded as the speaker of the feminist movement, Rich's politics are emphasized in most of the essays edited by Jane Cooper in *Reading Adrienne Rich* and in other research. Rich's dialogue with earlier women poets, such as H. D. (Susan Stanford Friedman in Cooper, 171–209, Montefiore, and Gelpi, "Two Ways") Dickinson (Erkkila), and other women in history (Marianne Whelchel in Cooper, 51–71), receive more attention than her dialogues with Shakespeare (Erickson) and John Donne (Profitt, Zivley), in part because of the political innovation of this enterprise.

Rich's contributions to the exploration of female identity are also investigated at length. Flowers discusses self-creation and identity and Kennard discusses the lesbian self. Numerous critics, such as Wendy Martin and Janis Stout, have also centered upon her poetic development, what Rich terms "the graph of a process still going on" (*PSN* xv), which parallels and directs that of conscious women in the latter part of this century.

Claire Keyes's Marxist study of Rich is most significant for its emphasis upon Rich's analysis of patriarchy and its use of power, and the possibilities of poetry to demonstrate a feminist alternative of creative power—a way of re-creating the world.

Criticism of Rich frequently focuses on her centrality in the feminist movement, although this is sometimes a limiting approach to her manifold interests and poetic intelligence. As Rich has become more vehement in her political convictions, the critics have tended to divide themselves sharply in their evaluations of the potential and significance of her poetic work. While many leaders in feminist criticism have focused on Rich and her influence in the movement, many scholars of poetry have found her political emphasis difficult to place in the poetic canon in the past few years, and at best they generally attempt to emphasize the way in which she transcends the limitations of feminist discourse. At worst, Rich is the subject of virulent attacks.

Most indicative of the disappointment of some academic readers is the criticism of the esteemed poetry critic Helen Vendler. "Someone my age was writing down my life" (237), she says, recalling her introduction to Rich's early poems, and this initial enthusiasm for Rich persisted into the seventies, even after other critics had begun their attack on what was considered a sacrifice of form and decorum for virulence and anger. "Better a change than the falsely 'mature' acceptance of the unacceptable" (253), Vendler noted. But with *Of Woman Born*, Vendler disengaged herself from this identification, claiming that Rich's tentative, exploratory vision had now become fixed and absolute. Acknowledging Rich's attempt at "inclusiveness," at what Emily Dickinson called "circumstance," Vendler nevertheless noted here and in reviews of later books as well that Rich remains blind to her own narrowness, sentimentality, propaganda. From her review of *A Wild Patience Has Taken Me This Far* to that of *An Atlas of a Difficult World,* Vendler has persisted in attacking Rich. Vendler's influence, her prolificness, and her representativeness make this criticism difficult to ignore, and, indeed, her arguments have been publicly and successfully countered only by a few critics, despite the fact that they are easily answered. For example, in her criticism of *A Wild Patience,* Vendler complains that the suffering of men is not considered in "The History of Human Suffering," ignoring Rich's point that the history of women is exclusively one of suffering, not that they are the only ones to suffer. Other critics such as Marjorie Perloff have made Rich the object of similar attacks.

Rich's work after *Diving into the Wreck* is also criticized on presumably formal grounds. Cary Nelson complains of "continual indirection" (146) because of her attempt to combine the individual and the political in her work. Altieri notes that "some of her ideas are little more than slogans" (167). Since so many other poets are simply ignored when they are disliked, this kind of attack indicates something of her major significance in American poetry, as well as the fact that she manages to hit raw nerves. This is indeed a poet impossible to ignore.

Almost no criticism makes any reference to the position of Rich in American poetry. Neither has she been considered within the context of Jewish writers, although she has been anthologized in collections of Jewish authors. Diaz-Diocaretz has examined Rich from a linguistic point of view, but a study of Rich's technical fluency and innovation remains to be done. Clearly, Rich's work can support a great deal more examination and contextualization.

BIBLIOGRAPHY

Works by Adrienne Rich

Poetry

A Change of World. New Haven. Yale University Press, 1951.
The Diamond Cutters and Other Poems. New York: Harper & Brothers, 1955.
Necessities of Life: Poems 1962–1965. New York: Norton, 1966.
Snapshots of a Daughter-in-Law. New York: Norton, 1967.
Leaflets: Poems 1965–1968. New York: Norton, 1969.
The Will to Change: Poems 1968–1970. New York: Norton, 1971: 1.
Selected Poems. London: Chatto & Windus, 1973.
Diving into the Wreck. New York: Norton, 1973.
Poems: Selected and New: 1950–1974. New York: Norton, 1975.
Twenty-One Love Poems. Emeryville, CA: Effie's Press, 1976.
The Meaning of Our Love for Women Is What We have Constantly to Expand. New York: Out & Out Books, 1977.
The Dream of a Common Language: Poems 1974–1977. New York: Norton, 1978.

A Wild Patience Has Taken Me This Far: Poems 1974–1977. New York: Norton, 1981.
Sources. Woodside, CA: Heyeck Press, 1983.
The Fact of a Doorframe: Poems Selected and New 1950–1984. New York: Norton, 1984.
Your Native Land, Your Life. New York: Norton, 1986.
Time's Power: Poems 1985–1988. New York: Norton, 1989.
An Atlas of a Difficult World: Poems 1988–1991. New York: Norton, 1991.

Prose

Of Woman Born: Motherhood as Experience and Institution. New York: Norton, 1976.
On Lies, Secrets, and Silence, Selected Prose 1966–1978. New York: Norton, 1979.
Blood, Bread, and Poetry: Selected Prose 1979–1985. New York: Norton, 1986.

Works about Adrienne Rich

Altieri, Charles. "Self Reflection as Action: The Recent Work of Adrienne Rich." *Self and Sensibility in Contemporary American Poetry.* Cambridge: Cambridge University Press, 1984. 165–191.

Bennett, Paula. *My Life, A Loaded Gun.* Boston: Beacon Press, 1986.

Christ, Carol P. "Homesick for a Woman, Homesick for Ourselves: Adrienne Rich." *Diving Deep and Surfacing: Women Writers and Spiritual Quest.* Boston: Beacon Press, 1980. 75–96.

Cooper, Jane. *Reading Adrienne Rich: Reviews and Revisions, 1951–1981.* Ann Arbor: University of Michigan Press, 1984.

Davidson, Harriet. "In the Wake of Home: Adrienne Rich's Politics and the Poetics of Location." *Contemporary Poetry Meets Modern Theory.* Eds. Antony Easthope and John O. Thompson. London: Harvester, 1991. 166–76.

Dennis, Helen. "Adrienne Rich: Consciousness Raising as Poetic Method." *Contemporary Poetry Meets Modern Theory.* Eds. Antony Easthope and John O. Thompson. London: Harvester, 1991. 177–94.

Des Pres, Terrence. "Adrienne Rich, North America East." *Praises and Dispraises: Poetry and Politics, the 20th Century.* New York: Viking, 1988. 187–224.

Diaz-Diocaretz, Myriam. *The Transforming Power of Language: The Poetry of Adrienne Rich.* Utrecht: HES, 1984.

———. *Translating Poetic Discourse: Questions on Feminist Strategies in Adrienne Rich.* Amsterdam, Philadelphia: Benjamins, 1985.

Erickson, Peter. "Adrienne Rich's Re-Vision of Shakespeare." *Women's Re-Visions of Shakespeare: On the Responses of Dickinson, Woolf, Rich, H. D., George Eliot, and Others.* Ed. Marianne Novy, Urbana: University of Illinois Press, 1990. 183–95.

Erkkila, Betsy. "Dickinson and Rich: Toward a Theory of Female Poetic Influence." *American Literature: A Journal of Literary History, Criticism, and Bibliography.* December 1984: 541–59.

Flowers, Betty S. "The 'I' in Adrienne Rich: Individuation and the Androgyne Archetype." *Theory and Practice of Feminist Literary Criticism.* Ed. Gabriela Mora, Karen S. Van Hooft, Ypsilanti, MI: Bilingual, 1982. 14–35.

Friedman, Susan Sanford, "I Go Where I Love: An Intertextual Study of H. D. and Adrienne Rich." *Coming to Light: American Women Poets in the Twentieth Century.* Eds. Diane Wood Middlebrook and Marilyn Yalom. Ann Arbor: University of Michigan, 1985. 233–53.

Gelpi, Albert. "Two Ways of Spelling It Out: An Archetypal-Feminist Reading of H.D.'s Trilogy and Adrienne Rich's Sources." *The Southern Review* 26.2 (Spring 1990): 266–84.

Gelpi, Barbara Charlesworth, and Albert Gelpi. eds., *Adrienne Rich's Poetry, A Norton Critical Edition: Texts of the Poems, The Poets on Her Work, Reviews and Criticism.* New York: Norton, 1975.

Kalstone, David. *Five Temperaments: Elizabeth Bishop, Robert Lowell, James Merrill, Adrienne Rich, and John Ashbery.* New York: Oxford University Press, 1977.

Kennard, Jean E. "Ourself Behind Ourself: A Theory for Lesbian Readers." *Gender and Reading: Essays on Readers, Texts, and Contexts.* Ed. Elizabeth A. Flynn and Patrocinio P. Schweickart. Baltimore: Johns Hopkins University Press, 1986. 63–80.

Keyes, Claire. *The Aesthetics of Power: The Poetry of Adrienne Rich.* Athens: University of Georgia Press, 1986.

Markey, Janice. *A New Tradition?* Frankfurt am Main, New York: P. Lang, 1985.

Martin, Wendy. "Adrienne Rich's Poetry." Monograph in *American Writers Series.* New York: C. Scribner's Sons, 1978.

———. *An American Triptych.* Chapel Hill: University of North Carolina Press, 1984.

Montefiore, Jan. " 'What words say': Three Women Poets Reading H.D." *Agenda* 25.3-4 (Autumn-Winter 1987–1988): 172–90.

Nelson, Cary. "Meditative Aggressions: Adrienne Rich's Recent Transactions with History." *Our Last First Poets: Visions and History in Contemporary American Poetry.* Urbana: University of Illinois Press, 1981. 145–76.

Proffitt, Edward. "Allusion in Adrienne Rich's 'A Valediction Forbidding Mourning.' " *Concerning Poetry* 15.1 (Spring 1982): 21–24.

Stout, Janis. "Breaking Out: The Journey of the American Woman Poet." *North Dakota Quarterly* 56.1 (Winter 1988): 40–53.

Vendler, Helen. *Part of Nature, Part of Us.* Cambridge, MA: Harvard University Press, 1980.

Werner, Craig. Hansen. *Adrienne Rich.* Chicago: American Library Association, 1988.

Zivley, Sherry Lutz. "Adrienne Rich's Contemporary Metaphysical Conceit." *Notes on Contemporary Literature* 12.3 (May 1982): 6–8.

ANNE ROIPHE (1935–   )

Carolyn Hoyt

BIOGRAPHY

Anne Roiphe has liberally used her life as material for novels, articles, and book-length essays that depict the anxieties and ambiguities of a Jewish generation whose parents had already "made it." In a piece about the act of writing, published by the *New York Times Book Review*, she describes her vision of the relationship between a writer's work and life:

> we writers expose our thoughts, our fears, our experiences. Often we cannibalize the lives of people we know. We are invaders of privacy, first and mostly our own, but also others'—bystanders who made the mistake of loving us or angering us or simply inviting us to dinner. ("This Butcher, Imagination" 3)

We find models for many of Roiphe's characters and plots in her biography.

Anne Roiphe was born December 25, 1935, to Eugene Roth and Blanche Phillips Roth in New York City, where she has lived most of her life. Roiphe's father had immigrated with his family to the United States at the age of six. Though the family was doing well in Hungary, Roiphe's grandfather feared losing his job because of anti-Semitism. In America, his son Eugene assimilated so successfully that "even John Quincy Adams would not have suspected that he had in truth been born on the other side" (*Generation Without Memory* 29). Eugene Roth attended Columbia Law School and, in the interest of attaining wealth and social status, cut himself off from his past. Roiphe describes her father as a man given to sudden fits of temper who kept himself aloof from wife and family. "Silent as a Yankee, his urban world required that he learn to move like a tiger, to trust no one, to need no one" (*Generation Without Memory* 30).

Roth's fortune was based on his wife's family's business, Van Heusen shirts, which became his major client. Founded by Roiphe's maternal grandfather on a Lower East Side pushcart, the business grew to support a luxurious lifestyle that included Fifth Avenue apartments, Palm Beach vacations, golf-club memberships, and multiple servants.

A budding bohemian dressed in sandals and black leotard, Anne Roiphe began college at Smith College in 1953 but received her B.A. from Sarah Lawrence College in 1957. After a year of travel in Europe, Roiphe married the gentile playwright Jack Richardson in 1958, a marriage that lasted until 1963. On January 20, 1967, Anne married Herman Roiphe, a well-known psychoanalyst in New York City. Their family would soon include five daughters, one from Anne's first marriage, two from Herman's, and two they had together.

Roiphe chronicles her upper-middle-class Jewish experience: Jewish had disappeared from my mind along with the swimming pool at the country club I no longer visited. . . . As my black leotard and sandals demonstrated, I was a citizen in good standing of bohemia, of beatnik turf. I thought of myself as tribeless, stateless, countryless, classless, religionless. (*Generation Without Memory* 79–80)

Roiphe felt caught among bohemian sexual mores, secular humanism, and a vague guilt at her rejection of Jewish culture. Her work replicates these feelings.

Roiphe's first novel (published under the name Richardson), *Digging Out* (1966), tells the story of Laura Smith as she thinks about her life and heritage while waiting out her mother's slow and painful death of malignant melanoma. Her second novel, *Up The Sandbox!* (1970) (made into a movie starring Barbra Streisand), focuses on Margaret Reynolds, who has wild fantasies incongruous with her existence as an urban housewife. In 1972 came *Long Division*, a mother-daughter travelogue.

Roiphe's fourth novel was published in 1977. *Torch Song* departs from the mother-child theme to examine an obsessive relationship between a beatnik Jewish girl and the self-destructive and sexually perverse writer she pursues and eventually marries. Published in 1987, *Lovingkindness* tells the story of Andrea's rebellion against her secular humanist mother, Annie Johnson. Andrea runs off to join an ultra-Orthodox sect in Jerusalem. Most recently, Roiphe published *The Pursuit of Happiness* (1991), a multigenerational family saga with a nineteenth-century-style narrator.

Roiphe wrote a book-length essay on assimilation, *Generation Without Memory: A Jewish Journey in Christian America*, published in 1981. Two additional works of nonfiction include *The Complete Book of Infant and Child Mental Health Care*, written with her husband, Herman Roiphe, in 1985, and *A Season for Healing: Reflections on the Holocaust* (1988), a more political book on issues facing contemporary Judaism.

An active journalist, Roiphe has written countless pieces for magazines as diverse as *Cosmopolitan*, *Commonweal*, *The New Yorker*, *Present Tense*, *Tikkun*, and *Vogue*. Her subjects range from typical women's magazine fare such as ''Daddy's Girls: Women Who Win,'' or ''Women Who Sacrifice for Their Man,'' to controversial pieces in the *New York Times Magazine* on subjects such as psychoanalysis and feminism, to Jewish-oriented political pieces about fundamentalism, and the Israeli-Palestinian conflict. A long-time contributor to *Tikkun*, Roiphe recently ended a stint as fiction editor at the progressive Jewish journal. For the last year she has been publishing regularly in the *New York Observer* and the *Jerusalem Report*.

MAJOR THEMES

Anne Roiphe's literary struggles with Jewish identity took on a painfully personal tone in December 1978, when she published what she had thought to be an unassuming lifestyle piece in the *New York Times* about her family's secular observance of Christmas. The public reaction to this article changed Anne Roiphe's belief system and left its permanent imprint on her writing.

"I have made misjudgments in my life but none so consequential for me as this one," Roiphe wrote two years later in *Tikkun*. She describes the emotionally charged reaction of her readers:

Housewives, rabbis, lawyers, doctors, businessmen, all but Indian chiefs phoned or wrote in, furious that the paper had published an article that advocated assimilation, displayed ignorance of Judaism, and seemed to express contempt for the Jewish way of life. ("Taking Down the Christmas Tree," 58)

In response, Roiphe acknowledged that her familiarity with Judaism was patchy and the article that she had blithely written for the *Times* revealed a deeply felt conflict, a "discomfort with the peculiar form my Jewishness had taken" (58). Thereafter, she began to educate herself about her heritage. Her fiction took on a new resonance as she let go of her resentment and began to reexplore her Jewish roots with a skeptical, but nevertheless, conciliatory viewpoint.

The evolution of her semiautobiographical protagonists reveal this change in attitude. The structure of *Digging Out*, alternating as it does between family history and Laura Smith's internal thoughts as she awaits her mother's death, schematizes the conflict between Jewish success and the incumbent deterioration in Jewish values. Roiphe's young heroines all react in similar ways to the shallow materialism they perceive in their elders, especially in the figures of their rich, comfortable, conformist Jewish mothers. The struggle over the meaning of Judaism becomes very personal, and painful, as it takes place in the personal relationships of mothers and their daughters. Roiphe interweaves the theme of a generation's ambiguous relationship with its Jewish heritage so subtly, with preoccupations about motherhood and feminism, that her work, taken as a whole, presents an evolving portrait of the quirky, intelligent, rebellious, and iconoclastic Jewish woman dealing with modernity.

Not only are the daughters in rebellion against mothers, but their mothers feel ambivalent, too. Though mothers are supposed to love their children unconditionally, the reality of parenting is otherwise, and Anne Roiphe bravely depicts the uneven texture of the mother-daughter relationship. In an interview after the publication of *Long Division* she stated:

A mother wasn't supposed to admit to anything but totally blissful feelings about a screaming baby that had kept it up for seven days straight. That's why I thought it was important to put the real feelings down where they could be seen and shared and recognized. (Ross 435)

In the final, riotous scene of *Long Division*, pre-adolescent Sarah Brimberg Johnson is stolen from her mother by a caravan of gypsies and, in the kind of parody that betrays a truth, her mother wonders if she really wants to get her daughter back:

The thought crossed my mind to leave her—impossible, but possible. Let her be her own person. Let her find her own way, gypsy or not. Cut the cords; like an animal, refuse responsibility past the first infantile moments. I would be without her, sparse, clean like a bone. Tomorrow would be mine to devour alone. (184–85)

In a Roiphe novel, neither the daughter nor the mother lives up to the other's expectations. Yet, as she writes in *Digging Out*, they are linked together, always. "A mother and a daughter are not entirely two separate entities. From the instant of conception on they are like a page of paper. Different anecdotes may be written on each side but there is only one single page" (67).

Surely Laura Smith loves her mother, but she does not respect the opulence and emptiness of her lifestyle or the ways in which her family acquired their wealth. Again, in *Up the Sandbox!*, the daughter, Margaret Reynolds, struggles to become a good mother on her own terms while breaking away from the image that her mother has for her. Margaret's mother criticizes everything about her daughter's chosen lifestyle, even going so far as to bring her maid along to clean Margaret's apartment.

The idea of a link that simultaneously cannot and must be severed is portrayed most poignantly in *Lovingkindness*. Roiphe depicts an ongoing battle between mother and daughter. The mother, Annie, watches her daughter, Andrea, get her stomach pumped and thinks, "It must have been unpleasant. I hoped it was unpleasant" (144). The daughter gets her licks in too. Andrea has three abortions, dyes her hair, gets kicked out of school, rides helmetless on motorcycles, and wears leather clothes and jewelry. She has a rattlesnake tatooed between her shoulder blades: "A blue rattlesnake with a bright red eye whose scales slithered and curved with the muscles of the upper spine." When mother Annie sardonically suggests a rose, Andrea replies, " 'A rose for Mother's Day . . . Maybe I'll have them do one on my ass' " (49).

Roiphe cautiously weighs a woman's longings to fulfill herself both in a career and in a family. Her conclusions are ambiguous and troubling. In the novel that proclaimed her a voice for feminism, *Up the Sandbox!*, Margaret

Reynolds remains ironic and ambivalent at the conclusion when she informs her husband of her pregnancy. "Paul, Elizabeth, Peter, the new baby and I will grow closer and closer in memories of days that promised more than they gave and love that offers everything and then like a mirage disappears as we get closer" (155). None of Roiphe's characters is willing to sacrifice relationship for ideology.

Roiphe's last two novels use Israel as a beacon for their disenchanted heroines, a place where they could live according to their values, where they could reclaim their historical ancestry and spiritual heritage all at once.

For Andrea of *Lovingkindness*, the religious life, while restricting her choices, also ensures the moral and emotional stability that her mother, an academic and a skeptic, could not provide. Critic Naomi Sokoloff comments that this "flight to Israel signals an impatience with self-centered values, exaggerated individualism, assimilation, sexual indulgence, and the failures of political liberalism at home" ("Imagining Israel" 66).

In *The Pursuit of Happiness*, a long and complicated family saga ends with Hedy, its contemporary narrator, waiting in the hospital for her daughter to come out of brain surgery. Namah was injured trying to defend an Arab child against outraged Jewish settlers, thus reflecting Roiphe's own beliefs about the moral ambiguity of Israel's occupation of the West Bank and the Gaza Strip and her incumbent support for the left-wing Israeli peace movement.

In fiction and in life, Israel then provides no easy answers for the Jewish woman trying to find meaning in her family history or her personal future. The search goes on.

SURVEY OF CRITICISM

Though Anne Roiphe has received unfailingly positive reviews from critics in the popular press, the academic response to her work has been sparse, limited to a few articles based exclusively on her novel *Lovingkindness*. Naomi Sokoloff criticizes the depiction of an Israel whose choices of Judaism are between Orthodoxy and assimilation. "The stances of the *haredim* [the ultra-Orthodox whom daughter Andrea joins] are too exaggerated for Annie to assimilate into her own thinking. Consequently, even as her encounter with this aspect of Israeli life brings her to a new self-criticism, it also allows her to discount much of the challenge to her beliefs, and so she evades any far-reaching transformation of her old outlooks" ("Imagining Israel" 73).

However, Miriyam Glazer argues that Annie's dream life subverts her conscious secularity. Glazer underscores Annie's recurring dreams about Reb Nachman of Bratslav, who haunts her lurid nightmares and then enables her to heal by playing on just those maternal instincts that her own daughter is struggling so hard against. According to Glazer, the Nachman visions become a source of "integration and healing" (90) while she is in Israel, though a "disturbing twist" (91) at the end of the novel leads Annie to live out her life in hypocritical denial of the dreams she had and the decision that she made to support her daughter's embrace of Orthodoxy. The depiction of Jewish values in *Lovingkindness* also occupies Lewis Fried, who sees the novel as "the quest for identity between the poles of the sacred and the profane" (179). He compares Roiphe to such important American Jewish writers as Anzia Yezierska and Henry Roth, because she continues their search for answers to a basic question that haunts the American Jew: "Can a sacramental life be achieved in America? Must the terms of redemption be secularly recast? Or theologically reconceived?" (179).

With the publication of *Digging Out*, Roiphe earned the praise of Stanley Kauffmann, who noted in *The New Republic* her "immediately perceptible talent" as well as the "compressed, oblique anguish" expressed in her narrative (22). As Roiphe's career progressed, reviewer Marylin Bender praised her "considerable gifts as a satirist, black humorist and piercing analyst of fuzzy white liberalism" (5).

Roiphe's next two novels met with less success, as did her efforts in nonfiction. E. N. Evans criticized *Generation Without Memory* as naive, a "disorganized patchwork," though he admitted that "her search deserves attention" (13). Roiphe's collection of reflections on the Holocaust provoked skepticism from all sides of the political spectrum. Berel Lang wrote in the *New York Times*, "Her attributing black anti-Semitism to Jewish emphasis on the Holocaust takes so shortened a view of American social history (and of all history) as to sound simply arbitrary" (7).

Though Roiphe considers herself to be a better writer of nonfiction than of fiction (Personal interview 19 Dec. 1992), her recent novels have fared well with the critics. *Lovingkindness* has been admired not only by academics but also by critics such as Blanche d'Alpuget of the *New York Times*, who called it "the keystone to a cause of 20 years: a novel that binds the author's entire work" (9).

Amy Wallace likens Roiphe's most recent novel, *The Pursuit of Happiness*, to "nothing less than the nature of human fulfillment seen through the eyes of a persecuted people" (9), and Richard Kaye is exuberant in his praise:

Restless, extravagantly overreaching, unable to shake off their Jewish souls, the Gruenbaums—as one of them remarks in another context—are all insomniacs unable to have the American Dream. Anne Roiphe succeeds in lifting their innumerable criss-crossing fables of achievement and woe into the realm of a true family epic. She understands that the gargantuan nature of her theme—the mixed blessing of Jewish America's "Hellenic" absorption in its adopted country's glittering prizes—requires a novelist's extravagant overreaching. The Pursuit of Happiness accomplishes this with tragicomic range and a lyricism that can only be described as, yes, triumphant and sweeping. (73)

BIBLIOGRAPHY

Works by Anne Roiphe

Fiction

Digging Out. New York: McGraw-Hill Book Company, 1966. (Published under the name Anne Richardson.)
Up the Sandbox! New York: Simon and Schuster, 1970.
Long Division. New York: Simon and Schuster, 1972.
Torch Song. New York: Farrar, Straus, and Giroux, 1977.
Lovingkindness. New York: Summit Books, 1987.
The Pursuit of Happiness. New York: Summit Books, 1991.
If You Knew Me. Boston: Little, Brown, 1993.

Selected Nonfiction

"Family Is Out of Fashion." *New York Times Magazine.* 15 August 1971: 10–11.
"What Women Psychoanalysts Say About Women's Liberation." *New York Times Magazine.* 13 February 1972: 12–13ff.
"Can You Have Everything and Still Want Babies?" *Vogue.* December 1975: 152–153ff.
"Christmas Comes to a Jewish Home." *New York Times.* 21 December 1978: C1, C6.
"Religious Void." *Commonweal.* 19 January 1979: 4–5.
Generation Without Memory: A Jewish Journey in Christian America. New York: Simon & Schuster, 1981.
The Complete Book of Infant and Child Mental Health Care. With Herman Roiphe. New York: St. Martin's Press, 1985.
A Season for Healing: Reflections on the Holocaust. New York: Summit Books, 1988.
"This Butcher, Imagination: Beware of Your Life When a Writer's at Work." With Philip Roth. *New York Times Book Review.* 14 February 1988: 3.
"Taking Down the Christmas Tree." *Tikkun.* November-December 1989: 58.

Interviews

With Jean W. Ross. *Contemporary Authors.* Detroit: Gale Research Company 1980: 434–36.
Personal interview, 19 December 1992.

Works about Anne Roiphe

Avery, Evelyn. "What's a Mother to Do?" *Midstream* (1988): 61–62.
Bender, Marylin. "Margaret Can Make a Human Being.' *New York Times Book Review.* 17 June 1971: 5.
d'Alpuget, Blanche. "A Daughter Lost to Faith." *New York Times Book Review.* 30 August 1987: 9.
Easton, Elizabeth. "*Up the Sandbox!*;" *Saturday Review.* 6 February 1971: 31.
Fried, Lewis. "Living the Riddle: The Sacred and Profane in Anne Roiphe's Lovingkindness." *Studies in American Jewish Literature.* 11.2, Fall 1992: 174–81.
Glazer, Miriyam. "Male and Female, King and Queen: The Theological Imagination of

Anne Roiphe's Lovingkindness.'' *Studies in American Jewish Literature*. Vol. 10.1. Spring 1991: 81–92.

Goldman, Ari. ''Trapped in Yeshiva.'' *New York Times Book Review*. 30 August 1987: 9.

Heldman, Irma Pascal. ''Love as a Bridge.'' *Time*. 25 January 1971: 74–75.

Henkin, Josh. ''Choosing Religion.'' *Tikkun*. May/June 1988: 98–100.

Horowitz, Sara R. ''Portnoy's Sister—Whose Complaining?'' *The Jewish Book Annual*, ed. Jacob M. Kabakoff. Vol 51. 1994. 26–41.

Kauffmann, Stanley. ''Welcome.'' *New Republic*. 4 March 1967: 22–23.

Kaye, Richard. ''Family Ties.'' *Tikkun*. May-June 1992: 73.

Lang, Berel. ''Man Did This to Man.'' *New York Times Book Review*. 13 November 1988: 7.

Lehmann-Haupt, Christopher. ''Descent of a People from Spiritual to Worldly.'' *New York Times*. 10 June 1991: C18.

Rosenfeld, Alvin. ''The Progress of the American Jewish Novel.'' *Response* Vol. 7 1973: 115–30.

Sayre, Nora. ''Breaking up and Working Loose: Long Division.'' *New York Times Book Review*. 4 November 1972: 5, 22.

———. ''Certain Aspects of Death.'' *Nation*. 11 September 1967: 219–20.

Sissman, L. E. ''Books: Second Time Around.'' *New Yorker*. 17 April 1971: 146–47.

Sokoloff, Naomi. ''Imagining Israel in American Jewish Fiction: Anne Roiphe's *Lovingkindness* and Philip Roth's *The Counterlife*.'' *Studies in American Jewish Literature*. 10, Spring 1991: 65–80.

Strickland, Ruth L. ''Anne Roiphe.'' *Dictionary of Literary Biography Yearbook*. 1980.

Wallace, Amy. ''Jitterbugging Through the Generations.'' *New York Times Book Review*. 21 July 1991: 9.

Weaver, Carole McKewin, ''Tasting Stars: The Tales of Rabbi Nachman in Anne Roiphe's *Lovingkindness*,'' *Mother Puzzles: Daughters and Mothers in Contemporary American Literature*, ed. Mickley Pearlman. Westport, CT: Greenwood, 1989. 131–39.

NORMA ROSEN (1925–   )

Susanne Klingenstein

BIOGRAPHY

Norma Rosen was born in Manhattan on August 11, 1925. She grew up in Borough Park (Brooklyn, New York). Her parents, Rose Miller and Louis Gangel, were American Jews; Norma was their only child. In her essay "On Living in Two Cultures" (1974), Rosen describes the family's relation to Judaism:

I was born of an immaculate Jewish conception. That is, my parents, who were Jews by birth, refrained from intercourse with the Jewish religion and proudly passed me, in an untainted state, into the world. Not that we were assimilated. No, we stood in a proud and terrible place outside the "two cultures." Some years, my father went to reform services on the extra-special "high" days. But not my mother, who could not stand even this skimpy slice of official Jewish life. I think now that she was an early women's liberationist, at least in Jewish matters. Even then I knew that she bitterly resented the treatment of women in her mother's orthodox synagogue—on the one hand, the denial of women's spiritual life, on the other, the physical wearing down of women under the burdens of homemaking. (*Accidents of Influence*, 126)

The family moved to Manhattan, where Norma attended Julia Richman High School. She proceeded to Mount Holyoke College, where she studied modern dance with José Limon and choreography with Martha Graham. Rosen was elected to Phi Beta Kappa and graduated *cum laude* in 1946. For the next three years, she taught English and dance at a private girls' academy.

In the early fifties, Rosen decided to continue her education, and in 1953, she earned a master's degree from Columbia University with a thesis on Graham Greene. She went on to study book designing at New York University, and in 1954, she was hired by the New York publishing house Harper and Row. Her job involved her in all stages of book production, hence her early characters' knowledge of typography, copy preparation, or jacket design.

In the late fifties, Rosen began to write seriously. In 1959, the year she left

Harper and Row, Rosen published her first two stories, one in *Commentary* and one in *Mademoiselle*. Her first novel, *Joy to Levine!*, was then taking shape. Rosen spent the summer of 1959 writing at the MacDowell Colony. In 1960, she received a Eugene F. Saxton Grant to complete the novel, which was published in 1962 by Alfred Knopf in New York.

After a brief first marriage, during which she published under the name Norma Stahl, she married Robert Samuel Rosen in 1960 and changed her name to Norma Rosen. Her husband, Robert Rosen, was born in Vienna in 1924. He had escaped to England on the famous children's transport in November 1938. His parents were murdered by the Nazis. Yet despite this fate, and as if to spite it, Robert Rosen insisted on a modicum of observance in his new American family, such as the observance of *kashrut* [dietary laws], of putting *mezuzah* on the doorpost of one's home, or of hearing the Torah on shabbat. Portraits of Robert Rosen appear in many of Norma Rosen's fictions. In her story "What Must I Say to You?" (1964), collected in *Green*, she writes: "My husband was born in Europe, of an Orthodox family. He is neither Orthodox nor Reform. He is his own council of rabbis, selecting as he goes" (200).

In 1961, Robert and Norma Rosen's daughter, Anne Beth, was born. The first days after this joy-filled but exhausting event are described in Rosen's short story of 1963, "Plaintain Shoot, It Want to Die." But as the title indicates, the joys of birth are muted by intimations of death. In 1962, her first novel was published, and in 1963, the Rosens' son Jonathan Aaron was born. A few years later, the family moved from New York City to Brookline, a suburb of Boston. Here, Norma Rosen was attracted to a variety of Jewish communities; once she even attended a women's *minyan*, an adventure she depicted in her essay "A Women's Service" (1973). More lasting influence, however, was exerted by Rav Joseph Soloveitchik, the author of *Halakhic Man* and *The Lonely Man of Faith*, whose *shiurim* [study hours] Rosen attended. The difficulties of relocating from New York City to Brookline and of writing in a new, unfamiliar environment are described in Rosen's short stories "Walking Distance" (1971) and "Traveling Toward the Inner Life" (1972).

In 1965, Rosen started her teaching career in creative writing with a fiction-writing workshop at the New School for Social Research in New York. Between 1965 and 1992, Rosen taught fiction-writing and analysis at thirteen institutions; among them are the University of Pennsylvania (1969), Harvard University (1972–73), Yale University (1982), Barnard College (1989–90), and Columbia University (1990). From 1986 to date, she has been teaching fiction-writing at New York University at the Tisch School of Dramatic Writing. Her first novel was followed in 1967 by a collection of short fictions, *Green: A Novella and Eight Stories*, and two years later by a second novel, *Touching Evil* (1969). Rosen spent the years 1971 to 1973 as a fellow at the Bunting Institute at Radcliffe College in Cambridge, Massachusetts. There she wrote more fiction and some of the essays recently collected in *Accidents of Influence: Writing as a Woman and a Jew in America* (1992). In 1982, Rosen published her third novel, *At the Center*, and began to write her ten-week column, ''Hers,'' for the *New York Times*. In the second half of the eighties, Rosen was particularly productive as literary essayist and book reviewer. In 1989, she published her fourth novel, *John and Anzia*. She is a member of Phi Beta Kappa, the American P.E.N., the Author's Guild, and Poets & Writers. She lives with her husband, a professor of Comparative Literature, in New York City.

MAJOR THEMES

Norma Rosen developed from a writer of stories depicting domestic scenes into a novelist who is not afraid to ask large moral and metaphysical questions. We can observe an odd split in Rosen's fictional writing: She permits her shorter work to form a running commentary on her life; whereas her four novels to date, *Joy to Levine!* (1962), *Touching Evil* (1969), *At the Center* (1982), and *John and Anzia* (1989), can be considered novels of ideas, despite their deceptively realistic style. They measure the impact of major historical events (such as the Holocaust or the legalization of abortion) on the daily lives of more or less ordinary people. In her essay ''The Holocaust and the American-Jewish Novelist'' (1974), which like all other essays referred to here is reprinted in Rosen's essay collection *Accidents of Influence* (1992), she indicates why she chooses to grapple with ideas in the medium of fiction. ''Fiction writers rely on ambiguity; they put their ideas forward behind the protection of characters' masks. Fiction writers find this congenial, not because they are afraid to speak the truth, but because they find truth to be slippery—or to put it more elegantly, truth is in the dialectic itself, in the interplay of ideas; ideas moreover that in life never express themselves purely but are always modified, sometimes grotesquely, sometimes nobly, by human behavior'' (*Accidents of Influence* 2). Rosen prefers the flux of life over the rigidity of ideas. The running commentary of her short fiction, however, demonstrates exquisitely how the necessity of coming to grips with political, philosophical, and even with theological ideas forced itself on Rosen. Although her novels fall stylistically into the category of psychological realism, Rosen weaves her fiction around the discussion of ideas and moral concerns.

The stories published before 1967 were collected in the volume *Green: A Novella and Eight Stories* (1967). ''Apples'' and ''The Open Window,' both published in 1959, ask questions about the parent-child relationship: How protective are parents allowed to be, and what do grown children owe to less-than-perfect parents? The two stories explore the delicate net of indebtedness, gratitude, liberty, and responsibility in which parents and children are entangled and which is further complicated by the knots of emotional and psychological abuse. *Joy to Levine!* belongs clearly to this period. The protagonist, Arnold Levine, is an employee of a run-down company that produces textbooks touting the British Rutborough shorthand, which its inventors call ''the most perfect system in the world.'' Although the system is obviously flawed, its inventors refuse to admit its fallibility. The company slowly deteriorates because of its rigid albeit deluded belief in the perfection of their product. Thus, the "most perfect system in the world" serves as an ingenious metaphor for the parental authority under which Levine suffers and which impedes the unfolding of his own personality and condemns him to indolence and indecision. "Levine," Rosen explained in 1974, "has an overprotective father, who fears for his son's luck out in the world. And so Levine concocts an elaborate lying pattern with which to keep his father misinformed. Levine falls in love with a girl who he thinks is not Jewish, and is delighted and appalled at this own adventurousness" (*Accidents of Influence* 6). The novel is funny and slightly sardonic; it is in part a satire on the American pastime of "getting ahead" and is full of fast, vivid dialogues that capture the quirkiness of different urban types. The tedium of office life (reminiscent of Walker Percy's 1961 novel, *The Moviegoer*) is disrupted by eccentric, life-hungry characters.

In the next phase of her writing career, Rosen explores what it means to be a woman, a mother, a writer, and a Jew. Her stories "Plaintain Shoot, It Want to Die" (1963) and "What Must I Say to You?" (1964) describe the relationship of a young American Jewish woman to her infant's Jamaican nurse. The young mother's ignorance about Judaism is revealed when she tries to explain to the pious nurse why the family does not have a Christmas tree; at the same time, the young woman herself refuses to observe any of the Jewish rituals, because after the Holocaust "there can be no mezuzahs" (*Green* 201). Her husband, however, who escaped the Nazi conflagration by a hair's breadth and who wants a life with Jewish symbols and traditions, tells her: "You don't know enough to discard them" (*Green* 202).

In the early sixties, Rosen was at work on her novel *Touching Evil*, which deals, as Rosen writes in a 1987 essay, "with the response of those not involved directly with the Holocaust except through imagination, and examines its impact on them" (*Accidents of Influence* 49). The writing of the novel was slow and painful; it took six years to complete, from 1961 to 1967. Although, as Rosen explains, she chose "non Jews to do the responding in order to extend as far as possible the reach of the Holocaust upon these witnesses-through-the-imagination," Rosen's feelings at the time of writing were certainly not universalist, but 'terribly and painfully particular, fixated, obsessed with the fate of Jews" (*Accidents of Influence* 49). It was as if the full impact of having married a man touched by the Holocaust was beginning to make itself felt.

In her important essay "The Second Life of Holocaust Imagery" (1987), Rosen sums up one of the themes in *Touching Evil*: "Two women have been stricken by knowledge of the Holocaust: one [Hattie Mews] through watching the Eichmann trial, televised daily in the early sixties; the other [Jean Lamb] through reading documents and seeing photographs of the death camps" (*Accidents of Influence* 49). In her 1974 essay, "On Living in Two Cultures," Rosen illuminates the narrative risks she took when she allowed Jean Lamb to be seduced by her college sociology teacher. He callously transmutes his own shock at the discovery of death camp photographs into sexual conquest. "I made my protagonist, at the time of discovery, young—and vulnerable to horror. I made the moment of discovery the precise moment of sexual seduction, almost of intercourse itself, so that everything should be open and the appearance of penetration complete" (*Accidents of Influence* 10).

For Jean Lamb, the double discovery is so traumatic that she vows not to have children and adopts a figure of the *Shoah* as her symbol. She chooses the woman who claws her way up from the bottom of a pile of corpses. Jean is abandoned by her lover and enters into an affair with a young Puerto Rican named Jesús. At the same time, she is befriended by Hattie Mews, a young pregnant woman, who persuades Jean to watch the Eichmann trial with her. Hattie, Rosen writes in "Notes Toward a Holocaust Fiction" (1990), "is overcome by terror, the child in her womb menaced by what has been loosed in the world. For her, the symbolic figure is the pregnant woman in the death camp, laboring on lice-infested straw, giving birth at the booted feet of a guard. I too was pregnant in 1961, watching the Eichmann trial every day . . . asking the question: How can we live now?" (*Accidents of Influence* 105). Rosen's novel attempts no answer beyond the low-keyed gesture of mutual assistance that the women render each other.

Rosen's next long work picks up on the theme of childbirth and assistance to pregnant women. *At the Center* is an ambitious novel that weighs the pros and cons of abortion as it narrates the everyday lives and personal histories of three doctors working at an abortion clinic. Although the omniscient narrator's stance is firmly proabortion, the novel demonstrates how the daily routine of performing the procedure affects and undermines the idealism of the three (male) doctors. The routine destruction of life, however unwanted these fetuses may be, seeps like a corroding evil into the complicated lives of the three physicians and upsets their domestic arrangements. Separations, adulteries, emotional and psychological cruelties are the perverse side effects of an originally idealistic enterprise, the founding of a family-planning center.

The narrative focus of the novel shifts gradually to Hannah Selig, an aide at the center. Her parents, Hasidic Jews who survived the death camps and came to America, were cruelly murdered in their New York apartment. This caused Hannah's complete lapse from faith. Like a modern Job, she argues in letters and in her journal with the rabbi and with God. Her work at the center as well as her love affair with one of the physicians are part of her rebellion against God's injustice. However, the longer she is exposed to the routine of death at the center, to its corroding, transformative influence, and to its power to harden and embitter the soul, the more she is led back to the moral certainty that faith and observance seem to hold out to her. In the journal entry that prepares her return to some agreement with God, she compares the murder of her parents to the *akedah*, the binding of Isaac by Abraham on Mount Moriah. "Even if there had been no ram, hadn't there been *something* that caused her . . . to thank God that they had never suffered ugliness from within, but only from without, had never returned evil for evil? . . . To suffer bitterly and yet the soul not to die of its poison—that was the ram" (*At the Center* 196).

Through the figure of Hannah Selig, a connection is established between mass abortion and the mechanical routine of murder in the death camps. The link remains in the realm of suggestion and is not further developed. A passage in Rosen's essay "Baby Making" (1982) shows, however, that the connection was on her mind. She writes:

Since legal abortion, it seems to me, is preferable to the evil involved in either illegal abortion or the birthing of unwanted children, I am firmly pro-choice. But sometimes I can sympathize with the anti-choice people. A million abortions a year in America alone seems too much like another one of those sickening numbers of the twentieth century, whose specialty has been mass death. (*Accidents of Influence* 171).

Rosen's short stories, "The Miracle of Dora Wakin's Art" (1985) and "Fences" (1986), also center around death. The earlier story is an allegory reminiscent of Hawthorne and James, in which the death of an artist transforms the perception of her art. The later story leads us back to a family that resembles Rosen's own. An aunt discovers a box containing the prayer shawl of her father who perished in the Holocaust. Her American-born nephew begs to see his grandfather's *tallis*. His parents fear that the *tallis* will raise painful questions. Eventually, father and son examine the shawl and wrap themselves in it. It is the family's boarder, however, who perceives the real issue: "'Grandchild of the Holocaust!'" he exclaims, "'Strange thing to be. All around there are electrified fences. As the grandparents could not get out, so no one else can ever get in. And he has after all an American mother'" ("Fences," 77). Rosen thus touches again on the theme of how the Holocaust can be adequately felt and remembered by those who did not witness it directly.

Rosen's last novel to date, *John and Anzia* (1989), seems almost an escape from all the heaviness. Varying her writer's theme of witnessing through imagination, Rosen re-imagines the brief love affair between a Jewish immigrant, Anzia Yezierska, and an American blue blood, John Dewey. We know that the affair between the writer and the philosopher happened around 1917 and did not last longer than a year. But documents are scarce. Rosen's reinvention brings to life, in the words of her preface, "an era of melting-pot heat, rage for Americanization, and grudge-filled boundaries" (*John and Anzia* ix).

SURVEY OF CRITICISM

Ruth Rosenberg, who wrote the first comprehensive essay on Norma Rosen for the *Dictionary of Literary Biography*, illuminated one specific aspect of Rosen's craft in an onomastic interpretation of the novel *At the Center*. She shows how the complex names of Rosen's characters contain, in fact, ironic comments on the events the novel unfolds. All aspects of naming are controlled in Rosen's fictions. But as I demonstrate in an essay on Holocaust fiction, Rosen's naming is a bit problematic in *Touching Evil*. I argue that the names of Rosen's Gentile protagonists, Hattie Mews, Jean Lamb, and Jesús, constitute a christological subtext that seems to hold out hope in the face of an all-pervasive evil, which is embodied concretely yet symbolically in the figure of Adolf Eichmann. Of course, all ideologies of redemption fail.

It is Rosen's treatment of the Holocaust and her efforts to come to grips with the question of evil as it arises from the systematic destruction of the European Jews that has attracted the most serious critical attention. In her book *By Words Alone*, Sidra DeKoven Ezrahi examines *Touching Evil* and concludes that Rosen achieves in this novel "a partial balance between the narrative of commonplace events in the lives of a few people in New York in 1961 and the subterranean forces of Holocaust evil and suffering which constantly threatens those events" (209–10). In *Crisis and Covenant*, Alan Berger points out that in *Touching Evil*, Rosen "wishes the Jewish experience [of the Holocaust] to be read as a cipher of the human condition" (172). Berger analyzes how Rosen's Gentile characters gain an authentic albeit vicarious knowledge of the Holocaust, and he perceives that Rosen pushes her characters to ask hard questions. "Rosen knows that any authentic post-Holocaust theology, Jewish or Christian, must account for an implicated deity" (174).

In the longest piece published to date on *Touching Evil*, S. Lillian Kremer argues that "the Holocaust has so permeated the lives of Jean and Hattie that it is indeed their Kantian category of reference. . . . Contemporary events, people, and conditions are correlated to Holocaust classifications and definitions. A personal betrayal is "like telling the police where Anne Frank is hiding" (218). Kremer then explores the theological dimensions of the novel, its indictment of God, and its rejection of faith. Like Berger, Kremer claims that Rosen does not consider the Holocaust to be a problem that affects only Jews. But Kremer goes beyond the theological, back to the worldly and human, which is, after all, Rosen's dimension. "One cannot simply curse the Germans," Kremer writes, "and forget them: 'their possibilities are always with us.' Rosen poses the crucial question of our time. Since the Germans '*passed* for human beings, what does that *say* about human beings?' " (221).

And what does it say about Rosen that she is haunted by such questions? In her aptly titled essay "The Soul-Searching of Norma Rosen," Marilyn Goldberg highlights some of the humane and writerly qualities that characterize Rosen's fictions and essays. Goldberg's premise is that "one of the tasks to which Norma Rosen set herself was to create within herself a Jewish soul" (202–03). In fact, Goldberg claims, "the record of [Rosen's] fiction provides an account of her search for Jewish authenticity" (203). From this angle, Goldberg examines the stories collected in *Green* as well as Rosen's three novels *Joy to Levine!*, *Touching Evil*, and *At the Center*. She concludes that an increasing awareness of the simultaneity of good and evil (as exemplified, for instance, in the work of an abortion clinic) transformed Rosen into a mature artist capable of dealing with moral ambiguity.

BIBLIOGRAPHY

Works by Norma Rosen

Joy to Levine! New York: Alfred A. Knopf, 1962.
Green: A Novella and Eight Stories. New York: Harcourt, Brace & World, 1967.
Touching Evil. New York: Harcourt, Brace & World, 1969.
"Walking Distance." *Commentary* (November 1971): 63–68.
"Traveling Toward the Inner Life." *Ms* (November 1972): 77, 111–12, 115.
A Family Passover. By Anne Rosen, Jonathan Rosen, and Norma Rosen; with photographs by Laurence Salzmann. Philadelphia: Jewish Publication Society of America, 1980.
At the Center. Boston: Houghton Mifflin, 1982.
"The Inner Light and the Fire." Forthcoming 1.3/4 (Fall 1983): 4–9.
"The Miracle of Dora Wakin's Art." *Lilith* 12/13 (Winter/Spring 1985): 22–25.
"Fences." *Orim* 1 (Spring 1986): 75–83.
John and Anzia: An American Romance. New York: E. P. Dutton, 1989.
Accidents of Influence: Writing as a Woman and a Jew in America. Albany: State University of New York Press, 1992.

Works about Norma Rosen

Berger, Alan. *Crisis and Covenant: The Holocaust in American Jewish Fiction.* Albany: State University of New York Press, 1985.
Ezrahi, Sidra DeKoven. *By Words Alone: The Holocaust in Literature.* Chicago: University of Chicago Press, 1980.
Goldberg, Marilyn. "The Soul-Searching of Norma Rosen." *Studies in American Jewish Literature* 3 (1983): 202–11.
Klingenstein, Susanne. "Destructive Intimacy: The Shoah Between Mother and Daughter in Fictions by Cynthia Ozick, Norma Rosen, and Rebecca Goldstein." *Studies in American Jewish Literature* 11.2 (1992): 162–73.
Kremer, S. Lillian. "The Holocaust in Our Time: Norma Rosen's *Touching Evil.*" *Studies in American Jewish Fiction* 3 (1983): 212–22.
Rosenberg, Ruth. "Norma Rosen's *At the Center:* A Literary Onomastic Interpretation." *Literary Onomastics Studies* 11 (1984): 165–77.
———. "Norma Rosen." *Dictionary of Literary Biography*, vol 28: *Twentieth Century American Jewish Writers* (Detroit: Gale Research Company, 1984), 248–52.

MURIEL RUKEYSER (1913–1980)

Janet E. Kaufman

BIOGRAPHY

Muriel Rukeyser was born in New York City, in 1913, on the eve of World War I. In her lifetime she witnessed and protested the Spanish Civil War, World War II, the Korean and Vietnam wars. She lived during the Sacco and Vanzetti executions, the Great Depression, and McCarthyism. All these compelled her to work for justice and freedom and to integrate her political life and the life of the psyche in her writing. Rukeyser began writing in adolescence; her first book, *Theory of Flight*, was published when she was twenty-one and was awarded the Yale Younger Poets Prize. At her death in 1980, Rukeyser left us sixteen volumes of poetry; biographies of the scientist Willard Gibbs, the explorer Thomas Harriot, and the political figure Wendell Willkie, a collection of essays exploring the role of poetry in society; translations of the Mexican poet Octavio Paz and the Swedish poet Gunnar Ekelof; six children's books, two novels, and uncollected journalism, essays, plays, and filmscripts.

The daughter of American-born Jewish parents, Rukeyser heard Yiddish at home, though her parents were, like many second-generation Americans, eager to assimilate. Though there was "no mark of Judaism" in their home except for a "silver ceremonial goblet, handed down from a great-grandfather who had been a cantor," and a legend that her mother's family was descended from the second-century Babylonian Talmudic scholar Rabbi Akiba, Rukeyser loved the Bible for its "clash and poetry and nakedness, its fiery vision of conflict resolved only in God." Assuming responsibility for being Jewish offered, she believed, a "guarantee" against the "many kinds of temptation to close the spirit" ("Under Forty" 26, 29).

Her father was a builder in New York. The images from his business of mixing, pouring, and building became central to Rukeyser's poetry. While her ethics and activism resisted her father's conservative politics, his work gave her metaphors for a language of reconciling differences and making peace. Rukeyser resented the lack of genuine dialogue in her family and wrote that the "poetry at home was only that of Shakespeare and the Bible. There were no books in the beginning." Her parents sent her to the Ethical Cultural and Fieldston schools. It is hard to determine to what extent her early educational experiences influenced her social vision. From 1930–32 she attended Vassar College, from which she withdrew due to her father's bankruptcy during the Depression.

Rukeyser's spiritual vision inspired her commitment to social justice, and at all ages, she found resources to nurture that vision. As an adolescent, she took ground-school instruction and, as an adult, flying lessons, for she was fascinated by the technology of aviation and the possibilities for communication and connection that it promised. In 1933 she was arrested for the first time when she traveled with friends to Alabama to witness and report the trial of the Scottsboro boys. Her life of activism involved reporting on and poeticizing the tragedy of silicosis for workers in the West Virginia Gauley Tunnel mining project in the early 1930s, and in the first decade of her career, she came to be associated with proletarian poets for her concerns for the working class. She reported on the anti-Fascist Olympics and the breakout of the Spanish Civil War, resigned from her position as writer for the Office of War Information in 1944, and lectured on poetry and politics at the California Labor School in 1945 and 1948. She traveled incessantly and lived on both coasts of the United States. In 1947, as a single woman, she gave birth to her son and remained a single mother throughout her life—a role which proved challenging in the decade of the 1950s, when her family and her colleagues at Sarah Lawrence College questioned her ability, as an unmarried mother, to provide moral leadership to students. Her poetry's attention to connections between dream life and the unconscious, and political life, offers evidence of her psychoanalysis with the Jungian analyst Frances Wickes through the decade of the fifties. In 1972, she went as a writer on an unofficial peace mission to Hanoi in 1972 with Denise Levertov and traveled as the president of P.E.N. to South Korea in 1975 to fight for a stay of execution and freedom for the imprisoned poet Kim-Chi Ha.

Rukeyser confronted the challenge of a range of illnesses throughout her life. Some of her last poems describe her efforts to teach herself to speak and walk again after suffering a stroke. Her son has commented that while she succumbed to self-doubts, the more fragile she felt, the more she insisted on strength. She always maintained her "belief in the love of the world" and her faith in human beings to repair and transform the world. By living "in full response to earth, to each other, and to ourselves," she believes we could become "more human" (LP 41). Though she never labelled her sexuality, her attitude toward it seems to have been, in the tradition of Whitman, democratic. In poetry and letters, she celebrates her intimate relations with men and with women. Her poetry draws from the experiences of birth and motherhood and the sexuality of old age. It was important to Rukeyser to bring together her identities as a poet, an American, a woman, and a Jew and to let each strengthen the other.

MAJOR THEMES

In her poetry, Rukeyser brought together those identities as poet, American, woman, and Jew by drawing upon the metaphors and the history of each and by finding intersections in the experiences of oppression or freedom that each offered. "The great devastating activity in life," Rukeyser once said, "is to shred all the unities one knows. It isn't that one brings life together—it's that one will not allow it to be torn apart" ("Craft" 32). The roles Rukeyser played in her life—pilot, mother, teacher, political activist, and defender of children's rights—help to explain the range and inclusiveness of her poetic vision. The realms of the political, the spiritual, and the erotic always inform each other in her poetry, and even the structure of her poems tells the story of a poet committed to showing the relationship between spirituality, politics, and art.

Poetry was Rukeyser's chosen form of bridging the realms of the spiritual and the political, the aesthetic and the erotic. Although it is tempting to treat these aspects of her writing chronologically, to show their development over time, the poetry resists this kind of organization, because Rukeyser did all things at all ages. Her poetry is sexual in her old age and philosophical in her youth. At twenty-five she dared to critique corporate America through her poetic rendering of a Union Carbide mining disaster, bringing to it her ethic of attempting to understand the forces that allowed tragedy to prevail. In mid-life she unsentimentally made pregnancy and motherhood a subject for poetry. The material object of the poem was a place where connections could be made and where the poet experimented with the fluid intersection of subject and object, war and the desire for peace, contradictory feelings within herself that, at times, unified in an experience of "transcendence" and the "constellations" of these factors that language negotiates.

Poetry, Rukeyser said, is "more like a transformation than anything I know." It carried "religious meaning" for her ("Craft" 31). Much of her poetry does have the quality of what Kenneth Burke in *Attitudes Toward History* calls "secular prayer" (220) and, as prayer, is one of the tools Rukeyser engages to "live for the impossible." Prayer entails a spiritual risk of participating in a conversation that offers no certainty of response. Poetry allowed Rukeyser to engage at least from one side of the conversation, to fill the silences on her end. From the beginning of her career, Rukeyser was committed to breaking through silences: The poem offers "a plough of thought to break this stubborn ground" (CP 11). She acknowledged that the "sources of poetry are in the spirit seeking completeness" and that "peace is completeness" (LP 224). This language invokes the Hebrew word for peace, *shalom*, and the word for complete, *shalem*, both derived from the same root letters. Her understanding of the way human transformation works parallels the Jewish notions of *tikkun*, or the belief that God created humanity to help repair and complete the world, to make the world whole.

Rukeyser's first published poetic lines reflecting on the meaning of being

Jewish appeared in *Beast in View* (1944), a volume of poetry struggling with the distress of war. A sonnet within the long sequence poem "Letter to the Front" declares that to 'be a Jew in the twentieth century / is to be offered a gift" (CP 239). This poem does not ignore the genocide of the Jews in Europe; rather it declares that the poet will not direct her life or work from the perspective of a victim: Personal power will develop by shaping reality through her own words and actions. The sonnet acknowledges: "The gift is torment." It is a particular kind of torture, a curse. To refuse it is to refuse life. To accept it is to accept "full agonies": ongoing persecution, resistance to that persecution, and the failures of resistance. It is to accept a God who does not fall from grace, but is reduced by humanity from being the "King of Kings" and the 'Host of Hosts" to a "hostage among hostages.' In accepting Judaism as a gift, even while circumstances would make it the greatest curse, Rukeyser accepts the responsibility for *tikkun*. This sonnet has been adopted into the Reform and Reconstructionist prayer books, a fact that "astonished" Rukeyser: "One feels that one has been absorbed into the line and it's very good" ("Craft" 20).

Claiming a distinct capacity for herself as a woman to interpret and prophesy, Rukeyser perceived herself as a contemporary seer in the tradition of women poets throughout history that began for her with Sappho, but also, as she said, with the Biblical prophets Miriam and Deborah who "dealt with triumph and justice." Her poems "Miriam: The Red Sea," and "Ms. Lot" appropriate the voices of those women in attempting to reconcile the aspect of the woman warrior with a heroic and nurturing model of the biblical woman. In "Akiba," Rukeyser questions the poet's role as a witness to personal, religious, and political history.

In her striving to become "more human," Rukeyser used the liturgical power of poetry to call herself forth to political and social action. Though she was "against war" and was classified early on as a social-protest poet, her political poems about war and social injustices are not simply protest poems. They offer a site for negotiating the contradictions that provoke such conflicts and thus offer possibility for envisioning resolution. War, in this poetry, constitutes a place or moment where people in opposition wrestle together. The possibility for making peace occurs in the process of "I" wrestling to respond to "You," or to the "Other." As an American poet, Rukeyser did not speak *for* all Americans, but found ways of acknowledging and accepting the "Other" who is different while staying her own course and bridging the space between herself and the "Other." In a poem like "The Book of the Dead" (CP 102), her poetic investigation of the 1930s Gauley Tunnel mining tragedies in West Virginia, she made poetry a place for the (re)formation of cultural and ethical practice. As an American she broke political and social silences: She would not forget the horrors of American history, nor keep silent, nor stand alone. Rukeyser considered herself to be a person who "makes things much more than a person who protests." Thus, she wrote in her poem "Wherever" that whatever she stands "against" she will "stand feeding and seeding" (CP 514). Her poetry could be seen as an attempt to respond to the question at the end of "The Gates," her concluding title-poem of her last volume of poetry inspired by her mission to Korea to save the poet Kim-Chi Ha: "How shall we speak to all those beginning to run?" (CP573). The dedication of *The Gates* to Kim-Chi Ha's son and to her own grandson suggest that, in this concluding question, Rukeyser was asking both how to explain injustice to children and how to end it. Recurring in this poetry is the implication that the meeting between "I" and "You" leaves the world stronger for those who inherit it. In "It is There," a poem evoking the horror of the Vietnam War, the poet asks what conditions would constitute a peace that could reach "all habitants, all children." The answer lies in the "change and tension of sharing consciousness" across the generations (CP 524). Poetry offered a way of forming transformational dialogue between herself and lovers, political events, historical moments, and, not least, between herself and her reader.

Implicit in Rukeyser's impulse to do the work of transformation is the knowledge that one does not do it alone. It happens in partnership. The multiple ways in which Rukeyser addresses her reader in her poetry suggest that she attempted to make the reader her partner by integrating the reader into the poetic process. For Rukeyser, the poem is not an object but a process, and the "giving and taking of a poem is . . . a triadic relation. It can never be reduced to a pair: We are always confronted by the poet, the poem, and the audience" (LP 187). In "H.F.D.," a poem honoring the stage director Hallie Flanagan, with whom Rukeyser produced her own stage play, she affirmed her sense that the audience is "the most important" ingredient of an artistic production, for its response brings an artistic work alive. Furthermore, she described the meanings of poetry not as something innate to the artifact of the poem, but as something established through the relations between the poet, the poem, and the reader. Because the poet and the reader are "changing, living beings," the experience of poetry constantly changes (LP 187). Rukeyser thought of the reader as a "witness," one who carries responsibility, as well as one who reveals the poem, who imbues it with the power to affect change. Poems fail, Rukeyser believed, if readers "are not brought by them beyond the poems" (LP 63). Therefore, in "What Do We See?" a poem about blindness to social injustice, Rukeyser addresses her audience through a large space between stanzas containing this line: "Cadenza for the reader" (492). Like a conductor, she directs the reader to respond and to be moved to action through the power of response. To establish communication, reaching out toward an "Other" in a personal relationship, such as in "Effort at Speech Between Two People," is one way Rukeyser attempts to break down barriers between people and create "meeting-places."

Her identity as a woman is vital to that process of making "meeting," a point she affirms in her poem "Searching/Not Searching": "I a live woman look up at you this day" (498). Locating herself as a woman in history, in politics, and in mythology in order to understand, critique, and make a place for herself in those arenas is one of the central activities of this poetry. Because for Rukeyser the "universe of poetry is the universe of emotional truth" (LP 21), being a "live woman" meant making oneself vulnerable to that universe. Thus, in her poem "The Poem as Mask," she confessed that when she wrote of the god Orpheus in an earlier poem "it was myself, split open, unable to speak in exile from myself" (CP 35). Here she proclaimed the line which became the title of Howe and Bass's anthology of women's poetry: "No more masks! No more mythologies."

Though she never called herself a feminist, in writing about the personal pain of childhood and the silencing of women in society, and in breaking taboos against women's expression and celebration of sexuality, Rukeyser broke ground for women writers to "explore further ways of reaching our lives" (CP 529) and to create possibilities for their lives by exploring their relationships to women in history. "What would happen if one woman told the truth about her life?" Rukeyser asked in her poem honoring the German artist Kathe Kollwitz. "The world would split open" (CP 482). Louise Bernikow's anthology of women's poetry, *The World Split Open*, took its title from these lines. Rukeyser's poems are filled with the courage it takes to ask such a question, and they offer, as Kate Daniels explained in *Out of Silence*, her thorough and rich introduction to the recently published volume of Rukeyser's selected poems, images of strength and honesty as a response.

The way Rukeyser conceives of intimate and erotic connections between people offers another reference point for understanding the way she sees creativity, power, and emotions operating in the sociopolitical as well as the personal world. While some of her poems suggest or describe a moment in lovemaking, her sense of the erotic goes far beyond that moment, taking into account the role of desire, power, social context, the personal spiritual experience, and even violence. For instance, the passionate moment that concludes the poem "Looking at Each Other" shows the power of desire to bring about "meeting" between two people, a meeting that in turn enhances their vision and enables them to see the coexisting "inner and outer oppression" surrounding them (CP 493).

In turning away from sentimentality, coyness, and modesty—the supposed virtues of women's poetry when Rukeyser came on the scene—Rukeyser found metaphors in the body to describe her perception as well as her poetic form. Daniels describes her as "uncanonical" and "fiercely individual" in that "she refused to bow to the confining influence of earlier conventions of poetry by women." She points out that Rukeyser once declared, "I write from the body, a female body" (xv). This is not to say that Rukeyser believed in an essentialist view of the woman's body, but that she trusted her own experience—which included the experience of her physical body in the world—to give her further ways of understanding and bringing together seemingly contradictory elements of life. Thus, she is "open like a woman" to the meaning of Akiba's story (CP 475) and in Kollwitz sees the "woman as gates" as a metaphor for the possibilities between people (CP 480).

Though Rukeyser's knowledge of traditional prosody and form is apparent in her poetry, she grounds her poetic rhythms and structures in those of the body as well. The repetitions of individual words and phrases in her poems she explained as her "rhymings. . . . The return once is not enough for me. . . . The phrase in a different position is new, as has been pointed out by many poets. . . . It's a time-binding thing, like the recurrence of the heartbeat and the breathing and all the involuntary motions as well. But in a poem I care very much about the physical reinforcement, the structure in a recurrence" ("Craft" 22–23). Punctuation, too, she saw as biological, like breathing: "It is the physical indication of the body-rhythms which the reader is to acknowledge. . . . Not least of all, we need a measured rest" (LP 123). For her printers who were wont to correct her colons and spaces that would appear as they do in the line below from "Effort at Speech," she had a rubber stamp made: "PLEASE BELIEVE THE PUNCTUATION."

> : Speak to me.   Take my hand.   What are you now? (CP 9)

This line is quintessentially Rukeyser, for throughout her poetry, she wrestled with and reached out to the "Other" in order to find a "meeting-place." In her poem "Waterlily Fire," Rukeyser tells a story from the teachings of Buddha. A student asks about the Buddha holding out a lotus flower, "Isn't that fragile?" The teacher responds, "I speak to you. You speak to me. Is that fragile?" (CP 309). Rukeyser seizes upon the knowledge in this story that language between us can be most fragile because it has the power to injure, reject, exclude. Yet just because the lotus is fragile does not mean the Buddha refrains from offering it; just because relationship and dialogue are fragile does not mean we do not speak, do not try to meet each other.

SURVEY OF CRITICISM

Rukeyser's work has received little critical attention since her death, though her books were widely reviewed as they were published. *Out of Silence*, the first volume of her work to be published since her death (all the others are out of print), carries an introduction by Kate Daniels. This introduction places Rukeyser's poetry in relation to her life history and explains precisely the expectations and conventions Rukeyser broke as a woman poet. Louise Kertesz's book, *The Poetic Vision of Muriel Rukeyser*, is the only comprehensive, chronological study of Rukeyser's work to date. Her work relies primarily on the reviews of Rukeyser's work to understand its reception. The book contextualizes Rukeyser's writing according to the literary, social, and political forces that affected it, such as the movement of proletarian writers of the 1930s, the New Critics of the 1940s and 50s, and especially the various wars of the twentieth century. Kertesz succeeds at tracking the development of what she sees as Rukeyser's major themes—vision, touch, speech—juxtaposed against the sociopolitical changes of her times.

An essay by M. L. Rosenthal entitled "Muriel Rukeyser: The Longer Poems'' (1953) discusses ''Theory of Flight,'' ''The Book of the Dead,'' ''The Elegies,'' and ''Orpheus.'' Because this essay came early in Rukeyser's career, it paved the way for further readings of her work. Rosenthal considers these poems according to what he sees as Rukeyser's effort to reconcile ''three sets of assumptions'': those of the ''world-oppressed sensibility,'' the democratic-pragmatic tradition, and scientific and revolutionary materialism (204). His explanation of Rukeyser's experimentation with documentary reporting and dramatic presentation shows how the poet ''met the challenge of centering a poem on a large social problem.'' Rosenthal notes the influence of Eliot, Yeats, and Crane on the then-young poet, as well as her ''universal, prophetic, organic'' romantic rhetoric that links her to poets like Shelley, Lawrence, and Whitman (229).

Virginia Terris's ''Muriel Rukeyser: A Retrospective'' (1974) offers a chronological, philosophical overview of Rukeyser's philosophical perspective. For Terris, Rukeyser's ''greatest creative strengths have manifested themselves in her poems of intimate human relationships and myth-making,'' an aspect of her work overlooked by early critics who built her reputation on the poems of social protest (10). While following the development of Rukeyser's poetic voice, Terris explores the Whitman-Transcendentalist roots of her poetry and explains that Rukeyser's belief in the unity of Being, and her reliance on the experience of the ''self,'' the body, and the senses as a source of truth, tie her to this tradition (10). Terris suggests that we consider Rukeyser a ''female counterpart'' of Whitman for her concern for the ''integration of the self and of the self with the world'' and in the ''power, sensuosity, and self-affirmation'' of her voice (11).

Rachel Blau DuPlessis, in ''The Critique of Consciousness and Myth in Levertov, Rich, and Rukeyser'' (1985), helps to place Rukeyser in context with her contemporaries, arguing that, for these three poets, the ''concern to investigate, to criticize, to protest against the commonplaces of perception and behavior that animates their poems about women leads the poets to examine political forces and power relations that inform individual consciousness'' (128). DuPlessis claims that the act of cultural criticism is the central lyric act of all three of these poets, whether they explore language and consciousness or the individual in history.

Personal essays and commentaries by Kate Daniels, Denise Levertov, Sharon Olds, Adrienne Rich, and Ted Solotaroff reflect the respect and admiration these contemporary writers have for Rukeyser as well as the inspiration she gave them. Daniels grapples with transcending her own life experience to understand and interpret Rukeyser's as she writes Rukeyser's biography, knowing that the poet, in fact, struggled to cross similar bridges. Olds remembers Rukeyser saying many times ''that a poem is not *about* something, a poem *is* something'' (56). Poems for Rukeyser were experiences; they were also actions. Portraying the breadth of Rukeyser's vision, Olds recalls: 'Muriel led us in twenty directions, but always there were three things: there was the personal effort at speech; there were the facts of the world; and there was the form that is the embrace of these two'' (57). Solotaroff writes of Rukeyser, ''Her experiments tended to be on the side of plenitude rather than restriction, of inclusiveness rather than refinement. For she had much to clarify, much to keep alive. In her body and in her mind, in her life and in her art, she fought against numbness'' (43–44). And Adrienne Rich helps us understand that, because Rukeyser ''had always pursued a complex political vision, she never joined the ranks of disillusioned Left artists and intellectuals. Secular and deeply spiritual Jew, sexually independent woman, she never fitted into the canon of Modernism, and has been largely unexplored by critics. American poetry of the past sixty years will be perceived very differently when Muriel Rukeyser is accorded her rightful place'' (''Under Forty'' 26).

BIBLIOGRAPHY

Works by Muriel Rukeyser

Theory of Flight. New Haven: Yale University Press, 1935.
U.S. 1. New York: Covici-Friede, 1938.
A Turning Wind. New York: Viking, 1939.
Wake Island. Garden City, NY: Doubleday, Doran, 1942.
Willard Gibbs. New York: Doubleday, Doran, 1942.
Beast in View. Garden City, NY: Doubleday, Doran, 1944.
The Green Wave. Garden City, NY: Doubleday, Doran, 1948.
Elegies. Norfolk, CT: New Directions, 1949.
The Life of Poetry. New York: Current Books, 1949.
Selected Poems. New York: New Directions, 1951.
Body of Waking. New York: Harper, 1958.
The Colors of the Day. Poughkeepsie, NY: Alumni Association of Vassar College, 1961.
Waterlily Fire: Poems, 1935–62. New York: Macmillan, 1962.
The Orgy. New York: Coward-McCann, 1965.
The Outer Banks. Santa Barbara, CA: Unicorn Press, 1967.
The Speed of Darkness. New York: Random House, 1968.
One Life. New York: Simon and Schuster, 1970.
The Traces of Thomas Hariot. New York: Random House, 1971.
29 Poems. London: Rapp and Whiting: London: Deutsch, 1972.
''Craft Interview with Muriel Rukeyser.'' *New York Quarterly* 11 (1972): 14–37.
Breaking Open. New York: Random House, 1973.
The Gates. New York: McGraw-Hill, 1976.
The Collected Poems of Muriel Rukeyser. New York: McGraw-Hill, 1979.
Out of Silence: Selected Poems, Ed. and introduction Kate Daniels. Evanston, IL: Triquarterly Books, 1992.

Works about Muriel Rukeyser

Bernikow, Louise. *The World Split Open: Four Centuries of Women Poets in England and America, 1552–1950*. New York: Vintage Books, 1974.

Daniels, Kate. "Searching/Not Searching: Writing the Biography of Muriel Rukeyser." *A Special Issue on Muriel Rukeyser*. Ed. Daniels. *Poetry East* 16/17 (1985); 70–93.

DuPlessis, Rachel Blau. "The Critique of Consciousness and Myth in Levertov, Rich, and Rukeyser." *Writing Beyond the Ending*. Bloomington: Indiana University Press, 1985.

Goldstein, Laurence. *The Flying Machine and Modern Literature*. London: Macmillan Press, 1986. 117–24.

Jarrell, Randall, *Poetry and the Age*. New York: Knopf, 1953.

Kertesz, Louise. *The Poetic Vision of Muriel Rukeyser*. Baton Rouge: Louisiana State University, 1980.

Levertov, Denise. *Light Up the Cave*. New York: New Directions, 1981. 189–94.

Marten, Harry. "Exploring the Human Community: The Poetry of Denise Levertov and Muriel Rukeyser." *Sagetrieb* 3.3 (1984): 51–61.

Mort, Jo-Ann. "The Poetry of Muriel Rukeyser." *The Jewish Quarterly* 28.4 (1980–81): 20–21.

Nichols, Kathleen. "A Woman's Odyssey: Muriel Rukeyser's 'Searching/Not Searching' " *Perspectives on Contemporary Literature* 8 (1982); 27–33.

Novak, Estelle G. "The Dynamo School of Poets." *Contemporary Literature* 2 (1970): 526–39.

Olds, Sharon. "A Student's Memoir of Muriel Rukeyser," in Daniels, 49–69.

Rich, Adrienne. "Muriel Rukeyser 1913–1978: Poet . . . Woman . . . American . . . Jew." *Bridges* 1.1 (1990): 23–26.

Rosenthal, M. L. "Muriel Rukeyser: The Longer Poems." *New Directions in Prose and Poetry* 14 (1953): 202–29.

———. *The New Poets: American and British Poetry Since World War II*. New York: Oxford University Press, 1967.

Rosenthal, Marilyn. *Poetry of the Spanish Civil War*. New York: New York University Press, 1975.

———. "Under Forty." *Contemporary Jewish Record* 7 (1944): 4–9. Rpt. in *Bridges* 1.1 (1990): 26–29.

Solotaroff, Ted. *A Few Good Voices in My Head*. New York: Harper and Row, 1987. 40–45.

Terris, Virginia. "Muriel Rukeyser: A Retrospective." *American Poetry Review* 3 (1974): 10–15.

Untermeyer, Louis. "The Language of Muriel Rukeyser." *Saturday Review* 10 August 1940: 11–13.

SUSAN FROMBERG SCHAEFFER (1941–   )

Dorothy S. Bilik

BIOGRAPHY

Susan Fromberg Schaeffer, Brooklyn-born and New York bred, spent her late adolescence and early young womanhood at the University of Chicago, where she earned a doctoral degree with honors by the time she was twenty-five. As of this writing, she is the author of nine novels, a collection of short stories, five collections of poetry as well as more than four hundred poems in many publications, two books for young people, the lyrics for a modern madrigal, at least nine scholarly articles, and more than one hundred book reviews. She is currently at work on a book of poetry, a novel, and some shorter fiction. She has been a full professor at Brooklyn College since 1974, and in 1985, she was appointed Broeklundian Professor of English. She teaches a full program in Creative Writing, she says, because it gets her out of the house. She lives with her husband Neil, a professor of eighteenth-century English literature at Brooklyn College, who after translating and editing the letters of the Marquis de Sade, is now working on a biography of de Sade.

The Schaeffers have adjoining studies in their large Victorian house. "It is an odd third floor up here, the two of us and our peculiar projects," observes Schaeffer (letter to the writer, 24 April 1993). They share the house with their two active teenage children and a more sedentary German shepherd. They also have a house in Vermont and recently have begun spending part of the year in England, where "for no sensible reason, I am always so much happier" (letter to the writer, 24 April 1993).

In January 1993, in response to a request from her publisher, Schaeffer wrote a memoir, *Memories Like Splintered Glass: Growing Up in New York,* which evokes haunting memories of place, including kitchens where mothers and grandmothers worked together while fathers went off to garment factory lofts. These recollections would be familiar to most second- and third-generation New Yorkers. At the same time, a number of Schaeffer's most compelling childhood memories are more anomalous yet recognizable to readers of her novels. For example, her immigrant grandfather, a pharmacist, once shot an armed intruder seeking drugs; he was killed himself, years later, by just such a criminal. The shooting occurred sometime after Schaeffer's grandmother had separated from her jealous husband who had threatened her with a gun. The grandmother, a particularly strong presence in the writer's life and work, lived with the Schaeffers until, according to Schaeffer's father, she came after him with a kitchen knife. What gives this operatic event a particularly Schaefferian character is that it was Susan's childhood misbehavior that provoked the conflict between mother-in-law and son-in-law.

Parts of Schaeffer's family history have been transformed into art or, in Schaeffer's words, "gilded by the alchemy of time" (Schaeffer, unpublished memoir 8). For example, the story of the charming uncle who spent time in Sing Sing has been assimilated into a number of her novels. Other details of her family background have not been transformed into the stuff of fiction. Both of Schaeffer's parents were well educated. Her father earned a B.A. and a Law degree, but then became a clothing manufacturer like his father. Her mother has a master's degree and taught Spanish at a Queens high school. Schaeffer recalls:

Much later, in a new house I find her Master's thesis in a white cardboard box, at the bottom of a closet. Even the attic is neat . . . Hanging above the cardboard box is her wedding dress, . . . When I see the dress brushing the sealed box, I shake my head and say, This will never happen to me. (unpublished memoir, 10)

Violent deaths other than her grandfather's have occurred in Schaeffer's family. Her formidable grandmother, who warned of the perils of eating fish, died of choking on a fish bone. Her father, who was afraid of heights, fell from a ski lift in Alaska in the middle of the summer. "Their deaths suit them: if the purpose of life is irony" (unpublished memoir, 13).

Rather than irony, the purpose of Schaeffer's life has been shaped by her commitment to the world of letters, as she eloquently and elegantly expresses it:

I don't know what drives me but I am driven. I've always said I would stop writing if I could and that, if someone would found a chapter of Writers Anonymous, I would attend the first meeting. But now I think that's not true. Writing is my best and truest way of expressing myself . . . probably my *only* way of expressing myself . . . When I'm writing I am as happy as anything on the face of the earth ever is . . . I suffer enough . . . before finding the entrance to the trail into the forest—but once I've begun, it's a kind of absolute reconciliation with the world and at such times it seems as if whatever goes wrong can't make any difference . . . .Naturally the instant I finish, write the last page, the ravens are back, heavy in the trees. (letter to the writer, 18 March 1993)

MAJOR THEMES

Schaeffer's fictional *oeuvre* is markedly broad, ranging in content from *shtetl* life before World War I, urban Jewish life in Poland before and during the

Holocaust, the war in Vietnam, photography and insanity in nineteenth-century Vermont, and the alternate life stories of a Hollywood star and her West Indian housekeeper. The novels sometimes grow out of scholarly research, interviews, newspaper files, old photographs, and other realia. The centers of consciousness in these novels are seemingly quite different from the more obviously autobiographical, contemporary narratives where the protagonist is a graduate student or, in the later novels, an established Jewish writer, wife, and mother. The Schaeffer-like heroines of these latter novels are ironic, self-deprecating, and funny.

Despite differences in time, place, and narrator, most of the fiction is marked by its attention to the intergenerational conflicts within families that, if not resolved, are at least accommodated. Although Schaeffer often focuses on three generations of women and employs predominantly female narrators, she radically departed from her usual practice in *Buffalo Afternoon*. Here she used a working-class Italian-American male central figure who battles with a brutal, unfeeling father only to undergo the carnage and horror of the Vietnam War. Even in this explosive, harrowing narrative Schaeffer is, as always, preoccupied with memory and time, with the uses of the past—the historic past and the personal past.

Inherent in her explorations of the construction of memory in her poetry and prose is a pervasive recognition of loss. The recognition may be simply expressed, as in a poem in which the irretrievable loss of love is compared in a homely simile to coins falling out of a hole in a purse (*Rhymes*, 54), or more complexly in the devastating losses of the Holocaust survivor of *Anya*. The novel *Time in Its Flight*, ostensibly about photography and three generations of family life in nineteenth-century Vermont, profoundly explores loss, mortality, and memory while simultaneously celebrating ordinary life.

While doing research for *Time in Its Flight*, Schaeffer found newspaper clippings about a murder trial of a young woman accused of killing another woman after discovering they were both engaged to the same man. The result, many years later, was *The Madness of a Seduced Woman*. The passionate, obsessive protagonist of *The Madness of a Seduced Woman* rejects her past. However, Agnes's attempts to reshape her life lead to madness and murder.

A number of factors contribute to the scope and complexity of Schaeffer's work, and they sometimes elude her critics. Her dissertation topic, "Folding the Patterned Carpet: Form and Theme in the Novels of Vladimir Nabokov," should alert the reader to the need for close attention to the intricate narrative shifts and underlying patterns of her prose. Like the fiction of Nabokov and Henry James, Schaeffer's works need to be read with awareness of the form that underlies the foreground of plot and character. Also contributing to the texture of Schaeffer's fiction is her use of folkloric and magical elements that go beyond the conventions of realistic fiction. Like Yeats, Isaac Bashevis Singer, and Cynthia Ozick, she dares to invoke the supernatural. The spirits of the living and the dead appear and mingle in Schaeffer's fictional worlds and in the dreams and nightmares of her protagonists.

One example of her daring is *Anya*, her novel of the Holocaust, which, despite its horrendous subject matter, takes the form of a romance depicting life as it ought to have been. The effect is the opposite of the reductivism of the banality of evil. Instead, by employing the literary conventions and allusions of the fairy tale, twentieth-century evil is rendered more ugly and inexplicable in a fictional context where courageous, admirable characters who live vivid, idealized lives are cruelly and wantonly destroyed.

In *The Queen of Egypt*, a collection of short fiction, Schaeffer experiments with a number of different modes, including fantasy and satire. "The Taxi," "Why the Castle?" and some of the other stories convey a Kafkaesque or Borgesian sensibility not always apparent in her fiction but more evident in her poetry.

Schaeffer's novels, especially those based on other people's memories, are notable for their dense and richly detailed textures. Holocaust survivors and Vietnam veterans are amazed at the authenticity of her descriptions of events she could not have experienced. She interviewed survivors and veterans for her material. But even when Schaeffer's novels are ostensibly based on "outside" sources, they are autobiographical in that the thoughts and emotions of the characters provide alter egos, disguises, and screens for the writer's inner life at the time of writing. In "The Unreality of Realism," Schaeffer differentiates between the surface of a novel—plot, characters, narrative structures—and its true subject. Using music as metaphor, Schaeffer notes that "the events of a novel, like the notes of a melody, do not constitute the story or the song; they exist to create the emotion which inevitably derives from a particular, though ageless, emotional vision of life" (736).

Her latest novel, *First Nights*, has a characteristically complex narrative strategy. The protagonists, a Garbo-like reclusive film star and her West Indian housekeeper, are the alternating narrators under the benign prodding of the one-time "most famous director in the world." Now a very old man, he is making this last "film" out of taped and written conversations, confessions, memories, photographs, and, above all, stories of the two now-dead women. The novel is fittingly cinematographic, with snippets of italicized film scripts, West Indian myths, fadeouts, abrupt transitions, and often-striking visual imagery. Though the warm, loyal aptly named Ivy Cook would seem to provide an emotional contrast to the icy actress, Anna Asta, there is no doubt about the affection and mutual regard between the women.

But the work is also about different ways of telling a story and, as always in Schaeffer, the importance of family, memory, and the gain and loss of love. Ultimately, *First Nights* is about the inhumanity intrinsic in the making of a work of art—film, fiction, or persona—where pattern is more important than people. (A more comic and manic variation of this theme may be found in her O. Henry Award-winning story "The Exact Nature of Plot"). The novel also raises questions about the nature of beauty, of guilt and expiation. As in most of Schaeffer's fiction, the intricate narrative pattern is meant to convey how fragmentary and ambiguous are our perceptions of others and of ourselves. The protean nature of truth is again emphasized in the frequent references to fairy tales, half-remembered, forgotten, misread, and, most colorfully, hand-crafted by a West Indian "story-tailor" to fit the listener's wishes.

SURVEY OF CRITICISM

In 1984, Susan Kress wrote that, despite her impressive imaginative range and her considerable success as an innovative poet and novelist, Susan Fromberg Schaeffer is "still awaiting an extended critical evaluation which will attempt to assess the importance of her total achievement" (276).

Since Kress's article, Schaeffer has written four major novels, two young adult books, and two critical introductions. Unquestionably, her novels have been widely and usually enthusiastically reviewed. However, with the exception of two articles by Katherine Gottschalk and Mickey Pearlman, Kress's comment on the dearth of extended criticism remains valid today. Nevertheless, it is a rare and fortunate writer whose first published works are favorably reviewed by Wayne Booth, as were Schaeffer's. "I cannot remember another first book of poems that appeared to me more exciting" was Booth's comment as cited on the back jacket of *The Witch and the Weather Report* (1972). Of Schaeffer's first novel, *Falling*, Booth said, "I love this novel—first reading, second reading, browsing" and compared it to "the best of Bellow" (56–57). Both Booth and Pearl Bell point out that Schaeffer is a "genuinely funny" writer, an attribute frequently overlooked by reviewers of her mainly serious fiction. Very serious indeed was *Anya*, Schaeffer's novel of the Holocaust, which won the Edward Lewis Wallant Award and the Friends of Literature Award in 1974.

In *Love*, Schaeffer reinterprets some of the history of a Jewish family that was a significant feature of her first novel. Susan Kress writes that "the compassion that Elizabeth Kamen of *Falling* must work for, the perspective she must earn is here achieved" (279).

Katherine K. Gottschalk, in a critical article, confronts the relationships of mothers and daughters in Schaeffer's fiction. Gottschalk, for the most part, focuses on the contemporary novels, with the woman writer as central character, but she also includes in her discussion *The Madness of a Seduced Woman*. Gottschalk points out that Schaeffer's contemporary women protagonists, Elizabeth in *Falling*, Eleanor in *Mainland*, and Iris in *The Injured Party*, are paralyzed when first encountered and will ultimately recover as writers, wives, and mothers, while Agnes of *Madness* ends up half-paralyzed, unmarried, and childless and recognizes how the past "has paralyzed her forever in the present" (154).

Mickey Pearlman also writes of the literary women protagonists and stresses the importance of mutability in Schaeffer's "dark comedies," and she concludes that "the author is an undervalued interpreter of the spatial relationships, familial disenchantments, and identity crises that, to some extent, are part of every contemporary reader's experience" (147).

Buffalo Afternoon, Schaeffer's eighth novel, with its male protagonist and Vietnam setting, has been hailed by Nicholas Proffitt as "one of the best treatments of the Vietnam war to date, and all the more impressive for the fact that its author never heard a shot fired in anger or set foot in that country" (7). Proffitt was *Newsweek* correspondent and bureau chief in Vietnam. In the *London Review of Books*, John Sutherland comments that "No one is going to accuse *Buffalo Afternoon* of pulling its punches and much of the novel is physically nauseating" (11). Sutherland concludes that "Schaeffer has written a novel which is extraordinarily tender and moving in its treatment of delayed casualty" (26).

First Nights, Schaeffer's latest novel, appeared in late April 1993. Reviewers, Belva Plain and Robert Plunket emphasize the Hollywood and Greta Garbo elements of the work. Says Plunket, "The problems faced by the most beautiful woman in the world are not the sort that trouble the average reader, and it is not until the conclusion of the book, in an ending both effective and affecting, that Anna becomes a real human being" (21).

Despite their complexities, several of Schaeffer's novels have enjoyed popular success. Both *Anya* and *The Madness of a Seduced Woman* have been widely translated, and both have been international as well as national best-sellers. *Madness* was a main selection of the Book of the Month Club in Sweden, and much to its author's surprise, her third novel, *Time in Its Flight*, was a main selection of the Book of Month Club in this country. An appreciative Clifton Fadiman writing in the *Book of the Month Club News* cautioned reviewers and readers who were looking for a conventional family chronicle in the manner of Galsworthy that *Time in Its Flight* was more akin to *War and Peace* (cited in Schaeffer, "Unreality," 735).

BIBLIOGRAPHY

Works by Susan Fromberg Schaeffer

Fiction

Falling. 1973. Rpt. New York: Ivy Books, 1991.
Anya. 1974. Rpt. New York: Ivy Books, 1991.
Time in Its Flight. New York: Pocket Books, 1978.
The Queen of Egypt and Other Stories. New York: Dutton, 1980.
Love. 1981. Rpt. New York: Ivy Books, 1991.
The Madness of a Seduced Woman. 1983. Rpt. New York: NAL/Plume, 1991.
Mainland. 1985. New York: Bantam Books, 1986.
The Dragons of North Chittendon. New York: Simon and Schuster, 1986.
The Injured Party. 1986. Rpt. New York: St. Martin's Press, 1987.

The Four Hoods and Great Dog. St. Martin's Press, 1988.
Buffalo Afternoon. 1989. Rpt. New York: Ivy Books, 1990.
First Nights. New York: Alfred A. Knopf, 1993.

Poetry

The Witch and the Weather Report. New York: Seven Woods Press, 1972.
Granite Lady. New York: Macmillan, 1975.
Rhymes and Runes of the Toad. New York: Macmillan, 1975.
Alphabet for the Lost Years. San Francisco: Gallumaufry, 1977.
The Bible of the Beasts of the Little Field. New York: Dutton, 1980.

Scholarly Articles

"The Unwritten Chapters in *The Real Life of Sebastian Knight*." *Modern Fiction Studies* 13 (Winter 1967–1968): 427–42.
"The Editing Blinks of Vladimir Nabokov's *The Eye*." *University of Windsor Review* 8.1 (1972): 5–30.
"Bend Sinister and the Novelist as Anthropomorphic Diety." *Centennial Review* 17 (Spring 1973): 115–51.
"Under the Chronoscope: A Study of Peter Redgrove's *Wedding at Nether Powers*. *Poetry Review*. London: Redgrove Special Issue. (Sept. 1981): 45–48.
"The Unreality of Realism." *Critical Inquiry* 6 (Summer 1982): 726–37.
Introduction. *Villette*. By Charlotte Bronte. New York: Bantam, 1986. 7–23.
Memories Like Splintered Glass: Growing Up in New York. Unpublished memoir, ts. 1993.

Interviews

"A Conversation with Susan Fromberg Schaeffer. With Harold U. Ribalow. *The Tie That Binds: Conversations with Jewish Writers*. Ed. Harold U. Ribalow, San Diego and New York: A. S. Barnes, 1980. 77–92.
"Susan Fromberg Schaeffer." With Mickey Pearlman. *Inter/View: Talks with America's Writing Women*. Eds. Mickey Pearlman and Katherine Usher Henderson, Lexington, KY: University Press of Kentucky, 1990. 58–63.

Works about Susan Fromberg Schaeffer

The following list does not include book reviews unless they are cited in the text.

Avery, Evelyn, Gross. "Tradition and Independence in Jewish Feminist Novels." *MELUS* 7.4 (1980): 49–55.
Bell, Pearl K. "From Brooklyn to the Bronx." *New Leader* (6 Aug. 1973): 15–16.
Bilik, Dorothy S. *Immigrant Survivors: Post-Holocaust Consciousness in Recent American Literature*. Middletown, CT: Wesleyan University Press, 1981: 101–11.
Booth, Wayne C. "Elizabeth's Fight for a Life of Her Own." *New York Times Book Review* 20 May 1973: 56–57.
Gottschalk, Katherine K. "Paralyzed in the Present: Susan Fromberg Schaeffer's Mothers or Daughters." *Mother Puzzles: Daughters and Mothers in Contemporary Amer-

ican Literature. Ed. Mickey Pearlman. Westport, CT: Greenwood Press, 1989. 141–157.

Kress, Susan. ''Susan Fromberg Schaeffer.'' *Twentieth Century American-Jewish Fiction Writers.* Ed. Daniel Walden. Detroit: Gale, 1984. Vol. 28 of *Dictionary of Literary Biography*, 28 vols.

Mazurkiewicz, Margaret. ''Susan Fromberg Schaeffer.'' *Contemporary Authors: New Revision Series.* Eds. Linda Metzger and Deborah A. Straub, eds. Detroit: Gale, 1986. Vol. 18. of 137 vols.

Pearlman, Mickey. ''Susan Fromberg Schaeffer: The Power of Memory, Family, and Space.'' *American Women Writing Fiction: Memory, Identity, Family, Space.* Ed. Mickey Pearlman. Lexington, KY: University Press of Kentucky, 1989: 137–152.

Plain, Belva. ''Close-up on a Cast of Two.'' *Washington Post Book World.* 18 April 1993: 6.

Plunkett, Robert. ''Garbo by Any Other Name.'' *New York Times Book Review.* 30 May 1993: 21.

Proffitt, Nicholas. ''Pete Bravado's War and Peace.'' *New York Times Book Review*, 21 May 1989: 7.

Sutherland, John. Rev. of *Buffalo Afternoon. London Review of Books.* 28 Sept. 1989: 11, 26.

LYNNE SHARON SCHWARTZ (1939–   )

Susan Meyer

BIOGRAPHY

Born in 1939 in Brooklyn, New York, to Jack M. Sharon, a lawyer and accountant, and Sarah (Slatus) Sharon, Lynne Sharon Schwartz grew up in what she describes as the stifling conventionality of Brooklyn in the forties and fifties. In the Brooklyn of her childhood, she writes, "urbanity and provinciality, incarnate in the decent, poignant ambitions and values of second-generation Eastern European Jews, made a troubling mix" (Colby 753). At the age of seven, Schwartz wrote her first stories, but she soon experienced the suppression of this imaginative childhood self by the pressures of Brooklyn conventionality. The first twenty-five years of her life were, she notes, "filled with everything that was Brooklyn in the 1950's" (Pearlman 190). In 1957, at the age of eighteen, she married her husband, Harry Schwartz, now a city planner, and together they had two daughters, Rachel Eve and Miranda Ruth. Schwartz attended Barnard and graduated in 1959; in 1961, she received a master's degree from Bryn Mawr. But as she described her life in this era in a recent interview: "I got married very young, and—I don't know, I stopped thinking . . . I followed my husband around, and wherever he got a job, I would get one of these odd jobs— I was an editor, translator, this and that" (Smith 69). Her work in these years included a position as associate editor for *Writer* magazine in Boston (1961– 63) and work as a writer for Operation Open City, a civil rights and fair housing organization. But looking back on this time, she sees her life as passive and aimless: "I didn't think," she says, "I must say, my brain was . . . mesmerized. I guess growing up in the 50's was just too powerful. I let myself drift and wait and do nothing—I don't know why. I was like lots of other women" (Smith 69).

Between 1967 and 1972, Schwartz studied Comparative Literature at graduate school at NYU, only to arrive, at the point of beginning the dissertation, at a crisis: "I couldn't face it; every topic I thought of was no good, and every time I went down in the NYU stacks I'd just get sick. Then suddenly it dawned on me: I was a little over 30, and if I was going to write, I'd better write. I had thought it would *happen*—I would wake up one day and be writer—but I didn't *do* it'' (Smith 69). She dropped out of the Ph.D. program and began to write. Her short stories were published in such magazines as the *Ontario Review*, *Transatlantic Review*, and *Redbook* and were received with much commendation. Several were chosen for anthologies, including the *Best American Short Stories* of 1978 and 1979 and the *O. Henry Prize Stories* of 1979. She won awards in the 1970s as well from Vanguard Press, for "Lucca," and from the Lamport Foundation, for "Rough Strife." At the encouragement of Ted Solotaroff, an editor at Harper & Row, she took that story, as well as several others with the same characters, and transformed them into a short novel, *Rough Strife*, which was published in 1980.

Rough Strife explores, with intimate intensity, the changing relationship between Caroline and Ivan over the course of twenty years of marriage. Her work on this novel was an important turning point in her career, because, Schwartz notes, "it really changed what I could be from a writer of short stories into a novelist" (Smith 68). *Rough Strife* was followed in 1981 by *Balancing Acts* (actually her first novel to be completed, although the second to be published). This novel focuses on the relationship between Alison Markman, a Westchester adolescent, and Max Fried, a former circus performer now resisting the constrictions of old age. In 1983, Schwartz went on to publish *Disturbances in the Field*, a novel of more epic proportions that traces the interconnected lives of Lydia Rowe and the college friends with whom she bonds in late-night philosophy discussions in a Barnard dormitory. Schwartz's two highly diverse collections of short stories and meditations, some of which use her own family as characters, *Acquainted with the Night and Other Stories*, and *The Melting Pot and Other Subversive Stories*, came out in 1984 and 1987. In 1985, she published *We Are Talking About Homes*, a nonfictional account of the destruction of her family's New York apartment building by fire and the subsequent struggle of the tenants to force the landlord, Columbia University, to restore their homes. Schwartz's most recent novel is *Leaving Brooklyn* (1989): More experimental in form than her earlier realist fiction, it explores questions about memory, vision, and story-telling through a plot in which Audrey, a Brooklyn adolescent, escapes the constraints of postwar Brooklyn through a series of sexual encounters with her Manhattan eye doctor. In the same year, Schwartz published a picture book. *The Four Questions*, a retelling of the Passover story for small children. Her translation from the Italian of Liana Millu's *Smoke Over Birkenau*, an account of women's experiences in the concentration camp, was published in 1991 and received the 1991 PEN Renato Poggioli Award. Lynne Sharon Schwartz has received considerable acclaim for her writing: she now lives with her family in New York City.

MAJOR THEMES

Lynne Sharon Schwartz's fiction is very much preoccupied with the nature of individual subjectivities. She dwells particularly on individualities of perspective and vision, often through an attention to literal vision: Eye problems and operations, flawed eyes, mismatched eyes, contact lenses, and mirrors recur repeatedly in Schwartz's *oeuvre* as metaphors for subjectivity, for the individual's relation to the external world. Individual modes of organizing experience are of central importance as well. Schwartz's characters often understand life through metaphors drawn from their careers: Caroline, a mathematician, wondering if she has expended too much of her life's energy on her marriage, contemplates her wedding ring with an attention born of her study of topology, thinking that a circle is ''a trivial knot'' (*Rough Strife* 79). Max Fried, meanwhile, feels the waning force of his life as the white light he once used to focus his center and balance as a young circus performer.

Yet, if the individual subjectivity is one focus in Schwartz's work, it finds its counterpoint in the fiction's equally intense emphasis on the ''rough strife'' of human bonds. The pull between the individual and the larger, less comprehensible movements of history provides an important tension in Schwartz's work. Her characters tend to live intense private lives while the larger events of the world swirl around them, only occasionally entering consciousness: As Caroline thinks, in Schwartz's first novel, playing on the popular slogan of the seventies, ''the political is so impersonal'' (187). Schwartz's characters struggle more successfully, although ambivalently, to connect with one another on an individual level, particularly within marriages and families. Imagery of blood and bleeding often marks significant moments of either complete or partial human bonding. Yet Schwartz's fiction also records failures of connection, particularly between generations. The writing is often characterized by a mood of yearning, nostalgia, and loss.

One of the losses experienced by Schwartz's characters, which is at the same time one source of the slippage between generations, is of a communal identity and shared sense of history. Many of Schwartz's characters are secular Jews: Her fiction explores the intricacies of their historical (and intellectual) position with force and poignancy.

Schwartz's first novel, *Rough Strife*, for example, is about a mixed marriage, between Ivan, the grandson of Jewish immigrants, and Caroline, of New England Protestant derivation. The novel devotes more attention to other ways in which their marriage is a union of contraries, if not opposites; at one point, Caroline and Ivan discuss their different ethnicities. Shortly after their marriage, Caroline asks Ivan if his parents will mind that she is not Jewish, No, he answers: his grandparents wanted American children and ''got them with vengeance'': his American-born parents, he says sadly, became like the people around them and have forgotten their history. When Caroline presses her question, asking whether Ivan himself will mind that she is not Jewish, he answers, ''It's not anything missing in you, so how could I mind? I only mind what is missing in me'' (65). As he says this, she feels him withdraw ''to some remote, hollow recess, a place within that her burrowing might never reach'' (65). As this passage implies, the various losses experienced by Caroline and Ivan, particularly of real connection with any people or history external to their marriage, both cause the intensity of their relationship and plague it.

Yet Schwartz's attitude toward the traditional Judaism of an earlier generation is not so romantic or idealizing as this passage in her first novel might seem to indicate. The complexities of her attitude are perhaps best encapsulated in he long story "The Melting Pot," which gives its title to her second collection of stories. In this story, Schwartz suggests the historical inevitability of the loss of the traditional cultures that have come together in America, as well as points out that advances for women are at odds with many traditions. Yet, at the same time, the story shows the painful costs of the loss of cultural identity. Rita, the protagonist, is the child of a Jewish father and a Mexican, immigrant mother who fatally stabs him in a fight when Rita is two yeas old. Her father dead, her mother first in prison and then vanished, Rita is brought up by her paternal grandparents, Orthodox Jews and Russian immigrants. She remains ignorant, until adolescence, of her parents' story. But even as a child, Rita feels like something of an outsider: Dark of complexion, she is always chosen to play Vashti, the alien and rebellious woman, in the Purim play, never Esther, the beautiful Jewish heroine. At the age of eighteen, Rita learns the story of her family and leaves to study at Berkeley: There she learns to speak Spanish like a native and wanders through San Francisco looking for her mother, whom she thinks may have been a battered wife. After college, she becomes an immigration lawyer and starts a relationship with Sanjay, an older Indian widower, who came to the United States thirty years before.

The story is about Rita's struggles to come to terms, psychologically, with who she is, and through he story, Schwartz comments on the problem of post-immigrant identity. On the one hand, the story suggests the generosity of spirit (and historical inevitability) in American mingling: Rita's Orthodox grandfather, the voice of an earlier generation, feels "the call of the blood" (19) only with other Jews, other Jewish immigrants, while Rita, whom he calls a "bleeding heart" (4), in her work as an immigration lawyer helps all kinds of immigrants into the country. The story also demonstrates the inequality with which women are treated in traditional cultures. As the story opens, Rita dreams that she causes a disaster at her grandfather's funeral by refusing to move to the women's side: all the mourners collapse in shock, "both sexes heaped together, mingling" (1). Rita's dream indicates her fear that her female independence will result in the destruction of the old traditions and chaotic mingling, while at the same time, it demonstrates her anger at the sexism of the traditional Jewish culture.

But without idealizing traditional Judaism, Schwartz's story shows the costs of the loss of identity produced by the intermingling of American immigrant history. In her halfness, Rita feels eternally like an outsider: Unable to belong to either culture, she feels "wispy vapors of another way she might once have been, another mode of feeling the world, as believers in reincarnation sense their past lives" (12). That her two halves are at war with each other is suggested by her father's violent demise. The tension between her two halves results in a loss of identity, a blankness: "there are times when she thinks of her name and who it stands for, and it is like looking in a mirror and seeing a blank sheet, the sheet covering a mirror in the house of the bereaved" (34). For Rita, identity is elusive—centrality seems always to be elsewhere, to belong to someone else. Searching for an authentic identity, she attempts, paradoxically, to find one in "otherness," by merging with her Indian lover's ethnicity. She eats his Indian food (prepared by his dutiful daughter) and, in the final scene, dresses in the sari of his dead wife. Only then, enacting the elusive "otherness" of identity by masquerading as a traditional, submissive Indian woman, does she feel centrally positioned in a culture; only then is she able to see a face in the mirror rather than blankness. In this final scene, she attempts to become, in a manic version of a Purim celebration, not the outcast, rebellious Vashti of her childhood, but the good Jewish woman: what she sees, paradoxically, in her sari-draped figure in the mirror is "Queen Esther, at last" (35). In this story, Schwartz makes clear that assimilation, the mixing of cultures, and even advancements for women, although all inevitable—there is no going back, except in masquerade—happen at a profound cost. Some of her other stories, particularly "Killing the Bees" and "The Opiate of the People," deal with similar issues.

Balancing Acts, Schwartz's second novel, touches, mockingly, on the blandness and absences that characterize the lives of Jews in an American suburbia from which ethnicity has been purged. The novel traces the conflictive friendship between Max Fried, a former traveling circus performer, who now lives in a "health-related facility" for the aged in Westchester, and Alison Markman, who suffers similar institutional incarceration of the stifling routine of a Westchester junior high. With the character of Max, Schwartz evokes the image of the Jew as nomad: Max still keeps a "wandering Jew" houseplant and has spent much of his youth as such a wanderer. By the time of Alison's generation, Jews have become firmly rooted in the American suburbs, but that this apparent historical progress is in fact a diminishment is suggested by Schwartz's parodic characterization of Alison's father. The only residue of the nomadic Jewish life that remains in this suburban generation is embodied in Josh Markman, traveling salesman, who trades in trailer homes. (The commodity Markman sells also marks the distant, diminished link between him and Max: a circus performer and true nomad, Max once inhabited such trailers.)

Alison's anomie, which drives her attempted friendship with Max, is partly a function of the assimilationist normativeness of her Westchester suburb (similar to the suburb to which Ivan's parents move in *Rough Strife*, exacerbating his sense of loss of history). Rather like Rita, Alison Markman fantasizes about discovering a more resonant identity through exotic "others": she dreams of living on an Indian reservation in the West, leading African archaeological digs, writing a book about famous vegetarians such as Gandhi. But above all, Alison wants to know Max, who has lived what she imagines to be the romantic wanderer's life of the circus performer and who consequently incarnates a more resonant, substantive identity. Max, however, has no intention of letting Alison into his life: The son of Ukrainian immigrants, he escaped his own family's wearisome Delancey Street history by ascending first to the roof of the tenement, where he amused himself by walking the ledge of the roof, and then to the trapeze and high wire of the traveling circus: "[s]econd-generation American, he became upwardly mobile, up and up, till he was scaling a rope to a metal bar hung in cavernous space . . . .He knew he was Urban Jew at play like Tarzan; but defying the social odds, he stayed up there half a life" (51). Max is suspended in this world apart (first in actuality and then in memory), and is married, until her death, to Suzy, another trapeze artist; without children, Max has attempted to escape from generational continuity and insertion in history, until Alison tries to claim him. Alison's attempted bond with Max is difficult for both, since Max resists, but it is perhaps more successful than other intergenerational struggles in Schwartz's fiction in that the end of the novel suggests the solitary Alison's achieved connection, through this bond, with the rest of the world. The novel ends, after Max's death, with Alison, her finger cut, bleeding in the ladies' room of an ice-cream parlor, her blood a suggestion of the cyclical women's bleeding which will link her ineluctably with cycles of humanity and mortality. Max's neighbor and friend in the health-care facility, Lettie Blumenthal, urges the bleeding Alison away from her solipsistic contemplation of her mirror image and out into the world: "so she went, reluctantly, into the sunshine and among the secretive people. There was no place else" (216). While the novel can provide no absolute solution to the isolation from history and identity which characterizes the lives of suburban Jews, it offers, in its ending, this fragile, redemptive moment in which Alison feels, through the immediacy of her own bodily vulnerability, her place in cycles of human history and generational continuity.

Disturbances in the Field, Schwartz's third novel, is not characterized by the same ironic representation of Jewish suburban life as is *Balancing Acts*: Instead, it follows the interconnected lives of Lydia Rowe, a New Yorker, and her friends and family, many of them like her, urban Jews. *Disturbances in the Field* is in part about the struggle of these characters to create meaning—through philosophy, through psychology, through music and art, through the forging of various communities—in a secular world. Their secular world is no longer guarded by the old beliefs, as the younger three of Lydia's four children are not guarded by the traditional Jewish red ribbon that is placed on an infant's crib to ward off the evil eye. When Lydia's family life is happy, she and her husband, Victor, lack a place to direct their gratitude: "not being believers we do not know where to address our thanks. Awkwardly, we address them to the void, to some rich source in the void" (65). And when life is cruelly arbitrary, when Lydia's youngest two children are killed in a bus accident, she lacks even the recourse of the historical meaning of a horror of vast proportions, of the kind voiced by the fruit man at her grocery, whose entire family was killed in the Holocaust.

Yet the lives of these characters are still influenced by their (largely secular)

Jewish identity. The novel returns significantly to the imagery of the Passover Seder, the yearly ritual that thematizes the passing on of Jewish communal meaning. As the youngest child present asks the ritual four questions and is answered, the meaning of Jewish history is passed down from generation to generation. And as the *Haggadah* describes the four types of children—the wise, the contrary, the simple, the one who does not know how to ask—the variety of possible new generational responses to Jewish history are imagined and pre-empted for each new generation. Each conceivable type of child is already written into a role and a kind of Jewish identity, thus assuring the continuity of Jewish identity against all possible contrariness and ignorance from generation to generation. The novel's first allusion to a Seder marks the bonds of loving community and shared meaning that were forged in Lydia's years at Barnard, as she and the three women friends (one Jewish, two not) with whom she has read and passionately discussed philosophy celebrate after their final exam. As Lydia tells what she has written for the optional essay on Aristotle's views on friendship ("a friend is another self"), she pours wine "slowly for all of us in turn, the way my father used to do at our Passover Seders with his teasing maverick expression." (59). Later in life, as an established musician and the mother of four, Lydia finds her life's meaning not so much through the abstractions of Greek philosophy as in the more heated and complicated immediacies of her struggles and bonds with her family as well as with her friends. The second, full-fledged Seder in the novel, at Lydia and Victor's apartment, with Lydia's sister and her Barnard friends, marks this joyous enmeshment: "[o]ur Seder may not have been faithful to the letter; we even had dry wine instead of sweet. Nonetheless, Elijah came and drank" (78). In the spring of the following year, Lydia eats an elaborate meal, including a salad of bitter lettuce (the "bitter herbs" of the Passover, marking life's sorrow), now completely alone, with no younger generation to whom to pass on meaning and bereft of community with which to forge it. Her four children are gone, contrary and simple alike—two dead in the bus crash and two gone their own ways—and she is without husband and friends.

The echoes of Jewish ritual, in Schwartz's third novel, mark a void that can no longer be filled by the faith of an earlier time. Lydia and Victor find their way back together in the fall, the time of the Jewish New Year; the novel subtly and quietly reminds the reader that time of reconciliations and new beginnings and thus the cycle of the Jewish year, is seen to have still a tenuous connection with their lives. But in *Disturbances in the Field*, the solution to the fundamental questions that lie behind the Passover Seder (What is my identity? What is my connection with the people around me and my ancestors? What is the reason for human suffering?) can paradoxically be solved in contemporary life only by an individual search, a search that is finally solitary and, strictly speaking, secular. Despite the insistence on the central urgency of the struggle of human relationships, meaning finally devolves from the solitary, contemplative individual. At the end of the novel, Lydia thinks of the Greek philosopher,

Thales, who discerned the height of the pyramids by measuring their shadows at the time of day when the length of his own shadow became equal to his height. In the final sentence, she imagines the philosopher turning from human communion (a shared drinking of wine, like that in the Seder) to the solitary reflection on the self necessary to an understanding of the world: "The old bachelor Thales waited too, perhaps sipping wine with his friends in the marketplace, till that right moment when a person's shadow grows to the person's size, when the body and its image, its burden, its imprint on the land, come together in harmony, and at that perfect moment of equivalence, he could take the measure of anything in the universe" (403).

Schwartz's most recent novel, *Leaving Brooklyn*, is more overtly than any of her other books a Jewish novel: Its title suggests, as one reviewer has commented, its archetypal nature as a novel about the postimmigrant experience, about the third generation's escape from the safe American haven created by the second (Hershman 67). Like other works by Schwartz, this novel meditates on individuality and community and on the different experience of Jewish identity and history by different generations. At the same time, this novel explores, with its fictional memoiristic form, the nature of memory and its distortion by storytelling, and it consequently calls into question the nature of history (our stories) and identity (the self we define through those stories). The novel explores these issues through the character of Audrey, a teenager who rejects the safety and complacency of her parents' postwar Brooklyn, its blandness established to protect its children from "carnage and deprivation and numbers" tattooed on arms (7). Audrey escapes through a series of sexual encounters with her eye ("I") doctor in cosmopolitan Manhattan, where there are churches and slim, fair people (62). Like Rita in "The Melting Pot," Audrey is a split daughter of the third generation, her division indicated here by the difference between her two eyes, one of which sees like everyone else in Brooklyn, one of which "wanders" and sees another world, the depths behind the surfaces.

Audrey's split vision results in a certain lucid critique, both of the limitations of the safety in middle-class normativeness and of the ideal of America itself: Looking out through the viewing machine at the top of the Empire State Building, a view of America's grandeur at which others gasp, Audrey, with her peculiar vision, can see "nothing extraordinary" (14). But the novel's ending points out the limitations of Audrey's adolescent scorn for her parents' Brooklyn (more goes on there than has met even Audrey's exceptional eye). And, the novel suggests, Audrey's two visions are hardly as distinct as she believes: Her normative eye sees with a stable vision which matches her parents' inclination toward a middle-class "settledness," caused by their more immediate experience of a horrifying Jewish past. Meanwhile, her "wandering" eye, the eye of one who wishes to move on, never to "settle," is equally the product of a Jewish identity (like Max Fried, she wishes to be the "wandering Jew"), but it is the result of the experience of Jewish history from a safer, generational position.

Schwartz's only book for children, *The Four Questions*, a simple, straight-forward retelling of the Passover story, was published in the same year as *Leaving Brooklyn*: it seems fitting that this author, so concerned with the gaps between generations caused by the different experience of Jewish history and the loss of Jewish identity, should write her one children's book to date about a ceremony in which Jewish history is passed down from one generation to the next.

SURVEY OF CRITICISM

Lynne Sharon Schwartz's fiction has been widely and often favorably reviewed since the appearance of her first novel. Of Schwartz's works, *Rough Strife*, *Disturbances in the Field*, and *Leaving Brooklyn* have received the most attention. *Rough Strife* was widely reviewed for a first novel, although the reviews were mixed. Those critics who most liked the novel repeatedly praised its wit and compassion, the economy of its prose, and the detailed precision of its emotional realism. Several critics commented, however, on the "narrowness" of the novel's focus on the emotional lives of the upper-middle class, emotional lives that seem constrained to a relentless focus on marriage (the "thirty- some-thing" phenomenon). As one reviewer commented: "[a]bout halfway through . . . my admiration for Miss [*sic*] Schwartz's gifts as a reporter of emotional weather turned to irritation at her lack of interest in anything else" (Pollitt 14, 22). A few critics noted as well that the women's movement is given an unjust representation in the episode in which Caroline experiences a brief flurry of feminist fervor: Since Ivan has carefully been set up as a highly atypical, egal-itarian husband, her sudden rage at him rings false. Yet, despite such criticisms, *Rough Strife* was widely termed "A fine first novel" and was nominated both for an American Book Award and for the PEN/Hemingway First Novel Award.

Balancing Acts fared less well with the critics. Due to the novel's surface resemblances to "young adult" fiction, a genre rarely accorded serious attention, this novel was by and large treated dismissively. While a few reviewers praised the painful realism of the book, demonstrated in passages such as those in which Max experiences the loss of the abilities of his once-powerful and athletic body, others found the characters only "cute" and "smug" and dismissed *Balancing Acts* as an "old-man-mourning-his-past/young-girl-in-search-of-a-better-father" young adult novel (*Kirkus* 457). The novel was far less widely reviewed than was *Rough Strife*.

With the publication of *Disturbances in the Field* in 1983, the critics resumed their attention to and frequent praise for Schwartz's work. With this novel's epic exploration of the many faces of Lydia's emotional life, Schwartz's fiction was no longer vulnerable to the charge of narrowness of focus, and she received accolades for having "the total quality of reality in all its untidiness and mud-dlement and mulish resistance to logic and formulae" (Cook 601). Of course, some critics, irritated by the same qualities, found the novel "long and sprawling'' (Gussow 61), and there were a few predictably snide comments about Lydia's Volvo and Upper West Side apartment. On the whole, reviewers found the novel impressive and moving, "noble in intent" (See 23). One critic found in the novel's "size and freedom . . . he 'immense and exquisite correspondence with life' that James maintained was the stuff and soul of fiction" (Cook 601).

Schwartz's two subsequent collections of short stories (1984 and 1987) were met with diminished critical attention. *Acquainted with the Night* received only limited praise: the stories tended to be described as flat and overly self-conscious. One critic felt that the problem lay in the diminished energies of the characters in Schwartz's stories, relative to her fiction: "Irony and poignancy are the sharp tools of Mrs. Schwartz's novelistic trade at its best. A blunter tone of helplessness and anger dominates the stories, blurring passions and perceptions" (Hulbert 9). The second collection, *The Melting Pot*, received much more favorable commentary: The stories were praised in particular for their sharp clarity and for their skillful use of "the small intimacies of daily life to tell stories about big subjects" (Klass 16).

Most recently, Schwartz's *Leaving Brooklyn* has been the recipient of an upsurge of critical attention, again mixed, but largely laudatory. Several reviewers described the "good eye-bad eye" motif as heavy-handed; one found it "the only creak in this otherwise stunning little book" (Birkerts 16). Another reviewer found considerably less emotional nuance and generosity in this novel's focus on Audrey's disgruntled, adolescent psyche than in Schwartz's earlier fiction (*Kirkus* 246). In general, however, critics have praised *Leaving Brooklyn* as a lyrical, vivid, and striking female coming-of-age story: As Anthony Quinn writes, Schwartz's most recent novel is "tightly cargoed, a rites-of-passage story which observes generic limits yet somehow rejuvenates its frazzled traditions" (Quinn 19).

BIBLIOGRAPHY

Works by Lynne Sharon Schwartz

Rough Strife. New York: Harper & Row, 1980.
Balancing Acts. New York: Harper & Row, 1981.
Disturbances in the Field. New York: Harper & Row, 1983.
Acquainted with the Night and Other Stories. New York: Harper & Row, 1984.
We Are Talking About Homes: A Great University Against Its Neighbors. New York: Harper & Row, 1985.
The Melting Pot and Other Subversive Stories. New York: Harper & Row, 1987.
Leaving Brooklyn. New York: Houghton Mifflin, 1989.
The Four Questions. Paintings by Ori Sherman. New York: Dial Books, 1989.
Trans. *Smoke Over Birkenau*. By Liana Millu. New York: The Jewish Publication Society, 1991.

Interviews

Interview. With Wendy Smith. *Publishers Weekly* 3 Aug. 1984: 68–69.
"Lynne Sharon Schwartz." With Mickey Pearlman. *Inter/View: Talks with America's Writing Women*. Eds. Mickey Pearlman and Katherine Usher Henderson. Lexington, KY: University Press of Kentucky, 1990. 199–194.

Works about Lynne Sharon Schwartz

Rev. of *Balancing Acts*. *Kirkus* 1 Apr. 1981: 457.
Rev. of *Leaving Brooklyn*. *Kirkus* 15 Feb. 1989: 246.
Berne, Suzanne. Interview with Lynne Sharon Schwartz. *Belles Lettres* 6 (Spring 1991): 32–35.
Birkerts, Sven. "A Girl and Her Eye Doctor." Rev. of *Leaving Brooklyn*. *New York Times Book Review* (30 Apr. 1989): 16.
Cook, Carole. Rev. of *Disturbances in the Field*. *Commonweal* 4 Nov. 1983: 590, 601–03.
Gussow, Adam. Rev. of *Disturbances in the Field*. *Saturday Review* Oct. 1983: 61.
Hershman, Marcie. "Leaving Brooklyn, Again." Rev. of *Leaving Brooklyn*. *Tikkun* 4.5 (1989): 67–69.
Hoffmann, Michael. "Heights of Fancy." Rev. of *Balancing Acts*. *New York Times Literary Supplement* 12 Mar. 1982: 277.
Hulbert, Anne. "Helpless, Angry, Insomniac Souls." Rev. of *Acquainted With the Night*. *New York Times Book Review* 26 Aug. 1984: 9.
Klass, Perri. "Keeping the Fat Rat Alive." Rev. of *The Melting Pot*. *New York Times Book Review* 11 Oct. 1987: 15.
Pollitt, Katha. "Twenty Years of Marriage." Rev. of *Rough Strife*. *New York Times Book Review* 15 June 1980: 14, 22.
Quinn, Anthony. "Audrey's Eye." Rev. of *Leaving Brooklyn*. *London Review of Books* 21 Feb. 1991.
Rae, Simon. "Feeling Bitter Together." Rev. of *Rough Strife*. *New York Times Literary Supplement* 7 Aug. 1981: 910.
"Schwartz, Lynne Sharon." *World Authors: 1980–1985*. Ed. Vineta Colby. New York: H. W. Wilson, 1991.
See, Carolyn. "Too Good to Be True." Rev. of *Disturbances in the Field*. *New York Times Book Review* 6 Nov. 1983: 14, 22, 24.

LORE SEGAL (1928–   )

Adam Meyer

BIOGRAPHY

Lore Segal was born Lore Groszmann in Vienna, March 8, 1928, to a middle-class Austrian family. Her father, Ignatz, was chief accountant at a bank, while her mother, Franzi, took care of the home. Young Lore received formal instruction in ballet and gymnastics, as well as "home tutoring" from her mother in music and from her Uncle Paul in politics and literature; she played with her friends in the park and summered in the Alps. She has reminisced that "I lived the first ten comfortable years as my parents' only child, my grandparents' only grandchild, my father's and mother's brothers' only niece—the center of attention, admiration, and the focus of great expectations" ("Lore," 311).

In 1938, however, all that changed. Following Hitler's annexation of Austria in March, the Groszmann family began to experience the effects of anti-Semitic persecution. They had to fire their German maid, as non-Jews were no longer allowed to work for Jews; Ignatz lost his position at the bank, as Jews were no longer allowed to work in non-Jewish organizations. Following an altercation with a group of Nazi students, Paul was expelled from the university, where he had been a medical student. Lore herself was attacked by some other children during the time in which she and her family, whose apartment had been commandeered by the SS, lived with her grandparents in the village of Fischamend.

In December 1938, Lore became one of the first post-Anschluss Jews to escape from the Nazis, when, as part of an experimental children's transport, she and 500 other schoolchildren were sent to England. She was to live in England for the next ten years, first with a succession of foster families and then for three years at Bedford College for Women. In 1939, her parents also escaped to England, although their lives there were far from what they had been in Vienna. Her father, who had always been somewhat frail, was forced to work as a servant and gardener and then, during the war itself, he was interned on the Isle of Man along with all German-speaking males over sixteen; he suffered a series of strokes and died in 1945. Her mother made the best of her new situation as a hired domestic. In 1948, Lore joined her mother in the Dominican Republic, and in 1951, they moved to New York City, where she has lived ever since. In 1961, Lore Groszmann married David Segal, an editor, with whom she had two children, Beatrice and Jacob; David Segal died in 1970. After having taught at several universities, Segal became associated with the University of Illinois at Chicago in 1978, staying there for more than a decade. She now teaches at Ohio State University.

Segal's experiences in Austria, England, the Dominican Republic, and, finally, New York City became the basis of her first book, *Other People's Houses*, which was partially serialized in *The New Yorker* before its publication in 1964. Although it is largely autobiographical, *Other People's Houses* is not entirely so and has often been classified as a novel; Segal's own epigraph for the text hints that it confounds genre distinctions:

The "Carter Bayoux" of my book once told me a story out of his childhood. When he had finished, I said, "I knew just where your autobiography stopped and fiction began."
He said, "Then you knew more than I."

To date, Segal has also published two novels, *Lucinella* (1976) and *Her First American* (1985), the latter a kind of sequel to *Other People's Houses*. She has also written a number of books for children, beginning with the award-winning *Tell Me a Mitzi* (1970). In collaboration with W. D. Snodgrass, Segal has translated the poetry of Christian Morgenstern, and on her own, she has translated the tales of the brothers Grimm and several books of the Bible. Most recently, Segal has been at work on a new novel, provisionally titled *An Absence of Cousins*. Several chapters of this work-in-progress have appeared in the *New Yorker* as short stories, one of these stories, "The Reverse Bug," was awarded third place in the 1990 O. Henry Awards.

MAJOR THEMES

Although Segal's writing contains little documentation of atrocities that we have come to expect in Holocaust or survivor literature—mainly because she herself escaped—there can be no doubt that her position as a refugee has had a dramatic impact on her writings and that exile has been one of her central themes. Indeed, the primary concern in Segal's *Other People's Houses* is to account for and portray the emotions of a young girl, Lore Groszmann, who is forced to leave her comfortable life behind her. The title itself is an indication of how awkward the girl's life becomes, as she constantly lives in other people's homes, never quite knowing how she should react to any given situation, all the while searching futilely for a place where she can feel a true sense of belonging. Lore is immediately attracted to Oxford, for example, because it "seemed everything that I was not: at one with itself, at one with its own past" (166).

After the first two chapters, which concern young Lore's life in Vienna and her trip to England aboard the children's transport, *Other People's Houses* is broken up into ten additional chapters, each taking its name from one of the various towns where she lived, either as foster child, student, or resident alien, during her long emigration from Austria to America. Even in the book's final chapter, the optimistically titled "New York: My Own House," Segal's sense of being a refugee has not entirely left her. The book concludes with the following passage:

> My husband is Jewish too, but he was born in America and accepts without alarm this normal season of our lives; but I, now that I have children and am about the age my mother was when Hitler came, walk gingerly and in astonishment upon this island of my comforts, knowing that it is surrounded on all sides by calamity. (309)

In her 1989 conversation with Cathy Earnest, Segal reiterated her view that "the refugee is more aware of present pleasures or comforts because of the improbability of it" (164).

The precariousness of the refugee is also a central theme in Segal's novel *Her First American* and in her novel-in-progress, *An Absence of Cousins*. Both of these works feature Ilka Weissnix, a somewhat fictionalized version of the Lore Groszmann of *Other People's Houses*. A refugee from Hitler's Europe, Ilka arrives young and very naive in New York City. Like young Lore, she doesn't quite feel at home or permanent in her new country. This uneasy position of the refugee is particularly emphasized in the story version of the chapter entitled "An Absence of Cousins." As the story opens, Ilka, older and somewhat wiser than she had been in *Her First American*, receives a job offer that involves the teaching of English to foreign students (something that Segal herself had done during her unhappy stay in the Dominican Republic). The position requires that she move to Connecticut, however, and the prospect of establishing a new home frightens her, as it has already taken her "a decade to find the right drawer to keep my spoons in and turn on the bathroom light without groping" (23). Even so, Ilka takes the job. While she is busy trying to meet the people among whom she will now be living and working, one of her students, Gerti Gruner, discovers that they are both Jewish refugees from Vienna and attaches herself to Ilka, much to the teacher's dismay. At the end of the story, however, Ilka comes to see that Gerti's pestering is really the manifestation of a desire for family, that "what Gerti Gruner could not learn was how to survive in an absence of cousins" (29). In conversation with Cathy Earnest, Segal said of this title phrase that it "also means an absence of place to live where you're at home with your cousins. . . . [M]ost people do not live among their cousins, in that extended sense, nor in their own neighborhoods. And it seems what we're all in the business of, is making ourselves a new place" (157). Clearly, the issue of the precarious refugee—and she reminds Earnest that the person in the Midwest who comes from New York is also a refugee—continues to be central to Lore Segal's writings.

Another of Segal's themes, related to her experiences as the victim of persecution, has been the problem of ethnic and racial discrimination. In *Other People's Houses*, an irony that the child learns in the processing camp in England is that those who are victims of prejudice are themselves prejudiced. The child notes that the counselor

> told us that a new transport of Jewish children from Germany was expected in camp. I understood from her that this was to be regarded as a calamity, because German Jews talked like Germans and thought they knew everything better than everybody else and would ruin the whole camp. I was surprised. At home I had learned that it was the Polish Jews who always thought they knew everything and were noisy and pushy in public and ruined everything for the *real*, the Austrian Jews. (43–44)

Here we see the innocent child both displaying and undercutting the effects of her education to prejudice. The kind of education that Segal feels is necessary to combat such an education *to* prejudice is one *about* prejudice: We must first acknowledge that we are all prejudiced, no matter how much we might try to deny it, and then we must learn to avoid acting on these baser impulses.

One of Segal's first published stories, "The Beating of the Girl," provides us with a very clear example of an education *about* prejudice, but not *to* it. Suzanne, a white woman, spends a weekend at the home of Lillian, a black former classmate. Lillian has recently been insulted by a white doctor, who assumed she was the maid rather than the mistress of her house, and she spends the entire first day "beating the boy," that is, bemoaning the insensitivity of whites to the feelings of African-Americans. Suzanne, however, soon comes to realize that she is really the one being beaten (as the story's title indicates), for she is forced to become aware of her own prejudices; the mistake that the white doctor made, Suzanne realizes, "was nothing more than a blunder and one she herself might have made" (54). She has gone to visit Lillian with the best of liberal intentions—at least, she says, she is "trying"—but Charles (Lillian's husband) explains to her that this is not enough. He knows that her first thought when she met him was how dark his skin was, and she must finally admit that she does, indeed, harbor prejudiced ideas. Nevertheless, Segal indicates that understanding this about herself, far from destroying her friendship with Lillian and Charles, will most likely improve the relationship, if she can use the knowledge appropriately.

The issue of racial prejudice is the central focus of *Her First American*. The title refers to Carter Bayoux, a black intellectual and drunkard who initially appeared in the final chapter of *Other People's Houses*, where he offered to give young Lore "an introductory course in Americana" (300); in the sequel, he does indeed teach Ilka Weissnix what it means to be an American, particularly a black American. When they first meet, Ilka is remarkably slow to pick up on the fact that Carter is black (both because he is light-skinned and because she does not yet understand the significance of race in America). She finally asks him, "Am I color-blind?" to which he replies, "You are a foreigner, but we're going to get you naturalized" (51). Her indoctrination, or acculturation process, is completed when, later in the text, she admits to Carter that she is a racist, only to have him respond, "Not to worry. Some of my best friends are racist" (206). As with Suzanne, Ilka comes to see that admitting one's prejudices does not mean endorsing them. Segal has said that "One of the things I learned from the original of Carter Bayoux is that people are simply racist. And if you find a thread of racism in yourself, relax. Just don't act upon it" (Earnest 160). This restraint is what separates Ilka and Carter from the Nazis.

The relationship between Ilka and Carter is an important educational experience that becomes an important personal one as well. By the end of the novel, though, their friendship has dissolved. This kind of failed relationship is something of a constant in Segal's writings, which frequently explore the difficulty of interpersonal communication and understanding. In *Other People's Houses*, for example, young Lore finds it very difficult to connect with her English foster families and they with her. *Her First American*, furthermore, contains an idyllic section, entitled "Summer," which describes a communal retreat set up by Ilka, Carter, and a number of their friends, both black and white. At first, Ilka finds everything wonderful, feeling herself and her friends to be in "a honeymoon of mutual accommodation" (193); by the end of the summer, however, the honeymoon is definitely over, as the group breaks up rather acrimoniously. The recent *New Yorker* stories also explore difficult loves and friendships, such as Nat and Nancy's failing marriage in "Money, Fame, and Beautiful Women" or Ilka's own brief marriage to Jimmy Carl in "Fatal Wish" and her affair with William in "William's Shoes."

Segal's novel *Lucinella* is concerned with writing itself and the party life of New York writers. The novel, Segal's most experimental, begins at the retreat for writers sponsored by the corporation of Yaddo (where Segal has herself spent some time) and goes on to trace the professional and social lives of the literary set. Lucinella's master plan—to "write a poem called 'Euphoria in the Root Cellar,' all about some poets who visit a root cellar in a Roethke poem" (6–7)—indicates both the metafictional nature of the novel, writing about writing, and the narrative's satirical bent. It is quite true that, for Lucinella, "writing is like brushing my teeth, without which . . . there's no way for god to get into his heaven" (101–02), but most of the other writers at Yaddo are significantly more jaded and cynical. Segal's satirical presentation of the writing establishment is also evident in the recent *New Yorker* stories, which take place in an environment somewhat like Yaddo's, a think tank called the Concordance Institute. One story in particular, "Money, Fame, and Beautiful Women," focuses on Nat Cone, a poet who believes that he has won a prize but is not entirely sure that he has because of some mixup about his name.

What Segal is satirizing in these pieces is the American writing environment, *not* the act of writing, a vocation that she takes quite seriously. Although Segal pokes fun at the Yaddo writers for being "seriously vain and silly," she also believes that they are very serious about their writing and that "one does not affect the other."[1] For Segal knows from personal experience how powerful writing can be. While she was in the refugee distribution camp in England, she composed a

tear-jerking letter full of sunsets. I sent it to the address of a refugee committee that my father had given me, and my letter moved them to procure the job, the sponsor, and the visa that brought my parents to England, proving that bad literature makes things happen. ("Bough" 241)

The writing of that letter is one of the key scenes in the early portion of *Other People's Houses*. In her essay "The Bough Breaks," Segal similarly recalls the response she received the first time she told the story that would become *Other People's Houses*: "it was my first experience of the peculiar silence of a roomful of people listening to what you are telling them" (245). Because storytelling contains such power, Segal stresses the importance of narrative in many of her works.

In fact, Segal's books for children, as well as her translations, similarly aimed at a juvenile audience, center around different kinds of storytelling. Her first children's book, *Tell Me a Mitzi*, consists of stories that she told her own children as they were growing up. Each of the three tales is prefaced by a child, Martha, asking her mother or father to tell her a story about the mythical Mitzi, after which the story begins, "Once upon a time there was a Mitzi." *Tell Me aTrudy* (1977) follows much the same format. These stories are patterned on fairy tales, a genre which is quite congenial to Segal, who has translated many of the tales of the Brothers Grimm. John W. Evans has argued convincingly that *Lucinella* is also based on fairy-tale motifs, although he notes that it partakes of the parable tradition as well. Two of Segal's other children's books, *The Story of Old Mrs. Brubeck and How She Looked for Trouble and Where She Found Him* (1981) and *The Story of Mrs. Lovewright and Purrless Her Cat* (1985), can indeed be seen as modern parables or fables, stories with a moral. Segal is also attracted to the stories of the Bible, and has translated several of them; she presents the books as adventure tales, emphasizing not the "hush of the sacred" but the "terrific story" (*King Saul* xv). As she noted in her article on the Second Book of Samuel, "story has the power to manipulate imagination . . . to reverse nature. It surprises us into imagining our neighbor" (124–25); interestingly, this is also the theme of her most recent *New Yorker* story, "The Talk in Eliza's Kitchen." For Segal, storytelling is the first important step in the proper kind of education. Writing, whether for children or adults is a way of presenting the world in an attempt to stave off its destruction.

SURVEY OF CRITICISM

Critics have, to date, taken relatively little notice of Lore Segal's works, although that is beginning to change. In addition to Cathy Earnest's very important "Conversation" with Segal, which appeared in 1989, the first scholarly article on Segal's writing appeared in 1992, with another following in 1993. The earlier of these essays, Alan L. Berger's "Jewish Identity and Jewish Destiny, the Holocaust in Refugee Writing: Lore Segal and Karen Gershon," focuses on the refugees of the children's transport and discusses *Other People's Houses* and "The Bough Breaks" in terms of the themes of "permanent exile" (84) and "refugee guilt" (89). The latter, Philip G. Cavanaugh's "The Present Is a Foreign Country: Lore Segal's Fiction," is a more wide-ranging introduction to some of Segal's central themes, particularly the problem of memory. He includes discussions of all of her works, making several particularly good points about *Lucinella* and the *New Yorker* stories. Cavanaugh's essay certainly lays a groundwork upon which future critics of Segal's works can build. Despite these two essays, however, we are still largely forced to rely on book reviews to get a sense of Segal's critical reputation.

Other People's Houses was generally well-received. Elie Wiesel, for example, stated that "few personal documents dealing with that period move us to such depths" (494); Cynthia Ozick concurred that "her book is unbelievably moving" (92). Richard Gilman noted that "this is Mrs. Segal's 'refugee' story, and in its cool, dry, accurate vision it makes almost all others, no matter how full of physical suffering, seem obvious and, what is most remarkable, irrelevant" (15). One aspect of the book which appealed to many critics is its unusual tone. Eveyln Torton Beck described and praised it as "nowhere self-pitying, always understated, slightly distanced and ironic" (16). Ozick also noted that "the subject-matter of these memoirs is rife with sentimental possibilities" (91) but that Segal's writing is "as far as possible from the maudlin" (92). Although a few critics faulted Segal's work, they were in the minority. Dan Jacobson complained that the writing is "sometimes pert, sometimes coy" (451), while Norman Weyand "regret[ted] the coldness and lack of compassion" (147).

Lucinella was reviewed neither as widely nor as favorably as its predecessor. Phyllis Birnbaum admired the tone of the novel, the way it "shifts between satire and fable to catch the tempo of the artistic life," but she ultimately felt that "the novel does not escape the limitations of its subject matter. The reflections on writing, not writing, and fame tend toward a suffocating sameness" (28). John Leonard asserted that the novel subdues many of the problems that it creates for itself, such as the limited subject matter. At the same time, though, he was bothered by such modernist touches as the three Lucinellas (the protagonist and projected older and younger versions of herself) and the introduction of Zeus and Hera, who are poets in Lucinella's circle as well as the actual Greek gods; "nothing much is gained by the device," he argued, "except a bothered reader" (20). Even so, Leonard concluded that *Lucinella* "remains a good book, a *likable* book'' (20). The novel does have some stronger proponents in Martin Washburn and, especially, John W. Evans. Evans found the book to be a ''brilliant example [of a] satirical fairy tale'' (460); he felt that Segal was ''perhaps at her best when satirizing literary and social pretentiousness'' (462).

If *Lucinella* is generally conceded to be Segal's weakest book, *Her First American* is widely considered her greatest achievement. Carolyn Kizer, for example, was most ecstatic in asserting that

> Lore Segal may have come closer than anyone to writing the Great American Novel. Essentially, the novel is about how we behave to one another, and the consequences of that behavior. It's about how we lose by winning, how we are educated by loving, how we change and are changed by everyone we know. (7)

Jacqueline Austin marveled at how ''Segal transforms the guilt, pain, hurt, the thoroughly stuck, negative attitude into something light, something which has spring breezes wafting through it'' (49). Segal's tragicomic tone once again earned her great praise; Laura Obelensky found the novel ''deceptively funny'' (41), while Christopher Lehmann-Haupt pointed out that it ''manages somehow to be good-natured all the way through to its sad ending'' (23). If nothing else, *Her First American* is one of the most important fictional accounts of Black-Jewish relationships yet produced in this country, as Shelly Usen noted in the fullest discussion to date of *Her First American*. It is clearly a novel worthy of more serious and in-depth study, as is the entirety of Segal's output.

NOTE

1. These comments come from marginal notes Lore Segal made on a copy of this essay's rough draft. I wish to acknowledge her help in explaining this point about *Lucinella*, as well as in clearing up several other questions for me.

BIBLIOGRAPHY

Works by Lore Segal

For adults

''The Beating of the Girl.'' *Saturday Evening Post* 23 Nov. 1963: 46–57.
Other People's Houses. New York: Harcourt, 1964. [References are to the paperback, New York: Fawcett Crest, 1986.]
Lucinella. New York: Farrar, Straus, 1976.
Her First American. New York: Knopf, 1985. [References are to the paperback, New York: Fawcett Crest, 1986.]
''An Absence of Cousins.'' *New Yorker* 27 Aug. 1987: 22–29.
''The Reverse Bug.'' *New Yorker* 1 May 1989: 34–40.
''Money, Fame, and Beautiful Women.'' *New Yorker* 28 Aug. 1989: 28–36.

"At Whom the Dog Barks." *New Yorker* 3 Dec. 1990: 44–49.
"Fatal Wish." *New Yorker* 1 July 1991: 26–37.
"William's Shoes." *New Yorker* 25 Nov. 1991: 48–54.
"Commencement." *Antioch Review* 50 (1992): 472–74.
"The Talk in Eliza's Kitchen." *New Yorker* 6 Apr. 1992: 28–37.

For children

Tell Me a Mitzi. New York: Farrar, Straus, 1970.
All the Way Home. New York: Farrar, Straus, 1973.
Tell Me a Trudy. New York: Farrar, Straus, 1977.
The Story of Old Mrs. Brubeck and How She Looked for Trouble and Where She Found Him. New York: Pantheon, 1981.
The Story of Mrs. Lovewright and Purrless Her Cat. New York: Knopf, 1985.

Translations

(with W. D. Snodgrass) Christian Morgenstern. *Gallows Songs.* University of Michigan Press, 1967.
Wilhelm Grimm and Jakob Grimm. *The Juniper Tree and Other Tales from Grimm.* New York: Farrar, Straus, 1973.
Wilhelm Grimm and Jakob Grimm, *The Bear and the Kingbird.* New York: Farrar, Straus, 1979.
The Book of Adam to Moses. New York: Knopf, 1987.
The Story of King Saul and King David. New York: Schocken, 1991.
"II Samuel." *Congregation: Contemporary Writers Read the Jewish Bible.* Ed. David Rosenberg. New York: Harcourt Brace, 1987. 106–25.
"Memory: The Problems of Imagining the Past." *Writing and the Holocaust.* Ed. Berel Lang. New York: Holmes and Meier, 1988. 58–65.

Non-Fiction

"The Bough Breaks." *Testimony: Contemporary Writers Make the Holocaust Personal.* Ed. David Rosenberg. New York: Times Books, 1989. 231–248.
"Lore Segal." *Something About the Author Autobiography Series.* Vol. 11. Ed. Joyce Nakamura. Detroit: Gale Research, 1991. 311–20.

Interview

Earnest, Cathy. "A Conversation." *Another Chicago Magazine* 20 (1989). 153–67.

Works about Lore Segal

Austin, Jacqueline. "Lore Segal's Usable Past." *Village Voice* 18 June 1985: 49.
Beck, Evelyn Torton. "What Writers Read." *Women's Review of Books* July 1987: 16.
Berger, Alan L. "Jewish Identity and Jewish Destiny, the Holocaust in Refugee Writing: Lore Segal and Karen Gershon." *Studies in American Jewish Literature* 11 (1992): 82–95.
Birnbaum, Phyllis. "Books in Brief." *Saturday Review* 16 Oct. 1976: 28.
Cavenaugh, Philip. "The Present Is a Foreign Country: Lore Segal's Fiction." *Contemporary Literature* 34 (1993): 475–511.

Evans, John W. "Lucinella." *Magill's Literary Annual.* Ed. Frank N. Magill. Vol. 1. Englewood Cliffs, NJ: Salem Press. 1977. 460–4. 2 vols.

Gilman, Richard. "One Refugee Child's Story." *New Republic* 12 Dec. 1964: 15–16.

Jacobson, Dan. "Lucky Ones." *New Statesman* 69 (1965): 451.

Kizer, Carolyn. "The Education of Ilka Weissnix." *New York Times Book Review* 19 May, 1985: 7.

Lehmann-Haupt, Christopher. "Books of the Times." *New York Times* 27 June 1985: 23.

Leonard, John. "Everybody a Writer." *New York Times Book Review* 24 Oct. 1976: 20–22.

Obelensky, Laura. "Odd Couple." *New Republic* 5 Aug. 1985: 41–2.

Ozick, Cynthia. "A Contraband Life." *Commentary* March 1965: 89–92.

Usen, Shelly. "Her First American." *Magill's Literary Annual.* Ed. Frank N. Magill. Vol 1. Englewood Cliffs, NJ: Salem Press., 1983. 416–420. 2 vols.

Washburn, Martin. "Literary Toxicity." *The Nation* 29 Jan. 1977: 122–4.

Weyand, Norman. untitled. *Review for Religious* Jan. 1965: 146–7.

Weisel, Elie. "From Exile to Exile." *The Nation* 25 April 1966: 494–5.

JO SINCLAIR (RUTH SEID) (1913–   )

Gay Wilentz

BIOGRAPHY

Jo Sinclair was born Ruth Seid on July 1, 1913, in Brooklyn, New York, to twice-displaced Russian immigrant parents. Ida and Nathan Seid, left Russia in 1895 during the pogroms to live in Argentina, then returned to Russia, only to emigrate a second time to New York in 1907. The history and her family's memories inform Sinclair's writings. The Seids, Ashkenazi (Eastern European) Jews, left the teeming Jewish environment of Brooklyn three years after Ruth's birth for the isolated, Midwest town of Cleveland, Ohio, where, they hoped, there would be more jobs. This triple displacement helps formulate the cultural trope of Sinclair's life and work.

As a child of the Depression and in a family of displaced Jews in the Midwest, Seid lived on the edge of poverty. She blamed both her family and her Jewishness for that fact. Her father, Nathan Seid, a carpenter, was never comfortable with English or with other aspects of his life in Cleveland. Sinclair's biographer, Elisabeth Sandberg, notes with some irony: "Nor did he embrace any of the ways of the New World including the possibility of good hygiene" (14). As a young child, Seid resented her father for what she saw as his ineffectualness (reflecting a common stereotype of Jewish men at the time) and felt pity for her mother. She considered her family, including her brothers and sisters, as "illiterates of the soul" (*Season* 32).

Despite her shame and isolation while growing up. Seid was an excellent student. However, without money for college, she attended a commercial school, John Hay High School, about which she exclaims: "Completely wrong school; not that there was ever a single question in her mind about attending college. In her rigidly traditional world, a decent child in a poor Jewish family always got a job immediately after graduating, to help with the food and rent and clothes" (*Seasons* 1). But Seid found a college in the Cleveland public library. There she began to see herself as a wrier. Her first published work was "Noon Lynching," printed in a 1936 issue of *New Masses*, which reflects her overall concerns with oppressed people. This published story led her to a job with the WPA, allowing her to write.

With her first published work, Seid takes on the pseudonym, "Jo Sinclair." Seid commented about this change: "Yes, she would hang on to that pseudonym she had made up as one more 'being different' for that Ruth trapped in a ghetto" (*Seasons* 3). It is noteworthy that this change both anglicizes her name—as many other Jewish writers at the time did—and raised questions as to her gender (at least when spoken). But for Seid, this pseudonym meant something else—a split in her personality between the ghetto worker Ruth and the writer Jo (*Seasons* 8). During this same time period, Sinclair met the most influential person of her life, her love and patron Helen Buchman. Because of Helen, whom she calls the "psychiatrist" who saved her, Sinclair was able to change from the dysfunctional "ghetto punk" into the writer. Leaving the restrictive pain and depressing poverty of her family (although she always brought part of her salary back to her mother), she moved in with the Buchmans—Helen, Mort, and their two children. Although Sinclair's comments evince a great love for Helen and there is often a strong lesbian motif in her writings, Sinclair does not indicate a lesbian relationship with Helen; in fact, she was taken in by the whole family and continued to live in the house with Mort after Helen's death. She called Helen her "dearest friend" and a "second mother" (*Seasons* 11), but this primary relationship and the powerful love between women has informed many of her works. Helen found Sinclair a job at the Red Cross; moreover, she helped Sinclair with the publication of her early short stories—many of which dealt with WPA and the Red Cross.

Sinclair's first novel is *Wasteland* (1946), which she wrote while living with the Buchmans. In *Wasteland*, Sinclair recreates the "wasteland" of her family's life and her shame/self-hate as a Jew while giving homage to Helen through the use of a Gentile psychiatrist. The novel concerns a young man, Jake Braunowitz, probably modeled after her photographer brother Herman, whose outside success relies (in his mind) on his "passing" as Gentile and changing his name to John Brown. This powerful novel deals with anti-Semitism, self-hate, and the ghettoization of those who are different. It also raises some interesting questions about Sinclair's life—why, after acknowledging in the novel that keeping one's name is important for one's emotional health and sense of self, does Jo Sinclair retain her "Gentile" pseudonym and not return to the identifiably Jewish Ruth Seid?

Nevertheless, *Wasteland* spotlights Sinclair as a major new talent. The novel won her the prestigious $10,000 Harper Prize for a new writer; with it, she began a longtime relationship with her editor, Ed Aswell, at Harpers. With a short story published by *Esquire*, and *Wasteland* acknowledged as a work by an important young author, Sinclair quit her job at the Red Cross and began work as a full-time writer. She commenced work on a new novel, *Sing at My Wake*, and a play, *The Long Moment*. Sinclair had great difficulty with this novel, and as her biographer notes, *Sing at My Wake* (1951) is considered "her least successful novel" (Sandberg 77).

In *Sing at My Wake*, Sinclair tried to do for Catholics what she did for Jews in *Wasteland*. Both Helen Buchman and Ed Aswell, her editor, felt the work was not as genuine as *Wasteland*, and Helen was "uncomfortable with how [she] presented Catholicism" (Sandberg 180). For Sinclair, however, this novel reflected her desire to expose ghettoes wherever they were. One interesting aspect of the novel is the interracial relationship Catherine has with the black sculptor, Paul Randolph. Sinclair's play, *The Long Moment*, performed in Cleveland in 1950, reflects this concern and examines black experiences in the United States in a tale of a fine musician whose dilemma is whether to be accepted into the classical arena by "passing" as white or make the difficult choice to be true to himself and his heritage.

After these endeavors, Sinclair returns to an earlier idea, a book the character Debby is reading in *Wasteland*. Sinclair revised the novel, formerly called "Now Comes the Black," to become her most impressive work, *The Changelings*. The ghettoes of Eastern Europe, the Holocaust, the history of slavery and oppression, the reality of "white flight," all work together to present a powerful work of cross-ethnic relations. Although this novel received more positive critical attention than *Sing at My Wake*, it was not nearly as commercially successful as *Wasteland*. So once again, Sinclair began work with trepidation.

Personal problems added to the author's anxiety. Both she and the Buchmans had money problems; her editor, Ed Aswell died of a heart attack in 1958; and her life-long companion and support, Helen Buchman, became increasingly ill with diabetic flair-ups. Moreover, the novel *Anna Teller*, based on Sinclair's long-time friends Oscar and Helen Ban, concerned her. She was fearful that Oscar would resent the scathingly honest portrait of him (which turned out to be true). However, Sinclair, committed to the vision in the novel, comments: "But I had to write the book. Some people call it betraying friendship and confidences. Not so. Writers don't betray. They use—and change, and build—and give to the world" (*Seasons* 178). *Anna Teller*, Sinclair's last published novel (1960), is long and complex, examining both personal and political ghettoes. Sinclair's lack of restraint in this work (cut down to 596 pages) was possibly due to her loss of Aswell as a firm but sensitive editor.

The next few years were very difficult for Sinclair. She had writer's block with her fifth novel, and in December 1963, Helen Buchman died of a stroke. Helen, who prodded and encouraged Sinclair to write, was her stability, and with this painful and protracted death, Sinclair was despondent. She further despaired when her fifth novel, *Approach to the Meaning*, was turned down by publishers. As she notes in her autobiography, *The Seasons: Death and Transfiguration*, these years became a "time to mourn" for both her mother (who died in 1960) and Helen. She was also at a loss because of the silence from publishers and magazines concerning her work (11). She wrote a play about the Jew as survivor, called *The Survivors*, but it was neither published nor performed. In 1969, Sinclair realized that she must give up mourning and decided to "choose life" (270). She began to write her book for Helen, *The Seasons*, which she calls a "kind of autobiography," documenting her life with the Buchmans and Helen's death. Sinclair moved to Jenkinstown, Pennsylvania, in 1973.

In "Some Biographical Notes on the Author (by the Author)," Sinclair comments that in her seventies, the silences are gone and the "singing begins anew" because two of her works, *The Changelings* (1985) and *Wasteland* (1987), were reissued, her autobiography was published in 1992, and *Anna Teller* was reissued the same year. For Ruth Seid/Jo Sinclair, there is a kind of transfiguration: "Both selves of the weary survivor feel overwhelmed, unreal. But slowly, an old joy begins again in Jo's soul, in Ruth's heart, as that renascence continues like a fantastic rebirth" (12). According to the author, Sinclair is presently "well into a new novel and planning next year's garden" (*Seasons* 13).

MAJOR THEMES

As evinced by the intense rush to reissue her work, the vision presented in Jo Sinclair/Ruth Seid's works resonates for modern readers. Sinclair is decidedly a literary antecedent to writers such as Adrienne Rich and Audrey Lorde, whose messages are to "affirm difference" and accept no labels. Writing her first novel in 1946, after the war and particularly the Holocaust, Sinclair examines ghettoes, not only external and forced ones, but the equally debilitating personal ghettoes—how one internalizes the prejudice and discrimination from without. She focuses on the issues of interpersonal familial relations, Jewish identity, and sexual orientation as her center, but she expands her discussion to include all the oppressed—all who suffer from ghettoes of the mind and society, especially African-Americans and those from the working class (often on the edge of poverty).

Wasteland, her first novel, explores all of the major themes in her corpus of works—the connection between personal wasteland and the ghettoes without, the interaction of family relations and ethnic identity, and the psychological toll of "otherness." The protagonist Jake Braunowitz, as the Gentile John Brown, is a successful photographer for a major newspaper, but his psyche is emotionally fractured and his life is a wasteland. The novel takes place in the psychiatrist's office and revolves around their weekly meetings. But the most important character is his sister Debby, based loosely on the author, who has been to this doctor and is Jake's liaison to health. At the time, the work was radical not only in its acceptance of psychiatry as a way to deal with discrimination and the effects of poverty, but also in the fact that the sister Debby, who brings Jake to a sense of himself, is a lesbian. By intersecting both Jewish and lesbian otherness, Sinclair exposes the complex workings of both individual and community desires—as well as addressing the conflicts of being a triple minority (Jewish, female, lesbian). Her powerful and sensitive portrayal of Jewish self-hate and the feeling of selfhood when one finally accepts oneself, is a significant contri-

bution to issues of ethnic identity and personal growth. Surprisingly, both biographers, Sandberg and R. Barbara Gitenstein, try to play down the Jewish
content in her work. Gitenstein remarks: "The question of Jewishness is part of
the background of Jake Braunowitz's self-hatred, but it is only part; his problem
could just as easily have been those of any second-generation immigrant . . . "
(297). Of course, many second-generation immigrants face problems in their
"new" world, but these problems are culture-bound. Precisely, the cultural specificity of Jewish life gives Sinclair's work their strength of meaning and emotion
as well as their ability to affect those from other backgrounds. Moreover, her
novel *Sing at My Wake*, her only published novel without major Jewish protagonists, is considered her least successful work.

Despite the problems associated with *Sing at My Wake*, Sinclair's writings
are exceptionally sensitive in detailing cross-ethnic relations, particularly between blacks and Jews, most explicitly expressed in *The Changelings*. Its theme
of interethnic strife, including Italians and other groups, prefaces contemporary
issues of economic racism and fear of difference. As its earlier title, "Now
Comes the black," indicates, the novel deals with the changing demographics
of a Cleveland suburb. Sinclair, concerned with personal and community ghettoes, could see what was happening to ethnic communities, primarily Jewish
and Italian, as black people tried to move into the neighborhood. Jewish residents, with the memory of both the pogroms in Russia and the Holocaust, see
their sense of security in their neighborhood dwindle as they are warned that,
when blacks move in, the property value goes down. Incorporating the prejudices of the dominant culture and afraid of difference, the rich Jews leave and
the poor ones wait to see who will finally rent to a black person. The "Changelings"—Judy Vincent, who is Jewish, and Clara Jackson, who is black—representing the possibility of change and a redefinition of society that is as
necessary today as it was in 1955 when the novel was published.

The conflict within the Jewish community is narrated by a constant battle
between Jules, a forward-thinking youth who is dying, and his mother Sophie,
who has an empty upstairs apartment to rent. Sophie takes the pragmatic view
that the blacks, by moving in, will take away what she has gained. But under-
neath her pragmatism is the fear of the unknown that becomes prejudice, that
Sinclair is quick to show us has been used against Jews throughout history. Jules
reinforced this view by representing the moral values of Jewish life in the novel,
and he constantly compares the situation of the blacks to what the Jews have
suffered. This ironic tension informs the book; its motif of how history controls
interpersonal relations and cultural conflict is an aspect of all of Sinclair's writings. By the end of the novel, the coming together of the changelings, Vincent
and Clara, presents the potential for change in the future. Sinclair's novels—
which expose the depths of self-hate, imposed ghettoes, and fear of otherness—
also open up a world to us of possibility, where there can be growth and people
can be made whole.

In *Wasteland*, it is Debby who presents a vision of inclusiveness that Sinclair further develops in *The Changelings*. At the end of the novel, Jake and Debby give blood for the war effort. As she gives her blood, Debby tells Jake and the reader how she feels: " 'When I give blood I feel as if I'm giving it for Jews, too. Jews like Ma, who never had a break. Never. And I'm giving a pint for Negroes. . . . For people like me. There are so many. It's like giving your blood against any kind of segregation there is in the world" (306). For Sinclair one can only evoke change if one has destroyed the ghetto in oneself. Change starts with your own group, your own family, your own self, but it must not end there. In both *Wasteland* and *The Changelings*, the powerful quality of human suffering is finally mitigated by this potential for personal and societal change. Each novel is reconciled, although not conclusively, with a reclaiming of self and a giving to others— sense of the potential for community beyond xenophobia. In this way, Sinclair's work remains contemporary, reflecting modern-day interest in ethnic identity and heritage while, at the same time, acknowledging the reality of the "other."

Sinclair's writings remain contemporary in another way: They examine in great detail the relationship of the historical moment to personal and ethnic identity—one's historicity. In *Wasteland*, the backdrop of the novel is the Holocaust and World War II; Jake's personal struggle with his Jewish identity is highlighted by the horror across the ocean and the misguided belief of German Jews that they were Germans first. *The Changelings*, published almost ten years later, reflects the changes in ethnic neighborhoods in the fifties by examining the subject position of each group as the country deals with the issue of civil rights for all Americans. Most pertinent, in regard to one's personal and community history, is Sinclair's "large" novel, *Anna Teller*. It spans time periods, geographical locations, and major historical events. But, in contradistinction, it is primarily about the relationship of mother and son. Through Anna's recounting of her personal and community history, Sinclair presents European Jewish wanderings in the twentieth century, from the mass migration to the United States throughout the first half of the century to the Holocaust and its aftermath. Moreover, Sinclair explores Jewish life on both continents after the devastation in Europe. Anna's son, Emil, emigrates to the United States before the attempted annihilation of the Jews and begins his life there; meanwhile, Anna remains in Hungary, living through the Holocaust, only to be a refugee once again during the Communist crackdown in Hungary after the 1956 uprising. The subjectivity of "history" and the sociocultural context of one's own historicity is evoked by Sinclair as Anna's refusal to listen to anyone but herself interferes with her ability to comprehend the threat of Hitler. As Sinclair writes of internal ghettoes, she also details how one lives as a survivor of historical concentration camps. How one survives one's history, personal and societal, is a major focus for Sinclair.

In addition to her published works, Sinclair has a corpus of unpublished works—a novel, short stories, and plays, all dealing with these major themes. Her short stories, some of which have been anthologized, reflect issues of sexual difference, interracial and ethnic relations (both in love and friendship), and the desire to throw off ghettoes and remake oneself whole. As Sinclair notes in her autobiography, ''The spirit can be the most intolerable ghetto of all'' (44). What Jo Sinclair and the ''ghetto punk'' Ruth Seid bring to us as readers are the connections between the external ghettoes, prejudices, and discriminations, and the internal fears, self-hatred, and loss of spirit that incapacitates. Moreover, Sinclair establishes the link between personal health and social responsibility.

SURVEY OF CRITICISM

Unfortunately, there is very little criticism on Sinclair's writings, but with the reissuing of her works, surely she will receive the critical attention she deserves. The novel that has had the most notice is *Wasteland*, probably because it won the Harpers Prize Novel Award, which recognized ''the author of a work of outstanding merit in the field of fiction.'' Yet critical attention to this work, a prize winner, has primarily been book reviews. Reviews of *Wasteland* at its publication are positive for the most part; some of what the critics saw as excesses are excused because it is a first novel. Most critics respond to the powerful intensity of the novel, and all critics comment on the structure or lack of it. The use of psychology is addressed, since it is an early work dealing with the intimacy of the psychiatrist's office. Richard Plant of *The New Republic*, while admiring the novel's ''forthrightness,'' comments that it ''appears more of a case history than a novel'' (844). In contrast, Gertrude Springer of the leftist *Survey Graphic*, states that Sinclair uses the framework of psychoanalysis extremely skillfully, ''avoiding the pitfalls both of over-elaboration and oversimplification'' (174). Although not a review per se, a letter to Seid from Richard Wright (who also wrote a prepublication review) extolled the novel: ''Honesty such as you put in your words is seldom seen. And the suffering you depict is rarely ever admitted. And the insight you possess is surely not common. . . . You have said about the Jewish family what I have been trying to say about Negro families'' (*Seasons* 140–41).

There are two sustained studies of *Wasteland* at this point—Vivien Gornick's introduction to the present edition, and ''John Brown (né Jake Braunowitz) of the *Wasteland* of Jo Sinclair (née Ruth Seid)'' by Ellen Serlen Uffen. In addition, Diane Esther Levenberg, in a larger study of Jewish American novels, explores *Wasteland* within the context of Jung's theory of individuation, especially in regard to the role of the mother and parent-child conflict. Gornick finds the novel ''problematic'' because of its prose and its simplification of psychoanalytic process, but she comments that the novel was startling for its ''boldness of social feeling that linked Jews, blacks and homosexuals as cultural outsiders in a time when very few were able to make that parallel'' (no p.n.). Unfortunately, Gornick places the novel within a matrix of male Jewish writers rather than presenting it in relation to Jewish women writers such as Anzia Yezierska (an obvious antecedent) and modern writers like Adrienne Rich, who explore

Jewish identity within a broad interethnic, gender-specific context. Uffen, in contradistinction to some reviewers and biographers, examines the novel within a specifically Jewish context. She comments on the use of the Sabbath as the chosen day for Jake to meet with his psychiatrist and Passover as a "recurring leitmotif" in the novel—a "paradigm for salvation" (43). At the end, Uffen raises a question that sheds light on the range of responses to the issue of Jewish identity in the novel: "Is it right to believe that a man who despised himself and his family for being foreigners and Jews, is 'cured' when he is able to see himself as an anonymous Everyman?" (49).

This apparent conflict in the novel, further complicated by the fact that Seid continues to keep her anglicized pseudonym, is the basis for my article, "(Re)Constructing Identity: 'Angled' Presentation in Sinclair/Seid's *Wasteland.*" I examine the narrative discourse of Jake, his (Gentile) psychiatrist, and his sister Debby through a Lacanian reading of the alienated self. By analyzing Debby's role as liaison to the psychoanalytic moment, I explore the subtext of the novel's discourse and focus on the (re)building of personal and cultural identity through the acceptance of sexual difference and the "otherness" in oneself.

The Changelings, probing the complexity of one's identity in relation to the other, has had very little critical response at this juncture. Except for the critical pieces attached to the new edition, there are only reviews, which are extremely positive. Most intriguing is the review by Anzia Yezierska in the *New York Times Book Review*. In "Landlords of a City," Yezierska critiques the generation of Jews after the immigrants she wrote about, commenting that Sinclair "knows the driving ambition of the poor to rise out of their poverty, their dehumanizing grip on the possessions which took a lifetime's toil to win, the threat (at the sight of the newcomers) of the misery that they have just escaped" (33).

It is from the point of view of these "newcomers" that the two critical additions to the 1983 edition are written. "On Racism and Ethnocentrism," by Cole and Oakes, responds to the interethnic strife in the novel from a sociological viewpoint. Renowned African-American literary critic Nellie McKay writes the "Afterword," and she presents a sensitive reading of the novel. She pays special attention to the role of Jules Golden, the dying visionary who can see beyond his street and his influence on the young Judy Vincent. McKay commends the author for "reinforcing the need for constant vigilance against those prejudices that diminish our humanity" (337). McKay's understanding of the aptness of the novel today may precipitate further critical studies on this important work.

Sinclair's other works have not been critically reviewed in any cohesive manner. *Anna Teller* has a few reviews and an introduction to the new 1992 edition by Anne Halley. At the time of its initial publication, reviews were mixed, seeing the novel as unwieldly and undisciplined. Granville Hicks, in a review for *Saturday Review*, comments that Sinclair "has tried to do too much," but he also states that Anna Teller is such a ''compelling figure'' that readers will enjoy meeting her ''so much that the novel's faults will be forgiven'' (16). Halley's ''Afterword'' examines the work within the contemporary framework of family models. She comments: ''Contemporary readers of *Anna Teller* will gain a passionate, particular view of forty years of American political and social history,'' seen through this Eastern European Jewish family (598). With the reissue of *Anna Teller*, the publication of *The Seasons*, and the topical relevance of Sinclair's work, there should be more critical attention in the future.

BIBLIOGRAPHY

Works by Jo Sinclair

Wasteland. 1946. Philadelphia: Jewish Publication Society, 1987.
Sing at My Wake. New York: McGraw-Hill, 1951.
The Changelings. 1955. New York: Feminist Press, 1983.
Anna Teller. 1960. New York: Feminist Press, 1992.
The Seasons: Death and Transfiguration. New York: Feminist Press, 1992.
The Complete Ruth Seid (Jo Sinclair) Collection, Boston University Special Collections, Boston, MA.

Works about Jo Sinclair

Cole, Johnnetta B., and Elizabeth H. Oakes. ''On Racism and Ethnocentrism.'' *The Changelings.* 339–47.
Connolly, Francis X. ''Rev. of *Wasteland.*'' *The Commonweal* 22 Feb 1946: 485.
Fields, Harold. ''A Personal Conflict and Victory.'' *Saturday Review of Literature* 16 Feb 1946: 18.
Gitenstein, R. Barbara. ''Jo Sinclair (Ruth Seid).'' *Dictionary of Literary Biography* 28: 295–97.
Gornick, Vivien. ''Introduction.'' *Wasteland.* n. pag.
Halley, Anne. ''Afterword: The Family in *Anna Teller.*'' *Anna Teller.* 597–612.
Hass, Victor P. ''Empathy on the Block.'' *Saturday Review* 1 Oct 1955: 21.
Hicks, Granville, ''Two Families in Trouble.'' *Saturday Review* 20 Aug 1960: 16.
Levenberg, Diane Esther. *Parents and their Children in the American Jewish Novel of Immigration.* DAI 48/11A (1987): 2874. New York University.
Lowry, William McNeil. ''Of Being and Belonging.'' *New York Times Book Review* 17 Feb 1946: 5.
McKay, Nellie. ''Afterword.'' *The Changelings,* 323–37.
Mitgang, Herbert. ''Big Mama from Hungary.'' *New York Times Book Review* 9 Sept 1960: 16.
Plant, Richard. ''The Ghetto Within.'' *The New Republic* 10 June 1946: 84.
Sandberg, Elisabeth. ''Jo Sinclair: Toward a Critical Biography.'' *DAI* 46/12A (1985): 3720. University of Massachusetts.
Springer, Gertrude. ''Rev. of *Wasteland.*'' *Survey Graphic* 35 (May 1946): 174.

Sugrue, Thomas. "Not Quite Immigrants, Not Quite Americans." *New York Herald Tribune Weekly Book Review* 17 Feb 1946: VII 3.

Uffen, Ellen Serlen. "John Brown (né Jake Braunowtiz) of the *Wasteland* of Jo Sinclair (née Ruth Seid)." *Midwestern Miscellany XVI.* Ed. David D. Anderson. East Lansing, MI: The Midwestern Press, 1988. 41–51.

Wilentz, Gay. "(Re)Constructing Identity: 'Angled' Presentation in Sinclair/Seid's *Wasteland.*" *Multicultural Literatures through a Feminist-Poststructuralist Lens.* Ed. Barbara Frey Waxman. Knoxville: University of Tennessee Press, 1993. 84–102.

Yezierska, Anzia. "Landlords of a City." *New York Times Book Review.* 25 Sept. 1955: 33.

TESS SLESINGER (1905–1945)

Harvey Teres

BIOGRAPHY

Her life was short. Born in New York City on July 16, 1905, Tess Slesinger was stricken by cancer at the age of thirty-nine and died in Los Angeles on February 21, 1945. She grew up with three older brothers in an acculturated, financially comfortable, Jewish household. Unusual for the time, both parents pursued careers, her mother more successfully than did her father. Anthony Slesinger arrived in America from Hungary as a child and he graduated from City College of New York in 1889. He went on to attend law school at Columbia University, but before receiving his degree, he married and went into his father-in-law's successful garment business. He remained there, modestly successful, the rest of his life. Tess's mother, Augusta Singer Slesinger, despite leaving school after the eighth grade, became active in the field of social welfare. She directed a guidance clinic for children, became executive secretary of the Jewish Big Sisters, helped to found the New School for Social Research, and at the end of her life, completed a manuscript on psychoanalytic technique. The marriage lasted a full fifty years, but not a day longer: The day after their fiftieth anniversary, Slesinger's parents separated and the two never saw one another again.[1]

Slesinger attended high school at the Ethical Culture Society School in New York, she went to Swarthmore College for two years, and, finally, to the Columbia School of Journalism, where she received her B.A. degree. She worked for several years as assistant fashion editor at the *New York Herald Tribune* and as assistant literary editor at the *New York Post*, where she wrote book reviews. In 1928, at the age of twenty-two, she married Herbert Solow, the assistant editor of the *Menorah Journal*. This small but influential left-wing magazine of secularized Jewish culture was edited by the charismatic Elliot Cohen. Cohen, who later founded *Commentary*, attracted a circle of soon-to-be influential Jewish intellectuals that included Lionel Trilling, Diana (Rubin) Trilling, Clifton Fadiman, Felix Morrow, Anita Brenner, Henry Rosenthal, and Albert Halper (on the periphery were Sidney Hook, Max Eastman, and Lewis Mumford). Slesinger contributed book reviews, and in 1930, the *Journal* published her first short story. Other stories soon followed—in *American Mercury, Forum, Modern Quarterly, The New Yorker, Pagany, Scribner's, This Quarter,* and *Vanity Fair.* In 1932, she gained a degree of notoriety for her subtly ironic story "Miss Flinders,' published in *Story Magazine,* in which the subject of abortion was broached before the broad American public. Slesinger expanded the story into a novel, *The Unpossessed* (1934), in which the politics and especially the sexual politics of the *Menorah Journal* circle and left intellectual circles like it were subjected to trenchant yet solicitous critique.

Slesinger (who retained her name) and Solow divorced in 1932, and shortly after the publication of her collection of short stories *Time: The Present* (1935; reprinted as *On Being Told That Her Second Husband Has Taken His First Lover and Other Stories,* 1971 and 1990), she moved to Hollywood where she began a second career as a scriptwriter. Enticed by MGM's Irving Thalberg's offer of $1,000 a week, Slesinger's first project was to write the script for *The Good Earth* (1937), most of which remained intact in the final version of the film. While working on the film she met, and soon married, the film's assistant producer Frank Davis. Slesinger and Davis had two children and remained happily married until Tess's untimely death. They collaborated on writing scripts for numerous films, including *Dance, Girl, Dance* (1940), *Remember the Day* (1941), *Are Husbands Necessary?* (1942), and *A Tree Grows in Brooklyn* (1945).

Always politically active, Slesinger supported the campaigns to free Tom Mooney and the Scottsboro Boys, worked on behalf of the Abraham Lincoln Brigade, joined the Hollywood Anti-Nazi League, and was an officer of the Motion Picture Guild, an organization that encouraged the production of progressive films. Janet Sharistanian reports that Slesinger became disillusioned with the Communist Party—of which she was not a member but a fellow-traveler—following the Moscow Trials (1935–38) and especially the Nazi-Soviet Pact of 1939. Her most enduring political work was her courageous public support for the embattled Screen Writers Guild, which was finally able to negotiate its first contract in 1941.

When she died, Slesinger was at work on her second novel, a depiction of Hollywood from the point of view of its overlooked rank-and-file artisans and professionals. Portions of the incomplete manuscript have been published under the title of "A Hollywood Gallery."

MAJOR THEMES

Long before the feminist movement adopted the slogan "the personal is the political" in order to transform leftist politics during the 1960s, Tess Slesinger was exploring with admirable insight and acerbic wit the androcentrism, instrumentalism, and damaged personal lives of intellectual leftists during the 1930s.

She did not confine herself to writing about this group—she wrote about servants, wealthy schoolgirls, department store clerks, society women, secretaries, black and white high-school students, and bohemian types as well—but she has always been known as a satirist of the New York intelligentsia. This was partly because the radical men and, occasionally, the women of the period tended to write or influence the reviews, and to these reviewers, what she had to say about *them* always seemed the more compelling.

Her chief work was *The Unpossessed*, a novel that depicted the trials and tribulations of a small group of intellectual leftists, the sum of whose political activity is endless planning for a new leftist journal that, not surprisingly, never sees the light of day. The six major characters—three men and three women—comprise three couples whose dynamics are to varying degrees shaped by the needs of the men. Elizabeth Leonard is an independent, sexually free artist who returns from the expatriate community in Europe and pursues a romantic relationship with her distant cousin, mentor, and leader of a circle of intellectual leftists, Bruno Leonard (who resembles Elliot Cohen). The sterile Bruno, an English professor with no real connection to the working class, is unable to provide Elizabeth with anything beyond his wry wit—little emotion and certainly no commitment. Nor is he able to inspire or lead others due to his self-absorption and paralyzing ambivalence about every major question he faces, personal or political. Norah and Jeffrey Blake (who resembles Max Eastman) are the more placid of the novel's two married couples, but only because the eternally nurturing Norah never fails to provide her narcissistic and philandering husband with comforting caresses. The other married couple. Margaret and Miles Flinders (who resemble Slesinger and her first husband, Herbert Solow) endure a marriage shaped by the repressed Miles's brittle New England morality, his disappointments with his career, and his perceived political obligations. In the powerful final chapter of the novel, ''Missis Flinders,'' the moody Miles convinces Margaret to abort their child so that they can devote themselves more completely to a political movement, with little regard for the personal, family, and emotional lives of its participants.

Whereas most political novels of the thirties centered around public events such as strikes, meetings, foreclosers, or dispossessions, Slesinger's was a leftist novel of manners: sexuality (homosexual as well as heterosexual), the construction of gender, marriage, family relations, sensibility, the unconscious—these comprised the real subject matter of a novel that insisted upon a broad definition of politics. In treating these themes, Slesinger employed a movable point of view, taking the reader inside the minds of various characters in order to render their inner speech. Evasion, rationalization, fantasy, and uncertainty were here given full and often ironic expression. In fashioning her fictions of consciousness, she owed a particular debt to Dostoevsky and his treatment of alienated intellectuals. Her title is itself a play on Dostoevsky's *The Possessed*, indicating that her radicals are rather more depressed than obsessed. One also finds in her work the imprint of Henry James, Katherine Mansfield, and Virginia Woolf and their intensive exploration of inner consciousness, especially where female sensibilities are concerned. There is, as well, the influence of James Joyce and his innovations in narrative point of view and stream of consciousness, and of Dorothy Parker, with her cheerful rather than mordant wit. In terms of Slesinger's own influence, it is worth noting that the fiction of her younger and more celebrated contemporary Mary McCarthy has much in common with Slesinger's (although no direct link has been established between the two writers). Certainly McCarthy's very witty novels, like Slesinger's, remain noteworthy for their bold explorations of female identity and sexual politics among the well-educated.

In her short stories, Slesinger explores such provocative subjects as class exploitation, racism, liberal guilt and unacknowledged snobbery, marriage and divorce, and masculine and feminine identity. She does so through the prism of personal impression and interior monologue, techniques that deflate whatever and whomever is portentous, self-important, or ideologically narrow. In *On Being Told That Her Second Husband Has Taken His First Lover,* for example, Slesinger depicts a vulnerable woman's complex response to her second husband's infidelity. Hardly a paragon of militant feminism, this twice-burned victim of masculine vanity struggles to suppress her emotions and perform the necessary roles that she believes will allow her to endure. ''White On Black'' is a rare example of a white author writing on black experience. The story charts the rise and fall of Paul and Elizabeth Wilson, black siblings who attend an exclusive and largely white private school on the West Side, whose early popularity gives way to isolation as the result of changing racial attitudes among whites. ''Jobs in the Sky'' dispenses with transitions and employs multiple narrative perspectives to lend a sense of confusion to the chaotic Christmas shopping season at a large department store whose employees are cynically exploited by the paternalistic owner and his managers. ''The Friedmans' Annie'' portrays a young, naive German housekeeper who must decide whether to marry her insensitive, unambitious working-class boyfriend or follow the advice of her employers who complacently assure her she can do better. Finally, the experimental ''A Life in the Day of a Writer'' brilliantly satirizes a childish male writer with writer's block who attributes his failures to his wife and who dreams that his work will be seminal in more ways than one.

SURVEY OF CRITICISM

By and large, Slesinger has been well served by her critics, most of whom have been appreciative of her talents—the problem has been a lack of critics. Her first book, *The Unpossessed*, was enthusiastically reviewed. Horace Gregory commented in *Books* that Slesinger ''is a writer of unquestionable ability'' (2). Writing in *New Outlook*, Robert Cantwell declared her book to be ''one of the very best of recent American novels'' (53). T. S. Matthews in *New Republic* described the ''extraordinary promise'' of the novel: ''[I]n its conscious sentimentality, its conscious self-mockery, in its fundamental unwillingness to be content with either, this novel is authentically of our day'' (52). J. D. Adams, writing in the *New York Times*, observed that ''*The Unpossessed* is an imperfect book, it is both clever and wise, which in a writer as young as Miss Slesinger is a rare combination'' (6). John Chamberlain, also writing in the *Times*, called the work ''quite simply and dogmatically, the best novel of contemporary New York City that we have read'' (17). In the *New Masses*, Philip Rahv praised Slesinger for her biting satire of Trotskyists, although he added that the novel failed to present radicals with a ''disciplined orientation'' (27). *The Unpossessed* enjoyed four printings within a month of its appearance, as well as a British edition. By the fifties, however, Kempton (1955) referred to the novel as ''almost forgotten.''

When it was reissued by Avon in 1966, it was accompanied by an ''Afterword'' by Lionel Trilling entitled ''A Novel of the Thirties,'' an essay of genuine importance for our understanding of American radicalism and the tumultuous decade of the 1930s. Although Trilling's views did not propel Slesinger to the higher ranks, his essay did strengthen her reputation as a writer still worth reading. (It should be mentioned that Slesinger was one of the very few female or noncanonical writers to whom Trilling devoted a major essay.) Having known both Slesinger and Solow as a fellow member of the *Menorah* group, Trilling contributed some personal impressions and biographical data. His focus, however, was on the lack of a moral life in the political culture of the day. Slesinger's novel, Trilling claimed, was not true to the specific political circle it portrayed, but no matter: Its enduring strength lay in its examination of what happens when ''the conscious commitment to virtue'' results in ''an absoluteness or abstractness which has the effect of denying some free instinctual impulse that life must have'' (1981, 20). Trilling argued that the novel was diminished by reading it as ''that so often graceless thing, a novel of feminine protest'' (23). He interpreted the novel's gendered stereotypes (men are linked to intellect and spirit, and women to instinct and the body—Norah, for example, is said to embody a ''mysterious private womanhood'') as contributing to the novel's larger intention, which was to ''set forth the dialectic between life and the desire to make life as good as it might be, between 'nature' and 'spirit' '' (23).

Turning away from the male critics' (Lionel Trilling, Philip Rahv, Murray Kempton) interest in whether Slesinger accurately portrayed the political left, Shirley Biagi and Janet Sharistanian reoriented Slesinger criticism in several ways. First, they gave greater emphasis to such subjects as female sexuality, gender construction, and the power relations between men and women in Slesinger's fiction. Second, they placed a new emphasis on Slesinger's short stories, showing her to be a more versatile and stylistically interesting writer than had been previously claimed. Third, they took seriously both her career as an accomplished scriptwriter and her political activism during her years in Hollywood. Finally, both scholars provided important new biographical data that has shed light on Slesinger's fiction. Janet Sharistanian (1979) has also introduced and edited portions of Slesinger's 150-page unpublished manuscript.

Alan Wald (1976) had given a thorough account of the *Menorah* group, and in *The New York Intellectuals*, he has inquired into how the group is represented in *The Unpossessed*. He has pointed out that several of the chief characters in the novel are actually composites: Miles Flinders, for example, said to be based solely upon Solow, is Irish Catholic, whereas Solow was Jewish, an important difference. Wald has called attention to the novel's failure to capture the dynamic and sophisticated political character of the group, but he has acknowledged that Slesinger's critique of the group's distance from ordinary Americans is accurate and central to the novel's overall meaning.

Paul Rabinowitz has provided yet a third approach to Slesinger, resisting the alternatives of placing her within the context of the male-dominated radicalism of the 1930s or within a bourgeois feminine literary history. Rabinowitz has instead placed Slesinger alongside other relatively neglected women writers of the 1930s who sought to "regender the revolutionary novel"—Tillie Olsen, Meridel Le Sueur, Josephine Herbst, and others.

Most recently, Philip Abbott has explored Slesinger's critique of dogmatism and male domination on the left in terms of its historical failure to construct organizations capable of attracting and sustaining a community of active citizens in a liberal society.

In 1977, Shirley Biagi ruefully observed that Tess Slesinger had been overlooked despite "the current flurry of rediscovery of gifted women writers." Today, she has not been overlooked—both her novel and her collection of short stories remain in print, and scholars mentioned above have contributed valuable work. But Slesinger has yet to be rediscovered by the public or, for that matter, by an academic culture enamored of politics but forgetful of the dangers of unlimited politicization and therefore in need of her gifts.

NOTE

1. These and other biographical details are derived from the work of Biagi and Sharistanian.

BIBLIOGRAPHY

My thanks to Janet Sharistanian, who has generously provided me with bibliographical data on Slesinger's uncollected work.

Works by Tess Slesinger

Fiction

"Young Wife." *This Quarter* 3.4 (April–June 1931): 698–708.
"Brother to the Happy." *Pagany* 3.1 (1932): 77–82.

"Kleine Frau." *Modern Youth* 1.2 (1933): 28–32.

The Unpossessed. New York: Simon and Schuster, 1934. New York: Avon, 1966. Old Westbury, CT: The Feminist Press, 1984.

"The Lonelier Eve."*New Yorker* 28 April 1934: 32–33.

"Ben Grader Makes a Call." *Vanity Fair* (June 1934): 40, 70.

"The Old Lady Counts Her Injuries." *Vanity Fair* (Oct. 1934): 23, 79.

Time: The Present. New York: Simon and Schuster, 1935. Reprinted as *On Being Told That Her Second Husband Has Taken His First Lover and Other Stories.* New York: Simon and Schuster, 1971. Chicago: Ivan Dee, 1990.

"After the Cure." *Vanity Fair* (Jan. 1935): 48, 65–66.

"Mr. Palmer's Party." *New Yorker* (27 April 1935): 30–32.

"The Best Things in Life Are Three." *Vanity Fair* (Aug. 1935): 16, 52b.

"For Better, For Worse," *Delineator* 28 (1936): 18–19.

"A Hollywood Gallery." *Michigan Quarterly Review* 18 (1979): 439–54.

Articles and Essays

"Memoirs of an Ex-Flapper." *Vanity Fair* (Dec. 1934): 26–27, 74, 76.

"Where the Dear and the Antelope Roam . . . ." *Vanity Fair* (June 1935): 42–43.

"How to Throw a Cocktail Party." *Vanity Fair* (July 1935); 46–47, 59.

Screenplays

With Talbot Jennings and Claudine West. *The Good Earth.* MGM, 1937.

With F. Bradbury Foote. *The Bride Wore Red.* MGM, 1937.

With Richard Sherman. *Girls' School.* Columbia, 1938.

With Frank Davis. *Dance, Girl, Dance.* RKO Radio Pictures, 1940.

With Frank Davis. *Are Husbands Necessary?* Paramount, 1941.

With Frank Davis and Allan Scott. *Remember the Day.* 20th-Century Fox, 1941.

With Frank Davis, additions by Anita Loos. *A Tree Grows in Brooklyn.* 20th-Century Fox, 1945.

Works about Tess Slesinger

Abbott, Philip. "Are Three Generations of Radicals Enough? Self-Critique in the Novels of Tess Slesinger, Mary McCarthy, and Marge Piercy." *The Review of Politics* (Fall 1991): 602–26.

Adams, J. D. Rev. of *The Unpossessed. New York Times* 20 May 1934: 6.

Biagi, Shirley. "Forgive Me for Dying." *Antioch Review* 35 (1977): 224–36.

Cantwell, Robert. Rev. of *The Unpossessed. New Outlook* June 1934: 53.

Chamberlain, John. Rev. of *The Unpossessed. New York Times* 9 May 1934: 17.

Ferguson, Mary Anne. "Tess Slesinger." *American Women Writers 4.* Ed. Lina Mainiero. New York: Ungar, 1979–1982: 94–96.

Gregory, Horace. Rev. of *The Unpossessed. Books* 13 May 1934: 2.

Kempton, Murray. *Part of Our Time.* New York: Simon and Schuster, 1955: 121–123.

———. "From the Depths of the Thirties." *New Republic* 5 Nov. 1966: 25–28.

Matthews, T. S. Rev. of *The Unpossessed. New Republic* 23 May 1934: 52.

Millett, Fred B. "Tess Slesinger." *Contemporary American Authors.* New York: Harcourt, 1943.

Rabinowitz, Paula. *Labor & Desire: Women's Revolutionary Fiction in Depression America.* Chapel Hill: North Carolina University Press, 1991: 137–50.

Rahv, Philip. Rev. of *The Unpossessed. New Masses* Sept. 1934: 27.

Sharistanian, Janet. "Tess Slesinger's Hollywood Sketches." *Michigan Quarterly Review* 18 (1979): 439–54.

———. "Afterword." *The Unpossessed.* Old Westbury, CT: The Feminist Press, 1984: 359–386.

Trilling, Lionel. "Young in the Thirties." *Commentary* May 1966: 43–51. Reprinted as the Afterword to *The Unpossessed.* New York: Avon, 1966. Also reprinted as "A Novel of the Thirties" in Trilling, *The Last Decade.* New York: Harcourt, 1981: 3–24.

Wald, Alan. "The Menorah Group Moves Left." *Jewish Social Studies* 38.3–4 (1976): 289–320.

———. *The New York Intellectuals.* Chapel Hill: North Carolina University Press, 1987: 64–74.

SUSAN SONTAG (1933–   )

Sherry Lee Linkon

BIOGRAPHY

Susan Sontag was born January 16, 1933, in New York City, and spent her early years there, living with her grandparents while her parents operated an export business in China. Her mother returned to the United States in 1938, after Sontag's father died of tuberculosis; in 1939, the family moved to Tucson, Arizona, in part because of Sontag's asthma. They later moved to southern California. Sontag's family was Jewish but not religious.

At fifteen, Sontag entered UC Berkeley and a year later she transferred to the University of Chicago, where she met and married her psychology professor, Philip Rieff. Once she completed her B.A. in 1951, they moved to Boston, where Sontag studied at Harvard University, completing M.A. degrees in both English and Philosophy. Soon after starting the Ph.D. program in Philosophy, she gave birth to their son, David. The couple spent two years apart while Sontag studied at Oxford and the University of Paris, and then they divorced in 1959.

Sontag taught at Sarah Lawrence College and the City College of New York and worked as an editor at *Commentary*. Abandoning work on her dissertation, she began writing essays and reviews and started her first novel. Published in 1963, *The Benefactor* received generally positive reviews. She continued writing essays on art and culture, which were collected in her most influential book, *Against Interpretation*. Her second novel, *Death Kit*, appeared in 1967, followed by *Trip to Hanoi* (1968), recounting her experiences in Vietnam, and another essay collection, *Styles of Radical Will* (1969). By this time, Sontag had become a sort of intellectual celebrity, appearing in *Rolling Stone* and *Playboy* as well as in *Partisan Review*.

In 1967, she began work as a filmmaker, writing and directing *Duet for Cannibals* (1969) and *Brother Carl* (1971). Sontag also made a documentary on the Yom Kippur war, *Promised Lands* (1974), her sole work dealing directly with Jewish issues. Along with her work behind the camera, she won a National Book Critics Circle Award for *On Photography* (1977).

In 1975, Sontag was diagnosed with breast cancer, resulting in a mastectomy and several years of chemotherapy. These experiences led her to write *Illness as Metaphor* (1978), an extended discussion of the language of disease and the use of disease as an image in Western culture. She published a short-story collection, *I, Etcetera* in the same year. Another essay collection, *Under the Sign of Saturn*, appeared in 1980. During the 1970s, she received additional grants and fellowships and was elected to the American Academy of Arts and Letters in 1976. Her contribution to American cultural criticism was marked by the publication of *A Susan Sontag Reader* in 1981.

Sontag continues her work in several media. *Unguided Tour*, her most recent film, appeared in 1983, and in 1985, she directed the premiere production of Milan Kundera's play *Jacques and His Master* at the American Repertory Theatre. She has written an additional volume on illness, *AIDS and Its Metaphors* (1989), as well as the fictional *The Way We Live Now* (1991). Sontag has been active in PEN International and became its president in 1987. Most recently, she has written essays for *The New Yorker* and a historical novel, *The Volcano Lover* (1992). She lives in Manhattan.

MAJOR THEMES

In both criticism and fiction, Susan Sontag explores the central concerns of modernism: the problematic nature of perception and interpretation, anxiety about self and death, and alienation. *The Benefactor* questions the connection between dreams and reality as the protagonist, Hyppolite, attempts, literally, to make his dreams come true. The story involves Hyppolite's efforts to end his relationship with his older mistress, Frau Anders. The first-person narrative relates both Hyppolite's dreams and his waking life, offering several versions of the protagonist's experiences and Frau Anders' fate. Through Hyppolite's dreams and recollections, Sontag raises questions about the nature of experience and reality.

Death Kit pushes the examination of reality further by creating a protagonist whose very name punningly asks the reader to question the veracity of his experience. Diddy (did he?) believes he has killed a train worker, but his blind lover, Hester, insists that he did not. The novel traces his relationship with Hester and his obsession with the murder. In the end, Diddy and Hester return to the train tunnel to reenact the opening scenes and explore the chambers of death they find there. Indeed, Tony Tanner has suggested that the entire narrative can be read as Diddy's exploration of the themes of life and death as he dies. Diddy's attempt to discern the truth reflects Sontag's critical concerns with the subjectivity and meaninglessness of interpretation, and his narrative raises questions about the experience and meaning of death.

The short stories in *I, Etcetera* explore the relationship of the self to art, history, and experience. Several stories employ a fragmentary style, such as ''Project for a Trip to China'' and ''Unguided Tour,'' which use short, note-like sections to present their narrators' perspectives on travel, history, and art. Sontag later wrote a filmscript and directed a film version of "Unguided Tour."

Sontag's most recent and most critically acclaimed novel, *The Volcano Lover*, examines the experience, meaning, and effects of aesthetic obsession in a re- telling of the real histories of Lord William Hamilton, his carefully cultivated wife Emma, and Lord Nelson. Emphasizing the characters' relationships with each other and their positions in history, Sontag identifies them, not by their names, but by labels: the Cavaliere, the Cavaliere's wife (most often referred to simply as "she"), and the hero. Through much of the novel, the narrator, speak- ing from a twentieth-century perspective, muses on the habits and sensibilities of the Cavaliere, a collector of fine art and ancient artifacts, who, like a critic, seeks to possess and even to have a hand in creating what he admires. In doing so, the collector both changes and risks losing what he desires to own. The Cavaliere first transforms Emma from a beautiful but lower-class, uneducated mistress into his accomplished wife, confidante to the queen, and a much- admired actress, known for her "attitudes," *tableaux vivants* based upon well- known statues and mystical figures. His efforts help her become the woman who could win Nelson's love, and as a collector, the Cavaliere recognizes that his possession gains value according to its desirability to others. Thus, while his- torical events swirl around them, he watches as the affair develops between his wife and Lord Nelson. This juxtaposition between the private history of these three characters and the public history of France, Italy, and England at the end of the eighteenth century highlights Sontag's sense of the inherent tension be- tween experience and reality. Where her earlier novels explored this tension within the lives and dreams of individual characters, *The Volcano Lover* posi- tions individual experiences in contrast with historical reality.

Although Sontag has said that she sees herself primarily as a fiction writer, she is best known for her essays on aesthetics, beginning with *Against Inter- pretation*. In the title essay, she argues that works of art should be experienced rather than interpreted; her later work on visual arts, literature, film, photogra- phy, and the politics of cultural discourse raise questions about how audiences experience art and how critics think about art in the twentieth century. Her work also explores the relationship between form, style, and content. She was among the first critics to take popular culture seriously in "Notes on 'Camp,' " which remains one of her most influential pieces.

Sontag does not draw directly on Jewish themes in her writing, but her essays reveal her strong connection with the European Jewish intellectual tradition. Angela McRobbie identifies Sontag as the "sole woman alongside a generation of great Jewish intellectuals" (7), and like many Jewish scholars and critics of the twentieth century, Sontag embraces serious secular discourse with the com- mitment of earlier rabbinic scholars. Acting as an intellectual liaison between Europe and the United States, she has introduced American readers to European Jewish critics such as Walter Benjamin and George Lukacs Starting in the 1960s, Sontag wrote essays critiquing and celebrating the ideas and personalities of these and other European critics long before they became central figures in academic criticism.

Sontag's three books on illness explore the relationship between discourse and experience. *Illness as Metaphor* examines the mataphorical uses of cancer and the problem of assigning agency to the disease or to its sufferers. In *AIDS and Its Metaphors*, she argues that the image of the plague distorts popular understanding of the disease. She also expresses her concerns about AIDS in *The Way We Live Now*, inspired by the illness and death of her friend Robert Mapplethorpe.

SURVEY OF CRITICISM

Reviews of Sontag's fiction have been mixed, and her novels and short stories have received little attention from literary scholars. While some reviewers have praised the ideas presented in her fiction, others have bemoaned its stylistic weaknesses. In a review of *Death Kit*, for example, Gore Vidal commented on Sontag's "well-known difficulties in writing English" (45). Richard Jenkyns, in his review of *The Volcano Lover*, similarly chastises Sontag for "fluctuation of tone," which, he says, "suggests not depth or complexity" but "uncertainty and a lack of control" (46). Other reviewers have praised Sontag's fiction for its insightful explorations of the nature of self and consciousness and have particularly noted how Sontag's style and form support the ideas of her work. Taylor, for example, values the artificial, constructed quality of Sontag's fiction (909), which, he says, makes readers aware of the self within texts that examine the nature of the self. For McCaffery, *Death Kit* is not "blatantly artificial"; rather, it is appropriately dream-like. Bassoff similarly praises Sontag for using a narrative approach that helps convey her ideas about alienation and the problems of interpretation in *The Benefactor*.

Many critics have seen Sontag's most recent novel, *The Volcano Lover*, as not only her best, but also as an important contribution to contemporary American fiction. It has achieved both critical and popular success, gaining best-seller status and reviews in *Time* and *Newsweek*, as well as being featured in popular book clubs. Michiko Kakutani celebrates the "intimate, friendly voice, erudite and knowing" that dominates the novel, claiming that it is "light years removed from the chilly, annoyingly abstract voice" of Sontag's earlier fiction. For Kakutani, *The Volcano Lover* is a "passionate and often radical novel of ideas that afford all the old-fashioned pleasures of a traditional historical novel." Alexandra Johnson, writing for *The Nation*, calls the book Sontag's "most successful statement" (365) and sees in it evidence of "a shift from the moral intelligence of the essayist to the intelligent heart of the novelist" (367). In her *Belles Lettres* review, Brenda Wineapple praises Sontag for successfully combining graphic descriptions of both the beautiful and the violent aspects of Neapolitan society with a narrative voice that sometimes remains appropriately distant and sometimes offers its own evaluations of the novel's events (60–61).

Other reviewers have been less enthusiastic, however. Jenkyns expresses doubts about the novel's characterization and Sontag's awkward, even lecture-like, combination of ideas and narrative. John Simon complains that Sontag often "contradicts herself" within the novel, and he cites a number of anach-ronisms and "gross errors" in the text. Moreover, he notes, the novel's central image "misfires, remains dormant" (65). In the *New York Times Book Review*, John Banville evaluates the novel as "impressive, at times enchanting, always entertaining," but also "curiously hollow" (27). While he praises Sontag for breathing life into "such a tired old genre as the historical novel" (26), he also notes that Sontag's "passionate moral intelligence" is "peculiarly damaging to her art" (27), a comment that echoes much of the criticism of Sontag's fiction.

The one book-length study of Sontag's work, Sonya Sayres's *Susan Sontag: The Elegiac Modernist* (1990), devotes one chapter to the two earlier novels and the remaining chapters to Sontag's aesthetics of silence and her attempts to articulate a modernist sensibility in an increasingly postmodern age. Sayres iden-tifies several "key terms" that she sees as essential in understanding Sontag's work: silence, the "spirit of negation," the "pathos or heroes," concerns with ethics and an "authentic moral spirit," political involvement, and a melancholy sensibility. According to Sayres, these themes reveal Sontag's allegiance to mod-ernism, even as some of her work employs postmodern themes and forms.

Elizabeth Holdsworth's unpublished dissertation, "Susan Sontag: Writer-Filmmaker" (1981), examines the contradictions as well as the unifying themes of Sontag's work. In her examination of Sontag's criticism, fiction, and film, Holdsworth traces the development of Sontag's ideas, especially her concern with individual consciousness.

Other criticism focuses on Sontag's contribution to contemporary critical dis-course. Cary Nelson argues that Sontag's criticism is less concerned with ex-ploring specific questions than with examining the nature of criticism itself by recording her own critical processes (1979). In a later piece, Nelson describes Sontag's criticism as self-reflexive, a "search for a text that is utterly unknow-able, . . . that cannot be contaminated by critical rhetoric" (1980, 709). Liam Kennedy identifies the parallels and disjunctions between Sontag's criticism and the work of poststructuralists such as Foucault and Derrida. While she shares the poststructuralists' doubts about the concepts of truth and the self, he claims, she will not relinquish the self at the center of her criticism. Like the poststruc-turalists, she questions dialectical thinking, but she is not satisfied with the play of difference as a critical end in itself. Kennedy identifies this resistance as the "humanist residue" in Sontag's work. Steve Light has criticized Sontag's claims about the integrity of American criticism.

Much of the criticism of Sontag focuses on her political ideas. Sontag's 1982 speech criticizing Soviet Communism as "fascism with a human face" (qtd. in Sayres 41) generated both criticism of her position and discussion of the role of writers in political life (see Branham, Lardner, Timmerman). Reflecting on

Sontag's 1969 essay about Cuba, Laura Kipnis questions her ideas about the relationship between aesthetics and foreign policy.

Feminists have both criticized Sontag's distance from the women's movement and embraced her ideas as useful. Angela McRobbie chastises Sontag for ignoring issues of gender in her criticism, but argues that feminist critics should not dismiss her. The modern mode Sontag explores is "a largely male condition" (8), McRobbie notes, and her lack of attention to gender reflects modernism's disregard for women. Writing from the perspective of feminist sociology, Joanne L. Finkelstein finds in Sontag's questioning of interpretive frameworks an alternative model of scholarship.

BIBLIOGRAPHY

Works by Susan Sontag

Selected Criticism

This list includes only Sontag's major critical writings.

Against Interpretation. New York: Farrar, Straus & Giroux, 1966; London: Eyre & Spottiswoode, 1967.

"Some Thoughts on the Right Way (for Us) to Love the Cuban Revolution." *Ramparts* 7 (April 1969): 6, 10, 14, 16, 18–19.

Trip to Hanoi. New York: Farrar, Straus & Giroux, 1968; London: Panther, 1969.

Styles of Radical Will. New York: Farrar, Straus & Giroux, 1969; London: Secker & Warburg, 1969.

"The Third World of Women." *Partisan Review* 40 (Summer 1973): 180–206.

On Photography. New York: Farrar, Straus & Giroux, 1977.

Illness as Metaphor. New York: Farrar, Straus & Giroux, 1977.

Under the Sign of Saturn. New York: Farrar, Straus & Giroux, 1980.

A Susan Sontag Reader. New York: Farrar, Straus & Giroux, 1981.

"Sontag on Mapplethorpe." *Vanity Fair* July 1985: 69–73.

Introductions/Prefaces

"Introduction." *Antonin Artaud: Selected Writings.* Translated by Helen Weaver, Susan Sontag, ed. New York: Farrar, Straus & Giroux, 1976. xvii-lix.

"Introduction." *A Roland Barthes Reader*, Susan Sontag, ed. London: Cape, 1981; New York: Hill & Wang, 1982. vii-xxxviii.

Fiction

The Benefactor. New York: Farrar, Straus & Giroux, 1963; London: Eyre & Spottiswoode, 1964.

"Man with a Pain." *Harper's* April 1964: 72–75.

"The Will and the Way." *Partisan Review* 33 (Summer 1965): 373–96.

Death Kit. New York: Farrar, Straus & Giroux, 1967; London: Secker & Warburg, 1968.

I, Etcetera. New York: Farrar, Straus & Giroux, 1978.

"The Letter Scene." *New Yorker* 18 Aug. 1986: 24–32.

The Way We Live Now. New York: Noonday Press, Farrar, Straus & Giroux, 1991.
The Volcano Lover: A Romance. New York: Farrar, Straus & Giroux, 1992.

Films

Duet for Cannibals. Prod. Goran Lingren for Sandrew Film and Theater (AB) Sweden, 1969 (distributed by Evergreen Films, USA). In Swedish, subtitles by Sontag. Black & white, 105 min.
Brother Carl. Prod. Goran Lindgren for Sandrew Film and Theater (AB) and Svenska Filminstitutet, 1971 (distributed by New Yorker Films). In Swedish, with English soundtrack. Black & white, 97 min.
Promised Lands. 1974 (distributed by New Yorker Films). Color, 87 min.
Unguided Tour. Prod. Giovannella Zannoni for Lunga Gittata Cooperative, RAI rete 3. Color, 72 min.

Selected Interviews.

Bellamy, Joe David. "Susan Sontag." *The New Fiction: Interviews with Innovative American Writers.* Urbana; University of Illinois Press, 1974. 113–29.
Boyers, Robert and Maxine Bernstein. "Women, The Arts & The Politics of Culture. An Interview with Susan Sontag." *Salmagundi* 31–32 (Fall 1975–Winter 1976): 29–48.
Cott, Jonathan. "Susan Sontag: The *Rolling Stone* Interview." *Rolling Stone* 4 Oct. 1979: 46–53.

Works about Susan Sontag

This list includes only major reviews and critical works, including those pieces cited above.

Banville, John. "By Lava Possessed." *New York Times Book Review* 9 Aug 1992: 1, 26–27.
Bassoff, Bruce. "Private Revolution: Susan Sontag's *The Benefactor.*" *enclitic* 3 (1979): 59–73.
Branham, Robert J. "Speaking Itself: Susan Sontag's Town Hall Address." *Quarterly Journal of Speech* Aug. 1989: 259–77.
Finkelstein, Joanne L. "Sociology and Susan Sontag: Reshaping the Discipline." *Women's Studies International Quarterly* 4 (1981): 179–90.
Gates, David. "There Is No Crater Love." *Newsweek* 24 Aug 1992: 63.
Holdsworth, Elizabeth McCaffrey. "Susan Sontag: Writer-Filmmaker." Diss. Ohio State University, 1981.
Jenkyns, Richard. "Eruptions." *New Republic* 7 Sept 1992: 46–49.
Johnson, Alexandra. "Romance as Metaphor." *The Nation* 5 Oct 1992: 365–68.
Kakutani, Michiko. "Historical Novel Flavored With Passion and Ideas." *New York Times* 4 Aug 1992: B2.
Kennedy, Liam. "Precocious Archaeology: Susan Sontag and the Criticism of Culture." *Journal of American Studies* 24 (April 1990): 23–39.
Kipnis, Laura. "Aesthetics and Foreign Policy." *Social Text* 15 (Fall 1986): 89–98.
Lardner, James. "Susan Sontag into the Fray." *Washington Post* 16 Mar. 1982: C1–9.

Light, Steve. "The Noise of Decomposition: Response to Susan Sontag." *Sub-stance* 26 (1980): 85–94.

McCaffery, Larry. "*Death Kit*: Susan Sontag's Dream Narrative." *Contemporary Literature* 20 (Autumn 1979): 484–99.

McRobbie, Angela. "The Modernist Style of Susan Sontag." *Feminist Review* 38 (Summer 1991): 1–19.

Nelson, Cary. "Reading Criticism." *PMLA* 91 (1976): 801–15.

———. "Soliciting Self-Knowledge: The Rhetoric of Susan Sontag." *Critical Inquiry* (Summer 1980): 707–29.

Roudiez, Leon S. "Susan Sontag: Against the Ideological Grain." *World Literature Today* 57 (Spring 1983): 219–23.

Sayres, Sohnya. "Susan Sontag and the Practice of Modernism." *American Literary History* 1 (Fall 1989): 593–611.

———. *Susan Sontag: The Elegiac Modernist.* New York: Routledge, 1990.

Sheppard, R. S. "Lava Soap." *Time* 17 Aug 1992: 66–67.

Simon, John. "The Valkyrie of Lava." *National Review* 31 Aug 1992: 63–65.

Tanner, Tony. "Space Odyssey." *Partisan Review* 35 (Summer 1968): 446–51.

Taylor, Benjamin. "A Centered Voice: Susan Sontag's Short Fiction." *Georgia Review* 34 (Winter 1980): 907–16.

Timmerman, Jacobo. "Moral Symmetry." *The Nation* 6 Mar. 1982: 261.

———. "Setting the Record Straight." *The Nation* 13 Mar. 1982: 292.

Vidal, Gore. "Miss Sontag's New Novel." *Reflections upon a Sinking Ship.* Boston: Little, Brown, 1969: 41–47.

Wineapple, Brenda. "Damn Them All." *Belles Lettres* 8 (Spring 1993); 2–3, 60–61.

BELLA SPEWACK (1899–1990)

Elizabeth Drorbaugh

BIOGRAPHY

Bella Spewack may be known best to the general public through her public relations legacy on behalf of the Girl Scouts. She claimed to have come up with the Girl Scout cookie as a promotional gimmick when she was a publicist for the organization. Much later in her life, in apparent exasperation, she described the cookie as "that heinous, heinous thing"; she preferred to be remembered for the plays and screenwriting that she and her husband, Samuel, coauthored over the course of several decades.

Bella Spewack (née Cohen) was born in the Transylvania region of what is now Romania (or, as has been variously reported, in Bucharest, Romania, or Budapest, Hungary). She emigrated to New York with her family when she was very young. Throughout her years at Washington Irving High School, from which she graduated in 1917, she was active in theatre as an actor and director. She helped out at the Provincetown Players, a renowned, experimental theatre company in Greenwich Village.

In 1922 Bella, who had been writing a column, "Pippa Passes," for the New York *Call*, met and married fellow journalist Samuel Spewack. Shortly thereafter, the couple moved to Berlin and then to Moscow, where Samuel was stationed as a correspondent for the *New York World*. During their four years overseas, Bella assisted her husband as a journalist, whole she continued to write fiction. One of her short stories, "The Laugh," was published in *The Best Short Stories of 1925*. The Spewacks later based some of their plays and filmscripts, including *Clear All Wires!*, on their experiences abroad.

When they returned to New York in 1926, Bella worked as a theatrical press agent for *The Miracle*, the revue *The Chauve Souris*, and the visiting music studio of the Moscow Art Theatre. "Seduced by the theatre," as Samuel Spewack put it (Gould 137), they began to write plays, beginning a close professional collaboration that lasted over forty years. Their first play to be produced was *Solitaire Man* (1926), a sentimental melodrama. This was followed by

Poppa and *War Song* in 1928, which opened to mixed critical reviews. In 1932 *Clear All Wires!* opened to generally good reviews, followed by a ninety-two-performance run, establishing the Spewacks on Broadway.

Responding to an offer from film producer Louis Weitzenkorn, who had been Bella's colleague on the staff of the *Call*, the Spewacks turned to writing screenplays. Their film adaptation of *Clear All Wires!* was released within a year of the play's opening. The Spewacks' romance with the movie industry was short-lived, however, for within three years, they returned to Broadway with their play *Boy Meets Girl* (1935), a farcical rendition of Hollywood. Nonetheless, they succumbed again to its blandishments and adapted their play *Boy Meets Girl* to film in 1938. In 1940, *Out West It's Different*, a spoof of the theatre this time—and one of the very few Spewack plays that did not have a Broadway production—opened at the McCarter Theatre in Princeton, New Jersey.

During World War II, the Spewacks temporarily stopped writing plays. Bella wrote a series of programs about war efforts for the American Broadcasting Company, while Samuel, as Bureau Chief of Motion Pictures for the Office of War Information, wrote and directed *The World at War*, the first full-length film on war to be produced by the United States government.

After the war, the Spewacks returned to script writing, generally earning greater commercial success in films [for example, *Weekend at the Waldorf* (1945)] than with plays, until 1948, when *Kiss Me, Kate* scored an enormous stage hit. The comedy, with its Cole Porter score, won a Tony Award for best musical. It played from 1948 to 1950 in New York, followed by a lengthy run in London and innumerable revivals worldwide. In 1953, *My Three Angels*, an adaptation of a French comedy about a trio of winning scoundrels, opened on Broadway to popular acclaim; its 344 New York performances were succeeded by 228 performances in London.

In 1955, *The Festival*, Bella and Samuel Spewacks' last original play for Broadway, opened to generally negative reviews, prompting Bella to take matters into her own hands. At the theatre the next night, she climbed on stage, surprising even the cast after their curtain call, and invited the audience to ignore the critics by telephoning five friends to encourage them to see the show. Fortified by her characteristic pluck and perseverance, Spewack utilized her experience as a publicist by taking her defense of *The Festival* to a dozen radio and television programs, thereby helping to extend the play's run for a few weeks.

After the death of her husband in 1971, Bella made public appearances and continued to write occasional scripts for benefit galas, pageants, and festivals. She died on April 27, 1990, of natural causes at ninety-one years of age.

MAJOR THEMES

The Spewacks' plays can be divided between serious dramas and light comedies. The dramas, which were less successful, attempt to probe social issues, particularly through representations of Jewish family life on New York's Lower

East Side. The more commercially successful comedies typically follow the exploits of wayward but likable protagonists.

The dramas, such as *Poppa*, *Spring Song*, and *War Song*, focus on generally serious subject matter for which treatment and tone spans the seriocomic to the tragic. In these plays, which were produced around the time of the Depression, poverty is a central issue. For example, in *Spring Song*, the elder daughter sacrifices herself to financial obligations of the family, while her rebellious younger sister desperately pursues fleeting self-gratification. In *Poppa*, the mother is distressed by her husband's irresponsibility and financial difficulties that prevent her making a favorable impression on the wealthy mother of her son's fiancée.

As the *New York Times* observed of *Poppa*, which is true of these plays in general, conflicting social and cultural values are expressed "in terms of family, neighborhood and racial customs [which] are at odds with the immigrant, who gulps down American idealism whole" (Atkinson, "Reverence" 1). For instance, the husband, Pincus Schwitzsky, unwittingly made an alderman by dishonest district leaders, tries to transform his vague idealism into purposeful action as he champions the rights of impoverished immigrant citizens to decent housing. Unfortunately, his reforms are undermined by the lawless politicians, with the result that his own constituency removes him from power.

When characters in the Spewacks' dramas have commerce with people from outside the neighborhood, the outcome is frequently the disruption of families and, metaphorically, the centrality of the Jewish neighborhood to their lives. In *Spring Song*, the younger sister roves daringly beyond her mother's wary eye. When she takes up with the fiancé of her duty-bound older sister, she sets in motion events that shatter the family and lead to her death.

Conflicts engendered by the failure of American idealism are expressed through the experience of another Jewish family in the play *War Song*, which explores how the quality of human life is compromised by war. The play, co-written by the Spewacks and George Jessel, focuses on the unheroic Eddie Rosen, whom Jessel played on Broadway. Rosen wants to stay out of the military, not for ideological reasons, but because he is more concerned with the welfare of his mother and his romance with Sally Moss. The play traces Rosen's misfortunates as a reluctant and not very good soldier as he is systematically abandoned by family members and other loved ones left behind.

Although the early plays like *Poppa* demonstrated the Spewacks' concern with representing Jewish American life on stage, they also left their authors vulnerable to criticism about blurring the boundaries of dramatic genre. Since *War Song* and *Poppa* contain elements of serious drama, comedy, and even burlesque, the thematic material was sometimes at odds with audience expectations of genre. The *New York Times* critic, Brooks Atkinson, chided the Spewacks for perplexing the audience of *Poppa* by "attempting to serve the two masters of human drama and ready-made burlesque" at the same time ("Alderman" 1). Heeding the critics, after *Poppa* the Spewacks tended to write more uniformly serious or comedic plays, turning increasingly to lighter fare. No doubt the commercial theatre's propensity for comedy was also a factor.

Nonetheless, in 1976, after the opening of the New York revival of the farcical *Boy Meets Girl*, Bella discounted the source of the Spewacks' fame. She told an interviewer that she actually preferred tragedies, even though they do not sell (Fraser). She said, "Sam did comedies, . . . I wanted to do tragedies, but I had to go his way" (qtd. in Fraser). It is likely that by tragedies, she meant significant, weighty literature as opposed to plays about tragic circumstances. In this sense, the Spewacks seem to have reserved more serious treatment for their portrayals of Jewish family life and comedic treatment for depictions of self-aggrandizement in Hollywood filmmaking, journalism, and other businesses.

Undisputedly, the Spewacks' fame rests on their comedies, particularly the hits, *Boy Meets Girl* (135) and *Kiss Me, Kate* (1948). It is worth noting that, in a departure from their usual collaborative process, Bella began writing the book for *Kate* alone, but when Samuel began contributing heavily to revisions, she changed the authorial ascription to include him. While she apparently did not write any other plays by herself, he wrote three. On most other accounts, the Spewacks worked so closely together that defining the exact contributions of each is tricky. It has been suggested by critic Jean Gould that since Bella was noted for her sharp wit, the fast-paced dialogue might be attributable to her, while Samuel might have been largely responsible for developing the plot and action (138). Bella frankly remarked once that, while her husband had "a marvelous writing mind," he lacked the ability to write good dialogue (qtd. in Arnold).

Frequently, the Spewacks placed writers and writing at the center of their comedies. In *Boy Meets Girl*, the Hollywood writers, who are appealing if roguish characters, instigate the plot in which an overbearing producer and assorted hangers-on are comically overpowered. In *Woman Bites Dog*, which lampoons irresponsible journalism, an intrepid journalist discovers a trumped-up story about a town's embracing Communism that had been disseminated as truth. The newspaper profession is again the subject of parody in *Clear All Wires!* in which an unscrupulous journalist creates news about himself to bolster his career, while publishing is caricatured in *Miss Swan Expects* and its revision, *Trousers to Match*. The play *Out West It's Different* centers on an essentially sane writer harassed by the aggressive, imbecilic behavior of his colleagues in the theatre. Given the Spewacks' customary praise for the theatre and denigration of Hollywood, it is unusual that the play's villain is a power-mad stage director while the voice of reason is a beautiful movie star. In this play, as in most of the other comedies, a recurring thematic idea is that megalomaniacs don't change. Only the mavericks and the ingenuous rise above the fray of the entrenched hierarchies of power that are parodied.

The perception of recurring themes and settings in the Spewack canon is due in part to the couple's practice of adapting their work. *Clear All Wires!*, for example, was adapted from *Swing High Sweeny*, its unproduced and little-known predecessor. Then it was made into a successful Hollywood film (1932) and finally adapted into a musical, *Leave It to Me!* (1938), which featured a Cole Porter score. (The score's hit song "My Heart Belongs to Daddy" was sung by Mary Martin in her Broadway debut.)

The theme of romantic love that is eventually requited found its proverbial expression in the Spewacks' play *Boy Meets Girl*. Here, two screenwriters boil down what they call the perfect plot to "Boy meets girl. Boy loses girl. Boy gets girl." The phrase has become idiomatic in the American theatre.

SURVEY OF CRITICISM

Criticism of the Spewacks' work primarily consists of abbreviated assessments in a few collections, brief encyclopedia entries, and reviews. No study on the life of Bella Spewack or the Spewacks' plays has been published. At present, the most useful resource, however limited, is the aggregate of several decades of play reviews, as well as a lesser number of articles written about, and infrequently by, the Spewacks.

Reviews show that criticism of the Spewacks' comedies has been varied. Some critics have saluted a comedy for being inventive while others have derided it for being unimaginative. For example, in reviewing *My Three Angels*, critic T. H. Parker wrote that the Spewacks

have compounded comedy that pushes brilliantly to the edge of fantasy that is filled with invention and, in the midst of some extraordinary wickedness, manages a curiously pointed morality. . . . The essence of the play . . . lies in the very paradox of justice brought about by murderers and swindlers, huge and gusty characters . . . themselves. . . . (33)

Writing about the same play, critic Walter Kerr takes issue with the Spewacks for not being inventive throughout, observing that characterization pales over the course of the play, which itself has "disturbing lulls."

While some reviewers fault what they perceive to be merely rapid-fire exchange, others regard the dialogue as witty and fast-paced, typical of the Spewacks' comedic craft. George Abbott, who directed the first production of *Boy Meets Girl*, wrote that the Spewacks "know how to write lines which are not only funny to read but which crackle when spoken in the theatre" (qtd. in Spewack, *Boy Meets Girl* 6). Frank O'Hara also commended the dialogue in the play, observing that the play is comprised of "[t]alk for the sake of more and better hilarity; action for the same good reason" (211).

While the Spewacks' serious dramas received mixed reviews from critics and the general public, they may have been judged more particularly for content than for craft. Consider, for example, the response of Max Gordon, who directed the first New York production of *Spring Song*.

Spring Song was not very successful in the theatre—why I shall never understand. I always thought it was one of the finest plays ever written, and I will always think so. I know it's true because I have known the people in it all my life. I was born and raised with them. I am afraid most of their first night audience were also raised with them but wanted to forget them. (qtd. in Spewack, *Boy Meets Girl* 113)

Since *Spring Song* is markedly concerned with social, economic, and cultural aspects of an early twentieth-century Jewish neighborhood on New York's Lower East Side, Gordon's assessment raises the troubling spectre of Jewish embarrassment or even self-hatred. Yet propriety of subject matter is not reserved for sensitive Jewish theatergoers. For instance, Arthur B. Waters, of *The Philadelphia Public Ledger*, vouches for the authenticity of the characters and what he calls "racial customs and expressions," but he downplays these elements at the same time, saying they "are not allowed to cloud the issue of the piece for non-Jewish playgoers" (qtd. in rev. of "Spring Song"). His somewhat backhanded assessment implies that representation of Jewish life on stage may be contentious.

Characterization in the serious dramas was often praised, sometimes nearly exclusively. The *New York Times* critic Books Atkinson observed of *Spring Song* that the playwriting was "pedestrian" while the characterization, tone, and authenticity were "touching and fine." While *War Song* received some positive notices, several reviewers, such as Wilfred Riley of *The Billboard*, credited George Jessel's acting skills for having surmounted the occasionally melodramatic but otherwise seriocomic script, thereby crediting characterization created by the performer rather than by the writers.

Overall, the Spewacks have received greater recognition for their comedies than for their serious dramas. In 1953, Elliot Norton, of the *Boston Post*, wrote that *My Three Angels* was a French comedy in "a Spewacky version" (qtd. in Spewack, "The Complete Text of *My Three Angels*" 32). Norton's coinage, "Spewacky," aptly describes the Spewacks' writing style and points to the genre that popularized their work. While the serious plays in the Spewack canon have been largely relegated to lists of the couple's complete works, their farces and comedies such as *Boy Meets Girl* and, especially, *Kiss Me, Kate* are their legacy to the theatre.

BIBLIOGRAPHY

Works by Bella Spewack

The following unpublished stage plays by the Spewacks may be found in the New York Public Library: *Leave It to Me!* (New York, 1938), *Miss Swan Expects* (New York, 1939), and *Out West It's Different* (New York, 1940).

Cohen, Bella. "The Laugh." *The Best Short Stories of 1925 and the Yearbook of the American Short Story*. Ed. Edward J. O'Brien. Boston: Small, Maynard, and Company, 1926.

Cohen, Bella, and Samuel Spewack. *Poppa*. New York: Samuel French, n.d.

Spewack, Bella, and Samuel. *The Solitaire Man: A Melodrama in Three Acts*. New York: Samuel French, 1934.

———. *Boy Meets Girl, Spring Song*. New York: Random House, 1936.

———. *Trousers to Match*. New York: Dramatists Play Service, 1941.

———. *Woman Bites Dog*. New York: Dramatists Play Service, 1947.

Spewack, Sam, and Bella. "The Complete Text of *My 3 Angels*." *Theatre Arts*. 38.6 (1954): 34–61.

———. *The Festival*. New York: Dramatists Play Service, 1955.

Spewack, Samuel, and Bella. "The Complete Text of *Kiss Me, Kate*." Book by Samuel and Bella Spewack, lyrics by Cole Porter. *Theatre Arts*. 39.1 (1955): 34–57.

Spewack, Bella. "My Life with Shakespeare." *Show*. February 1964: 70–72.

Selected Films

Clear All Wires!. Dir. George W. Hill. MGM, 1933.

Boy Meets Girl. Dr. Lloyd Bacon. With James Cagney, Pat O'Brien, Marie Wilson, Ronald Reagan, others. Warner, 1938.

Weekend at the Waldorf. Dir. Robert Z. Leonard. With Ginger Rogers, Walter Pigeon, Van Johnson, Lana Turner, others. MGM, 1945.

Selected Television Writing

The Enchanted Nutcracker. Music and lyrics, Sol Kaplan and Edward Elisco. Chor. Carol Haney. Prod. Marlo Lewis. Dir. Jack Smight. With Carol Lawrence, Robert Goulet, Pierre Olaf, others. Westinghouse Special. WABC-TV, New York, 23 Dec. 1961.

Kiss Me, Kate. Mus. and Lyr. Cole Porter. Chor. Ernest Flatt. Dir. and Prod. George Schaefer. With Alfred Drake, Patricia Morison, Julie Wilson, others. Cond. Franz Allers. Hallmark Hall of Fame. KRCA-NBC, Hollywood/L.A., 20 Nov. 1958.

My Three Angels. Prod. Bretaigne Windust. Dr. Windust, Gordon Rigby. With Walter Slezak, Barry Sullivan, George Grizzard, others. Comp. and Cond. Sol Kaplan. Ford Startime. KRCA-NBC, Hollywood/L.A., 8 Dec. 1959. Based on Albert Husson's *La Cuisine des Anges*.

Works about Bella Spewack

"My 3 Angels" and other reviews may be found in *New York Theatre Critics' Reviews* in years corresponding with productions.

Arnold, Elliott. "Two Heads Are Better." *New York World Telegram* 2 Dec. 1938: n.p.

Atkinson, Brooks. "Alderman Schwitzky Goes Free." *New York Times* 25 Dec. 1928: 311.

———. Rev. of "Spring Song." *New York Times* 2 Oct. 1934:18.

———. "Reverence Ill at Ease." *New York Times* 30 Dec. 1928: sec 8, 1.

Fraser, C. Gerald. "Bella Spewack, Comedy Author, Prefers Tragedy." *New York Times* 15 Apr. 1976: 24.

Gould, Jean. *Modern American Playwrights*. New York: Dodd, Mead and Company, 1966.

H. B. " 'War Song' Brings Jessel's Talent to Serio-Comic Play: Another Version of

Humor and Agonies of Conflict Bared at National Theater.'' *New York Times* 25 Sept. 1928: n.p.

Hevesi, Dennis. ''Bella Spewack, Author, 91, Dies; 'Kiss Me, Kate' Is One of Her Hits.'' *New York Times* 29 Apr. 1990: 36.

Kerr, Walter. Rev. of ''My 3 [sic] Angels.'' *New York Herald Tribune* 12 Mar. 1953: n.p.

Klain, Jane. *International Motion Picture Almanac.* vol. 61. New York: Quigley Publishing Company, 1990.

Krutch, Joseph Wood. ''Drama: A Coward's League for Peace.'' *The Nation* 127.3302 (1928): 406.

Leonard, William Torbert. *Theatre: Stage to Screen to Television.* Metuchen, NJ, and London: The Scarecrow Press 1981.

Norton, Elliot. ''Spewack.'' *Boston Post.* Rpt. in *Theatre Arts* (1954): 32.

O'Hara, Frank. *Today in American Drama.* Chicago: University of Chicago Press, 1939.

Parker, T. H. ''Bella and Samuel Spewack.'' *Boston Post.* Rpt. in *Theatre Arts* 1954: 33.

Riley, Wilfred. Rev. of ''The War Song.'' *The Billboard* 40 (1928): 42.

''Bella Spewack, Broadway, Hollywood Author.'' *Newsday* 30 Apr. 1990: 28.

Rev. of ''Spring Song'' in Philadelphia tryout. *New York Times* 14 Aug. 1932, sec. 9, 1.

GERTRUDE STEIN (1874–1946)

Linda Wagner-Martin

BIOGRAPHY

Born February 3, 1874, in Allegheny, Pennsylvania, to Daniel and Amelia Keyser Stein, Gertrude was the seventh and youngest child (two died in infancy). Gertrude's father and maternal grandfather were Austrian Jews, who settled in Maryland. Soon after Gertrude was born, Daniel and Amelia moved to Austria and then to Paris, where Gertrude learned German and French as well as English. When the family returned to America, they lived with Gertrude's maternal grandparents in Baltimore for a year. There, the Stein children learned the customs of their faith.

In 1880, hungry for financial success, Stein took his family to California, where he managed investments and a street railway company. From East Oakland, the Steins sporadically attended the Reform services of Rabbi M. S. Levy. Gertrude fondly remembered the freedoms of California's open lands and classless society. After her parents' deaths in 1888 and 1891, Gertrude dropped out of school, reading daily in San Francisco's major libraries, and soon she, Leo, and their older sister, Bertha, returned to Baltimore to live with Aunt Fanny Keyser, the wife of photographer David Bachrach, a member of the Har Sinai Reform congregation. In 1892, Leo went to Harvard; in 1893, Gertrude followed him to study at Radcliffe with William James, George Santayana, Hugo Munsterberg, and Josiah Royce. In 1898, she graduated *magna cum laude* in Philosophy and Psychology.

While she was a junior at Radcliffe, Gertrude wrote an essay, "The Modern Jew Who Has Given Up the Faith of His Fathers Can Reasonably and Consistently Believe in Isolation." Echoing conversations she had with classmates, she wrote that "Jew" means "a belief in a personal or quasi-personal God . . . a belief in the Revelation of the law by the Lord through Moses," and "the people of Israel are the chosen people of the Lord." She defined "isolation" in the context of marriage, writing that it means no inter-marriage with an alien. The Jew shall marry only the Jew. He may have business friends among the Gentiles; he may visit with them in their work and in their pleasure, he will go to their schools and receive their instructions, but in the sacred precincts of the home, in the close union of family and of kinsfolk he must be a Jew with Jews; the Gentile has no place there.

In closing, she stated that one was "a Jew first and an American only afterwards . . . race feeling" was kinship, "an enlargement of the family tie." She also said that Cambridge was the place "where to be a Jew is the least burden . . . of any spot on earth" (Yale Stein Collection).

The outgoing Gertrude, who loved theater, tennis, and long walks, had a number of Cambridge friends: Margaret Walker, Beulah Dix, Arthur Lachman, Leo Friedman, Adele Oppenheimer, Mabel Weeks, and others. With Leon Solomons, the brightest of James's graduate students, she published "Normal Motor Automatism" in *The Harvard Psychological Review* (1896). In 1898, she published her senior project essay, a study of the effect of fatigue on the attention of ninety-one men and women ("Cultivated Motor Automatism: A Study of Character in Its Relation to Attention").

By the time she began Johns Hopkins Medical School, Gertrude was confident of her ability, her talent, and her capacity to be good friends with (and often, to counsel) people. She resumed friendships with Claribel and Etta Cone and their family and with the other women in "The Sociables," daughters of the Guggenheimer, Frank, Bamberger, Federleicht, and Gutman families. While Gertrude did not accept the mandate that all Jewish women were to marry well and become homemakers, she understood that women needed to stay within their class and ethnic group. By 1897, she was involved in a lesbian liaison.

Being one of only eleven women in the medical school class of sixty-three students chastened Gertrude, and friends reported that some professors disliked her because she was Jewish—and outspoken. Whether her male professors were, indeed, anti-Semitic or simply antifemale, Gertrude had conflicts with enough of them—particularly one in women's medicine, the field in which she had wanted to specialize—that she did not graduate with her class. When she was told that she could take a summer course and then graduate, she traveled to Europe instead, though she returned to take a year of post-graduate work on brain anatomy. In 1903, Gertrude joined her brother Leo at 27 rue de Fleurus in Paris, and began writing fiction (*Q.E.D., Fernhurst, Three Lives*, and the early version of *The Making of Americans*) while she learned about painting.

Gertrude and Leo, with their older brother Mike and his wife Sarah "Sally" Samuels now also living in Paris, began buying the Renoir, Cézanne, Matisse, and Picasso works that shocked the international art community. So many people wanted to see their paintings that "The Stein Corporation" began their famous Saturday salons. While many of their visitors were family members or friends from the United States and many were Jewish, more were art collectors, writers, and artists such as Picasso, Matisse, Apollinaire, Max Jacob, the Delaunays,

Picabia, Jo and Yvonne Davidson, and others. Among Stein's European friends were the Bernard Berensons, the Alfred Whiteheads, and Mildred Aldrich.

In 1906, Picasso painted the portrait of Gertrude that marked one beginning of Cubism. In 1907, when Alice B. Toklas and Harriet Levy, San Francisco friends of Mike and Sally's, arrived in Paris, Gertrude saw her life of art collecting and writing take form. She felt that, with Alice to encourage her, she could become an important writer; the relationship between the two well-born Jewish women gave each passion and permanence. Due to their increasing disagreements on art and lifestyle, Leo moved to Italy in 1913, taking his half of the art collection with him.

During World War I, Gertrude and Alice worked in Perpignan, Nimes, and Alsace for the American Fund for the French Wounded, with Gertrude learning to drive the donated Ford truck. After the war, many of the visitors to their salon were Jewish friends from the United States or new young friends who were artists and writers. Some of the problems Gertrude had with various of her guests were directly connected with anti-Semitism. Much as she liked Ernest Hemingway, his jealousy over Stein's friendship with Harold Loeb, about whom she had written a flattering portrait, led to his unappealing characterization of Robert Cohn in *The Sun Also Rises*.

Occasionally, when a review or an interview emphasized her family's Jewishness, Stein was likely to undercut that affiliation or to make some wry comment about it. In conversation with friends and family, however, she would say, as she did to her nephew Arthur in 1928, "I am the most famous Jew in the world." Within the Stein family, particularly between Mike and Leo, jokes about being Jewish were common, and many of the women friends who wrote to Alice and Gertrude in Paris sent the long Jewish jokes Stein loved. In her notebooks, Gertrude comments on Jewishness, saying "Jews mostly run themselves by their minds, now they have good minds but not great minds" (NB, A-3); in her charts about people's traits in those same notebooks, she usually divided subjects into the categories of "Jewish" and "Anglo-Saxon" (NB, "Book of Diagrams"). And in her love poems, she sometimes referred to herself as "your little Jew" (as in "A Sonatina Followed by Another").

When Stein wrote *The Autobiography of Alice B. Toklas* in 1932 and found that the memoir brought her money and acclaim, she returned to the United States on a speaking tour. During the nine months of their 1934–35 visit, their first return to America in thirty years, Gertrude and Alice enjoyed being lionized. They realized, however, that their small incomes from family trusts—even when augmented by royalties from Stein's books that Random House promised to publish—were inadequate for life in the United States. They settled back into their French routine, spending winters in Paris, now at the rue Christine apartment, and summers in Belley, with their efforts focused on Gertrude's writing. She wrote the second of her memoirs (*Everybody's Autobiography*), as well as the unclassifiable *Four in America*, plays, libretti, and numerous essays about writing.

During the late 1930s, friends warned them to leave Europe, but they stayed on in the country near Lyon, in Vichy France, throughout World War II. Several times enemy troops were quartered in their home; they seldom had enough food. Stein kept writing (*Wars I Have Seen*, *Brewsie and Willie*, *The Mother of Us All*) and walking, though whether she worked for the French Resistance—as was rumored—remains unknown. In any case, the survival of the two American ladies seems to have been a miracle. And when the Allied victory came, Gertrude was once again a celebrity; she enjoyed a last year of visits and acclaim from American GIs. After her unexpected death from abdominal cancer on July 27, 1946, Alice delayed her funeral service until October 22, when Stein was buried in Pere Lachaise Cemetery after "special ceremonies" for her Jewish faith at the American Cathedral Church of the Holy Trinity (Mellow, *Charmed Circle* 471).

MAJOR THEMES

Beginning with Stein's magnun opus, *The Making of Americans*, her theme was often the power of family. Her generational saga stressed that family feeling, based on loving kinship, stemmed from women's place in families. Starting with four strong grandmothers, Stein ordered her plot to show how women's choices in marriage, which they saw as the only suitable career, shaped their lives. Contrasting the Orthodox Eastern branch of the family with the Californian Reformists, with whom she identified, Gertrude named the latter line *Hersland*, suggesting matriarchal strength. Because Stein was fascinated with the way immigrants became part of American culture, much of her novel explored the ways the children of her families achieved success in the United States.

Stein's work on *The Making of Americans*, from its inception as a short book in 1903 through its completion in 1911 as a 1,000-page work, dominated nearly a decade of her writing life. Its publication, finally, in 1925, followed by her revising and shortening the long version during the 1930s, meant that it dominated much of her writing career. In it she stated and restated what Mary Dearborn has called the essential theme of ethnic fiction, the search for one's own identity set against that for the father (190–93). Gertrude's identification with her older brother Leo linked her with the patriarchy, and when she broke with him, much of her poetry, portraits, and plays concerned not only the difficulty of living with him, but also the difference between male and female (*Two*, "He Didn't Light the Light," "Publishers, The Portrait Gallery and the Manuscripts at the British Museum," "He Said it. A Monologue").

Gertrude's most realistic writing occurred in her first fiction, *Q.E.C., Fernhurst*, and in the three portraits that were published as *Three Lives* in 1909. Although none of the characters is defined as Jewish, Adele in *Q.E.D.* admits, "I have the failing of my tribe. I believe in the sacred rites of conversation even when it is a monologue." And in variations of women trapped in conventional, impoverished lives, "The Good Anna," "The Gentle Lena," and "Melanctha,"

Stein voiced her conviction that women deserved the same freedoms that men enjoyed. Her texts were admonitory, as she showed that women who accepted social codes died without finding personal fulfillment. Certainly for Gertrude, the youngest daughter of a traditional German Jewish family, to marry and have children was the fate her family desired for her; by going against those wishes, she cut herself off from the kinship that was so central in her life.

Another of Stein's themes was the joy to be found in lesbian love; in the poems of *Tender Buttons* and many of her early plays, she wrote about her love for Alice in what she called a cubist style. Her use of disassociational language disguised what she was saying. When she wrote about empowered and sexual women, her style fell into puns, wordplay, and seeming nonsense ploys. Much of it echoed the prose poetry of her French writer friends, Apollinaire, Blaise Cendrars, and Max Jacob, or the dissonance of the German *Klange* group; but more of it was her own invention. (See "Ada," "A Sweet Tail," "Bee Time Vine," "Sacred Emily," "Pink Melon Joy," "All Sunday," "Lifting Belly," *Tender Buttons*, and, later, *Lucy Church Amiably*.) Because of her frequent use of disguise and pun, specific Jewish references (such as "Yet Dish" for "Yiddish") are rare.

The love of play that masked a consistent undercurrent of morality and her need to define her Americanism in ways that included Jewishness remained a touchstone throughout Stein's writing, especially in her longer plays, *Four Saints in Three Acts*, *Daniel Webster Eighteen In America A Play*, *Dr. Faustus Lights the Lights*, and *The Mother of Us All* (about Susan B. Anthony). Wresting language into tone without relying on literal meaning was Stein's great accomplishment in drama, and her attention to women characters (even in *Dr. Faustus*) showed her continuing interest in gender.

Her plays paralleled in some ways the nonfiction prose she considered her primary work. Her exploration of American history continued in 1933 with the difficult portrait-essays of *Four in America*. Here, she described Ulysses S. Grant as a religious leader, Wilbur Wright as a painter, Henry James as a general, and George Washington as a novelist. Stein's power to create a person through portraiture melded with the effects of history. With *The Geographical History of America, or the Relation of Human Nature to the Human Mind* (1936) she returned to philosophy, a field she drew from only intermittently in her thirty years of writing.

The exploration of self, or of self in the context of others, was the motive in part for Stein's writing the three autobiographies: *The Autobiography of Alice B. Toklas* (1933), whose humorous—and authoritative—narration was Stein's contribution to the various discourses about twentieth-century life in Paris; *Everybody's Autobiography* (1937), an account of Stein's 1934–35 U.S. tour and her life afterward, when she was situated in France and feeling even more the expatriate after seeing America; and *Wars I Have Seen* (1942), a meditation on the ways in which war had marked the century. The latter book was, in some ways, a resolution to her philosophical writings in the 1930s and was linked with her *Paris France* (1939), in which she wrote that "life is tradition and human nature." In *Mrs. Reynolds* (1940), Stein explored Hitler's charismatic appeal for ordinary people; in *Brewsie and Willie* (1945), she created natural-sounding dialogue between two American G.I.'s as a means of locating their value system. Whatever kind of writing she did, Stein valorized the permanence of kinship relations and of Americanism, reifying that solid role of family and ethnic culture that she had respected so consistently throughout her career.

SURVEY OF CRITICISM

There has been very little attention paid to Gertrude Stein as a Jewish writer. Critics who have praised her work have connected her with modernism, purposely avoiding ethnic identification. Because criticism tends to repeat and reify itself, if Stein's ethnicity was not emphasized early, there is little reason it would have appeared later. Like her lesbianism, her Jewishness was something critics knew about but did not often mention in commentary. The modernist writer aimed to be universal, above political alliances, washed clean in the purity of serious and innovative aesthetics, and Gertrude certainly wanted to play that game well. She would have gained nothing in high modernist Paris by describing herself as a Jewish American lesbian.

Katherine Anne Porter's ambivalent 1927 review of *The Making of Americans* emphasizes that "Gertrude Stein is an American Jew," discussing the firmly entrenched morality she finds in this "deeply American book" as characteristic of both Jews and Americans (*Days Before* 39). Similarly, in 1925, Hemingway wrote to a friend that Stein was behaving like a "kike" by not reviewing one of his recent books (Mellow, *Hemingway* 316).

Milton Hindus deals with the problem of Stein's Jewishness in a 1974 *Midstream* essay, noting that while she never denied her birth (and, he assumes, her allegiances), she also never emphasized it ("Ethnicity" 69–70). He comments that it is possible to read the "playful" *Autobiography of Alice B. Toklas* without being conscious that either Gertrude or Alice was Jewish. Typical of Stein, who often wrote playfully, the reference to being Jewish is made in what seems an anti-Semitic context. That kind of "in" humor is also an ethnic trait; those inside a group can make remarks that might be offensive if an outsider expressed them.

Mary Dearborn's discussion of Stein as Jewish writer focuses on *The Making of Americans* as ethnic text. She admits that Gertrude's "perception of herself as Jewish is very difficult to puzzle out" because it is at all times connected "with her perception of herself as an outsider by virtue of her homosexuality and expatriate status" (*Pocahontas's Daughters* 166), but she says that Stein's writing proves how involved she was in a consideration of ethnic issues. And by defining "American" to include the marginalized, Stein was able to insist on her *Americanness*—which she did consistently throughout her career—without specifically mentioning either her Jewish belief or her lesbianism.

Hindus also asks why Stein was so often omitted from surveys of Jewish writers once the category was privileged in criticism of American letters, suggesting that those academic exercises of the 1960s and 1970s were intent on charting Jewish *male* writing; most early courses in "Jewish literature" included no women. For Gertrude Stein to be omitted from a number of important directories of Jewish families, Jewish celebrities, and Jewish literary figures may also be evidence of the discomfort the compilers of those guides and directories felt about her sexual preference. It is more likely, however, that her work was so little read, and what was read was so difficult to decipher, that her omission was unintended. If Gertrude Stein was truly "the Mama of Dada," and her writing a joke, then there would be little reason to include her.

BIBLIOGRAPHY

Works by Gertrude Stein

Fiction

Three Lives. New York: Grafton Press, 1909.
The Making of Americans. 1925. New York: Something Else Press, 1966.
Ida. New York: Random House, 1941.
Brewsie and Willie. New York: Random House, 1946.
Fernhurst, Q.E.D., and Other Early Writings. New York: Liveright, 1971.

Poetry

Tender Buttons: New York: Claire Marie Press, 1914.

Plays

Geography and Plays. 1922. New York: Something Else Press, 1968.
Operas and Plays. 1932. Tarrytown, NY: Station Hill Press, 1987.
Four Saints in Three Acts. New York: Random House, 1934.
Last Operas and Plays. 1949. New York: Vintage, 1975.

Autobiography

The Autobiography of Alice B. Toklas. New York: Random House, 1933.
Everybody's Autobiography. New York: Random House, 1937.
Wars I Have Seen. New York: Random House, 1945.

Essays and Other Nonfiction Prose

Composition as Explanation. London: Hogarth, 1926.
How to Write. Paris: Plain Edition, 1931.
The Geographical History of America or the Relation of Human Nature to the Human Mind. 1935. New York: Vintage, 1973.
Lectures in America. New York: Random House, 1935.
Paris France. London: Batsford, 1940.
Four in America. New Haven, CT.: Yale University Press, 1947.

"The Modern Jew Who Has Given up the Faith of His Fathers Can Reasonably and Consistently Believe in Isolation." Unpublished essays. Yale American Literature Collection.

"Notebooks for *The Making of Americans.*" Unpublished. Yale American Literature Collection.

Collected Works

The following volumes published by Yale University Press consist of previously uncollected or unpublished poetry, fiction, and plays.

Two: Gertrude Stein and Her Brother and Other Early Portraits, 1908–1912. New Haven, CT: Yale University Press, 1951.

Mrs. Reynolds and Five Earlier Novelettes, 1931–1942. New Haven, CT: Yale University Press, 1952.

Bee Time Vine and Other Pieces, 1913–1927. New Haven, CT: Yale University Press, 1953.

As Fine as Melanctha, 1914–1930. New Haven, CT: Yale University Press, 1954.

Painted Lace and Other Pieces, 1914–1937. New Haven, CT: Yale University Press, 1955.

Stanzas in Meditation and Other Poems, 1929–1933. New Haven, CT: Yale University Press, 1956.

Alphabets and Birthdays. New Haven, CT: Yale University Press, 1957.

Works about Gertrude Stein

Agee, James. "Woman with a Hoe," *Time* 40 (27 July 1942):83–84.

Barnes, Djuna. "Matron's Primer," *Contemporary Jewish Record* 8 (June 1945):342–43.

Benstock, Shari. *Women of the Left Bank: Paris, 1900–1940*. Austin: University of Texas Press, 1986.

Bridgman, Richard. *Gertrude Stein in Pieces*. New York: Oxford University Press, 1970.

Burke, Carolyn. "Gertrude Stein, the Cone Sisters, and the Puzzle of Female Friendship," *Critical Inquiry* 8 (Spring 1982):534–64.

Chessman, Harriet Scott. *The Public Is Invited to Dance: Representation, the Body, and Dialogue in Gertrude Stein*. Stanford, CA: Stanford University Press, 1989.

Dearborn, Mary V. *Pocahontas's Daughters, Gender and Ethnicity in American Culture*. New York: Oxford University Press, 1986.

DeKoven, Marianne. *A Different Language: Gertrude Stein's Experimental Writing*. Madison: University of Wisconsin Press, 1983.

Gallup, Donald, ed. *The Flowers of Friendship, Letters Written to Gertrude Stein*. New York: Alfred A. Knopf, 1953.

Hindus, Milton. "Ethnicity and Sexuality in Gertrude Stein." *Midstream* 20 (January 1974):69–76.

Katz, Leon. "The First Making of *The Making of Americans*: A Study Based on Gertrude Stein's Notebooks and Early Versions of Her Novel (1902–8)." Ph.D. dissertation, Columbia University, 1963.

Kazin, Alfred. "From an Italian Journal," *Partisan Review*, 15 May 1948:555–57.

Kellner, Bruce, ed. *A Gertrude Stein Companion: Content with the Example*. Westport, Ct: Greenwood, 1988.

Levy, Harriet. *920 O'Farrell Street*. 1947 Rpt. New York: Arno Press, 1975.

London, Blanche. "The Career of a Modernist," *New York Jewish Tribune*, 6 March 1931:2, 6.

———. "Gertrude Stein," *New Palestine*, 5 April 1929:298–300.

Mellow, James R. *Charmed Circle, Gertrude Stein & Company*. New York: Praeger, 1974.

———. *Hemingway, A Life Without Consequences*. Boston: Houghton Mifflin, 1992.

Porter, Katherine Anne. *The Days Before*. New York: Harcourt, Brace, 1952.

Raffel, Gertrude Stein. "There Once Was a Family Called Stein," *A Primer for the Gradual Understanding of Gertrude Stein*, ed. Robert Bartlett Haas. Los Angeles, CA: Black Sparrow Press, 1971, 127–38.

Rather, Lois. *Gertrude Stein and California*. Oakland, CA: Rather Press, 1974.

Richardson, Brenda. *Dr. Charibel & Miss Etta*. Baltimore, MD: Baltimore Museum of Art, n.d.

Rogers, W. G. *When This You See Remember Me: Gertrude Stein in Person*. New York: Holt, Rinehart, 1948.

Simon, Linda. *The Biography of Alice B. Toklas*. Garden City, NY: Doubleday & Co., 1977.

Stimpson, Catharine R. "Gertrice/Altrude, Stein, Toklas and the Paradox of the Happy Marriage." *Mothering the Mind, Twelve Studies of Writers and Their Silent Partners*, ed. Ruth Perry and Martin Watson Brownley. New York: Holmes and Meier, 1984, 122–39.

Thomson, Virgil. "Remembering Gertrude," *Columbia Library Columns*, Feb. 1982, 3–16.

Toklas, Alice B. *What Is Remembered*. New York: Holt, Rinehart, and Winston, 1963.

Wilson, Edmund. *Axel's Castle: A Study in the Imaginative Literature of 1870–1930*. New York: Charles Scribner's Sons, 1931, 237–56.

ELIZABETH SWADOS (1951–)

Dorothy Chansky

BIOGRAPHY

Elizabeth Swados was born in Buffalo, New York, in February 1951, the younger child of Robert Orville and Sylvia Maisel Swados. Her father is a lawyer; her mother was a former actress and poet who committed suicide in 1979. Swados's brother Lincoln, seven-and-a-half years her senior, was a major influence in her early life and later figured in her prose and dramatic writing. An eccentric child, Lincoln was diagnosed in his teens as schizophrenic, became a street musician in New York's East Village, refused to vacate his storefront after eviction, and died under uncertain circumstances at age forty-six.

The family, whose name was originally Swiadisch, has roots in Vilna, Lithuania. Swados's maternal grandfather was a violinist in Russia and her paternal grandmother was a concert pianist. The late novelist Harvey Swados was a second cousin. The family observed major Jewish holidays and attended services at a Reform synagogue, but for her musicals based on biblical themes and characters, Swados sought information and assistance from translators, scholars, and rabbis to provide insight that her limited Jewish education did not.

Music and writing figured prominently in Swados's early life. She began playing piano at age five, guitar at ten, and performing as a folk singer by age twelve. She also wrote short stories and accumulated a collection of rejection slips from the *New Yorker* as a teenager. She enrolled in Bennington College at age sixteen. While a student, she spent two summers singing and playing guitar with Pete Seeger, and she lived with an Appalachian family, where she made a public protest against black-lung disease. Swados left Bennington to work in New York at Cafe LaMama and there she achieved early success as a composer. Swados wrote music for avant-garde director Andrei Serban's productions of *Medea*, *Agamemnon*, and *The Cherry Orchard* and submitted the *Medea* score as completion of her work at Bennington. She was awarded a degree in 1972. In the early 70s she traveled through Africa with Peter Brook's troupe and created the music for his *Conference of the Birds*.

Swados is best known for *Runaways*, the 1978 musical about alienated young-sters for which she created both text and score. In the, 1980s her theatre work focused on political satire and an exploration of Jewish rituals, texts, and iden-tification. The latter area includes *The Haggadah, Esther: A Vaudeville Megil-lah*, and *Jerusalem*. Her theatre work has won five Obie awards and five Tony nominations. Swados has written music for numerous films and public television specials and is the author of several children's books, a novel, a family memoir, and a nonfiction book about the vicissitudes of beginning a career in music. Journalists have frequently identified her with the Age of Aquarius and have consistently cited her artistic eclecticism. She has obliged by eschewing main-stream, commercial theatre and by continuing her prolific and varied writing, which includes, roughly, a musical theater work a year from 1978–1992.

Acknowledging the emotional and behavioral precedents her family has set, Swados is firm about her commitment to engagement and productivity. "I can choose to be unstable. I have all the makings for a nervous breakdown, but I want to *do* a lot of things. I work most of the time. The way to survive is to work and to live entirely in the moment" (Gussow, "Elizabeth Swados," 54).

MAJOR THEMES

Principal themes in Elizabeth Swados's work in all genres are social dys-function, especially in the young and the disenfranchised, and "survival with a vengeance" (Swados, personal interview). She has reworked biblical stories with an eye to contemporary spiritual quickening and frequently issues calls for joy and for an exercise of our capacities to revel in sound and celebration. A plea for sensitivity to each other and to something that might be called an inner self also permeates her work. The musical variety with which she challenges her audiences' listening and hearing habits in her theatrical collages is both a trademark and a trope. The styles she freely and frequently mixes include rec-itative, the percussive use of unpitched sounds, the clicks and flutters associated with birds, rap, rock, reggae, salsa, country western, disco, samba, blues, gospel, flamenco, punk, and cantorial chant. Her scripts include segments in Hebrew, Yiddish, Spanish, and occasionally in other languages, and those listing original casts indicate her preference for working with ethnically diverse performers.

Swados's first New York show, *Nightclub Cantata* (1977), sowed the seeds for the reception and analysis of her later theatre work. The piece treats a com-mon theme in songs and sketches without relying on a plot; it comprises twenty segments for which Swados wrote the score and compiled the text from works by Pablo Neruda, Syliva Plath, Carson McCullers, Muriel Rukeyser, Isabella Leitner, Frank O'Hara, Nalzim Hikmet, Delmore Schwartz, and herself. The recurrent concerns in the work are family, couples, women's autonomy, and "secular optimism" (Munk). The title itself is indicative both of Swados's in-terest in collapsing genres and of the difficulty of assessing her work in terms of traditional theatre expectations.

Runaways investigates the interior lives of children who leave home and cope with pain and abandonment in a variety of ways. As with most of Swados's contemporary, non-biblical works, the setting is urban. The play, which evolved from a lengthy workshop under the auspices of Joseph Papp and the New York Shakespeare Festival, has been compared with *A Chorus Line* because of its use of workshop participants' stories to develop a show that is often first-person and confessional. Again, Swados wrote both music and text. *Runaways* shows repeatedly that indifference and insensitivity on the part of adults and institutions lead to fear and withdrawal on the part of children. A child prostitute character talks about how she learned to be relatively invisible. A generic child survivor reports that:

He or she never admitted that he or she was born.
He or she said that he or she just got here.
      . . .
Therefore this twelve or nine or six years old little
    boy or girl was never no longer a child.

                                  ("Once Upon a Time")

A child who learned early about rote attention to physical needs minus a concern for the spirit declares, "Now I'm in an orphanage for grownups. The world" ("Spoons"). A child who is terrified of rejection and punishment conflates family fights with publicly reported violence as he delivers a school report with the refrain "Please don't flunk me" ("Current Events"). The play's final plea is "Let me be young before I get old, let me be a kid." However, Swados does not suggest that this will be easy. She indicts both the realm of consumer comfort and the antiestablishment movement of the sixties as means of easing life's difficulties. In a segment titled "The Untrue Pigeon," a girl declares that she has been left a "defective fairy tale" since "Hollywood's done gone and bought it all up": The song "Where Are the People Who Did *Hair*?" answers that: "They're a corporation big as IBM and they subsidize lost and phony visions."

Runaways expresses hope, but Swados's vision is gritty. The suggestion is not that the world should be a place without pain nor that childhood should lack fear and demons. Rather, she seems to be saying that attention must be paid and that we proceed at societal peril if emotions and immaturity are not heeded.

Two later shows also use similar techniques to explore the problems of being young, disenfranchised, scared, and surviving in an American city. *Swing*, later retitled *The Red Sneaks*, uses "swings of fate, swings of mood, swings of luck and swings of fashion" as a metaphor for "a confused, crazy world that too often leaves young people alone, accompanied by just their longings" (Brown). Its central concerns are the breakup of the nuclear family and children becoming inured to violence. *The New Americans*, presented as a work-in-progress early in 1992, brought together a multinational cast of young people to explore a social issue, this time immigration, problems of adapting to a new country, and coming to terms with the American dream.

Swados's first overtly Jewish culture-based theatre piece was *The Haggadah*, in which she combined texts by Eli Wiesel, Gabriela Mistral, Kadia Molodowsky, and herself with passages from the Haggadah and the Old Testament. *The Haggadah* juxtaposes questions about oppression, ghettoization, and genocide under the Nazis with traditional Seder passages and references to Pharaoh's ethnic policy. Swados's purpose is to invite viewers to consider the familiar Passover celebration as a means of interrogating and enriching contemporary life. She urges faith in the Jewish community, and following Moses's example of celebrating that community, even if one will not be alive when one's prayers for the common good are answered. One key passage describes a seven-week wait for God's revelation of his law. Finally God speaks, not about his mystery or majesty, but about people's obligations to each other, suggesting that human relations rather than theology guide responsible Jewish living. The piece playfully places a group of women reading cookbooks alongside a group of rabbis discussing religious law. The text indicates that, in the original production, the rabbis were represented by puppets manipulated by speaking actors. The original cast featured an Asian boy and an old actor who began his career in the Yiddish theatre, suggesting that the playwright/composer (who also served as director) envisions Jewish ethics embracing and respecting cultural diversity.

Jerusalem picks up the latter theme. Using the device of a tourist being taken on a guided walk through the holy city, Swados's oratorio, inspired by her own trip to Israel, portrays Jerusalem as the home site of four major religions. Swados's text incorporates poems by Yehuda Amichai, and the liturgy is sung in fifteen different languages. *Esther: A Vaudeville Megillah* retells the Purim story by means of shtick, slapstick, and audience participation, concluding with the directive, ''Go forth and speak of peace to thy children.'' By portraying Esther as a Wonder Woman heroine and sending up a beauty contest early in the play, Swados casts the historically distant tale in immediate terms, thereby both making it accessible and holding it up for reexamination. *Job: A Circus* does much the same thing, although, of course, the theme of the story is different. If *Esther*'s message is peace, *Job*'s is *carpe diem*, as one never knows with what cosmic pie she or he will next be hit in the face. While the use of Hebrew words and cantorial chant codes these shows as Jewish, their playfulness and use of popular entertainment forms invites general interest.

Several of Swados's books are autobiographical, and the title of one of her children's books, *The Girl with the Incredible Feeling*, was used as the title of a documentary film bout Swados herself. Her 1982 novel, *Leah and Lazar*, uses material from her own life, especially her relationship with her brother, as the basis of a work of popular fiction. In the novel, the character based on her brother is found dead in his East Village hovel, a young victim of physical injury, mental illness, paranoia, and neglect. Lincoln Swados's real death in 1990 fulfilled very much his sister's eerily prescient vision. Her 1991 family memoir *The Four of Us* explores instability, manipulation, and the search for identity among the members of her immediate family. Swados's nontheatre writing also explores the difficulties of powerful emotions, especially those of a child in a profit-driven, patriarchal, mass-culture society.

Political and social commentary were the basis for her two collaborations with cartoonist Garry Trudeau, *Doonesbury* and *Rap Master Ronnie*. Similarly, the musical *Groundhog* deals with homelessness, civil rights, the fine line between schizophrenia and possible genius, and the pain of loving an outcast.

SURVEY OF CRITICISM

The overwhelming majority of criticism of Elizabeth Swados's work has appeared in the theatre sections of the daily and weekly newspapers in New York City, with the most in-depth writing occurring in the *New York Times* and the *Village Voice*. Book reviews have appeared in other newspapers in major cities and in *Publishers Weekly*. Despite her status in the theatre community, no major piece has ever been written about her, either by *The Drama Review*, the premier American journal of nonmainstream theatre and performance, or by *American Theatre*, which concerns itself mostly with regional theatre.

Early criticism of Swados's work in the seventies made much of her youth, exotic eclecticism, and intensity (Munk; Barnes 1977; Stasio). Some writers found her output galvanizing, others were offended or bored, and some were respectful and challenged (Gottfried, Watt, Feingold). By the eighties, reviewers were calling her work self-congratulatory, bland, and derivative (Rich, Review of *Rap Master Ronnie*; Barnes, Review of *Rap Master Ronnie*; Solomon, Review of *Rap Master Ronnie*). In his 1989 review of Swados's book *Listening Out Loud*, *New York Times* arts critic Michael Kimmelman reports that the author ''[a]fter enjoying early success, . . . met with a barrage of criticism that left her devastated and confused'' (1989:10). Response to her 1991 book *The Four of Us: The Story of a Family* was mixed and frequently mentioned the author's self-centeredness and amateur psychologizing (Yardley; Stabiner). However, reviews of the 1992 musical, *Groundhog*, which featured fictionalized versions of herself and her deceased brother, were generally favorable and respectful (Russo; Gussow 1992).

Among the most thoughtful and informed critiques of Swados's work is Alisa Solomon's essay on *Esther: A Vaudeville Megillah*. Solomon was troubled by Swados's failure to consider the sexism in the story and by the show's neglect of the implications of Jews triumphantly slaughtering their enemies in light of ongoing, late-twentieth-century tensions between Israel and its neighbors. However, Solomon took seriously Swados's efforts to represent a key Jewish legend in a fresh, timely way (Solomon, ''Not the Real''), honoring the social purpose that Swados has publicly said she intends in her work (Brown; Delatiner; Gussow, ''Elizabeth Swados'' 22).

Swados's absence from Broadway for nearly a decade is probably best explained by her impatience with the world of commercial musicals, which she calls ''still back in the '40s and '50s, ignoring the music of our times, characters who reflect modern-day people, and a political conscience'' (Delatiner). Her commitment to her work and her prolific output continue unabated.

BIBLIOGRAPHY

Works by Elizabeth Swados

Scripts/Libretti/Lyrics

This is a partial list. It includes the theatre pieces and books for which Swados is best known. Where no publication information is included, the text is not publicly available. Except for *Doonesbury*, collaborations in which Swados served exclusively as composer are not included here.

A tape of *Runaways* was done by the Theatre on Film and Tape Project and is available for viewing at the New York Public Library in the research division of the Lincoln Center Branch.

A tape of *Esther: A Vaudeville Megillah* is available for viewing at the New York Public Library in the research division of the Lincoln Center branch of the library.

Nightclub Cantata, 1977.
Dispatches, A Rock Musical. Typescript. New York: New York Shakespeare Festival. Libretto and music, 1979.
Runaways. New York: Samuel French, 1980.
Alice in Concert. New York: Samuel French, 1981.
The Haggadah: A Passover Cantata. New York: Samuel French, 1982.
Rap Master Ronnie. Lyrics cowritten with Garry Trudeau. New York: Broadway Play Publishing, 1985.
Doonesbury. Text by Garry Trudeau, score by Elizabeth Swados. New York: Samuel French, 1986.
Jerusalem. New York: Broadway Play Publishing, 1988.
Esther: A Vaudeville Megillah. New York: Broadway Play Publishing, 1989.
The Red Sneaks. 1989.
Song of Songs. 1989.
Jonah. 1990.
Job: A Circus. 1992.
The New Americans. 1992.
Groundhog. 1992.

Books

The Girl with the Incredible Feeling. New York: Persea Books, 1976.
Leah and Lazar. New York: Summit Books, 1982.
Listening Out Loud: Becoming a Composer. New York: Harper & Row, 1989.
Inside Out: A Musical Adventure. Boston: Little, Brown, 1990.
The Four of Us: The Story of a Family. New York: Farrar, Straus & Giroux, 1991.

Recordings

Runaways. Original Broadcast Cast. Jacket notes by Elizabeth Swados. Columbia, JS3540, 1978.
Doonesbury. MCA Records, MCA6129, 1986.

Interview

Personal interview, 18 November 1992.

Works about Elizabeth Swados

This is a selective and partial listing. An extensive and accessible collection of clippings and reviews for all of Swados's New York shows is available at the New York Public Library, Lincoln Center for the Performing Arts Branch, in the research division. The material is catalogued by show, and generally there is a bound volume containing reviews and a separate folder with feature articles for each play.

Barnes, Clive. Rev. of *Nightclub Cantata.* Village Gate, New York. *New York Times* 10 January 1977:29.

―――. Rev. of *Rap Master Ronnie.* Top of the Gate, New York. *New York Post* 4 October 1984:38.

Brown, Patricia Leigh. "*Swing*: Songs of Innocence and Experience." *New York Times* 18 October 1987:Section 2:5.

Delatiner, Barbara. "Bible Serves to Inspire Elizabeth Swados." *New York Times Long Island Weekly:* September 1991, 15.

Feingold, Michael. Rev. of *Nightclub Cantata.* Village Gate, New York. *Village Voice* 17 January 1977:83.

Gottfried, Martin. Rev. of *Nightclub Cantata.* Village Gate, New York. *New York Post* 10 January 1977:19.

Gussow, Mel. "Elizabeth Swados—A Runaway Talent." *New York Times Magazine 5 March 1978:19.*

―――. *Rev. of Jerusalem.* LaMama, Etc., New York. *New York Times,* 26 May 1984: C14.

―――. "A Homeless Man Confronts the System." Rev. of *Groundhog.* Manhattan Theatre Club, New York. *New York Times* 4 May 1992, Section C:14.

Kimmelman, Michael. "Scheme and Variations." Rev. of *Listening Out Loud. New York Times Book Review* 22 January 1989:10.

Munk, Erik Rev. of *Nightclub Cantata.* Village Gate, New York. Village Voice 24 January 1977:79.

Publishers Weekly. Unsigned Rev. of *The Four of Us.* 19 July 1991:42.

Rich, Frank. Rev. of *Rap Master Ronnie.* Top of the Gate, New York. *New York Times* 4 October 1984:C16.

―――. Rev. of *Esther: A Vaudeville Megillah.* Mosaic Theatre at the 92nd Street YMHA, New York. *New York Times* 24 February 1988:C24.

Russo, Francine. Rev. of *Groundhog.* Manhattan Theatre Club, New York. *Village Voice* 12 May 1992:98.

Solomon, Alisa. Rev. of *Jerusalem.* LaMama, Etc., New York. *Village Voice* 5 June 1984:66.

————. Rev. of *Rap Master Ronnie*. Top of the Gate, New York. *Village Voice* 16 October 1984:114.

————. "Not the Real Megillah." Rev. of *Esther: A Vaudeville Megillah*. Mosaic Theatre of the 92nd Street YMHA, New York. *Village Voice* 1 Mar. 1988:94.

Stabiner, Karen. Rev. of *The Four of Us. Los Angeles Times* 1 Sept. 1991: Book Review Section:6.

Stasio, Marilyn. Rev. of *Nightclub Cantata*. Village Gate, New York. *Cue* January 22–Feb. 4, 1977:26.

Wallach, Allan, "Triviality and Forced Jollity in *Esther*." Rev. of *Esther: A Vaudeville Megillah*. Mosaic Theatre of the 92nd Street YMHA, New York. New York *Newsday* 24 February 1988: Part II:9.

Watt, Douglas. Rev. of *Nightclub Cantata*. New York *Daily News* 10 January 1977:17.

Yardley, Jonathan, "One Family, Darkly." Rev. of *The Four of Us. Washington Post* 9 October 1991: Section C:2.

WENDY WASSERSTEIN (1950–   )

Iska Alter

BIOGRAPHY

Born in Brooklyn on October 18, 1950, the youngest of four children, Wendy Wasserstein grew up in the comfortable circumstances of an upper-middle-class Jewish family whose foibles and idiosyncrasies she continues to comment on and dramatize in her plays. Her father, Morris Wasserstein, a prosperous textile manufacturer, patented several fabrics, including velveteen, which becomes Holly's signifier in *Uncommon Women and Others*. Her mother, Lola, remains passionately interested in dance and theater and continues to take dance classes, much like Tasha Blumberg in *Isn't It Romantic*. Her sisters are themselves uncommon women (and doubtless are models for two of the sisters Rosensweig): Sarah Meyer, presently head of corporate affairs at Citicorp and among the first women to break into senior management; and Georgette Levis, owner of the Wilburton Inn in Manchester Village, Vermont. Her brother is Bruce Wasserstein, whose company, Wasserstein Perella, engineered some of the major hostile takeovers in recent business history.

The family moved to Manhattan's affluent Upper East Side when Wasserstein was twelve. After graduating from the Calhoun School, she went on to Mount Holyoke College where she majored in history. After graduation, she returned to New York City and received an M.A. from City College. Wasserstein then went to Yale University's School of Drama, which she chose over Columbia University's Graduate School of Business. Although "frightened to death" at Yale (Betsko and Koenig 427), she thrived nevertheless, writing as her master's thesis a one-act version of what would become *Uncommon Women and Others*: "I made the decision to write a play with all women after seeing all that Jacobean drama, where a man kisses the lips of a woman's skull and drops dead. . . . I wanted to write a play where all the women were alive at the curtain call" (Betsko and Koenig 425–26).

Since *Uncommon Women and Others* (1977), Wasserstein has produced a growing body of work—*Isn't It Romantic* (1981/1983, the revisions made to focus better on the development of Janie Blumberg), *The Heidi Chronicles* (1989, winner not only of the Pulitzer Prize and the Tony Award, but also of the New York Drama Critics Circle, Outer Critics Circle, and the Drama Desk "Best New Play" honors), *The Sisters Rosensweig* (1992)—that has reinforced the promise and the success of her first play.

In moves that took her from Brooklyn and the Yeshiva Flatbush to Yale's School of Drama, Wasserstein lived the complicated, seemingly chaotic dislocations of gender and ethnicity that would determine the behavior of so many of her characters. Growing up in an upper-middle-class family she describes as "a sort of traditional family, eccentric but traditional" (Maychick 58), dominated by a powerful mother who insisted upon intellectual and professional achievement, but who also valued marriage, motherhood, and domesticity, the playwright embodies the conflicting pressures such a familial system constructs. This energizing idea of family is also critical to Wasserstein's professional development. Her talent seems to be most effectively nurtured by the nonprofit theater group Playwrights Horizon and its director André Bishop, who re-create a similar family constellation that Wasserstein herself often has referred to as "a home" ("Acknowledgments," *The Heidi Chronicles and Other Plays*).

MAJOR THEMES

From her first success, *Uncommon Women and Others*, through *Isn't It Romantic*, the multiaward-winning *The Heidi Chronicles*, and, most recently, *The Sisters Rosensweig*, Wendy Wasserstein has created comedies of feminine survival that explore the ambiguous effectiveness of the women's movement during the past quarter of a century. Using the pattern of her own life as paradigm, she has dramatized with a sharply satiric wit the problematic intersection of the individual experience and the collective feminist ideology that would explain and transform it.

Written "from the vantage point of the slighted . . . the underachiever who . . . fashioned a life based on anticipated exclusion" (*Bachelor Girls* 193–94), and fueled by the autobiographical impulse, Wasserstein's plays chart the processes by which the outsider—in this case, the Jewish woman—must uncover, negotiate, deny, or reject the existing contract between the female self and the male-directed culture. In order to produce a viable adult identity, her protagonists must choose among the oppositions imposed by ethnic assumptions, familial expectations, patriarchal traditionalism, and the unstable promises of historical change. Not to do so is to remain forever a child. Nor does chronological maturity necessarily ensure the pleasures of certainty or the comforts of inertia, no matter how much they are deserved. The middle-aged Rosensweig sisters are little different from the uncommon collegiate women in this regard: Choices remain revisionary; options can be refigured.

The Jewishness that Wasserstein represents is ethical and secular: a fact of character, a linguistic marker, the condition of family, community, and culture rather than the theological discipline of a practiced faith. Nevertheless, to acknowledge such an identity is an act of resistance, however problematic, against the claims of effacement and homogeneity. Indeed, the Jewish American protagonists who inhabit Wasserstein's evolving comic universe are never more Jewish (or more American, for that matter) than when they are mediating the boundaries of ethnicity and the limits of assimilation required to maintain both individual integrity and social cohesion. Even the tonalities of Yiddish and its vocabulary occasionally emerge as essential components of the playwright's language and method of characterization to support this process of dramatized juggling. The audience hears clearly the self-deprecation that is at once the voice of Wasserstein's female protagonists, the speech of Wasserstein herself as she writes "in order to express myself, my thoughts, my individual voice" (*Bachelor Girls* 122–23), and the reflexive mockery of traditional Jewish humor—the use of "wit for those you're scared of" (*Uncommon Women, The Heidi Chronicles and Other Plays* 5)—to control, determine, or forestall the consequences of felt or actual victimization: "I don't spend much time thinking about being funny. For me it's always been a way to get by, a way to be likeable, yet to remain removed" (*Bachelor Girls* 184).

Although both the commitment and the promises offered by assimilation produce equivocal responses in these theatrical representations of female experience, traditionalists seem to occupy a particularly ambiguous space on Wasserstein's stage, accepting, as they often do, behavior defined by comforting restraint rather than determined by provocative openness. Gorgeous Teitlebaum, one of the sisters Rosensweig, remains a figure of mockery in part because of her suburban religiosity, notwithstanding audience sympathy or the sincerity of her convictions. Dr. Marty Sterling (*Isn't It Romantic*) purposefully, if smugly, reclaims name and place becoming Dr. Murray Schlimovitz and returning to Brooklyn "where people have real values" (110). In doing so, however, he also claims another more questionable inheritance of patriarchal Judaism: belief in the domesticity of female existence and the maternalism of the feminine self: "All I want is a home, a family, something my father had so easily. . . . Sure I want to know where I'll live, who'll take the children to the nursery, but I wanted something special too" (138).

It is not until *The Sisters Rosensweig* that Wasserstein is able to construct a Jewish American figure who is entirely comfortable within the skin of his or her own hyphenated character. Mervyn Kant, a politically correct furrier who manufactures "synthetic animal protective covering," teaches Sara Rosensweig Goode that adopting the assimilationist agenda that dismisses the value and validity of difference leads to functional social blindness. His lessons point out to Sara that not only is she unable to challenge the polite anti-Semitism of her adopted home and upper-class British lover, but also that she cannot recognize its ugly, dangerous recrudescence in the present historical moment. And he demonstrates Sara's evasions without imposing traditional Jewish gender ideology on Sara's prickly independence. Although it may be that such an accommodation comes from Wasserstein's "own heightened consciousness of her Jewish identity, gleaned from her post-Heidi travels abroad" (Darling 12), yet it is a curious irony that she creates this act of ethnic reconciliation for a male to whom she gives a name suggesting both insincerity and incapacity in addition to the more obvious German exponent of philosophical idealism. Wasserstein's plays reveal the Jewish female's desire for an individual self able to choose and to act in the world complicated by the shifting relationship among familial demands, matrilinearity, and Jewishness. The daughter's need for separation becomes difficult, because feminine identity both rebels against and reconciles with the mother, symbolic possessor of the power to shape the conflicted expectations of the Jewish ethnic and religious environment. Janie Blumberg (*Isn't It Romantic*), comparing her preference to the ideology of maternalism as well as to the realities of Tasha Blumberg's existence, points out:

Mother, think about it. Did you teach me to marry a nice Jewish doctor and make chicken for him? You order breakfast from a Greek diner every morning. Did you teach me to go to law school and wear gray suits at a job that I sort of like every day from nine to eight? You run out of here in leg warmers and tank tops to dancing school. Did you teach me to compromise and lie to the man I live with and say I love you when I wasn't sure? You live with your partner; you walk Dad to work every morning. (149–50)

In spite of the near-inevitability of such antagonism apparent in these quasicomic works that dramatize women's lives, the women's behavior and experiences incorporate elements of the maternal tradition, even as the younger women seek a world of limitless possibility and negotiable social contracts.

Although Holly Kaplan of *Uncommon Women and Others* finally emerges from the protective skin of her collegiate raccoon coat into chronological adulthood, she remains the only one of her Mount Holyoke classmates still financially and psychologically tied to familial (and therefore maternal) prescriptions of decorum and desire. She has become trapped in a cycle of postponement, moving from graduate school to graduate school, that at once signifies futurity and stasis.

If Holly Kaplan is permitted to inhabit the childhood of indecision sheltered by paternal allowance, Janie Blumberg, the Jewish protagonist of *Isn't It Romantic*, is initially resentful of "having to pay the telephone bill, be nice to the super, find meaningful work, fall in love, get hurt" (82)—signs of an adult and independent life. Her discomforts with adulthood bring her back to New York to reenact the role of daughter within the paradoxes of the Blumberg family comedy. To satisfy her mother's requirements, she becomes involved with the traditional Jewish prince, a specialist from Mount Sinai Hospital. At the same time, in order to be her mother's child, she also is attempting to become, with considerable irony, a "free" lance writer, with more obvious irony, for "Sesame Street." But in order to create Janie Blumberg, she must reject Dr. Sterling/

Schlimovitz who calls her "Monkey," believes her to be "sweet" and "real," and makes her decisions for her.

Unlike Holly, Janie also is allowed to choose because the comic structure of her matrimonial dilemma ensures that she cannot lose: Whether it is marriage or individual self-fashioning, she always will retain parental acceptability, support, and love. Janie's decision, however, is not a negation of Tasha Blumberg's way; it is the process by which Janie includes the appropriate maternal heritage. The play closes with Janie's adopting her mother's dancing persona, a sign of filial respect and admiration, and also a commitment to a life of risk and contingency.

But Wasserstein is not concerned simply with depicting family in ethnically narrow terms. She also dramatizes the more general structural dialectic produced by the oppositions between the static ideology of familialism and the destabilizing forces of change that would modify, subvert, or eliminate its power. The Jewish family, represented by the Kaplans, the Blumbergs, and even by the Rosensweigs, needs to replicate its system of values in the next generation. This poses special problems for women whose choices can remove them from participation in public action, necessitating alternative female networks to counter the family's effacement of the feminine self.

The comfortable, tradition-bound environment of Mount Holyoke, the primary setting for *Uncommon Women and Others*, establishes a space of feminine privilege and possibility where young women can assume intellectual poses, try on personae, and enact roles in the process of making a workable self. The sustaining, compassionate sisterhood that has developed among the characters in Wasserstein's play is meant to serve as an example—the family of preference, not of blood—for the organization of women's lives. But the institution, itself caught in a period of transition, represents a utopian moment in the lives of these women, not a permanent condition, frozen unchanging in time, once they graduate into the shifting forms of history. When they meet for their first reunion in six years, they all are changed save Holly, and the college has become memory, not model.

Harriet Cornwall, the Protestant half of *Isn't It Romantic*, uses her friendship with Janie Blumberg as another version of the family to fill the absences left by her own nontraditional upbringing. However, this relation is amended when Harriet accepts the contemporary dictate that women can have it all. In virtually the same language she earlier employed in assessing the significance of her connection with Janie, only now more conventional in its resonance, she explains: "Joe makes me feel like I have a family. I never had a family. I had you and Lillian, but I never felt I could have what other women just assumed they would get" (143). Acknowledging the authority of the cultural definition of family, Harriet has come to associate Janie's choices with a reluctance to enter adulthood; in so doing, she further diminishes the validity of alternative feminine systems of support.

Heidi Holland's ambiguous personal history is firmly anchored to, and in part explained by, Wasserstein's problematic representation of the public history of the women's movement during the twenty-four years spanned by *The Heidi Chronicles*. Heidi's decisions about what constitutes a worthwhile life are made early in the play; they are generated and sustained by the collective vision of sisterhood whose liberating impulses are the heart of the movement and whose energies fuel its activism.

Yet even as Heidi attempts to hold fast to the movement's utopian commitments, this idealized gendered community is questioned, subverted, and ultimately dissolved in scenes of disappointed mockery by the desire to please men, to follow political fashion, and to exercise the power of the marketplace. The last scenes find Heidi increasingly alone, abandoned by a mutable system whose promises are subject to time and the vagaries of history, isolated by choices that are no longer acceptable within the feminine collective that once guaranteed the value of her identity. Forced to reconsider what had seemed so certain, Heidi feels betrayed: ''I thought the point was that we were all in this together'' (232).

In order to rescue the uncertain self from the deceptions of the historical process, Heidi returns to the ideology of familialism and adopts a child—a daughter, of course. So it would appear, as *The Heidi Chronicles* concludes, that if politicized sisterhood is inherently unstable, choosing motherhood is a conserving act; and the unconditional love required to raise a child can guard against the seductive transformations offered by history.

But it is not only *The Heidi Chronicles* that asserts the playwright's dismay at the power of public circumstance to undermine the utopian enterprise. Deliberately giving the lie to history, the uncommon women of Mount Holyoke, students during a most tumultuous political time (1968–1972), appear more concerned with undermining tea and Gracious Living than with confronting the Vietnam War and the rage it produced. In her account of the genesis of *Uncommon Women and Others*, Wasserstein indicates that originally ''Mark Rudd came to Mount Holyoke. In that version, Susie Friend had a strike speech and even organized a strike for Mark Rudd'' (Betsko and Koenig 426). But the playwright's explanation seems at the very least incomplete: ''There used to be pieces in the play that were very political. . . . I took it out because I thought it would open the play up to all the questions of Vietnam, and that's another play. I really wanted to do something so that women's voices could be heard'' (Betsko and Koenig 426).

Janie Blumberg, Harriet Cornwall, their friends, lovers, and families are permitted to inhabit a world emptied of history, concentrating instead on those issues of personal growth and resolving the crises of personal identity. Even *The Sisters Rosensweig* trivializes the explosive events in Eastern Europe by making a running joke of Tess Goode's adolescent wish to participate in the revolutionary activity in Lithuania. Her final decision to remain in London rather than to travel eastward with her radical Lithuanian boyfriend is meant, in fact, to signify a growing maturity. Indeed, the only historical events to carry serious meaning for the characters in this play are those associated with the Holocaust and the revival in parts of Europe of violent anti-Semitism.

The Sisters Rosensweig further extends Wasserstein's dialogue between the familial terrain of unconditional love and the authority of the historical to include the claims of mortality as her women grow into middle age. The single Jewish American female protagonist of the earlier plays has been divided into three differently Jewish sisters (Wasserstein's version of Chekhov's trio), each of whom has taken a different route to Moscow, only to discover that once there, Moscow may not be what they had dreamed.

Sara, Gorgeous, Pfeni, née Penny—"A Mainstream corporate executive, a New England homemaker, and a solo artist" (*Bachelor Girls* 16; it is no accident that this description originally refers to Wasserstein and her own siblings)— seem to have satisfied to a greater or lesser degree the needs of the self, the expectations of family, and the varying demands of culture; yet they remain discontented. This sense of unkept promises has intensified because each is acutely aware that growing older has begun to deprive her of the opportunities that once were available to fulfill wishes, a recognition that makes all three edgy, fearful, and angry.

They have come together in Sara's London house for the first time as sisters without also being daughters, and the death of their mother releases them into the undiscovered country of genuine adulthood. During the dramatic time of the play (about twenty-four hours), the sisters must reconstruct out of rivalry, re-crimination, envy, and affection that capacity for unconditional love that will allow them to live such choices that remain: Pfeni might return to the practice of a socially committed art; Gorgeous might restore that wholeness of family that her radio broadcasts praise; and Sara might recover her lost Jewish identity through the tentative relationship with Mervyn Kant—but these are hopes, not surety. All that remains certain is that they are the daughters of Rita and Maury Rosensweig, a message about kinship that is inherited by Sara's daughter, Tess, in the closing of the play. These three separate sororal identities are able to offer one another momentary but invaluable shelter against time and mortality.

SURVEY OF CRITICISM

With the exception of Susan Carlson's essays, "Comic Textures and Female Communities in 1937 and 1977: Clare Booth and Wendy Wasserstein," which discusses not only the feminine/feminist behaviors that separate Booth's *The Women* from Wasserstein's *Uncommon Women and Others*, but also the cultural forces that produced them, Wendy Wasserstein's work has attracted little scholarly attention thus far; but there are reviews of specific plays, interviews with the author, and more general articles, essays, and profiles about her place in contemporary or women's drama, her life and her celebrity that appear in the popular press immediately prior to or following the opening of a new play.

The reviews by Mel Gussow (*New York Times*), Clive Barnes (*New York*

Post), Douglas Watt (*Daily News*), and even the usually irascible John Simon (*New York*), among others, tend to be generous to the playwright's comic flair and witty lines, although less comfortable with the episodic structure of the first three plays. But Gerald Weales, writing in *The Georgia Review* and *Commonweal*, as well as some of the more politicized feminist critics such as Alisa Solomon writing for the *Village Voice* have been more acerbic about her willingness to make easy, even sentimental, and surprisingly unpolitical choices for her presumptively "feminist" characters.

The critical response to *Uncommon Women and Others* generally praises the comic action and language of Wasserstein's first professionally produced play, even as critics acknowledge the play's problematic structure. The reviewers recognize the playwright's ability and her promise. Commentators who reviewed the first version of *Isn't It Romantic* continue to admire her comic flair but are disappointed in the play's conventional presentation of the clichés of Jewish family life. The critics found the revision of *Isn't It Romantic* a more focused play. As Edith Oliver notes in the *New Yorker*, in losing "its innocence," the comedy "acquired muscle and form." However, some of the reviewers such as John Simon find the play a disappointment, one in which "the promise continues to be brighter than the delivery" ("The Group").

All critics view *The Heidi Chronicles* as Wasserstein's most mature play to date, as it delineates a generation's loss of faith as ideals are transformed into greedy narcissism through the presentation of art historian Heidi Holland's journey from the promise of the 1960s to the defeats and losses of the 1980s. Yet there remain those who continue to be dissatisfied with the direction taken by *The Heidi Chronicles* and who see the trivialization of issues such as feminism, political activism, and AIDS where others see satiric honesty. The more political feminists are disturbed by Wasserstein's presentation of the feminist movement as it culminates in a most controversial ending—Heidi's adoption of a child. Wasserstein's 1992 *The Sisters Rosensweig* has received excellent reviews as many critics note especially the ways in which tighter and more traditional structure controls the playwright's characteristic excesses.

BIBLIOGRAPHY

Works by Wendy Wasserstein

Plays

"The Sorrows of Gin" (1980, PBS *Great Performances*, adaptation of John Cheever's short story).

"The Girl from Fargo: A Play" (with Terence McNally). *New York Times* 8 March 1987:Sec. 2, 5.

"The Man in the Case" in *Orchards, Orchards Orchards: Seven American Playwrights Present Stories by Chekhov*. New York: Broadway Play Publishers, 1987 (adaptation).

Bachelor Girls. New York: Alfred A. Knopf, 1990.
The Heidi Chronicles and Other Plays. New York: Harcourt Brace Jovanovich, 1990.
    [Includes *Uncommon Women and Others* (1977), *Isn't It Romantic* (1983), and
    The Heidi Chronicles (1988).]
"Tender Offer." *Antaeus* 66 (Spring 1991), 452–58.
The Sisters Rosensweig. New York: Harcourt Brace & Company, 1993.

Unpublished Plays

"Any Woman Can't" (1971).
"Montpelier Pa-Zazz" (1973).
"Maggie/Magalita" (1986).
"Miami" (1986, with Jack Feldman and Bruce Sussman).

Articles and Interviews

"Wendy Wasserstein," Interview with Kathleen Betsko and Rachel Koenig, eds., *Interviews with Contemporary Women Playwrights.* New York: Beech Tree Books, 1967, 418–31.
"Theater Problems? Call Dr. Chekhov," *New York Times* 24 January 1988:Sec. 2, 5, 26.
"An Unconventional Life: Q & A with Wendy Wasserstein," Interview with Carol Rosen, *Theater Week* 2 November 1992:17–27.

Works about Wendy Wasserstein

Backes, Nancy. "Wendy Wasserstein." in *Notable Women in the American Theater*, Eds. Alice M. Robinson, Vera Mowry Roberts, and Milly Barranger, Westport, CT: Greenwood Press, 1989. 901–03.
Brustein, Robert. "*The Heidi Chronicles.*" *New Republic* 17 April 1989:34.
———. "Women in Extremis." *New Republic* 17 April 1989:32–34.
Carlson, Susan. "Comic Textures and Female Communities in 1937 and 1977: Clare Booth and Wendy Wasserstein." *Modern Drama* 27:4 (Dec. 1984):564–73.
Feingold, Michael. "Prisoners of Unsex." *Village Voice* 3 November 1992:109–10.
Gussow, Mel. "A Modern-Day Heffalump in Search of Herself." *New York Times* 12 December 1988:C13.
———. "Wasserstein: Comedy, Character, Reflection." *New York Times* 23 Oct. 1992: C3.
Hoban, Phoebe. "The Family Wasserstein." *New York* 4 Jan. 1993:32–37.
Hodgson, Moira. Rev. of *The Heidi Chronicles.* *The Nation* 1 May 1989:605–06.
Kramer, Mimi. "Portrait of a Lady." *New Yorker* 26 Dec. 1988:81–82.
Miller, Judith. "The Secret Wendy Wasserstein." *New York Times* 18 Oct. 1992:Sec. 2, 1, 8.
Nightingale, Benedict. *Fifth Row Center: A Critic's On and Off Broadway.* New York: Times Books, 1986.
Oliver, Edith. "The Day before the Fifth of July." *New Yorker* 22 June 1981:86–87.
———. Rev. of *Isn't It Romantic.* *New Yorker* 26 Dec. 1983:68.
———. Rev. of *Uncommon Women and Others.* *New Yorker* 5 Dec. 1977:115.

Richards, David. "Wendy Wasserstein's School of Life." *New York Times* 1 Nov. 1992: Sec. 2, 5.

Shapiro, Walter. "Chronicler of Frayed Feminism." *Time* 27 Mar. 1989:90–92.

Simon, John. "Failing the Wasserstein Test." *New York* 29 June 1981:36–37.

———. "The Group." *New York* 12 Dec. 1977:103.

———. "Jammies Session." *New York* 27 Mar. 1989:66, 68.

Solomon, Alisa. Rev. of *The Heidi Chronicles*. *Village Voice* 20 Dec. 1989:121.

Stuart, Jan. "If Chekhov Sisters Had Lived in Brooklyn." *New York Newsday* 23 Oct. 1992:77, 63–64.

"Wendy Wasserstein." *Contemporary Literary Criticism Yearbook 1989*. Ed. Roger Matuz. Vol. 59. Detroit: Gale, 1990.

"Wendy Wasserstein." *Contemporary Literary*, Criticism Yearbook, 1989. Eds. Jean C. Stine and Daniel Marowski, vol. 32. Detroit: Gale, 1985, 439–43.

"Wendy Wasserstein." *Current Biography Yearbook 1989*. Ed. Charles Moritz. New York: H. W. Nelson, 1990. 610–13.

Weales, Gerald. Rev. of *The Heidi Chronicles*. *Commonweal* 5 May 1989:279–80.

Winer, Laurie. "Christine Lahti as an Angry Heidi in 'Chronicles.' " *New York Times* 9 Oct. 1989:C13, C16.

RUTH WHITMAN (1922–   )

Miriyam Glazer

BIOGRAPHY

"Nothing in the world seems to me more beautiful than the way that a concrete fact or object suddenly leaps beyond itself into metaphor," Ruth Whitman has written, describing her lifelong "obsession with poetry." That obsession was kindled in her earliest childhood. Born in 1922, she grew up hearing her grandfather's Yiddish and Russian lullabies, in a richly polyglot first-generation Russian-Jewish household. "I can still remember some of the words and tunes" (*World* 882).

She wrote her first poem when she was nine and sold her first poem when she was eleven. With the prize money, she bought Louis Untermeyer's anthology of American poets:

> I read every word, thinking
> I want, I want, I want
> to be one of them. (*Hatshepsut* 21)

Whitman sensed that she was "one of the last romantics" and so sought to temper her romanticism by immersion in the poetry of "Williams and Pound, Eliot and Auden, Levertov, Creeley, Rich, Kunitz and Ammons" (*World* 882). A heady summer on scholarship at the Bread Loaf Writers' Conference in 1941 introduced her to "granddaddy/ of us all" Robert Frost, as well as to John Crowe Ransom, Theodore Roethke, and to the man who was to become her first husband, Cedric Whitman. The young couple eloped to prewar Cambridge; she earned her B.A. at Radcliffe in 1944, majoring in Greek and English, and an M.A. from Harvard in 1947. By the 1950s, she was the mother of two daughters with "a household to run, a husband in graduate school, money to earn, and, like 'rowing against the tide,' the drive to write poetry" (*World* 882). She describes this era as one in which she suffered "a crisis of gender identity." "Women were generally regarded as second-class citizens," she writes in the preface to *Hatshepsut*. "I felt guilty about my ambition to be a writer and at the same time anxious about my identity" (11). Divorcing in 1958, she later remarried, gave birth to her third child, a son, and completed her first book of poems during a two-week retreat at the MacDowell Colony (*Blood & Milk Poems* 1963). After her second divorce, she married painter Morton Sacks in 1966. She wrote *The Marriage Wig and Other Poems* (1968), her second collection, while on a fellowship to the Bunting Institute at Radcliffe.

During the decades that followed, Whitman published both her own poetry and her highly praised translations from modern Greek, French, and Yiddish. From 1969–1989 she lectured at Radcliffe and taught at Harvard, Holy Cross, and the University of Denver. She was also on a Fulbright Writer-in-Residence at the Hebrew University in Jerusalem. These were years devoted to "bearing witness" to the lives of extraordinary women. Moved by the tragic story of the Donner wagon train, Whitman received a grant from the National Endowment for the Humanities to travel the route taken by Tamsen Donner in 1846, recreating that pioneer's voice in *Tamsen Donner: A Woman's Journey*. *Tamsen Donner* was followed by *The Testing of Hannah Senesh*, based on the life and poetry of the young paratrooper who was captured and tortured by the Nazis in 1944.

The third woman about whom Whitman was drawn to write is Hatshepsut, the only woman pharoah of Egyptian history. While in the earlier books, Whitman herself assumes the voice of her subject; *Hatshepsut, Speak to Me* (1992) is, rather, a dialogue. "I wanted to juxtapose our two lives across the twenty-five centuries between us," she explains in the Introduction to the book, "and see what parallels might emerge. I wanted to examine her life and tell her about mine" (12).

Ruth Whitman is currently a Visiting Professor of Poetry at Massachusetts Institute of Technology (MIT) and divides her time between her homes in Boston and on the Rhode Island seacoast.

MAJOR THEMES

In the introduction to *Laughing Gas*, Whitman describes her poetic career as reflecting "the common experience of a woman living during the second half of the twentieth century": from the "repression and vulnerability" of the 1950s; the rebelliousness of the 1960s; the "growing self-empowerment" in the 1970s; and the "confrontation with loss and aging" in the 1980s and 1990s.

She engages this "common experience" through a revelation of self that is at once intimately personal, emotionally intense, rooted in family, aware of its Jewishness, and alive to history. Romanticist or not, she is to an almost startling degree capable of what the poet John Keats called "negative capability": In *The Passion of Lizzie Borden*, *Tamsen Donner: A Woman's Journey*, and *The Testing of Hannah Senesh*, she becomes the women in whose imagined voices she writes. Perhaps not coincidentally for a contemporary woman poet whose career was launched in a determinedly male, Gentile, and anti-Romantic era, all three of Whitman's women are selves *in extremis*. Suffocating in the August heat and in the airlessness of her own tightly corseted life, Borden traps "rage in her like a cage/trapping a bear" (*Passion* 16); ironing handkerchiefs, she feels herself having to "slash air so she can breathe,/ take life to make life, break/the blind wall open with her fist" (*Passion* 15). Borden's rage and repression gave way in Whitman's opus to the acute sensitivity of Tamsen Donner, who begins the cross-country trek with her family and friends imagining that this band of humans will give the land "birth"—but who discovers, instead, "the anger of the land," its "immensity and loneliness": "We change in relation/ to the land," writes Whitman in Tamsen Donner's voice. "We become smaller" (*Laughing Gas* 153). Whitman captures the growing desperation of the Donners' plight, as Tamsen describes how the journey demands, Lear-like, that she discard all those accoutrements of civilized life with which she set out: her books, her desk, the "great fourposter," until she is left only with "one sketchbook one journal" (*Laughing Gas* 162–63). At the end, in the relentless snowfall, refusing to leave her dying husband, she surrenders her own life.

The Testing of Hannah Senesh again picks up the theme of the doomed woman. But if Borden is a victim of her own murderous repression, and Donner succumbs to death, Senesh consciously chooses her mission fully aware of its deadly risks. "There's a fire in me:/ it must not go to waste," she insists (74). Even when she is captured and tortured by the Hungarian Nazis, Senesh remains defiant, "insubordinate, incorrigible" (104): "Not to despair, not to be diminished" (202). Published in 1986, the Senesh sequence inscribes an eloquent and determined courage that itself deepens Whitman's own claim that she moved from feelings of repression and vulnerability to rebelliousness and "self-empowerment" as a woman. One is tempted to suggest, too, that such self-empowerment is also reflected in her choosing, in *The Testing of Hannah Senesh*, to enter the soul of a heroic *Jewish* woman.

Like a true Romanticist, Whitman does not avoid passionate intensity; she invites it. Such intensity, evident in the poems written in the personae of Borden, Donner, and Senesh, also characterizes those she has written in her own voice, many of which focus on aspects of the Jewish-American immigrant experience. Fascinated with the ties that bind others, Whitman's poetry explores as well the ties that bind her: ties to the men she has loved, to her children, her uncle, her grandparents, all expressions of continuity between the self and culture, the self and its past, selves and other selves, the individual self, and collective history. Both as Jew and as woman, Whitman continually remembers and reconstitutes. She is sensitive to the palpable presence of the past in the present moment, in the gesture, the expression, the cry. In "Her Delirium," for example, from her 1968 collection *The Marriage Wig and Other Poems*, "The old lady" cries out in her sleep, reliving a beating by the police in a "dark cellar" when she was seven. "Which is me," the woman struggles to know, "which body is mine."

With her "wrinkled arm" and her "withered knee," she is yet a "little girl," who cannot fathom why they are beating "an old lady of eighty-nine."

Permanent Address: New Poems 1973–1980 includes "Bubba Esther, 1888" who, "still ashamed, lying/ eighty years later/in the hospital bed," pours out her pain at the sexual molestation she suffered as a girl of seventeen in exchange for her ticket to America. Similarly, ninety-three-year-old "Uncle Harry at the La Brea Tar Pits" bemoans his unwilling exile as a boy from Russia in 1907, still as submerged in his loss as "the lifelike mastodon . . . half-submerged in tar . . . [in] the "black museum" (*Laughing Gas* 248). Human memory dissolves chronological time.

Clearly, too, throughout her career, Whitman's poetry has engaged both the drama and the historical anguish of the Jewish experience. She writes about more than the Jewish American immigrant experience. Anthologized in the feminist collection *The World Split Open*, her well-known "Cutting the Jewish Bride's Hair," from her 1968 collection *The Marriage Wig and Other Poems*, challenged that traditional custom, warning "that this little amputation/ will shift the balance of the universe" (*Laughing Gas* 65). Among the poems included in her 1990 collection, *Laughing Gas*, are those that penetrate fleeting moments of present encounters in Israel—between a mother and her grown son, between herself and a woman with "numbers on her arm" in a Jerusalem bakery, between herself and an Arab poet, between herself and a "bearded Russian painter" in a Jerusalem suburb—to reveal a European-Jewish history of war and suffering and a contemporary Israeli condition of war, alienation, and fear. Thus, for Whitman, even in the confrontation with one's own aging, even in the most private of all moments—face to face with one's own image in a mirror—all of one's collective history is present. "Who is this woman in my mirror?" she asks in wonderment, "Who is this interloper?" She studies her own "dark eyes," her own "high cheekbones"; she perceives in them echoes of ancestors "ravished by the Mongols" on the steppes of Russia. And she concludes that, "in the end," face to face with the self alone, "it's the bones that tell who you have been" (*Laughing Gas* 281).

SURVEY OF CRITICISM

The reception afforded Ruth Whitman's poetry, to some extent, mirrors the changing perceptions of women's writing in general over the course of the last thirty years. In 1963, poet James Dickey noted that "there are a great many American women poets, more and more all the time," and he suggested that a "kind of uniquely feminine poetry" was evolving (4). "Uniquely feminine" to Dickey meant a "certain new delicacy of perception, a feeling of personal and unanalyzable continuity with the natural world, an acceptingness, a flowing-into quality surprisingly like that described by the Zen masters" (5). Along with Denise Levertov, Ruth Whitman in *Blood & Milk Poems*, Dickey commented, "has this quality to a marked degree" (5). He summed it up as a "womanly mysticism'': "that of a wife and mother who can hear the faint sound of the stars trying to sing while sitting with her hands in her lap.'' (5).

The consciousness of Whitman as a "feminine" voice is echoed in Robert D. Spector's review of her 1968 collection, *The Marriage Wig and Other Poems.* "Her feminine sensitivity responds warmly and wittily to the demands made upon womanhood,'' he notes (34). But whereas Spector perceives a "deceptive simplicity" in the verse, "hiding allusiveness behind a straightforward style and unaffectedly uniting rhythm and subject matter,'' Mona Van Duyn faults that style, seeing in it "some sort of lack of effort, a misplaced confidence . . . that simply by printing her feelings or thoughts on a page she will 'catch and hold' a reader's interest, empathy, admiration'' (438). Spector finds Whitman's lyrics "no model of sweetness and light'' (34); Van Duyn faults them for their "falsely naive . . . coy-playful'' tone.

What Dickey called "womanly mysticism" in 1963 evolves into a poetry "of magic or epiphanal moments'' for Richard Damashek in 1985. Noting that such moments tend to be "personal, subjective, and strongly formal,'' Damashek comments that Ruth Whitman "seems to spy out cracks in the great unknown, and then, as if to capture them before they close, dashes words on a page to hold them'' (*Contemporary Poets* 923). " . . . brilliant moments,'' for him, are "primarily the substance of Whitman's work.'' But in his assessment of Whitman, Damashek also considers *The Passion of Lizzie Borden* (1973), *Tamsen Donner: A Woman's Journey* (1977), and *Permanent Address: New Poems 1973–1980* (1980); he finds in these books not only the search "for the proper role and mode of self-actualization in a new world where freedom to achieve self-fulfillment comes into continual conflict with deeply embedded psychological, historical, and traditional societal and religious restraints,'' but also and crucially, a celebration of freedom. In such poems, he perceives "a level of precision, of craft molded with exquisite passion, that few of her contemporaries can match'' (923).

Recent critics echo this assessment of Whitman's more mature work. For Laurel Blossom, *The Testing of Hannah Senesh* (1986) offers a "steady eye [that] reveals the stillness at the heart of heroism'' (24). For Maxine Kumin, *Hannah Senesh* "rekindles both our despair in the presence of human depravity and our hope aroused by human selflessness. *The Testing of Hannah Senesh* makes us ask ourselves what we would die for'' (6). Finally, Blossom points to "The Drowned Mountain,'' a new fourteen-poem elegy to Whitman's first husband included in *Laughing Gas* (1990) as an exploration of "the territory of memory and dream at a depth few of us ever reach.'' "It is magnificent,'' she writes. "While we may quibble with her shorter lyrics, we will return again and again to 'The Drowned Mountain' and the other long poems she has had the quiet courage to write'' (24).

BIBLIOGRAPHY

Works by Ruth Whitman

Poetry

Blood & Milk Poems. New York: Clarke & Way, 1963.
The Marriage Wig and Other Poems. New York: Harcourt Brace Jovanovich, 1968.
The Passion of Lizzie Borden: New and Selected Poems. New York: October House, 1973.
Tamsen Donner: A Woman's Journey. Cambridge, MA: Alice James Books, 1977.
Permanent Address: New Poems 1973–1980. Cambridge, MA: Alice James Books, 1980.
The Testing of Hanna Senesh. Detroit: Wayne State University Press, 1986.
The Fiddle Rose: Poems 1970–1972 by Abraham Sutzkever. Detroit: Wayne State University Press, 1990.
Laughing Gas: Poems New and Selected 1963–1990. Detroit: Wayne State University Press, 1991.
Hatshepsut, Speak to Me. Detroit: Wayne State University Press, 1992.

Translations

Selected Poems of Alain Bosquet. Translation, with others. New York: New Directions, 1963.
An Anthology of Modern Yiddish Poetry. New York: October House, 1966. 2nd ed., Workmen's Circle Education Department, 1979.
Short Friday. I. B. Singer. Translation, with others. New York: Farrar, Straus, 1966.
The Seance. I. B. Singer. Translation, with others. New York: Farrar, Straus, 1968.
The Selected Poems of Jacob Glatstein. New York: October House, 1973.

Nonfiction

Poemmaking: Poets in Classrooms. Boston: Massachusetts Council of Teachers of English, 1975.
Becoming a Poet: Source, Process, and Practice. Boston: The Writer, 1982.

Film

Sachusest Point. Television documentary. Written and narrated by Ruth Whitman. Filmed and directed by Peter O'Neill and Lee Gardner under a grant from the Rhode Island Committee on the Humanities, 1977.

Essays

"Four Modern Yiddish Poets." *Antioch Review* (Summer 1966):205–12.
"Teaching the Sources of Poetry." *American Poetry Review.* (March–April 1973):50–51.
"The Translator as Juggler." *Jewish Quarterly* (Spring–Summer 1978):n.p.
"Finding Tamsen Donner." *Radcliffe Quarterly* (Spring 1978):40–41.
"Why I Live Here and Not There." *The Writer* (December 1979):16–17.
"The Divided Heart." *In Her Own Image: Women Working in the Arts.* Edited by Elaine Hedges and Ingrid Wendt, Old Westbury, NY: Feminist Press, 1980: 151–55.

"Motor Car, Bomb, God: Israeli Poetry in Translation." *The Massachusetts Review* (Spring 1982): 309–28.

"What Is Your Permanent Address?: Questions and Answers." *Iowa English Bulletin* 35.1 (1987):35–42.

"History, Myth, and Poetry: Writing the Historical Persona Poem." *Iowa English Bulletin* 35.1 (1987):65–73.

"The Last Dark Violet Plum on the Tree: Modern Yiddish Poetry." *Associated Writing Programs Chronicle* (September 1990):2–5.

"The Bitter Taste of Freedom." *American Book Review* (June–July 1991):15, 19.

Works about Ruth Whitman

Blossom, Laurel. "Quiet Courage." *American Book Review* (Feb.–Mar. 1992):23–24.

Damashek, Richard. "Ruth Whitman." *Contemporary Poets*. New York: St. James, 1985. 923–24.

Dickey, James. "Tactics of Shock, Discoveries of Innocence." *New York Times Book Review* Sept. 1963:4–5.

Kumin, Maxine. "Three's Company." *Women's Review of Books* (July–August 1987): 6.

Spector, Robert D. "Poetry Quarterly," *Saturday Review* 15 March 1969:32–35.

Van Duyn, Mona. "Seven Women." *Poetry* March 1970:430–39.

"Ruth Whitman." *World Authors 1980–1985*. Ed. Vineta Colby. New York: H. W. Wilson Company, 1991. 882–85.

EMMA WOLF (1865–1932)

Barbara Cantalupo

BIOGRAPHY

Emma Wolf was born in San Francisco on June 15, 1865, to Simon and Annette (Levy) Wolf, who had emigrated from France in the 1850s. Emma was the fourth of eleven children, Emma and her sisters and brother came under the sole care of her mother at her father's death. Considered "one of the most important Jewish pioneers of [Contra Costa] county" (Tornheim, 5), Simon Wolf died suddenly of a heart attack in 1878, when Emma was thirteen. Although the family was left insolvent, Emma's mother prevailed in keeping the family's place in society both secure and respected: Emma's sisters married men of wealth and position, and her brother Julius (one year Emma's junior) became a prominent influence in the economic life of San Francisco as president of the Grain Exchange. As William Tornheim (author of "The Pioneer Jews of Contra Costa County") recounts, "when Julius died in 1923, The Board of Trade closed in his honor—a unique event in its history." Emma's younger sister, Alice Wolf, the prototype for the main character in Wolf's first novel, *Other Things Being Equal*, was also a writer who published short stories and a novel, *A House of Cards* (1896).

Emma attended both grammar and normal schools, but, like her sisters, she never actually taught. She was an active member of the Philomath Club, "the only Jewish literary club in the city" (Gradwohl, 12), until the effects of polio, a childhood affliction, grew worse and kept her from meetings. As Rosa Sonneschein, editor of *The American Jewess*, notes in 1895: "Her literary genius developed at a tender age, which she has cultivated continuously since her thirteenth year. Not being very robust, the author enters little into society except that of a small beloved circle" (295).

Rebekah Kohut, a high-school classmate and close friend, describes Emma in "My Life in San Francisco":

handicapped from birth by a useless arm, there was no defect in her mentality. Her memory was the most remarkable I have ever encountered. She could quote with equal facility the texts of long poems or the fatality statistics of each of the world's greatest battles. (503)

Polio aftereffects, nevertheless, restricted Wolf to a relatively insular life and, unlike her sisters, she never married.

Her family, part of the French/German Jewish community of San Francisco, were members of Temple Emanu-El. Describing the condition of Jews living in California in a letter dated June 20, 1858, Daniel Levy (cantor in the temple and prominent educator of the time) notes that much had changed in San Francisco over a short span of ten years:

Instead of social chaos . . . [you] would find a thousand Jewish families with pure morals and with homes that contained all the conditions necessary for comfort and even luxury . . . .These families are linked by bonds of neighborliness and friendship . . . the influence of family feeling has restrained the former passionate fervor and led men back to the true path in which human society should move . . . family life. (110–11)

This environment and these values were part of Wolf's everyday life, and they found their way into her characters' lives as well.

In 1910, the editor of *Emanu-El* describes Emma as "the well known California writer, whose works, by the way, are much appreciated in the Eastern States and in England." Yet Emma seems not to have pursued literary notoriety though her novels were reviewed in San Francisco newspapers and the *New York Times* and in such journals as *The Overland Monthly*, *The Jewish Messenger*, and *Literary Digest*. Her short stories and a novella appeared in *The Smart Set*, along with such prominent writers as H. L. Mencken and Ezra Pound; her five novels were published by H. L. McClurg of Chicago and Harper & Bros. and Henry Holt of New York.

Her great-nephew, Richard Auslen, remembers his aunt Emma as quiet, sensitive, and unobtrusive, sitting most often in her wheel chair by the bay window of their parlor. Emma's modesty is clearly evidenced in a 1930 interview with Helen Piper of the *San Francisco Chronicle*: "A shut-in's adventures can't possibly be exciting. . . . One sits by one's window and watches the parade. There is time to think. There is time to enjoy much that others are too busy to see." Yet a distinguishing characteristic of Wolf's work is precisely this sensitive observation of the intricacies and involutions of intimacy and the environment that shapes it. The quiet quality of her descriptions draws the reader into the comfort and security that intimacy and home can provide, yet they're drawn without the distraction of sentimentality; the interiors of place and heart are written about with a distant yet passionate reverence.

Wolf lived in San Francisco all her life. In her last fifteen years, she was bound to a wheel chair and was taken care of by her older sister, Linnie (Celeste) Kauffman and her mother at their home at 2100 Pacific Avenue. She died in Dante Sanatorium on August 30, 1932, at the age of 67.

MAJOR THEMES

The setting for all of Wolf's novels is California, mainly San Francisco's upper-middle-class neighborhood, Pacific Heights. As a review of Wolf's work in the 2 April 1916 *San Francisco Chronicle* confirms: "San Francisco is writ large . . . the local color is faultless" (35). Her novella "The Knot" (1909) details the fright and horrors of the San Francisco earthquake—

for the wind had changed and now all Loki's forces had entwined arms, pirouetting from Market Street, ablaze from end to end, and Hayes Valley and Chinatown and so, together, marched a triumphant band, two miles wide, sweeping and whirring and purring and soaring and roaring, agile and invincible, unassailable, in terrible, godlike godlessness . . . ."San Francisco was." Such was the burden of the strangely hushed note of mourning. (33)

Yet her fiction does not depend on local detail for its poignancy. Rather, Wolf's acute atmospheric rendering applies not only to the scenery surrounding her characters, but also to their inner perceptions and interpersonal engagements.

Wolf's fiction embraces three major themes: problems associated with Jewish American identity, implications of conventional morality especially in relation to women's roles, and complications born of financial status. All of these evolve from and revolve around the question of marriage.

Complicating these themes is Wolf's perception of love, "the mantle of Elijah" (from "Eschscholtzia")—its consuming intensity, its irrefutable force, its indiscriminate nature, its grace, and, most of all, the belief that it happens only once in a lifetime. This last aspect transforms the lives of many of her characters, leaving them victims of loneliness as a result of unrequited love or, as in her last novel, showing them the vanity of believing in such a sentimental ideal. Barbara Gerrish, a college-educated woman in *The Joy of Life*, gives up the love of one man for the romantic memory of his dead brother; Constance, a dedicated mother to her siblings in *A Prodigal in Love* makes her lover marry her sister out of moral necessity, forcing her own love underground; and Louis, a dedicated cousin in *Other Things Being Equal* is left alone in his unobtrusive enduring, but fruitless love. Always, Wolf's characters struggle with conventional morality and its implications; often intermarriage, abortion, divorce, extramarital affairs, and out-of-wedlock motherhood are given serious attention, calling into question the mores of "modern life."

Wolf also engages issues that concerned feminists of her time: the rest cure, universal suffrage, motherhood, and the role of the "new woman"; however, her consideration of these issues does not fit neatly into any ideology. Unlike Charlotte Perkins Gilman's "The Yellow Wallpaper," *Other Things Being Equal* and *Fulfillment*, for example, portray the rest cure as an effective method of relieving emotional exhaustion rather than an oppressive, destructive tool of patriarchy. In fact, in the earlier novel, the doctor who uses this method falls in love with his patient's daughter who admires his strength and his "reverence to women" (85) enough to fall in love and want to marry him despite the fact that he's a Christian.

Barbara Gerrish in *The Joy of Life*, in many respects a "new woman" [though she hates the term: "of all the tawdry, run-to heel phrases that strikes me the most disagreeably," (121)] maintains that no woman should be denied the right to vote based on her sex if she were qualified to vote, yet she does not believe in universal suffrage: "there are as many women as capable of casting an intelligent vote as there are men incapable of doing so" (120). She also suggests that motherhood and certain kinds of work can go hand in hand: "You can't be a mother and a President, but you might be a mother and a school-director" (120) and adds that certain women are "desirous and capable of extending their influence beyond their homes" (121). Like Barbara, Wolf's female characters do not fit neatly into any one category; they reflect contemporary conflicts confronted by middle-class women and involve a mix of "traditional" and "feminist" values.

Class is certainly a concern for Wolf. Her own life showed her how vulnerable women were to the constraints of economic status. Her female characters' self-esteem is often tied to economic circumstances. In *Fulfillment*, Gwen marries impulsively because she is unwilling to be seen as "needing to work"; in doing so, she compromises both her self-respect and the respect of others. On the other hand, in *The Joy of Life*, Nellie's self-abnegation comes from having wealth: "We rich girls, who think ourselves the salt and pivot of the world, are only its ornaments . . . and don't amount to much, after all" (199). In *The Joy of Life*, Wolf, through the character of Barbara Gerrish, seems to come to the pragmatic conclusion that "poverty, or even gentility, is very piquant for an experiment, but for a permanent state, give me downright, all-powerful riches" (200).

Fulfillment, Wolf's last novel, provides an alternative to that somewhat cynical conclusion; her female characters grow beyond the social expectations that demand that "ladies" not work, that "ladies" find fulfillment in marriage. Deb, the symbol of "law and order," with practical grace, engages completely with her role as social worker, going off to Chicago to learn from Jane Addams. Gwen comes to value the independence and self-respect that a vocation provides, even though she never has to act on that realization because her marriage finally turns around and she finds fulfillment in her relationship.

Wolf's short fiction, published mostly in *The Smart Set*, could almost be considered the equivalent of the late twentieth-century "popular romance." The main characters are mostly women who struggle with their desires—for a more romantic life than marriage to a "steady" man seems to provide ("The Conflict" and "A Still Small Voice"), for a life independent of marriage ("The Courting of Drusilla West" and "A Study in Suggestion"), for a new marriage after divorce ("Tryst"). Yet other fiction describes the determination of an illegitimate child to know his unknown father ("The End of the Story") and the feelings of abandonment that divorce brings to children ("The Father of Her Children"). All written after the turn of the century, they engage issues that "modern" life opened up for scrutiny: divorce, adultery, the romantic life of the artist, "the new woman."

Of Wolf's five novels, only two portray Jewish characters. As a review in *The Jewish Messenger* of December 14, 1900, notes:

[Wolf] is to be expressly omitted from the category of Jewish novelists who exploit their religion and special class of people and call the result literature. . . . Her delicacy, spirituality, intellectuality are not restricted to Jewish subjects. (1)

Nevertheless, Wolf is best known for *Other Things Being Equal*, a novel that expressly concerns itself with the dilemma of a young Jewish woman who wants to marry a Christian yet who feels committed to her Jewish faith and, most adamantly, to the need for her father's approval. Her struggle with the implications of difference and the question of assimilation are not resolved in the novel, since the marriage that ends the novel merely begins the social complications associated with intermarriage. Although her father initially refuses to grant approval for this proposed marriage, he has, after many years, a revelatory experience that shows him "character and circumstances are not altogether of our own making . . . only God can weigh such circumstantial evidence . . . final judgment is reserved for a higher court" (256). Consequently, on his deathbed, he realizes that his not having blessed his daughter's engagement has been selfish and foolish.

I stood convicted; I was in the position of a blind fool who, with a beautiful picture before him, fastens his critical, condemning gaze upon a rusting nail in the wall behind— a nail even now loosened, and which in another generation will be displaced. (257)

Whether that nail is now completely rusted and replaced or whether such relinquishing of personal judgment brings the possibility of successful intermarriage but also extends beyond this concern to the conclusion that all laws (both religious and legal) are negotiable remains to be seen.

Wolf's vision comprehended such complications, and as her writing matured, these concerns became more problematic. Furthermore, Wolf's sustaining belief that "love conquers all" seems to override even the most difficult convolutions, making way for the possibility of woman happiness within the constraints of law.

SURVEY OF CRITICISM

The first more than cursory critical assessment of Wolf's fiction was written by Louis Harap in *The Image of the Jew in American Literature* (1974). Although Harap's chapter, "Early American Jewish Novels," begins with reviews of two of Wolf's novels, (*Other Things Being Equal* and *Heirs of Yesterday*), he finally considers Wolf merely a "competent, though minor, writer" (472). Harap also suggests that Wolf's main character Ruth in *Other Things Being Equal* "(and the author) have ... to some extent and quite unconsciously, become insensitive" (474) to stereotyping. Yet, Harap agrees, "there is no doubt of [Ruth's] wholehearted acceptance of her Jewish identity" (474). Since the two novels Harap chooses to review deal directly with issues related to Jewish identity, his questioning Wolf's own sensitivity seems particularly poignant.

Contextualizing *Heirs of Yesterday* as "a frontal attack" (474) on "the new, more intense quality of anti-Semitism in the United States" (474), Harap seems to redeem Wolf from his previous criticism. He does, however, read *Heirs of Yesterday* as reflecting what he conjectures as Wolf's "hav[ing] undergone disillusioning experiences with non-Jews" (476), suggesting that the novel concludes with the belief "that the Christian world regards Jewishness as an ineradicable stigma" (476). This interpretation is open to question.

Unlike Harap, Diane Lichtenstein suggests that Wolf's work is an important part of the tradition of American Jewish women writers. In her 1988 article in *Studies in American Jewish Literature*, Lichtenstein uses all five of Wolf's novels to contextualize Fannie Hurst's work, placing Wolf's stance in between the fairy tale idealism of her predecessor Rebekah Hyneman (1812–1875) who "wrote almost exclusively about Jewish subjects in her poetry and fiction of the 1850s and 1860s" (27) and Hurst's 1920s realistic ambivalence. Although Lichtenstein argues that Wolf's *Other Things Being Equal* presents a "modified fairy-tale ending" (32) to the problem of intermarriage, she also suggests that Wolf's approach "reveals how ideals of Jewish womanhood and questions about assimilation have changed from 1860 to 1960" (27). Lichtenstein sees Wolf as assimilated into American culture and suggests that her novels imply that "Jews could live among non-Jewish Americans, and even marry them ... if they did not try to 'pass' or deny their Jewish identities" (37), that assimilation through intermarriage is possible since "love resolves all differences" (32).

Lichtenstein sees Wolf's work as tackling problems associated with changes in the expectations of women's roles. Wolf's female characters seem able to maintain traditional values of Jewish family life as they untangle the emotional struggles of what it means to be a "new woman."

BIBLIOGRAPHY

Works by Emma Wolf

Novels

Other Things Being Equal. Chicago: A. C. McClurg, 1892, 1893, 1895; revised 1916.
A Prodigal in Love. New York: Harper & Bros., 1894.
The Joy of Life. Chicago: A. C. McClurg, 1896.

Heirs of Yesterday. Chicago: A. C. McClurg, 1900.
Fulfillment: A California Novel. New York: Henry Holt, 1916.

Novella

The Knot. New York: Ess Ess, 1909.

Poetry

"Eschscholtzia (California Poppy)." *American Jewess* 2.4 (January 1896):195.

Short Stories

"One-Eye, Two-Eye, Three-Eye." *American Jewess* 2.6 (March 1896):279–90.
"A Study in Suggestion." *Smart Set* 6.3 (March 1902):95–100.
"A Still Small Voice." *Smart Set* 8.2 (October 1902):157–60.
"The Courting of Drusilla West." *Smart Set* 9.2 (February 1903):69–81.
"The End of the Story." *Smart Set* 14.4 (December 1904):137–46.
"Tryst." *Smart Set* 16.3 (July 1905):109–16.
"Farquhar's Masterpiece." *Smart Set* 18.3 (March 1906):101–11.
"The Conflict."*Smart Set* 20.3 (November 1906):1–45.
"Louis d'Or." *Smart Set* 22.4 (August 1907):94–104.
"The Father of Her Children." *Smart Set* 34.2 (June 1911):135–40.

Interviews

Auslen, Donald. Personal interview, 18 June 1992.
Auslen, Richard. Telephone interview, 19 June 1992.
Lowe, William. Telephone interview, 14 October 1992.
Wolf, Emma. Interview with Helen Piper for "Who's Who in San Francisco." *San Francisco Chronicle* (3 December 1930):47.

Works about Emma Wolf

Danziger, Gustav. "The Jew in San Francisco." *Overland Monthly* (April 1895):403.
Rev. of *Fulfillment. Overland Monthly, Second Series* 67.5 (May 1916):ix–x.
Glanz, Rudolf. *The Jewish Woman in America: Two Female Immigrant Generations, 1820–1929, vol. 2.* New York: KTAV and National Council of Jewish Women, 1976:163.
Gradwohl, Rebecca. "The Jewess in San Francisco." *American Jewess* 4.1 (October 1896):10–12.
Harap, Louis. *The Image of the Jew in American Literature from Early Republic to Mass Immigration.* Philadelphia: Jewish Publication Society of America, 1974. 472–76.
Rev. of *The Joy of Life. Overland Monthly, Second Series* 29.172 (April 1897):454.
Kohut, Rebekah. "My Life in San Francisco." *Memoirs of My People Through Thousands of Years.* Ed. Leo Schwartz, Philadelphia: Jewish Publication Society, 1943.
Levy, Daniel. "Letters About the Jews of California: 1855–1858." Trans. Marlene Rainman. *Western States Jewish Historical Quarterly* 3.2 (January 1971):86–112.
Lichtenstein, Diane. "Fannie Hurst and Her Nineteenth-Century Predecessors." *Studies in American Jewish Literature* 7.1 (Winter 1988):26–39.

————. *Writing Their Nations: The Tradition of Nineteenth-Century American Jewish Women Writers.* Bloomington: Indiana University Press, 1992: 78–80, 84–85, 113–17.

Marcus, Jacob. *The American Jewish Woman 1654–1980: A Documentary History.* New York: KTAV, 1981.

Mighels, Ella Sterling (Clark). *The Story of the Files: A Review of California Writers and Literature.* San Francisco: World's Fair Commission, 1893.

"Miss Wolf's New Story." Rev. of *Heirs of Yesterday. Jewish Messenger* 88, 24 (December 14, 1900):1.

Reely, Mary Katherine. Rev. of *Fulfillment: A California Novel. Book Review Digest: Reviews of 1916 Books.* Ed. Margaret Jackson. New York: H. W. Wilson, 1917: 598–99.

"San Francisco Setting of New Emotional Romance." Rev. of *Fulfillment: A California Novel. San Francisco Chronicle* 2 (April 1916):35.

Sonneschein, Rosa. "Emma Wolf" in *American Jewess* 1.6 (September 1895):294–95.

Tornheim, William. "Pioneer Jews of Contra Costa." *Western States Jewish History* 16.1 (October 1983):3–22.

SUSAN YANKOWITZ (1941–   )

Len Berkman

BIOGRAPHY

Born on February 20, 1941, in what she terms "the Philip Roth section of upperward Jewish Newark,"[1] Susan Yankowitz grew up, the second of three children, within a household that bridged law and the arts. With father and brother both lawyers, Yankowitz and her sister, a thriving visual artist, were to extend the path begun by their mother, an actress in amateur theatricals who, upon marriage, turned to U.N. organizational work. Sent to Hebrew elementary and high schools, Yankowitz was confirmed at thirteen. Her maiden publication at age twelve, an essay on prejudice in the local *Jewish News*, symbolized to her both the start of her writing career and what was to become her lifelong support of societal victims. Freer than in her suburban environment to be "myself, the kook" at Sarah Lawrence College, she studied short-story writing there with Harvey Swados. The year after graduation from Sarah Lawrence (1963–64) she lived in Madras, India, where she wrote her first plays.

Lured to dramatic structure by its needs for economy, its disciplined countering of what she saw as her "adjectival" self, Yankowitz, in 1964, at The New School in New York signed on for four lecture/demonstrations by a young, experimental ensemble, the Open Theatre, with exercises led by its director, Joseph Chaikin. Entranced, she secured permission to attend Open Theatre work sessions several times a week. Her script *The Ha-Ha Play a.k.a. And The Hyenas Laughed* earned her admission to Yale Drama School for fall 1965. In November 1970, *The Ha-Ha Play* would premiere at New York's Cubiculo Theatre.

Viewing Yale as a mix of clamped tradition and inspired stimulus, Yankowitz studied playwriting with a critic/teacher of one generation, John Gassner, and a dramatist of another, Arnold Weinstein. She attributes to faculty critic Richard Gilman special fostering of her quirky spirit. "Write about what you know" is standard pedagogic wisdom, but Yankowitz prized imagination beyond experiential limits: "I never wanted to write about what I knew." A film fellowship afforded her a post-M.F.A. year at Yale, 1968–69, to study with filmmakers

Mike Roemer and Bob Young, and with theatre/film critic Stanley Kauffmann. She divided her time between New Haven and New York City.

When Yankowitz submitted *Slaughterhouse Play*, written at Yale, to the Open Theatre in 1969, Joseph Chaikin contacted her, not to work on *Slaughterhouse*, but on a new ensemble piece, *Terminal*. *Slaughterhouse Play*, with musical score by Robert Dennis, had its premiere, nonetheless, in New York at Joseph Papp's Public Theatre in 1971. Yankowitz's text for *Terminal* was to evolve after a full year of Open Theatre collaboration. Performed at St. Clement's Church in New York, it toured the United States and Europe (1971–73) and led to offers that Yankowitz accepted, to collaborate with ensembles such as the Omaha Magic Theatre (*Transplant*, 1971), the National Theatre of the Deaf (*Sideshow*, 1971), the Academy Theatre of Atlanta, Georgia (*Acts of Love*, 1973), and Los Angeles's Provisional Theatre (*America Piece*, 1974). She worked briefly, as well, with Andre Gregory's Manhattan Project. Always she felt collaboration's creative tension: her individual identity enhanced but dissolved within a group process. To balance this collectivity with a purely individual thrust, she began her first novel, *Silent Witness*, in 1973.

By 1976, Yankowitz had completed *Silent Witness*. This period was especially dramatic and transitional for her, marked by her father's death and her meeting of Herb Leibowitz, poetry critic and publisher/editor of *Parnassus*, whom she would marry in 1978 and who would father her son, Gabriel, in 1979.

At this time, too, Yankowitz turned to television and visual-centered projects. For the PBS series *Visions* (from KCET, Los Angeles), she wrote a teleplay, *The Prison Game*, which aired nationally in 1977. At *Visions*, she met film/TV director Shirley Clarke, with whom she adapted her 1969 screenplay, *The Land of Milk and Funny [Or] Portrait of a Scientist as a Dumb Broad*, into a TV script, *Milk and Funny*. Both film and TV versions mix live action and animation, a mode that would not become popular in films and music videos for more than a decade. Yankowitz's next stage work, *Still Life*, was also a visual-performance piece. Its 1977 premiere at Women's Interart Theatre in New York was directed by former Open Theatre colleague Rhea Gaisner, and its subsequent productions included one at Toronto's comparably adventurous Factory Theatre Lab. On the cusp of the 1980s, Yankowitz would complete yet another teleplay, *Charlotte Perkins Gilman: Forerunner*, for WGBH (1979, PBS, Boston), adapt *Silent Witness* for Michael Jaffe (film) Productions (1980), and write an original screenplay for Jaffe/MGM, *The Amnesiac* (1982).

Continuing to alternate fiction with drama, Yankowitz put five years of labor into her second novel, *Taking Liberties*. Its central character is the daughter of a Holocaust survivor. Although all but one chapter of *Taking Liberties* remains unpublished, Yankowitz drew a play from it that premiered in 1986 as a work-in-progress at Lawrence Sacharow's River Arts Repertory in Woodstock, New York. Meantime, just as her early work with the Open Theatre had led to other ensemble invitations, so, too, did *Silent Witness*, *The Prison Game*, and *Charlotte Perkins Gilman*. With their intense exploration of female-centered issues, these plays led to friendships with such feminist writers as Andrea Dworkin and Karen Malpede, and led to calls for Yankowitz to work on material specific to women's perspectives. Her late '70s and early 80s stage plays are wide-ranging in this regard, from a musical partially and whimsically inspired by an evening spent with playwright John Guare, *True Romance* (1978, Mark Taper Lab, Los Angeles; Elmer Bernstein composer), to her adaptation of her satiric, fierce *Prison Game* for the French stage as *Qui Est Anna Mark?* (1979, TEP Theatre, Paris). Two projects grew consciously out of her childbearing experiences: (1) her work for over two years with writer/lyricist Richard Maltby and composer David Shire on the hit musical *Baby*, and (2) *A Knife in the Heart*, a startling play spurred by a rash of headline murders and attempted murders the year her son outgrew infancy (for example, Wayne Williams/Atlanta youths, John Hinckley/President Reagan). *Knife* focused not on an assassin within the drama of his crime but on his mother's tumultuous experience of his social impact. *Knife* debuted at the O'Neill Playwrights Conference in 1982 and was the new play in Williamstown Theatre Festival's 1983 mainstage season.

Yankowitz's feminist involvements also led her, in the mid-80s, into contact with the British women's theatre ensemble, Monstrous Regiment. *Alarms* was the commissioned result, a modern version of the Cassandra tale influenced greatly by the nuclear disaster at Chernobyl that had occurred during the development of *Alarms*. After its 1986 London run, *Alarms* toured England and had several U.S. performances.

With her husband inspiring a new passion for music, Yankowitz was drawn increasingly to opera. Tackling several projects simultaneously, she adapted George Eliot's novel *Daniel Deronda* (1986) for Moshe Cotel's operatic score. Then she embarked on several versions of *Monk's Revenge*, a nonmusical adaptation of *Rigoletto* based on Nahma Sandrow's literal translation of the original Victor Hugo source. With Alvin Epstein in the lead, *Monk's Revenge* received its first staged reading at Williamstown the same summer of *Knife*'s production there. Revived at CSC in New York with F. Murray Abraham in the lead (1988), *Revenge* has had staged readings elsewhere, benefitting from the sustained nurturance of its director Gordon Rogoff and from Yankowitz's energetic redraftings.

While completing her third novel, *Taking the Fall*, Yankowitz continues to write for TV and film. *Sylvia Plath*, a PBS documentary, 1988, received a Writers' Guild nomination for Best Documentary of the season. Yankowitz's most recent major staged venture, *Night Sky*, brings her full circle in her work with Joseph Chaikin. In 1984, Chaikin suffered a stroke that left him aphasic but still able to function as a director. After guiding a drama workshop on aphasia at San Francisco State, Chaikin turned to Yankowitz to develop a script that would satisfy certain given not previously linked to this subject: It would have a simple story and be accessible and educational. *Utterances*, which centers on a woman, an astronomer, who has an accident that causes her aphasia, was Yankowitz's response. Under Chaikin's direction, it was performed as a workshop in the

American Conservatory Theatre's Plays in Process Series (1990, San Francisco). Then it was revised and retitled *Night Sky,* and it premiered in Julia Miles's 1991 Women's Project season in New York. International interest was swift, resulting in a 1992 production at the Market Theatre in Johannesburg, South Africa. Yankowitz has also been developing her latest play, *Real Life,* with drafts that had readings in early 1992 at New Dramatists in New York and within the New York Stage and Film Company's summer 1992 New Play Festival at Vassar College (both directed by Melia Bensussan). She has also embarked on a musical piece on the subject of the Jonestown cult and massacre, to be developed with director Hilary Blecher.

MAJOR THEMES

From *Terminal* of the early 1970s to *Night Sky* and *Real Life* of the early 1990s, Yankowitz's command of theatrical language and brave stage vision have thrust her into the forefront of writers for our American theater. She explores experiences of death, illness, public policy, societal violence, injustice, and sheer human survival, with complex precision, depth, and a compassion that especially unsettles critics who do not associate such compassion with writers as gripped as she is by scientific discoveries (for example, in brain research, astronomy, military weaponry, even embalming).

How we distance ourselves from ourselves and how we dehumanize ourselves and others is a recurrent concern in her plays and novels alike. In so much of *Terminal,* for example, in its post-Brechtian monologue on saying YES when we should have said NO, and in the embalming section's grotesquely comic details of "lip slip," Yankowitz offers searing images of our acceptance of authority and violence that denies our soul. The unspoken shadow of the Holocaust is everywhere in *Terminal,* as it is also in the less abstract setting of her *Slaughterhouse Play,* which symbolically fuses butcher shop, slaughterhouse, living room, and street. The slaughterhouse owners/operators, tellingly, are whites, and the meat sold is not of animals or Jews but blacks. Likewise in *Boxes* (with its oblique dramatizing of Malvina Reynolds's 1960 satiric song "Little Boxes"), Yankowitz sustains focus on urban anonymity and confinement. In *Boxes,* however, we see how people restrict their own human potential. The overarching impact of all of these early plays is of death-in-life and of the refusal of the living to weigh and grieve death and its losses. The Yiddish mourning song of *Terminal,* contributed to and sung in the Open Theatre production by Shami Chaikin as she staggers forward with a large chunk of wall strapped to her back and thudding on the ground, conveys the magnitude of that denial.

This essentiality of imagination (call it "art") over sheer physical experience in defining the vitality, the reality, of human life is at the core of *Still Life,* which invests things normally inanimate with more animation than things animate. A pogo stick or wheelchair, for example, become capable of movement usually attributed to a person. Yankowitz's interest in the technical mix of live action with animation in her *Portrait of a Scientist/Milk and Funny* shooting scripts is further testament to her questioning of borders between assumed reality and the application of art.

The related issues of truth, as it bears upon justice, and of fact, as it defies belief, emerge in Yankowitz's novel *Silent Witness*. Through the unjust imprisonment for murder of its deaf and mute heroine, the novel conveys Yankowitz's absorption with the interplay of guilt with innocence and of criminal with noncriminal behavior as defined by our legal and penal systems. This concern would also be reflected in her experiences in the 1970s and 1980s of offering writer workshops to prison inmates. One of these workshops inspired a monologue by Sarah Jane Moore that focused on what Moore planned to wear on the day of her intended assassination of President Gerald Ford. Another workshop led to Yankowitz's success in getting prisoner Jimmy Walker released from serving further time for a crime he did not commit. Yankowitz explores different interweavings of imagined/real, murderer/innocent in *The Prison Game/Qui Est Anna Mark?*, a subversion of the long-run TV game show *To Tell The Truth*. In *Prison/Anna*, three women in a game show each claim to be the actual Anna Marks who killed her husband, under differing circumstances that each woman reenacts. The climax, the moment when only the "real" Anna Marks is to rise from her panelist seat and sort fiction from fact, turns, instead, into a stark revelation of solidarity among oppressed women.

Facing the truth takes comic forms in Yankowitz's work as well. In her fable, *The Ha-Ha Play*, hill-dwelling hyenas kidnap a child from its crib, not to devour it but to teach it to laugh. *True Romances* flips its very form—musical comedy— on its head when a "misfit" girl finds her misfit guy as both expose their inability to dance or sing while everyone around them can.

Yankowitz admits the autobiographical importance of the outsider theme that pervades her work. She links it not only to growing up Jewish apart from both a dominant Christian culture and many aspects of Jewish culture, but also to feeling alienated from all larger human communities and thereby identifying with all whom those larger communities view as "the other." Though she designates few of her characters as explicitly Jewish, many of them reflect her perceptions of her own multidimensioned Judaic self: Composed of a span of social-class variants, they incorporate both her serious side—the prophetic tradition, social consciousness, and the *chutzpah* to speak up for societal victims— and her self-caricature, with its awkward physical gestures, loud brash phrases, and self-conscious dress and makeup.

It is ironic that Yankowitz's outsider figures are primarily women with maternal and interdependent impulses. A prime example of such a mother is Mrs. Holt of *A Knife in the Heart*, who must confront the total upheaval of her life when her son fatally stabs the state governor and five other arbitrary victims. Yankowitz's incorporation of expressionist exchanges to heighten audience engagement with Mrs. Holt's internal/societal dilemma is a technique she employs in *Alarmas* as well. Here, her unheeded prophet, a modern Cassandra in the guise of a doctor, strives to prevent a radiation disaster that her colleagues will not help her avoid. The aphasic Anna in *Night Sky* also combines an internal and social fight: to reconnect to language, to her career as reputed astronomer, and to her responsibilities as mother and wife. The burden particular to women within the framework of a male-centered culture that educates women to identify with men's struggles as well as (if not more than) their own also sharpens the ironic edges of Yankowitz's *Real Life*. In this play, a lawyer tries to convert his mid-life crisis by defending an alleged serial killer of women. Relegating his wife and daughter to being mere supportive spectators of his quest, with minimal "real life" of their own, the lawyer aims to pursue his case objectively, as though it were a singular and impersonal event, ignoring how violence against women and those deemed "the other" permeates his culture.

SURVEY OF CRITICISM

Critical focus on Susan Yankowitz's writings has been scant and disproportionate to her earned status as an influential playwright within avant garde and feminist spheres. Perhaps, early on, her relative anonymity within an ensemble, her being, in her own words, "the author of an 'authorless' piece" (Sainer 149) contributed to this. Jack Kroll's review of *Terminal*, for example, overrides the Open Theatre's "text by Susan Yankowitz" credit by referring to the piece as "a collective work created by everyone in the company" (89). Still, Kroll's praise of *Terminal*'s "amazingly wide emotional range, from clinical horror to irony and warm humor," and his regard for its "resourceful use of clear and distorted speech" (89) could also characterize *Night Sky*. Similarly, Kroll's regard for *Terminal*'s "sharp sense of contemporary fatality and the necessity for unpolluted feeling and expression" (89) could be accurately applied to *Qui Est Anna Mark?*, *A Knife in the Heart*, and *Real Life*.

Karen Malpede calls *Terminal* the Open Theatre's "most timeless work, and most tormented" (16). Harold Clurman sees it as a mix of "existentialist pessimism" with the "quasi-mystic" and is especially struck by the ironic humor, "man's inability to understand God treated as funny" (765–66). Arthur Sainer, too, refers to its "choral-mythic quality . . . at times lovely, at times chilling, always haunting" (107). Though Sainer argues that "the play never really comes to grips with the complex feelings of our culture toward death," he sees *Terminal* representing the Open Theatre "in full maturity" and calls it "nevertheless extraordinarily passionate and demanding both of its performers and of the audience" (107).

Henry Hewes underscores the starkness of *Terminal*'s perspective, "the living individual's inexplicable willingness to suffer the humiliations that precede death," and the power of its artistic means, "an unforgettable sequence of simply executed images, an experience that will jar you out of your half-life if anything can'' (12). From her prose interweave of linguistic method and evoked images in *Silent Witness* and *Taking the Fall* to her links of carved dialogue with real/surreal stage imagery in virtually all her plays, the elements in *Terminal* that these critics attribute to the Open Theatre at large impressively prefigure Yankowitz's entire *oeuvre*.

In her review of *Silent Witness*, Katha Pollit affirms the book's rich authenticity. ''Yankowitz shows us Anna's world: visual impressions, gestures, intuitions, silence . . . what could have been sensational exploitation of human misery and viciousness is redeemed by the moral passion that informs, sometimes clumsily but often with great delicacy, every page'' (29). Critical applause for Yankowitz's conceptual, linguistic, and imagistic range in *A Knife in the Heart* and *Night Sky* is comparably strong. Of *Knife*, Robert Bell writes, ''Yankowitz has superb dramatic gifts, both verbal and visual; her play succeeds through metaphoric language, telling gesture, indirection, and connotation'' (13). Frank Rich points to *Knife*'s ''almost surreal, stream-of-consciousness style,'' its ''one unexpected scene after another'' and its ''find[ing] its dramatic soul in images that bleed as profusely as its protagonist's actions'' (C4). Rich further observes, ''One might expect Miss Yankowitz to write a courtroom drama, or something resembling a docu-drama, or maybe a problem play about the controversial insanity defense that her protagonist pleads in his trial. But this writer has indeed let her imagination run wild, to the point where *A Knife in the Heart* does create its own, totally theatrical reality . . . '' (C4).

Reviewing *Night Sky*, Mel Gussow charts its multiple scale ambition: Aphasia is the subject, astronomy the metaphor, he observes, providing *Night Sky* ''with fluctuating success in several simultaneous philosophical planes'' (C24). The South African critics are uniformly enthusiastic: Raeford Daniel calls *Night Sky* ''a searching, grueling play . . . not only rich in histrionic opportunities but also fired by poetic analogy'' (12). Brenda Van Rooyen notes that in this ''superbly crafted play . . . [t]he depth of Yankowitz's research enables her to spin wonderful metaphors'' (3), while Jenny Dowthwaite finds *Night Sky* ''a fascinating and moving play, interweaving human tragedy and emotion with the enduring mystery of the cosmos'' (9). Michael Feingold is the sole critic of *Night Sky* struck by its formalistic paradoxes in relation to Yankowitz and Chaikin's previous work: ''Remarkably, these two artists who have so often broken the mold of realism, with towering abstract or imagistic representations of grandeur, seem quite comfortable encased in it, fluidly painting strokes of detail, atmosphere, domestic convention in a manner one would have thought quite alien to them'' (111).

NOTE

1. Quotations in this section are drawn from my personal interview with Susan Yankowitz at her New York City apartment on May 24, 1992.

BIBLIOGRAPHY

Works by Susan Yankowitz

Plays

Slaughterhouse Play. *New American Plays 4*. Ed. William Hoffman. New York: Hill and Wang, 1971.

Terminal. *Scripts* (November 1971):17–45. Rev. ed. *Three Plays by the Open Theatre*. Ed. Karen Malpede. New York: Drama Book Specialists, 1974. 38–89.

The Ha-Ha Play. *Scripts* (October 1972):81–92.

Boxes. *Playwrights for Tomorrow* 11. Ed. Arthur Ballet. Minneapolis, MN: University of Minnesota Press, 1973.

The Land of Milk and Funny or Portrait of a Scientist as a Dumb Broad. Screenplay. *Yale/Theatre* (Fall 1974):8–59.

Alarms. *Female Voices*. London: Playwrights Press, 1988.

Night Sky. New York: Samuel French, 1992. Rev. ed. *Plays from the Women's Project*. Ed. Julia Miles. Portsmouth, NH: Heinemann, 1992.

Novels

Silent Witness. New York: Knopf, 1976. New York: Avon, 1977.

"Taking the Fall." *Parnassus: Poetry In Review* 15.2 (1989):139–52.

Interviews with Susan Yankowitz

Personal Interview. New York: 24 May 1992.

"Susan Yankowitz." Kathleen Betsko, and Rachel Koeing eds. *Interviews With Contemporary Women Playwrights*. New York: Morrow & Co./Beech Tree Books, 1987. 432–49.

Sainer, Arthur. *The Radical Theatre Notebook*. New York: Avon, 1975. 147–53.

Works about Susan Yankowitz

Bell, Robert. Rev. of *A Knife in the Heart*. *Williamstown Advocate* 24 August 1983:12–13.

Chinoy, Helen Krich, and Linda Walsh Jenkins, eds. *Women in American Theatre*. Rev. ed. New York: Theatre Communications Group, 1989.

Clurman, Harold. Rev. of *Terminal*. *The Nation*. 22 June 1970:765–66.

Daniel, Raeford. Rev. of *Night Sky*. *Johannesburg Weekly Mail*. 16–23 April 1992:12.

Dowthwaite, Jenny. Rev. of *Night Sky*. *Johannesburg Star Review*. 12 April 1992:9.

Feingold, Michael. Rev. of *Night Sky*. *The Village Voice*. 4 June 1991:111.

Gussow, Mel. Rev. of *Night Sky*. *New York Times*. 23 May 1991:C24.

Hewes, Henry. Rev. of *Terminal*. *Saturday Review*. 2 May 1970:12.

Keyssar, Helene. *Feminist Theatre*. London: Macmillan, 1984.

Kroll, Jack. Rev. of *Terminal*. *Newsweek*. 4 May 1970:89.

Leavitt, Dinah Luise. *Feminist Theatre Groups*. Jefferson, NC: McFarland, 1980.

Malpede, Karen, ed. *Three Plays by the Open Theatre*. New York: Drama Book Specialists, 1974:38–89.

Pollit, Katha. Rev. of *Silent Witness*. *New York Times Book Review*. 27 June 1976:29.

Rich, Frank. ''Where Writers Mold the Future of Theater.'' *New York Times*. 1 August 1982:C1, C4.

Sainer, Arthur. *The Radical Theatre Notebook*. New York: Avon, 1975. 107–08.

Van Rooyen, Brenda. Rev. of *Night Sky*. *Praetoria News*. 10 April 1992:3.

ANZIA YEZIERSKA (1880–1970)

Tobe Levin

BIOGRAPHY

The youngest of nine children, Anzia Yezierska emigrated from the Russian-Polish *shtetl* of Plinsk in approximately 1890. Neither her date of birth nor date of landing is known. However, Mary Dearborn suggests 1893 for entry (36), while Jules Chametzky places her birthday with near certainty in 1880 (personal interview, 1 July 1992).[1]

Immigration authorities appropriated the eldest child, Mayer's, first name, making it into the family's last name. Thus, on disembarking, Anzia became Harriet, shortened to Hattie Mayer. An overcrowded tenement on New York City's Lower East Side became her first American home. The girl, with no formal education, could attend elementary school for no more than two years before being sent to work selling homemade paper bags, sewing buttons, rolling cigars, and doing domestic chores.

In 1900, clashes with her Orthodox father led the teenager to move into the Clara de Hirsch Home for Working Girls. There she won a scholarship to study domestic science at Teacher's College, Columbia University, from 1901 to 1905, earning her degree in a subject that apparently held little interest for her. New York City records show her as a substitute teacher. In 1909, the Board of Education granted her a leave of absence so she could attend the American Academy of Dramatic Arts, but after one year, she returned to the classroom, where in 1911, she taught full time. Only in 1913, at about thirty-three, did she funnel her expressive impulses into writing fiction (Dearborn 37).

Her marriage in March 1911 led to a first brush with publicity. She left her husband the day after the ceremony, and six months later, with the annulment approved, Yezierska appeared in the papers, quoted on her quixotic views of matrimony as a communion of souls. She claimed ignorance of the more physical side of the relationship. Later that year she would marry Arnold Levitas in a religious but not civil ceremony, and a daughter was born in 1912. Yezierska was by all accounts a "New Woman," not one to bend to male authority.

Domestic quarrels over money and housekeeping led to her precipitous flight to the West Coast, where in 1916, she served briefly as a social worker for the Hebrew Charities in San Francisco, complaining in a letter to her Socialist friend Rose Pastor Stokes that the work was "the dirtiest, most dehumanizing . . . a human being can do. I see how people are crushed and bled and spat upon in the process of getting charity and I must keep my mouth shut or lose my job . . . " (Henriksen 71). Desperate to be self-supporting and to keep her beloved daughter, "Tynkabel," Yezierska found herself forced to place five-year-old Louise in her father's household. The decision to "tear [her] heart from her body" in relinquishing the child was made in the early years of her career. She could not carry the single mother's economic burden while struggling desperately to master her craft.

In 1915, *Forum* magazine rewarded Yezierska's efforts with $25 for publication of "The Free Vacation House," and in 1918, *Metropolitan* took "Where Lovers Dream." But demand for her stories was created only after "Soap and Water and the Immigrant" found favor with the *New Republic*'s editor, who read it on John Dewey's recommendation. The professor entered Yezierska's life when, on her return to the East in 1917, she wished to resume full-time teaching but found only part-time work. Suspecting class discrimination, she complained to Dewey, then dean of Columbia University's Teachers College. Having observed her lecture and having read her published story, he gave her a typewriter and encouraged her to write. He also invited her to join his graduate seminar and then to translate for a group studying Polish immigrants in Philadelphia. His regard for her, expressed as infatuation in letters and poetry she cherished for years after his interest faded, led to creation of the "Dewey" figure, Yezierska's male American muse. Henriksen writes: "His character . . . portrayed repeatedly in her fiction . . . influenced and haunted her throughout her long life." (308).[2]

John Dewey's belief in her talent strengthened Yezierska's resolve. After he severed their friendship, withdrawing abruptly for a three-year lecture tour to the Far East, Yezierska enrolled in a writing course at Columbia University Extension. The homework she submitted. "The Fat of the Land," would later be chosen by Edward O'Brien as the best short story of 1919; Yezierska's first collection, *Hungry Hearts* (1920), found a publisher shortly thereafter. Although it was critically acclaimed, the collection failed to sell. Displeased with her publisher's advertising efforts, Yezierska visited syndicated columnist Dr. Frank Crane. Several weeks later, his front-page column in three hundred newspapers noted how "she walked into [his] office one day and brought the Old World with her." He celebrated her rise "from a sweatshop worker to a famous writer!" (Henriksen 149). Thanks to this exposure, *Hungry Hearts* reached the desk of Samuel Goldwyn, who offered Yezierska $10,000 for the movie rights. She accepted, went to Hollywood for several months, but refused to sign when William Fox wrote up a three-year contract; she feared she would be unable to produce under pressure. Nonetheless, her first novel, *Salome of the Tenements* (1922), would also be sold to the movies.

Once again in New York City, Yezierska published another collection of short stories, *Children of Loneliness* (1923). That same year she followed the Lost Generation to Europe, calling on Havelock Ellis and Gertrude Stein. Two more novels appeared in the twenties: *Bread Givers* (1925) and *Arrogant Beggar* (1927). In 1929, a University of Wisconsin Zona Gale Fellowship enabled her to continue writing. Impoverished by the Depression, she rented an inexpensive house in Arlington, Vermont, in 1931 and finished her fourth novel, *All I Could Never Be* (1932). Since she qualified as a pauper, the New York WPA writer's project made a place for her in the mid-thirties, as documented in her last book, *Red Ribbon on a White Horse* (1950).

Yezierska's vitality never waned. During her so-called eighteen-year silence she was ceaselessly revising *Red Ribbon*. In her final decades, she also wrote more than fifty book reviews for the *New York Times* and published several stories about aging. She died in California in 1970.

MAJOR THEMES

Louise Levitas Henriksen titled her 1988 book *Anzia Yezierska: A Writer's Life*, highlighting her mother's dedication to craft and directing the critic to those aspects of Yezierska's experience most important for her art: her foreign origin implying the need to master English as a second language, her father's Orthodoxy, her gender, her poverty, and, more generally, her struggle to publish. Henriksen defines her primary themes: the American dream, generational conflict, female self-realization, the ethical tensions in upward mobility, and the artist's responsibility to her community. Her spectacular rise to prominence in the early 1920s generated a myth of "the sweatshop Cinderella," a rags-to-riches saga; the reality is much more ambiguous, for success measured in dollars is incompatible with Yezierska's inherited values. "Poverty becomes a poor man like a red ribbon on a white horse." This epigraph to her last book suggests the incompatibility of wealth and happiness, and yet, Yezierska notes: "Critics [complain] I have but one story to tell . . . in different ways each time I write. That is true. My one story is hunger. Hunger driven by loneliness" (*Children* 136).

For Mary V. Dearborn, however, Yezierska's "work sounded [another] theme repeatedly: that of the immigrant misunderstood and betrayed by America" (140). The two themes are in fact one. Hunger measures America's fulfilled or broken promises. Literal hunger gnaws at the children in many stories and scars the memories of those just emerging from want. In Yezierska's work, hunger for food is real, as sweatshop wages and inadequate "bread-givers" provide too little sustenance. But success itself, in American terms, satiating body but not soul, remains elusive even in its fulfillment. Best illustrated by her most-often-anthologized prize-winning tale, "The Fat of the Land," a vital Hannah Breineh, first-generation mother of five American children, bargains for hours in Part 1 to save a penny, but still cannot offer her family enough: She witnesses the famished brood symbolically skirmish for a potato that has slipped onto the kitchen floor. In Part 2, her offspring grown and producing Broadway plays or supplying hats to the city elite, the *baleboste*, now displaced to Riverside Drive, lives in luxury but cowers before her maid, detests the plentiful but bland American food, and finds herself mocked for her immigrant ways by her embarrassed children. The story, told from the first generation's point of view, presents an excruciating irony in Jewish immigrant experience: When they fulfill their parents' dreams, the young leave the old behind, alone and alien again. The fat of the land is withheld from their plates.

Equally disruptive of oral pleasures is the need to suppress the mother tongue. Yezierska's heroines, often aspiring writers, replicate their author's struggle with the foreign medium and muse. Illustrative of a pattern, Sophie, in "My Own People," turns from Emerson to Hannah Breineh to the chanting Schmendrik, from English to Yiddish to Hebrew, as her inspirational source and thus emerges from a writer's block. The resulting English is not English; it is evidence of mutation occurring when cultures meet. A displaced woman's accession to writing and the not-yet-existing language she invents link theme and form. The Yiddishized speech of the tenements, the original speech itself absent, erased by an Anglo-American audience's ignorance of Yiddish, is inseparable from the immigrant writer's political agenda: to place herself and her people's ethnic specificity on the New World's cultural stage. In an unpublished manuscript, a young woman takes an alias to get a job but strongly resents the subterfuge because "the day [she] gave up her Jewish name, [she] ceased to be [herself] ....[Cut] off from [her] people, ... [she had] become a shell, a cipher, a spiritual suicide" (quoted in Schoen 7). Yezierska's literary language preserves a distinctive minority identity while mediating it for the majority.

Themes that appeal specifically to feminists cluster around heroines who fight to earn a living at work they enjoy, before *and* after marriage. For instance, in Yezierska's most popular novel, *Bread Givers: A struggle between a father of the Old World and a daughter of the New* (1925), teenager Sara Smolinsky, nicknamed "Blut-und-Eisen" (blood and iron), leaves home to pursue a degree in education. Aware that success requires isolation, Sara rejects Max Goldstein, a wealthy but egocentric suitor who had, however, engaged her affections. In the sadness following his departure, she remembers her father, a Talmudic scholar, whose other worldliness seems to make him the only one capable of understanding her intellectual craving. As though summoned by telepathy, Reb Smolinsky does indeed materialize at her door, but not to confirm the similarity between patriarch and offspring. Instead, he thunders: " 'What's a woman without a man? Less than nothing—a blotted-out existence. No life on earth and no hope of Heaven' " (205). In his eyes, the gender divide remains unbridgeable, the sex roles immutable. Intellect is not a female quality: "Women had no brains for the study of God's Torah, but they could be the servants of men who studied the Torah. Only if they cooked for the men, and washed for the men, and didn't nag or curse the men out of their homes; only if they let the men study the Torah in peace, then, maybe, they could push themselves into Heaven with the men, to wait on them there'' (9–10). Having left the community of servile housewives, the protagonist achieves both profession and mate at the novel's close—the teacher marries her principal—but conveys a feeling of tempered achievement. In part, this is due to conditions her father—now destitute and ailing—has placed on Sara's invitation to join her household. Agreeing to his Orthodox demands, she steps into her mother's shoes and fulfills the Jewish expectation of the dutiful daughter after all. Thus, *Bread Givers'* three sections, ''The Old World,'' ''Between Two Worlds,'' and ''The New World,'' attempt to dissociate temporally what remains thematically interwoven, as suggested by the story's ambiguous closure: The old does not disappear from the new but rather takes up residence within it.

This is not to deny departures from tradition. Yezierska's *oeuvres* accepts a WASP male model for women's career aspirations. In *Salome of the Tenements* (1923), based on Rose Pastor Stokes's life, Salome, desperate to escape the literal ugliness of poverty, vamps and wins John Manning, millionaire philanthropist. But Manning's emotional distance, cold correctness, and implied sexual inadequacy send her packing. Escaping from her isolation, Salome finds fulfillment as a dress designer. Only then can she join Jacques Hollins, né Jaky Solomon, as both a business and a matrimonial partner. Similarly, in *Arrogant Beggar* (1927), Adèle Lindner falls in love with Arthur Hellman only to reject the secularized Jew for the egocentrism he shares with others of the ruling class. Jean Rachmansky, Hellman's pianist protégé, also escapes Hellman's patronage to share Adèle's endeavor. Together, they run Muhmenkeh's coffee shop, hub of the ghetto's artistic life. And again, in *All I Could Never Be* (1932), the Dewey figure Henry Scott is replaced by Vladimir Pavlowich, with whom writer Fanya Ivanowna shares not religion but an immigrant past.

Female independence carries over into the theme of aging. Entering the world of the elderly as an immigrant to yet another foreign culture, Yezierska published tales in the 1960s protesting the conditions under which those advanced in years were forced to live. Most galling were the lack of respect from others, the seniors' own diminished agency, and the inability of both sides to effect change. For instance, in ''10,000 Pages of Research,'' reproduced in *The Open Cage*, a group of women above sixty-five return to college, taping their views of isolation, increasing physical fragility and artificial uselessness. Not their handicaps, but society's indifference to their potential contribution forces them into idleness. Yezierska asks the radical and still relevant questions: Why aren't the talents and remaining energies of these qualified people tapped? Why aren't they employed at tasks commensurate with their abilities? Having entered the professor's class with high enthusiasm, feeling that at last they will have something to contribute and hoping to alter what is wrong, they leave gravely disappointed. The quires of data are nothing but paper, research divorced from life and, thus, like old people themselves, superfluous.

Yezierska's narrators thus speak for various constituencies without evading the complexity of conflicting interests. They appear within realist fictions of an upwardly mobile immigrant class.

SURVEY OF CRITICISM

Alice Kessler-Harris opens her introduction to *Bread Givers* by quoting an opinion of the 1920s: " 'There wasn't anybody who didn't know Anzia Yezierska' ....Today,'' she goes on, ''there is hardly anyone who does'' (v). Although it was true in 1975, this statement is now outdated. With the ground broken by a number of dissertations, full-length studies followed. How ironic it is, Dearborn writes, that ''today Anzia Yezierska's difficult name is in many circles more familiar than John Dewey's. For the slight resurgence of interest that she experienced in her later years has blossomed into a full-blown renaissance'' (176).

Representative of the tone of Yezierska's initial reception is a *New York Tribune* article (19 November 1922): " 'Probably as romantic a figure as contemporary American literature affords is that of Anzia Yezierska ... a frail ... Polish-Jew immigrant girl ... who now has won her way through dreary hours in sweatshop and scullery to a place among the [day's] successful authors' '' (Henriksen 1). Babette Inglehart, covering contemporary reviews, notes how encomiums greeted Yezierska's authentic Jewish East Side voice. Yale Professor William Lyon Phelps, for one, found her tales ''desperately true to life'' and penned as though ''her heart would set the paper aflame'' (quoted in Henriksen 201). That passion, conveyed by brief, dashing strokes, fascinated crucial readers. Instrumental in attracting Sam Goldwyn to *Hungry Hearts* was columnist Frank Crane, who praised the author for ''dip[ping] her pen in her heart'' (Schoen 36). But *Bread Givers* (1925) garnered mixed reviews. Some critics ''praised its blistering intensity and translucent prose. They talked about its 'crisp' quality, its vitality. 'One does not seem to read,' commented ... Phelps. 'One is too completely inside' '' (Kessler-Harris xvii). Others maligned its documentary intention, flat characterization, and assimilationist drive (Ferraro 548). Susan Jacoby explains: ''Yezierska's power as a narrator is [that] of the old-time war correspondent pounding out stories in a battle zone. Her works are not great literature; they are great combat dispatches'' (159). And by the end of the decade, appreciation had soured. Accounting for Yezierska's falling popularity, Schoen points to the faddish interest in ethnic writings and her treatment of materials in such a way that both WASP and ghetto audiences might take offense. ''The newly arrived Jewish immigrants resented her critical attitude toward their manners, their language, their mores, while her condemnation of ... the Americanized Jewish community and Americans in general undoubtedly antagonized them as well'' (76). Drawing up the decade's balance sheet, Dearborn adds: "Her novels were first welcomed by native-born America, but as she continued to play the same tune the reviewers began to find her overemotional, hysterical, even—some . . . were explicit—'too Jewish' " (132). Waning enthusiasm greeted Yeziersha's 1927 *Arrogant Beggar*, and still less accepting were the audiences for her 1932 novel *All I Could Never Be*. Her next manuscript searched for eighteen years before finding a publisher. As Kessler-Harris notes, "In the forties and fifties she was out of vogue" (xi).

Nonetheless, more recently she has been viewed as "a visionary foremother, radicalized and politicized before her time" (Golub, 51). Thanks to Kessler-Harris, *Bread Givers* returned to the world of books-in-print in 1975. "In the light of the emerging women's movement," Kessler-Harris notes, "[this novel] has become more meaningful than ever. . . . For freedom is at [its] pivot . . . as it was the driving force in Yezierska's life. Half a century after she wrote, the power and intensity of her message remain intact" (xvii, xviii).

Charlotte Goodman welcomes Carol Schoen's 1982 study of *Anzia Yezierska* in the Twayne Series, appreciating its emphasis on "Yezierska's feisty female protagonists and the compassion with which [she] portrayed the experiences of immigrants and of the elderly." Schoen "demonstrates why Yezierska's best work deserves to reach a wider audience" (238). Chapters devoted to events in the author's life, including summaries of plot and characterization for all her major works, plus a helpful bibliography, make Schoen's study an invaluable introduction.

Ellen Golub (1983) deepens prevailing sociological approaches with her psychoanalytic viewpoint. She notes the inability of Yezierska's heroines, having attained financial comfort, to dispel their sense of alienation. Although sated, they remain hungry. Golub accounts for this by arguing that Jews have become "inured to exile and to homelessness. Always desiring, the Jew continues to yearn, eventually evolving a nostalgia for his [sic] own desire . . . typically expressed in oral terms as hunger for hunger" (54). Thus, Golub goes on, "Yezierska's metaphor is of chronic oral dissatisfaction which derives from the locus of mother-child interaction, the getting and giving of food. Orality means mother, her loss, and the insatiable longing for her. For a hunger which is not hunger, for food which is not food. The novelist has located in these themes a libidinal language which speaks for her generation's great angst" (55). Rose Kamel (1988) attributes malaise to the warring dichotomies fueling Yezierska's prose: "Jew/Gentile, native born/immigrant, man/woman." (63). She concludes that the author "never came to terms with the import of these contrasting sets" (77), never mediating the resulting fragments. Gay Wilentz (1991–1992) narrows the grounds for this rupture: operating "within the historicity of the immigrant self-made American compounded by the scholarly traditions of Judaism" the female protagonist opts for "symbols of fulfillment . . . inscribed as male" (37). Unresolved gender polarities trouble her work. Susan Hersh Sachs (1983) evaluates differently the effect of such oppositions. Listing "youth-age, rich-poor, modern-traditional, assimilated-Orthodox, accepted-rejected, isolated-part of the community, and, certainly, love-hate'' (66) as the poles between which the author navigates. Sachs judges these to be a source of nourishment, not impoverishment, for Yezierska. ''Because the tensions in her experiences were never as completely resolved as she would have liked, they continued to spark her creativity'' (66).

Illuminating experiential ''tensions'' as they flow into narratives. Louise Levitas Henriksen offers a balanced study of her mother's life. ''[A]though Anzia Yezierska's seemingly autobiographical work was always fictional, it incorporated small chunks of *verité*,'' which Henriksen highlights in her biography (vii). Melanie Kaye/Kantrowitz sees it as ''so even-handed that one continually forgets . . . the author is the subject's daughter'' (15). Quoting extensively from private files, contemporary reviews, and unpublished stories, Henriksen set herself the task, in Helen Yglesias's view, of ''recast[ing] the myth [of the public relations product, the sweatshop Cinderella] in the mold of truth'' (18). Yet the daughter's evaluation of her mother's fiction and behavior, both at times embarrassing in their foreignness, is not without ambivalence. As a preteen, Louise was recruited, like so many others, to help edit manuscripts, a task she didn't care for. Yet the reader senses the pair's closeness, their meetings once every seven days are the highlight of young Louise's week. Nonetheless, in the ''writer's life'' Henriksen mutes herself and, instead, as a professional biographer, focuses on linking her mother's individualistic struggle for recognition in America with her responsibilities as an author.

Mary V. Dearborn in *Love in the Promised Land: The Story of Anzia Yezierska and John Dewey* (1988) reads both the Yezierska archives and her narratives as autobiography, an approach troubling to literary scholars, yet Melanie Kaye/Kantrowitz welcomes the Columbia professor's book. ''If Henriksen's triumph is the re-creation of a struggling feisty literary matriarch, Dearborn's is the situating of Yezierska—and the immigrant experience—in the tumultuous context of the progressive era, including the settlement houses, the trade union movement, a vibrant socialism, first-wave feminism, and the sexually liberated economically autonomous new woman'' (16). Dearborn places Yezierska among influential friends—Rose Pastor Stokes, Zona Gale, Henrietta Rodman, and, most importantly, John Dewey. Alternating chapters devoted to the two personalities, Dearborn's biographical study illuminates Yezierska's recurring fascination with the native-born (white) male as key to acceptance by America. As Sam B. Girgus points out, we can trace the idea of the immigrant's ''responsibility to be the creative impulse of 'America to be' '' to Dewey's warm encouragement (108).

Thus, most Yezierska criticism takes a sociological or historical approach. For instance, Thomas J. Ferraro (1990) views Yezierska as intersecting ''Russian-Jewish immigration, women's experience, and labor history,'' but he cautions against judging her *oeuvres* as ''a terrain of authentic Otherness removed by ethnicity, gender and class from 'the dominant culture' ''(548). Instead, he shows how *Bread Givers* enters the mainstream, allowing Judaism to flow into and be preserved within a receptive bourgeois context. Focusing on economic metaphors and modest prosperity rather than dwelling on the ghetto scenes, he feels the novel "should be understood as an inquiry into the contribution of ethnicity to the triumph of the middle class" (552). Betty Bergland also holds out a promising lens through which to view Yezierska. Influenced by Bakhtin, she offers "a chronotopic analysis of . . . immigrant women's autobiographies" (432–33). Distinguishing among "historical, authorial, and autobiographical subjects," she finds that Yezierska "*disidentifies* with prevailing cultural discourses, resisting alliances that deny the multiplicity of subjectivities in her life" (426). In this assessment she seconds Vivien Gornick. Calling Yezierska "one of the great refuseniks of the world," Gornick notes: "She refuses to accept life's meanness and littleness. . . . She refuses to curb emotional ambition. She's an immigrant? She's a woman? Her hunger is voracious? intrusive? exhausting? *Still* she refuses. And on a grand scale. We cannot turn away from her. Obsessing as grandly as the Ancient Mariner, her words continue . . . to grab us by the collar. . . . The performance is astonishing" (xi, xii).

NOTES

1. The importance of age at arrival cannot be overstressed as it affects language assimilation and alienation. Yezierska appears to have retained an accent and immigrant trappings throughout her life, making it much more likely that she had emigrated at thirteen rather than ten.

2. Norma Rosen fictionalized the affair in her novel *John and Anzia: An American Romance*. New York: E. P. Dutton, 1989.

BIBLIOGRAPHY

This listing privileges publications in English, but it should be noted that studies of Yezierska have begun to appear in French, German, and other European languages.

For comprehensive bibliographic references, including contemporary criticism, letters in collections, and some of Yezierska's more than fifty book reviews, see Henriksen, 317–18.

Works by Anzia Yezierska

Hungry Hearts, New York: Houghton Mifflin, 1920.
Salome of the Tenements. New York: Boni and Liveright, 1922.
Children of Loneliness. New York: Funk and Wagnalls, 1923.
Bread Givers: A struggle between a father of the Old World and a daughter of the New. New York: Doubleday, Page and Co., 1925. Rpt. with Intro. by Alice Kessler-Harris. New York: Persea, George Braziller/Venture, 1975 and London: The Women's Press, 1984.
Arrogant Beggar. New York: Doubleday, Page and Co., 1927.
All I Could Never Be. New York: Brewer, Warren and Putnam, 1932.

Red Ribbon on a White Horse. New York: Charles Scribner's Sons, 1950. Rpt. New York: Persea, 1981.

The Open Cage: An Anzia Yezierska Collection. New York: Persea, 1979.

Hungry Hearts & Other Stories. New York: Persea, 1985.

How I Found America: Collected Stories of Anzia Yezierska. New York: Persea, 1991.

Works about Anzia Yezierska

Books

Dearborn, Mary V. *Love in the Promised Land: The Story of Anzia Yezierska and John Dewey.* New York: The Free Press, 1988.

Henriksen, Louise Levitas, with Jo Ann Boydson. *Anzia Yezierska: A Writer's Life.* New Brunswick, NJ: Rutgers University Press, 1988.

Schoen, Carol. *Anzia Yezierska.* Boston: Twayne, 1982.

Chapters in books

Auden, W. H. "Introduction." *Red Ribbon on a White Horse.* By Anzia Yezierska. New York: Charles Scribner's Sons, 1950. Rpt. NY: Persea, 1981.

Boydston, Jo Ann, Ed. "Introduction." *The Poems of John Dewey.* Carbondale: Southern Illinois University Press, 1977, ix–lxvii.

Chametzky, Jules. "Anzia Yezierska." *Notable American Women* (1980).

Gelfant, Blanche. "The City's 'Hungry' Woman as Heroine." *Women Writing in America: Voices in Collage.* Hanover and London: University Press of New England, 1984.

Girgus, Sam B. " 'Blut- und Eisen:' Anzia Yezierska and the New Self-Made Woman." *The New Covenant: Jewish Writers and the American Idea.* Chapel Hill, N.C.: University of North Carolina Press, 1984. 108–17.

Gornick, Vivian. "Introduction." *How I Found America: Collected Stories of Anzia Yezierska.* By Anzia Yezierska. New York: Persea, 1991.

Harris, Alice Kessler. "Introduction." *Bread Givers.* By Anzia Yezierska. New York: Persea, 1975.

Henriksen, Louise Levitas. "Afterword." *The Open Cage.* By Anzia Yezierska. New York: Persea, 1979. 253–62.

Kamel, Rose Yalow. "Anzia Yezierska, Get Out of your Own Way: Narrative Distance in Yezierska's Autobiographical Fiction." *Aggravating the Conscience: Jewish-American Literary Mothers in the Promised Land.* New York: Peter Lang, 1988. 59–79.

Stinson, Peggy. "Anzia Yezierska." *American Women Writers* 4 (1982):480–82.

Articles and Reviews

Adler, R. "Mothers and Daughters. The Jewish Mother as seen by American Jewish Women Writers." *Yiddish* 6.4 (1987):87–92.

Avery, Evelyn. "Tradition and Independence in Jewish Feminist Novels." *MELUS* 7 (1980):49–55.

———. "In Limbo. Immigrant Children and the American Dream ('Bread Givers' by Anzia Yezierska; 'Jews Without Money' by Michael Gold; 'Christ in Concrete' by Pietro Didonato; and 'The Fortunate Pilgrim' by Mario Puzo).'' *MELUS.* 8.4 (1981):25–31.

Dearborn, Mary V. ''Anzia Yezierska and the Making of an Ethic American Self.'' *The Invention of Ethnicity.* Ed. Werner Sollors. New York: Oxford University Press, 1989.

Drucker, Sally Ann. ''Yiddish, Yidgin, and Yezierska. Dialect in Jewish-American Writing,'' *Yiddish* 6.4 (1987):99–113.

Ferraro, Thomas J. '' 'Working Ourselves Up' in America: Anzia Yezierska's *Bread Givers.*'' *The South Atlantic Quarterly* 89.3 (1990):547–81.

Golub, Ellen. ''Eat Your Heart Out: The Fiction of Anzia Yezierska.'' *Studies in American Jewish Literature* 3 (1983):51–61.

Goodman, Charlotte. ''Carol B. Schoen: Anzia Yezierska,'' *Studies in American Jewish Literature* 3 (1983):236–38.

Inglehart, Babette. ''Daughters of Loneliness: Anzia Yezierska and the Immigrant Woman Writer.'' *Studies in American Jewish Literature* 1 (Winter 1975):1–10.

Kaye/Kantrowitz, Melanie. ''An Immigrant Life.'' Rev. of Louise Levitas Henriksen with assistance from Jo Ann Boydson. *Anzia Yezierska: A Writer's Life* and Mary V. Dearborn. *The Story of Anzia Yezierska and John Dewey. The Women's Review of Books* July 1988:15–16.

Levin, Tobe. '' 'How to Eat Without Eating': Anzia Yezierska's Hunger.'' *Cooking by the Book.* Ed. Mary Ann Schofield. Bowling Green: Bowling Green University Popular Press, 1989. 27–36.

———. ''Aesthetik einer erzwungenen Fremd/sprache: Anzia Yezierskas Immigrantin als Schriftstellerin und Muse.'' *Jüdische Kultur und Weiblichkeit in der Moderne.* Ed. S. Schilling, I Weigel, S. Weigel. Cologne: Böhlau Verlag, 1994. 131—40.

Regenbaum, Shelly. ''Art, Gender, and the Jewish Tradition in Yezierska's *Red Ribbon on a White Horse* and Potok's *My Name Is Asher Lev.*'' *Studies in American Jewish Literature* 7.1 (1988):55–66.

Sachs, Susan Hersh. ''Anzia Yezierska. Her words dance with a thousand colors.'' *Studies in American Jewish Literature* 3 (1983):62–67.

Satlof, Claire R. ''History, Fiction, and the Tradition. Creating a Jewish Feminist Poetic.'' *On Being a Jewish Feminist: A Reader.* Ed. Susannah Heschel. NY: Schocken, 1983. 186–206.

Schoen, Carol B. ''New Light on the 'Sweatshop Cinderella'.'' *MELUS 7.3 (1980):3–11.*

Wilentz, Gay. ''Cultural Mediation and the Immigrant's Daughter: Anzia Yezierska's Bread Givers'' MELUS 17.3 (1992) 33–41.

———. ''The Immigrant's Daughter: Tradition and Identity in Anzia Yezierska's *Bread Givers.*'' *Women's Studies International Forum* 10.5(1987):34.

Yglesias, Helen. ''Cinderella of the Tenements.'' Rev. of *Anzia Yezierska: A Writer's Life* by Louise Levitras Henriksen with Jo Ann Boydson. *New York Times* 3 April 1988:18ff.

Dissertations

Bergland, Betty. ''Disidentification and Dislocation: Anzia Yezierska's *Red Ribbon on a White Horse*'' and ''Conclusion'' in *Reconstructing the ''Self'' in America: Patterns in Immigrant Women's Autobiographies,* Diss. University of Minnesota,

1990. 169–244; 426–33.

Drucker, Sally Ann. *Anzia Yezierska: An Immigrant Cinderella.* Diss. SUNY Buffalo, 1988.

Laufer, Pearl David. *Between Two Worlds: The Fiction of Anzia Yezierska.* Diss. University of Maryland, 1981.

HELEN YGLESIAS (1915–   )

Lewis Fried

BIOGRAPHY

Helen (Bassine) Yglesias was born on March 29, 1915, in Brooklyn, New York. Her parents, Solomon and Kate (Bassine) Yglesias, emigrated from Europe by way of England; her father came from Russia; her mother, from Russia-Poland. Her parents had been furriers, but in America, her father became a grocer, trying to support his wife and six children.

Yglesias attended James Monroe High School and graduated in 1931. While Helen was there, her fifth-term English teacher arranged for her to hear Gertrude Stein. As Yglesias recollects, Stein "was a Jew, a woman and a writer, or a woman, a Jew and a writer, or a writer, a woman and a Jew, whichever condition was troubling me most at the given moment" ("A Way In and a Way Out" 25). After graduation, Yglesias began to write an ambitious novel "telling what it was like to be an adolescent girl in an American public high school," but one of her brothers humiliated her into shredding the work (*Starting* 23).

Afterward, this same brother, already a financial success, paid for a trip to Europe and Palestine for Yglesias, a sister, and her parents. The contrast between the impoverished Arabs and Palestine's prosperous urban dwellers fueled her sense of social justice. When she returned to America, she became drawn to the Left and joined, first, the Young Communist League and, later, the Communist Party in about 1937. (She left the Party, she remembers, in 1952.)

In 1937, she married Bernard Cole, with whom she had two children, Tamar, and Lewis. During their marriage, she was a branch organizer of the Communist Party and, during the early forties, for approximately three or four months, she recalls, she was cultural editor on the staff of the *Daily Worker*. In 1950, she and Cole were divorced. That year, she married Jose Yglesias, the writer. They had one child, Rafael; Helen and Jose were divorced in 1992.

During the sixties, she worked under Warren Miller of the *Nation* and, on his death, became literary editor of the journal, from 1965 to 1969. When she was fifty-four, she decided to commit herself to writing, and in 1972, won the

Houghton Mifflin Literary Fellowship for her first novel, *How She Died*. This work was followed by *Family Feeling* (1976); *Starting: Early, Anew, Over, and Late* (1978), a work examining both her own and others' new ventures in life; the novels *Sweetsir* (1981) and *The Saviors* (1987), and the study of the artist Isabel Bishop in the book of that name (1988). At present, Yglesias is at work on a novel dealing with the politics of the times.

MAJOR THEMES

Yglesias's memories of the public parks, schools, and libraries of the city as pathways beyond an immigrant background find their way into her urban fiction as criteria of a democratizing community. So do the structures of the metropolis—the subways, highways, and the skyscrapers remind us of the city as an artifact, made to serve and enhance human needs. The city allows its inhabitants to test the values of their lives against those of a wider environment.

At the center of Ygesias's novels is a woman, usually urban and Jewish, invariably the product of a parochial and parochializing background, whose life is an attempt to gain an independent place in the outside community. This theme is nourished by the broad traditions of American realism in which characters struggle to comfort their psychological needs with the facts a metropolitan culture provides. As a result, the dissatisfactions of Yglesias's protagonists are less with their past than with the difficulties of finding a genuinely satisfying community that respects the integrity of their autonomy.

How She Died explores a dying young woman's attempt to redefine what a practical life and community might be against the background of the then-contemporary politics. Mary Moody Schwartz's cancer, and its misdiagnosis during her pregnancy, become the metaphors of politics and renewal, metaphors that also speak to the frailty and regeneration of the feminist imagination. Beginning the book in a hospital ward, and alternating the narrative voices between Mary and her friend, Jean, Yglesias describes the accommodations women have made throughout their lives to satisfy their given roles. Mary, the daughter of a spy convicted of stealing atomic secrets, Isabella Vance Moody, must assert her will against that of the ''Committee'' as well as against her husband. Throughout the book, Mary's insistence on ''no more mistakes'' and her obsession with charting a satisfactory human settlement speak to her belief that the world and her disease can be made rational. As she says early in the book, ''I had to think about the spot I was in, how to get out of it and whose fault it was. . . . Find out who's to blame. Put it all down on paper. *Organize this thing*. Analyze it'' (15).

Yglesias points out that the task of *doing* is not romantic. Jean is hired by the ''Committee'' to be Mary's companion. Jean's own life, marked by divorce, the problems of raising three children, and a career of unexciting secretarial jobs is now interrupted. As she desperately becomes Mary's husband's lover, she also discovers that she must integrate her obligations to self and to others.

Mary's plan for new communities is such an attempt at integration. Writing against the onslaught of a deteriorating marriage and death, she offers a vision as much utopian as it is *eutopian*. Her solutions do not begin, she argues, with the seizure of the economy; rather, they start "at the source of society, the family structure, the virtual enslavement of women and the use of power in personal relations." "Don't you see," she asks, that you have to "take power, coercion, economic bullying out of the human situation first?" (88).

In this novel, as in her others, Yglesias is concerned with humanization as well as with politicization. Mary argues that the base of Leftist movements is marred by exclusion; human beings are conceived of as categorical and useful and understood only in that manner. She insists that the movement has to embrace those on the periphery of ideology itself: the sick, the dying, the poorest of the poor. Of course, this is Yglesias's plea as well, since in this novel, disease functions literally and metaphorically.

Similarly, Yglesias is interested in the pathos of resignation: a recognition of the understood limits of effort, conduct, and good will. In communitarian fashion, Jean lets things that she cannot control take their own course. The novel ends with the act of acceptance itself: Jean and Mary's husband resume their stations at Mary's bed.

Family Feeling deepens Yglesias's search for the center of American politics: in this case, the daughter of an immigrant Jewish family enacting and interpreting the substance of American dreams. With this work, Yglesias dramatizes how the family domesticates the promises of American culture and how these are responded to on an individual level. As a result, members of the Goddard (formerly Yagoda) family see each other as variants of American success and failure.

For the most part, the novel concerns itself with Anne Goddard's life and, specifically, with her need to develop her own freedom in relation to the psychologically and financially dominating figure of her brother Barry (Baruch). Her success is hard won. Moving from trivial jobs through an unfortunate marriage to a Communist Party educational-director-turned-lawyer, to an editorial post with the *National Tribune*, and, finally, to marriage with Guy Rossiter, its New England publisher, Anne traverses the arc of acculturation. Unlike Abraham Cahan's eponymous protagonist of *The Rise of David Levinsky*, Anne not only gains a commanding sense of herself, but she also comes to speak to and for the nation. In the novel, Anne recollects the achievements and life of F. L. Olmstead, the great park planner and antislavery writer. In Olmsted, she finds an individual who wanted to create a democratic public by creating a democratizing landscape. She discovers a man who both envisioned and ultimately realized a public good. Against her recollections of her often luckless father, she speaks of Olmsted, whom she calls "My legendary grandfather, my real American hero . . . " (259).

Guy Rossiter's senseless murder by slum kids looking to steal a bicycle results in Anne's inheriting his fortune, but it forces her to realize that the American dream of upward mobility and opportunity is denied to the underclass of New

York. Bereft and looking for comfort, she seeks the meaning of her family's history. She meets Barry in the "Goddard" building, where atop New York, he speaks of his progress and power. He derides those who critique technological prowess while speaking of what he thinks are his accomplishments. In this encounter, Anne recognizes that, like her brother, she has achieved autonomy. She thinks, "I pull myself back to positions I've won for myself, and we approach one another, smiling, from our separate corners of the ring that bounds us" (309).

Yet Barry's declamation, carrying her back to her origins, is both a sentimental tribute and a triumph. Brother and sister have not been lost to or within the city of their birth and dreams. They have wrested some form of mutual recognition and a share of public good from their origins.

With *Sweetsir*, Yglesias turned to New England for a new setting. Just as cancer, she believed, was an appropriate metaphor for urban politics, so domestic violence and murder were appropriate to a modern, impoverished New England. Thus, Yglesias is part of a tradition that contests the pastoral image of New England.

As in her previous work, Yglesias depicts a character on the margin of society. *Sweetsir* deals with a woman's growing consciousness about her role as a wife at the same time that she becomes aware of her needs as an individual. Sally Stark, a pregnant teenager, marries Vin Ciomei, a quarry worker. She marries him, although he is twice her age, because he is her "ticket out of troubles." As a result, she enters a marriage in which she is dubious of love, unsure of her place in an Italian, immigrant family dominated by a patriarch, Papa Ciomei, and estranged from the new life around her. Vin's debts and gradual disinterest lead her to seek a divorce.

She meets and marries Morgan Beauchamp Sweetsir, thirty-four, a road builder. Her life now consists of adjusting to his behavior, which involves beating her. As the marriage deteriorates, Sally begins to lose sight of herself as a human being. On their last day together, she is told she has a positive Pap smear (indicating possible cervical or uterine cancer); he accuses her of lying to gain his sympathy; he has planned to sell her car to a neighbor. They fight and she kills him.

The novel begins with this fight—Sally's right to a decent life. When Sally is arraigned, she is defended by Ellen Mahoney, a middle-aged Ph.D., graduate of Yale Law School, mother, and wife. It is Mahoney who provides Sally with a different perception of what she can be; in effect, a different perception of what a woman can be apart from the conventional and dehumanizing roles that life in Eatonville suggests. When Sally is pushed into going to a feminist consciousness-raising group, she is perplexed, but this, too, is an introduction to women creatively and ritualistically dealing with their sense of power or the loss of it. Sally, with her growing awareness of the difference between role and human nature, pleads not guilty rather than *nolo contendere*. Her trial becomes for her and the reader not so much about her relations with Morgan, but about the disabilities she has had forced upon her in her roles as daughter and wife. She is found innocent.

Sweetsir is a novel in which judgment is passed about the way social conventions and individuality collide. The verdict of not guilty confirms what Sally already knows: She has been victimized by a role that is both dysfunctional and conventional. Even though she had tried to better herself by working as an executive secretary, her life was reduced to being either a sexual or economic unit, depending upon her late husband's fortune. Tragically, she had not learned what alternatives could be created; instead, she accepted what possibilities were socially granted to her. The novel draws to a close with a sense that this cycle of victimization is being carried on: Sally's daughter, a teenager, decides to commit herself to a boy who has no skills or prospects.

With *The Saviors*, Yglesias dealt with how varying *idealisms* could lead to a larger community, one based on hope as well as on the fullness of human nature. In this novel, Yglesias studies how an individual chooses a social role and how that role may serve as a pathway to the world. The novel begins with a group of elderly people on a peace march toward the United Nations Plaza. These individuals reflect upon the present political crisis and the aspirations of their youth—most of which were bound up in one way or another with the Universal Society of Brotherhood.

The Saviors focuses on the youth of Maddy Brewster Phillips, born Bessie Bernstein in the Bronx. Her parents deliberately de-Judaicize themselves before they move to Iowa City, where her father has accepted a faculty position. They choose the name Brewster for themselves; Bessie chooses Madeleine. Her parents, later killed in an automobile accident, entrust her in 1927 to the Society, and it is at its headquarters on Hampstead Heath that Maddy receives her adolescent education. The Society centers on the figure of Vidhya, supposedly possessing a remarkable aura and groomed by Bishop Nysmith to be the coming Savior of the World.

The novel deals with Maddy's coming of age; her discovery that good and evil are not simple, discrete categories but are part of the stuff of experience itself. Secretly engaged to Vidhya, she suffers his sexual betrayals of her; she has several affairs, all of them lessons in commitment and opportunism. Her confusion about sexuality, love, and need is *precisely* her education. Coming to grips with curiousity and eros, she also comes to grips with herself. A young woman returning with the nucleus of the Society to New York, she discovers that the press announces that she and Vidhya are engaged. He informs the press that Maddy is a habitual liar and tells Maddy he is doing this to clear his reputation. In fact, he will renounce the humbug of the Society and start the New Vidhya Foundation.

The Saviors ends with the comfort of what might be called the deceptions of the party of goodness—Maddy's astonishment that Vidhya would deny knowing her. In the last chapter, in New York for the conclusion of the peace march, Maddy wonders what her life has amounted to. She reflects that even if she can't point to concrete accomplishments, she "had struggled to protect life in its spiritual, societal and natural spheres" (301–02). Maddy's youth has been a struggle to separate the richness of experience from its conventional categories. Part of this struggle is a response to her deracination; she is pulled back to the memory of her grandmother in the Bronx. Part is a response to surrendering to the ambiguity of experience itself. Looking at the Parthenon, she wonders, "Who made the rules of good and evil? What if it were all a senseless mess, and what one did or didn't do was of no consequence? What then?" (252).

Certainly, both she and Vidhya are invented people: she, by her parents; Vidhya, by Bishop Nysmith. Yet her creative illusions about social values are not Vidhya's deceptive claims about the past. Maddy's reminiscences, at times candid and embarrassing, indicate a willingness to accept her life as whole: How many times has she "confessed" that she is Jewish? Her memory rescues her life, and the moral uses of memory make her a beloved figure.

What should we make of this quest for a worldly, rational community, this search for the role of emarginated in American life in Yglesias's works. Yglesias has talked about her need to familiarize herself with the cultural past: "I look at history to make myself at home in it and in the world" ("Invoking America" 22). Her childhood, as she recollects it, was characterized by the longing to escape the limited cityscape she inhabited and to become acquainted with a nation populated by "real Americans . . . descendants of the actual heroes and heroines who landed with the Mayflower . . . established a peaceable kingdom . . . in a blessed land called New England" (22). Emerson reminds her of a Talmudic figure, easily found at a seder, and F. L. Olmsted, of an "Old Testament character" because of his public projects. Similarly, Henry James is a figure to reckon with because his female characters were large and had "profound authority"; they could "sidestep defeat."

Yglesias's work participates in a dialogue with Americas other than those of her heroines' immediate backgrounds. Her books invoke communities open to the influence of universal and universalizing currents; her works speak, on the social level of American realism, to the perdurable struggle of humanization.

SURVEY OF CRITICISM

There is little sustained criticism of Yglesias's novels. Part of this may be attributed to the tradition of social realism she works in. Her novels, dealing with timely, political occasions and events, are not seen as expressing common themes, and reviewers often focus on the immediacy of the work. For example, Dean Flower, speaking of *Family Feeling*, praises the skill of her narrative and points out that Marxian solutions are "hovering" in the book, threatening the integrity of Anne's "family feeling for America" (272). Rosellen Brown, writing of *Sweetsir*, praises Yglesias for the fidelity of Sally's voice, "a real, anguished voice in the act of self-discovery" (3). The lack of longer criticism may be partly attributable to the sheer currency of the work itself. Perhaps with

Yglesias's next novel, her books will be seen more clearly to form a whole. Yglesias receives critical attention in Evelyn Avery's "Oh My 'Mispocha'!" which argues that *Family Feeling*, along with *Oh My America!*, are, in a sense, "the realistic conclusion" to *The Promised Land* and *Bread Givers*. In *Mother Images in American-Jewish Fiction*, Abbey Poze Kapelovitz suggests that *Family Feeling* "shows us how a child embarrassed by her mother matures into a woman who appreciates her" (243).

BIBLIOGRAPHY

Works by Helen Yglesias

How She Died. Boston: Houghton Mifflin Company, 1972.
Family Feeling. New York: Dial Press, 1976.
Starting: Early, Anew, Over, and Late. New York: Rawson, Wade, 1978.
"A Way In and a Way Out." *New York Times Book Review* (14 June 1981):3, 24–26.
Sweetsir. New York: Simon and Schuster, 1981.
"Invoking America: A Gitche Gumee Memoir." *New York Times Book Review* (5 July 1987):1, 22.
The Saviors. Boston: Houghton Mifflin, 1987.
Isabel Bishop. New York: Rizzoli. 1988.

Interviews

"Helen Yglesias." With Nancy Bunge. *Finding the Words: Conversations with Writers Who Teach* by Nancy Bunge. Athens, Ohio: Swallow Press/Ohio University Press, 1985:182–89.
"Contemporary Authors Interview." With Jean Ross. "Yglesias, Helen," *Contemporary Authors*, Ed. Linda Metzger. New Revision Series, vol. 15. Detroit: Gale Research Company. 1985:471–74.

Works about Helen Yglesias

Avery, Evelyn. "Oh My 'Mishpocha'! Some Jewish Women Writers from Antin to Kaplan View the Family," *Studies in American Jewish Literature*. 5 (1986):44–53.
Brown, Rosellen. "Breaking the Circle of Destructive Love," *New York Times Book Review* 5 April 1981:3, 28–29.
Chevigny, Belle Gale. Review of *Family Feeling*. *New Republic* 8 May 1976:27–29.
Flower, Dean. "Fiction Chronicle,' in *Hudson Review*. 29 (Summer 1976):270–82.
Haynes, Muriel. Rev. of *How She Died*. *Saturday Review*. (18 March 1972):74–75.
Kapelovitz, Abbey Poze. "Mother Images in American-Jewish Fiction." Diss. University of Denver. 1985.
Lehmann-Haupt, Christopher. "The Novel as an Anxious Dream," *New York Times*. 8 February 1972:31.

Prose, Francine. "The Truth Is Out," *Vogue*. August 1987: 194, 196.

Talbot, Tony. "There's More to Life Than Astral Voyages." *New York Times Book Review*. 16 August 1987:14–15.

Wood, Michael. "Betrayals." *New York Review of Books* 6 April 1972:25–28.

JEWISH AMERICAN WOMEN'S AUTOBIOGRAPHY

Barbara Shollar

The Jewish American woman has made a distinctive contribution to the distinctive American genre of autobiography. The circumstances that made this possible derived from a confluence of Jewish and American cultures at the turn of the century that was particularly liberating for women: The abrupt break from tradition in the modern age, rendered even more emphatic by the trauma of immigration, resulted in both a clash and a synergy of cultures; the proletarianization of labor and the related rise of modern political movements produced women who were self-conscious of their roles as social actors; the relatively high status of women in both cultures positioned women to take advantage of and instigate the women's movement; the respect for learning and literacy dovetailed with the needs of an emergent capitalist economy and a society dominated by middle-class values.

Many of these sometimes contradictory as well as overlapping elements served as the impetus to *all* women who set out to inscribe the new identities that they were creating for themselves, which thus made the autobiography a major genre for women in America. However, in a genre identifiable as one in which the writer inscribes her individuality *in relation to* the collective, the Jewish American woman contributed to the florescence of women's autobiography out of proportion to her numbers. She created a text that captured the multiple and frequently divergent selves of female as against the male definition, ethnic/subaltern as against nationalist/hegemonic cultural definitions. In the process, the genre in large measure created the hyphenated American and the new woman. At the same time, the texts reshaped the Ur-genre of American autobiography to convey new dimensions of gender and ethnicity.

In sheer numbers, some 200 titles produced in the twentieth century since the first text was published in 1912 are identifiable as Jewish American women's autobiographies—that is, those in which ethnicity and gender are significant touchstones for the writer's identification and (self-)creation. Notwithstanding their numbers and significance, the corpus of Jewish American women's autobiographies has been marginalized by both literary scholars and feminist critics

as well as by Jewish historians. The reasons for this are complex, and the explanations here are meant to be merely suggestive. As the following discussion
will make clear, very few—if any—of these texts fit the literary or ethnic mold
into which scholars, critics, and historians would cast them. Many are also the
works of public figures, who have frequently been taken to task for the imper-
sonality of their writings. These standards depend on a circumscribed range of
ideological demands, narrow definitions of literary style, and stereotypic views
of what constitutes the personal or "autobiographical." Such standards have
operated to exclude *women* writers and to restrict consideration to those works
that display a particular perspective and a specific repertoire of stylistic techniques for symbol-making and indirection. The result has been the critical in-
visibility of these autobiographies.

This chapter is intended to remedy the exclusion of Jewish American women
from the autobiographical canon and from the canon of Jewish American literature. It focuses on those autobiographies with literary aspirations and historical and thematic significance. I emphasize those texts that seem best to capture
the archeology of women's autobiography, marking those attributes that are
distinctive in the autobiographical tradition that Jewish women created in less
than a century. (A great number of popular works written by media personalities—actresses of the stage and screen, opera singers, and journalists—exist and
are deserving of a chapter unto themselves.) While I have also attempted to
retain a chronological outline based on the dates of publication, these dates are
not necessarily correlated with the *weltenschaung* or period that the text centrally
evokes. In this case, the characteristics intended to clarify the classification
scheme have taken precedence. At the same time that I hope to establish a
taxonomy, I also raise questions and define literary and other issues that are
implied by the very categories that I have established.

The immigrant autobiography initiates the Jewish women's autobiographical
tradition and remains a staple of life-writing up until the present time. Interestingly, the original immigrant autobiography has its roots in the Russian Jewish
immigration rather than in the earlier immigrations of Sephardim and the
German Jews (although, oddly enough, its earliest examples derive not from
those living in the largest community that settled on the Lower East Side of
New York, but from those who made their homes in ghetto communities in
Boston and Pittsburgh, respectively). This historical fact points to the multiple
determinants of the genre's appearance. That is, its appearance is in part a
marker of the new role of women in American society at the turn of the century.
In addition, however, it is a marker of the emergence of a new working class
and the tensions attendant upon the extensive immigration of Central and Eastern
Europeans to the United States, itself a token of the economic and social upheaval resulting from the establishment and growth of capitalism. From that
point of view, autobiographical reproduction may be understood as an expression of the American culture's effort to come to grips with and resolve the costs
of that upheaval. Moreover, the numbers of Jewish immigrants were sufficient

so as to make possible group cohesiveness, which then became the basis of an ethnic politics.

As a genre, the autobiography reflected a new kind of "cultural work," as Jane Tomkins has termed it, in defining a new, that is to say, ethnic identity (3). Jewish women were the likely agents of this endeavor, first, because Jewish women were in some measure prepared by Jewish culture to become literate and, second, because previous social/economic histories of work made them receptive to the economic promise that capitalist society offered them, and therefore most willing to articulate a view of reality different from that prescribed by the traditional religious, patriarchal culture from which they had come. In doing so, they took on a role from which they were previously banned. Jewish women, instead of men, became the carriers of culture, responsible for educating the coming generation to the dominant values of American life. At the same time, they offered a variety of resistances (sometimes muted) to those values.

Mary Antin's *The Promised Land* (1912) has been canonized as the archetype for all subsequent immigrant autobiographies.[1] Early commentators argued that she optimistically (some say traitorously) suppressed ethnicity and exalted assimilationist values.[2] While the priority of Antin's text makes her location in the canon as the first published Jewish autobiography seem natural, the reality is that her text was never the paean that title of her work or traditional literary histories suggest, nor the paradigm that critics implied. The narrative that describes her ascendancy also details the painful descendancy of her father; implicitly, the one is paid for by or built on the other. Moreover, the crisis of the plot (symbolized by Antin's adolescent breakdown) is resolved by a desire for metaphysical transcendence: The universe replaces America as the metaphysical "home" for her new-found sense of identity and security. The maneuver tacitly rejects an easy, simplistic reading of her patriotic loyalty.

The two autobiographical works written by Elizabeth Gertrude Stern, published in 1917 and 1926, suggest even more poignantly the tensions experienced by immigrants of living in two worlds, the costs of assimilation, and the persistence (or manifestation) of anti-Semitism. If the first text suits the immigrant paradigm even better than Antin's in celebrating not merely assimilation but what might be termed embourgeoisification, the second points to the failure of bourgeois as well as feminist ideals.[3] Stern, as autobiographer, also raises metaphysical and metanarrative questions with regard to what it means to write the self; in recasting her life in two separate texts, she points to the essentially fictive nature of autobiography, to autobiography as a means of revisioning the self, and therefore to the role of autobiography in creating an identity. The anxiety that surrounded the publication of her work (reviewers in both the Jewish and the "mainstream" press by turns questioned the veracity of her account or doubted its fictionality) is itself indicative of the tensions attendant on Jews and women who made a public place for themselves in American culture even as it expressed the dominant culture's uneasy reconciliation with that identity.[4]

The texts that document the life of the impoverished working class in the

New York ghetto are marked by greater trauma and greater narrative incoherence than either Antin's or Stern's works. They include Rose Cohen's *Out of the Shadow* (1918) and Elizabeth Hasanovitz's *One of Them: Chapters from an Immigrant Autobiography* (1918), written only two years after Hasanovitz's arrival here in this country(!). Increasingly, this subgenre of ghetto autobiography was subject to nostalgia, especially as the writer became more alienated from the communal sources of her inspiration in the Old World and the New World and more distant from her subject matter.

If this tradition became subject to trivialization, it also produced works of significant literary merit. Recent critical and biographical work has sorted out the autobiographical elements in Anzia Yezierska's fictional writing; critics have also commented on the apparent omissions and distortions of critical life elements in her autobiographical writing, including her failure to acknowledge her child. Yet the age of postmodernism is perhaps more prepared than modernists to sympathize with Yezierska's *Red Ribbon on a White Horse* (1950) as a narrative of her encounter with Hollywood and its demands for a *shtetl*-heroine that renders Yezierska's self-construction increasingly elusive and problematic. In this autobiography, Hollywood itself becomes a symbol, an intensified version not only of the more general tendency of American culture to insist on personalities defined in terms of success, but of personality as itself the byproduct of a mediated reality.

Another work, that of the unknown Pauline Leader, in contrast, submits the autobiographical project to the crucible of literary modernism. A startling work of the imagination, *And No Birds Sing* (1931) recounts the story of the protagonist's loss of hearing as a child, her flight from an abusive family, and her thwarted efforts to make her way in the Lower East Side and Greenwich Village communities, a worker by day and a bohemian by night. Inspired by the imagism of writers like Ezra Pound, the depiction of small-town life by writers like Sherwood Anderson and Evelyn Scott, and portraits of independent women by authors like Zona Gale and Ellen Glasgow, this *künstler-roman* represents the underside of the myth of success; at the same time, it introduces a class politics into considerations of gender that had not previously been articulated. In its stylistic experimentation and social critique, the text bridges the gap between the aesthetics of the 1920s and the literary politics of the 1930s.

Within this formative tradition of Eastern European-Russian Jewish immigrant autobiography, a major subgroup of political autobiography emerges, one whose permutations can be tracked throughout the twentieth century. In the first period of its emergence, it documents Jewish American working-class women's shaping of and contribution to anarchy and socialism from the beginning of the century through World War II. While many of the works discussed thus far often have as a key trope a meeting with a sympathetic and supportive patron, such as Lillian Wald or Jane Addams, who offers the hope of a different life and a "glimpse into a different world" (Cohen 233), political autobiographies are marked by an incident in which the "glimpse" serves to establish the disparity between worlds, the gap between the rich and the poor, and to move their viewers/writers to anger and rebellion. The classic in this mold is Emma Goldman's *Living My Life* (1931). Goldman's life, if not her autobiography, inspired other women either to emulation or rivalry. One of the most problematic examples of this subgenre is the work of Marie Ganz. The central portion of *Into Anarchy—And Out Again* (1919) describes the wretched conditions of work and the desperate struggles of the poor to avoid starvation and homelessness, which drive the protagonist to direct action and increasingly extremist protest.

The writer's growing concerns about the impact of anarchist terrorist activities on the lives of innocent victims and her sense that dedicated revolutionaries committed themselves to actions that ignored human needs contribute to her eventual disillusionment. (This trajectory marks political life-writings of a later era as well.) Yet Ganz's transformation from anarchist to renegade is disconcerting: She celebrates the irony of finding herself on the same platform with John D. Rockefeller, who, as the owner and strikebreaker of the Colorado mines, was the archenemy of the anarchist movement; she herself has been arrested after leading a march to his offices at Standard Oil and threatening to kill him. Her text concludes with a jingoistic tableau in support of the Great War— describing the throng of men from the ghetto in which she had lived and worked parading off to join the draft. It is not so much her pride that is disturbing, but the lack of any self-consciousness that she has betrayed her own ideals; she does not see any inconsistency between her support of socially sanctioned violence and her rejection of anarchist terrorism.

In contrast, Rose Pesotta was continually inspired by Goldman and remained deeply committed to anarchist and socialist, ultimately communist, ideals, carrying them into the labor movement, whose broad base and mass politics she hoped would provide for their realization. Following an autobiographical chapter focused on her early life and the origins and evolution of her political identity, *Bread Upon the Waters* (1944) inscribes her activist years as labor organizer and leader of the ILGWU. As vice president, she was the only woman on the union's executive board, a token position she sacrificed to return to work with the rank and file. Another activist nurtured by Goldman is Lucy Robins Lang. *Tomorrow Is Beautiful* (1948) recounts her involvement in the tumultuous events of anarchism as well as her ensuing commitment to socialism. Her book offers an interesting and lively account of the many dedicated and colorful personalities who formed these movements. Lang captures the sense of community these people created (and the horror when it was violated by informers), one that stretched across the country and permitted women like her to feel at home from Chicago to New Orleans to San Francisco.

Perhaps the most well-known of the political works that have their roots in the Russian Jewish period of immigration is Rose Schneiderman's *All for One* (1967). In this autobiographical memoir, Schneiderman recounts the mentorships of the anarchist Bessie Brauer and later of uptown patron Mary Dreier and other members of what she termed the ''mink brigade'' (6). Already a leader of the labor movement at the age of twenty-two, she joined the Women's Trade Union League to forge alliances between laboring women and socialites, between the labor movement and the women's movement and its struggle for the vote. Schneiderman subsequently abandoned her socialist leanings and worked with Samuel Gompers to establish the ILGWU. Later she became close to Eleanor Roosevelt and, through her, influenced Franklin Roosevelt's political education. Other works rooted in the socialist and communist political traditions are those of Hilda Satt Polacheck and of Rose Pastor Stokes, respectively.

Many of these women were ardent feminists who became anarchists and socialists precisely because they believed these political movements were in part defined by a commitment to gender equality and sexual liberation. Yet their autobiographies deal with these elements only peripherally and omit discussion of critical dilemmas of their personal and public lives: sexual preference and identification, sexuality and its relation to affectional ties and the restructuring of society. These issues did not receive attention until a later generation charged them with ultimate significance under the rubric of the personal is political. Their absence and omission in these texts raises questions of the degree to which autobiographies by women are hedged in by cultural limits. The gaps, omissions, and silences in autobiographies become as meaningful as their inclusions.

Another group of works initiated after the turn of the century might be classified as autobiographies of the Progressive Era, set off from the initiating tradition by generational, cultural, and class differences. In contrast to the working-class origins and identification of those texts described above, for example, these autobiographies were usually the work of the daughters of a well-to-do merchant class who constituted the first great wave of Jewish immigration impelled to America by the failure of the 1848 revolutions.

Among other things, Progressive autobiographies document the movement of this first generation of women into the public sphere. As members of the first American-born generation of an upper middle class for whom college was generally not yet an option (for either Jewish or Gentile women), their authors educated themselves largely through the women's club movement and turned to scientific philanthropy (as the combination of the then-new discipline of sociology and social work was called) and civic reform as outlets for their ambitions and energies. They used their knowledge to feminize Judaism by creating ethnic organizations of self-help.

The earliest autobiography to be written in this mode was Lillian Wald's *The House on Henry Street* (1915). This work, by its very title, points to the submergence of the self within an institution, and establishes the institutional autobiography as an important variant within this category. (Its author is also anomalous in having graduated from nursing school and having pursued a professional career.) Another work in this vein is Hannah Solomon's posthumously published *Fabric of My Life* (1946), documenting the founding of the National Council of Jewish Women in 1893. Like Wald's, Solomon's text is probably inspired by and modeled after the work of their common friend Jane Addams, whose life also inspired their own. Yet unlike Wald's text, Solomon's is also in some measure an implicit critique of and counterstatement to Addams's *Twenty Years at Hull-House* (1910). In describing the founding of the women's educational, religious, and philanthropic organization, as well as subsequent activities in the areas of education, social and public welfare, and urban politics, Solomon delineates the specifically Jewish character and spirit of the organization as well as recording the specific contributions of particular Jewish women.

Between the publication of these two texts stands that of Rebekah Kohut's *My Portion* (1925). Though herself an immigrant, her status, as the daughter and wife of rabbis important to the ferment and reorganization of the Jewish religion going on from the turn of the century through the 1920s, placed her in a position to exert power and influence in formulating a new role for women within Judaism, not only in the United States, but internationally as well. As an advocate for Russian Jewry, she accomplished in New York City what her cohort Solomon accomplished in Chicago. Appearing with regularity in the *New York Times* from 1895 through the 1930s, Kohut also forged links between Judaism and the secular world of reform. In personalizing these activities, that is, in setting them in the context of her personal struggles, her text is itself pioneering, symbolic of women's movement into the public sphere.

Other writers who sought to document their role as "pioneers," as Maud Nathan put it, "in going outside of Jewish philanthropy and communal work" (102) and engaging in the work of "political housecleaning" (167) included Sara Hart (Hannah Solomon's cousin) and Nathan's sister Annie Nathan Meyer, as well as Nathan herself. These writers frequently depict with pride their initial efforts to break free of traditional women's roles, emphasizing their activities as public speakers, legislative lobbyists, and political campaign organizers. They also provide histories of their contributions in establishing organizations for women and children and their participation in suffrage movements. Thus, in *The Pleasure Is Mine* (1947), Hart describes her work as head of the Juvenile Court Commission, her successful campaign to elect her friend Mary Bartelme as judge of the Circuit Court of Cook County, Chicago, and her leadership of the Women's and Children's Hospital and the various innovations in the medical and health-care fields created under her auspices.

Nathan describes organizing the New York Exchange for Women's Work, the Women's Municipal League, the Women's Auxiliary of the Civil Reform Association, and the Consumer's League, as well as her work with the Progressive Party and in the woman's suffrage movement in *Once Upon a Time and Today* (1974). Meyer is eager to recount her own effort to pursue a collegiate course and her desire to ensure that other women could gain an education equal to men's by helping to found Barnard College. In addition, her text, *It's Been Fun* (1951), inscribes her career as novelist, playwright, and art critic among the earliest to draw on African-American material (in her play *All God's Chillun Got Wings*) and to insist on an American aesthetic that might adequately define the distinctive qualities of American art.

Literary historians valorized the works of Russian immigrant Jews. From their vantage point, Jews were ethnically defined as Russian immigrants, middle-class children of the ghetto. The texts I have been discussing inevitably complicate or undermine this reductive view of Jewish ethnicity. If its major contributors are German Jews, Annie Nathan Meyer and Maud Nathan define a Sephardic Jewish tradition within American life, while Kohut documents the progressive intellectual traditions of Hungarian Jews. Although all three women were identified with New York, their lives in some measure reflect the influence of the Midwest and the Far West.

The aristocratic Nathan family encountering financial losses withdrew to Green Bay, Wisconsin, and after that to Chicago; Kohut's family moved from Baltimore to San Francisco, where she grew up the daughter of a rabbi, doctor, and civic reformer forced to be respectful of the more conservative and wealthy German Jewish congregation her father served. The status struggles of these women, as well as the liberation from convention they sometimes experience in finding themselves outside the social hierarchy and in places less confined by tradition, are other bases for characterizing the shape their autobiographical texts took.

Many of these Progressive texts have as their subtexts the fruitful collaboration and tensions between Gentile and Jew on one hand and between native-born upper-middle-class German Jew and immigrant Russian Jew on the other. Another text born of this era is less self-consciously political, but perhaps more moving as a loving and tender critique of "the German merchant world" of San Francisco out of which it emerged. In *920 O'Farrell Street* (1947), Harriet Lane Levy depicts an insular world divided by subtle social cleavages based on class, ethnic origin, and, above all, wealth, at once complacent and anxious. These tensions often played themselves out within the microcosm of the family and the incompatibilities of husband and wife. In addition to its astringent wit and literary brilliance in using the house as metonym for the community, this minor classic is also notable for the portrait it offers of Levy's friend and neighbor, Alice B. Toklas.

If these texts sometimes display the anxieties of assimilation, a later, American-born generation's texts express a desire for "cultural roots" (Powdermaker 22). The aims of this group of writers are both to define themselves professionally and to declare their Jewish identity. Sometimes their Jewish identity is understood as the formative basis, direct and indirect, of their professional development; other times, this ethnic identification is a declaration of allegiance in the face of the rising tide of anti-Semitism and the Nazi threat that increasingly cast its shadow up to World War II. In addition, the writer's artistic and intellectual identity is seen as a source of salvation, a refuge from the barbarism that threatened civilization.

Part of this category, Edna Ferber's first autobiography, *A Peculiar Treasure* (1939), is marked by a life-loving vitality and high-spirited feistiness. The text takes its title from a passage in Exodus that awards the Jews this epithet for their loyalty to a monotheistic god; in a rhetorical strategy originating with the earliest American, Puritan autobiographers and also characteristic of other Jewish autobiographers (Antin and Solomon use it extensively), Ferber transfers the epithet to identify America and its enterprise, hoping to recall Americans who have strayed from their true course to renew their commitment to those ideals of equality and democracy on which the country's greatness has been built. By conflating Jews and Americans, Ferber also implies their essential sameness and reaffirms their unity.

Tracing her personal and professional evolution offers still another strategy for affirming her ethnic identity as an integral aspect of American life and culture. Hers was a midwestern childhood and adolescence; her work as a reporter gave her entry into all levels of American society; her subsequent work built on its empirical method—observation, experiential and documentary research— as the basis of the imaginative reconstructions of American life. (She carefully notes that her books cover New England and more generally the North, the South, the Midwest, and the West; at the same time she points to her frequent use of ''Jewish'' material.) Nonetheless, Ferber's work avoids directly condemning fascistic, pro-Nazi, and anti-Semitic activities in the United States, even while this condemnation constitutes the subtext of the autobiography.

Another text whose motive derives from the need to counter the madness of Hitler is Goldie Stone's *My Caravan of Years* (1945). The work of a member of the older immigrant generation, its power and haunting sadness are measured in the metaphoric distance traveled between her original migration and the end of her life. For Stone, the journey to America was a descent from the wealth and comfort of the Lithuanian gentry into the maelstrom of domestic and economic disintegration, before marriage restored her status. Struggling to overcome the view ''that the life of man is little more than a dream and that his brief story is of little or no importance'' (93–94), she succeeded through her identification with impoverished immigrants in the desire to assuage ''the gnawing hurt of a cruel welcome'' (109). Active on behalf of Orthodox Jewry, Stone finds the values by which she has lived, the meaning on which she rebuilt her life, indeed, her very sanity, threatened still again, this time by ''revolution and war''—and the death camps. The text is darkened by madness, both personal and social, and, like Ferber's, marked by the reticence with which it indicts American society.

Like Stone, Hortense Powdermaker was the product of a well-to-do family. However, in her case, her parents' assimilation to a world ruled by material values also led her to a renewed ethnic identification. *Stranger and Friend* (1967) details her fieldwork with the Lesu, a Melanesian people, as well as the black and white communities of Mississippi, and the very different contemporary community encompassed by Hollywood. Powdermaker was among the first anthropologists to train her skill on contemporary American life, believing as she did that anthropological study must paradoxically come out of the professor's ''passions'' and sources of identification. Concerned with professional and ethical issues of detachment and involvement, Powdermaker offers a variety of meditations on "passing"—that is, on being taken or not taken for a woman (as differently defined by various societies), a Jew, a white person. The book's title itself has a variety of related meanings; referring primarily to the participation-observation method of the anthropologist, it also suggests her own personality, as well as the status of the Jew in American life.

However, there is a further irony here, as Powdermaker indicates, since her own life-choices partly involved the rejection of "an Americanized business culture . . . which bored me" and concomitantly, the reclamation of that Jewish culture that her highly assimilated parents had disavowed. Thus, she self-consciously rejected "insider" status in favor of "outsider" status, working with Russian Jews as a labor organizer in her early years, and eventually committing herself to a profession that values "outsider" status as a source of objectivity and knowledge.

Other books that offer significant assessments of the relationship between life and work include those written by people whose lives were rendered chaotic by the Russian revolutions and civil wars and later imperiled by Hitler. These are the writings of a "generation in turmoil," an apt phrase, which is the title of musician Frida Kahn's autobiography. The works depict the profound havoc and trauma wreaked by the need to flee their homes, the constant move from one country to another (or from one part of a country to another) that makes nomads of them all. Living, as Lore Segal notes, in "other people's houses," their political status in these countries is uncertain, their social and economic positions disrupted. For them, " 'the departure from Europe is acknowledgment of defeat' " (Woytinsky 150), defining then as emigrants rather than immigrants. Not only their political motivation, but their middle-class culture also distinguishes this category of autobiographers from the earlier generation of immigrant writers.

Despite the betrayals and dislocations they experienced, what pervades their texts is their humanity and love of life: their commitment to art, to the life of the mind, and to the betterment of mankind is ultimately dominant. The fusion of love and work acts as a dike against the chaos that threatens like a deluge to inundate them. In Woytinsky's *Two Lives in One* (1965), as in Kahn's *Generation in Turmoil* (1960), autobiography also doubles as biography, depicting not only the writers' lives but those of their husbands. Woytinsky's title suggests the ways in which she conceived that the marriage of heart and mind enlarged and enriched the possibilities of living; more skeptically, it suggests the antithesis as well—that is, the ways in which even highly educated career and otherwise independent women subordinated themselves in relationship to the other. More poignantly, the title points to the ways in which these writers lived two lives—if not more—in a single lifetime, when they suffered the disruption created by world events.

These texts merge into what is defined as the Holocaust literature of "survivors"; ironically, many of these have been denominated novels, perhaps because the writers have drawn on the narrative techniques of fiction or perhaps because they wished to draw the veil of fiction so as to prevent further suffering that exposure or reliving this part of their lives might bring to some individuals. Others have insisted on the documentary nature of autobiography; for these writers, the personal narrative or life-writing is a moral act of record keeping. Their works are the raw material of history. In such writings as *I Will Survive* (1962) by Sala Kaminska Pawlowicz, *In the Hell of Auschwitz: The Wartime Memories of Judith Sternberg Newman* (1963), *Where Are My Brothers?* (1965) by Sarah Bick Berkowitz, and *Seed of Sarah: Memoirs of a Survivor* (1991) by Judith Magyar Isaacson, autobiography is transformed into an ethical genre of witness.

They are texts that are also marked by unusually intense ironies. In *Dry Tears* (1984), for example, Nechama Tec describes the family's scrutiny, identification, and avoidance of those traits that are considered "Jewish" that is a grotesque but precise parody of the Nazi idea; she and her sister survive only at the price of passing as Christians. Her narrative thematizes duplicity, as painful when she begins to be the person she plays as when she bears the burden of knowledge that she must constantly suppress the truth of her identity; the text itself must be seen as an expression of the promise she kept to herself once she left Poland, "never again to pretend to be someone else" (241). Heda Margolius Kovály's account, *Under a Cruel Star*, is burdened by a different but no less tragic series of ironies. Having escaped from Lodz and apparently from her deportation to Auschwitz, she returns to Czechoslovakia to confront all those who failed to oppose the Nazis and to build a new life—only to be forced to submit to the terrors of Stalinism. Surviving the execution of her husband in a purge trial and her own official ostracism, virtually an internal exile, she allows herself again to hope during the Prague Spring of 1967, and finally to hope no more, to be at home in the land of her birth, at last abandoning the country in which, she remarks, no relative of her child had died a normal death.

The postwar renascence of personal narrative writing has its origin in the Holocaust in still another way. This decisive event was a turning point for many who experienced a variety of conversions, if not to traditional religious belief then to the need to identify as Jews. It was also related to the creation of a Jewish homeland in Palestine, and the establishment of the Israeli state is, in different ways, the focal point of a number of significant works—notably, Irma L. Lindheim's *Parallel Quest: A Search of a Person and a People* (1962) and Golda Meir's *My Life* (1975).

If the Holocaust generated the renascence of autobiography in the postwar period, the feminist movement was perhaps the single most important factor contributing to the resurgence of life-writing beginning in the 1970s, and a feminist sensibility characterizes the important works produced in the most recent period. In such writings as Kim Chernin's *In My Mother's House* (1983) and Vivian Gornick's *Fierce Attachments* (1987), we can trace one version of the movement's thrust to recover our mothers; in Kate Simon's *Bronx Primitive*

(1982), we can discern the effort to desentimentalize the ghetto and reframe the abuse of male power.

The leaders of the mainstream feminist movement, however, have been somewhat reluctant to bridge the personal and the public. Both Gloria Steinem and Betty Friedan have written only fragmentary autobiographical narratives, channeling most of their energies into journalistic essays that focus on defining the movement and various aspects of sisterhood; only Letty Cottin Pogrebin has sought to give narrative shape to her life through a full-scale autobiography. Moreover, *Deborah, Golda, and Me: Being Female and Jewish in America* (1991), as its title suggests, derives its impetus not from feminism per se, but from Pogrebin's disillusion with the feminist movement and the fruitful struggle to resume her Jewish identity; the text is shaped by inscribing her Jewishness within the feminist community and her feminism within the Jewish community. (In this, she is perhaps linked to the tradition of Progressive autobiography established by Solomon and Kohut. Kohut, too, invokes Deborah and other biblical heroines and rereads them in light of the woman's movement of her own age; she, too, must come to grips with her father in order to return to the faith of the Fathers.)

In other writings, women's coming of age and emergent feminist identity is linked to the involvement with and often reevaluation (rather than total rejection) of the radical and progressive politics of the period. *The Autobiography of an American Communist* (1977) by Peggy Dennis is an important work in this tradition of political autobiography identified above. Written by a woman of an earlier generation, her text forms a link between the older anarchist and socialist life-writings and those New-Left narratives that follow. While keeping faith with her passionate ideals, she renounces the party that she once believed had served as their repository, finding its institutional practices at odds with its professed commitments. Similarly, *Growing Up Underground* (1981; 1990) by Jane Alpert forswears the New-Left terrorism that she believes violated the ideals that it was meant to further. Her text tracks her gradual realization that violent acts were the social expression of psychic madness, and her own acquiescence in them was a manifestation of her need to be part of a community and a perversion of her desire for a better world.

Yet these texts are by no means recantations; they represent the best examples of the effort to make sense of the relationship between the political and the personal, which was the source of their inspiration and is the touchstone of their originality. They indicate how ethnicity becomes a textual marker for "outsider" status that has enabled their authors to develop a social and political critique. Finally, these works also reflect the continuing ethical impulse embedded in the Jewish American autobiographical project.

NOTES

1. For the most recent statement of this, see Werner Sollors, *Beyond Ethnicity: Consent and Descent in American Culture*, New York and Oxford: Oxford University Press,

1986. 45–46. Reviewers of works discussed subsequently and cited later in the text achieved this by conflating Antin's work with the one under review.

2. See, for example, reviews in the *New York Times* 4 April 1912:228; *The Nation* 94 (1912):517; *The Dial* 52 (May 1912):348–50; *The American Hebrew* (19 June 1912): 358–59; *Literary Digest* 44 (1912):1261–62. These reviewers generally supported her assimilationist strategy, while subsequent historian-critics have condemned it; for this, see *Encyclopedia Judaica* 3.67; Mary Dearborn, *Pochontas's Daughters: Gender and Ethnicity in American Culture*, 41, 43; New York and London: Oxford University Press, 1986; Sarah Blacher Cohen, "Mary Antin's *The Promised Land*: A Breach of Promise," *Studies in American Literature* 3 (1977–78):28–35; and Richard Tuerk, "The Youngest of America's Children in *The Promised Land*." *Studies in American Literature* 5 (1986): 29–34.

3. For a detailed elaboration of this statement, see Barbara Shollar, "Writing Ethnicity/Writing Modernity: Autobiographies by Jewish-American Women." Diss. City University of New York, 1992, 129–202.

4. See especially the reviews in the *New York Times* (8 July 1917):255, 258, and 13 March 1927:12; *The Nation* 105 (30 August 1917):224–25; and *The Menorah Journal* 3 (1917):304–05 and 13 (1927):331–32.

WORKS CITED

Alpert, Jane. *Growing Up Underground*. 1981. Carol Publishing Group. New York: Citadel, 1990.

Antin, Mary. *The Promised Land*. Foreword by Oscar Handlin. Sentry Edition. Boston: Houghton Mifflin, 1969.

Berkowitz, Sarah Bick. *Where Are My Brothers?* New York: Helios Books, 1965.

Chernin, Kim. *In My Mother's House: A Daughter's Story*. New York: Harper, 1983.

Cohen, Rose. *Out of the Shadow*. New York: George H. Doran Company, 1918.

Dennis, Peggy. *The Autobiography of an American Communist*, Westport, CT: Lawrence Hill, 1977.

Ferber, Edna. *A Peculiar Treasure* 1st ed. New York: Doubleday, Doran & Company, 1939.

Friedan, Betty. *It Changed My Life: Writings on the Women's Movement*. New York: Random House, 1976. 187–254.

Ganz, Marie. *Rebels: Into Anarchy—and Out Again*. 1919. Millwood, NY: Kraus Reprint Co., 1976.

Goldman, Emma. *Living My Life*. 1931. 2 vols. New York: Da Capo, 1970.

Gornick, Vivian. *Fierce Attachments: A Memoir*. 1987. New York: Simon and Schuster, 1988.

Hart, Sara L. *The Pleasure Is Mine: Autobiography*. Chicago: Valentine-Newman, 1947.

Hasanovitz, Elizabeth. *One of Them: Chapters from an Immigrant Autobiography*. Boston: Houghton Mifflin, 1918.

Isaacson, Judith Magyar. *Seed of Sarah: Memoirs of a Survivor*. Urbana/Chicago: University of Illinois Press, 1991.

Kahn, Frida. *Generation in Turmoil*. Great Neck, NY: Channel, 1960.

Kohut, Rebekah. *My Portion*. Foreword by Henrietta Szold. New York: Seltzer, 1925.

Kovály, Heda Margolius. *Under a Cruel Star: A Life in Prague, 1941–1968*. Trans.

Franci Epstein, Helen Epstein, and Heda Margolius Kovály. New York: Penguin Books, 1986.

Lang, Lucy Robins. *Tomorrow Is Beautiful*. New York: Macmillan, 1948.

Leader, Pauline. *And No Birds Sing*. New York: Vanguard, 1931.

Levy, Harriet Lane. *920 O'Farrell Street*. Illust. Mallette Dean. 1947. The Modern Jewish Experience. Ed. Moses Rischin. New York: Arno, 1975.

Lindheim, Irma Levy. *Parallel Quest: A Search of a Person and a People*. New York: T. Yoseloff, 1962.

Meir, Golda. *My Life*. New York: G. P. Putnam's, 1975.

Meyer, Annie Nathan. *It's Been Fun*. New York: Henry Schuman, 1951.

Morton, Leah [Elizabeth Gertrude Stern]. *I Am a Woman—and a Jew*. Introd. by Ellen Umansky. 1926. Masterworks of Modern Jewish Writing. Ed. Jonathan Sarna. New York: Markus Wiener Publishing, 1986.

Nathan, Maud. *Once Upon a Time and Today*. 1933. New York: Arno, 1974.

Pawlowicz, Sala Kaminska. *I Will Survive*. With Kevin Rose. New York: W. W. Norton, 1962.

Pesotta, Rose. *Bread Upon the Waters*. Ed. John Nicholas Beffel. With a new intro. by Ann Schofield. 1944. New York: ILR Press/New York State School of Industrial and Labor Relations, Cornell University, 1987.

Pogrebin, Letty Cottin. *Deborah, Golda, and Me: Being Female and Jewish in America*. New York: Crown Publishers, 1991.

Polacheck, Hilda Satt. *I Came a Stranger. The Story of a Hull-House Girl*. Ed. Dena J. Polacheck Epstein. Preface and afterword by Dena J. Polacheck Epstein. Intro. Lynn Y. Weiner. *Women in American History*. Urbana/Chicago: University of Illinois Press, 1989.

Powdermaker, Hortense. *Stranger and Friend: The Way of an Anthropologist*. New York: W. W. Norton, 1967.

Schneiderman, Rose. *All for One*. With Lucy Goldthwaite. New York: Paul S. Eriksson, 1967.

Segal, Lore Groszmann. *Other People's Houses*. New York: Harcourt, Brace & World, 1958.

Simon, Kate. *Bronx Primitive: Portraits in a Childhood*. 1982. New York: Harper & Row [Harper Colophon], 1983.

Solomon, Hannah G. *Fabric of My Life: The Story of a Social Pioneer*. 1946. New York: National Council of Jewish Women/Bloch Publishing Company, 1974.

Steinem, Gloria. *Outrageous Acts and Everyday Rebellions: Collected Essays*. New York: New American Library [Signet Book], 1983. 1–168.

Stern, E[lizabeth] G[ertrude]. *My Mother and I*. Foreword by Theodore Roosevelt. New York: Macmillan Company, 1917.

Stokes, Rose Pastor. *"I Belong to the Working Class": The Unfinished Autobiography*. Ed. and intro. Herbert Shapiro and David L. Sterling. Athens and London: The University of Georgia Press, 1992.

Stone, Goldie Tuvin. *My Caravan of Years: An Autobiography*. New York: Bloch Publishing, 1945.

Tec, Nechama. *Dry Tears: The Story of a Lost Childhood*. With a New Epilogue. New York: Oxford University Press, 1984.

Tompkins, Jane. *Sensational Designs: The Cultural Work of American Fiction, 1790–1860*. New York: Oxford University Press, 1985.

Wald, Lillian D. *The House on Henry Street.* New York: Holt, 1915.

Woytinsky, Emma Shadkhan. *Two Lives in One.* New York: Praeger, 1965.

Yezierska, Anzia. *Red Ribbon on a White Horse: My Story.* Intro. by W. H. Auden. New York: Persea Books, 1950.

SUGGESTIONS FOR FURTHER READING

Adler, Polly. *A House Is Not a Home.* New York: Rinehart, 1953.

Antin, Mary. *From Plotzk to Boston.* Translated from the Yiddish. Foreword by Israel Zangwill. 1899. Upper Saddle River, NJ: Literature House/Gregg, 1970.

Baum, Vicki. *It Was All Quite Different: The Memoirs of Vicki Baum.* New York: Funk & Wagnalls, 1964.

Bengis, Ingrid. *I Have Come Here to Be Alone.* New York: Simon and Schuster, 1976.

Berkowitz, Sarah Bick. *In Search of Ashes.* New York: Shengold Publishers, 1984.

Deutsch, Helene. *Confrontations with Myself: An Epilogue.* New York: W. W. Norton, 1973.

Ferber, Edna. *A Kind of Magic.* Garden City, NY: Doubleday, 1963.

Fisher, Florrie. *The Lonely Trip Back.* As told to Jean David and Todd Persons. Garden City, NY: Doubleday, 1971.

Gabor, Georgia M. *My Destiny, Survivor of the Holocaust.* Arcadia, CA: Amen Pub. Co., 1981.

Gruber, Ruth. *Israel on the Seventh Day.* New York: Hill and Wang, 1968.

Hartman, May Weisser. *I Gave My Heart.* New York: Citadel, 1960.

Heifetz, Julie. *Too Young to Remember.* Detroit: Wayne State University Press, 1989.

Hoffman, Eva. *Lost in Translation: A Life in a New Language.* New York: Dutton, 1989.

Hurst, Fanny. *Anatomy of Me: A Wanderer in Search of Herself.* Garden City, NY: Doubleday, 1958.

Jones, Hettie. *How I Became Hettie Jones.* 1990. New York: Penguin Books, 1991.

Katzenstein, Caroline. *Lifting the Curtain: The State and National Woman Suffrage Campaigns in Pennsylvania as I Saw Them.* Philadelphia: Dorrance, 1955.

Kern, Janet. *Yesterday's Child.* Philadelphia: Lippincott, 1960.

Kimball, Gussie. *Gitele.* First Edition. New York: Vantage, 1960.

Klein, Gerda Weissmann. *All But My Life.* New York: Hill and Wang, 1957.

Lamport, Felicia. *Ermine on Sundays (Mink on Weekdays).* Boston: Houghton Mifflin, 1950.

Leitner, Isabella. *Saving the Fragments: From Auschwitz to New York.* With Irving A. Leitner. New York: New American Library, 1985.

Lerner, Tillie. *In Retrospect.* New York: Vantage, 1982.

Levertov, Denise. *The Poet in the World.* New York, New Directions, 1973.

Lowenstein, Andrea Freud. *The Worry Girl: Stories from a Childhood.* Ithaca, NY: Firebrand Books, 1992.

Malina, Judith. *The Diaries of Judith Malina. 1947–1957.* New York: Grove, 1984.

Mandler, Anica Vesel. *Blood Ties: A Woman's History.* With Sarika Finci Hofbauer. Berkeley, CA: Moon Books, 1976.

Moskowitz, Faye. *A Leak in the Heart: Tales from a Woman's Life.* 1985. Boston: David R. Godine, Publisher, 1987.

Nadler, Susan. *Butterfly Convention.* New York: Dial, 1976.

Newman, Judith Sternberg. *In the Hell of Auschwitz: The Wartime Memories of Judith Sternberg Newman.* New York: Exposition, 1963.

Ochs, Vanessa L. *Words on Fire: One Woman's Journey Into the Sacred.* New York: Harcourt Brace Jovanovich, 1990.

Penzik, Irena. *Ashes to the Taste.* New York: Universal Publishers, 1961.

Popkin, Zelda. *Open Every Door.* New York: E. P. Dutton, 1956.

Randall, Margaret. *Part of the Solution: Portrait of a Revolutionary.* New York: New Directions, 1973.

Roiphe, Anne. *Generation Without Memory: A Jewish Journey Through Christian America.* New York: Linden Press/Simon & Schuster, 1981.

Sender, Ruth Minsky. *To Life*; 1988. New York: Puffin Books, 1990.

Sher, Eva Goldstein. *Life with Farmer Goldstein.* New York: Funk & Wagnalls, 1967.

Shick, Malte Gordon. *The Burden and the Trophy.* Trans. Mary J. Reuben. New York: Pageant, 1957.

Sidransky, Ruth. *In Silence: Growing up Hearing in a Deaf World.* 1990. New York: Ballantine Books, 1991.

Simon, Kate. *Etchings in an Hourglass.* New York: Harper & Row, 1990.

Sinclair, Jo. *The Seasons: Death and Transfiguration.* The Cross-Cultural Memoir Series. New York: Feminist Press, 1993.

Stern, Susan Harris. *With the Weathermen: The Personal Journal of a Revolutionary Woman.* Garden City, NY: Doubleday, 1975.

Trupin, Sophie. *Dakota Diaspora: Memoirs of a Jewish Homesteader.* Berkeley: Alternative, 1984.

Viertal, Salka. *The Kindness of Strangers.* New York: Holt, Rinehart & Winston, 1969.

GLOSSARY

Agada (*Aggada*). Hebrew. Jewish allegory, folklore, anecdote, and fable found in the Talmud

Baleboste. Yiddish. The consumate housekeeper

Bashert. Yiddish. Inevitable, predestined

Brit (*Bris*) *Milah*. Hebrew. Ritual circumcision

Challah (*Challa, Challeh*). Hebrew. A braided loaf of white bread traditionally eaten on the Sabbath and holidays

Chuppa (*Huppa*). Hebrew. Wedding canopy

Dybbuk. Yiddish. An evil spirit who takes possession of someone causing mad or corrupt behavior

Golem. A legendary creature created by a human to do his/her bidding

Haggadah. Hebrew. The narrative that is read aloud at the Passover Seder describing Israel's bondage and the flight from Egypt

Halakhah (*Halachah*). Hebrew. Jewish law and jurisprudence

Hashem. Hebrew. One of the words used for God so as not to utter a sacred name

Kabbalah (*Cabbala, Cabala*). Jewish mysticism or classical book of Jewish mysticism

Kaddish. Aramaic. Mourner's prayer

Mama-loshen (*Mame-loshn*). Yiddish. Mother tongue. Also Yiddish itself

Mechitza (*Mekhitzah*). Hebrew. Partition in Orthodox synagogues separating the women from the men

Megillah. Hebrew. Generally the Book of Esther, read in the synagogue during Purim

Mensch. Yiddish. A good human being

Mezuza (*Mezuzah*). Hebrew. A rolled parchment inscribed on one side with texts from Deuteronomy and on the other side with the name of God, put in a case and attached to the doorpost of the house as literally commanded in the text

Midrash. Hebrew. Parables, allegories, stories, and interpretative narratives commenting on biblical texts

Mikveh (Mikva, Mikvah). Hebrew, Yiddish. Ritual bath traditionally used by a Jewish woman before her wedding and after menstruation thereafter; also occasionally used by Jewish men

Minyan (Minyon). Hebrew. Quorum of ten Jews (traditionally only men) required for religious services

Pilpul. Aramaic. Intensive argumentation about passages in the Talmud, sometimes regarded as argument to display brilliance rather than illuminate issues

Shabbos (Shabbes, Shabbat). Hebrew. Sabbath

Shaygets. Yiddish. Gentile man

Shema (Shma). Hebrew. Prayer affirming faith in God

Shiurim. Hebrew. Study hours, especially related to holy texts

Shiksa (Shikseh). Yiddish. Gentile woman

Shoah. Hebrew. Holocaust

Shtetl. (Shtetlach, pl.). Yiddish. Small town or village, especially the Jewish communities of Eastern Europe before World War II

Tallis (Talith, Tallit). Hebrew. Prayer shawl used at religious services

Talmud. Hebrew. A massive compendium of sixty-three books that include commentaries and interpretations of the Bible written between the fifth century BCE and the second century

Tefillin (T'fillin). Hebrew. Phylacteries or small boxes containing parchments inscribed with biblical passages that are worn by Orthodox males during weekday morning prayers

Tikkun. Hebrew. Repair of the world through good deeds

Tsadeket. Yiddish. A righteous woman

T'Shuva. Hebrew. Repentance denoting a return to God

Yeshiva. Hebrew, Yiddish. A rabbinical seminary or college; in the United States, a secondary Hebrew or elementary school in which both religious and secular subjects are studied

Yiddishkeit. Yiddish. Customs and traditions of Yiddish-speaking Jews; Jewishness

Zemirot. Hebrew. Sabbath songs

NOTE

Although the definitions contained here came from several sources, I am especially indebted to Leo Rosten for his two books, *The Joys of Yiddish* (New York: McGraw-Hill, 1968) and *Hooray for Yiddish: A Book About English* (New York: Basic Books, 1976).

FOR FURTHER READING _____

The following titles are suggested in addition to those cited earlier.

Adler, Rachel. "A Mother in Israel: Aspects of the Mother Role in Jewish Myth." *Beyond Androcentrism: New Essays on Women and Religion*, Ed. Rita M. Gross. Missoula, MT: Scholars Press, 1977. 237–55.

Alter, Robert. *After the Tradition: Essays on Modern Jewish Writing*. New York: Dutton, 1969.

———. *Defenses of the Imagination: Jewish Writers and Modern Historical Crisis*. Philadelphia: Jewish Publication Society, 1977.

Ashton, Diane C., and Ellen Umansky, eds. *Piety, Persuasion, and Friendship: A Sourcebook of Women's Spirituality*. Boston: Beacon, 1991.

Baskin, Judith, ed. *Jewish Women in Historical Perspective*. Detroit: Wayne State University Press, 1991.

Baum, Charlotte, Paula Hyman, and Sonya Michel: *The Jewish Woman in America*, 1976. New York: NAL, 1977.

Berger, Alan. L. *Crisis and Covenant: The Holocaust in American Jewish Fiction*. Albany, SUNY Press, 1985.

Biale, Rachel. *Women and Jewish Law: An Exploration of Women's Issues in Halakic Sources*. New York: Schocken, 1984.

Blicksilver, Edith, ed. *The Ethnic American Woman: Problems, Protests, Lifestyle*. Dubuque, IA: Kendall/Hunt, 1978.

Burstein, Janet. "Jewish-American Women's Literature: The Long Quarrel with God." *Studies in American Jewish Literature* 8.1 (Spring 1989):9–25.

Cantor, Aviva. *The Jewish Woman 1900–1985: A Bibliography*. Fresh Meadows, NY: Biblio, 1987.

Cohen, Sara Blacher, ed. *From Hester Street to Hollywood: The Jewish- American Stage and Screen*. Bloomington: Indiana University Press, 1983.

———. *Jewish Wry: Essays on Jewish Humor*. Bloomington: Indiana University Press, 1987.

Cohen, Steven, and Paula E. Hyman, eds. *The Jewish Family: Myth and Reality*. New York: Holmes and Meier, 1986.

Elwell, Sue Levi, and Edward R. Levenson. *Jewish Women's Study Guide*. New York: Biblio, 1982.

Fishman, Sylvia Barack. "American Jewish Fiction Turns Inward." *American Jewish Yearbook*. Eds. David Singer and Ruth Seldin. Philadelphia: Jewish Publication Society, 1991.

Glanz, Rudolph. *The Jewish Woman in America: Two Female Immigrant Generations, 1820–1829*. 2 vols. New York: Ktav, 1976–77.

Guttmann, Allen. *The Jewish Writer in America: Assimilation and the Crisis of Identity*. New York: Oxford University Press, 1971.

Harap, Louis. *Creative Awakening: The Jewish Presence in Twentieth-Century American Literature, 1900–1940s*. Westport, CT: Greenwood, 1987.

———. *The Image of the Jew in American Literature*. Philadelphia: Jewish Publication Society, 1974.

———. *In the Mainstream: The Jewish Presence in Twentieth-Century Literature, 1950s–1980s*. Westport, CT: Greenwood, 1987.

Hellerstein, Kathryn. "Songs of Herself: A Lineage of Women Yiddish Poets." *Studies in American Jewish Literature*. 9.2 (Fall 1990):138–50.

———. "Women Poets in Yiddish." *Handbook of American-Jewish Literature*, 195–238.

Kaufman, Debra Renee. *Rachel's Daughters: Newly Orthodox Jewish Women*. New Brunswick, NJ: Rutgers University Press, 1991.

Klepfisz, Irena. "Anti-Semitism in the Lesbian/Feminist Movement." *Off Our Backs*, April 1982.

Knopp, Josephine Zadowsky. *The Trial of Judaism in Contemporary Jewish Writing*. Urbana: University of Illinois, 1976.

Liptzer, Solomon. *The Jew in American Literature*. New York: Block, 1966.

Ozick, Cynthia. "America: Toward Yavneh." *Judaism* 19 (1979): 276.

Pinsker, Sanford. "New Voices and the Contemporary Jewish-American Novel." Jewish Book Annual. Ed. Jacob Kabakoff. New York: Jewish Book Council, 1991. 6–20.

———. *The Schlemiel as Metaphor: Studies in Yiddish and American Fiction*. Carbondale: Southern Illinois University Press, 1991.

Plaskow, Judith. *Standing Again at Sinai: Judaism from a Feminist Perspective*. San Francisco: Harper, 1990.

Pogrebin, Letty Cottin. "Anti-Semitism in the Women's Movement." *Ms.*, June 1982.

Pratt, Norma Fain. "Culture and Radical Politics: Yiddish Women Writers, 1890–1940." *American Jewish History*. 70 (September 1980):68–90.

———. "Transitions in Judaism: The Jewish American Woman Through the 1930s." *American Quarterly*. 30 (1978):681–702. Rpt. in *Women in American Religion*. Ed. Janet James. Phila.: University of Pennsylvania, 1980. 207–28.

Rothenberg, Jerome, et al., eds. *A Big Jewish Book: Poems and Other Visions*. New York: Anchor, 1978.

Schechner, Mark. "Jewish Writers." *Harvard Guide to Contemporary American Writing*. Ed. Daniel Hoffman. Cambridge: Belknap Press of Harvard University Press, 1979.

Schiff, Ellen. *From Stereotype to Metaphor: The Jew in Contemporary Drama*. Albany: State University of New York, 1982.

Schneider, Susan Weidman. *Jewish and Female—Choices and Changes in Our Lives Today*. New York: Simon & Schuster, 1985.

Schwartz, Howard, and Anthony Rudolph, eds. *Voices Within the Ark: The Modern Jewish Poets*. New York: Avon, 1980.

Szold, Henrietta. "What Has Judaism Done for Woman?" *Judaism at the World's Parliament of Religions*. Cincinnati: Union of American Hebrew Congregations and Robert Clarke, 1894.

Walden, Daniel, ed. *On Being Jewish: American Jewish Writers from Cahan to Bellow*. Greenwich, CT: Fawcett, 1974.

———. *Twentieth-Century American-Jewish Fiction Writers*. Detroit: Gale, 1984. Vol. 28 of *Dictionary of Literary Biography*. 28 vols.

Wenkart, Henry, ed. *Sarah's Daughters Sing: A Sample of Poems by Jewish Women*. New York: KTAV, 1990.

Wisse, Ruth R. *The Shlemiel as Modern Hero*. Chicago: University of Chicago Press, 1971.

INDEX

CONTRIBUTORS _____

VICTORIA AARONS is Associate Professor of English at Trinity University. She wrote *Author as Character in the Works of Sholom Aleichem* and has recently completed a book manuscript, *A Measure of Memory: Storytelling and Identity in American Jewish Fiction.*

KAREN ALKALAY-GUT is a lecturer at Tel Aviv University. She is the author of *Alone in the Dawn: The Life of Adelaide Crapsey* and two books of poetry, *Mechitza* and *Ignorant Armies.*

ISKA ALTER is Associate Professor of English at Hofstra University. She is the author of *The Good Man's Dilemma: Social Criticism in the Fiction of Bernard Malamud* and articles on Anzia Yezierska, Arthur Miller, modern drama, and Shakespeare.

EVELYN M. AVERY is Professor of Ethnic and Jewish Literature at Towson State University. She is the author of *Rebels and Victims: The Fiction of Richard Wright and Bernard Malamud*, the literature section for *Sex and the Jewish Woman*, and many articles on Jewish writers. She is working on a book on Jewish American women writers tentatively titled ''Divided Selves: Jewish Women Writers in America.''

SHARON DEYKIN BARIS teaches in the English Department at Bar-Ilan University in Israel. She has published essays on Hawthorne, Melville, Stevens, Malamud, Henry James, and the biblical Book of Daniel. She is currently working on a book about the Book of Daniel in American literature, film, and art.

CAROL BATKER is Assistant Professor of Ethnic American Literature at Florida State University in Tallahassee.

LEN BERKMAN is Hesseltine Professor of Theatre at Smith College. His plays include *Voila! Rape in Technicolor*, *These Are Not My Breasts*, *Two Demon Plays*, and *Missing Children*, produced both in the United States and Canada. In addition, he has contributed essays to *Massachusetts Review*, *Modern Drama*, *Parnassus*, and the book *Upstaging Big Daddy*. He also works as playwright/ dramaturg at Robert Redford's Sundance Institute, the New York Stage and Film Company, and other theatres developing new plays.

DOROTHY S. BILIK is Associate Professor of Yiddish at the University of Maryland. Author of *Immigrant-Survivors: Post-Holocaust Consciousness in Recent Jewish-American Fiction*, she recently contributed entries on Yiddish language and literature for the 1994 *World Book Encyclopedia*.

LUDGER BRINKER is Professor in English at Macomb College. He is the author of a forthcoming book on Alfred Kazin's autobiographies and has published essays on Marlowe, Kazin, Wharton, Cahan, and Jewish American gay and lesbian literature.

DEBORAH LAMBERT BROWN is Associate Professor of English at the University of New Hampshire in Manchester. Her original poetry and essays have been published in a number of journals, including *American Literature*, *Massachusetts Review*, and *The Women's Review of Books*.

C. BETH BURCH is Assistant Professor of English Education at the University of Alabama, Tuscaloosa. She has published articles on American and Jewish American authors, including an article on American Jewish women writers in the *Oxford Companion to Women's Writing in the United States*.

BARBARA CANTALUPO is Assistant Professor of English at the Pennsylvania State University Allentown Campus. She has published on Tillie Olsen, Yvonne Rainer, Poe, and Melville, and is working on a literary biography of Emma Wolf to accompany a reprinting of one of her novels.

DOROTHY CHANSKY is a doctoral candidate in Performance Studies at New York University. Her criticism has appeared in *Theatre Journal*, *TheatreWeek*, *Women and Performance*, and *Ariel*. Her musical, *The Brooklyn Bridge*, ran off-Broadway in 1983.

ANNIE DAWID is Assistant Professor of Creative Writing and Fiction at Lewis and Clark College and the author of essays, poetry, and a novel, *York Ferry*.

ELIZABETH DRORBAUGH is a dictoral candidate in the Department of Performance Studies at New York University and an adjunct faculty member at

York College and the Borough of Manhattan Community College. A playwright, performer, and director, she is also a member of the Editorial Board of *Women and Performance: A Journal of Feminist Theory.*

JERILYN FISHER is Assistant Professor of English at Hostos College. She is coediting a volume of critical essays that use feminist psychological theory about women's development to interpret literary texts.

SYLVIA BARACK FISHMAN is Senior Research Associate and Assistant Director at the Cohen Center for Modern Jewish Studies at Brandeis University. She is the author of *Follow My Footprints: Changing Images of Women in American Jewish Fiction* and *A Breath of Life: Feminism in the American Jewish Community* as well as coeditor of *Changing Jewish Life: Service Delivery and Planning in the 1990's.*

LEWIS FRIED is Professor of American literature at Kent State University. He is editor-in-chief of the *Handbook of American Jewish Literature.*

KAREN WILKES GAINEY is Liberal Arts Division Chairman at Tulsa Junior College. She has recently completed a manuscript tentatively titled ''Semiotic Fiction'' on the work of Anne Tyler, Bobbie Ann Mason, Jayne Anne Phillips, and Grace Paley.

MIRIYAM GLAZER is Associate Professor of Literature and chair of the Department of Literature at the University of Judaism. A poet, she edited *Burning Air and Clear Mind: Contemporary Israeli Women Poets* and has written many articles on contemporary Jewish American women writers.

BRUCE HENDERSON is Assistant Professor of Speech Communication at Ithaca College. He is coauthor of *Performance: Texts and Contexts.*

SARA R. HOROWITZ is Director of the Jewish Studies Program and Assistant Professor of English Literature in the Honors Program at the University of Delaware. She is coeditor of *Kerem: A Journal of Creative Explorations in Judaism* and is completing a book on muteness in Holocaust fiction, *Voicing the Void.*

CAROLYN HOYT is a doctoral student in English literature at New York University. She has taught writing and literature at New York University, Kean College, and the New York Institute of Technology. Recent publications include essays, articles, and stories on Jewish life as well as women's issues.

BABETTE INGLEHART is Professor of English at Chicago State University. The editor of *Walking with Women Through Chicago Literature*, she has published a number of articles on women and ethnic writers, including a recent article "Comedy as Healing Art" in *Saul Bellow Journal.*

JANET E. KAUFMAN teaches at the University of Iowa. A published poet, she is working on a study of Muriel Rukeyser.

BLOSSOM STEINBERG KIRSCHENBAUM is Researcher in Brown University's Department of Comparative Literature. She has translated Giuliana Morandini's *I cristalli di Vienna* as *Bloodstains*, Paola Drigo's *Maria Zef*, stories by Marina Mizzau in *New Italian Women* and other short fiction from Italian, Yiddish, and Slovak sources.

SUSANNE KLINGENSTEIN is Assistant Professor of Writing and Humanistic Studies at the Massachusetts Institute of Technology. Author of *Jews in the American Academy, 1900–1940: The Dynamics of Intellectual Assimilation*, she is currently at work on a biographical history, *Enlarging America: The Cultural Work of Jewish Literary Scholars, 1930–1990.*

S. LILLIAN KREMER is Assistant Professor of English at Kansas State University. Author of *Witness Through the Imagination: The Holocaust in Jewish American Literature*, she is writing a critical analysis of literature by women on women's Holocaust experience.

RONIT LENTIN is a doctoral candidate at Trinity College, Dublin. She has published six novels, including *Night Train to Mother*, and has just completed a seventh. In addition, she is the author of two radio plays, a number of translations into Hebrew, and several nonfiction books and articles, including several articles on Jewish women writers.

TOBE LEVIN is a member of the English Department of the University of Maryland European Division and teaches Holocaust and American ethnic women's literature at J. W. Goethe Univeristat Frankfurt am Main. A cofounder of WISE (Women's International Studies Europe), she edits the association newsletter and coedited the special issue of *Women's Studies Quarterly* (1992) on Women's Studies in Europe.

DIANE LICHTENSTEIN is Associate Professor of English and Co-Chair of Women's Studies at Beloit College. She is the author of *Writing Their Nations: The Tradition of Nineteenth-Century American Jewish Women Writers.*

SHERRY LEE LINKON is Assistant Professor of English and Women's Studies at Youngstown State University. She is coeditor of *Revisioning the 30s: New Directions in Scholarship.*

MARCIA LITTENBERG is Assistant Professor of English at the State University of New York at Farmingdale. A specialist in American women writers, she has published reviews in *Legacy* and is currently working on Elizabeth Ashbridge's Quaker narrative.

BARBARA PITLICK LOVENHEIM is Instructor at Monroe Community College.

ADAM MEYER is Assistant Professor of English at Fisk University in Nashville. A contributor to MELUS and other journals, he is currently working on two book-length studies—one on Raymond Carver and another on the theme of black-Jewish encounters in the works of contemporary black and Jewish writers.

SUSAN MEYER is Assistant Professor of English at Wellesley College. As a Fellow at the Bunting Institute at Radcliffe College, she completed a book, *Gender and Empire: Figurative Structures in the Fiction of Charlotte Bronte, Emily Bronte, and George Eliot.*

DEVON MILLER-DUGGAN is a doctoral candidate in English at the University of Delaware, where she teaches contemporary poetry and fiction. Her poems have appeared in a variety of journals, including *The Indiana Review*, *Gargoyle*, and *Yellow Silk*.

JAYE BERMAN MONTRESOR is Assistant Professor of English at Villanova University and the author of *The Critical Response to Ann Beattie*.

KAY HOYLE NELSON is Assistant Professor of English and Humanities at Aurora University School of Nursing at Illinois Masonic Medical Center, Chicago, Illinois. She is coeditor of *The Critical Response to Tillie Olsen*.

GERDA S. NORVIG is Visiting Assistant Professor of English at the University of Colorado in Boulder. A poet whose work has appeared in *Response*, *The Massachusetts Review*, and *The Iowa Review*, she is also the author of *Dark Figures in the Desired Country: Blake's Illustrations to "The Pilgrim's Progress."* She is currently coediting a book tentatively titled Blake and Women.

RENA POTOK is a doctoral candidate in Comparative Literature and Literary Theory at the University of Pennsylvania, where she has taught courses in English and Women's Studies. A published poet, Potok also writes fiction and drama and translates Israeli literature.

CINDY ROSENTHAL is a doctoral candidate in Performance Studies at New York University, where she teaches expository writing. She has been a member of the Equity acting ensemble at the Bread Loaf School of English in Vermont since 1986.

CLAIRE R. SATLOF teaches in the English Department of the University of Pennsylvania. The author of several articles on Jewish literature, she explored the emergence of a recognizable canon of Jewish feminist fiction in ''History, Fiction, and the Tradition: Creating a Jewish Feminist Poetic.''

ELLEN SCHIFF is Professor Emerita of French and Comparative Literature. She is the author of *From Stereotype to Metaphor: The Jew in Contemporary Drama* and many articles and essays on Jewish plays and playwrights. A consultant to the National Foundation for Jewish Culture's Council of Jewish Theatres, she is working on a two-volume anthology of plays.

MERYL F. SCHWARTZ is Assistant Professor English at the University of Hartford. A doctoral candidate at the University of Wisconsin, she is completing her dissertation, ''Contemporary Women's Political Awakening Novels: Narrative Strategy, Reader Response, and Utopian Desire.''

ANN R. SHAPIRO is Professor of English at the State University of New York at Farmingdale. She is the author of *Unlikely Heroines: Nineteenth-Century American Woman Writers and the Woman Question* and various articles and reviews on Jewish American women writers and nineteenth-century American women writers.

BARBARA SHOLLAR currently teaches at Queens College and serves as a consultant to the New York City Board of Education. She coedited *The Longman Anthology of World Literature by Women, 1875–1975* and is working on a book, Writing Ethnicity/Writing Modernity: The Autobiographies of American Jewish Women.

MAEERA Y. SHREIBER has been a Visiting Assistant Professor at Reed College and is currently a Finkelstein Fellow at the University of Judaism in Los Angeles. She is working on a study of contemporary American Jewish women poets.

CAROLYN ARIELLA SOFIA is a doctoral student in English at the State University of New York at Stony Brook and also teaches literature at Hofstra University.

ELIZABETH Q. SULLIVAN is Assistant Professor of English at the State University of New York at Farmingdale. She is a frequent contributor to *Beacham's Guide to Literature for Young Adults* and *Beacham's Guide to Popular Fiction in America.*

HARVEY TERES is Associate Professor of English at Syracuse University. He is the author of *Remaking American Radicalism: Episodes in the History of the New York Intellectuals, 1930–1970*.

LINDA WAGNER-MARTIN is Hanes Professor of English and Comparative Literature at the University of North Carolina, Chapel Hill. Author of sixteen books and editor of another thirteen, she is working on a revisionist biography of Gertrude Stein and her family. In addition, she is coeditor of *The Oxford Companion to Women's Writing in the United States* and section editor for Contemporary Writers for the *D. C. Heath Anthology of American Literature*.

DANIEL WALDEN is Professor of American Studies, English, and Comparative Literature at Pennsylvania State University. He is the author of four books and more than fifty articles. His most recent works are *On Being Jewish: Jewish American Writers from Cahan to Bellow* and *Twentieth-Century American Jewish Writers*. In addition, he is the founder and editor of *Studies in American Jewish Literature*.

KIRSTEN WASSON is Assistant Professor at Hobart and William Smith colleges. She is writing a book on Mary Antin, Elizabeth Stern, and Anzia Yezierska. Her essay, "A Geography of Conversion: Dialogical Boundaries of Self in *The Promised Land*" is included in a collection, *Autobiography and PostModernism*.

GAY WILENTZ is Associate Professor of English at East Carolina University and the author of *Binding Cultures: Black Women Writers in Africa and the Diaspora*.

MERLA WOLK is a senior lecturer at the University of Michigan, Ann Arbor, where she teaches nineteenth- and twentieth-century British and American fiction and writing. She is the coauthor of *Arenas of the Mind: Critical Reading for Writers* and is currently at work on a cultural study of Jewish women writing in English, Offerings: the Voices of Jewish Women Writers.

ISBN 0-313-28437-7

HARDCOVER BAR CODE